Praise for *Nelson A. Miles and the Twilight of the Frontier Army*

"Wooster's readable book gives us a full portrait of Miles, analyzing his defects as well as his virtues. At the same time, Wooster keeps Miles in proper perspective in relation to the army and the nation of his time. Wooster's approach, solidly based on his exhaustive research, gives us the definitive biography of this controversial general." — *Journal of American History*

"Clearly written and judicious in its analysis, Wooster's biography sheds considerable light on Miles's career, as well as on the internal world of the 'old army' and the values and perceptions of the professional officer corps in the second half of the nineteenth century." — *American Historical Review*

"A meticulously researched and well-written work that breathes life into the man Theodore Roosevelt called a 'brave peacock.' At the same time, the author vividly recreates the old army with its intense rivalries and frustrations, stemming from lack of money and public appreciation and limited opportunities for promotion. Finally, Wooster presents an excellent analysis of the army's deficiencies as it entered an era when progressive reformers sought modernization." — *Western Historical Quarterly*

"An excellent biography of Miles, along with an insightful look at the frontier army Miles helped shape and eventually commanded. . . . For anyone interested in the history of the American West, this book is must reading." — *Montana The Magazine of Western History*

"An even-handed portrait, based on wide use of primary materials, of Miles and his career. . . . [Wooster's] assessments of Miles's role as commanding general and activities after retirement are particularly valuable." — *Southwestern Historical Quarterly*

"A stimulating narrative of Miles's life, cast against the backdrop of U.S. military history from the Civil War through the Spanish-American War. . . . The author's enlightened views stem from the U.S. Military History Institute's recently acquired collection of Miles's papers, augmented by an impressive array of other source materials. With Wooster's entertaining style, the reader experiences a rollercoaster-like effect of alternately cheering and booing Miles, not unlike his contemporaries. . . . an excellent perspective on one of the Indian Wars' most notable figures." — *Journal of Arizona History*

"Wooster's fine book is a fitting reminder of the days of the Old Army and a life story of a fascinating personality." — *Journal of Military History*

"Based on exhaustive primary research, including some recently discovered Miles papers, this is a superb biography." — *International Bibliography of Military History*

"An exceptionally well-written, brilliantly paced biography that illustrates fifty years of American military history through the story of the Army's last commanding general." — *Washington Times*

"[Wooster] carefully analyzes Miles's military prowess, political blunders, Indian relations, and combative personality. . . . useful, informative, and well worth the wait." — *New Mexico Historical Review*

"Wooster writes in such a way as to give the reader insights into the whole era of the settling of the West as well as into the politics of the day." — *Choice*

"[T]he reader comes away with a good understanding of the command-level weaknesses of the U.S. Army during the late nineteenth century and the importance of individual personalities and egos within that system." — *North Dakota History*

"[An] important contribution to our understanding of the post–Civil War army and the personalities involved in the final phases of western expansion." — *Civil War History*

By Robert Wooster

NELSON

University of Nebraska Press *Lincoln & London*

A. MILES

AND THE TWILIGHT OF

THE FRONTIER ARMY

First Bison Books printing: 1996

Most recent printing indicated

by the last digit below:

10   9   8   7   6   5   4   3   2   1

Library of Congress

Cataloging-in-Publication Data

Wooster, Robert, 1956–

Nelson A. Miles and the twilight of the frontier

army / Robert Wooster.

p.   cm.

Includes bibliographical references.

ISBN 0-8032-4759-1 (cl: alk. paper)

ISBN 0-8032-9775-0 (pa.)

1. Miles, Nelson Appleton, 1839–1925.

2. Generals—United States—Biography.

3. United States. Army—Biography.   4. Indians

of North America—Wars—1866–1895.   I. Title.

E745.M54W66   1993

973.8'092—dc20

[B]   92-25510

CIP

To my

Friends, Students,

and Colleagues

at Corpus Christi

State University

CONTENTS

ILLUSTRATIONS

MAPS

ACKNOWLEDGMENTS

I have always maintained that the author's most enjoyable job comes in writing the acknowledgments to a completed book. Musing over the past five years indeed brings back pleasant memories. I continue to marvel at the work done by librarians and archivists across the country. Almost without exception, they provide their time and expertise in a most generous fashion. I thank each and every one of those individuals who assisted me. A special note of gratitude, however, goes to those at the U.S. Army Military History Institute, Carlisle Barracks, Pennsylvania. There Richard Sommers and his excellent staff went out of their way to allow me to use the recently acquired Nelson A. Miles collection, although the papers were unprocessed and still in a dusty old trunk.

I am grateful to the following libraries and societies, which have assisted my research in their collections and, in many cases, have granted permission to quote: the Arizona Historical Society, Tucson; the Bancroft Library, University of California, Berkeley; the Beinecke Rare Book and Manuscript Library, Yale University; Bowdoin College, Brunswick, Maine; the Huntington Library, San Marino, California; the Illinois State Historical Library, Springfield; the Kansas State Historical Society, Center for Historical Research, Topeka; the Library of Congress; the Massachusetts Historical Society, Boston; the Perkins Library, Duke University, Durham, North Carolina; the New-York Historical Society, New York City; the New York Public Library; the Proctor Free Library, Proctor, Vermont; the Rutherford B. Hayes Presidential Center, Fremont, Ohio; the Southern Historical Collections, Library of the University of North Carolina at Chapel Hill; Stanford University Libraries; the Sterling Library, Yale University; University of Oregon, Eugene; the U.S. Army Military History Institute; the Virginia Historical Society, Richmond; and the William L. Clements Library, University of Michigan, Ann Arbor.

Fellow historians have been equally generous. Ronald James Barr and Dudley Acker lent their unpublished manuscripts. Thomas Van Sant went out of his way to send me a copy of a privately published biography. Gregory J. Urwin provided expert commentary and a close reading of my original manuscript, saving me from numerous factual and interpretative errors. Robert M. Utley provided a typescript copy of letters between Nelson Miles and his wife, collected by Sherman Miles. Bob also read my manuscript, offering encouragement tempered by constructive criticism. Indeed, the reader's reports of Urwin and Utley epitomized the professionalism toward which academics should always strive. At the University of Texas at Austin, the advice and counsel of John E. Sunder, my supervising professor, continues to have a positive influence on my teaching and publications. And Lewis L. Gould, who originally suggested that I write a biography of Nelson A. Miles, offers a fine model of an active, supportive scholar. Captain Dale E. Wilson and his former colleagues at the U.S. Military Academy allowed me to spend parts of two summers at West Point, New York, where I escaped some of the Texas heat and met a number of fellow historians while attending and working for the R.O.T.C. Military History Fellowship.

Several years ago, I had the good fortune to work for James A.

Michener and his able assistant, John Kings. They taught me much about writing and publishing. More important, however, they instilled in me a sense of confidence I had often lacked. I shall always remain grateful to these remarkable men for their advice, inspiration, and guidance.

Corpus Christi State University has for the past five and one-half years furnished an environment well suited to my professional and personal needs. Along with a Travel to Collections Grant from the National Endowment for the Humanities, CCSU's Organized Research Fund provided a generous stipend that allowed me to tour the country in search of materials on Nelson A. Miles. Fellow historians Patrick Carroll, Joe B. Frantz, and Paul E. Orser have been cooperative, talented colleagues who have assisted me at every opportunity during my career at CCSU. Thomas Kreneck and James E. McClellan have been boon friends, the latter also making revealing suggestions about Lewis Henry Morgan. Dorothy McClellan and Robb Jackson have through their warmth and friendship made the bad times tolerable and the good times even better. Pat Thomas and Lisa K. Hill read my manuscript, made uniformly good suggestions, and provided fine companionship. And Catherine I. Cox has over the past year provided a combination of advice, warmth, comfort, and love I have never before experienced.

Although I have dedicated this book to my students and friends at Corpus Christi State University, my parents deserve a special note of thanks. Through it all, Edna and Ralph Wooster have been the best mother and father a son could ever hope for.

1 : THE BOY FROM WESTMINSTER

Nelson Appleton Miles, who would later become a Civil War hero, the captor of Chief Joseph and Geronimo, and the last commanding general of the United States Army, was born on August 6, 1839. His parents, Daniel and Mary Curtis Miles, lived about fifty-five miles west of Boston in the rural township of Westminster, Massachusetts. Nelson inherited solid Yankee roots; his forebears had arrived in America two centuries earlier. His mother claimed a direct lineage to William Curtis, who came to Boston in 1632 aboard the *Lyon*.[1]

Nelson's paternal ancestors had played an even more significant role in colonial New England development. The Reverend John Myles, first of the clan to come to the New World, had sailed from Wales in 1634. The minister taught the wide array of grammar, arithmetic, and classical languages common to a late Renaissance education. With the outbreak of King Philip's War, he shed his clergyman's robes for a captaincy in the local militia. One of his sons, Samuel, graduated from Harvard nine years later. Following his father into the clergy, Samuel received his orders in the Anglican church and served as rector of King's Chapel, Boston, for twenty-nine years. He then left Boston for Pomfret, Connecticut, before settling in central Massachusetts near what ultimately became Petersham.[2]

As its colonial roots deepened, the family replaced its Old English surname with the more Americanized Miles. They participated early and often in the American Revolution: three of Nelson's great-uncles, along with his great-grandfather Daniel, took up arms against the British. Consumed by patriotic zeal for his new country, Daniel, like many of his contemporaries, lost much of his fortune with the swift depreciation of Continental currency following the Revolutionary War.[3]

Seeking to recoup these losses, Daniel's son, Daniel, Jr., moved to Westminster, Massachusetts, where several relatives had already established the family's good name. Settling onto a farm in the Berkshire Hills, he and Mary Curtis, both devout Baptists, announced their intention to marry in late January 1825. Their first child, Daniel Curtis Miles, was born two years later, followed by daughters Mary Jane and Anna Maria in 1831 and 1836, then Nelson in 1839. The family thrived in their new Worcester County home. By 1850, Daniel, age fifty-one, and his wife had amassed a comfortable estate of forty-four hundred dollars. His four children all attended school that year; their eldest son claimed property of his own valued at sixteen-hundred dollars.[4]

Nelson later recalled that he enjoyed "an innocent and happy childhood" on the farm near picturesque Wachusett Mountain. The forests, streams, and rolling hills encouraged outdoor activities. His father taught him to ride a horse, and at age six Nelson received his own pony. Accompanied by his dog, the rambunctious lad roamed across the nearby countryside. Sledding, skating, hunting, and swimming were his favorite sports. He and his boyhood chums also dreamed of military adventure. "Some of the boys were necessarily assigned to play the part of the odious Britisher, the bloodthirsty Indian or the unfortunate Mexican," the nationalistic Nelson reflected later, "and these were invariably defeated in the desperate encounter and put to ignominious rout."[5]

Yet outdoor frolicking did not consume all the young man's energies, for Daniel Miles proved a stern taskmaster. As selectman, assessor, and member of the school committee, he staunchly supported prohibition and civic boosterism. Nelson, already exhibiting a smug self-assuredness reinforced by his family's status, attended John R. Gaut's academy, a thriving institution run by the local Congregational church, but his atrocious spelling of later years suggests that formal education held little appeal. As a classmate remembered, "The study in which he seemed to take most delight was fighting." Tales of his family's military exploits seemed more interesting than recitation or multiplication. Like many of his generation, the pugnacious teenager dreamed of the patriotic adventure that might propel him to true manhood. But when his sisters married and his brother stood to inherit the farm and his parents' white frame house, Nelson wondered what the future might hold for a second son.[6]

With only two churches, three general stores, and assorted small mechanic shops, Westminster offered limited options. Not attracted to farming or the small family lumber business, Nelson decided to leave. Boston, the nation's fifth-largest city, at 177,800 people, seemed ideal for a man on the make. Even better, several of his mother's relatives lived in the Boston area. By July 1857 he was working up to thirteen hours a day in a small city fruit market. "Bisness has been very good," he informed his older brother, "cherrys are all gone most but all kinds of berrys are in the market and some fruit."[7]

By 1858, the gangly, blue-eyed lad, six feet tall but weighing less than 150 pounds, had gone to work as a clerk in the John Collamore, Jr., and Company crockery store at 190 Washington Street. Although his uncle John Curtis was one of the proprietors, Nelson received few special favors. Concerned but still optimistic, he confided, "I have not succeeded in getting any more wages yet but am hoping for some soon." "My prosperity . . . has not amounted to much. I have some hard time to go through," he admitted. "But as it was my choice to come into this city I mean to put it through if I can."[8]

Long hours of toil did not intimidate Miles, who was convinced that his Protestant values and American birth destined him for success. Having been baptized at thirteen, he attended the First Baptist Church of Boston. "Try and do all you can to keep up meetings there for you can do a grate deal of good," he instructed his older brother in Westminster. With large numbers of foreign-born immigrants arriving in

Boston, Miles's Massachusetts heritage proved an advantage during an era often dominated by nativist rhetoric. Further, the Collamore store's enviable location among the bustling shops along Washington Street encouraged business growth. Nelson's move to a rather fashionable boarding house at Temple Place, overlooking Boston Commons, signified his improved financial status. In 1860 he confidently paid to have his name placed in the city's business directory and started drawing a regular salary.[9]

Meanwhile, Miles doggedly resumed his education at Comer's Commercial College. Though a lifelong skeptic when it came to formal academic training, he encouraged his brother to correct his spelling and grammar, a task that sorely tried Daniel's energies and patience. But the exertions paid off, and the young man's writing showed marked improvement during the Boston years. At his brother's behest, Nelson also began to read more widely. "I now have access to 3 different librarys the Mercantile, Young Mens Christian Association, & the Public Library," he boasted. Histories of the United States, Britain, and France, along with biographies of Napoleon Bonaparte, Daniel Webster, and the merchants and philanthropists Stephen Girard and Amos and Abbott Lawrence held much appeal, as did a particularly inspirational volume titled *The Richest Men of Massachusetts*.[10]

The move to Boston did much to reconcile the trivial disputes—only hinted at in Miles's correspondence and later writings—that sometimes divide even the closest of families. Still, reverence rather than love characterized his relations with his parents. Nelson recalled a "sense of obligation" to his mother, whose "loftiest ambition [was] to guide her children by good example, pure thought, upright and praiseworthy life to honorable and noble purpose." As for his father, Nelson owed him, as he put it, "whatever of aptitude I have possessed in meeting the stern realities of a somewhat tumultuous life." He found occasional visits to Westminster rewarding now that he had left the family home. Miles got along more comfortably with brother Daniel and his family—wife Lucy Ann and children Mary, George Herbert, and Arthur—even submitting himself, uncharacteristically, to friendly teasing from his nieces and nephews. The young clerk also visited his Roxbury uncles, George and Nelson Curtis, on a frequent basis.[11]

It was in Boston that Nelson's fascination with politics and power first blossomed. Upon encountering several state legislators at Boston's Old South Church, he observed, "Some look as if they knew how to make the laws & others as if they knew how to make Boots." He heard fiery abolitionist oratory at Tremont Temple and Faneuil Hall. The ominous controversies of the presidential campaign of 1860 further whetted his appetite for political debate. Aware of the unsuccessful Democratic convention at Charleston, South Carolina, Miles took keen interest in the Republican meeting at Chicago. Fired with the excitement of the times, he declared his intention to spend a vacation at a Republican club meeting in nearby Worcester.[12]

The year seemed too hectic for routine amusements. Although Boston buzzed over a "Great Prize Fight in England" that spring, Miles said he took little notice, admitting only his pride "that [the] Stars & Stripes 'gave it to his m[ajesty].' " Military training, by contrast, offered him a more interesting diversion. He and fellow enthusiasts organized a drill club under the tutelage of a former French army colonel.[13]

While Miles drilled, secession tore the nation apart. Years of controversy over the slave question had deeply divided the country. Many Southerners believed the election of Abraham Lincoln signaled an end to life as they knew it. Terrified by the prospect of a Republican president, seven slave states seceded from the Union in late 1860 and early 1861. After the firing at Fort Sumter, South Carolina, four additional slave states joined the Confederacy. Miles concluded that his military training might now have practical value. "*War* is all the talk and nothing else is to be thought of at this time," he told his brother. He urged Daniel to form a Westminster volunteer group, confidently offering to lend his expert assistance during his next visit home.[14]

But like most Americans, Nelson did not immediately sign up for service—only after the shocking defeat at the First Battle of Bull Run did he act. As he later recalled, "My time & mind was all taken up for weeks." Spending one thousand dollars given to him by his father and borrowing another two thousand from an uncle, Miles organized and outfitted a company at nearby Dudley Hall, Roxbury. By September 7, seventy men had joined the unit, which ultimately became Company E of the Twenty-second Massachusetts Infantry Regiment. Not surprisingly, the men elected their twenty-two year-old benefactor as captain. But political patronage and fears about Miles's youth took precedence over the enthusiastic acclaim of a few young Massachussans. Governor John A. Andrew refused to commission Miles, whose family enjoyed little political influence, as a captain, offering him only a first lieutenancy. Miles resentfully accepted the lower rank on October 7, 1861, but

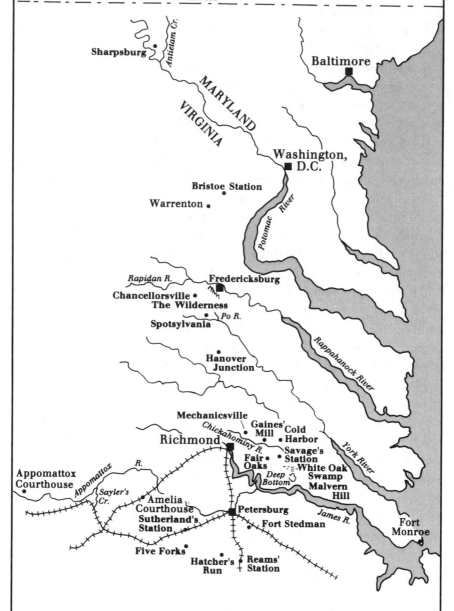

Huntingdon

Gettysburg

Sharpsburg

Antietam Cr.

MARYLAND

VIRGINIA

Baltimore

Washington, D.C.

Bristoe Station

Warrenton

Potomac River

Rapidan R. Fredericksburg

Chancellorsville
The Wilderness

Spotsylvania *Po R.*

Rappahanock River

Hanover Junction

Mechanicsville

Chickahominy R. Gaines' Mill Cold Harbor

Richmond

Savage's Station

Fair Oaks

White Oak Swamp

Deep Bottom

Malvern Hill

York River

Appomattox Courthouse

Appomattox R.

Sayler's Cr.

Amelia Courthouse
Sutherland's Station

Petersburg

Fort Stedman

James R.

Fort Monroe

Five Forks

Hatcher's Run

Reams' Station

NELSON MILES AND THE CIVIL WAR

would never forget the incident. "I was cheated out of it," he concluded bitterly. It would not be the last time that politics checked his martial ambitions.[15]

Temporarily shattered by the setback, Miles took his place among the officers of the Twenty-second Massachusetts. His six-foot frame had finally filled out and his intense blue eyes and well-defined features made the clean-shaven young man an impressive physical specimen. The first colonel of the Twenty-second was Henry Wilson, more politician than soldier, who would soon resign his command in favor of a seat in the United States Senate. Lieutenant Miles's personal rival and immediate superior was Captain William S. Cogswell, the man who held what Miles believed to be his rightful command. In assessing Cogswell critically, Miles proved an accurate judge of character—the captain would resign on July 11, 1862, only nine months after joining Company F.[16]

Armed with Enfield rifles, the men of the Twenty-second Massachusetts began their military careers outside Lynnfield at Camp Schouler. In early October Robert C. Winthrop, former speaker of the United States House of Representatives, welcomed them into the army and presented the regimental flag on Boston Commons, a ceremony repeated countless times across the continent. The regiment then took the train to New York City, where the Fifth Avenue Hotel treated the officers to a complimentary breakfast. A women's group presented the Twenty-second with still another flag at Madison Square. Cheering crowds ushered the regiment off by boat to Philadelphia, where they landed on October 10.[17]

The recruits soon found war to be more than elegant flag presentations. Two of their number, who had undoubtedly celebrated a little too boisterously, fell overboard during the short trip to Pennsylvania. And the citizens of Philadelphia and Baltimore gave the regiment a cool reception as the troops wound their way to Washington. Only inside the capital city did the members of the Twenty-second again find themselves the object of adoring crowds; a parade down Pennsylvania Avenue helped restore their sagging spirits. Their arrival held a special poignancy for Lieutenant Miles. His brother Daniel had accompanied the regiment to this point; now, as the troops crossed the Potomac River, Nelson confided, "It was hard to part with him as he had come so far with me and was the last one to part with[,] . . . he to friends and a pleasant home, I to cross the river to meet the enemies of my country in a strange land without a *single friend,* with nothing to depend upon except my sword."[18]

On October 13, the Twenty-second Massachusetts bivouacked at Hall's Hill, just outside Falls Church, Virginia. Dubbed Camp Wilson (for Colonel Henry Wilson) by its occupants, the site offered enough wood and water to suit the needs of even chronically wasteful recruits. The men scoured the area for bricks to construct rough ovens and logs to protect their flimsy tents from the elements. To improve morale, one officer furnished a football and several checkerboards. Singing added to the social activities.[19]

Life took on an increasingly martial air amid the regimental band's sentimental medleys. Inspired by the popular new commander of the Army of the Potomac, Major General George B. McClellan, drills, patriotic addresses, and full-dress parades, the Army of the Potomac rose from the ashes of First Bull Run. Springfield rifles replaced the older Enfields and the Twenty-second Massachusetts found itself grouped into General Fitz-John Porter's division. By late October, Nelson Miles, supremely confident in McClellan, believed the army could shield the capital city against the Confederate hordes. "With the present force and the fortifications it is an impossibility for them to take Washington from this side," he ventured.[20]

But a mere lieutenancy in an undistinguished regiment did not satisfy Miles. A brief stint as aide to Brigadier General Silas Casey only whetted his appetite for higher command. Tired of Miles's constant grumbling, a fellow officer asked him if he knew any generals. After a moment's reflection, Miles reported an acquaintance with Brigadier General James S. Negley of Pennsylvania. "Well," retorted his comrade, "you borrow a horse and go over to Negley, and ask him to get you detailed on his staff." Failing to get an appointment there, Miles won the attention of the commander of the First Brigade, Brigadier General Oliver O. Howard, a deeply religious West Point graduate who on November 10, 1861, appointed him as an aide-de-camp. Thus began a tumultuous relationship of thirty-five years, during which the two would be the closest of friends as well as the bitterest of enemies.[21]

Work on Howard's staff appealed to Miles. "The General lets me do just as I like," he chortled, happy to have left the Twenty-second Massachusetts behind. Training and picket duty under his new division commander, the grizzled old war-horse Brigadier General Edwin V. ("Bull") Sumner, were demanding, but reviews of the unit by

McClellan lifted the soldiers' morale. As did most in the Army of the Potomac, Lieutenant Miles adored McClellan. In contrast to the country's senior military officer, Winfield Scott, whom Miles dubbed "too old," McClellan kept up incessant activity that buoyed the army's spirits. Miles did, however, express reservations about McClellan's broad authority: "He has as much responsibility entrusted to him as any one man ought to have."[22]

For Miles, as for many of his comrades, military service marked the first venture that far from home. The northern Virginia surroundings aroused his curiosity. He deemed the local men "very dull" and lacking in "enterprise." The women, however, caught his eye. As he informed an aunt, "the ladies are *very gay* think much of a dress and the better class are even more accomplished than the northern ladies." Keenly interested in technological developments, Lieutenant Miles wandered over to the camp of "aeronaut" John La Mountain, who promised to take him on a balloon ride. Miles also bought a horse, which he named Excelsior.[23]

Habitually mindful of finances, Miles directed that his bounty money, or enlistment bonus, be used to begin paying off the debts incurred in raising his company. He now regretted having spent so little time with friends and family before traipsing off to war. But year-end celebrations and a visit from his father eased the pangs of homesickness. The enlisted men's races, boxing matches, fencing contests, and football games provided fine entertainment that Christmas. Miles admitted a special fondness for the greased-pig contests. He also toured Mount Vernon with his new-found friend, Lieutenant Colonel Francis C. Barlow of the Sixty-first New York.[24]

Lieutenant Miles had secured a talented and powerful ally in Barlow, a twenty-seven-year-old lawyer who had graduated at the top of his Harvard class. A member of the *New York Tribune*'s editorial staff, he enlisted as a private shortly after the firing on Fort Sumter and ultimately rose to rank of major general. Barlow, a talented, aggressive leader who cared for the welfare of his men in camp and field, frequently used the broad side of his saber to discourage straggling. Miles and Barlow had mutual associates in Boston who vociferously pressed Miles's abilities, leading Barlow to wonder if "Miles' Boston friends" were "a permanent encumbrance." But Barlow hastened to add, "I should miss the society of that excellent young man." Despite Miles's overly zealous supporters, Barlow sponsored his cause before Governor

Edwin D. Morgan of New York. "I am anxious to have Mr. Miles made either Lieutenant Colonel or Major," urged Barlow. "Officers and men know, respect and obey him."[25]

As the Army of the Potomac matured, the lack of action frustrated Lieutenant Miles. "We are not here to play soldier," he wrote. "All we want is *orders* to let us move on to victory or death." Diplomatic disputes with Britain added to the lieutenant's concerns. Of the October 1861 incident involving Confederate diplomats to Britain and France, James M. Mason and John Slidell, forcibly removed from the British steamer *Trent* but later released in the face of heavy diplomatic pressure, Miles reflected the views of many other young Yankees when he sighed, "It looks a little cowardly." He admitted that the nation could not take on both Britain and France, but argued, "With England alone I think we could at least [have] sustained our national honor."[26]

In the spring of 1862 diplomatic maneuvering gave way to force as McClellan began his Peninsular campaign. Hoping to take Richmond, the Confederate capital, from the southeast, McClellan landed his army on the York Peninsula and began a slow overland push toward that city. Though fancying himself a "Young Napoleon," McClellan had none of his idol's aggressiveness, and his undue caution allowed the Confederate General Joseph E. Johnston to race south from the Rappahannock River and block the Northern advance. The two armies clashed just to the east of Richmond at the Battle of Fair Oaks on May 31, 1862. Miles, as one of Oliver O. Howard's aides, found himself attached to the First Brigade, First Division. Casualties left several companies in the Eighty-first Pennsylvania without field officers, so the untested Miles was dispatched to rally the men "and to make the best disposition of it he could." Ignoring a foot wound, Miles halted the regiment's retreat and checked subsequent Confederate assaults.[27]

Accolades for Miles's conduct poured in to headquarters. Though the mismanaged conflict at Fair Oaks had ended in a bloody stalemate, Miles had performed brilliantly in his first test under fire. Howard noted his "entire satisfaction and approval" for his aide's efforts. Another officer reported that the lieutenant, "fresh from civil life, showed there, to the admiration of all beholders, that address and gallantry which were . . . to make the name of Nelson A. Miles the pride of the volunteer soldiers of the Union."[28]

Despite his foot wound, Miles had performed courageously. But he also witnessed firsthand the horrors of the Civil War battlefield. His duties had required him to cross and recross a field upon which eleven thousand men had fallen. "A more gruesome scene cannot be imagined," he later remembered. General Howard was himself badly wounded and his right arm had to be amputated. Lieutenant Miles had a full view of this macabre spectacle; he held Howard's right arm during the operation.[29]

General Johnston was also a casualty at Fair Oaks and was replaced as the Confederate commander by Robert E. Lee. Lee's previous construction of fieldworks across the approaches to Richmond had earned him the nickname "King of Spades." But a passive defense was not his object; he hoped the works would allow him to attack McClellan's massive army, which was spread from Mechanicsville on the north to White Oak Swamp on the south and divided by the Chickahominy River.

On June 26, Lee's hammer fell on the exposed Union right flank at Mechanicsville. Although a tactical defeat for Lee, the fighting nonetheless confirmed McClellan's misguided notion that the Confederates enjoyed an overwhelming numerical superiority. The Rebels again pressed the attack on the Federal right at Gaines' Mill the following day. Lieutenant Miles now found himself attached to the staff of Brigadier General John C. Caldwell, commander of the First Brigade, which was in the Union center.[30]

McClellan deemed the Confederate pressure too heavy and fell back south to the James River. On the twenty-ninth, the Confederates engaged the Second Corps rearguard at Savage's Station and Allen's Farm. Miles volunteered to help cut a road between exposed Union artillery at those two points, thus saving three batteries from falling into Confederate hands. Yet the Union retreat continued that evening through a driving rain. On June 30, with his division now on the Yankee right flank, Miles commanded the Eighty-first Pennsylvania during the fighting at White Oak Swamp. The action next shifted south to Malvern Hill at the James River, where McClellan's army used prepared positions to throw back Lee's legions but received heavy losses.[31]

Bloodied in the fighting from Mechanicsville through Malvern Hill—known collectively as the Seven Days' Battles—the Army of the Potomac remained unbroken. Francis Barlow believed that if it were not for the "damned miserable creatures" who led the army, the push against Richmond could be resumed. McClellan had indeed been outgeneraled; he had refused to capitalize on his superior numbers and he blamed the failure on everyone but himself. A beaten Young Napoleon held his army along the James River through July, at a prudent distance from Confederate forces.[32]

In contrast to his commanding general, Miles had performed with distinction. Brigade chief John C. Caldwell reported, "[Of] Miles I cannot speak in terms of sufficient praise. His activity was incessant." Though General Sumner nominated Miles for a commission in a new Massachusetts regiment, the state failed to follow through. Barlow, however, added his usual support, for Miles had secured a cannon for his command during the fighting at Malvern Hill and brought in reinforcements despite heavy fire at White Oak Swamp. He persuaded Governor Morgan to appoint Miles lieutenant colonel in the Sixty-first New York, retroactive to May 31, 1862. Miles immediately resigned his position in the Twenty-second Massachusetts.[33]

McClellan called for more men, reorganized on the James Peninsula, called for still more men, and in August finally began a slow withdrawal. Lee turned his attention to the short-lived Union Army of Virginia, led by the bombastic Major General John Pope. As Miles and his comrades in the Army of the Potomac boarded transports and sailed back to Washington, Lee defeated Pope at the Second Battle of Bull Run in late August 1862. In early September the Confederates pushed into Maryland. McClellan, following warily, kept between the Southerners and Washington, D.C.

As Lee's divisions scoured the countryside for supplies and laid siege to Federal troops at Harper's Ferry, McClellan received an enormous piece of luck: a Union sergeant unwittingly discovered a copy of Lee's operational plans. "Here is a paper," trumpeted a jubilant McClellan, "with which if I cannot whip 'Bobbie Lee,' I will be willing to go home." Though previously prudent when it came to advancing, McClellan now mustered his resolve and his command to fight Lee's scattered army. Surprised by McClellan's unusual aggressiveness, Lee pulled his forces together at the Maryland village of Sharpsburg.[34]

During a skirmish on September 16, a Confederate artillery shell mortally wounded Miles's horse, Excelsior, which had carried him from the outskirts of Richmond to the cornfields of Maryland. "It was like losing a devoted friend," Miles later remembered. He would lose many comrades the following day along Antietam Creek, where Mc-

Clellan squandered his two-to-one numerical superiority by launching three uncoordinated assaults against Lee's thin gray lines.[35]

Lieutenant Colonel Miles took part in the second of these attacks, that conducted by Sumner's Second Corps against the Confederate center. Rebel defenders dug in along a sunken road smashed the frontal assaults of Brigadier General William French's division, but a low rise in the ground allowed Major General Israel B. Richardson's troops, including Barlow's recently combined Sixty-first and Sixty-fourth New York regiments, a relatively unscathed approach. They opened an enfilading fire into the Confederates, who were exposed on the road forever after known as Bloody Lane. The Confederates' efforts to extricate themselves soon turned into a disorganized flight. Capturing two hundred prisoners and a stand of Rebel colors in the brutal struggle, Barlow's New Yorkers swept inexorably ahead.

But Richardson was mortally wounded, and Barlow was also injured. With his senior officers thus out of action, twenty-three-year-old Nelson Miles inherited the combined New York regiment. He boasted little formal military training. But Civil War soldiers, immersed in society's belief that real manhood included a healthy portion of raw courage, demanded bravery and common sense rather than schoolbook excellence from their officers. Instinctively, Miles attacked. Through a nearby cornfield and apple orchard rolled the men in blue, thirsting to regain their honor after so many embarrassing retreats. "Lee's army was ruined, and the end of the Confederacy was in sight," concluded a Confederate artilleryman. But panicky superiors ordered Miles and the other Yankees who had moved ahead to fall back. He and the others spent the rest of the day in frustration as Lee restored his embattled center. Uninspired attacks by the Union left wing finally petered out against eleventh-hour Confederate reinforcements.[36]

The night rang with ghastly pleas from the wounded and the dying. Heavy casualties left Lee with scarcely thirty thousand combatants after the Battle of Antietam, the bloodiest single day of fighting in the war. But Union losses had also been severe. Satisfied at having repelled Lee's invasion, McClellan allowed the Rebels to fall back to Virginia virtually unimpeded. For Nelson Miles, the battle meant new plaudits and a full colonelcy. Brigadier General Caldwell reported "[Miles] added to the laurels he has acquired on every battle-field" and handled his men "in a masterly manner." Barlow's praise was typically effusive.

"Miles behaved splendidly and is unhurt," he wrote his mother. In his official report he elaborated, "The voice of every one who saw him in this action will command better than I can his courage, his quickness, his skill in seeing favorable positions, and the power of his determined spirit in leading on and inspiring the men."[37]

President Lincoln seized the opportunity provided by Lee's strategic defeat to announce plans for emancipating slaves in areas under Rebel rule. He also hoped for aggressive action against Lee. But overcaution again undid McClellan. Neither cajoling, fatherly advice, nor a direct order would spur him into combat. In November, Lincoln removed McClellan in favor of Major General Ambrose Burnside, despite Burnside's protests. "[I am] not fit for so big a command," warned Burnside, who had twice refused Lincoln's previous offers. Pressured to attack the Confederate Army of Northern Virginia, Burnside settled on a frontal thrust across the Rappahannock River at Fredericksburg, Virginia. There he proved the wisdom of his words.[38]

On December 10, 1862, Federal troops began crossing the Rappahannock under cover of darkness. Three days later, the "grand division" of Major General William B. Franklin, a veteran of the Peninsular campaign, hit the Confederate right flank. As Franklin's assault stalled, another attack took place against Marye's Heights, at the base of which the Southerners held a stone wall. Broken terrain channeled the advance of what ultimately included fourteen Yankee brigades. Major General French's division was again shattered against the solid gray lines. About 11:00 A.M., fresh troops, including Miles's infantry, passed through the torn remnants of French's division to continue the fight. With a mile of open ground ahead of them, Miles's New Yorkers pushed to within forty yards of the enemy. There Miles urged brigade commander Caldwell to press onward, declaring that "it only needed a spirited charge with the bayonet." Caldwell, however, wisely deemed the suggestion "a wanton loss of brave men" and ordered a halt.[39]

Bristling at Caldwell's decision, Miles moved to screen the brigade's open right flank, where a group of riflemen had engaged a Confederate battery. Suddenly, a bullet tore open Miles's throat. As blood poured from his gaping wound, new units of bluecoats continued a fruitless charge against the Confederates. Though injured, Miles urged upon General Howard a new deployment of his men. But the troops' raw courage was not enough. When the slaughter finally ended just before dusk, Federal casualties stood near thirteen thousand; Lee's losses to-taled fewer than five thousand. Southerners still held the high ground dominating Fredericksburg as the Army of the Potomac retraced its steps across the Rappahannock.[40]

Despite the disaster, superiors again sang the praises of Nelson Miles. Caldwell, who had rejected Miles's request for another assault, nonetheless called attention to his "coolness, judgment, and intrepid-ity." Division commander Winfield Scott Hancock noted Miles's "ad-mirable and chivalrous manner," adding, "His battalion behaved with steadiness unsurpassed by any troops."[41]

Although Miles eventually took a thirty-day convalescent leave, the day after the battle he was strong enough to help compile his official report. The failed assault confirmed his belief "that nothing but the strictest discipline . . . [would] enable any commanding officer to handle his troops while under fire." Though awed by their command-er's bravery, his men seemed less certain of the virtues of the attack in which they had suffered 108 casualties out of 432 men engaged. One sardonic veteran later remembered that the "accommodating" Rebel bullet that hit Miles had added "to the longevity of the Sixty-firsters there present." Another concluded that a renewed advance would merely have pushed Miles "a little nearer than other regiments to the invincible lines of the enemy," thus securing a promotion for the colo-nel at the cost of human lives. And a staff officer later pointed out that even if the Yankees had taken the stone wall, they would have had to clamber up Marye's Heights against Confederate reserves.[42]

Like the Army of the Potomac, Miles spent the winter recovering from the Fredericksburg blood bath. He convalesced in his brother's home at Westminster, visited relatives, and grew a trim goatee to hide the scars left by his recent wound. On his way back to Washington, Nelson stopped at Albany and New York City to lobby for promotion to general. But he was puzzled by the continuing lack of assistance from Massachusetts and still bitter about having lost his captaincy a year and a half before. "I don't believe there is a Col. in the Army who has better recommendations than mine but I am not a politician," he explained to his brother. He called on relatives to press Senator Wilson. "It all goes by political favor," he explained.[43]

In the spring of 1863 Miles returned to his unit as dramatic changes swept the Army of the Potomac. "Fighting Joe" Hooker replaced the overmatched Burnside. Hooker brought fresh bread, better sanitation, and long-overdue pay and furloughs to his veterans. His introduction of corps and division insignia further enhanced the troops' morale. Though Miles's face reflected the death and destruction of the past year, he was spiritually rejuvenated and believed the army to be in peak condition. He and his men, now part of the First Brigade (led by Caldwell), the First Division (under Hancock), the Second Corps (led by Major General Darius Couch), were convinced that Hooker would lead them to victory. The new campaign opened impressively in late April as Hooker and seventy thousand men forded the Rappahannock west of Fredericksburg while Major General John Sedgwick and forty thousand troops held Lee's attention along the heights above Fredericksburg.[44]

By April 30, Hooker had passed the crossroads hamlet of Chancellorsville. Though still in the densely forested Wilderness, he was a mere nine miles west of Fredericksburg. "Our enemy must ingloriously fly," proclaimed an exuberant Hooker. But General Lee now recognized the threat to his left. Leaving ten thousand men to screen Sedgwick, he shifted some fifty thousand soldiers to face Hooker. Indecisive skirmishing on May 1 convinced the Union commander to fall back to Chancellorsville. Miles was in the thick of the fighting, his regiment filling a gap left by the premature retreat of units belonging to the Twelfth Corps. Impressed by Miles's cool handling of the situation, Hancock gave him command of all of the division's skirmishers. Miles immediately directed his men to dig rifle pits and erect timber abatis, further improving a fine defensive position.[45]

On May 2, Federals around Chancellorsville beat back Lee's demonstrations. Urging his men on, Miles assumed an aggressive defense in the thick underbrush behind Mott's Run and broke up Confederate probes well before they reached the main Union lines. Hancock marveled at Miles's efforts. "Ride down and tell Colonel Miles he is worth his weight in gold," he told an orderly. Of more practical significance was Hancock's selection of reinforcements for his beleaguered skirmishers—the ranking officers of the fresh troops were junior to Colonel Miles, thus ensuring that the latter retained command.[46]

But the main Confederate threat that day came not toward Chancellorsville but against the Union right flank, east of the Wilderness Tavern, held by Major General Howard's unlucky Eleventh Corps. Rushing out from what were thought to be impenetrable woods, Lieutenant General Stonewall Jackson's reinforced wing surprised Howard's men. Jackson's troops rolled up the Union line until dark. Though Jackson and his second-in-command, Major General A. P. Hill, both fell wounded (the former mortally injured by his own men's fire), Jackson's audacious move stunned Hooker. Thinking only of the defensive, despite his substantial numerical superiority, Hooker held back, allowing Lee to reunite the two wings of his army and renew his assaults the next day. Reinforcements reached Miles about 9 A.M. on the third, just in time to receive a fresh Rebel onslaught against Chancellorsville.[47]

Colonel Miles encouraged his troops by horseback as the shot and shells rained about him. About ten o'clock, a minié ball fired from the direction of the Tenth Georgia deflected off Miles's metal belt plate and entered his body near the navel, passing between the lining of his bowels before lodging near the point of his left hip. "The result," he remembered, "was an instant deathly sickening sensation. . . . I was completely paralyzed below the waist." The impact tore off his scabbard and belt; his sword dropped from his right hand. Soldiers carried him back to the Chancellor mansion, a crossroads house transformed into a crowded makeshift hospital. Someone pulled a corpse off a couch to make room for the new arrival.[48]

Here Miles found only brief respite. Assistant Surgeon Calvin P. W. Fisher dressed the wound but feared it would be fatal. A bursting shell turned the house into a fiery inferno; stretcher-bearers carried the colonel five miles into the Wilderness that night. On the fourth, as Lee turned his attention to the Federals who had finally broken through at Fredericksburg and a dazed Hooker established a defensive perimeter along the Rapidan River, an ambulance conveyed Miles twelve more miles over a jarring plank road to a field hospital. Still paralyzed below the waist, Miles filed his official after-action report on the fifth from the Lacey House Hospital in Falmouth, Virginia. He was subsequently moved to Washington, where his brother took him home to Massachusetts. Two weeks after the battle he finally mustered enough strength to move his right foot; the bullet was later extracted from his hip.[49]

Accolades from fellow officers eased some of the pain. General Caldwell, in recommending yet another promotion, described Miles's handling of the picket line as "masterly." In a personal letter to Miles he wrote that he had seen Hancock, Couch, and Hooker on Miles's behalf. "God speed your recovery," he added. "Your promotion is certain." Hancock described Miles's services as "brilliant." Couch reportedly told a group of officers, "I tell you what, gentlemen, I shall not be greatly surprised to find myself some day serving under that young man." From the regiment, subordinates decried the absence of their "beloved and highly esteemed colonel" and prayed for his recovery.[50]

Little in Miles's background had foreshadowed his military success. Although he had ambition, military forebears, and an affinity for the army, these scarcely guaranteed military distinction. His decision to risk his financial future by raising a company after First Bull Run was a stroke of genius, for even though he lost his captain's bars to political intrigue, he did guarantee his commission.

Now painfully aware of the role of politics in the army, Miles soon proved himself on the battlefield. He possessed courage in abundance. His troops knew that he would be at the forefront of any engagement. But his heroics, though inspirational, had often endangered his and his soldiers' safety. As General Sumner once observed: "That officer will get promoted or get killed." Indeed, Miles had much to learn about tactics; his foolhardy insistence on continuing the assault at Fredericksburg even earned the temporary enmity of his own men. But with experience he mastered the intricacies of selecting suitable terrain, as witnessed in his outstanding defense at Chancellorsville, for which he later received a Medal of Honor.[51]

Miles also possessed a great deal of soldier's luck. Had he not been stripped of his captaincy in the Twenty-second Massachusetts, he might not have benefited from the sponsorship and experience of men like Barlow and Howard. Too, the move to Barlow's regiment brought Miles under the division command of Israel B. Richardson. Dubbed "Fighting Dick" for his exploits during the war against Mexico, Richardson conducted rigorous military training tempered with an informality suitable for volunteer soldiers. Miles also served under Winfield Scott Hancock, who succeeded the fallen Richardson and became one of the North's ablest generals. Though Miles's brigade commander John Caldwell sometimes absented himself from the thick of the action, Colonels Barlow and Edward E. Cross, another veteran of the bloodbath at Antietam, were solid combat leaders. "All in all," one historian has written, the division "was as formidable as any in the Army of the Potomac." Surrounded by men such as these, Miles could indeed go far.[52]

2 : DIVISION COMMANDER

Though Nelson Miles had established his reputation as a combat leader, he had yet to command large formations. Like others in the Army of the Potomac, he had displayed exceptional feats of bravery. But courage alone could not defeat Robert E. Lee's Army of Northern Virginia. Supremely confident in themselves, their cause, and their leaders, the Confederates readied for yet another invasion of the North that summer. Meanwhile, confusion and discontent spread through the Union lines. General Darius Couch, the able leader of the Second Corps, was disgusted with recent failures and resigned his command for an independent station in the Department of the Susquehanna.[1]

Still on crutches from his Chancellorsville wound, Miles left Massachusetts in June 1863 in a futile effort to rejoin his command. "We miss you in the Regt.," wrote one subordinate. "We want your cheerfull countenance and humour, to relieve the camp of its tedious monotony, as well as your cool & deliberate council and direction in keeping things well ballanced." But the wound was too painful. Even though he was unable to withstand active duty, he could at least help Couch organize Pennsylvania militia against the invading Confederates.[2]

Miles assumed command of 73 officers and 1,514 men at Huntingdon, where he readied to block mountain passes into central Pennsylvania should Lee's legions continue their advance. Though anxious to return to the army, Miles needed time for healing and reflection. Although his recent stay in Massachusetts had been too short, the mountains of Huntingdon County provided a beautiful backdrop for his convalescence. Miles boarded at a pleasant house and enjoyed the support of a cooperative staff. "But a soldier's life is not one of luxury and I fear I am indulging myself to[o] much for my good," he admitted. He observed later that "the only trouble was that no enemy was near." Nor did the Confederate threat materialize close by. The Army of the Potomac, now under the competent if uninspired leadership of General George G. Meade, won a three-day battle some fifty miles southeast of Huntingdon at Gettysburg, where approximately fifty thousand Americans fell.[3]

Miles well knew the importance of politics and took pains to visit the capital before returning to the Army of the Potomac. Never one to miss a career opportunity, he called at the White House, only to find President Lincoln out of his office. Yet Barlow and Hancock did not forget their talented young protégé. With their help, Miles assumed command of a brigade in Barlow's First Division, Second Corps. His First Brigade consisted of his old Sixty-first New York Regiment, now led by the Swedish-born Lieutenant Colonel Knut O. Broady, a solid subordinate; the Eighty-first Pennsylvania, commanded by a trusted friend, Colonel Harry Boyd McKean; and the 148th Pennsylvania, under Colonel James A. Beaver, recently a fellow convalescent in the Department of the Susquehanna.[4]

"I had a very pleasant time among the mountains of Penn . . ., but my post is at the front there I am at home," explained Miles. But many familiar faces were missing. New conscripts, "far below the grade of *volunteers*," could not replace the veterans lost during the Gettysburg blood bath. Miles worried that his brigade, its ranks swollen with draftees and substitutions, might not perform well under fire.[5]

Bodily aches and personal crises complicated Miles's return to the Army of the Potomac. He refused to allow surgeons to reopen his abdominal wound, but briefly contemplated going north for special saltwater treatments. News from home was equally disheartening. In early August he received word that his father and mother had separated (the former eventually resettled in Brattleboro, Vermont). A disconsolate Miles told his aunt, "I fear it will not seem like home again." Matters went from bad to worse in late September, when a female admirer stopped writing. "I have not had a letter," worried the would-be suitor, "*for a week.* I do not know what the trouble is."[6]

But the melancholy soon passed. Westminster citizens took up a collection to replace the sword he lost at Chancellorsville, and his father brought the new one during a brief visit. The routine of camp life also buoyed his spirits. Training, drills, and work on various boards of officers helped pass the time between campaigns. Miles, now seasoned by two years of war, wisely winked at minor transgressions by his veterans. One soldier remembered that Miles, upon learning that some of his men had grabbed "a good-sized pig," let them go with a caution that they never allow themselves to "be *caught* again." The grateful men sent him "a neat roast from a hind quarter."[7]

The interlude between battles extended into the fall of 1863 as both armies licked the wounds they had received at Gettysburg. Miles proclaimed the Warrenton area "the finest country . . . to be found in Virginia." A stately grove of trees graced the fine house used as brigade headquarters. The grandeur of neighboring plantations and the nearby resort of Sulphur Springs further enhanced the pleasant setting; the local church reminded Miles of his serene Westminster childhood. Yet the lull could not hide the war's carnage. "There was a sadness about it," Miles admitted. "There is scarcely a male citizen in the town and almost every lady is dressed in mourning."[8]

Failures of the Yankee high command proved increasingly frustrating to Miles and his comrades as they girded themselves for further action. The Second Corps' excellent showing during a minor encounter at Bristoe Station, Virginia, on October 14 strengthened his desire to fight again. Miles criticized Meade for failing to pursue Lee. "I have not the least doubt but we might have been in Richmond," wrote Miles.

"The rebels I think are not so strong as we have met them on former occasions." His speculations about strategic affairs during that fall evidenced his growing military acumen. He admitted that Meade, in being forced to operate on exterior lines, faced built-in disadvantages. Yet the general remained, in Miles's view, far too cautious to win the war.[9]

In late November the Union's Mine Run offensive buoyed its morale as the Army of the Potomac crossed the Rapidan River. The First Brigade led the advance, driving the enemy *"pell-mell"* for three miles. Yet because of Meade's overcaution the army had, in Miles's words, missed a *"golden opportunity"* by not rolling up the Confederate line when presented with the chance. "This is now the second time we have retreated before the enemy with a force inferior to our own and without a battle," Miles complained. "One victory gained now by this army would have ended the war." But the campaign ground to a halt.[10]

Miles also displayed a greater awareness of the western front. Renewed pressure on Lee, he theorized, would prevent Lee from reinforcing the Confederate Army of Tennessee. He blasted Major General William S. Rosecrans's leadership at Chickamauga and reported a rumor that Lee himself was going west. "I hope this is so for Lee is a hard *old nut*," he joked. News of Ulysses S. Grant's smashing victory at Chattanooga led Miles to conclude that Lee might, if pressured, evacuate Virginia. Miles's only regret: "Our failing to whip Lee this fall will prolong the war at least a year."[11]

Following a month-long recruiting stint in New York City, Miles witnessed numerous changes when he returned to field duty in early 1864. On March 12, Grant was named General in Chief of the Armies of the United States. Meade remained at the head of the Army of the Potomac, but Grant would accompany that force and direct its strategic operations. Hancock again led the Second Corps; Barlow, by this time a general, returned from his convalescent leave to resume command of the First Division. Colonel Miles still headed the First Brigade, which now included the Sixty-first New York; the Eighty-first, 140th, and 183d Pennsylvania; and the Twenty-sixth Michigan regiments. As the two armies sparred along the Rapidan River, Miles tested his new command by seizing some enemy pickets on March 26.[12]

"A united North is sure to overpower them unless we make some grand mistakes this fall," Miles had predicted six months earlier. Though mistakes had been made, none had been serious enough to break Union resolve. With Grant's emergence as chief strategist, the Army of the Potomac would attempt in the spring of 1864 to coordinate its operations with other armies along the Red River, the Shenandoah Valley, the James River, and against Georgia. Though campaigns in Louisiana, western Virginia, and south of Richmond soon bogged down, the unified effort represented a major break from previous Federal strategy.[13]

Grant initially moved against Lee's extended left flank, west of Fredericksburg. Bolstered by Barlow's return, Miles's brigade broke camp during the evening of May 3, and crossed the Rapidan with the rest of Hancock's Second Corps. In an eerie replay of the events of 1863, the First Brigade bivouacked on the Chancellorsville battlefield about 5 P.M. the next day. Blooming dogwoods, huckleberry bushes, and wild roses only partially covered the unburied bones of the previous year's gruesome contest. On the fifth, the Second Corps resumed its march southwest of the Chancellor mansion. Lee, however, struck Grant's army before it could disentangle itself from the thick underbrush. Falling upon the Federal Fifth and Sixth Corps, the Confederates handed Grant a serious defeat in the Battle of the Wilderness.[14]

Hancock meanwhile had countermarched to link up with the exposed Union left. Although the corps as a whole suffered grievous losses, Miles reported only twenty-four casualties in his brigade. On the evening of May 7, having failed to turn Lee's left flank, Grant began moving southeast toward Spotsylvania Court House. Hancock dispatched Miles in the meantime to investigate rumors about a Confederate assault to the west. The probes stirred up trouble; Miles conducted a fighting retreat during which he repulsed two Rebel attacks "with great skill and success," according to Hancock.[15]

But the Confederates won the race to Spotsylvania Court House. West of the Spotsylvania crossroads Hancock subsequently threw three divisions across the narrow, heavily wooded Po River. Meade, not wanting to fight south of the Po, on May 10 ordered Hancock's withdrawal. Occupying a crest on the stream's south bank, Miles's rear guard again threw back two Confederate assaults as the corps retired that afternoon.[16]

The drive against Lee's right flank having failed, Grant shifted his attention to the Confederate center. On the eleventh, as Miles demonstrated along the Po River, the Federals assembled for a major thrust against an exposed Rebel salient known as the "Mule Shoe" for its odd shape. The men of First Brigade, exhausted by the previous day's skirmish, now embarked on a forced march to position themselves for the attack. Riding blindly at the head of the column, General Barlow and his fellow officers protested the proposed strike, which was to be made with little knowledge of either terrain or enemy dispositions. As Barlow later recalled, Miles in particular "was so emphatic in his indignation that I was at last compelled to . . . tell him to be quiet." The assault having been scheduled for 4 A.M., Miles's troops got little sleep in the damp, chilly weather.[17]

Dense fog delayed the attack until 4:35. The Confederate lines lay up a hill nearly a mile away, but woods covered all save the last four hundred yards. Barlow's division, with Miles and Colonel John R. Brooke leading the advance and two more brigades in reserve, composed the left wing. Using innovative storm tactics successfully employed by Colonel Emory Upton two days earlier at Spotsylvania Court House, Barlow massed each regiment in a double column rather than the traditional linear assault formation. Miles sent his horse to the rear and placed himself at the head of his men as the attack began.[18]

The division advanced at quick time for several hundred yards. In a tremendous stroke of good fortune, the Confederate artillery had been removed from the salient for a counterattack elsewhere. The Federals sliced across a shallow draw through sleepy Rebel pickets, then broke "into a tremendous cheer, and spontaneously taking the double-quick, they rolled like an irresistible wave into the enemy's works." Capturing two generals, thirty stands of colors, four thousand men, and twenty pieces of artillery that had only just been returned to the area, the jubilant Second Corps struggled to re-form and deliver a death blow to the Confederacy.[19]

But the Army of Northern Virginia was made of sterner stuff. Reserves threw up a second line of earthworks at the base of the salient. Lee, feeding in every available man, checked the Northern thrust and pushed Hancock's men back to the original Rebel lines. Fighting at pointblank range through a cool, drenching rain until midnight, blue and gray struggled with unparalleled frenzy. Cannon poured in round after round of shell and canister; rifle fire cut down trees; bayonets jabbed through the entrenchments. Dead and wounded bodies were trampled in the muck as reinforcements joined the melee, known forever after as the Bloody Angle. The Southerners retreated to the base of the salient that evening but their line remained unbroken.

Miles remembered the awful carnage as "a spectacle of horror without a parallel." "So desperate was the struggle that after the battle was over," he later declared, "it was impossible to walk over the field near the line of earthworks without stepping upon the dead bodies of soldiers." His own brigade lost six hundred of the twenty-two hundred engaged.[20]

Although the fighting had turned into a bloody quagmire, the initial success at Bloody Angle remained one of the war's most remarkable feats. With virtually no information on enemy dispositions, the Second Corps had captured an entire Confederate brigade. Nelson Miles played a prominent role in the conflict. As a subordinate wrote, "he did not seem to mind the bullets and shells buzzing past him any more than if they were so many bees." General Barlow redoubled his efforts on Miles's behalf, as did Hancock. General Meade in turn requested that Miles be promoted "for distinguished gallantry on several occasions in the face of the enemy." The Senate agreed, confirming Miles as a brigadier general of volunteers retroactive to May 12, 1864.[21]

Grant, meanwhile, braced for continued action. "I propose to fight it out on this line if it takes all summer," he wired Washington. He ordered another assault at Spotsylvania, against what he presumed to be weakened defenses. On May 17, Barlow's division again moved forward. But twelve days of nearly continuous action had exhausted many in the Union ranks. Sickened by the sights and smells of the bloated, decomposing bodies at Bloody Angle, the Federals failed to crack the line held by the Rebels.[22]

Grant now opted for another effort against Lee's right flank, with Hancock's Second Corps spearheading the drive against the strategic railroad interchange of Hanover Junction, twenty-two miles south of Spotsylvania. But Lee again won the race. Confederate positions seemed impenetrable. On May 25, an exhausted Miles found a few minutes to write home. "I have been spared thus far by kind providence," he wrote. "We have been marching & fighting almost every day for almost a month and this is the hardest campaign I ever was in." But the contest had just begun; Grant, still seeking to outflank Lee, again swung south and east.[23]

Skirmishing along the Totopotomoy Creek on May 30 and June 1 revealed to Grant the strong Confederate positions, so he shifted southeast toward Cold Harbor. The Second New York Heavy Artillery joined the First Brigade, thus replacing some of the casualties suffered earlier that spring. The brigade broke camp about ten on the evening of the first, having been further reinforced by the Fifth New Hampshire, fresh from a long leave. Though boasting a proud record, the Fifth got off to a bad start—during that night's arduous march, a frightened mule set off a panic among their ranks. The long trek, combined with further skirmishing on June 2, served to delay the assault against Cold Harbor until the morning of the third.[24]

Grant hoped to parley his two-to-one numerical advantage into a final shattering blow. Forming the Union left, the divisions of Barlow and Brigadier General John Gibbon composed Hancock's first wave in the daylight assault. The brigades of Miles and Brooke assumed their customary role in the vanguard. With little intelligence about enemy positions, the lead brigades set off at the double quick through the mud caused by the previous night's rains. They briefly breached the Confederate lines, but enfilading fire forced the First Brigade back to a low crest fifty yards from the Rebel works. Here, despite severe pressure, they dug in and held their advanced position.[25]

Barlow's troops had done better than most of their comrades in blue. Though the division "showed a persistency rarely seen," the frontal assault at Cold Harbor failed disastrously. Union casualties were put at seven thousand; Confederate losses were less than fifteen hundred. Hancock acknowledged the defeat as "a blow to the corps from which it did not soon recover." Reeling from the past month's losses (the North had lost some fifty thousand men and the South about thirty-two thousand), the two armies, front lines one hundred yards apart, paused to gather their second wind. Only on June 7, four days after the debacle at Cold Harbor, did a truce allow the dead and wounded to be cleared. The hard fighting, heroism, and staggering losses had seemed for naught; General Miles again reflected on missed opportunities of the past.[26]

But still another chance soon presented itself. Blocked at Cold Harbor, Grant planned a looping swing south of Richmond against the railroad junction at Petersburg. On June 12, the Army of the Potomac began crossing the Chickahominy River. Major General William F. Smith, commanding the Eighteenth Corps and a detachment from Hancock's Second Corps, missed a golden opportunity by failing to take the thinly held Petersburg three days later. The delay proved fatal, for on the sixteenth reinforced Confederate positions threw back uncoordinated Union attacks. Miles reported that Grant's maneuvers were "splendid"; he blamed the failures on Generals Smith, Burnside, Meade, Ben Butler (responsible for the fiasco on the James Peninsula), and Quincy A. Gillmore (a participant in the as yet unsuccessful efforts to catch Jubal Early in the Shenandoah Valley).[27]

Miles's First Brigade had done well at Petersburg, seizing the first Rebel line of rifle pits. But renewed attacks by the Army of the Potomac two days later miscarried, as did a final push on the twenty-second. The most recent assaults had lacked the vigor of earlier thrusts. As Barlow frankly admitted, the "loss of commanding and other officers, exhaustion and other causes have so affected the three concerned in these operations, Second, Third, and Fourth Brigades, that they cannot just now be relied on to meet critical emergencies with much determination and spirit." Only by calling up Miles's First Brigade had he repulsed a Confederate counterattack. Though in better shape than any other brigade in the division, the First also needed rest. "You cannot imagine how worn out and tired the army is," wrote Miles in a moment of weary reflection, again thanking Providence that he was still alive. He asked for more letters from home and apologized for not having written. Considering the constant marching, skirmishing, and fighting, Miles explained, "In this campaign I think if I send word that I am alive every few days I am doing well."[28]

Emotionally spent, Miles reviewed the horrors of the past eight weeks. Since the opening of Grant's summer offensive on May 5, Miles's brigade (now further reinforced by the Twenty-eighth Massachusetts) had lost 2,110 men—nearly two-thirds of its original strength. His own horse had been shot; a bullet had split the new sword his father had brought him, and his wounds still pained him. His best friend, Colonel Harry B. McKean, had fallen at Cold Harbor. And in the recent fighting around Petersburg, a cannonball had decapitated the man next to him, as he described it, "blowing his brains all over my coat cap & face. I thought it a pretty close call." Miles, now aged beyond his years, concluded, "About the only solice I have is my Brigade Band."[29]

Although shattered by the fighting, the Second Corps dug in as the siege of Petersburg commenced. Rebel sharpshooters lent an air of danger to the tedious proceedings. Behind the front lines, soldiers experimented with various forms of recreation—Colonel Broady, for example, organized a slate of horse races. Through Hancock's auspices, Miles finagled a dinner engagement with Grant, whom he admired. Miles quickly distinguished the bulldog-like Grant from the more politically minded Ben Butler, another invitee. Though Miles thought him "a very pleasant man," Grant seemed to him to be "more of a lawyer than General." Butler's lone advantages—his charming wife and daughter—were not present. "[I] would not mind taking *a sneeze at his daughter*," admitted Miles. And his family matters were not forgotten. He promised to try to secure a commission for his brother Daniel. But military life had lost much of its former glamor. He warned his brother, "I do not think you would be as well of[f] as you are now."[30]

After two weeks off the line, the Second Corps again swung into action in late July. Some coal miners from Burnside's Ninth Corps had hatched an ambitious new scheme to blow a hole in the Confederate lines by tunneling beneath enemy trenches and setting off four tons of explosives. To divert attention, Hancock moved north of the James River against the Confederates at Deep Bottom. On the morning of July 27, Miles's brigade spearheaded the attack. Union troops seized four Confederate Parrott guns, but in the face of heavy opposition the advance soon faltered. Though the four regiments that had captured the heavy artillery received special commendations, most other Federals had shied away from making frontal assaults. Skirmishing the following day also proved inconclusive.[31]

The men returned from the Deep Bottom failure in time to witness Burnside's attack against Petersburg. In fact, one observer reported that a spent Rebel cannonball came "to rest in a very respectful manner directly beneath a stretcher upon which General Miles was resting." The explosives set by the miners created a huge crater in the Rebel lines, but the attackers turned into a disorganized mob while their division commander sipped medicinal rum. Overcoming their initial shock, the Confederates counterattacked and transformed the Crater into a killing field. Miles later joined Hancock on a board of officers appointed to investigate the bloody fiasco; initially delayed by fighting along the Deep Bottom line, the board eventually censured Burnside and four other officers for the botched Crater offensive.[32]

While the board considered the evidence, intervening probing attacks at Deep Bottom reflected the diminished combat effectiveness of Hancock's corps. Clumsy attempts by the Second Corps at subterfuge postponed the attack but failed to deceive the Confederates. Badly managed, the lead troops from the Second Corps finally swung into action late in the afternoon of August 14. Again, however, the men, drained by the summer heat, the loss of a night's sleep in the poorly conceived effort to mislead the enemy, and the staggering losses of recent months, refused to press the fight. "None of the troops that came under my observation that day behaved with their usual vigor and gallantry under fire," commented Barlow, himself wracked by the pain from wounds incurred at Antietam and Gettysburg. Skirmishing on the sixteenth also included Miles's brigade, which suffered 274 of the division's 434 casualties.[33]

On the seventeenth, Barlow handed divisional command over to his best subordinate—Brigadier General Nelson Miles. His health broken, Barlow would not resume permanent command for nearly nine months. Hancock and Miles proposed another attack on the nineteenth, only to be deterred by Grant. Down to some six thousand men, Hancock's riddled corps was instead assigned the job of destroying railroad lines south of Petersburg at Reams' Station.[34]

Although the assignment was meant to give the Second Corps a break from combat, the long marches through the humid Virginia summer exacted a brutal toll. On the twenty-fourth, Hancock noted, "[Miles] reports his men as tired out." The corps occupied a previously erected U-shaped defensive position after hearing reports that large bodies of Confederate infantry were nearby. Though several officers later commented on the poor design of the works—the sides of the perimeter were too close together, and friendly artillery gunners were exposed to Rebel sharpshooters—little was done to strengthen the site. Miles, holding the northern face, did his best to cajole his exhausted soldiers to slash timber for protection and to improve communication by cutting new roads.[35]

At noon on August 25, Confederate assaults indeed commenced. Miles drove back three attacks. During the fourth, however, units in the center and on the right flank collapsed. General Miles coolly called up his reserves. But their commander was nowhere to be found and his men had either surrendered or fled. Attempts to plug the gap failed when the 152d New York also broke. By this time, Miles admitted, "the panic had become somewhat general, and it was with the greatest difficulty that any line could be formed." Seeking to stem the retreat, Miles led his old Sixty-first New York in a desperate counterattack that recaptured several cannon, while Hancock and staff officers restored a semblance of order.[36]

Furious at the behavior of his men, Miles suggested an evening attack. Hancock rejected this option and instead took stock of the situation. His Second Corps, once the pride of the Army of the Potomac, had been dishonored on the field. Miles's troops had at least driven off three assaults; on the southern face of the line, John Gibbon's division had broken with scarcely a fight. Only the charismatic leadership of Generals Miles and Hancock had rallied a few stalwarts and averted even greater disaster. The Federal killed and wounded numbered some six hundred men; Confederate casualties exceeded seven hundred. But the Second Corps also lost nine guns and twelve colors and two thousand of its men were taken prisoner.[37]

Hancock blamed the debacle on the lack of experienced junior officers, the failure of others to reinforce the salient, and the poor quality of recent recruits. Though well aware of his outfit's declining effectiveness, Miles could not bring himself to recognize that both he and his troops had been pushed beyond human endurance. Instead, he found a convenient scapegoat in his immigrant draftees. Miles maintained that his men had brushed aside the attacks until the Confederates hit "a few dutch [German] cowards." Not above a bit of self-promotion for his old command, he told the now-departed Barlow that "the *glorious* 61st was the only *cool* regiment on the field." He concluded, "The battle was lost by cowardice." Despite the failure, Miles earned a brevet major generalship for his determined leadership.[38]

Following the disaster at Reams' Station, the Second Corps returned to siege duty outside Petersburg. Miles and his men built artillery redoubts, strongpoints, and secondary lines of defense along the Union right, near Fort Stedman and the Appomattox River. On October 3, Hancock issued an indirect reprimand against Miles, whose First Division, along with Gibbon's Second, had not been fully under arms at daylight. Determined to impress his superior, Miles redoubled his vigilance, later requesting that an engineer officer sink shafts to detect suspected enemy mines.[39]

Meanwhile, Grant continued to probe Lee's flanks. In late October, Hancock pulled two divisions out of line to join a thrust against the Confederate right. Miles's First Division thus assumed the front formerly held by the entire corps. Hancock regretted wasting Miles's talents in a static defense, but he feared that the high proportion of green troops rendered Miles's unit unfit for field duty. Smarting from the defeat at Reams' Station, Miles determined to regain his stature and to deceive the enemy as to his strength. After nightfall on the twenty-seventh, one hundred men from the 148th Pennsylvania made a demonstration against the Rebels. This audacious move brought in forty-four Confederate prisoners before Miles's men fell back to safety.[40]

But the laurels won on the twenty-seventh could not hide the division's inexperience. During the evening of October 30, more than 80 surprised pickets from the Sixty-ninth New York, believing the men in blue caps and light blue overcoats who had infiltrated their position to be a Yankee relief force, allowed themselves to be captured by Confederates. General Miles declared that deserters had given his position to the enemy. Treason could have indeed contributed to the loss; also noteworthy, however, was the presence of 190 recruits among the 230 men on the line.[41]

Miles needed time to invigorate his shaken command. But as the recruits were slowly transformed into soldiers, he could afford to devote more attention to his personal affairs. Although his battle wounds still troubled him, particularly in damp weather, and a mid-October fever left him weakened for several days, his two horses—a black stallion, "as useful as ever and full of his tricks," and an elegant gray, "as fine a parade horse as there is in the army"—offered pleasant diversions. Following the departure of his personal servant, Miles found and hired "a 'colored individual'" who he described as "a very fancy duck."[42]

The general continued to send much of his pay to his father to invest on his behalf. But ever the pragmatist, Nelson asked his uncle, to whom he had drawn progressively closer, to confirm that his father had carried through with his financial obligations. The money, as Nelson explained truthfully, "was dearly earned." On December 7, 1864, he sent his cherished appointment papers that granted his brevet major generalship for his action at Reams' Station to his uncle and aunt for safekeeping, a further sign of his deteriorating relations with his parents.[43]

While suffering through the alternating tedium and tension of the front lines, Miles continued to follow the diplomatic, military, and political developments further afield. In September he again predicted war with England or France. As for events closer to home, he now blamed the Union's inability to take Richmond on the failures of Meade and a legion of corps commanders. He approved of General

William T. Sherman's western campaigns and delighted in Phil Sheridan's spectacular success in the Shenandoah Valley. Sheridan's narrow victory at Cedar Creek would, in Miles's view, "decide the [upcoming presidential] election in Lincoln's favor." Lincoln's Democratic opponent, George McClellan, once "the pride & ideal of the army," had, according to Miles, "become very unpopular by mingling with the enemies of his country." For once Miles proved an accurate political forecaster. On election day the First Division, like the army as a whole, voted overwhelmingly Republican.[44]

Despite Lincoln's victory, the immediate future offered to the men of the Army of the Potomac only more of the skirmishing, sniper fire, bomb proofs, dugouts, and rats of Petersburg. Miles suffered a fourth wound during the siege when a bullet ricocheted off his sword and hit his shoulder, penetrating the flesh but causing no serious injury. During a two-and-a-half-month period ending November 10, the division was off the front lines for only two days. But the Second Corps would now fight without General Winfield Scott Hancock, who departed to raise a new corps of veterans. Major General Andrew A. Humphreys, formerly Meade's chief of staff, assumed command of Hancock's old corps.[45]

Conditions made it difficult to assimilate incoming recruits, who by December 6 composed one-half of the First Division's 6,336 enlisted men. Miles labeled these untested men a "hard set," but Humphreys deemed them ready. On the ninth, Miles took three brigades of his infantry, three cavalry regiments, and several artillery batteries to test enemy positions at Hatcher's Run, south of Petersburg. The recently dammed river, four feet deep and fifty feet wide, presented a formidable obstacle. Fallen trees and rifle pits further strengthened the Confederate works.[46]

General Meade worried that the raid might expose the division to a flank attack. "I hope Miles will be on the alert," he fretted. But Grant ignored Meade's caution, ordering Miles to use whatever methods he deemed appropriate to force a crossing. His initial efforts having failed, Miles wheeled up two cannon and asked for volunteers from the Second New York. Receiving none, he ordered Captain George A. Armes and two companies to ford the cold waters. Furious with Miles for his having refused a recent request for a leave, Armes complied nonetheless, and in the face of heavy fire his men seized a foothold on the opposite bank. Miles fed in reinforcements, enlarged the lodgment, and swept the other side of Hatcher's Run with cavalry scouts until he was ordered to retreat the following day. At a cost of fewer than thirty-five men, the effort, Miles believed, "proved that any position, however difficult, could be carried by determined men if led by brave officers." He recommended Armes and two other officers from the Second New York for promotion.[47]

As the army readied for a spring offensive in 1865, Miles continued to assert himself. He presided over the corps board that set policy on battle-flag inscriptions, and suggested that orders explaining the North's humane treatment of Confederate deserters "be printed on very thin paper, and in high winds be let off from the signal stations," so as to spread them among the Rebels. This, he theorized, might encourage more Southerners to abandon their cause. More importantly, Miles briefly assumed command of the Second Corps in mid-February during Humphreys's leave of absence. But controversy marked his temporary increase in duties, for the day after Miles received his new assignment, the Senate confirmed the appointment of Brevet Major General Gershom Mott, Third Division, retroactive to August 1, 1864. Because Miles's brevet rank dated August 25, 1864, Mott assumed corps command by virtue of his seniority. The army reversed itself two days later, undoubtedly having noted Miles's superior fighting record. Mott's promotion was postdated to September 9, according to the War Department's most recent interpretation of the date of Miles's promotion. With that change, Brevet Major General Nelson A. Miles assumed the job.[48]

He immediately pushed out skirmishers to straighten his picket line. Because he failed to warn his superiors of his intentions, the initiative was not entirely appreciated by army command. "The change was so slight that I did not deem it of sufficient importance to be reported," explained Miles. Meade's worried chief of staff responded, "It was sufficient to force [Confederate] General [Henry] Heth to put under marching orders three-fourths of his command. Had it been known that you had advanced your picket-line the cause of this action of General Heth would have been apparent." Undeterred by this minor rebuke and anxious to improve the quality of life for his tired men, Miles demanded an increase in the bread ration.[49]

Humphreys returned in time to command the Second Corps during what would be the final campaign of the eastern theater. Lee opened the action on March 25 with an assault against Federal works around

Fort Stedman. Although they surprised the fort's sleepy defenders, the soldiers in gray were too weak to exploit their breakthrough. Confederate demonstrations against the Second Corps later that afternoon disrupted the hoopla resulting from a three o'clock presidential review but failed to penetrate Miles's front. "Scarcely a skulker or coward was noticed in the rear of the line of battle," he proclaimed.[50]

Determined to exploit the victory, Grant prepared his own assault. Miles, with the war's end tantalizingly near, was so busy that he could not even escort his friend Major Albert A. Pope on a tour of his own command. The brigade had "fought splendidly" and "handsomely whiped" the Rebels. "I think this campaign which opens tomorrow may be the final one," Miles predicted on March 28. Instructions to his men reflected this optimism. "The troops should rely more upon the bayonet, which is the most powerful weapon," read his general orders. Any regiments that broke under fire would suffer the ignominy of disbandment. Skirmishers were to contest every foot of ground. Finally, all available men, including cooks, attendants, and hospital patients, would be in the front lines.[51]

On the twenty-ninth, the Union advance commenced. Humphreys's Second Corps and Major General Gouverneur K. Warren's Fifth Corps slogged forward through heavy rains and rough terrain to support Phil Sheridan's thirteen thousand cavalrymen as they threatened the Confederate right. Eager to boost morale, Miles, in an action that surely would have nettled his prohibitionist father, requested permission to issue a ration of whiskey and to bring up the division band. On the morning of March 31 a surprise Confederate counterthrust temporarily pushed the Fifth Corps back. Miles, acting "in the promptest and most spirited manner," fell upon the exposed Rebel left flank. Taking several hundred prisoners, Miles called on the Fifth Corps to help exploit his breakthrough.[52]

But the opportunity was lost. Warren, who as staff engineer at the Battle of Gettysburg had instantly grasped the significance of taking and holding the crucial Little Round Top, proved more sluggish here in the fields south of Petersburg. Indeed, Sheridan relieved him the following day for not pressing a similar advantage. And within the First Division, elements of the First Brigade had inadvertently swerved into those of the Third, thus preventing even Miles from capitalizing on the situation.[53]

Sheridan did, however, finally secure the strategic crossroads at Five

Forks, southwest of Petersburg. The collapse of Petersburg seemed imminent. Grant pulled Miles, known for his aggressive record, out of line to reinforce Sheridan. Upon Miles's arrival at daylight on April 2, Sheridan threw his troops against thinly held Confederate positions at the junction of the White Oak and Claiborne roads. Miles pressed the attack home and drove the enemy back toward Sutherland's Station, Petersburg's lone remaining railroad link with the rest of the South. "I am close behind the enemy who are flying in perfect disorder," he scribbled hastily. "Please send forward all my ambulances, teams, ammunition, &c."[54]

Without pausing for his artillery, Miles launched two brigades into the teeth of strong Rebel breastworks at Sutherland's Station. But Henry Heth's stubborn defenders threw back the Yankees. Miles organized a second thrust, this time supported by a few guns, just after noon. Again the attack miscarried. Undaunted, Miles sent a reinforced line of skirmishers against the enemy's right flank. Heth's attention now diverted, Miles launched his reserve Fourth Brigade against the Confederate left. "At 2:45 p.m. the brigade advanced at double quick, with a hearty cheer and in magnificent order," reported Miles, as the third charge overwhelmed the enemy. A thousand prisoners, two pieces of artillery, and another Rebel battle flag fell to the triumphant First Division.[55]

Sheridan hoped to throw the Fifth Corps behind Miles in a battle of annihilation around Petersburg. A dispute with corps commander Humphreys, however, forced Sheridan to send the Fifth Corps back toward Five Forks, away from Lee's line of retreat. Disappointed, Sheridan also relinquished command of Miles's division as Lee temporarily eluded the Union noose. Still, the end seemed near, with Miles again having displayed exceptional abilities. Meade dubbed Miles's attack at Sutherland's Station "brilliant"; Grant seemed even more pleased. "Miles has made a big thing of it and deserves the highest praise for the pertinacity with which he stuck to the enemy until he wrung from them the victory," he wrote.[56]

Dangerously close to being trapped, Lee fled west with fewer than thirty thousand underfed soldiers. Petersburg and Richmond fell as Lee cajoled his men toward Amelia Courthouse. Eager to finish off the Rebels, Miles strove to ensure that his men received proper rations for the task. The opportunity to win the war must not be lost. "Every officer must use his utmost endeavors to encourage the troops and keep his command in hand, and it is hoped that the troops will submit to the inconvenience cheerfully in order to disperse or capture the enemy," Miles instructed.[57]

On April 6, the Second Corps caught Lee's rear guard protecting the Southern supply train as it crossed Sayler's Creek. "Nothing could have been finer than the spirit of the officers and men," wrote Humphreys. With a great cheer, the Federals breached the Confederate line; Miles's troops grabbed two cannon, four flags, and 250 supply wagons. That evening saw Miles's division bivouac amid the loot, feasting on Southern crackers and coffee and dividing up the remnants of the Confederate treasury. Exuberant Yankees wagered worthless Rebel money in joyous card games. "The veterans proceeded with the comedy," remembered Miles, "and such preposterous gambling was probably never before witnessed," as millions in Southern greenbacks exchanged hands.[58]

The pursuit continued the following day, with Miles still nipping at the Rebel left. Heavy enemy fire and broken terrain checked a First Brigade attack that afternoon. Even as Grant and Lee began exchanging notes concerning possible surrender terms, Miles believed the end had come. "I can send a communication through my picket to the enemy to-night," he told his superiors on the seventh. "The lines are very close together here and the enemy's pickets have called over, asking if a flag of truce would be received."[59]

On the eighth, Miles's division marched from 6 A.M. to 4 P.M., then tramped another five miles after their evening meal as the two armies neared Appomattox Courthouse. Lee attempted one last breakout the following morning. The Confederates struggled through clouds of cavalry only to find rank upon rank of Federal infantry in place. Outnumbered by over five to one, Lee knew the game was up. "There is nothing left for me to do but go and see General Grant," he rued, "and I would rather die a thousand deaths." The war in the east was over.[60]

Amid the strains of "Hail Columbia," Miles's First Division celebrated the final triumph. "The shouts of victory and peace swelled from a hundred thousand throats and above all reechoed such continued thunder from double-charged cannon, firing blank cartridges, as has seldom been heard on any battlefield," Miles remembered later. "At the same time the air was full of hats, canteens, haversacks, cartridge boxes; everything that could be detached from the person and thrown overhead." Only the assassination of President Abraham Lincoln five short days after the surrender quieted the jubilant veterans of the Army of the Potomac. As they trudged back across old battlefields to Washington, men from the Second New York dug up a tree severed in half by rifle fire at Spotsylvania. Ever alert to a bit of publicity, Miles ordered the stump presented to Secretary of War Edwin M. Stanton as a grisly memento of the fearsome firepower of the Civil War infantryman.[61]

Rising from the ashes of a political demotion, Nelson Miles had displayed a natural flair for things military. The grievous human casualties and the arrival of less-than-enthusiastic recruits and draftees during the dog days of 1864 had been indeed disheartening. But Miles shook off his despair. Brave and willing to take the initiative, he exhibited a growing tactical prowess at Sutherland's Station and Sayler's Creek. Though alert to the everyday needs of his men, his innate aggressiveness never waned in the face of heavy losses. Like Grant, Miles knew that death and destruction inevitably accompanied combat. In subsequent reminiscences, he proudly reported that the Second Corps suffered more killed and wounded in battle than any corps in the Army of the Potomac; his First Division had the highest number of casualties in the corps.[62]

Army associates recognized Miles's talent for war. "Other men let up once in a while," wrote one, "but he kept at it always." General Howard called attention to his "remarkable gallantry" and "efficiency," adding that he always found Miles to be "perservering, self-reliant and fearless." Francis Barlow described his friend as "a man of untiring & sleepless energy who does not wait to be told to do a thing, or when & how to do it, but who uses all the means in his power to attain success without waiting to be urged or quickened by any one." It was not surprising, therefore, that Nelson Miles was later appointed major general of volunteers. The Civil War had transformed Miles the soldier from a boy into a man. He was a long way from the quiet Westminster family farm.[63]

3 : RECONSTRUCTION

As Lee and Grant danced the final steps of their deadly waltz, President Jefferson Davis and his close advisers and family had fled Richmond in a desperate attempt to piece together the remnants of the Confederacy. To the north, President Andrew Johnson, cognizant of Davis's rumored involvement in the recent assassination of Abraham Lincoln, placed a one-hundred-thousand-dollar bounty on the Confederate president's head. Near Abbeville, Georgia, in the early morning of May 10, 1865, Davis, his wife Varina, and Clement C. Clay, a former Confederate Senator and diplomat to Canada, were captured by a squadron of Union cavalry.[1]

Wearing a badge of mourning for the fallen Lincoln, Nelson Miles had in the meantime accompanied his command as it retraced its steps through northern Virginia. He and his fellow officers concentrated on preventing straggling and the destruction of property, and their tired veterans talked of home. But the Union high command had a much bigger job in store for Miles, whose political reliability and military talents seemed to mark a bright future. "Order General Miles to report to my headquarters without delay to receive special orders," demanded Ulysses S. Grant on May 19. "He should come in to-night prepared to leave Washington at once." There Grant informed Miles of his new command: the Military District of Fort Monroe, Virginia.[2]

Begun in 1819, Fort Monroe was intended to shield the entrance to Hampton Roads, Virginia, from naval attack. Union troops had occupied its formidable stone walls and casemates throughout the Civil War. Now it seemed a safe prison for Jefferson Davis and Clement Clay. Major General Henry Halleck, commander of the Military Division of the James, and Assistant Secretary of War Charles A. Dana greeted Miles upon his arrival at Fort Monroe on the twenty-second of May. At 1:00 that afternoon, Miles left by tug to retrieve the prisoners from the steamer *William P. Clyde*, anchored just offshore. With guards swarming over the Engineers Wharf, General Miles led Davis ashore. "Not a single curious spectator was anywhere in sight," reported Dana, who noted that the former president, dressed in gray with a thin overcoat, "bore himself with a haughty attitude."[3]

Security was airtight. Davis and Clay were allowed no communication with their dependents on the departing *Clyde*. Miles inspected their linens and clothing; he was to issue new materials "only as required." Each prisoner occupied the inner room of what had been until recently an artillery casemate. A sentry guarded the interior door, with two more guards posted outside of another gate. An officer checked the prisoners every fifteen minutes; lamps lit the cells at all times. Extra sentinels guarded adjoining rooms, cut off access to the casemates, patrolled the overhead parapets, and watched the moats on the counterscarp opposite the cells.[4]

Dana and Halleck took no chances. They forbade enlisted personnel from communicating with either prisoner—only officers could respond to questions or requests. Unauthorized persons were kept away from the casemates. Dana explained, "[I have] not given orders to have them placed in irons, as General Halleck seemed opposed to it, but General

Miles is instructed to have fetters ready if he thinks them necessary." Halleck in turn authorized Miles "to take any additional precautions he . . . deem[ed] necessary for the security of his prisoners."[5]

The possibility of an escape haunted Union officials, who fully expected Davis to undergo trial as a party to Lincoln's murder. Rumors of elaborate conspiracies swirled around Washington; should a breakout occur, anyone associated with Fort Monroe would see his career ruined. An element of revenge for the long, costly struggle was also evident. Secretary Dana thus left final instructions. "Brevet Major-General Miles is hereby authorized and directed to place manacles and fetters upon the hands and feet of Jefferson Davis and Clement C. Clay whenever he may think it advisable in order to render their imprisonment more secure."[6]

A distraught Varina Davis quizzed Miles about her husband's health the following morning. The interview seemed amicable enough, since Mrs. Davis thanked Miles for his "courtesy and kind answers." But Miles fretted about security arrangements. After all, the escape of his prisoner might prolong the Civil War; Confederate units west of the Mississippi were still fighting. Heavy grated doors had not yet replaced the lighter fixtures outside the main cells, so Miles decided to leave nothing to chance. He instructed the officer of the day, Captain Jerome E. Titlow, to chain the former president's legs.[7]

Titlow and two blacksmiths found a listless Davis lying on his cot, his food untouched on tin plates on the floor. The captain uttered a brief word of apology, then ordered his blacksmiths to secure the anklets. Lurid contemporary accounts (which Davis later labeled "fiction distorting fact") had him springing to life, desperately battling efforts to rivet the manacles around his ankles. Miles reported the incident matter-of-factly. "Yesterday I directed that irons be put on Davis' ankles, which he violently resisted, but became more quiet afterward."[8]

Ambitious, inexperienced in all but the ways of war, nervous about the task ahead of him, and eager to please his superiors, Miles went about his work as commander of the Military District of Fort Monroe. His duties far exceeded those of a simple jailor, for as commander of a military district that included Northampton and Accomac counties he took an active interest in Reconstruction. He sought pardons for selected Confederate veterans and tried to help the Bureau of Refugees, Freedmen, and Abandoned Lands assist former slaves in securing legal rights, jobs, and education. But Miles believed Southerners would stop at nothing to subordinate blacks and "clog the wheels of progress." It was indeed a bittersweet period for him. Honored to have been entrusted with such awesome responsibility, he nonetheless missed the comradery of his First Division veterans. While Miles oversaw his valuable prisoner, the Army of the Potomac celebrated the war's conclusion in a spectacular parade down Pennsylvania Avenue. Subordinates sent him a horse and a gold watch as a testimony of their esteem and admiration.[9]

On the morning of May 24, Surgeon John J. Craven entered Davis's stark casemate, which now included a hospital bed and iron bedstead, one chair, a table, a small stool closet, and a Bible. A New York native and distinguished war veteran, Craven quickly grew fond of Davis, who in his view "presented a very miserable and afflicting aspect." At the surgeon's behest Miles secured tobacco, a prayer book, and a dietary change for the former president. Craven also asked that Davis be unchained.[10]

With the new grate doors firmly in place on the twenty-eighth, Union soldiers removed the fetters from Davis's ankles. But the *Philadelphia Telegraph* had already broken the story. Secretary of War Edwin Stanton soon queried Miles. "Please report whether irons have or have not been placed on Jefferson Davis. If they have been, when was it done, and for what reason, and remove them." In response, Miles explained that "light anklets" had been fixed about Davis's legs until secure doors had been installed.[11]

Orders from Washington grew more restrictive. Officials approved Miles's request to furnish writing materials to the prisoner, with the provision that they be used only in allowing Davis to secure legal defense. Only those persons bearing written passes from the adjutant general or secretary of war could see Davis; specifically, the Reverend Mark L. Chevers of Hampton, the post chaplain since 1838, was prohibited—presumably because of his Southern sympathies—from visiting the prisoner. On July 14, Stanton cautioned Miles about a Canadian-based attempt to free Davis and Clay. "The Government has implicit reliance on your vigilance," he advised.[12]

Because of these tougher regulations, relations between Davis, Craven, and Miles soon deteriorated. Craven protested the lack of fresh linens. He and Davis complained that the constant light and nighttime tramping of the sentinels outside Davis's cell hampered his sleep. Miles refuted the charge. "His usual answer on being asked how he had slept was invariably 'very well,'" according to Miles. Nevertheless, in late July he ordered the guards to stand at ease.[13]

"The statements made in the papers that his [Davis's] health is declining under his imprisonment are utterly false," Miles had written on June 27, "and in my opinion are intended to excite sympathy in the North." Despite such protestations, Dr. Craven fretted about the prisoner's poor appetite, double vision, nervousness, and weak pulse. Miles attributed Davis's declining health to news of the executions of Lincoln's alleged assassins. But he recognized the need for adjustments, and secured permission from Secretary Stanton to dim the lights, to remove some of the guards, to supply additional reading materials, and to escort the prisoners on daily walks along the ramparts.[14]

The improvements notwithstanding, Davis and Craven resented Miles's unbending vigilance. Understandably, Davis wanted to contact his grieving wife. But Washington feared a conspiracy. "Any letters which Mr. Davis desires to send his wife must relate only to family matters and be first submitted to the Attorney General's inspection," directed Adjutant General Edward D. Townsend. Sporadic communication between Mr. and Mrs. Davis finally opened in late August. But when Miles asked if he could answer Mrs. Davis's requests concerning her husband's health, the War Department dictated but a terse letter that expressed no sympathy for Davis's plight. It was in Miles's name.[15]

Miles and Davis developed a mutual aversion. Davis resented the general's censorship and refusal to return a valise confiscated at the time of his captivity. He also disliked having the Yankee, "a heartless vulgarian" whose lack of formal education, opposition to slavery, and brusque self-confidence offended Davis's aristocratic tastes, accompany him on his daily walks. Miles was equally critical. He respected Davis's intelligence, but, he wrote, "Intimate acquaintance has not changed my opinion . . . that he is a most ambitious man, and unscrupulous, and I doubt if he would hesitate at any crime to carry out his traitorous designs."[16]

In August Davis's health, long poor, deteriorated further. Having been in chronically poor health for most of his later years, his left thigh now became inflamed and his face swelled bright red. Craven, finding him "very feeble" and "extremely reduced in physical structure," asked Miles to move Davis from the damp casemate. Miles promptly requested permission from Washington; on September 4, President Johnson directed Miles to select more suitable quarters. The general found a site eight days later, but the final decision to move Jefferson Davis came only after a special inspector's report later that month. On October 2 Miles oversaw Davis's transfer, under a strong guard, to a larger and better-ventilated room.[17]

Miles seemed more sympathetic to the plight of Clement Clay, who initially responded graciously. He corresponded with Clay's wife on several occasions throughout the summer, informing her that her husband was "quite cheerful." Although his attempts to give Clay new reading material went slowly, he told her, "You may be assured that while your husband is within the limits of my command, he will not suffer." Clay assured his captor that he would leave the country if allowed; Miles in turn told superiors that this would be a good risk. And in contrast to Davis, Clay attributed the frustrating mail censorship and delays to Washington officials rather than Miles, granting that Miles was "allowed no discretion."[18]

But relations between Clay and Miles soon cooled. An anonymous source warned Clay not to trust Miles. In a response apparently smuggled past his captors that fall, Clay scribbled, "Thank you for your caution as to Genl. Miles. As soon as I ascertained his character, my disgust for him prevented [me] from talking to him." On another occasion, he described Miles as "extremely ignorant and unrefined. . . . [He is] not fit for anything better than a turnkey; which is all they make of him."[19]

Meanwhile, the alliance between Craven and Davis grew stronger. Craven believed Miles was eager to profit at Davis's expense, and often disagreed with the military commander. Mrs. Craven and her daughter delivered clothes and food to the former president. "I am deeply indebted to my attending physician, who has been to me much more than that term usually conveys," wrote Davis. And Mrs. Davis promised she would "teach [her] children to pray for dear Dr. Craven all his life." Fed up with what he perceived to be Craven's manipulations, Miles in mid-November ordered the surgeon to confine his discussions with Davis to professional matters.[20]

Just after Christmas Miles uncovered what he believed to be the makings of an escape attempt. A large window in Davis's cell, secured by iron doors, overlooked the interior of Fort Monroe. During a routine search, guards uncovered small pieces of cloth tied together to form a thirty-six-foot-long cord. Miles directed that this "red tape" be removed from the cell. Davis protested vigorously: "The ass! Tell the damned ass that it was used to keep up the mosquito net on my bed. I had it in the casemate and he knew it. The miserable ass!" Miles, however, asserted that Davis's enraged response merely proved that the prisoner had "desired it for improper uses."[21]

War Department officials commended Miles for securing the long cord. "You cannot at this time be too vigilant," Adjutant General Townsend assured Miles, "especially in regard to vessels arriving at night off Fort Monroe." Townsend also alerted Miles to watch for suspected rebel sympathizers within the garrison. In January 1866, intrigued by matters of espionage, Miles discharged several former Confederate veterans and offered to set up a districtwide net of informers. And Major George E. Cooper, the assistant surgeon at Fort Monroe, replaced Craven as Davis's physician.[22]

Scrutinized by Washington, vilified by many newspapers, despised by Davis and Clay, and uncertain of his future, Miles soon tired of his lot at Fort Monroe. Ever sensitive to any real or perceived slight and convinced that his rank did not befit his achievements, he considered leaving the army. In a December 12 note to his old mentor Oliver O. Howard, Miles sought a testimonial of his abilities—"I should wish to volunteer my services in any foreign war," he wrote. Miles also contemplated politics, but concluded that he lacked the money or connections to run for office. Letters of support from Senator Henry Wilson, General Andrew Humphreys, and General Henry Halleck only partly alleviated his concerns about his future.[23]

Davis's health fluctuated throughout the spring of 1866, as Congress and President Johnson sparred over the proper course of Reconstruction. The administration eased its restrictions on Davis when it became clear that the Confederate president had no role in Lincoln's assassination. At Miles's suggestion, Clay was paroled within the fort and later freed. Davis also received additional time outside his cell and Varina Davis was allowed to come to Fort Monroe. Though she later blasted Miles for trying to house her "with the camp women" rather than the officers' wives, Mrs. Davis moved into her own casemate on May 3.[24]

Despite the new conditions, wrangling between Miles and the Davises continued. (Varina later alleged, "[He] visited upon me and upon my husband all the insults and petty tyranny a vulgar mind could devise.") Dr. Cooper's medical report of May 9 sparked further controversy. A "considerably emaciated," "debilitated," and "excessively irritable" Davis suffered from vertigo, acute neuralgia, and severe skin inflammation. The tramping of sentinels still kept him from getting enough sleep. In his weakened condition, he would likely die if stricken by any of the diseases common to the Virginia tidewater region.[25]

Newspapers seized on extracts from Cooper's report. Miles frantically sought to reverse the public relations disaster, asking to allow reporters to visit with Davis and thus reveal the "gross misrepresentations" in the surgeon's review. Miles admitted that he had not made Davis his "associate and confidant or toadied to his fancy." Instead, he said, "[I] endeavored to do my duty and have acted in implicit obedience to my orders." He attributed Davis's poor health to age, previous infirmities, and recent disappointments rather than to bad food or guards; he accused Cooper, whose wife was allegedly a secessionist, of being "entirely under the influence of Mr. and Mrs. Davis."[26]

In June, publication of *The Prison Life of Jefferson Davis* provoked even more public outcry. During his stint as Davis's physician, Dr. Craven had taken notes of his conversations with his star patient. He agreed to allow Charles G. Halpine to ghostwrite a book based on his accounts. A prominent Democratic editor, Halpine saw political gain from such a project—not only could it assist President Johnson's conservative Restoration policies, it would neutralize a pro-Republican volume that Nelson Miles, "the special pet & protege of Senators Sumner and Wilson, Gen. Butler, Gov. Andrew and so forth," was reputedly preparing to release. *Prison Life* painted a flattering portrait of Jefferson Davis as an intelligent, fair-minded, reasonable individual who bore malice against only extreme radicals.[27]

Debate about Davis continued throughout the summer. Surgeon General J. K. Barnes checked the prisoner in early June and found Davis's health to be "remarkably good," considering his age and circumstances. Miles provided a "wholesome and nutritious" diet and allowed plenty of exercise. "The prisoner's own statement was distinctly to the effect that his health is and has been much better than has been represented," reported Barnes. But Dr. Cooper, who acknowledged that Davis's health improved temporarily in June, argued six weeks later that his patient suffered from a high pulse, poor appetite, and general debilitation. "Mr. Davis complains but little and is very reticent concerning his ailments, and it is with difficulty I can discover from him when he is more unwell than usual," explained Cooper in indirect response to the Barnes diagnosis.[28]

But political controversies were not Miles's sole concern that summer, as army reorganization bills slowly wound their way through Congress. Seeking a regular army commission, Miles believed he had assurances from Stanton about such a position by July 31. But with reductions threatening to slice the army from over a million volunteers to fifty-four thousand regulars, Miles determined to further his career on his own. Upon hearing that a fellow volunteer had already secured an appointment, he called upon Senator Henry Wilson. "I hope you will make my case a personal one," he requested unabashedly.[29]

August brought disquieting news about Miles's future in the U.S. Army. On the second, Secretary Stanton promised to "spare no effort" in placing him. "How would you like to command a colored regiment?" queried Stanton the following day. But Miles still lacked a formal appointment when he received mustering-out orders for September 1. With only a week left at Fort Monroe, Miles, still uncertain about whether a permanent commission awaited him or not, struck out against what he described as "the base slanders and foulest accusations which the disloyal press have heaped upon me." He asserted that Davis had received "as much leniency as the dignity of the Government would justify."[30]

In notes of August 24 and 30, Miles pleaded to be allowed to retain his Fort Monroe command until October 5, which would mark his fifteenth month there. Unsure about his military future, he considered attacks on his regime "unjust and an injury to [his] reputation." But Miles was in the end awarded with a full colonelcy in the Fortieth Infantry Regiment; official orders dated September 3, 1866, called him to Washington to recruit his regiment.[31]

An act of July 28, 1866, had set the army at ten cavalry, five artillery, and forty-five infantry regiments. Of these, two cavalry and four infantry regiments, including Miles's Fortieth, would consist of black enlisted personnel and white officers. Letters from Sheridan and Meade assured Miles of their support; just prior to his appearing before the examining board that would approve his appointment, Miles received an especially encouraging note from General Hancock. "I have never met an officer," to whom "I would rather trust a Regiment, Brigade or Division in a campaign or on the field of battle than yours." Though a colonelcy seemed a major disappointment after the dizzy heights he had known during the war, it was in fact in line with general grade reductions necessitated by the smaller army.[32]

By December 1866, Miles had passed his exams and was superintending regimental recruiting. Drawing from the Washington D.C. area, the Fortieth assembled at Camp Distribution, Virginia. Like much of the army, the Fortieth was slated for Reconstruction duties. In late February 1867 most of the regiment left Alexandria by steamer for North Carolina. The headquarters, staff, band, and three companies soon followed. Miles would command the post of Smithville, North Carolina, and oversee defenses along the Cape Fear River.[33]

The Fortieth made an inauspicious North Carolina debut. On March 1, five companies were shipwrecked off Fort Fisher, near Cape Fear. Though no lives were lost, most of the outfit's clothing, supplies, and ordnance sunk. And just as Miles began setting up headquarters at Smithville, new orders relieved him of command of local defenses in favor of duty as assistant commissioner in the Freedmen's Bureau. This necessitated a transfer to the state capital at Raleigh, where Major General Daniel Sickles, commander of the Second Military District, prepared to implement the provisions of the Reconstruction Act of March 2, 1867.[34]

The Reconstruction Act was passed by a Republican-dominated Congress that had determined to take a stronger hand in Reconstruction as violent attacks against freedmen became more common and friends of secession regained political control in the South. The new legislation carved the former Confederate states (except Tennessee, which had already complied with congressional demands) into five military districts. It also required that each state write a new constitution that provided for black suffrage and ratification of the Fourteenth Amendment. In duties more fully amplified by subsequent legislation, the army and the Freedmen's Bureau would register eligible voters, protect the civil rights of blacks and white unionists, and assist in the formation of provisional governments. Reform, rather than reconciliation, seemed the new order.[35]

Miles, long an advocate of federal intervention in the unreconstructed South, fit the congressional mold. As commander of the District of Fort Monroe, he had recognized the plight of destitute freedmen and supported one group's planned move to Florida, where they hoped to use the Homestead Act to procure land. To combat the influences of a "swindler" who warned the freedmen against such action, he had sought the assistance of Oliver O. Howard, a supporter of black rights who headed the Freedmen's Bureau. Miles concluded that the Freedmen's Bureau must take a "strong hand" in supporting former slaves. He also championed political change. "I would like to see every office [in the South] filled by ex officers and one armed soldiers of our army as the surest and best foundation for the Union party now forming in every Southern state," he explained to a fellow Republican. Miles later insisted that conservative state officials be removed in favor of "men of undoubted loyalty, whose patriotism [could] be relied upon."[36]

In an April 26 circular, Miles outlined his interpretation of his new Freedmen's Bureau position. Hoping to "overcome" the "prejudices" against his agency, he wanted to use the bureau "to protect, comfort and elevate the oppressed and destitute, encourage energy and enterprise, [and] afford the blessings of education and religious instruction to a people." All officers and agents were to submit the names of three people as potential district voting registrars. One was to be a local resident, another was to be a bureau agent or army officer, and a third was to be a black "of intelligence and sufficient education."[37]

This circular helped to fuel a fierce struggle for political control of North Carolina. William W. Holden, a former Democratic governor who had broken with his party by calling for a separate peace with the Union in 1863, now edited the *Raleigh Standard,* which championed quick reconciliation and moderate reform. "This is a good movement," wrote the *Standard* of Miles's order. "The colored people were entitled to at least this much power in the work of enrolling." Governor Jonathan Worth, however, took a different view. Dubbing Holden "the most malignant, mean, unscrupulous Radical the Devil has raised up to affect our people," Worth suspected that Dan Sickles had approved Miles's handiwork. The conservative governor protested the "ultra radicals nominated by Genl Miles," and sponsored his own alternative slate of registrars. But Worth's suspicions of Sickles's duplicity were proved false when the general, whose restrained approach to reconstruction clashed with Miles's views, sided with Worth.[38]

Convinced of the propriety of his convictions despite the criticism, Miles strove to improve the freedmen's lot. He urged bureau agents to inform blacks of their rights to register, vote, secure an education, and hold jobs. He urged that lists of employment opportunities and those seeking work should be forwarded every ten days to Raleigh, where laborers could be matched with employers. Agents should investigate attempts to defraud or break contracts with black laborers. Drawing on his strong Baptist upbringing, Miles also directed his subordinates to organize "Lincoln Temperance Societies" among the freedmen.[39]

Miles believed economic recovery to be crucial to success of Reconstruction, and that the Freedmen's Bureau and the army could help expedite financial development. To this end, he solicited charitable contributions and sought to expand the bureau's authority. Assisted by the Boston fund raiser William Gray, Miles and Holden administered the privately financed Boston Fund. The charity, "designed for the aged and infirm and delicate children and for purchase of flour, coffee, sugar, calico, sheeting and muslin," collected several thousand dollars in money and supplies to be used at Miles's discretion. Disturbed by charges of corruption within the Freedmen's Bureau, Miles also demanded accountability from his agents. At the same time, he condemned the "rebuffs" from the "little post commanders" who refused to use their troops to assist his efforts.[40]

The energetic new program received its first popular test in North Carolina in November 1867, when voters chose delegates for the congressionally mandated constitutional convention. Whites retained a solid majority of the electorate, even when allowing for the disfranchisement of several thousand former Confederates. With strong support from the army and the Freedmen's Bureau, however, a coalition of blacks, Unionists, yeoman farmers, and former Whigs gave the Republicans a smashing victory. The following spring North Carolinians ratified the new constitution and elected William Holden as governor.[41]

But intraparty factionalism and the vengeful reaction by white supremists and conservatives prevented the Republicans from consolidating their position. Although the constitutional convention thanked Miles "for the efficient impartial and faithful manner in which he . . . discharged his duties," neither the army nor the Freedmen's Bureau could quell the political and racial violence, persecution, and intimidation. Ominously, the Ku Klux Klan became a major force in several North Carolina counties.[42]

Though unsuccessful in eradicating these opposition groups, Miles strove to fulfill his assignment. In his view, the Freedmen's Bureau provided "wonderful assistance" to blacks and Unionists. He feared that without the Bureau's continued presence the new state government would collapse and blacks would be forced into virtual slavery. He protested funding cuts and in early 1868 proposed an ambitious new series of bureau programs. Miles reminded agents to monitor contracts between freedmen and landowners, urged the planting of cereals rather than cotton, and discouraged sharecropping. He advised citizens to take advantage of the Freedmen's Savings Bank, chartered in 1865 by Congress to encourage savings. "Put every cent you can spare into the Bank and coming years will show the wisdom of such a course," he counseled them.[43]

Oliver O. Howard commended Miles's efforts. In December 1867, Miles had asked him for a transfer to the agency's central offices. Howard, however, had urged his friend to stay in North Carolina. "I do not know of anybody I can trust so well in that state," he explained, "and your influence will be unbounded for good." The general added that Miles had "to a considerable extent succeeded in relieving the Colored people of unjust exactions and in restoring public confidence throughout the State."[44]

But not all of Miles's time was spent on professional matters. At Fort Monroe, for example, he had urged his brother Daniel to come south to take advantage of postwar opportunities. Though Daniel declined, he and Nelson did speculate in Southern timber. And Nelson's ten-day visit to his ailing father in July 1866 had at least briefly relieved the stress stemming from his military responsibilities. Never forgotten was his military career. Miles frequently reminded his superiors that officers with less-distinguished Civil War records than his had received higher rank and more prestigious postings.[45]

Eager to cultivate political ties, Miles also managed to steal away to Washington on several occasions. His association with Massachusetts senators Henry Wilson and Charles Sumner provided special inroads into capital society. On one such trip Miles visited the home of Senator John Sherman of Ohio. Here he met an attractive (and eligible) house guest: Mary Hoyt Sherman, daughter of District Court Judge Charles T. Sherman and niece to the senator and his brother, General William T. Sherman. Nelson and Mary soon fell in love.

The Sherman family scrambled to find information on the young war hero. John Sherman, though he had no personal knowledge about Miles, assured his niece: "I have no doubt Gen. M. is honorable and worthy." By August 1867, the blossoming relationship led Judge Sherman to query Senator Sumner about Miles. Sumner responded, "General Miles was in the habit of visiting my house last winter, and I always found him intelligent, pleasant and of agreeable manners. He seemed to be a favorite with the young ladies. . . . I think he was in business— left business for the war and was successful."[46]

That September, Miles asked Judge Sherman for his daughter's hand in marriage. "I confess I have felt less trepidation in meeting our enemy than I do in addressing you on the subject when your answer involves my life interest and future happiness," he wrote. The judge having agreed to the match, marriage plans were made that fall. John Sherman contributed a thousand dollars to defray expenses. Miles made trips to Washington in February and April 1868 so the young couple could finalize arrangements for a June wedding. Brigadier General Alfred Terry, a wealthy Yale Law School graduate and like Miles a volunteer with a strong Civil War record, agreed to serve as best man.[47]

Nelson and Mary planned a glittering ceremony. The guest list, replete with a Supreme Court justice and Generals Grant, Sherman, and Sheridan, illustrated the Sherman family's national prominence. Although deeply in love with Mary, Nelson also relished the prospect of having such connections. "I expect there will be a number of distinguished generals of the army present," he explained when inviting Oliver Howard. The groom also included Generals Hancock and Barlow among those he invited. But as the wedding neared, the nation's business took precedence. Duties on the Indian Peace Commission of 1868 prevented Terry from coming. "As a soldier you know too well what that means," explained Terry. Senator John Sherman also added his regrets, but sent a sizeable cash wedding gift. Despite the absence of a few they had invited, Nelson and Mary Sherman were married in Cleveland's Trinity Church on Tuesday evening, June 30, 1868. All the officers save Sherman wore their full-dress uniforms, with Sheridan stepping in as best man. Six bridesmaids accompanied Mary, whose satin white dress was complemented by diamonds, pearls, and orange blossoms. An elaborate reception at Judge Sherman's home followed the ceremony.[48]

By early August, the newlyweds had returned to North Carolina, where Nelson resumed his Freedmen's Bureau duties and Mary made her debut in North Carolina society. Governor Holden's daughter Laura described the "charming bride": "[She is] handsome, middle-sized, rather thin, [has] brown eyes and hair, straight nose, and an exquisite mouth. Her manners are gentle, and polished; I take her to be a perfect lady." Laura added: "She is so winning in her manner, so sweetly dignified in her carriage."[49]

Yet even marital bliss could not keep Miles from skirmishing with his superiors. In August 1868, General George Meade assumed command of the newly formed Department of the South. Miles received the District of North Carolina in the resulting administrative shuffle. Governor Holden promptly asked that Meade authorize Miles to use his troops to enforce laws and to prevent violence in the upcoming elections, a proposal that Miles supported. Meade, however, took a more conservative tack. "I have no right to interfere or use the military forces under my command, except when instructed to do so from superior authority," he explained. Since North Carolina had recently regained its statehood, the army could not be used for policing functions as it had during reconstruction. The troops, he believed, should remain concentrated to counter any major resistance rather than take an active part in the daily affairs of the state.[50]

In late September, Meade ordered Miles to draw up new plans for concentrating troops in North Carolina. Disregarding Meade's wishes, Miles, in consultation with Governor Holden, planned to scatter companies in nine different cities. Proud of his postwar record, Miles reasoned that although the Freedmen's Bureau was transferring its responsibilities to civil authorities, Governor Holden had granted wide discretionary powers during the transition period. Thus the army should, in Miles's view, remain active. On the twenty-ninth, he reported that opponents of the federal government at Wilmington had collected a large arms cache. He wanted permission to seize the weapons. Meade refused the request, noting that no one could prove that the arms were to "be used for improper purposes." He went on to restate his determination to avoid army involvement in civil matters whenever possible. Civil authorities, he believed, must assume control.[51]

Miles disagreed with this policy, arguing that rebel sympathizers had violated their paroles by accepting arms and rioting. Pseudomilitary organizations like the Ku Klux Klan, whose movements were "clouded in mystery" and whose ranks included "remnants of the rebel army, guerillas, bandits, and rebels," had sprung up throughout the state. "These men have formed themselves into an armed organization in my opinion hostile to the Federal and State governments," he wrote. Since such activities exceeded their constitutional right to bear arms, Miles believed the army must take vigorous action. Governor Holden supported this stance, and the Republican-dominated *Raleigh Standard* published Holden's request for military assistance.[52]

Miles's protests and thinly disguised appeal for popular support infuriated Meade. Though he respected Miles's war record, Meade argued that the army's delicate position in the South demanded strict obedience and "harmony of judgment" from subordinates. "General Miles not only differs in total with me as to the authority given by the Law, and instructions of the War Department—but that after the clear and positive enunciation of my views, he continues to make labored arguments in opposition to the case," complained Meade. "I have to ask a decision on the issue raised and that the officer whose judgment is not approved, whether it be myself or General Miles, be relieved from further command in this Department."[53]

Meade and Miles established a temporary truce on the eve of the 1868 elections. On October 13, Meade withdrew his request that Miles be relieved. Miles relinquished his duties with the Freedmen's Bureau the following day. Later that month, however, Miles could not resist taking one parting shot. "Not the slightest intention existed to raise any issue with the Commanding General whose orders and instructions will always be cheerfully observed and enforced."[54]

Despite the controversy, Miles made every effort to ensure smooth elections. He directed his subordinates to be sure "that no cause for complaint be permitted from the indiscretions of the troops." Soldiers should camp outside the cities, avoid dramshops, and respect personal property. Working closely with Governor Holden, Miles also dispatched small units to assist civil authorities in maintaining law and order. The election went well; even the staunchly conservative *Raleigh Sentinel* described it as "one of the most quiet we had."[55]

The Republican party maintained its hold over the North Carolina electorate in the November 3 balloting. In the presidential contest, Ulysses S. Grant received roughly 54 percent of the votes; Republicans also took six of seven congressional seats. Jubilant Raleigh Republicans celebrated later that week as Miles honored Governor Holden with a fifteen-gun salute. In his address to the cheering crowd, Miles described Grant's victory as "a triumph of ideas; a triumph of loyalty over treason, a triumph of patriotism over rebellion and secession."[56]

But the work of Reconstruction brought few professional rewards. Miles seemed genuinely interested in the South's economic and political recovery. Yet even his best efforts seemed unable to quell the violence or to protect Unionists, blacks, and moderates. Within his own Fortieth Infantry, racial tensions between white officers and black enlisted men obstructed military discipline and training. One anonymous soldier complained that officers cursed and condemned the men because of their race. "If this be the regulations," he concluded, "I think that we better be slaves." Miles also complained about the poor quality of subordinates in the Freedmen's Bureau. "When I first assumed charge of the Bureau my first duty was to get rid of some of the drunkards," he recalled.[57]

Many white North Carolinians found it difficult to cooperate with a Massachusetts-born officer who led black troops and married a woman named Sherman. The petty slights proved increasingly difficult for Nelson and Mary to endure. Mary pleaded with her Uncle William to transfer them to a more congenial setting. But the general, who tried to ignore personal favoritism when making decisions, refused to promote Miles without proper cause. He instead advised patience; a move to a staff position in Washington, for example, would prove a dead end for any field commander.[58]

Undeterred, Miles in January 1869 continued his campaign for promotion, enlisting the aid of Governors Holden and Robert K. Scott of South Carolina. Eager to cut spending and military influence, however, Congress reduced the number of infantry regiments from forty-five to twenty-five in March 1869, thus precluding any notion of a brigadier generalship for Miles. His bid to secure command of the Fourth Military District (Mississippi and Arkansas) also failed. As something of a consolation, Miles in mid-March managed to wangle a transfer to the Fifth Infantry, an all-white outfit stationed in Kansas. He would thus exchange the uncertain duties of Reconstruction for the equally volatile, yet potentially more glamorous task of patrolling the western frontiers.[59]

M iles's postwar years had been fraught with controversy. Each of his assignments—warden for Jefferson Davis, commander of a black regiment, and assistant commissioner for the Freedmen's Bureau—had tested his resolve to make the army his career. In particular, the decision to place Davis in irons would always haunt him. A hero of four years of bloody civil struggle, Miles had no idea of the enormity of this fateful decree. Considering the government's insistence on security and Miles's vigilant quest for promotion, his determination to place "light anklets" about the legs of Jefferson Davis seemed justified. But the decision to do so also revealed the political naiveté of both Nelson Miles and the United States government. For the sensitive position at Fort Monroe, the army needed someone whose career reflected more balance than did that of Miles, who was more accustomed to charging headlong into Rebel lines than finessing political subtleties.[60]

Once the controversial chains had been removed, Miles's judgments at Fort Monroe are less questionable. Granted, he made no effort to ingratiate himself with the former president; little evidence remains that Miles sought to comfort Mrs. Davis as he did Mrs. Clay. But the legions of those testifying to his humane treatment of Davis is impressive, even considering Miles's self-interest in ferreting out such support. Nine fellow Union officers at Fort Monroe went on record as crediting Miles with treating Davis as well as conditions allowed. Wrote Brevet Colonel Joseph Roberts, on duty at Monroe during the first six months of Davis's confinement, "His [Davis's] physical comforts were all that could be expected or desired." Another officer swore that Miles, in urging Dr. Craven to make any recommendations he deemed advisable, had insisted: "I do not wish they should suffer in health on account of treatment or fare." Subsequent charges by Mrs. Davis concerning alleged mistreatment of her husband also led a number of observers to rush to Miles's defense.[61]

Yet the Clay and Davis families never forgave Miles. Upon his release, Clement Clay complained that Miles had not allowed him even to bid Davis farewell. "If nothing else can be had, let his jailor be supplanted by one who does not *hate* him & who is not of the *radical* school," he insisted. And Varina Davis, in assembling forces to oppose Miles's promotion thirty years later, continued to attack her nemesis in the most venomous of terms, accusing Miles of being an ignorant, ambitious brute, equally deficient in intellectual abilities and social graces.[62]

When considering Jefferson Davis's swift decline—from the president of a powerful confederacy to a prisoner denied virtually all privileges—the family's motives in blocking the career of the man they held responsible, Nelson Miles, seem almost instinctive. Others also hoped to manipulate events for their own purposes. Through the publication of *Prison Life*, for example, President Johnson and fellow conservatives sought to reap political benefits from Davis's degradation.

Miles never fully grasped the depths of this hatred. In a note to Mrs. Clay in September 1866, for example, he gallantly, if somewhat naively, offered his services on her husband's behalf. He continued, "I presume you are aware of the unpleasant light Dr. Craven has endeavored to place me in . . . but his misrepresentations will be answered when the passions of the people subsided enough to believe the candid truth." Frustrated at his inability to influence the course of politics as easily as he did the course of battle, Miles eagerly left the South behind him.[63]

4 : THE RED RIVER WARS

Nelson Miles, nearing his thirtieth birthday as he rode the train out West, could look back at the last decade with pride. As a teenager he had left his Westminster home for the uncertain rewards of a Boston crockery shop. The war had given him ample opportunities to display his ambition, courage, and initiative. But certain traits—jealousy, contentiousness, and political naiveté—had rendered Miles less effective in handling the complexities of the postwar South. His new assignment as commander of the Fifth Infantry Regiment promised relief from the controversies of Reconstruction, where actions designed to assist one segment of society only alienated another.

It was his first trip to the West, which was popularly seen as a land of romance and adventure, inexhaustible resources, and savage Indians.

Espousing a nationalistic view of expansion, Miles did not question the righteousness of the country's western march. Accordingly, he believed non-Indians could occupy any lands deemed desirable and that the government could remove Indians who opposed such measures. Nelson Miles hoped the transfers of Native Americans would proceed smoothly, but, like most of his colleagues, he thought their quick removal to be more important than the Indian's well-being.[1]

In the spring of 1869, the Fifth Infantry kept watch over western Kansas and eastern Colorado Territory. Two companies, plus the regimental headquarters, were housed at Fort Hays, Kansas. Another three units held Fort Wallace. The remaining five companies occupied Camp Belcher and Forts Lyon, Reynolds, Leavenworth, and Harker. The small outposts guarded emigrant trails as well as construction teams for the burgeoning Kansas Pacific Railroad, now approaching the Colorado border from the east, against Indian attack.[2]

Miles assumed his new command on April 21, 1869. His predecessor, Colonel Daniel Butterfield, had been away from the regiment on recruiting detail for the past three years; as a result, junior officers had grown accustomed to an independence they would lose with Miles's arrival. All fourteen captains, majors, and lieutenant colonels listed on the regimental returns that spring were Civil War veterans; five had earned wartime brevets. The list also boasted four West Point graduates, two future brigadier generals, and four future Medal of Honor recipients. But the regiment also included its share of laggards and malcontents. Five of the fourteen would either be cashiered, mustered out, or transferred within two years of Miles's arrival. The jealousies associated with the relative merits of a West Point education, Civil War experience, and seniority that disrupted the Fifth Infantry mirrored similar discord in every unit in the army. At Fort Hays, Miles's domineering personality would exacerbate these tensions.[3]

The concurrent consolidation of the old Thirty-seventh Infantry with the Third and Fifth regiments, necessitated by recent army reductions, added to the upheavals. As one officer confessed, the Thirty-seventh included "the worst element" from the older volunteer force. The action did, however, bring to the Fifth Lieutenant Frank D. Baldwin, a hero of the Civil War Battle of Peach Tree Creek, Georgia. The ambitious Baldwin was delighted to come; one colleague later advised him that promotion would surely follow if he kept "a tight hold on Genl. Miles' coat-tails."[4]

At the Fort Hays headquarters, Miles mingled with the dashing Lieutenant Colonel George A. Custer. Like Miles, Custer was a boy general of the Civil War and his recent campaigns against the Kiowas, Cheyennes, Arapahos, and Comanches of the southern plains had reinforced his controversial image. His supporters pointed to Custer's destruction of Black Kettle's Cheyenne village at the Battle of the Washita; his critics denounced his failure to ascertain the fate of Major Joel Elliott and nineteen troopers before leaving the scene of combat. But Miles shared none of the latter concerns. When Custer's weary cavalrymen concluded their operations and returned to Fort Hays, they were met by a special greeting party, organized by Miles, as the band struck up "Garryowen," the Seventh's favorite.[5]

Though relishing the chance to hunt big game with Custer, Miles found accommodations at Fort Hays decidedly inferior. He soon transferred his headquarters to Fort Harker, seventy miles east of Hays and closer to "the confines of civilization." Miles's insistence on cleanliness and good order, unusual for a military frontier where health and military efficiency often seemed to be in perpetual conflict, won plaudits from the surgeon at Harker.[6]

As Nelson attended to his military duties, Mary set the tone for polite society. In her near-regal status as the post commander's wife, she entertained visiting dignitaries and select garrison members with refined grace. And Mary learned to enjoy the outdoor activities that broke the monotony of western duty. She and Elizabeth Custer, the lieutenant colonel's wife, had accompanied their husbands on at least one elaborate buffalo hunt while at Fort Hays. Mary also found time to champion her husband's career with her powerful relatives, a cause only temporarily delayed by her return to Cleveland to give birth to their first child, Cecilia, in September 1869.[7]

Nelson and Mary lived comfortably on his colonel's income, which, with regular salary, allowances for food and servants, and miscellaneous emoluments totaled over four thousand dollars per year. Devout Baptists, they still contributed to the Westminster Baptist Church. The couple also hired a housekeeper, a nurse, and a soldier-servant, or "striker." Exploiting his inside connections with military and political brass, Miles, using his savings and Mary's dowry, was well prepared to capitalize on the western move. Within a year of his arrival in Kansas he had contacted Generals Hancock and John M. Schofield regarding lands in Kansas and Colorado Territory. Speculative ventures with his uncle-in-law, Senator Sherman, which initially included real estate investments on the northern plains, would prove even more profitable.[8]

But even the financial comfort, new baby, and occasional association with Custer did not compensate for the lack of action. Scattered in tiny packets along the Kansas and Colorado frontiers, the Fifth could rarely take effective action against Indians deemed hostile by the federal government. The southern plains peoples commonly avoided the bluecoats; they had accepted reservation life during the campaigns of 1868–69 only after Phil Sheridan had resorted to using formations of converging columns, hordes of allied Indian auxiliaries, and winter campaigns to force their submission.

Bored and ambitious, Miles turned to army intrigue. He had a quarrel with Major Lewis Merrill, a noted Custer antagonist who commanded the Seventh Cavalry detachment at Harker, which led to the removal of the former at Miles's insistence. With this potential challenger disposed of, Miles sought out new opportunities within the army. "My ambition is not extravagant, but simply for a command in accordance with my rank," he explained to General Sherman in June 1870. The general tried in vain to appease Miles, pointing out that Indian troubles "always break out where we least expect it." After briefly toying with the notion of going abroad to observe the Franco-Prussian War, Miles initiated another flurry of personal communiqués with Sherman. Transfer to a mounted regiment would surely offer exciting new career challenges. "I do not advise it," telegrammed Sherman, whose response, combined with the rumors of upcoming operations along the Kansas Pacific Railroad, changed the colonel's mind. "Please accept my thanks for the interest you manifest in my behalf," wrote Miles, who admitted that his position left him "well satisfied."[9]

Despite the promise of greater action, deteriorating buildings and expanding railroads rendered Fort Harker nearly obsolete. In April 1871, Miles moved his regimental headquarters and band to Fort Leavenworth, a bustling post with an attendant civilian community. But the presence there of the Department of the Missouri headquarters, commanded by the bombastic Brigadier General John Pope, made Miles long for an independent posting. Pope, equally willing to find fault in others, chided the colonel about a series of petty incidents. Miles treated any criticism as a personal challenge, however common such critiques might have been in army procedure. A thirty days' leave in February 1872 temporarily removed him from Pope's watchful glare. But his routine duty promised Miles neither excitement nor promotion. Upon the army's renewal of hostilities against Indians in the Southwest, Miles asked his Uncle William for command of the District of New Mexico, a "good field to work," for which he was "willing to sacrifice for a time [their] present delightful surroundings." Sherman refused to comply, explaining that Pope, as department commander, held such authority. Still, Sherman added that he admired Miles's "ambition and desire to do real work."[10]

Unfulfilled ambitions again marred the following year. The recent army cutbacks rendered the meteoric promotions of the Civil War a thing of the past, but Miles, who had tasted the glories of commanding a full corps of battle-hardened veterans, could hardly be expected to relish the prospect of a long career in command of a single regiment. To his old friend and confidant Oliver Howard, Miles complained that Sherman's failure to free him from the confines of Leavenworth left him "greatly disappointed and disgusted." But Sherman remained the colonel's trump card. Miles was convinced that Pope sought to sabotage his career and he peppered Sherman with requests. In November 1873 he requested a transfer to General Hancock's Department of the Lakes, which included the Great Lakes region. Sherman suggested a trip around the world instead; Miles explained that his father-in-law needed Mary to remain closer to home. "Besides," explained Miles, "we may have use for the army before another summer."[11]

Lieutenant General Philip H. Sheridan, commanding the sprawling Division of the Missouri (which at that time stretched from Illinois on the east to present Colorado on the west and from Minnesota on the north to Texas on the south and Arizona on the southeast), had indeed contemplated a major offensive nearly a year earlier. The slaughter of the buffalo, the continued migration of non-Indian settlers, the inadequate government-issue rations to peoples on the reservations, and the illegal trade in guns and alcohol with Indians had spawned a new wave of violence by Indians in Kansas and Texas. Blaming the Indians, Sheridan believed a winter campaign similar to those of 1868–69 would forever break the military power of the Kiowas, Comanches, and Southern Cheyennes. Miles, whose work Sheridan had admired during the final days of the Civil War, was to transfer to Fort Sill, in present Oklahoma, by January 1, 1873, to participate in the attack. The plan fell through, however, when Secretary of the Interior Columbus Delano refused to grant the army permission to enter Indian reservations.[12]

Miles chafed as negotiations between the War and Interior departments stalled. Beautification plans at Fort Leavenworth, though pleasing to the eye, did not make up for the inaction. That spring's issue of the all-important *Army Register,* which erroneously listed him after John E. Smith and Galusha Pennypacker among infantry colonels in length of service, precipitated a minor crisis. With promotion often based on seniority, and the upper echelons bulging with young officers boasting fine Civil War records, such a mistake could delay a brigadier generalship for years. Miles's vehement protest resulted in a correction in the next edition. He also challenged new army cutbacks that threatened to reduce to forty the number of enlisted men per infantry company. Not forgotten, of course, was the need to keep his uncle, General Sherman, informed of his loyal support and unappreciated military genius.[13]

The noncombat assignments continued when in May 1873, Miles, who had dodged an earlier such appointment, was selected to replace Lieutenant Colonel August V. Kautz as head of a board formed to compile plans for a military prison. After a visit to the proposed site at Rock Island, Illinois, the five-man committee instead suggested as an alternative the abandoned arsenal buildings at Fort Leavenworth. The board also recommended that the prison, in accordance with the latest theories on penal institutions, seek to reform rather than simply punish its inmates. A chaplain, surgeon, and educational instructor should be available, and cleanliness and sanitation should be emphasized. Prisoners would work eight to ten hours per day, six days a week, but were to be treated "in a kind and humane manner." Mandatory attendance at religious services and four hours of weekly school instruction, ruled the board, would encourage inmates to become productive citizens on their release. The report concluded, "All officers and noncommissioned officers are enjoined to keep constantly in view the fact that the reformation of its inmates . . . was one of the chief objects of the Government in establishing the institution."[14]

Congress temporarily delayed funds for the Leavenworth prison and later that year Miles found himself appointed to a blue-ribbon panel to investigate Oliver Howard's alleged involvement in Freedmen's Bureau scandals. As a former aide to Howard, Miles sided with the accused. Though the Bureau had not been without financial misappropriations, the board cleared Howard of any malfeasance. Miles rejoiced over the fall of those who had accused Howard. "I think you must realize that 'the Lord reigns,' " Miles wrote as he and Howard celebrated the latter's legal victory.[15]

In the summer of 1874, as the Howard court concluded its docket, the army secured the Interior Department's permission to cross reservation lines. Hurried plans were made to take advantage of the unusual freedom of action. From Fort Sill, Lieutenant Colonel John W. Davidson, six troops of the Tenth Cavalry, and three companies of the Eleventh Infantry tried to separate Indians near Fort Sill termed "friendly" from those dubbed "hostile." Four companies of Fifth Infantrymen and one troop of the Sixth Cavalry would help Lieutenant Colonel Thomas H. Neill pursue a similar course at the Cheyenne and Arapaho Agency. All Indians seeking a safe haven were to be enrolled by mid-August; those declining were declared hostile.[16]

Four other columns would operate against those tribes who defied the government edict. From the Department of Texas, Colonel Ranald S. Mackenzie, six times wounded in the Civil War, would lead thirteen companies north from Fort Concho. Lieutenant Colonel George P. Buell also took eight companies from Fort Griffin. From the west, Major William R. Price led 250 horsemen from Fort Union, New Mexico Territory. And Colonel Miles, with eight troops of Sixth Cavalrymen and four companies of his Fifth Infantry, would drive south from Fort Dodge, Kansas. If all went according to plan, the converging columns would force the Indians to fight a major engagement in the Texas Panhandle.[17]

As head of the Department of the Missouri, John Pope oversaw the Miles and Price columns. Pope believed that the late summer start doomed the effort to failure. "I fear if we begin now we shall only use up our cavalry," he protested. His orders, typical of those issued during the Indian campaigns, left matters largely to the discretion of field commanders. Though Miles was told, "Be guided by circumstances as they arise," the general suggested that it would be "desirable" if he operated west of the Wichita Mountains. Price would, "if circumstances permit[ed]," join Miles west of the Antelope Hills. Pope did insist that if the Indians were defeated, it would be at the hands of troops from his department rather than those from Texas.[18]

Well aware of interdepartmental rivalries and anxious to further his career, Miles named Lieutenant Baldwin chief of scouts. On August 11, a swarm of civilian frontiersmen, Delaware Indian auxiliaries, and regulars left Fort Dodge with Baldwin for Palo Duro Creek and Adobe Walls. Baldwin was to locate the enemy but avoid any pitched battles, establish contact with Major Price, and ensure *"that [they] not leave any large forces of Indians to the right."* A Civil War veteran, Major Charles E. Compton, leading four troops of cavalry and an infantry company, departed the same day. With a pack of dogs tagging along, Miles and the main body, which included a ten-pound Parrott rifle and a Gatling gun, set out on August 14, one day ahead of Pope's original timetable. But Miles shared his superior's pessimism about immediate victory, privately predicting that little could be achieved before winter.[19]

Though fearing the campaign might be for naught, Miles relished his return to the field, as he and his setter, Jack, led the column. But disaster nearly ended the expedition before it really began. As the column wound its way south toward Camp Supply, Indian Territory, the barren country showed the effects of a recent drought. The canteens were soon empty and scouts scoured the horizon in vain for watering holes. "One man endeavored to open a vein to drink his blood and another tried to drink his urine," one veteran later remembered. Exhausted soldiers ditched their equipment in desperate efforts to lighten their loads. Miles admitted that he was hotter and thirstier than ever before in his life. Only Jack had done well, sniffing out a tiny water hole for a lucky few. Miles had learned a valuable lesson that he put to use as his command headed south following a brief refitting at Camp Supply. Subsequent marches began before sunrise to avoid the blistering heat. He found that many of his junior officers, though well-meaning, seemed befuddled by the environmental limitations of the Great Plains, which demanded attention to minute detail. Miles thus assumed progressively greater responsibilities. As spirits rose with the commander's personal involvement, Baldwin's scouts, who had struck a fresh Indian trail southwest of Sweetwater Creek, rejoined the main column.[20]

Pursuit began on August 24. The high temperatures and rough terrain, broken by innumerable dry ravines, increased the dangers of ambush as the column cut loose from its supply train and headed southwest. No word on Price was forthcoming as man and beast pushed onward, despite the salty, alkaline-filled water on the trail. On August 30, several hundred Indians fell upon Baldwin's scouts, who

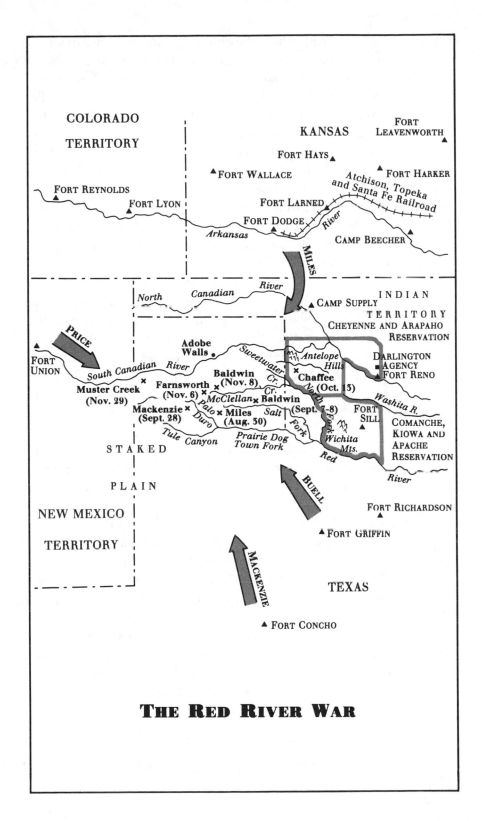

COLORADO
TERRITORY

KANSAS

FORT
LEAVENWORTH ▲

FORT HAYS ▲

▲ FORT WALLACE

FORT HARKER ▲

Atchison, Topeka
and Santa Fe Railroad

FORT REYNOLDS ▲

FORT LYON ●

FORT LARNED ●

FORT DODGE ▲

Arkansas   River

CAMP BEECHER ▲

MILES

North   Canadian   River

INDIAN

▲ CAMP SUPPLY

TERRITORY
CHEYENNE AND ARAPAHO
RESERVATION

PRICE

FORT
UNION ▲

South Canadian   River

Adobe
Walls ●

Sweetwater
Cr.

Antelope
Hills

DARLINGTON
AGENCY ■
FORT RENO ▲

Muster Creek
(Nov. 29) ×

Baldwin
(Nov. 8) ×
Farnsworth ×
(Nov. 6)

× Chaffee
(Oct. 13)

North Fork

Washita R.

Mackenzie ×
(Sept. 28)

McClellan ×
× Miles
(Aug. 30)

Palo

Duro

Cr.
Baldwin
(Sept. 7-8)

Salt

FORT
SILL
▲

COMANCHE,
KIOWA AND
APACHE
RESERVATION

S T A K E D

Tule   Canyon

Prairie Dog
Town Fork

Fork

Wichita
Mts.

Red

River

P L A I N

BUELL

FORT RICHARDSON ▲

NEW MEXICO

TERRITORY

▲ FORT GRIFFIN

MACKENZIE

TEXAS

▲ FORT CONCHO

THE RED RIVER WAR

repulsed the charge with a hail of gunfire. The ten-pound Parrott and Gatling guns belched forth covering fire for Miles's counterattack. "If any man is killed, I will make him a corporal!" shouted an excited Captain Adna R. Chaffee as his men swept forward. The enemy fled across the drought-ravaged Red River, by then little more than a stagnant pool of alkali and gypsum, up Tule Canyon, and onto the Staked Plain. Cursing bluecoats scrambled up the sides of the canyons in vain pursuit. Casualties had been light—official army reports listed one soldier wounded and three Indians killed—but supply shortages restricted Miles's range. A tremendous thunderstorm soon transformed the dry creek beds into raging torrents and rendered chase impossible. Miles fired off petulant diatribes against the twin shortages of supplies and qualified subordinates as he awaited fresh provisions.[21]

On September 7 and 8, Lieutenant Baldwin and three scouts fought through a large party of Indians along the Salt Fork of the Red River on their way to Camp Supply. In another action, several hundred Kiowas and Comanches surrounded Miles's supply train south of the Washita River. A relief force from Camp Supply and the belated arrival of Major Price's New Mexico column finally rescued the beleaguered escort after a three-day siege. And a six-man mail party, detached from the main column, held out against over one hundred Indians by scooping out a buffalo wallow. With his communications threatened and food stores exhausted, Miles had no choice but to fall back to the Washita. An accompanying newspaperman declared, "The whole country is alive with Indians. . . . The pursuit to the Red river was certainly not satisfactory."[22]

Despite the army's victory at Tule Canyon, the Indians had infested Miles's supply lines and forced a 140-mile retreat. Small expeditionary forces groped for signs of the enemy while Miles organized base camps along the Washita and South Canadian rivers and Sweetwater Creek. In the meantime, conflicting messages from Pope baffled the colonel. "It is wholly out of the question to secure complete results in a summer campaign against Indians. It is too easy for them to scatter like partridges all over the plains," General Pope consoled him in one note. But other communications criticized Miles's handling of supplies and his failure to mount another offensive. "The object of your movement is to find the hostile Indians," scolded Pope. "They seem to be all around you."[23]

Frustrated by the torrential rains and what he believed to be undue meddling from above, Miles furiously assailed subordinates, army quartermasters, and even his superior. Other than Baldwin, most junior officers, particularly those from the regular army rather than Civil War volunteers, had grown too accustomed to the leisures of post life. They had performed reasonably well during good weather, but found it too easy to make excuses and complain when the rains came. Incompetent quartermaster officials at department headquarters had failed to secure adequate supplies. But Miles saved his sharpest barbs for Pope. The general's determination to allow Price a free hand, his inability to rectify the supply crisis, and his official criticisms embittered Miles, who charged that his superior had robbed him of any credit for the Tule Canyon affair. Pope was too far away from the fighting, so he was unable to forward adequate intelligence reports and was instead dispatching useless advice, declared the colonel, who made certain that superiors heard his side of the story. "I do not think he [Pope] has much sympathy with this movement," charged Miles.[21]

Pope countered with his own spirited defense. "[Miles] seems to want wagons enough to haul supplies and half forage to great distances which it is impractical to furnish him and impracticable for him to get along with if he had them." Miles believed that troops from Camp Supply, commanded by Lieutenant Colonel William H. Lewis, should guard the supply routes, thus freeing his own column for pursuit duties. Though Pope first supported this scheme, the overtaxed garrison at Camp Supply could not hope to comply. The general decided that because Lewis must keep open the line between Supply and Dodge, Miles would have to protect his own trains and camps.[25]

Still decrying the lack of support, Miles dispatched several troops of cavalry to guard his rear. Each day's delay grew more difficult to bear, for the colonel feared that rivals would snatch away his glory while he waited for supplies. His worries were justified, for thirty-four-year-old Colonel Mackenzie, who boasted a Civil War record comparable to Miles's own, was hot on the trail. As dawn broke on September 28, Mackenzie's cavalrymen descended a narrow path down Palo Duro Canyon to surprise Iron Shirt's Cheyenne, Ohamatai's Comanche, and Mamanti's Kiowa villages, numbering several hundred lodges in all. In the pandemonium that followed, one army trumpeter was wounded and at least three Indians killed as the soldiers destroyed most of the tribes' homes, winter stores, and ponies. Two weeks later, Lieutenant Colonel Buell's Eleventh infantrymen burned a large number of Kiowa lodges along the Salt Fork of the Red River.[26]

Miles feverishly worked to get back into action. His detachments scoured the plains; on October 13 Chaffee destroyed five Indian lodges and captured a hundred ponies. Miles geared up for a winter offensive, requesting that Mary send warm woolen stockings, buffalo overshoes, a portable camp stove, and a gallon of rye whiskey. Confident that the Indians would weaken as temperatures fell, he pushed into the far reaches of the Staked Plain in late October, hoping to smash the Indians against Major Price's troopers waiting to the east.[27]

But his enemies had plenty of fight—on November 6 a hundred Cheyennes ambushed Captain Henry J. Farnsworth and twenty-five cavalrymen at the headwaters of McClellan Creek, killing two and wounding four of his men. Two days later, Lieutenant Baldwin, escorting an empty wagon train back to the Washita base, stumbled upon Grey Beard's Cheyennes on the north bank of McClellan Creek. Baldwin loaded his outnumbered footsoldiers onto a double line of wagons, threw out his small force of mounted men on either flank, and rushed the village. A twelve-mile pursuit ensued, as the Cheyennes, low on ammunition, fled the unorthodox onslaught. Major Price, with five troops of cavalry, was at one point within a mile of the action, but he mysteriously failed to join the contest. Grey Beard's people, though routed, made good their escape.[28]

Although complete victory still eluded his colonel, Baldwin had at least rescued two white captives—Julie and Adelaide German, survivors of a Cheyenne attack the previous September, in which their parents had been killed. Aged five and seven, the girls' pitiful condition (Baldwin described them as being "nearly starved to death and naked") rekindled the sensational tales of Indian captivity so popular among nineteenth-century readers. The soldiers redoubled their efforts to save the eldest German sisters, Catherine and Sophia, also believed to be alive. With the children bearing heavily in his calculations, Miles planned another campaign toward the headwaters of the Red River, a determination backed by Sheridan at division headquarters. The southern plains "should be swept of these miserable savages and opened to settlements," he advised Sheridan. "There is scarcely any part of it not adapted to pastoral or agricultural purposes."[29]

Miles complained that Price's incompetence had nearly ruined his campaign, but he determined to remain active. Bitterly cold weather magnified his difficulties. A four-day ice storm killed a hundred horses and left twenty-six men from Davidson's column with severe cases of frostbite. A captured pony intended for Miles's daughter Cecilia also perished. The arctic conditions and supply shortages forced Mackenzie, Buell, and Davidson to break up their commands in late November and December. Although scattered Indian bands had surrendered throughout the fall, over two thousand Cheyennes, Kiowas, and Comanches remained defiant. On November 29, an Eighth Cavalry column attacked but failed to destroy about fifty Cheyenne warriors along Muster Creek, a tributary of the Canadian.[30]

Colonel Miles, believing his men were better able to withstand the ice and snow than the Indians, brushed aside Pope's suggestion that he abandon his Panhandle cantonments and launched another three-company sortie on January 2. His spirited veterans, now better acclimated to the subzero temperatures and proud of their growing reputation, sang the incongruous "Marching through Georgia" as they slid across the icy plains west of Fort Sill. Desperate to save the missing German sisters, Miles dispatched Indian messengers with a final ultimatum to the enemy chiefs—their surrender depended upon the safe return of Sophia and Catherine. Turning up nothing and suffering minor frostbite damage to his left ear, he led his weary soldiers back to the relative comforts of the Washita cantonment in early February.[31]

But the Red River campaigns of 1874–75, with their endless pursuits, demand for constant vigilance on the part of the Indians, and numbing cold, had rendered most of the southern plains people destitute. In late February, the Kiowas surrendered. The Cheyennes, including Grey Beard, turned themselves over to Lieutenant Colonel Neill the following month. With them came Catherine and Sophia, barely alive after their long ordeal. The exhausted Kotsoteka and Kwahadi Comanches finally gave up in April and June at Fort Sill.[32]

As the Indians came in, Miles presented a wide-ranging report on the previous seven months. In addition to a detailed summary of the military operations, he discussed the nature of the country, the problem of supplies, the need for good communications, the decline of the buffalo, and the character of his enemies. Miles enthusiastically proclaimed the southern plains suitable for white occupation. Government ox trains rather than the contract transportation or the mule trains favored by many of his rivals seemed more economical for use in

Indian campaigns. Carrier pigeons and flares would improve communication and the forthcoming destruction of the bison herds would open up vast new lands for stock raising. Finally, concluded Miles, Indians should be disarmed, dismounted, and taught trades useful in white-dominated society.[33]

As for his men's performance, the victorious Miles could afford to be generous; he praised no fewer than seventeen officers in his official report. He was particularly lavish in his praise for Baldwin. Within the month, he recommended that the lieutenant be breveted to captain for his actions at the Salt Fork of the Red River and to major for his work at McClellan Creek. Though the army had temporarily ended the system of awarding brevet appointments, Miles never forgot his trusted subordinate, later helping to secure for him two Medals of Honor for his heroism during the Civil War and in recapturing the German girls.[34]

Miles also extended his good offices to the orphaned German sisters. The eldest, Catherine, was of legal age, but the colonel was appointed guardian for Sophia, Julia, and Adelaide. Congress diverted five thousand dollars from Cheyenne annuities for the care and upbringing of the two youngest girls. Miles worked tirelessly to secure equal funding for Catherine and Sophia. Army band benefits raised money and attracted public support in the meantime. He resigned his guardianship when he left Kansas, but Miles continued to press the case of the elder girls among national legislators. In 1879, Congress belatedly appropriated another five thousand dollars for Catherine and Sophia.[35]

Pope and Miles also enjoyed something of a reconciliation. Pope's direct personal correspondence had always expressed confidence in Miles's abilities. But official communiqués from the Department of the Missouri reflected a more critical tone. Frustrated by the lack of consistency and never patient with censure, Miles aired his complaints to General Sherman. Why, wondered Miles on December 27, 1874, did he continue to receive negative reports from Pope's headquarters and at the same time "private and strictly confidential letters from the same officer . . . filled with flattering praise"?[36]

A more rational analysis became possible as it became obvious even to Miles, whose delicate sensibilities required careful handling, that all commands had experienced near-crippling supply deficiencies. The tension between Pope and himself, he concluded, could be attributed to a staff officer, Lieutenant George Smith Anderson, who had sabotaged their relations. "How any honorable gentleman [Anderson] can remain on the staff . . . and do nothing but make disparaging criticisms and belittle every honest effort, is more than I can understand. . . . I think he has misrepresented you. . . . Your personal letters and many assurances that I receive from Fort Leavenworth convince me of your hearty friendship," Miles wrote to Pope.[37]

Whatever Anderson's real role, blaming a junior officer provided a convenient excuse for both Miles and Pope. General Pope was stung by his subordinate's sniping and proclivity for appealing to higher authorities. But both realized the advantages of cooperation. Because of Miles's relationship with General Sherman, widely thought to be of more practical value than it probably was, Pope thought Miles might put in a good word on Pope's behalf. By the same token, a promotion for Pope would open up a brigadier general's slot for an energetic colonel like Miles.[38]

Even as Miles and Pope mended fences, jealousies between Miles and the irascible Ranald Mackenzie intensified. Mackenzie, less verbal but just as anxious for promotion as Miles, received command of the strategic Fort Sill. Shortly thereafter, the department was enlarged to include an important new cantonment along Sweetwater Creek, Texas. Mackenzie saw the move as a thinly veiled effort by Miles, also ensconced in the Department of the Missouri, to vie for control of the Indian Territory. "While I like Miles," protested Mackenzie to Sheridan, "I think that this ought not be done and was very much hurt by even such a proposition being made."[39]

Mackenzie's immediate fears went unrealized. In late March, Miles's father died. Though their recent relations had not been close, he went to Boston to help settle the estate. He enjoyed several options on his return west. Pope had asked him to take command of Camp Supply and Sheridan queried about his interest in the District of New Mexico. Seeking advice from Sherman, Miles wondered if the latter transfer was worth the loss of "all personal comfort." Sherman, who still believed the arid Southwest an expensive headache for the army, with little to attract an ambitious colonel, advised against such a move. Miles thus resumed his duties as post commander at Leavenworth.[40]

Meanwhile, the army dealt with the recently surrendered Indians. Lieutenant Richard Henry Pratt escorted seventy-four chiefs, "ringleaders," and assorted warriors to Florida for three years of confinement. The remainder were relegated to their reservations. But Miles realized that exiling a few malcontents would not address the deeper problems resulting from mismanagement of the agencies, the government's failure to fulfill its treaty obligations, and the clash of cultures. Miles, whom Pratt believed was "greatly interested" in the case of Grey Beard, unsuccessfully interceded on the chief's behalf.[41]

Miles maintained no such sympathies for Major Price, whom he blamed for his failure to secure complete military victory. General Pope had championed Price, an Ohio native three times brevetted for service in the Civil and Indian wars, in the face of Miles's vigorous assaults. Securing support from Sheridan and Sherman, Pope asked his junior to drop the issue. But conciliation was foreign to the uncompromising Miles, who demanded a court-martial. Hearings against Price dragged on through the spring and summer of 1875, leaving the accused's reputation tarnished but his career intact.[42]

Troubles in New Mexico Territory disrupted an otherwise quiet fall at Leavenworth. At the Cimarron Agency, rancor between local non-Indians, the Jicarilla Apache and Muache Ute inhabitants, and Indian agent Alexander G. Irvine had been building for several months. The causes—white trespassing, illegal whiskey trade, and inadequate government rations—seemed all too common. Irvine had lost control of his charges and the Indian Bureau had requested a detachment of soldiers there as early as June 1875. In November the well-meaning Irvine, though "a good man in every respect," shot three intoxicated Indians and was himself wounded in the hand in a final imbroglio. Although he was slated to take a similar post at the Navajo Agency, Irvine instead resigned from the service.[43]

Pope dispatched Miles and a squad of cavalry to quell the disturbances while the new civilian agent, John Pyle, transferred south from Montana. Resorting to the olive branch rather than the sword, Miles met with several chiefs on December 6. Miles acknowledged in his report the validity of Indian grievances and criticized what he believed to be incompetent management and fraud within the Interior Department. Clothing and supplies promised by treaty had not been delivered and food that had reached the tribes was virtually inedible. The distribution of fresh rations and the promise of better conditions persuaded more than 250 Indians to return to the agency. With Agent Pyle safely in place, Miles, who had handled the affair with tact and patience, headed back to Kansas within the month.[44]

On returning to Leavenworth, he had to come to grips with the death of his mother, who had died while he was in New Mexico. In early

January 1876, he found time to tie up a few matters at his post before returning to Massachusetts. Hardened by nearly fifteen years' military service, Nelson imperiously dominated his older brother, Daniel. He dictated funeral arrangements, by mail, like a military command. In no uncertain terms, he asked for his mother's family Bible, issued instructions concerning his mother's remaining estate, and picked out a headstone and suitable inscription. The forty-eight-year-old Daniel complied.[45]

Nelson Miles was now a westerner. The hills of Massachusetts and the internecine slaughter of the Civil War seemed far removed as he and the regulars helped, as they saw it, to conquer a continent. Like so many others on the frontier, he found time to speculate in real estate and begin a family. Outsiders like president-to-be James Garfield, on an extended western tour, found him "a good talker and very bright." But Miles craved more. His campaigns against the Indians of the southern plains—despite drought, monsoon rains, blazing heat, subzero cold, and constant supply shortages—fulfilled his obligation to duty as well as his own ambitions.[46]

Miles had learned much; campaigning against Indians, where the long chase became an end in itself, was vastly different from the fighting he had known against the Confederates. He had soon recognized that a successful western officer left nothing to chance. Hardy soldiers, good scouts, an adequate supply and transportation system, and tenacious pursuit in the face of physical hardships were critical. His superiors agreed that he had adapted well; Sheridan, for example, noted that Miles had "exceeded [his] expectations."[47]

Miles was not afraid to suggest changes in the postwar army. Quasi-independent bureau chiefs wielded almost feudal control over the army's ten departments—the Adjutant General's Office, the Inspector General's Department, the Judge-Advocate General's Office, the Quartermaster's Department, the Subsistence Department, the Ordnance Department, the Corps of Engineers, the Medical Department, the Signal Bureau, and the Pay Department. The division of authority between the secretary of war and the commanding general also remained unclear. As Miles noted cogently when testifying before a blue-ribbon congressional panel, this Bacchic system created "a conflict of authority and multiplicity of channels of communications, resulting in the impossibility of fixing responsibility, laxity of discipline, and indifference in administration." He urged the consolidation of the quarter-master, commissary, and pay departments into a single corps and an increase in the responsibilities of the commanding general to resolve these problems. Finally, those who performed well in the field should be given special consideration regarding promotion.[48]

His recent experience had also convinced Miles that the government's Indian system needed much reform. The tragedies of reservation life seemed all too unnecessary. As he proclaimed to Howard, "You will see that I do not believe in the old army theory of destroying the whole race, neither do I approve or hesitate to denounce the mismanagement that in my opinion has caused much of the trouble." Adopting a view popular among contemporary officers, Miles blamed the Indian wars on corruption, mismanagement, and inexperience within the Indian Bureau, which he believed was a convenient tool for patronage-minded politicians. Congress had long considered the possibility of restoring sole control over Indians to the War Department, and Miles supported the transfer before Congressman Henry B. Banning's Committee on Military Affairs. The colonel also lobbied Senator Sherman and William C. Church, editor of the influential *Army and Navy Journal,* to reform the Indian system. Though Congress decided against an immediate change, Miles and others continued to advocate such reform.[49]

Miles's frontier experience also highlighted less attractive sides of his persona. Though he was by no means an advocate of the physical slaughter of the tribes, his admonitions that the "wild savages" had been "taught that murder is noble and labor degrading," and his belief that they needed the army's firm hand and a healthy dose of "the benefits, advantages and blessings of civilization" betrayed an inability to see any virtues in Indian culture.[50]

And critics questioned Miles's motives. His hiring of a newspaperman as a scout for the Red River expedition, though not unusual for commanders during the era, seemed little more than a heavy-handed publicity stunt. Further, his determination to strike south to defeat the Indians before Mackenzie could attack, rather than to move north to protect his own supplies, suggested that enhancing his own career was more important than protecting the lives of his men. In a similarly controversial move, Miles had refused a plaintive request from Lieutenant Colonel Buell for a loan of supplies. "You and I are both soldiers and of course working for the same interest. We should meet in my judgment and form some plan of co-operating," Buell had reasoned.[51]

Plagued by his own supply troubles, Miles had refused Buell's offer of cooperation. In so doing, he acquired a reputation as an ambitious climber who would advance his own interests at any cost. Even a presumed ally like George Custer feared a cabal, predicting that Miles would use his relationship with General Sherman to ignore official channels and secure one of the coveted mounted regiments. Sherman, Custer asserted, "would gladly advance Miles' interests and would give little thought to the outcry such a transfer would be on us." Such infighting was endemic to the postwar army; it remained to be seen whether the talents and bravery of men like Miles and Custer would outweigh the problems and controversies stemming from their personal ambitions.[52]

5 : VICTORY AGAINST THE SIOUX

Patriotic celebrations and gala exhibitions commemorated the nation's centennial year. But 1876 opened on a disappointing note for Colonel Nelson A. Miles. Congress had two years earlier limited the regular army to twenty-five thousand men. Angry at the army's involvement in Reconstruction, House Democrats now looked to renew the attacks, passing bills that would cut the pay of officers and reduce the army by another three thousand. Senate Republicans blocked the reductions, but the dark political clouds boded ill for the ambitious colonel.[1]

The possibility that his army rivals might secure new laurels further threatened Miles's designs. Waves of non-Indian migration had accompanied the discovery of gold in the Black Hills, which lay deep within lands promised in perpetuity to the Sioux and Northern Cheyennes. As violence between whites and Indians intensified, Secretary of the Interior Zachariah Chandler authorized the army to take the offensive and enter Indian reservations on February 1, 1876. From divisional headquarters in Chicago, Phil Sheridan envisioned two columns penetrating deep into Sioux country and the Northern Plains. Brigadier General Alfred Terry, Miles's first choice as groomsman, was slated to push west from Fort Abraham Lincoln, in the Department of the Dakota. George Crook, a successful Indian fighter whose promotion from lieutenant colonel to brigadier general earned him the undying enmity of Nelson Miles, was to command a column from Fort Fetterman, in the Department of the Platte.[2]

Heavy Montana snows dissuaded Terry from leaving Fort Lincoln. Crook's expedition, with Colonel Joseph J. Reynolds as titular commander, limped back to Fort Fetterman, Wyoming Territory, after less than a month in the field. "These winter campaigns in this latitude should be prohibited," shivered Reynolds. "Cruelty is no name for them." The winter strikes having failed, columns under Terry, Crook, and Colonel John Gibbon resumed the war that spring. Safely in Kansas, Miles seized the opportunity to remind General Sherman of Crook's failures. Urging that Sherman "explode that Black Hills humbug," Miles asked to be allowed to strike the Sioux, promising to "make their country so uncomfortable for them" that they would sue for peace.[3]

Miles took small comfort in the fact that Crook had earned no new accolades in mid-June at the Battle of the Rosebud, where the Indians fought his troops to a standoff. But Miles's jealousy turned to horror in early July when he learned of the fate of Lieutenant Colonel George A. Custer. In a detached column from Terry's command, Custer and five troops of the Seventh Cavalry had been cut down along the Little Bighorn River by a large coalition of Sioux and Northern Cheyennes. Nelson and Mary had adored the rakish Custer and enjoyed the company of his wife Libbie; the sudden defeat proved a tragic reminder of the dangers inherent to every column that took to the field.[4]

Plans to reduce the size of the regular army were laid aside amid the national horror over the disaster. Instead, Congress increased the number of privates per cavalry troop from sixty-four to one hundred

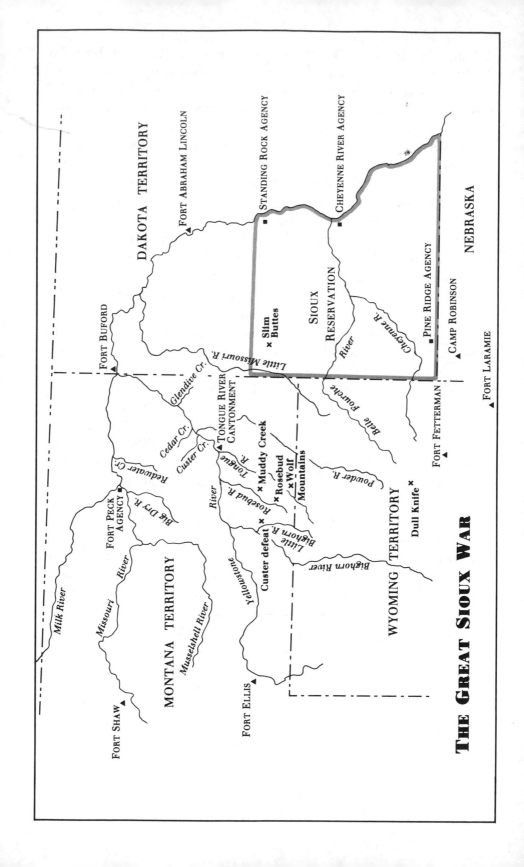

THE GREAT SIOUX WAR

and funded two big new forts for the Yellowstone River region. Meanwhile, Sheridan funneled in reinforcements to Custer's shaken comrades. The Fifth Cavalry moved up to assist Crook, as did Ranald Mackenzie and most of the Fourth. Elements of the Fifth and Twenty-second Infantry regiments would support Terry and Gibbon.[5]

As Miles's troops prepared for the northern plains, the Custer defeat weighed heavily on soldiers and dependents alike. Lieutenant George W. Baird's pregnant wife was particularly distraught; as Mrs. Alice Baldwin (wife of Frank Baldwin) sympathized, "This makes the third time when she has been in this condition that her husband has been away from her." Even William Sherman warned of the rigors of the upcoming campaign. "I admired your spunk & spirit in responding so promptly to the call, but I see in the long future a pretty hard career for you . . . and it may be a long time before you will again have the pleasant home you had at Leavenworth." Rejecting any notion that Lieutenant Colonel Joseph Whistler, a battle-hardened veteran of the Mexican and Civil wars, would lead the Fifth Infantry into the fray, Miles departed Fort Leavenworth in late July without even waiting to greet his nephew George, who had come from Massachusetts looking for fame and fortune.[6]

As the column rode a river steamer up the Missouri River, past Fort Lincoln, Miles found time to pay his respects to the mourning dependents of the Seventh Cavalry. Among the twenty-seven widows then at the post was Libbie Custer, who the colonel feared would not recover from her grief. The enlisted personnel adopted a more practical approach to their upcoming duty, discarding their bayonets and cartridge boxes in favor of lighter cartridge belts more suited to long marches.[7]

The situation grew increasingly ominous as the Fifth wound its way toward its Yellowstone River rendezvous with Terry. Seeking to understand his tribal foes, Nelson asked Mary to have her father forward information about the nation's past relations with the Indians. He reminded his wife to discount rumors, trying to comfort her by repeating reports that suggested the Indians would flee the region long before his column arrived. But as the steamer plowed up the Missouri, he privately admitted that the Standing Rock Agency tribes, well-armed with Spencer and Henry rifles, appeared to be extremely hostile to the army. Traders licensed by the government, declared the colonel, had sold the Indians these weapons—"another establishment in what the Belknap creatures were interested," complained Miles in reference to

William Belknap's scandal-wracked tenure as secretary of war. Early indications that Miles and his men would again be relegated to garrison duties only magnified Miles's uncertainties.[8]

The steamer's frequent stops to take on wood gave the command time to shape up with a few drills and last-minute conferences. Yet their arrival at Terry's main camp at the mouth of the Rosebud on August 2 offered no encouragement. The command officers there seemed totally shaken, he confided to Mary on the fourth. Though amiable to Miles, Terry seemed disheartened and unenthusiastic about encountering any enemy Indians. The reputation of Indian leaders like Sitting Bull, a Hunkpapa chief whose keen political skills and adamant resistance to intruders had been a rallying point for many Plains peoples, grew to fearsome proportions among frightened whites.[9]

Miles found little reason to question this conclusion as he pieced together the summer's events. Army leadership had been poor at all levels. In May, Sheridan had assured Terry as to "the impossibility of any large numbers of Indians keeping together as a hostile body for even a week." Although Sheridan's prediction usually rang true, that summer thousands of Northern Cheyennes and Sioux formed into a loose coalition of six circles—Cheyenne, Hunkpapa, Oglala, Minneconjou, Sans Arc, and Blackfoot. Even when allowing for the erroneous advice, the army's three columns seemed sufficient to handle any contingency. In April, Colonel Gibbon had left Fort Ellis, Montana Territory, with ten companies. Crook, eventually assembling a thousand soldiers, 250 Indian auxiliaries, a pack train of 250 mules, 106 wagons, and five journalists, had pushed north from Fort Fetterman the following month toward the Yellowstone and Bighorn rivers. From the east, Terry had mustered over nine hundred regulars, forty Arikara scouts, three Gatling guns, a cattle herd, and 150 wagons. Following the stalemate at the Battle of the Rosebud, Crook had fallen back to his supply wagons on Goose Creek, south of the battlefield. Pushing west in June, Terry's Dakota column had also groped to find the main Indian camp. Seeking to trap the enemy, Terry had dispatched Custer to enter the Little Bighorn valley from the south while Gibbon blocked a northward escape. Shaken by the Custer defeat of June 25, Terry and Gibbon had opted to await reinforcements before searching for any more Indians.[10]

Observing the rattled commands, Colonel Miles condemned both his inadequate ordnance and the paralysis that gripped general officers now in the field. The Napoleon guns attached to his infantry he deemed too immobile for service against Indians. But then, he speculated, what could be expected from an Ordnance Department whose chief, Stephen V. Benet, had spent most of the Civil War away from the action at West Point, and whose junior officers never accompanied the regulars into the field. Sheridan cared about only the cavalry, sulked the colonel, and Sherman did not intervene as needed. The entire campaign, Miles predicted, would end in an embarrassing failure to the army.[11]

Most of these complaints were justified. Although all the troops were operating in the Division of the Missouri, Terry's Dakota column remained independent from Crook's soldiers, who were from the Department of the Platte. The divided departmental structure had been maintained at Sheridan's insistence; Miles found it ridiculous that Terry and Crook acted with so little coordination. The separately administered columns violated a basic military maxim—unity of command—fumed Miles, who was resentful at being temporarily placed under Gibbon's command. On August 10, Miles shook his head in disgust as the Dakota and Platte columns blundered into one another in the Rosebud River valley.[12]

Crook and Terry decided to combine forces. Miles believed the very size of the joint expedition, now thirty-two hundred strong, precluded any success. If the Indians had wanted to fight, he reasoned, they would have challenged Terry or Crook before their accidental junction. He also found time to dash off a strong defense of Custer's memory to the *Army and Navy Journal.* Anxious to disassociate himself from a chase he correctly gauged to be futile, Miles suggested that he take six companies and guard the fords of the Yellowstone between the Powder and Tongue rivers.[13]

On approval of the move, Miles fairly leaped at the chance for an independent command. His sturdy infantrymen marched thirty-four miles in twenty-four hours to cut off any Indian attempts to cross the Yellowstone en route to Canada. "The march was as hard as any I ever knew or have read of," he declared, as the heat, dust, and rugged terrain took their toll. Yet the men "went through to the River in the best of spirits, though utterly exhausted. Nearly all of the officers held up until the last few miles." By mid-August his patrols, supported by the steamboat *Far West* and two light howitzers, were combing the region.[14]

True to Miles's prediction, the Terry-Crook combination was short-lived. Crook, junior to Terry in seniority, chafed at being relegated to a subordinate's role. Supplying the huge column seemed problematic as water levels on the Yellowstone dropped, rendering it unnavigable. After a desultory march east to the Powder River and Miles's supply base there, the two generals parted company on August twenty-fourth, Crook to pursue the trail south and Terry to investigate reported sightings of Indians north along Glendive Creek. A brief meeting with these men did nothing to soften Miles's criticism. None of the commanders had analyzed the unique military problems associated with Indian fighting, he charged. Terry seemed the best of the lot, but even that officer, inexperienced in western campaigning, had allowed himself to come under the influence of dullards like Gibbon.[15]

Save for a dinner party to celebrate the arrival of his nephew George to the command, Miles found little relief from his frustrations on the barren plains. A young bachelor could tolerate the long Civil War campaigns. But a married man approaching his fortieth birthday had bigger responsibilities. He contemplated resigning rather than enduring another thankless, poorly-conceived campaign like the most recent summer fiasco. Long waits between postal deliveries compounded his anxiety; he finally dispatched a squad to go downriver and pick up the regiment's mail.[16]

New duties came later that month as driving rains drenched the command. On August twenty-sixth, General Terry had received orders to occupy the Yellowstone Valley throughout the upcoming winter. To do so, a new post would be needed at the mouth of the Tongue River. Lieutenant Colonel Whistler and two companies of the Fifth steamed up the Yellowstone to begin construction and Miles arrived in time to christen the cantonment on September 11. As quartermasters labored to supply the army's growing presence in the northern plains, Terry disbanded his expedition and Crook's men nearly starved in a vain attempt to chase down the Indians in the Black Hills. Crook's disappointing campaign culminated in an inconclusive fire fight at Slim Buttes.[17]

With most of his Fifth Infantry and two companies of the Twenty-second, Miles began settling in for the winter at the Tongue River Cantonment. The alkali cliffs, lava beds, and ravine-broken prairies presented a stark backdrop as the troops, slowed by maddening shortages of construction equipment, threw up rude picket buildings of

cottonwood logs chinked with mud. Remembering all too vividly earlier winters on the southern plains, the troops "applied themselves
zealously" in securing heavy coats, masks, and buffalo moccasins.
Woolen blankets were crafted into crude underclothing. Miles urgently
requested regulation winter uniforms, pack animals, Sibley tents,
mounted troops, and better artillery.[18]

Good reconnaissance was essential if he hoped to locate the Sioux
and Northern Cheyennes in their winter haunts. Miles thus hired a
swarm of allied Indians and scouts, including Luther S. "Yellowstone"
Kelly, a rugged frontiersman who won his job by presenting the colonel
the paw of a huge bear as a calling card. "Buffalo Bill" Cody, with
whom Miles would also form a long relationship, was also enlisted
during the coming months.[19]

Supplies posed a thornier problem. Ice and low water blocked the
Yellowstone River, on which the new cantonment depended for trans-
porting the bulk of its provisions, for several months every year. As a
result, an existing road to Fort Buford, at the junction of the Yellowstone and the Missouri, was shortened to prepare for the additional
traffic. But overland travel remained precarious at best. On October 16,
Miles advised General Sherman, "Tonight I am somewhat concerned
about a wagon train out from Glendive as it has been seven days
enroute and should have come in today. I shall start down to meet it
tomorrow morning if my scouts do not bring me word of it tonight."[20]

Miles left the Tongue River cantonment with most of his regiment
the following day. His hunch proved correct. In the wee hours of
October 11, several hundred Hunkpapas, Minneconjous, and Sans
Arcs had attacked the ninety-four wagon supply train, escorted by
Captain Charles W. Miner and four infantry companies, west of Glendive Creek. Capturing forty-seven mules in the initial skirmish, the
Indians forced Miner to retrace his steps to Glendive. Here Lieutenant
Colonel Elwell S. Otis took command, replacing the panicky civilian
teamsters with regular soldiers, increasing the escort to 185 men, and
adding a battery of Gatling guns. The supply train set out again, but the
Indians harassed it with long-range sniping. Otis received a message
from Sitting Bull, offering friendship, asking for food, and demanding
that the bluecoats leave the Sioux hunting grounds. The lieutenant
colonel could not meet such terms, so the brief parley soon broke up.
Miles, following sketchy reports that "hostile" Indians were moving
north toward the Yellowstone River, bivouacked at Custer Creek before

meeting the beleaguered supply train on October 18. Otis then proceeded on to the Tongue River Cantonment as Miles followed the Indians' trail to the northeast.[21]

Miles overtook the coalition two days later. Hungry and tired of war, the tribes requested further talks. A wary Sitting Bull, whom Miles later dubbed "a wild, reckless warrior," met the colonel that day. "He desired to know why the soldiers did not go into winter quarters," reported Miles, who had outfitted himself in a fur cap and long overcoat trimmed with bear fur, "and in other words he demanded an old-fashioned peace for the winter." The Sioux called for trade and an end to white trespass; the colonel and his aides, who despite an agreement that they should come unarmed had in fact brought revolvers under their winter coats, required that the tribes return to their government agencies. Having reached an impasse, the talks ended about sundown on the twentieth. Miles then edged his command farther north along Cedar Creek to cut off a possible flight to Canada by the Indians.[22]

Another peace council, which included Sitting Bull, Pretty Bear, Bull Eagle, Standing Bear, Gall, and White Bear, met the following day. Concerned about his ebbing strength, Sitting Bull desperately sought terms—"he desired to live as an Indian," according to Miles—that would enable the tribes to remain free of government domination. Miles, haunted by dreams of being assassinated (as General Edward R. S. Canby had been during negotiations with the Modocs in April 1873), was equally apprehensive, but firm. He demanded that Sitting Bull "should camp his tribe at some point on the Yellowstone under the troops, or go into some Government agency and place his people under subjugation to the Government." Though several chiefs seemed to waiver, Sitting Bull rejected such a solution.[23]

"An engagement immediately followed," reported Miles matter-of-factly. The Indians, who numbered between eight hundred and a thousand warriors, seemed surprised by the stubborn advance of Miles's 398 regular infantrymen, who opened up a steady fire with their single-shot Springfield rifles. A model 1861 artillery ordnance rifle, expertly handled by Captain Simon Snyder, discouraged the Indians from pressing too closely, though one counterattack forced the bluecoats to form a defensive square. The Indians finally set the prairie afire; amid the haze of early evening and smoke from the grass fires, Miles halted the chase after overrunning the Indian campsites.[24]

Few slept that night, as soldiers watched for an attack and Indians sought to salvage their winter stores and equipment. The pursuit continued the following day, with Miles finally calling a halt on the south side of the Yellowstone River, forty-two miles from the site of the initial engagement. As was often the case during flights between regulars and Indians, reported casualties had been light—five dead warriors were found, along with three wounded bluecoats. But the soldiers had captured a good deal of stores and camp equipage; in addition, they had overcome their own fears of Sioux invincibility.[25]

Tired and cold but thirsting for victory, Miles shared his feelings with those who meant most to him—his wife Mary for her love and devotion, and Sherman for his power within the army. On the twenty-fifth he promised to write Mary more frequently and blamed his previous silence on the pressures of the campaign. One mistake, he reminded her, might cause a massacre. Sleep came only fitfully, he complained, but he admitted that the rigors of the pursuit had allowed him to shed several pounds. Buoyed by the recent success, he wrote letters to General Sherman, mixing promises to continue the pursuit with complaints about a supposed conspiracy within the army against his interests. The Indians were low on ammunition and supplies. "I believe we can wear them down," Miles determined. But the want of cavalry, which he blamed on Crook's wastefulness, had prevented him from completing his victory. He asserted, "it is not easy for Infy to catch them although I believe we can whip them every time."[26]

On October 26, Miles received new peace feelers from segments of the crumbling coalition. He could not feed the inhabitants of the four hundred Minneconjou and Sans Arc lodges involved, so on the following day five chiefs surrendered themselves as hostages. Their people were supposed to turn themselves over to authorities at the Cheyenne Agency within thirty days. Always eager to give advice, the colonel urged that all the Indian captives be accorded firm but fair treatment. "My endeavor has been to convince them, first—of our superior power, and second—that we will deal fairly and justly with them," he explained. Miles suggested that once the followers of the surrendered chiefs had turned themselves in, their property should be sold and the proceeds invested in domestic stock. He believed that a pastoral life would suit them well.[27]

Until such recommendations could be implemented, Miles determined to follow Sitting Bull north toward the Fort Peck Agency, 120 miles from the Tongue River Cantonment. He called the Indians "the worst set of rascals I have ever seen together," and wrote that he hoped to strike these "outlaws" from the west. On November 6, after pausing to refit and pick up incoming shipments of winter gear, Miles and 434 soldiers (20 of whom were mounted), 7 scouts, 38 six-mule teams, and 2 ambulances took the field. With thirty days' rations, 250 rounds per man, every available scrap of warm clothing, and instructions that additional supplies be made available at Fort Peck, the colonel believed he could outlast any Indians who dared defy him.[28]

All hailed the Fifth and its tenacious commander. "We are all pleased to hear of the Genls [Miles's] fight," wrote Alice Baldwin, "and think he has done more than either Crook or Terry." "General Miles has displayed his usual earnestness and energy," applauded commanding general Sherman, "and I hope he will crown his success by capturing or killing Sitting Bull and his remnant of outlaws." With an eye toward reliving her husband's experiences and aware of the fame and fortune that a published account of the campaign might bring, Mary suggested that Miles record his thoughts and actions in a diary.[29]

But these accolades could not hold back the formidable conditions of a northern plains winter; a driving snowstorm soon covered Sitting Bull's trail. Long before, Sherman had warned, "Winter on the Yellowstone is another matter from winter on the Red River." By November 13, temperatures had fallen to ten degrees below zero, but Miles managed to bundle himself within silk underclothing, buffalo moccasins, overshoes, and mammoth buffalo robes. The troops marveled at the colonel's energy as they scrambled to wrap gunny sacks around their shoes and sustain the quest. When they reached Fort Peck, Miles divided his force, on the assumption that Sitting Bull remained south of the Missouri River. Captain Snyder took four companies and a cannon back south along the Big Dry, and Colonel Miles and the remainder marched along the north bank of the Missouri to the mouth of the Musselshell River.[30]

It was too cold and official demands too pressing to compile a journal, Miles explained to Mary. But confident that Sitting Bull's followers were demoralized, the colonel did find time to write a long letter to Sherman on November 18. His success, he reminded Sherman, had come without the benefit of cavalry. "I can hunt them on foot," he explained, but cautioned, in only a slight exaggeration, "It is not easy for ten small Infy companies with broken down mules & four scouts to confine the whole Sioux nation." Miles believed that such a feat merited big rewards—either command of a department or a cabinet position as secretary of war.[31]

As Miles and his hardy infantrymen plodded across Montana Territory, General Crook launched a twenty-two hundred-man sortie into the Powder River valley from the south. Leading the cavalry and the Indian scouts in an advance guard, Colonel Mackenzie struck the village of Dull Knife, a Northern Cheyenne, at daybreak on November 25. Seven soldiers died in the onslaught. Indian losses, though relatively light in terms of human life, included seven hundred ponies and two hundred lodges. Shaken by the destruction of their material possessions and cultural artifacts, the Northern Cheyennes made good their escape and found succor among Crazy Horse's Oglalas. The reclusive Mackenzie blamed himself for failing to complete the pursuit. Crook ended the Powder River campaign in late December when temperatures dropped to fifty below zero.[32]

Plowing through the snow and ice of the upper Missouri River valley, Miles encountered just as many difficulties. "I cant describe the country it is so wretchedly poor & worthless," wrote Lieutenant Baldwin. After hearing reports that Sitting Bull was now to the east, Miles hoped to dispatch Baldwin to block any attempted flight to Canada. But first the entire command needed to get across the Missouri River. Treacherous ice drifts turned the crossing into a dangerous comedy of errors. With supplies running low and tempers running high by November twenty-ninth, even the faithful Baldwin concluded, "I never saw the Genl more x x x x with everything." Already exhausted from the normal pressures accompanying a field command, Miles had good reason to be upset. His raft broke loose during one vain attempt to cross the river and began to drift downstream, finally coming to rest on a snag where it remained for the better part of a day. Efforts to throw out ropes having proved fruitless, an enlisted man finally swam out with a cable and released the " 'shipwrecked Colonel.' The Gen. was so well pleased," remembered one veteran, "that he gave the lad thirty days' furlough."[33]

With the Missouri impassable, Miles altered his plans. He crossed farther upstream and returned to the Tongue River on December 14, having tramped over five hundred miles. Snyder's column, detached in mid-November, had come in three days earlier. Baldwin and three companies had in the meantime marched east and traversed the Missouri at Fort Peck. On December 18, following up one last rumor after making Fort Peck, the indefatigable Baldwin intercepted Sitting Bull's

122 lodges near the headwaters of Redwater Creek. Neither side reported casualties, but Baldwin captured most of the enemy's winter provisions. Reaching the Tongue River post five days later, his resolute battalion had marched 716 miles through the Montana winter.[34]

The most recent expeditions further divided the nonreservation Indians. In mid-December, five Minneconjou chiefs, representing many of those who had previously surrendered but then drifted away from the agencies, approached the post on the Tongue. On the way to the cantonment the chiefs passed a camp of Crow Indians, bitter enemies of the Sioux and now allied with the bluecoats. Several Crow scouts "approached them in a friendly manner, said 'How,'" then killed them in "an unprovoked, cowardly manner," reported Miles. The guilty warriors scampered away. Undoubtedly inflating the totals, Miles declared that a thousand fighting men might have surrendered had this assassination not taken place; not surprisingly, the slaughter convinced any wavering Sioux that peace was a poor option.[35]

As Miles sorted through rumored sightings of "hostile" tribes, his men enjoyed a freezing Christmas respite at the Tongue River Cantonment. December twenty-third, wrote George Miles, who had accompanied the column back to the Tongue, was "a little cool—35 below." Eager to catch up on current affairs after their long sojourn, the troops awaited the results of that year's disputed presidential contest between Rutherford B. Hayes and Samuel Tilden. Others found the sutler's alcoholic refreshments especially tempting, and the resulting crush in the guard house led Miles to forbid liquor sales on the post. Enterprising capitalists, however, promptly opened up new saloons just off the base.[36]

In late December, Miles launched a new campaign, directed against Crazy Horse and an assortment of Oglalas and Cheyennes. Five companies of the tireless Fifth and two from the Twenty-second Infantry composed the column of 436 officers and men. Two cannon were disguised as supply wagons. Shortages of horses, mules, grain, and regulation winter clothing led Miles to urge his men to purchase additional garments from the sutler before leaving. The possibility that his rival George Crook had received more supplies than he gnawed at his ego, but Miles consoled himself with the idea that an official investigation might later ruin his enemies.[37]

After a week of herculean marches up the Tongue, food shortages threatened to force the campaign's premature end. "I believe I can fight

& whip them even if they run three or four to one," boasted the colonel to General Sherman, "but the danger of getting blocked up in two feet of snow without food is some thing that I have to be careful about." The bitter cold froze mercury thermometers; the ice and difficult terrain— "ground that a mountain goat would have trouble in getting over"— dispirited even Miles. But on January 7, scouts captured a teenaged warrior, four women, and three children. A rescue attempt made later that evening by other Indians in the area alerted the soldiers and brought forth a hail of artillery fire.[38]

Fighting, later known as the Battle of Wolf Mountains, broke out early the next morning in the hills of the upper Tongue River. Led by Crazy Horse, five to six hundred dismounted Sioux and Cheyenne warriors pushed through knee-deep snow to within five yards of Miles's lines. But the bluecoats, with inferior numbers, held in the face of heavy fire and a late-morning blizzard. Just after noon the Indians, with their ammunition running low, the big army cannon booming, the soldiers threatening to outflank them, and their morale destroyed by the death of an influential medicine man, retreated. Three enlisted men had been killed and eight wounded in the five-hour battle. Miles later claimed fifteen enemy dead and at least thirty wounded.[39]

Miles had again displayed tremendous bravery. "I remonstrated with him for exposing himself unnecessarily," wrote an awe-struck Lieutenant James W. Pope, a West Point graduate of 1868. At Miles's recommendation, Captains James S. Casey and Edmund Butler later received Medals of Honor for their heroism. Lieutenant Baldwin also won acclaim in some quarters for his capture of a crucial hill. Yet Fifth Infantry officers split into rival camps when attempting to assess the battle. Butler later sought to minimize Baldwin's role; others, including Lieutenants Baird and Pope, tended to minimize Butler's efforts. Baldwin added another critical assessment, "With the exception of Pope & Dickey there was not an officer on duty with companies who *seemed* to comprehend the character of the engagement beyond blindly defending the point they were assigned, or by chance might drift to."[40]

Crazy Horse fell back east toward Powder River. Low on supplies but still holding the prisoners he had captured before the Wolf Mountains battle, Miles retired to the Tongue-Yellowstone junction. Reaching the cantonment on January 19, Miles dashed off letters to Mary to vent his criticism of alleged conspirators behind his own lines. Terry never seemed to read his reports or requests, he declared. Miles also blamed

Otis and Major Benjamin Card, quartermaster for the Department of the Dakota, for his predicament, and threatened to go to the press if the situation were not improved. He dispatched the trusted Baldwin to voice his complaints at department headquarters in St. Paul, Minnesota.[41]

Miles unleashed a full-scale barrage on General Sherman. Despite bitter cold and rugged terrain, he had cleared the region of hostile Indians until forced by the "criminal neglect" of scheming bureaucrats to take winter quarters. Only a department command would enable him to defeat his Indian foes and overcome the conspirators. "I . . . have fought and defeated larger and better armed bodies of hostile Indians than any other officer since the history of Indian warfare commenced, and at the same time have gained a more extended knowledge of our frontier country than any living man," declared Miles. "A perfect spy system," he bragged later, had enabled him "to know the strength & design of [the] enemy, to always find, defeat & follow him."[42]

Sheridan meanwhile struggled to prepare another spring campaign, when Indian ponies would be weak from the long winter and the Missouri and Yellowstone rivers would be navigable. Though neither Crook nor Terry had performed with much distinction, Sheridan rejected Sherman's suggestion that the irascible Miles be given overall command. "To give all the troops to Col. Miles would be putting too much on him," explained Sheridan. Nonetheless, the latter did want to expand Miles's area of command to include the Powder River country. He planned to give the colonel nearly five regiments, the Pawnee Indian scouts, and authority to ignore administrative boundaries. Mackenzie and a smaller column would operate on Miles's eastern flank, along the Little Missouri and Belle Fourche rivers. General Terry would stay in St. Paul to ensure that Miles received adequate supplies; Crook would go to Omaha or Cheyenne to supply Mackenzie.[43]

Caught between an ambitious nephew-in-law, a stubborn divisional commander, and a parsimonious Congress, General Sherman strove to maintain a degree of harmony among his own ranks while at the same time defeating the Sioux and Cheyennes. He urged Sheridan to reduce expenses and to end the war before Congress released the emergency troops raised in the aftermath of the Little Bighorn. Though exasperated by Miles's braggadocio, Sherman supported his being selected to head the main column. Finally, Sherman reassured Miles that winter weather and the focus on the disputed presidential election, not a conspiracy, had slowed supplies. "There ought to be but one Department over all that country," he acknowledged in agreement with one of Miles's many proposals, "but I cannot at present accomplish so radical a change." In a ploy surely designed to appeal to Miles's ambition, he added: "I advise you not to tarry but to work hard this year, for whoever brings this Sioux war to a close will be in the fairest way to promotion."[44]

As the army scrambled to resupply and reinforce Miles, the situation among the tribes deteriorated even more appreciably. Months of running and skirmishing had taken their toll. The cumulative effects of Mackenzie's strike against Dull Knife's Northern Cheyenne village and Miles's action at Wolf Mountains had sapped tribal resolve. Hundreds of Indians had already turned themselves in; Sitting Bull had opted to head for Canada. The climate seemed ripe for negotiation. On February 1, Miles sent out his oldest captive, Sweet Woman, to assure the main body of Oglala and Brule Sioux and Cheyennes now camped along the Little Bighorn of fair treatment. Accompanying Sweet Woman were a small escort of soldiers, several pack animals loaded with gifts, and the mysterious Johnnie Bruguier. A mixed-blood scout and interpreter who had in 1875 fled government service after killing a man, Bruguier, also known as Big Leggins, subsequently established himself as a special assistant to Sitting Bull. Miles's promises that he would protect Bruguier from legal action had recently lured the latter back into government employment. With the intercession of Sweet Woman and Bruguier, several Indian chiefs opened further negotiations with "Bear Coat," as Miles was now known, in reference to his enormous winter robe.[45]

Following four days of discussions at the Tongue River, the peace delegation departed on February 23. The colonel asserted that he had convinced the Indians of his authority and that all was proceeding according to design as the leaders returned to their villages. But then, complained Miles, George Crook interfered. At Camp Robinson, Crook had opened rival negotiations with the influential Brule leader, Spotted Tail. Crook's runners hinted that the Indians might retain their ponies and arms if they came in to Camp Robinson. Still uncertain about Miles's sincerity, the Indians decided to seek out this better deal.[46]

On March 16, about 150 warriors, mostly Cheyennes but including a smattering of Oglalas, and 16 leaders cautiously approached the Tongue River Cantonment for further talks. Bruguier had warned the nervous tribesmen that Miles rode two horses. If Bear Coat rode out on the roan, it meant he sought war. But a white horse meant he was offering peace. Miles indeed trotted out atop the lighter horse and the negotiations proceeded, even though Miles's initial gesture—while shaking hands he inadvertently made the Indian sign for prisoner— did nothing to assuage their fears. The Indian leaders, though inclined toward peace, remained skittish. Miles claimed to have made no concessions, but the Indians found promises that they could chose their own reservation site and work as government scouts, which was much to their liking. The satisfied chieftains left White Bull, head warrior of the Cheyennes, and eight other delegates as hostages while the remainder departed on March 23 to bring in their families.[47]

The wait now seemed interminable to Miles. To help pass the time, he extolled the virtues of stock raising to the newly arrived tribesmen. The unit's band and a traveling acrobatic troupe held their attention, as did illustrations cut out of recent issues of the London *Graphic*. Miles assured General Sherman, "These prominent men say they would prefer to surrender here as they believe the power that can whip them can take care of them."[48]

True to Miles's prediction, 300 Indians, mostly Cheyennes, surrendered at Tongue River Cantonment on April 22. But others had opted for different solutions. Several hundred Minneconjous and Sans Arcs had already turned themselves in at the Cheyenne River Agency. In March more than 2,200 Indians had come into Crook's Department of the Platte. On May 6, Crazy Horse and 889 additional followers also surrendered there.[49]

A few Minneconjou, led by Lame Deer, still remained defiant to the army. With four cavalry troops, six companies of infantry, and a squad of recently surrendered Cheyennes enlisted as army scouts, Colonel Miles departed his cantonment on May 1. After several days' march up the Tongue, Miles left his supply train under a strong escort and headed west across country. The scouts having locating Lame Deer's camp along Muddy Creek, a tributary of the Rosebud, the colonel hurried ahead with the cavalry and half the infantry, thundering into the sleeping village of fifty-one lodges at sunrise on the seventh. One troop corralled the pony herd while a running fight broke out in the pine-covered bluffs west of the encampment.[50]

Lame Deer and a cluster of warriors were cut off from the rest of their people. Following a brief verbal exchange through an interpreter,

Miles rode ahead and shook hands with Lame Deer while his adjutant, Lieutenant George Baird, greeted the head warrior, Iron Star, who warily refused to give up his weapon. A white scout rode up, and, fearing for his colonel's safety, instinctively covered the Indian leaders with his gun. One of the allied Cheyennes lunged at Iron Star's rifle and Lame Deer grabbed his own rifle from the ground and fired at Miles from point-blank range. The colonel saved himself when he instinctively jerked his horse's reins; the bullet whistled past, killing Miles's luckless orderly, Private Charles Shrenger.

"This necessarily ended that mode of peace-making," panned Miles later, and a general melee ensued. A hail of gunfire cut down Lame Deer as he clambered up a hill. Iron Star, cresting the rise, ran into G Troop. Captain James W. Wheelen killed him with a pistol shot. The Battle of Muddy Creek raged on as most of the Sioux escaped eastward, leaving behind fourteen dead. With their own casualties totaling four dead and seven wounded, the troops destroyed the Minneconjou lodges with all of their stores and rounded up 450 ponies, with which Miles mounted four companies of his Fifth Infantry.[51]

General Terry later pronounced the victory at Muddy Creek as "the best thing that has been done since hostilities commenced." But a tremendous deluge washed away the trail of fleeing Indians and forced Miles to return to the Tongue River Cantonment in mid-May. Though most Indians declared hostile had now either surrendered or fled to Canada, army reinforcements poured into the Yellowstone Valley to finish the job. Occasional skirmishing and tedious marches marked the season as columns under Captain Snyder, Major Henry M. Lazelle, Captain Edward Ball, and Major James S. Brisbin patrolled the Powder and Little Missouri rivers in search of the recalcitrant followers of Lame Deer, now led by his son Fast Bull. In mid-June, Miles left by the steamer *Ashland* to confer with Terry, but he returned with the long-overdue paymaster in time to begin a final sweep between the Yellowstone and Missouri rivers on July 4. With the bluecoats in the field to stay, small parties of Indians began coming in by late July. The largest remaining band, numbering 224, gave themselves up at Camp Sheridan, Nebraska, on September 10.[52]

For those Indians who had defied the government's attempts to reduce their reservations, the previous twenty months had been truly harrowing. By October 1877, Sitting Bull and some four thousand Sioux had fled to Canada. Their migration created enormous pressures on the diminishing buffalo herds of the far northern plains. Crazy Horse, chief of the "southern" Sioux and Miles's able antagonist at the Battle of Wolf Mountains, was murdered while in captivity at Camp Robinson. After much debate, those Oglalas who accepted the government's terms settled in southern Dakota Territory on the Pine Ridge Reservation. The Brules opted for a site farther east, along the South Fork of the White River, at Rosebud Agency.[53]

But the suffering had just begun for the Northern Cheyennes. A homesick year in the Indian Territory brought death and gloom. In September 1878, three hundred made a desperate break for their traditional lands along the Powder and Tongue rivers. The bluecoats caught most of the escapees near Camp Robinson. After a four-day hunger strike, the Indians made another frantic dash for freedom on a moonlit January night. Killing their guards, the men, women, and children began making their way across snowy fields, only to be caught by the remainder of the garrison. Sixty-four Indians were killed, as many as ten were never found, and upwards of fifty others were returned to Indian Territory or to the Pine Ridge Agency. Another large party surrendered near Fort Keogh. Only in 1884 did the Northern Cheyennes secure their own reservation along the Tongue River.[54]

Colonel Nelson Miles and the Fifth Infantry basked in the praise given them for their efforts to bring the Indians in. "You are ahead of every one else who has taken a hand in the Indian campaigns north of the Platte," applauded General Pope. In his official report for 1877, Sheridan credited the "constant pounding and sleepless activity on the part of [the] troops, (Colonel Miles in particular) in midwinter" with having forced many Sioux and Northern Cheyennes to surrender. Sherman recognized the colonel as having shown "extraordinary pluck and talents." Terry, whom Miles had criticized so severely, also gave praise. "I have no doubt that McKenzie's action last winter with Crazy Horse's band contributed to these results, but I repeat that, in my judgment it is to your operations that they are *mainly* due, and, I think, it is right that you should have this expression of my opinion as your Department Commander."[55]

Celebrations at the Tongue River Cantonment sweetened the triumph. On July 11, a steamer brought Mary and the regiment's dependents to the post. Another vessel bearing Sherman and Terry landed there five days later. After a day of inspection and a formal reception at the colonel's quarters, on the eighteenth a regimental review was conducted in Sherman's honor. As darkness closed in, Sherman awarded "badges of honor" to thirty enlisted men. A visit by Sheridan, Crook, and their staffs on the twenty-fourth, including the usual attendant ceremonies, seemed almost routine by comparison.[56]

6 : CAPTURING CHIEF JOSEPH

Sitting Bull, Lame Deer, Crazy Horse, and their followers had been formidable antagonists. Their temporary alliance had destroyed the ill-fated Custer and frustrated the efforts of most of the other army commanders who faced it, particularly Terry and Crook. "The fact of the case is," admitted Sheridan, "the operations of Generals Terry and Crook will not bear criticism, and my only thought has been to let them sleep."[1]

Never one to let things sleep, Nelson Miles had lambasted his fellow officers throughout the recent campaigns. He seethed when comparing his own Civil War record against that of Crook, a West Point graduate who had suffered the embarrassment of capture by Confederate cavalrymen late in the conflict. Miles was resentful of Crook's lofty status as brigadier general, and believed that Crook's insinuations that Miles had received too much credit for defeating the Sioux came "with very poor grace from a man who was a failure during the war and has been ever since." He complained, "It is a somewhat remarkable fact that for seven months, not a single important request or recommendation of mine has been favorably considered and nearly all of my communications have been treated with silent contempt."[2]

Miles clamored for recognition commensurate with his success. Appointment as secretary of war would be ideal; promotion to brigadier general was long overdue. Generously, however, he suggested that department command might be an alternative. "If you can give me a department you will give me *more* than ample means of closing this Sioux war *and do me the greatest kindness,*" he informed Sherman. Eager to be helpful, Miles offered a means for engineering such a move—"Genl. Pope would be pleased to go to New York [the Department of West Point] and Genl. Terry to Leavenworth [the Department of the Missouri]"—thus creating a vacancy in the Department of the Dakota. "By giving me such a command," explained Miles, "you give me control over my own resources and a fair field for all my energies or abilities for a number of years."[3]

Sherman abhorred such personal lobbying but did not want to anger his most effective colonel. Ignore the press speculation about army reorganization, he advised Miles; a cabinet-level position was "out of the question." As for a brigadier generalship, President Grant would probably appoint his personal favorite, Ranald Mackenzie. "I will be rejoiced if you succeed," Sherman admitted, but cautioned Miles against counting on a star in the near future.[4]

Sherman conceded that the colonel deserved commendation. Unfortunately, Miles's scheme to acquire a departmental command did not take into account Major General John M. Schofield. A stately regular who had displayed his multiple talents as a field officer in the Civil War, as military emissary to France during Emperor Maximilian's short-lived regime in Mexico, and as temporary secretary of war, Schofield could scarcely be ejected from command at West Point to fulfill a colonel's whimsy. In early August, Sherman therefore proposed to Secretary of War George W. McCrary an alternative. Miles and Brevet Major General August V. Kautz, whose stint as commander of the Department of Arizona had been less than impressive, could switch regiments. Miles would receive the latter department as part of the transfer, using his brevet rank of Major General.[5]

Before such machinations could be implemented, events in eastern Oregon's Wallowa Valley distracted the army from its routine politicking. Ideal for natural grazing, the area was home to Chief Joseph's band of the Nez Perce Indians. Handsome, dignified, and respected by whites as well as his own people, Joseph in 1863 had refused to accept a treaty that ceded nearly seven million acres of land in the Wallowa Valley in exchange for an Idaho reservation one-tenth the original's size. When the government opened surrounding lands to non-Indian settlement incidents between natives and newcomers became more and more frequent.[6]

In 1874, Miles's Civil War mentor Oliver O. Howard had assumed command of the Department of the Columbia. Earnest, well-intentioned, and inured to controversy, the general was duly impressed with Joseph's six-foot-two-inch frame and courtly bearing. Though initially sympathetic to Joseph's protests, Howard insisted that it was the government's right to remove the Indians. But in June 1877, after Joseph and the others bid farewell to their homeland, three young Nez Perces emboldened by alcohol killed four whites noted for their anti-Indian prejudices. This act put the countryside in a frenzy, and Captain David Perry, with two companies of the First Cavalry and a mob of local volunteers at his side, eschewed last-minute diplomacy and charged the Nez Perces camped near White Bird Canyon on June 17, 1877. But the Indians reacted quickly and fought back with vigor. Perry, narrowly escaping Custer's fate, left thirty-four dead on the field. The Nez Perces admitted three wounded.[7]

General Howard, who had been assembling an expeditionary force at Fort Lapwai, took the field five days later. Reinforcements soon brought his command up to four hundred men. But the pursuit turned into a nightmare for the bluecoats. Skirmishing along the Cottonwood Creek in early July saw a body of volunteers defeated and an eleven-man scouting party of regulars annihilated. A week later, Howard nearly ended the campaign at the Battle of the Clearwater by scattering three hundred Nez Perce warriors, only to call off the pursuit before completing his victory.[8]

Howard then spent two weeks awaiting reinforcements and refitting his command, which now included over five hundred regulars, twenty-

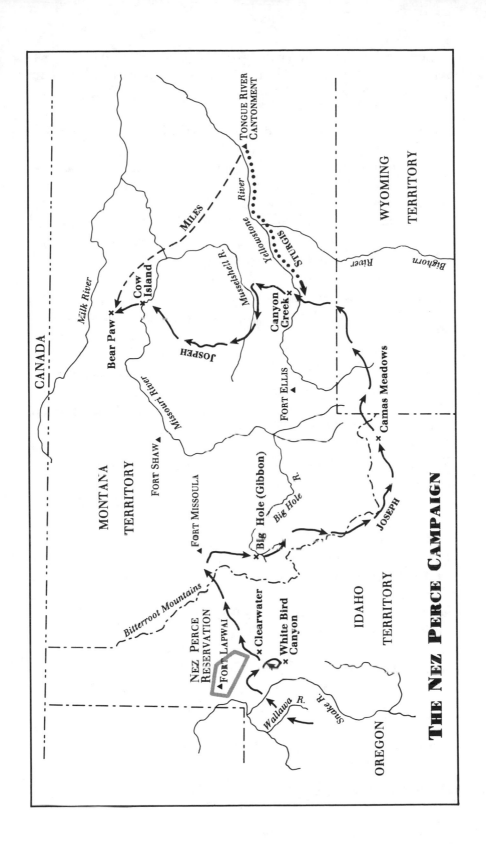

THE NEZ PERCE CAMPAIGN

CANADA

MONTANA TERRITORY

WYOMING TERRITORY

IDAHO TERRITORY

OREGON

Milk River

Missouri River

Musselshell R.

Yellowstone River

Bighorn River

MILES

Bear Paw ×

Cow Island ×

JOSEPH

Canyon Creek ×

STURGIS

Tongue River Cantonment ▲

Fort Shaw ▲

Fort Ellis ▲

Fort Missoula ▲

Big Hole (Gibbon) ×

Big Hole R.

Camas Meadows ×

JOSEPH

Bitterroot Mountains

NEZ PERCE RESERVATION

▲ Fort Lapwai

× Clearwater

× White Bird Canyon

Snake R.

Wallawa R.

five Bannock scouts, 150 civilian packers, and 350 mules. The Nez Perces fled east into the Bitterroot Mountains, then south along the Big Hole River valley in a meandering journey to Canada, where they hoped to find respite from the U.S. government. Safely ahead of Howard and in pleasant surroundings, the weary tribespeople slowed their pace. The delay nearly proved fatal. On August 9, 160 regulars and forty-five volunteers under Colonel John Gibbon stunned the Indians with a sunrise attack. The infantrymen overran the camp, only to find themselves nearly decimated by recovering Nez Perce marksmen. For the next thirty-six hours, the warriors laid virtual siege to Gibbon's embattled command as the women and children made good their escape.[9] Gibbon could do little but lick his wounds—his seventy casualties amounted to a third of his original force. But the Nez Perces had left behind eighty-nine bodies, many of them children slain during the initial melee. On the eleventh, Howard finally came up to meet Gibbon.[10]

That same day, Colonel Miles dispatched Colonel Samuel D. Sturgis and six companies of the revamped Seventh Cavalry to block Joseph's eastern flight. Conflicting orders from Miles, however, complicated the difficult task. Sturgis was initially assured that Sitting Bull would not venture south to interfere. Within the week, though, Miles warned his subordinate to prepare for just such a contingency. On August 26, he instructed Sturgis to send a party of Crow auxiliaries and white scouts to induce the surrender of the Nez Perces. But several days later, he again reversed his course. A preemptive strike should precede any negotiations.[11]

His horses shoeless and his men out of rations, a disconsolate Sturgis gave up the chase on September 13. "I fear you will be greatly disappointed," he told Miles, "when you learn that the hostiles have, by a sudden and unexpected turn, . . . thrown us hopelessly, I fear, in their rear. . . . I have no suggestions to offer."[12]

Howard was also having difficulty keeping up the chase. On August 24, he had wired Sherman: "What I wish is from some eastern force, the hostiles be headed off. . . . My command is so much worn by overfatigue and jaded animals that I cannot push it much farther. If Miles or Sturgis is near by . . . I think I may stop near where I am, and in a few days work my way back to Fort Boise slowly." Shocked by the general's lethargy, Sherman first encouraged him to continue the chase, then detailed Lieutenant Colonel Charles C. Gilbert as a substitute field commander. Gilbert, however, could not find Howard's column, thus leaving Howard in command by default.[13]

Howard now turned to Miles. "I earnestly request you to make every effort in your power to prevent the escape of this hostile band and at least to hold them in check until I can overtake them."[14]

Miles needed no further urging. Receiving Howard's report on the evening of September 17, he left the Tongue River Cantonment the next morning. Miles showed his usual energy in pushing his command—a squad of Cheyenne scouts, four mounted companies of his loyal Fifth, six troops of cavalrymen, a foot company to guard his mule and wagon train, and two pieces of artillery—toward the junction of the Missouri and the Musselshell rivers. He offered Howard words of advice and encouragement. "Do not let *anything* influence you to turn the command over to some one else, for you will soon drive them into submission, or out of the country. I know you are very tired and deserving of rest, but I am convinced you should see it out." Calling the press's criticism of Howard's slow pursuit "outrageous and shameless," he went on, "I congratulate you on making one of the most vigorous and successful campaigns against Indians and one of the most laborious and persistent pursuits that has ever been made after Indians."[15]

Seemingly regenerated, Howard felt confident enough by September 20 to assure Miles, "There is no one here to relieve me from command and I am strong and well and not weary." The general also offered up a new plan. His animals needed to rest before he could march against Joseph. "The moment we check pursuit they stop 30 or 40 miles ahead and rest till their scouts discover our forward movement," he reasoned. "We shall not hasten the pursuit overmuch, in order to give you time to get into position," he advised Miles, who was to confront the Indians before they reached Canada. Howard knew from personal experience that Miles would make every effort to seize this chance for glory.[16]

Miles reached the Missouri River on the twenty-third. On the same date the Nez Perces crossed upriver at Cow Island, the head of navigation for steamboats plying the Missouri. There four civilians and a dozen regulars guarded thirty-six tons of government supplies awaiting overland transport. Long-range skirmishing enabled the hungry Nez Perces to replenish their stores at federal expense. They ransacked a freight train the following day. The Nez Perces easily brushed aside Major Guido Ilges and forty volunteers, but the tribe, now under the sway of Looking Glass, a prominent Nez Perce leader known for his moderate views, again slowed perceptibly.[17]

Miles, after arriving at the Missouri, cut loose from his supply train and headed north, reaching the northern ranges of the Bear Paw Mountains by September 29. Scouts discovered the Nez Perce trail that evening as Miles, still uncertain if he could catch Joseph, asked Howard to continue the chase. Maintaining the easy relations of their Civil War days, the colonel noted, "We have had good weather except today, it is now raining as it used to in Virginia."[18]

Miles was back on the trail by four o'clock the next morning. The Nez Perces, less than forty miles from the Canadian border, were feeling the effects of their three-month, seventeen-hundred-mile trek across the Idaho and Montana territories, and they failed to react to the new threat. Upon discovering the Indian camps among the tangled coulees and hollows of Snake Creek, Miles organized an attack. Captain Owen Hale led three troops of Seventh Cavalrymen directly against the Nez Perce camp. To cut off the enemy from their ponies and any escape to Canada, Miles dispatched Captain George H. Tyler, a squadron of the Second Cavalry, and most of the Cheyenne scouts to hit the rear of the village. He held Captain Simon Snyder and the mounted infantrymen in reserve.[19]

The tactics—a frontal assault against the village, accompanied by an effort designed to block any attempted flight—were standard to the frontier army's most audacious leaders. Though the military rarely formalized Indian-fighting doctrine, men like Miles knowingly divided their forces in hopes of gaining complete victory. George Custer had used this tactic to win the Battle of the Washita in 1868; but he had also employed such an attack, with disastrous results, at the Little Bighorn.[20]

Almost as if reluctant to believe they had been caught, the Nez Perces formed their defenses and opened a deadly fire when the soldiers came within about two hundred yards. With uncanny marksmanship belying their exhaustion, the Indians singled out the officers and noncommissioned officers as targets. Captain Hale and Lieutenant Jonathan W. Biddle, along with seven sergeants, were killed; Captains Myles Moylan and Edward S. Godfrey fell wounded, as did three sergeants and two corporals. In all, sixteen cavalrymen lay dead as the shattered squadron withdrew. "I'm the only damned man of the Seventh Cavalry wearing shoulder straps who's alive," screamed one officer as Miles reformed his command.[21]

Captain Tyler's drive against the pony herd met with greater success. Joseph, about seventy warriors, and most of the women, children, and old men had reached their mounts just as the cavalrymen and their Cheyenne allies galloped up. In a wild, swirling melee, clusters of Nez Perces battled their enemies for control of the panicky animals, while others scrambled to safety. The troopers gathered up about seven hundred horses and mules but failed to break the Indian defenses, now solid among the rocks and ravines.[22]

Meanwhile, Snyder's mounted reserve rushed through the depleted ranks of the Seventh Cavalry. The mounted infantrymen of the Fifth were a tough, veteran bunch, but found in the Nez Perces a skilled foe holding superb defensive positions. Dismounting under heavy fire, the soldiers could not pinpoint the Indian marksmen. Lieutenant Henry Romcyn remembered that "from their concealment they sent shots with unerring aim at every head exposed." Romeyn, along with adjutant George Baird, were wounded as the attack stalled.[23]

Lieutenants Mason Carter and Thomas W. Woodruff spearheaded a smaller detachment of the Fifth down a slope toward the west end of the village. Suffering heavy casualties, the attackers managed to maintain a tiny foothold until Miles called off the assault. Joseph later admitted that eighteen Indian men and three women had been killed in the opening engagement. The bluecoats lost fully 20 percent of those engaged. Miles had exhibited his usual heroism; adjutant Baird recalled, "He must have been a sorry soldier who could not fight under the inspiration of the leadership and example of Gen. Miles on that field." The junior officers also performed well—Miles later helped secure Medals of Honor for seven captains and lieutenants, including the wounded Moylan, Godfrey, Romeyn, and Baird, along with Lieutenants Carter, Edward J. McClernand, and Robert McDonald.[24]

But courage alone was not enough. Miles's subsequent explanation of the events suggests a bit of rationalization as well as good tactical sense, for the Indian position was too strong for any more frontal assaults. "Having inflicted a severe loss in dead and wounded upon the Indians, and placed the troops in such position as commanded their camp, and having secured the principal part of their herd," he wrote somewhat more confidently than events warranted, "I determined to maintain the positions secured, prevent the escape of the Indians, and make preparation to meet the re-enforcements from the north that the Nez Perces evidently expected."[25]

Miles wheeled up his Hotchkiss gun that evening as soldiers, scouts, and Nez Perces dug in for a siege. Both sides suffered from the biting northerly winds; occasional well-aimed shots from the Nez Perces dissuaded any thoughts of a renewed assault. But having lost most of their horses, the Indians dared not risk the lives of the women and children in a breakout. Six warriors thus crept through the soldier lines to seek out Sitting Bull, their only remaining hope.[26]

On the morning of October 1, five inches of fresh snow blanketed the stalemated battlefield. Artillery fire failed to disrupt the Nez Perce warriors, seemingly impregnable in their rifle pits. Colonel Miles now faced something of a quandary—if he waited too long, Sturgis and Howard might arrive and steal the credit for a final victory. And though Miles had as late as September 3 discounted the possibility of Sitting Bull's intervention, the colonel had grown more concerned about such a threat as the month wore on. Could his regulars maintain the siege and at the same time fend off Sitting Bull? Shortly before noon, then, talks between Miles and the Nez Perce leaders commenced.[27]

Conflicting reports shroud the circumstances leading up to these preliminary discussions. Miles later implied that the enemy had initiated the negotiations; the Nez Perces adamantly denied this. The Cheyenne scouts, by contrast, happily assumed responsibility. Remembering Miles's desire to capture rather than kill the enemy, they explained the hopelessness of the situation to the Nez Perces. According to the Cheyenne account, "High Wolf [one of the Cheyenne scouts] rode back to tell Miles, and Big Leggins [Miles's trusted scout Johnnie Bruguier] interpreted. Miles got mad and asked who had gone in talking to the enemy that way; and High Wolf grabbed his collar and said, 'You told us to try to get these people to come in and not be harmed. They are Indians like us. Why don't you talk to them?' "[28]

"The shooting was still going on," continued the Cheyenne version, "but soon white flags went up, and the Nez Perce chiefs met Miles and his officers in the middle of the battlefield." Against the advice of war chiefs White Bird and Looking Glass, Joseph met with Miles at least once in the colonel's tent. Miles promised Joseph that his people could spend the coming winter at the Tongue River Cantonment but insisted that they turn over their weapons. Joseph demurred, demanding that his tribe retain half of their guns for hunting. Frustrated by the stalled negotiations and concerned about the possible arrival of Howard, Sturgis, or Sitting Bull, Miles dispatched the mixed-blood interpreter Tom Hill back to the Nez Perces but refused to allow Joseph to leave.[29]

As the Joseph-Miles talks proceeded, Lieutenant Lovell H. Jerome wandered over to the Nez Perce camp. On realizing that Miles still held Joseph, the Nez Perces promptly detained Jerome, thus negating the colonel's ill-gotten advantage. A furious Miles finally exchanged his captive for the sheepish lieutenant the following afternoon. "Joseph gave me his solemn pledge yesterday that he would surrender, but did not, and they are evidently waiting for aid from other Indians," wrote Miles on the third. "They say that the Sioux are coming to their assistance." For his part, Joseph denied having made any promises.[30]

Although the belated arrival of the supply train helped the army's wounded weather the worst effects of the snowstorm, Miles remained pensive. Even his twelve-pound Napoleon gun, converted to a makeshift howitzer by placing its tail carriage in a hole, seemed to be inflicting little damage. The spectre of Sitting Bull thundering up to relieve the siege loomed ever greater to the impatient colonel. At one point, observers spotted a large column on the distant horizon. Hasty plans for blocking this potential threat were abandoned only when the "column" turned out to be a herd of buffalo. And the Nez Perces maintained their stubborn resistance. "They fight with more desperation than any Indians I have ever met," reported Miles. He asked the government to enlist British assistance in preventing any more escapees from crossing the international boundary, a request that clearly indicated the gravity of the situation.[31]

Sporadic firing continued through the afternoon of October 4, when General Howard arrived at Miles's camp. Howard was accompanied by Lieutenant C.E.S. Wood; the interpreter Arthur Chapman; Captain John and Old George, two Nez Perces who had already signed a treaty with the government; and a small escort of regulars. The two commanders, old friends and comrades, must have experienced mixed emotions as they rode out to meet one another. Criticisms of his failure to catch Chief Joseph still nagged Howard. Now his subordinate seemed on the verge of outshining him once again. As for Miles, the prospects of sharing any credit after a bloody fight and five days of tedious siege duty were less than appealing. "We have the Indians corraled down yonder in the direction of the firing," shouted Miles.[32]

Following a brief battlefield tour, Howard and Miles hammered out their lines of authority. The tension eased only with Howard's twin assurances that he would not assume command until Joseph had surrendered and that he would help Miles secure a brigadier's star. Afterwards, Lieutenant Wood drew Howard aside to question the latter's acquiescence to the ambitious colonel. The general, according to Wood, laid a soothing hand on his aide's shoulder and replied, "Wood, you are wrong to distrust Miles. Why, I would trust him as fully as I would you. He was an aide-de-camp on my staff during the Civil War, just as you are now. I got him his first regiment. I would trust him with my life." Howard's report that evening reflected similar sentiments. "Colonel Miles keeps bright his well-earned record. This successful march, to intercept, of three hundred miles could not be excelled in quickness of conception and promptitude of execution."[33]

Although watching for Sitting Bull and protecting his reputation had caused Miles many anxious moments, the cold and prolonged vigilance had exacted a more tangible toll on the Nez Perces. Sleep had been difficult and blankets were running short. On October 4, a direct hit on one of the Indian dugouts killed a woman and her granddaughter. The influential leaders Toohoolhoolzote, Ollokot, and Poker Joe already lay dead. So when Howard and Miles initiated discussions on the morning of the fifth, a weary Joseph seemed inclined to end the conflict.[34]

The terms were consistent with those offered earlier by Miles. Joseph was to take his followers to the Tongue River for the winter, after which they could return to the Northwest. Whether that meant the Wallowa Valley, from which Joseph's people had started their remarkable journey, or the reservation in Idaho to which the government had sought to move them, was uncertain. But all accounts set the Northwest as the final destination. "I believed General Miles or *I never would have surrendered*," insisted Chief Joseph the following year. With a dignity and presence that impressed all witnesses, 87 men, 184 women, and 147 children thus turned themselves in that afternoon.[35]

Not all had concurred with Joseph's decision. Still defiant, Looking Glass and White Bird pledged to lead their people to find Sitting Bull. That night White Bird and a large number of followers stole away from the camp; including those who had escaped during the first day's fighting, over two hundred had eluded Miles's clutches. But Looking Glass never found his earthly freedom. As deliberations were concluding, he was killed by a stray bullet to the forehead, the battle's last official casualty.[36]

With characteristic bravado, Miles dispatched news of the surrender to General Terry. "We have had our usual success," he wrote. "We made a very direct and rapid march across the country, and after a severe engagement, and being kept under fire for three days, the hostile camp of Nez Perces, under Chief Joseph, surrendered at two o'clock today." Almost as an afterthought, Miles acknowledged Howard's role in the campaign. "It is an added source of congratulation that General O.O. Howard, who has so persistently waged a war against these hostile Nez Perces and driven them from the slopes of the Pacific into this remote country, was present to witness the completion of this arduous and thankless undertaking." Most newspapers, however, failed to publish this passage.[37]

At first, Howard seemed reluctant to share the glory. In a letter dated October 7, he congratulated Miles "with all [his] heart." He continued, "It is *the* co-operation with my overworked column which I coveted, and knew beforehand, from your past history and well-known promptitude, that I should receive. . . . A forced march of nearly 300 miles, quick attack, successful battle, ending with capture of the main body of enemy, their chief and main camp, and driving of the remnant across the boundary of the United States, afford a meager outline of the achievements of your command. I am gratified to have been present and to have contributed ever so little to facilitate the surrender."[38]

Howard soon changed his outlook. The two commanders had agreed on a joint communiqué following Joseph's capitulation. Miles then handed the message to a subordinate for dispatch. According to Wood, whose subsequent recollections were inevitably affected by the mutual antipathy arising between him and Miles, "Howard said to me: 'I knew Miles could be trusted. His telegram to Sheridan, which he showed me, said: General Howard and his whole command present and assisting at the surrender.'" But newspaper accounts of the telegram's contents omitted Howard's role. Wood and Howard both suspected that Miles had tampered with the message. Howard recalled twenty years later: "The telegram that arrived in my presence and at my request should not have been altered so as to leave out the fact of my being there. Who changed the telegram I do not know. Gen. Miles was my devoted friend till then."[39]

Disappointment at negative press reports ("Oh! Oh! Howard!" cackled one headline, "The trouble with O.O. Howard is that he is an ass") soured the general, whose earlier faith in Miles's motives now seemed misplaced. Howard's concern about "garbled dispatches" led him to explain his movements in a lengthy letter to Sheridan as early as October 19. His own congratulatory order to his command barely mentioned Miles. And vital segments of his extraordinarily long report on his operations also minimized Miles's efforts, emphasizing instead the link between his decision to slow his own command and the Nez Perce delay.[40]

Howard, who had endured severe criticism from his superiors even before Miles entered the campaign, also authorized that "a true account of the surrender" be given to the press. Wood promptly sold such a dispatch to a Chicago newspaper. The subsequent Wood publications flabbergasted Miles, whose first letters to Mary, though typically self-serving, expressed sympathy with Howard because of the censure cast on him. Published newspaper interviews also suggested that Miles had at first been reluctant to assume sole credit.[41]

General Sheridan sharply criticized the Wood releases. Sherman, with perhaps a better understanding of Miles's propensity for picking a fight and with an eye to what the controversy might do to the army's image, urged his nephew-in-law to avoid any public wrangling. He skirted the issue in his annual report by explaining that though Miles had won the Battle of Bear Paw Mountain, Howard's tireless pursuit had made the fight possible. "Keep quiet," advised Sherman. "Don't seem to contend for the honors. Let Howard Gibbon & Sturgis dispute if they must. It is sufficient that you overtook overcame and captured the whole."[42]

Neither Miles nor Howard heeded such counsel. On January 8, 1878, the colonel, unwilling to share the limelight with a colleague he deemed ungrateful, challenged Howard to elaborate on claims made in official reports and the press. Miles found the general's assertions that his own calculated delays and the return of the Seventh Cavalry to Miles's command had "enabled" Miles to "strike Joseph" particularly troubling. Miles fired a second salvo on the thirty-first. Howard's congratulatory orders had done "an injustice to those who were killed and wounded days after [Howard] had abandoned the pursuit."[43]

A February 21 letter from Wood to Miles that exonerated Howard satisfied no one. Howard received Miles's second letter in mid-March. "I am astonished at your accusations," answered Howard, who again proclaimed his innocence. "You fought the battle and succeeded and if there is any language in which I can state it to the credit of yourself, your officers and your men I was willing, and remain willing to do so. I do not think it necessary for an old friend to use such language as you have to me." Miles responded in early June, charging, "You [Howard] virtually gave up the pursuit." The colonel further asserted that he had never asked Howard to slow his column.[44]

Both soldiers continued the bitter war of words. Implicitly at least, Howard encouraged his more verbally minded aide, Lieutenant Wood, to prosecute his case. Stiffening his own position, Miles now allowed Howard only a minor role in the victory. In later years, Wood would accuse Miles of persecuting him for his role in the controversy. When Wood sought to avoid a transfer from splendid Vancouver Barracks (overlooking the Columbia River) to Boise Barracks, Idaho Territory, the lieutenant pleaded ill health and requested permanent assignment at Vancouver. Miles blocked the move, declaring that Wood merely wanted to continue his private business. Labeling these charges "an absolute falsehood," Wood recounted, "I called him a liar and resigned."[45]

However damaging to its contestants, the Miles-Howard dispute paled in comparison to the sufferings of the Nez Perces. Like Howard, Miles came to respect the people and their leader, showing an attitude that was a far cry from his earlier decision to violate peace negotiations and hold Joseph after the fight at Bear Paw Mountain. "Fraud and injustice," contended Miles, had caused the war. "I believe that Joseph is by far the ablest Indian on the continent and if they can be fairly treated will rank as loyal friends of the govt. as they have been dangerous enemies," he concluded in a note to Sherman.[46]

Despite such declarations of faith in the Nez Perces, General Sherman determined that they must not be allowed back to their homeland. After reaching Miles's cantonment on the Tongue River, Joseph's followers were removed to Fort Leavenworth rather than returned to the Northwest. Miles protested the change but concluded that his resignation would be futile. If he quit the army, he explained to Joseph, another officer would simply carry out the order. The chief, at least publicly, believed Miles's sincerity. "I do not blame him for what we have suffered since the surrender," concluded Joseph. The government's action seemed but another in a long line of broken promises. "I can not understand how the Government sends a man out to fight us, as it did General Miles, and then breaks his word. Such a Government has something wrong with it," charged Joseph.[47]

After a terrible winter at Fort Leavenworth, Joseph's people were moved first to the Quapaw Reservation and then to a dusty reservation in Indian Territory that they dubbed "Eikish Pah," or hot place. In 1879 they moved to the Ponca Reservation, where tribal deterioration continued. Babies and young children, including the chief's daughter, died by the droves because of the poor land and demoralization, and reformers pressured the government to allow the Nez Perces to go home. Miles remained an outspoken advocate of their removal, reminding outgoing President Rutherford B. Hayes, in January 1881 of their enfeebled condition. The following month, the *New York Daily Tribune* supported the removal of the tribe back to the Northwest and pointed out, "[Miles] feels his own [honor is] involved in this matter, and is sparing no effort to bring about the redemption of his pledge to Chief Joseph."[48]

In 1885, the government allowed 118 people to rejoin at the Lapwai Reservation, Idaho Territory, fellow tribespeople who had not followed Joseph. Joseph and 149 compatriots were placed on the Colville Reservation in Washington Territory. The chief continued to lobby for a return to his beloved Wallowa River valley homeland; in 1897 and 1903 he visited Washington, D.C., in unsuccessful efforts to obtain presidential support. Miles supported Joseph's cause, but the chief died at the Colville Reservation in 1904, still in exile.[49]

7 : DISAPPOINTMENT

For the moment, Miles basked in the glory of his triumph over the Nez Perces and savored the praise of his contemporaries. Retired General Gouverneur K. Warren, hero of the Battle of Gettysburg, wrote: "I am sure the Army of the Potomac survivors all feel as I do. . . . It is an honour to us, that one we thought of so highly should make himself the most successful fighter of the indians." Colonel John Gibbon asked Miles to provide a personal account for an article he was writing on the recent campaign. Commissioner of Indian Affairs Ezra A. Hayt added his congratulations for the "gallant achievement," which, he declared, "has had a decided and beneficial influence on other hostile tribes."[1]

As Nelson enjoyed the praise, Mary Miles struggled to adapt to western military life. Fort Leavenworth had introduced her to the frontier army. Though her elite social status—wife of a colonel and member of the powerful Sherman family—eased many mundane concerns, Mary found the constant worrying over Nelson's safety a terrible burden. Her association with other officers' wives and the occasional visit by a relative provided her some relief, although as the colonel's mate she was expected to set a strong example for other regimental dependents. "I hate to have her go," confided Alice Baldwin to her husband, Lieutenant Frank Baldwin, as Mary departed for a brief eastern visit in 1876. "It seems as if another link that binds all we forlorn wives together was broken if she leaves."[2]

Through the winter of 1876–77, their families had made the best of life at Leavenworth as the men of the Fifth pursued the Sioux and hacked out a new cantonment on the Tongue River. General Pope assured Miles that he would watch out for Mary, but Nelson knew that the army made little official provision for wives. Chronic housing shortages might force newly arrived officers to oust the women and children from their quarters at any time. "With Miles at the Yellowstone for an indefinite time and some old colonel with his family at Fort Leavenworth," lamented General Sherman to his niece, "your quarters will be demanded as a right & cannot be refused."[3]

"I certainly did positively discourage Mary and all applicant wives from attempting to reach you this winter," explained Sherman to a lonely Nelson in October 1876. "Had Mary gone, every wife would have gone in spite of the trouble, expense & increased labor imposed on your command." At her uncle's urging, Mary and little Cecilia split the winter between the family home in Cleveland and the commanding general's quarters in Washington, D.C. There she pled for her husband's promotion or a change of station. "You may be assured that I personally am well informed of his [Miles's] special merits," sighed the general.[4]

Only as the Missouri and Yellowstone rivers thawed could the wives proceed upriver to the Tongue River Cantonment. In the interim, the command hastened to finish preliminary work on the post. In February, 1877, Miles exclaimed that the regimental band had nearly completed a crude performance hall. His own quarters would have four rooms in addition to a small dining room and kitchen. That he was clearly enjoying the respite from the Sioux campaigns was evidenced by the fifteen pounds he had already gained since the Battle of Wolf Mountains.[5]

Mary often wrote her husband, but the sporadic mail service frustrated attempts to maintain regular contact. Finally, she and the other wives boarded the steamers *Don Cameron* and *General Sherman* in mid-May. Disaster struck forty miles below Sioux City when the *Cameron* hit a snag and sunk within twenty-five minutes. No one was killed, but most of the officers' personal effects were lost, causing the commissioned personnel much hardship. Lieutenant Baird, for example, would not receive compensation for his property, valued at eight hundred dollars, until 1885.[6]

Entangled in the furor resulting from the recently disputed presidential election, politicians soon dealt those officers, along with the rest of the army, another fateful blow. After acrimonious debate, the Forty-fourth Congress adjourned without passing an army appropriations bill, which meant an interruption in pay at the close of the fiscal year on June 30, 1877. This, along with the steamboat accident that spring, posed a terrible hardship for those at Tongue River. "You will be in a bad way in that remote Region without house furniture or pay," pointed out General Sherman.[7]

Mary, her daughter Cecilia, her sister Elizabeth Sherman, and the other dependents arrived at the Tongue River Cantonment on July 11, safe but shaken by their ordeal. There they found the rude beginnings of a military community, with its accompanying comforts and annoying nuisances. Sherman, whose concurrent visit recognized the exploits of the Fifth Infantry, described the colonel's quarters as "a good log house with flat dirt roof, but really most comfortable considering the surroundings." Miles had already skirmished with the plethora of civilian hangers-on who followed the army. Excessive sales of alcohol particularly troubled the colonel, who periodically forbade the liquor trade. And it was fortunate that Elizabeth Sherman stayed that summer, as Nelson, Mary, and several other garrison members fell ill with the "whoops" (whooping cough) in late July.[8]

Campaigning against the Sioux and the Nez Perces continued in the summer and fall of 1877 as the colonel mustered enough energy to select a permanent post site two miles west of the cantonment. "The river was just alive with boats," recalled one inhabitant as construction materials poured in. Dubbed Fort Keogh (after Captain Myles W. Keogh, killed at the Little Bighorn), the position became a center for military operations on the northern plains. "Comparatively commodious quarters," wrote Miles, replaced the rude huts, temporary buildings, and tents of the cantonment. With most commissioned personnel still on detached duty following the Chief Joseph campaign, the officers' wives, assisted by enlisted men who served as personal servants, occupied the new housing in early November 1877. Even so, eagerly-awaited shipments of carpeting and curtains could not make up for the depressing solitude. The death of one of Nelson's prized foxhounds further soured the occasion. And Captain David H. Brotherton seized the opportunity to retaliate against Miles, with whom he had feuded for the past two years, by ordering Mary's striker back to the ranks.[9]

Exhausted by her fear for Nelson's safety and the strain of the move to Fort Keogh, Mary turned for support to her friend Alice Baldwin. "Mrs. Miles was in," wrote Mrs. Baldwin to her husband on November 4, "& she shed tears, said she never felt so forlorn in her life before & wished we had both gone with you & so do I." Mary returned the favor a week later. Ambitious for her husband's promotion and concerned about the dangers he might encounter in the field, Alice broke down when Mary assured her of the colonel's support for Frank. "I was so touched when she told me," explained Alice to her husband, "I could not help but cry for joy & gratification."[10]

Nelson shared this loneliness. Although he was rarely willing or able to confide his true feelings, the hardships and long periods of separation he had endured during the past eighteen months had rendered him uncharacteristically frank in his letters to Mary. Despite his difficulties, however, he could not resist the temptation to complain about his lack of a promotion. A brief meeting with Sheridan, who had grown dissatisfied with Brigadier General E.O.C. Ord's handling of disputes along the Mexican border, raised his hopes for a transfer to command the Department of Texas. Ord, who advocated a more vigorous prosecution of affairs along the Rio Grande, had on several occasions dispatched U.S. troops across the river. Miles assured Sheridan that, in contrast to Ord, he was not looking to provoke a war with Mexico. On leaving the meeting, the colonel wired John Sherman, recently appointed secretary of the treasury by the newly elected President Rutherford B. Hayes: "I believe you can secure me the Department of Texas by moving at once in my interests."[11]

But problems along the forty-ninth parallel made transfer of the invaluable Miles extremely unlikely. By October 1877, some four thousand Nez Perces and Teton Sioux had crossed the border into Canada. Although the red-coated North West Mounted Police did what they could to maintain order, the declining buffalo herds could scarcely support the resident Blackfeet, Crees, and Assiniboines, much less the newcomers. Canadian officials thus joined their U.S. counterparts in encouraging the tribes to return south. Lieutenant Colonel James F. Macleod of the North West Mounted Police arranged meetings north of the border at Fort Walsh between General Terry and leading Indian chiefs. Yet the conferences only highlighted the Sioux's distrust of United States representatives; Sitting Bull remained north of the border.[12]

Miles traveled to Washington in November and December of 1877 to testify before the House Military Affairs Committee and to relay his criticisms of Terry's mission. The colonel also asked General Sherman for "discretionary power and force to overpower and govern all the Indian tribes" of the upper Missouri. Maintaining that the Indians had "used the British territory as a recruiting depot and arsenal," Miles requested permission to take his regiment, now mounted on captured Indian ponies, "to move up to the line and in conjunction with the British authorities compel that miserable savage [Sitting Bull] to choose his country and abide by its laws." The Indians should, he argued, be forced to exchange their ponies and guns for domestic cattle.[13]

Though Secretary of War George W. McCrary seemed inclined to reinforce Miles, Sherman feared his impetuous nephew-in-law might precipitate an international incident. On February 9, 1878, he reprimanded Miles for ignoring Terry and Sheridan in the chain of command and warned the colonel not to cross the Canadian boundary without a direct presidential order. Renewed Democratic threats to reduce the army, along with new violence along the Rio Grande and on the Ute Reservation in Colorado, dictated a peaceful policy in the north, where negotiations with the Mounted Police might prove fruitful. "Keep your men well in hand," ordered Sherman, "and don't venture out too far—encourage settlers all along the valley & in time we will give the Sioux North of the Missouri all the fighting they want."[14]

Sherman monitored the situation closely throughout the spring and early summer of 1878. Cognizant of renewed attacks on the military budget, he reminded Miles, "Everybody should economize." The latter responded by asking once again for promotion. His growing host of enemies (Miles listed Generals Sheridan, Crook, and Terry, along with Colonels Mackenzie, Gibbon, Wesley Merritt, William B. Hazen,

Thomas H. Ruger, and George W. Getty as being among the conspirators) would undoubtedly oppose him. Prepared for the machinations of these cabals, Miles forwarded the names of own supporters, including seven United States senators. "In my opinion what is needed is for some friend in Washington to interest himself fortunately in my interest," suggested Miles. "I do not expect you to do this but . . ." The implication was clear.[15]

The lobbying infuriated Sherman, who had in April notified Miles, "There is no vacancy now and none likely to occur except by death, and none of them seem disposed to die to accomodate us." The general shared his anger with Sheridan. "Miles was racing off with the bit in his teeth, determined to ignore Terry, you and me, for the purposes of making a little personal fame & capital. Every thing connected with the Army is now working so smooth that it would be a shame for Miles to run wild a hornets nest of his own creation." The colonel must not anger the Canadians or the British, who had promised to ensure the new dominion's independence. On July 30, Sherman told Miles bluntly, "You have done all that man could do and should be content."[16]

Belatedly recognizing that any precipitous movements to the north could endanger his career, Miles threw his energies into other endeavors. In August, he submitted a plan for building new army posts. The elaborate model featured his attempts to overcome the major problems of frontier military architecture: capricious design, fires, and insufficient quarters. But his blueprint proved totally unfeasible. Even his own new cantonment, by his own admission, did not follow the recommendation because of "irregular ground." Army bureaucrats labeled the plan "useless" and quietly filed it alongside similar works of other bored officers.[17]

Miles also organized two travel junkets that summer. The first, a June excursion to the Little Bighorn, reaffirmed his belief that subordinate officers, especially Major Marcus Reno, had betrayed Custer, a view that Miles would espouse for the rest of his life. A second trip promised to combine business and pleasure. With one hundred soldiers Miles would reconnoiter a wagon road and telegraph line west of the Tongue River post and then lead a tour of the Yellowstone country. Mary, Cecilia, six other women and children, ten officers, and four male civilians accompanied the column.[18]

On August 29, the entourage reached the Crow Agency, where they learned that a number of Bannock Indians were heading toward Canada and a possible juncture with Sitting Bull. Hunger and illegal white encroachment had excited the Bannocks and Paiutes of southern Idaho Territory; in late May and early June some 450 warriors had slipped away from their reservations. Ready for such a confrontation, General Howard skillfully directed the ensuing chase through the heat and rugged terrain of southeastern Oregon. A smaller group of Bannocks, now approaching Montana Territory, were among the last to remain out.[19]

Sending the noncombatants scurrying back to Fort Ellis, Miles organized his escort to block Yellowstone's eastern passes. He dispatched Lieutenant William Philo Clark with forty troopers toward Boulder Pass. To cut off escape through Clarke's Fork, Miles himself led thirty-five soldiers; en route, promises of food, ammunition, and all the horses they could capture persuaded seventy-five Crow Indians to join his command. While Miles's men were setting up camp outside Clarke's Fork Pass, lookouts spotted the Bannocks on September 3. Miles positioned his troops for a daybreak attack the following morning, when he routed the surprised Bannocks, killing eleven and capturing thirty-one of their number. Among Miles's column, Captain Andrew S. Bennett, a Crow auxiliary, and a civilian interpreter died in the brief fight, and one regular was wounded.[20]

This victory further bolstered Miles's reputation among Montana residents, who renewed their call for a separate department and a larger military presence. Additional troops would help defeat the Indians and be an economic boon; Colonel Nelson Miles seemed ideally suited to command this force. Benjamin F. Potts, a Republican who served as governor of the territory from 1870 to 1883 and who owed his appointment in part to Senator John Sherman, championed both the colonel and the wars against the Indians. He would, vowed Potts, cooperate with Miles "in all matters." However, Secretary of War McCrary maintained, "Montana is not as important a post as is now filled by General Miles on the Yellowstone," and he and commanding general Sherman resisted such lobbying.[21] Miles had been given command of the District of the Yellowstone, a subunit of the Department of Dakota that included forts Keogh and Custer as well as the detachment at Fort Peck, but McCrary and Sherman refused to gerrymander yet another independent department.

Governor Potts refused to concede defeat. "Our people are clamorous for Miles to command all Montana troops," he exclaimed. "He is a terror to the hostiles because he gives them no peace," wrote the governor to President Hayes. Meanwhile, Miles made frequent trips to Helena to strengthen his ties with other Montana officials. Army construction of telegraph lines in eastern Montana and the growth of civilian settlement around Fort Keogh reinforced these bonds. "Cattle get fatter in Montana than in Colorado or Texas," proclaimed the colonel before a congressional committee. Forwarding an extract from his annual report to the long-time territorial delegate Martin Maginnis on October 18, 1878, Miles reminded his recipient that voters along the Tongue-Yellowstone junction had returned a solid majority in Maginnis's favor. Miles pointed out that Maginnis's support for a new department and Nelson Miles as its commander would encourage settlement and economic development.[22]

That same day, Miles informed Sherman that Montana officials would soon make "a very strong effort . . . to have a Department made of this northwest country," with himself as commander. "Now I am told that the President Secretary of War & Lieut. General [Sheridan] are either favorable or do not oppose such a measure but that the General opposes it. Now I hope you will not continue to oppose such a change. The feeling on this matter is stronger than you imagine."[23]

Stung by the threat, Sherman forwarded a copy of this letter to Sheridan. "[Miles] constantly implies that because he married my niece whom I love very much that I approve his ambitious views—I surely encourage him in his activity, but don't want him or any subordinate to be chafing in harness like an unbroken colt," thundered Sherman. The general also informed both his niece and her husband that far from adding a new department, the army was looking to reduce one to match them with the number of brigadier generals. Sheridan's response vindicated Sherman, who passed along a copy to Miles. Though recognizing Miles's "great energy and force of character," Sheridan, too, concluded that another department would simply increase expenses. Sherman wrote to Miles, "I thought you were mistaken in saying that Genl Sheridan approved of a new Department. You will see that you were entirely misinformed. In like manner I tell you that the President and Sec of War never intimated such a wish to me."[24]

But Montanans continued to promote the twin causes of Nelson Miles and a separate military department. Maginnis spoke with Secretary McCrary and General Sherman. Governor Potts secured the aid of Samuel T. Hauser, a shrewd Montana capitalist, and young William

McKinley, an Ohioan who held some influence with the president. Potts also vowed to "put [President] Hayes on the right place on Gibbon," whose "copperhead proclivities" and rivalry with Miles made him an enemy. At the governor's behest, the territorial legislature resolved that Colonel Miles be awarded command of a new military department in Montana. Despite these persistent efforts, the army remained firm: the districts of Montana and the Yellowstone would not be combined to form an independent command.[25]

Ironically, Miles had challenged Sherman just as the general had awarded him a choice posting—presidency of a new equipment board scheduled to meet that winter in Washington, D.C. Bringing the colonel to the capital for the winter of 1878–79, wrote Sherman to Mary, "would I think be pleasing to you." The locale would allow the colonel to expand his enviable political connections, made even stronger by the recent marriage of Mary's sister Elizabeth to James Donald Cameron, the former secretary of war and heir to his family's dominant position in Pennsylvania politics. Though but half her husband's age, Lizzie was accepted in his political and literary circles, thereby offering Nelson another way to mix with the nation's elite.[26]

Mary took Cecilia back east by mid-October of 1878; Miles left Fort Keogh on November 25 and convened the board three weeks later. But the late arrival of a fellow committee member, Mackenzie, who had been fighting a bout with typhoid fever, delayed the proceedings. And on January 1 (the day before Mackenzie's arrival), Mary's father, Judge Charles Sherman, died in Cleveland. Mary was already there; Nelson and Lizzie Sherman Cameron rode out together to attend the funeral, again stalling the committee's deliberations.[27]

The board finally settled down to work in mid-January. Meeting six times weekly between 10 A.M. and 2 P.M. at the mammoth but still-incomplete State-War-Navy Building, the board studied a wide range of ordnance and military equipment. Wagon wheels, company account books, whistles, cutlery, infantry and cavalry equipment, shoes, bayonets, sabers, uniforms, revolvers, and rifles all came under their scrutiny. Miles, proud of his knowledge of military technology, took a keen interest in the deliberations. During the past decade, troops under his command had tested a wide range of experimental weapons developed by the Remington, Sharps, and Ward-Burton armories. In an attempt to solve the jamming problems in army firearms, he had recommended a shell extractor suitable for releasing faulty metallic cartridges.[28]

As for the army's larger weapons, Miles believed that Gatling guns were "worthless for Indian fighting," mountain howitzers had too little range, and other artillery pieces in the army arsenal were "too heavy for rough country." In 1876 Miles had called for development of a light rifled cannon similar to that used by colonial armies. Ordnance Department officials had responded indifferently to his flurry of requests and recommendations. After all, they, not some flashy colonel who chased after wild Indians, were the experts. Miles had seethed at their patronizing correspondence. He had made no friends in the Ordnance bureau when he told a congressional committee, "The Ordnance Department could, in my judgment, be reduced one-half and be quite as efficient as, and far less expensive than, at present."[29]

Spurred by Miles's curiosity, the board received thirteen hundred communications and examined 180 models of various equipment. "Threatened troubles with Indians" led McCrary to order the board to adjourn by April 1. In order to expedite the committee's conclusion, the secretary overruled General Sherman and allowed the members to study production facilities at Philadelphia; Rock Island, Illinois; and the Watervliet Arsenal, New York. In late March, Colonel Mackenzie removed a final stumbling block to adjournment—the detailed investigation of dress uniforms—by reminding his fellow board members of the more practical need to study the worth of special summer clothing.[30]

Miles's equipment board called for sixty-one changes in uniforms, equipment, and weaponry. Better shoes, summer uniforms featuring white cork helmets and linen- or cotton-duck clothing, a combination knife-bayonet, new Whitman saddles, canvas overcoats, increased pay allowances for enlisted men, and the introduction of the Lee magazine rifle highlighted their recommendations. In forwarding their proposals to Secretary McCrary, Sherman admitted that the board had made recommendations "which hardly fell inside the province of their inquiry. But in the army," he explained, "changes are necessary and inevitable and can only be met as they arise." Still, Sherman rejected sixteen changes outright and approved six others, including the Lee rifle, for testing alone. The general also reminded the secretary of war that the board's actions, if fully implemented, overran Congress's nine hundred thousand dollar appropriations for new equipment by 55 percent. On the whole, the War Department accepted Sherman's recommendations that the magazine rifle be adopted on only an experimental basis, that summer uniforms were unnecessary, and that the combination knife-bayonet be rejected.[31]

The army's failure to enact the board's recommendations disappointed Miles. On April 24, he asked Adjutant General Edward D. Townsend to supply his regiment with the Lee magazine rifle and the combination knife-bayonet. This "would render my command better able to meet an enemy armed with the most modern firearms," explained Miles. Townsend forwarded the request to Chief of Ordnance Stephen V. Benet, a conservative West Pointer who had seen little Civil War combat. Benet ignored Sherman's call for a new study of magazine weapons and rejected Miles's proposal out of hand.[32]

Miles stubbornly defended his requests. Of the 398 rifles currently in his regiment, 336 were "more or less defective," wrote the colonel. "I am more interested in this matter than the Chief of Ordnance can possibly be. . . . I think the Chief of Ordnance would not care to go into an engagement with a command so armed if he could obtain more effective weapons." Miles went on to attribute the disaster at the Little Bighorn to inferior weapons.[33]

In response, Benet blasted Miles's "rambling and incoherent" attacks on the Ordnance Department. Steadfast in his judgment that production of the Lee rifle was illegal, Benet argued that his nemesis had "neglected his duty" in failing to requisition functional weapons for his men. Further, he demanded that Miles "be admonished." Miles responded that November, disclaiming "any unfair reflection upon the Ordnance Corps." He went on to note, however, "It must be admitted that the Ordnance Corps do not have to risk their lives fighting in line with troops the same as other officers." Charging that Ordnance officers had contrived to take the decision regarding the Lee rifle "out of the hands of the President," he demanded a congressional investigation.[34]

The army did not appreciate such internecine warfare. General Sherman proclaimed that Miles "was not warranted in making such sweeping charges against the Ordnance Department." Silencing the feud after eight months of controversy, Adjutant General Townsend labeled the correspondence between Miles and Benet "fruitless." It "should be discontinued," he ordered.[35]

M iles had returned to Fort Keogh on June 2, 1879, having been delayed by the removal of a small growth near his right shoulder blade. He immediately reinforced his reputation as an army malcontent by protesting the recent posting of the Eighteenth Infantry Regiment (commanded by Colonel Thomas H. Ruger, Miles's senior) to Montana Territory as "the severest injury that has been done me by any official or friend." Already apprehensive about letting the impetuous colonel anywhere near the Canadian border, Sherman launched into a bitter tirade against Miles. "I have repeatedly in every form expressed and acted as your personal friend," stormed Sherman. Just because Ranald Mackenzie had in 1873 wrongfully crossed the Mexican border, continued the general, "is no reason why I should imitate so bad an example" by authorizing a Canadian crossing.[36]

Despite Sherman's fulminations, skirmishing along the northern boundary led the department commander, Terry, to call upon Miles "to clear out the straggling bands of hostile Sioux which [had] come across the line to hunt." But caution remained essential; "it will be desirable to force the Sioux back rather by a display of force than by actual conflict," instructed Terry. That July, Miles organized a command of 33 officers, 643 enlisted men, and 143 Indian auxiliaries at the Fort Peck Agency.[37]

Two days out from Fort Peck at Beaver Creek, an advance guard encountered Sitting Bull and four hundred Sioux. A running fight ensued and the bluecoats followed the Sioux through the mud to the Canadian border; on July 23, Miles met with Major J. M. Walsh of the North West Mounted Police. Here Miles received assurances that the Sioux had no intention of starting another war with the United States. Under orders to act cautiously, Miles fell back south of the Milk River. In the process, he arrested and expelled from the United States several hundred Canadian Métis he believed had supplied the Sioux with ammunition.[38]

In late August, Miles retraced his steps to Fort Keogh. Terry applauded his actions, which, "by a most happy union of enterprise and audacity, prudence and foresight," had cleared the upper Missouri of Sioux hostile to the government. Sherman was less certain. Newspaper accounts that played up the threat of war, along with correspondence from Canadian authorities that discounted the hostile intentions of the Sioux, reinforced his doubts. "General Miles is too apt to mistake the dictates of his personal ambition for wisdom and I am sorry to say that he is not just and fair to his comrades and superiors," wrote the commander. "He will absorb all power to himself . . . if not supervised and checked." For his part, Miles believed the operation to be a failure that resulted from impractical orders issued by his superiors.[39]

Concerned that his failure to capture Sitting Bull might damage his reputation, the colonel threw his energies into more mundane affairs at Fort Keogh, which, with its four- to six-hundred-man garrison, was one of the nation's largest military establishments. As was the case at every fort, a caste system divided enlisted men and commissioned personnel as well as their dependents. Alice Baldwin, for example, when company laundresses moved into quarters near hers, reported wryly, "You can see I have a swell neighborhood." Life took on a cyclical routine. The short open season on the Yellowstone River brought supplies, visitors, and general excitement and a sense of gloom fell over the command in the fall as the last boat took away summer visitors and children going off to school.[40]

Outdoor sports provided a major source of entertainment and relaxation. Horseback riding and ice skating attracted men and women alike. In October 1879, Miles took eight officers, twelve soldiers, and five Indians on a six-day hunt along the Rosebud. Presumably, the post commander's pack of fine hunting dogs assisted in the operation. Ten six-mule wagon teams hauled in the spoils—sixty deer, three antelopes, a mountain sheep, five elk, seventeen buffalo, seventy prairie chickens, and six ducks—enough game for the four-hundred-man garrison to enjoy a memorable feast. Sleighing and skating helped ease the winter isolation, and full-dress inspections added military pomp to the growing settlement.[41]

Amateur theatricals, evening musicals by the regimental band, and the post library provided additional diversions. Indians living near the post performed ceremonial dances in exchange for trinkets from the garrison. Officers and their wives could also expect an invitation to an occasional "soiree musicale" at the commanding officer's quarters. Miles, his hair now sprinkled with gray, had taken to smoking big cigars in the style of President Ulysses S. Grant. With his brilliant wartime record, his penchant for storytelling, and his imperious military bearing, Miles had a special knack for impressing young officers. Mary seemed equally adept at such functions. Lavishly provisioned, courtesy of the colonel's careful financial investments during and after the war and the efforts of the family's black servant, Kentucky-born Harriet Mobley, the events highlighted post society. Mrs. Miles "is a beautiful lady," observed an awe-struck young lieutenant the morning after one such gala. Of the event, he added, "There is a good deal of talk and heart burning over it today of course."[42]

Civilians established the bustling community of Miles City just outside the military reservation. With the big garrison providing a captive market and a newly flourishing cattle industry pumping in capital, Miles City became the economic center of southeastern Montana. Miles had reported by spring 1878 that there was "quite a rush for land" as merchants competed with official post traders for government business. The colonel saw to it that his nephew George Miles received a variety of government sinecures and snapped up choice land tracts throughout the region. George later parleyed these advantages into a significant personal fortune.[43]

Miles City attracted its share of entrepreneurs and ne'er-do-wells as it blossomed into an important cow town. George Miles concluded that it was "the headquarters for the frontier rough element," and the colonel became embroiled in at least one lawsuit over lost cattle. In town, the Cosmopolitan Theater and the Gray Mule Saloon attracted cowboys seeking a good time, a fact not lost on the more staid locals who sometimes resented the wild intruders. "Nice people in Miles City," reported one sage, "would as soon have thought of inviting a rattlesnake into their homes as a cowboy."[44]

By now Nelson Miles had become a popular source of information on Indian affairs. In his letters to politicians and reformers, congressional testimony, newspaper interviews, speeches, and an essay published by the prestigious *North American Review*, Miles tempered his racism. This growing affinity for Indians could be attributed in part to his familiarity with tribal members. He knew and had depended on Crow and Northern Cheyenne auxiliaries throughout the latter 1870s. Further, during treaty negotiations several chiefs had won his respect. The colonel's insatiable thirst for promotion also helped to explain his expedient changes in outlook. Reformers enjoyed wide political support; it might make practical sense to join their ranks.

Like most of those interested in changing the nation's Indian policy, Miles never accepted the principal of racial equality. He instead agreed with the conclusions of the acclaimed anthropologist Lewis Henry Morgan, whose frequent contributions to leading periodicals and publication of *Ancient Society* in 1877 won wide readership. Morgan organized societies into three major stages—savagery, barbarism, and civilization. Miles accepted Morgan's conclusion that the majority of American Indians had passed from savagery to barbarism. The Indians, argued Miles in a letter to Senator Alvin Saunders in 1878, must now be guided "from barbarism to civilization."[45]

Miles contended that Indian groups had reached various levels of barbarism. In testimony before a congressional committee in December 1877, he maintained that "localized" tribes like the Creeks and Choctaws who could read and speak English were capable of self-government and should be accorded citizenship. Other bands, however, needed more development. These less advanced persons, he argued, "must first be made a pastoral people before they can become agriculturalists. That is the stepping stone by which every civilized race has passed from barbarism to civilization." They should be stripped of their guns and provided with stock and "heavy draught horses unsuited for war" in order to hasten this process. Schools should teach them English and the rudiments of cultivation.[46]

Changes in government policy might expedite this process. Miles blamed the constant warfare with Indians on the government's "bad faith and mismanagement." To set matters right, the corruption-ridden Indian Bureau must be transferred back to the War Department. Only the army, its officers honed by years of frontier experience, could provide Christian moral authority "strong enough to control them and just enough to command their respect." He reinforced this theme in an address before the prestigious New England Society, a contemporary literary and philanthropic group: "With us it is not a question of destroying them or being at war with them perpetually, but whether we are competent and able to govern them not only with a strong and firm hand, but also with entire justice."[47]

The colonel gleaned many lessons from the Canadians' experience with the Indians. Their "permanent, decided, and just" system meant less violence. The Canadians carried out their treaty promises, were "positive and despotic," and acted under a unified command structure rather than the mixed army–Indian Bureau system. In Canada special courts punished individual criminals rather than entire tribes. Finally, the slower pace of white immigration into western Canada allowed more time for negotiations.[48]

Contemporaries counted Miles firmly among the ranks of Indian reformers. Captain Richard H. Pratt, who infused many of the movement's values into his Carlisle Indian School, believed that Miles would do "justice to the Indians," who respected his power and honesty. "General Miles has to do so much of the fighting himself that it is only fair to allow him to suggest how a good part of it might be prevented," suggested the *New York Daily Tribune.* Though he had long ago lost influence with Mary's Uncle William, Miles did influence Senators Sherman and Henry L. Dawes and Secretary of the Interior Carl Schurz.[49]

But the Indians must first accept the authority of the United States government, by force if necessary. "At some future time we may have to fight these Sioux," General Sherman concluded on August 2, 1879, "but at this moment our orders are to be peaceful and economical, and leave the Indian Bureau a free field to find out the sheep from the goats." The general failed to reckon with deteriorating conditions in Canada, where diseases among the Indian pony herds had combined with the declining buffalo and inadequate resources of the Canadian government to render the migrant Sioux destitute by spring 1880. Miles asserted that by mid-March fifteen hundred Sioux had surrendered at Fort Keogh alone. The North West Mounted Police estimated that fewer than two hundred lodges from the United States remained north of the forty-ninth parallel. The July departure of the Superintendent of the Mounted Police, J. M. Walsh, a man respected for his courage, careful negotiations, and honesty, further demoralized the Sioux. With Colonel Miles's bluecoats patrolling the border, there seemed no escape, and Sitting Bull's influence waned as he vainly awaited an honorable solution.[50]

At Fort Keogh, Miles chafed at his superiors' refusal to let him take the field. "Gen. Miles is perplexed and disgusted," wrote a junior officer in August 1880. Secretary of the Interior Schurz, dispatched to Montana to investigate the situation, met with Miles the following month. The two became good friends, despite initial misunderstandings stemming from Miles's sharp critiques of the Indian Bureau. Impressed with the way the colonel had handled those Sioux who turned themselves in, Schurz hoped that Miles would be given a free hand to deal with the Sioux "according to the original plan discussed between us."[51]

The U.S. government redoubled its pressure that fall. Sitting Bull realized his people might not last another winter. At Fort Buford, Major Brotherton, a long-time antagonist of Miles's recently transferred from the Fifth to the Seventh Infantry, sent a scout, E. H.

Allison, to secure their final surrender. At about the same time, Colonel Miles dispatched his own agent, Willis E. Everette, on a similar mission. Everette later asserted that he was on the verge of securing Sitting Bull's capitulation when Allison arrived with four wagonloads of provisions. According to Everette, a notoriously unreliable source, the new arrival warned the Sioux that "Bear Coat" would kill them. Thus Allison, "actuated by the envious and malicious wishes of his patron," according to Everette, scuttled the negotiations.[52]

Sitting Bull ventured south of the border that December, and finally surrendered to Brotherton in July 1881. One hundred eighty-seven hungry, sullen, destitute souls were all that remained of his once-formidable legions. The surrender to Brotherton was a bitter disappointment to Miles, who had hoped to add Sitting Bull to his list of conquests. Terry's annual report for 1881 further infuriated Miles: "To Major Brotherton is due the credit of having originally suggested the course of action which resulted in the surrender or capture of Sitting Bull. . . . No term less strong than 'invaluable' would fitly characterize the service which he rendered."[53]

The recent years had not yielded the fruits that Miles had hoped to pluck. They did, however, suggest that his contentiousness worked against professional advancement. Though his record outshone that of every other officer of the Indian wars, his stubborn, quarrelsome attitude and insatiable quest for publicity and power counterbalanced this success. In spite of his personality, he did earn a grudging respect from some. "He is a good pushing officer . . . I should like to have when there is a necessity for an action near," explained an astute Phil Sheridan, who also noted in an equally telling comment. "Miles has no idea of economy; but very little for the regulations, also ambitious."[54]

Though unjustified in their tenor and length, many of Miles's complaints were understandable. Relatively young Civil War veterans dominated the higher ranks of the army and they were bitter and somewhat stagnant after severe reductions in force; until they died or retired, junior officers like him suffered. Promotions, usually made on the basis of seniority, included enough cases like that of George Crook, who had been bumped from lieutenant colonel to brigadier general, to exasperate those not on the receiving end of such boons.[55]

Equally infuriating was the attitude, widely held in army circles, that the Indian wars were simply "a fleeting bother." Stephen Benet, with whom Miles had tangled in the ordnance controversy, certainly shared this view, a fact not lost to Miles as he endured the hardships of campaigns against the Comanches, Cheyennes, Sioux, Nez Perces, and Bannocks. Lieutenant Colonel Emory Upton, a Civil War hero, respected theorist, and rival for a brigadier generalship that was coveted by Miles, also expressed this opinion: " 'Bushwacking' and Indian fighting with one or two companies do not qualify an officer for the position as General."[56]

Miles rightfully saw himself as a superb combat officer who cared for the physical welfare of his men. Though his tirades against staff officers were often unfair, they promoted regimental esprit de corps, and his subordinates agreed with Miles's claims that jealous rivals had conspired to minimize the Fifth's accomplishments. He made the sufferings of his regiment well known; in 1877, for example, he informed the secretary of war that his men had been forced "to march through blinding snow storms, in piercing winds, with insufficient underclothing, and feet bound up in grain sacks, and in skins of wild animals." To Sherman, he ranted, "I concider it refined cruelty to compel troops to remain out in this country" without proper tenting. "The failure of the army to keep supplies of troops up here is a great disgrace."[57]

His requests seemed endless. Following his first campaign against Sitting Bull, he called on Congress to appropriate an extra issue of clothing to the men of his Fifth and six companies of the Twenty-second in gratitude for their superhuman efforts. He also sought congressional support for those of his command who had lost goods on the *Don Cameron* when that steamer sunk. And Miles fought long and hard to secure medals and promotions for deserving junior officers; he worked stubbornly in an unsuccessful bid to procure the army's adoption of a knife-bayonet, designed by an officer in his regiment. Likewise, Miles battled the influence of the Indian Bureau, an organization in which corruption seemed unusually widespread, even in an era hardly known for good government.[58]

This sort of personal lobbying was common to the old army. In 1874, Sherman had moved his headquarters from Washington to St. Louis to protest the machinations of then Secretary of War William Belknap. But Miles's calls for preferment and special treatment, never-ending in number and brazenly critical of his superiors, seemed especially blunt. Miles was an able though irritating officer whose great ambition rivaled only his great talent. It was unclear which of these traits would dominate his career, and in the end, his life.

8 : NORTHWESTERN INTERLUDE

Nelson Miles had watched assorted other developments even as the Sioux drifted in from Canada. In June 1880, in an ironic twist, the self-educated soldier gave the commencement address at the United States Military Academy. He also pondered the upcoming presidential race, in which his old ally, Winfield Scott Hancock, was making a bid for the Democratic nomination.[1]

Though himself a Republican and in no way at odds with either the party machinery or its candidate, former Brigadier General James A. Garfield, Miles had good reason to be interested in Hancock's candidacy, for he believed his old mentor would look favorably on his best division commander. The possibility of Miles's promotion looked particularly ripe that summer, as Generals E.O.C. Ord and Irvin McDowell both neared the usual army retirement age of sixty-two. Itching for a change (one Miles City citizen noted, "Genl Miles has been acting a little queer lately"), Miles reminded his uncle John Sherman, now treasury secretary, that he still desired promotion. Sherman spoke to President Rutherford B. Hayes; "I believe he is earnestly desirous of promoting you," reported the secretary. The August 24 death of Brigadier General Albert J. Myer, the army's chief signal officer, created still another vacancy. Colonel Miles nominated himself as a candidate for Myer's job, which with its engineering, meteorological, and communications work would open "a wide field of usefulness." The major obstacle seemed to be General William T. Sherman, whose "nonsupport," charged Miles, "may amount to actual opposition."[2]

Secretary Sherman, perhaps unaware of the Miles-Hancock alliance, cautioned his nephew-in-law about seeking the highly politicized chief signal officer's post. As a Republican, Miles risked being "legislated out of office" should a Democrat be elected president. But buoyed by the recommendations of several governors and senators, Interior Secretary Carl Schurz, and Generals Sheridan, Hancock, and Pope, the colonel reiterated his desire for advancement. Because of the kind of work the job involved, its accompanying promotion to brigadier general, and its Washington base, it seemed too good for Miles to pass up.[3]

Ord's retirement came as expected. Even General Sherman's intercession had failed to save the outspoken Ord, whose Democratic politics, coupled with his advocacy of more aggressive action in the southwestern borderlands, had angered Republican officials. But the apolitical McDowell remained in his Division of the Pacific, thus reducing by one the number of vacant brigadier's slots. And many believed Miles, who lacked formal scientific training, to be too valuable as an Indian fighter to be cooped up in the Washington-based office. The last-minute efforts by the president's wife, Lucy Webb Hayes, to push a rival candidate, Colonel Thomas L. Casey, posed another hurdle to Miles's accession to the chief signal officer position.[4]

Time resolved all, but not to Miles's complete satisfaction. Hancock lost the election by a minuscule popular majority. Later that month several New York and Philadelphia newspapers reported that Miles had been appointed chief signal officer. Such accounts, however, proved premature. Colonel William B. Hazen, a caustic opponent of the now discredited Secretary of War William Belknap, had also pushed hard for the position, and his willingness to use his inside connections with president-elect Garfield dwarfed even that of Miles. Hazen also boasted a good Civil War record and a wide range of frontier experience. The combination proved unbeatable; Hazen secured the chief signal officer's position in December. As something of a consolation, Miles received the generalship vacated by Ord, an appointment blessed by president-elect Garfield. With the promotion came command of the Department of the Columbia.[5]

Since Miles ranked only seventh among colonels in terms of seniority, his advancement sparked bitter protest among army circles. Sherman attributed the selection to the determination of outgoing President Hayes "to create a vacancy for General Miles on the openly expressed theory that the army was not gratified enough to the Republican Party." Senator John A. Logan, a noted critic of the regular army, added, "It was done entirely on personal grounds, he being a relative of General Sherman." Though unsubstantiated, the charges of nepotism reinforced the negative opinions often engendered by the blunt colonel.[6]

Miles left Fort Keogh to receive his star in official Washington ceremonies. There the proud brigadier, in the prime of his life and invigorated by his robust frontier adventures, rubbed shoulders with the great and the near-great, distributing souvenir Indian moccasins to admiring women in the process. But an onerous task also awaited, for Miles was detailed to preside over the court-martial of U.S. Military Academy cadet Johnson C. Whittaker. A black South Carolinian, Whittaker had endured the racial slurs of fellow West Pointers for two-and-a-half years until he was found one morning, bound and beaten, on the floor of his room. Incredibly, a court of inquiry charged that Whittaker had staged the entire incident in order to win public sympathy.[7]

Army protocol and the publicity generated by the case demanded an official court-martial. The court's deliberations quickly took an ugly turn. Though he had been an abolitionist and an active supporter of black economic rights during Reconstruction, Miles, reflecting the views of most white Americans of his time, did not believe in racial equality. Miles also wanted to please his superiors who sought Whittaker's prosecution, and he undoubtedly knew that his name had been mentioned as a candidate for the superintendency of the Military Academy. The case lingered into early June 1881 as temperatures and pressure rose. Torn by conflicting emotions, Miles sought removal from the court. But General Sherman refused to let Miles squirm free, advising him "to control the managing lawyers" and to resolve the case quickly.[8]

The court-martial supported earlier verdicts in finding Whittaker guilty of attempting to deceive the Academy and lying at the court of inquiry. However, the board did recommend that a one-year sentence of hard labor be remitted. Judge Advocate General D. G. Swaim later compiled a scathing criticism of the entire case; in early 1882, President Chester A. Arthur voided the court's decision and sentence. Consequently, however, army authorities dismissed Whittaker from West Point for having failed a course.[9]

Indian affairs also claimed General Miles's attention. Reformers and government officials, with an eye toward speeding assimilation of the tribes while at the same time reducing costs, had accelerated a program designed to concentrate the Indians on a few large reservations. This process took little account of the Indians' pain and suffering as they left their homelands, to which the tribes had deep economic, cultural, and psychological attachments. One such group, the Poncas, had been removed from their homes in northern Nebraska to the Indian Territory in 1877. A small, peaceful tribe, the Poncas quickly deteriorated on the southern plains.[10]

In early 1879, some Poncas left the reservation and made their way north to Nebraska. They blocked government attempts made in federal district court to force them back to Indian Territory. The Poncas attracted widespread support; Rutherford B. Hayes appointed a special commission to investigate the affair in late 1880. Chaired by George Crook, the Ponca Commission also included Miles, William Stickney (of the Board of Indian Commissioners), and William Allen, a prominent Boston attorney. The group questioned the Poncas in Nebraska as well as those in the Indian Territory. With President Hayes prodding them to reach a decision and Miles and Crook forming an unusual alliance, the commission recommended that both groups of Poncas be allowed to remain where they were.[11]

In so doing, Crook, Miles, and Stickney accepted the wishes expressed by those Poncas they had interviewed. The majority report also concurred with a delegation of leaders representing those Poncas still in the Indian Territory who declared their desire to remain in place. In a subsequent newspaper interview, Miles blasted the initial removal as "simply inexcusable." The treatment of this peaceful tribe "was a serious mistake, resulting from mismanagement, incompetency or selfish motives. They were wronged." Congress approved the new arrangement, appropriating to the Poncas $165,000 in indemnities.[12]

It had been a difficult case, and in recommending that some of the Poncas be kept in the Indian Territory Miles angered radical reformers, who demanded that all the tribe be returned north. But despite the public controversies, at least the Ponca and Whittaker investigations had allowed Miles to remain in the east. Here the general mingled with influential people like John Jacob Astor, whose family fortune was built on the fur trade, and the historian Henry Adams, regaling his listeners with stirring tales of his wartime exploits. Circumstances also permitted him to further the cause of prohibition. Having been genuinely concerned since his childhood about the evils of strong drink, Miles joined a fellow Massachussan, Major Thomas F. Blair, in pressing the issue in a late-February visit to the White House. This conversation, according to Miles, convinced the lame-duck president Hayes to issue an executive order that forbade the sale of hard liquor on military posts.[13]

His detached service concluded, Miles caught a train to San Francisco and then took a steamer to Vancouver Barracks, Washington Territory. On August 2, 1881, the general assumed command of the Department of the Columbia. His administration included Oregon, the Washington and Idaho territories (excepting a slice of eastern Idaho, which belonged to the Department of the Platte), and the district of Alaska. Miles would retain this command of over fifteen hundred men distributed on eleven military posts for five years.[14]

Excited about the assignment he had sought so long, Miles vowed to resist the boredom that had ruined many a promising frontier regular. Strong drink, frustration, frequent transfers, and loneliness might destroy what Confederates and Indians had not. He thus threw himself into the affairs of his far-flung command—inspecting troops, reducing desertion, improving roads, laying out telegraph lines, and resolving minor Indian disputes. To improve morale he instituted a regular system of calisthenics and exercise at Vancouver Barracks. Post canteens, intended as a more regulated alternative to the often raucous sutler's bars, also won his support. Still fascinated with weapons and technology, he came into contact with the inventors Alexander Graham Bell and Thomas A. Edison during frequent trips back east. More directly, the general oversaw experiments with the new Hotchkiss "revolving cannon" and corresponded with John Ericsson, the engineer-inventor most noted for his work on the Civil War ironclad, the *Monitor.*[15]

Though Mary bore their second child, Sherman, in 1882, the restless father longed for new experiences and challenges. In 1881 he had made a brief visit to San Francisco, with its splendid Palace Hotel; the following September, "the death of a near relative and other personal reasons" led Miles to take leave for Boston and Washington. Occasional outings to the opera highlighted that journey, and an "important civil suit in Boston" extended the visit through April 1883. That summer he was elected a corresponding member of the Military Historical Society of Massachusetts and he helped organize a West Coast reunion of the Grand Army of the Republic, the powerful organization of Civil War veterans. Another two months' leave came that September. When one of his children was taken "rather seriously ill," Miles was three days late reporting back to duty; the adjutant general's department ruled him absent without leave and docked him three days' pay.[16]

Nelson also delved into politics. Lingering disputes over Civil War exploits and the army bill of 1882, which mandated retirement at age sixty-four, demanded considerable time and energy on his part. He offered advice on various political affairs to anyone willing to listen, predicting that the Republicans would nominate John Sherman for president in 1884. James G. Blaine's primary victory surprised Miles, who was even more disappointed when Grover Cleveland and the Democratic party won the presidency. The latter election meant that Miles's candidate for the Montana territorial governorship, Martin Maginnis, also failed to secure office.[17]

Though Mary remained a somewhat reluctant westerner, Nelson enjoyed his tenure at the comfortable Vancouver Barracks headquarters. "I have found it exceedingly interesting and am very much pleased with my command," he assured General Sherman. Miles doggedly championed his region's future prospects. Non-Indian settlement would complement the area's distinctive natural beauty, he believed; as department commander, Miles could speed this development by improving railroad and telegraph links, bringing in additional troops, constructing new military facilities, and securing funds for exploration.[18]

The army had long allied itself with railroad interests, which, explained their military proponents, reduced quartermaster costs and allowed rapid deployment of reinforcements during emergencies. Miles

Nelson Appleton Miles, age ten.

Courtesy Massachusetts Commandery Military Order of the Loyal Legion and the U.S. Army Military History Institute, Carlisle Barracks, Pennsylvania.

Brigadier General J. C. Caldwell and staff near Fair Oaks, Virginia, June 1862. First Lieutenant Nelson A. Miles, second from left, strikes a defiant pose. Caldwell is seated to Miles's right.

Courtesy Massachusetts Commandery Military Order of the Loyal Legion and the U.S. Army Military History Institute, Carlisle Barracks, Pennsylvania.

This photo shows Brevet Major General Nelson A. Miles at the end of the Civil War. On his left arm Miles wears a black band in tribute to the recently assassinated President Lincoln.

Courtesy Library of Congress.

Miles at age thirty-six. Here he boasts part of his heavy winter
clothing.

The snows of Montana did not deter Miles and his Fifth Infantry
from pursuing Indians deemed hostile by the federal government. In
1876, just before leaving the Tongue River Cantonment in pursuit of
Crazy Horse and Sitting Bull, several officers braved the winter
weather for a photograph. From left: Lieutenant Oscar F. Long,
Surgeon Henry R. Tilton, Lieutenant James W. Pope, Colonel
Nelson A. Miles, Lieutenant Frank Baldwin, Lieutenant Charles E.
Hargous, and Lieutenant Hobart K. Bailey.

In November 1887 the citizens of Arizona presented Miles with a
ceremonial sword. Miles is pictured at Levin's Park, Tucson,
responding to a speech of Judge W. H. Barnes.

Courtesy Arizona Historical Society/Tucson, photo accession no. 7219.

Miles cultivated the friendship of many famous westerners, among them William F. ("Buffalo Bill") Cody. Here Cody joins a clean-shaven Miles in reviewing an Indian camp near Pine Ridge, South Dakota, just after the close of the Wounded Knee Campaign.

Courtesy National Archives and Records Administration.

Commanding General Nelson A. Miles.

Courtesy Arizona Historical Society/Tucson, photo accession no. 1156.

During the war against Spain, Miles and Major General William R. Shafter (U.S. Volunteers) enjoyed less than amiable relations. Here the two are consulting during the Santiago Campaign.

Courtesy National Archives and Records Administration.

Major General Nelson A. Miles, near the turn of the century.

Courtesy Massachusetts Commandery Military Order of the Loyal Legion and the U.S. Army Military History Institute, Carlisle Barracks, Pennsylvania.

(Above) Commanding General Miles and Colonel Charles Morton reviewing the Seventh Cavalry and Third Battery Field Artillery, July 4, 1903, at Chickamauga Park, Georgia.

Courtesy Arizona Historical Society/Tucson, photo accession no. 44701.

(Below) Miles and a veterans' parade. With the press and an audience present, Miles, even at age eighty-two, was in his element.

Courtesy National Archives and Records Administration.

General Miles's funeral procession, May 19, 1925.

Courtesy Arizona Historical Society/Tucson, photo accession no. 189.

worked hard to cultivate good relations with the Northern Pacific Railroad, soon to become the region's first transcontinental line. In 1880 he had vigorously backed federal support for railroads in letters to appropriate congressional committees, seeing to it that the Northern Pacific received a copy of his message. "It ought to do our enterprise a great deal of good to have such a clear statement from one so peculiarly qualified," responded Frederick Billings, then the president of the Northern Pacific. Miles maintained a constant vigil on company affairs, encouraging Senator John Sherman to assume the line's presidency in 1884. Though Sherman opted to retain his senate seat, Miles's efforts to secure influence paralleled those of many of his army peers. In return, company officials supported Miles's promotion.[19]

Noting the area's vast size, Pacific defenses, and lingering Indian troubles, General Miles also pressed for better regional communications, reinforcements, and improved department facilities. Telegraph lines and heliograph stations multiplied. Whether as a result of Miles's complaints or actual need, his department saw an 8 percent increase in troops stationed there—from 1,667 in 1881 to 1,804 in 1884—a significant growth, considering that the army's total strength remained stable. His superiors also supported his determination to replace old Fort Colville with Fort Spokane as the major army base in eastern Washington Territory. His calls for improvements at Vancouver Barracks, however, received only sporadic funding.[20]

Interested in further national expansion, Miles dreamed of moving north of the forty-ninth parallel. British Columbia, he thought, seemed destined to become part of the United States. He also took a special interest in Alaska, then under the loose police of Treasury Department revenue cutters and a Sitka-based naval vessel. In 1881, he sailed up the Inland Passage and asked the War Department to sponsor an exploration of the Alaskan interior. "Whatever its treasures," explained Miles, "they are beyond the reach of private enterprise." Lieutenant Frederick Schwatka, "an officer highly distinguished and experienced," would lead the team at a cost of sixty-eight thousand dollars. General Sherman and Secretary of War Robert T. Lincoln rejected the proposal on the grounds that Captain Charles W. Raymond had already traversed the district in 1869. Not so, responded Miles; the Raymond expedition had not gone inland. "The industrial and commercial resources of that territory are attracting the interest and attention of the Pacific Coast," he insisted.[21]

Undeterred by War Department skepticism, Miles convinced Congressman Melvin C. George and Senator Sherman to sponsor new bills, whose sixty-eight-thousand-dollar price tags mirrored original projections. Congress again tabled the proposals, but Miles refused to give up, taking a more creative tack in 1882. As he later rationalized, "Frequent reports of disturbances of the peace between the whites and Indians in Alaska" led him to dispatch Schwatka, then serving as his personal aide, to investigate the region.[22]

No stranger to the far north, Lieutenant Schwatka had in 1878 led a team in the international search for the ill-fated Sir John Franklin expedition. Miles ordered the lieutenant and his six-man party to assess the number, character, and military potential of the native peoples of Alaska. "Strict economy" was to govern his moves, which were to remain "especial and confidential." In May 1883, Schwatka left Portland "like a thief in the night." Though Schwatka's trip up the Yukon River produced little new scientific information, his subsequent publications rekindled public interest in the region.[23]

Fascinated by Alaska, Miles dispatched two expeditions in 1884 and another in 1885. Former scout Willis E. Everette made a rather timid effort to explore the area between the White and Copper rivers, and Lieutenant William R. Abercrombie unsuccessfully attempted to travel the length of the Copper River. Although Abercrombie named a glacier after his commander, Miles replaced the lieutenant with still another aide, Lieutenant Henry Allen, in 1885. The handsome, Kentucky-born Allen had thoroughly researched his Alaskan assignment. Although his careful reports failed to generate the excitement resulting from Schwatka's, a beaming General Miles compared his epic fifteen-hundred-mile journey into northern Alaska with the work of Meriwether Lewis and William Clark. "For . . . four years I have tried to have that unknown region explored and I should have been pretty disappointed had you failed. It was my last effort," wrote Miles.[24]

Having risked official censure, Miles never forgot the lieutenant's efforts and promoted his career for the next two decades. Fascinated by intrigue and misdirection, the general had freed Schwatka, Abercrombie, and Allen by assigning them to his personal staff. Alaska's size and frontier potential no doubt piqued his interest. But Miles also voiced other motives that, if made public, would have reinforced Canadian fears that the U.S. acquisition of Alaska was merely the first step in an American campaign to grab the entire Pacific Northwest. "I think it too soon to occupy the Boundary line now, when we are ready for that the North Pole may be the boundary," he had advised General Sherman in 1881. "A majority of the people of British Columbia would vote for annexation tomorrow."[25]

Miles also dabbled in speculative ventures. In Washington, D.C., a group spearheaded by Senator Sherman was developing the Columbia Heights, two miles north of the Executive Mansion. The senator brought in Miles as an investor in 1883; to his existing property on Fourteenth Street, the general added a rental house and seven new lots. Miles agreed to pay Sherman and his "Columbia Heights Association" $22,638 (at 5 percent annual interest) for the new real estate. In the hope of raising property values in the area, Miles was to spend another $5,000 to improve his new building.[26]

"We all wish that you shall own that property & are quite willing to meet your wishes," Sherman assured the new partner. But the Washington real estate market changed just as Miles was completing his purchase. Columbia Heights fell temporarily out of fashion in lieu of the even more promising development of Massachusetts Avenue to Rock Creek. Prospective buyers, from whom he had hoped to secure an $18,000 profit, lost interest in the Miles tracts. Two wings rendered the rambling old rental house too expensive to heat or furnish. Extensive remodeling was necessary and the other partners blamed Miles's ramshackle house for their inability to sell their own lots.[27]

Pressed by other investors, Senator Sherman encouraged Miles to begin the promised improvements. "Marked and radical changes" were necessary. "I have been afraid that in some way the fashion would drift away from it and leave it an elephant on your hands, and that you might think that I was responsible," explained the senator, who offered to assume one-half of Miles's obligations as a show of good faith. "I am determined to get some prominent man to occupy that house if we have to let him have it free of rent," wrote the senator on September 1, 1884. Sherman finally engineered the sale of the house and several lots for $20,000. Though strained, relations between the senator and his nephew-in-law remained unbroken.[28]

Miles managed to retain several prime Washington, D.C. properties in spite of the disappointment. He also used the associated financial connections for his own schemes, which ranged from stock and timberland acquisitions to his broader plans to develop the Department of the Columbia. Like most of his army colleagues, Miles found it unnecessary to separate personal profit from professional development. If his military department expanded in size and importance, his stature as an officer would increase, as would the value of any investments he might make along the way.[29]

Miles also remained interested in Indian affairs. Upon appointing Miles to command the Department of the Columbia, President Hayes, at the suggestion of Interior Secretary Schurz, had directed that some of the Nez Perces might be returned to the Northwest upon Miles's "reasonable assurance" that he could protect the Indians from the possible vengeance of whites. Still under the impression that every inhabitant in Idaho Territory would kill Chief Joseph on sight, the Indian Bureau balked at this proposal. Only with great difficulty were small groups returned to the Lapwai Reservation in 1883 and 1885. Joseph and his supporters, however, were sent to the Colville Reservation in northeastern Washington Territory.[30]

In less-publicized incidents, Miles supported several bands of Paiutes in their determination to leave the Yakima Reservation in Washington Territory, to which they had been removed following the Bannock-Paiute outbreak of 1878. The Paiutes wanted to either rejoin their friends and cousins near Camp McDermit, Nevada, or move to the Warm Springs Reservation in north central Oregon. His reasoning was simple—the Paiutes were destitute. In a slightly different vein, Miles helped adjudicate disputes between several bands on the Colville and Columbia River reservations, with the tribes in question often accepting land in severalty (allotments of land given to individuals or families) in exchange for their reservation claims.[31]

Miles now placed great stock in the idea of assimilating Indians into the larger population. Like the anthropologist Lewis Henry Morgan, he always emphasized the tribal nature of Indian society. For the race to progress to civilization, however, clannish ties must be reduced. He argued in 1881 that families should not be moved to large reservations in alien terrain but be given small land grants where they currently lived. Since they were already surrounded, he told a *New York Daily Tribune* reporter, they "must become a part of our population." By 1885, as the land-in-severalty movement gained momentum, Miles wanted to abolish existing reservations and distribute the lands to individual families. "The Indian Territory is now a block in the pathway of civilization. It is preserved to perpetuate a mongrel race far removed from the influence of civilized people; a refuge for the outlaws and indolents of whites, blacks, and Mexicans," Miles wrote.[32]

In 1884, upon reaching the mandatory retirement age of sixty-four, William T. Sherman left the United States Army. The old war-horse had long anticipated such a move; only the need to secure his full pension had kept him in the service. "All Army officers should have in mind the rights of Juniors to promotion and command," he had reasoned. Miles, however, viewed the move with some bitterness, and concluded that an ungrateful Congress had ousted his uncle-in-law. The incident thus reinforced Nelson's mania for securing political allies. Sherman had frequently denounced any links between army officers and politics; to Miles, this seemed a foolish disregard for the American system of government.[33]

Upon Miles's promotion to brigadier general, Major General Hancock had advised his younger protégé, "Now is the time for rest, and for study." An extensive program of military reading would prepare Miles for new challenges, thought Hancock. But such cerebral activities held little interest for the goal-oriented Miles. And Mary longed to return east. However publicly he boosted the Northwest, privately he put out feelers about a transfer as early as 1882. But not just any new posting would do; suggestions that he take over duties in Texas or Arizona, for example, did not appeal to him.[34]

In 1885, the imminent retirement of Brigadier General Christopher C. Augur opened new horizons. In the resulting shuffle Miles demanded either the Department of the Dakota or Augur's sprawling Department of the Missouri. The latter command, which contained several large Indian reservations, seemed particularly well suited to Miles's purposes. As William Sherman commented from his home in St. Louis, "This will bring his family nearer to their Home, for which his wife Mary my niece has yearned, from her station at Vancouver." Miles received his desired post. Sheridan assured him that President Cleveland himself had made the decision. Characteristically, Miles attributed the assignment to an hour-long meeting he had had with Cleveland that spring.[35]

Miles sought to exploit his perceived connections within the new administration with a prompt acknowledgment. He thanked the president for the transfer and included some advice on the Cheyenne and

Arapaho Agency, where the peace of his new department seemed threatened. The Cheyenne Dog Soldiers, a warrior society long noted for its opposition to white expansion, had become virtually intractable toward the U.S. government. In addition, most of the Cheyennes believed that the leasing of reservation lands to white cattlemen threatened tribal culture. Miles blamed the turmoil on "mismanagement and a defective system of Indian affairs." The Cheyennes, he explained, "have wrongs that I trust will soon be righted." Offering land in severalty seemed to Miles the proper response, and he attached a copy of his *North American Review* essay on Indian affairs with his letter to Cleveland.[36]

Congress would not enact the much-heralded land-in-severalty program until the Dawes Act of 1887 was passed. In the meantime, events required more immediate action. Threats, thefts, and acts of defiance led the army to reinforce the garrison at Fort Reno in the summer of 1885. One official estimated that the Cheyennes could assemble fifteen hundred warriors "well armed and mounted." Indian inspector Frank C. Armstrong made a special visit to the Cheyenne and Arapaho reservation. He reported in emphatic terms: "These Indians must be made to submit. . . . Nothing but an overpowering force to awe them into submission will prevent trouble and bloodshed."[37]

After a brief Chicago meeting at divisional headquarters, Sheridan, now the commanding general, and Miles went to the reservation in mid-July to take a closer look and consult with tribal leaders, cattlemen, and agents. Sheridan and Miles sided with the Indians, recommending that reservation leases be canceled and food distribution improved. They also determined that the military must assume control over reservation affairs. Reported one junior officer of the peace talks: "Our going was timely and averted a terible bloody Indian war." Though eviction posed a "hardship" on the cattlemen, the actions brought peace to southern Kansas.[38]

After the investigation, General Miles arrived for duty at Fort Leavenworth on July 28, 1885. His family joined him in early October, having been delayed by final moving arrangements and baby Sherman's ill health. Offering spacious quarters befitting a brigadier, the post also allowed Miles easier access to William Sherman in St. Louis. Sherman found dealing with his nephew-in-law more pleasant now that he was not part of the army's decision-making process and thus not subject to Miles's petulance. He extended a generous invitation to the annual St. Louis Agricultural and Mechanical fair that fall, an act that symbolized their cozy new relationship. "All the hotels are full," reminded Sherman, "but we can take good care of you at the Hotel Sherman."[39]

With the Miles family now settled in at Leavenworth, violence in Arizona and New Mexico caught Nelson's attention. Here small bands of Apaches had bedeviled intruders for nearly three centuries. George Crook, who had compiled an impressive record during an earlier southwestern stint in the early 1870s, had returned to the Department of Arizona in 1882. But Crook's later efforts to control the tribes seemed futile. Geronimo, an Apache leader; forty-two warriors; and ninety-two women and children had the following May left the reservation once again. The raiders terrorized the residents of southern Arizona and New Mexico territories while eluding Crook's teams of Indian auxiliaries and regular officers. General Miles could scarcely conceal his glee over the mounting criticism of his long-time rival.[40]

As Crook floundered, other brigadiers speculated about the retirement of Major General John Pope. Slated for March 1886, Pope's departure would mean promotion for either Howard, Terry, Miles, or Crook. The former pair enjoyed seniority; the latter two had better records as Indian campaigners. Miles concentrated his efforts against Crook. "If the selection is made by seniority I have no fault to find," he maintained, but Crook "has never succeeded to my knowledge in sending away Indian trouble." A former aide to Miles, Oscar Long, known for his bravery during the Battle of Bear Paw Mountain as well as his intense loyalty to Miles, worked to secure for his patron the support of Pope, Hancock, and Francis Barlow. One of Crook's most bitter detractors, New Mexico's territorial governor, Edmund G. Ross, who wanted the army to open new lands for white settlement, also joined several Pacific Coast politicians in backing Miles.[41]

Debate concerning Pope's retirement soon became entangled with escalating criticism of Crook's performance in Arizona, where his reliance on Indian scouts dissatisfied General Sheridan and President Cleveland. Many speculated that Miles would replace Crook. Friends in both camps mounted strong lobbying campaigns for their favorites, fanning the flames to a white heat by planting newspaper stories laced with disinformation. Publicly, Miles assumed a lofty disinterest. "I have not tried to get Ariz.," he declared to Sherman in early 1886. Still, Miles assured him, "If called upon, I believe those Apaches can be destroyed by the U.S. troops."[42]

His enemies told a different tale. Captain John G. Bourke, a frontier veteran and ally of Crook's who enjoyed great rapport with many southwestern tribes, charged that Miles had sent a staff member to Arizona in an effort to convince Geronimo to surrender to him rather than to Crook. Bourke and another ally of Crook's, W. H. Llewellyn, also accused Miles of having promised to transfer the departmental headquarters to Albuquerque in exchange for Governor Ross's support. According to this account, Ross backed the plan in the hope that the new military presence would increase the value of his Albuquerque real estate.[43]

True to form, Miles personalized the controversy. He believed that only an unethical combination could have dictated the transfer of New Mexico from his Department of the Missouri to Crook's Department of Arizona. Though the adjustment made administrative and strategic sense, Miles took it as a personal affront and blasted Sheridan's most recent annual report as containing "unwarranted" praise for Crook. He had no desire to exchange his comfortable Fort Leavenworth posting for Arizona, but he did not want Crook and his friends to dominate the army. Miles pressed Oscar Long to do some quiet lobbying in the capital. "Be careful who you talk with in Washington," he warned. "It would be well to keep your ears open & a close[d] mouth."[44]

Speculation concerning the major general's slot and the situation in Arizona intensified early in 1886. Crook's dependence on Indian scouts led by white officers—knowledgeable men like captains Emmet Crawford and Wirt Davis and lieutenants Charles B. Gatewood and Britton Davis—continued to rankle Washington officials. While commanding a squad of Apache scouts that went after Geronimo deep into Mexico, Crawford was killed by Mexican militiamen on January 11, which only increased Washington's skepticism about Crook's methods. But the tragedy scarcely deterred the lobbyists as Pope's retirement neared. "It probably lies between Miles and Crook," concluded Francis Barlow, who reminded friends of the former's superior military record, service in a New York regiment, and deep interest in Indian affairs. "I have made no effort to go to Arizona," maintained Miles on February 5, but he made little effort to conceal his opposition to Crook's promotion.[45]

The unexpected death of General Hancock on February 9 interrupted intrigue about promotions, if only temporarily. Miles and a host of Civil War comrades took part in the funeral ceremonies honoring the gallant warrior. With two major general's slots now open, the War Department promoted Terry and Howard by virtue of their seniority in rank. Disappointed with the decision (he claimed superiority, by brevet, over Terry), Miles took comfort in the fact that Crook had also been passed over.[46]

Consistent with his earlier assertions, Miles reiterated his desire to remain in the Department of the Missouri. His attempt to avoid a direct confrontation with Crook over the latter's handling of the campaigns in Arizona seems genuine enough; why not allow Crook to continue to squirm amid the dreary Arizona deserts and mountains? In assuming this stance, Miles unwittingly established some personal credibility with Secretary of War William Endicott, who still resisted the "constant clamor" for Crook's removal. "[I] have been satisfied that he was the best man we could have there," he confided to a friend. Though events later forced Endicott to go along with Crook's transfer, Miles's reticence deviated from his usually outspoken approach. Had he maintained this more restrained style, Miles might well have avoided the controversies that would mar the remainder of his career.[47]

9 : GERONIMO

Spanish, Mexican, and American encroachments had long been met with violent resistance from the fiercely independent Indians of the Southwest. Although the Pueblos and Navajos had capitulated by the late 1860s, many Apaches continued the struggle. George Crook had been the most effective U.S. commander against the Apaches, but even he had secured only intermittent truces rather than complete victory. Poor land, inadequate rations, frequent trespasses by whites, weak agents, and the government's attempts to consolidate rival tribes engendered poisonous enmity between tribes on many reservations. Particularly devastating were the sporadic Chiricahua raids on the surrounding populace, ably led by men like the gigantic Juh and the scowling Geronimo.[1]

144

During a three-day meeting with Geronimo in March 1886, Crook had very nearly ended the conflicts. The general initially insisted on the Indians' unconditional surrender; Geronimo, tired but stubborn, refused these demands. Finally, the Apaches accepted Crook's promise that they and their families would be returned to their Arizona reservations after two weeks' confinement in the east. A jubilant Crook raced ahead to Fort Bowie, where he wired the news to Washington, while a loose escort shepherded Geronimo and about one hundred others along. But the general had failed to reckon with a possible change of heart by some of the reluctant prisoners. Emboldened by a cache of potent mescal, Geronimo and over forty followers bolted from their guards.[2]

An impatient Sheridan, who had already ordered Crook to cancel any promises made to the Apaches, attributed the breakout to treachery among the government's Indian scouts. Crook defended his use of the scouts and offered his resignation from the Department of Arizona. A day later, April 2, 1886, Sheridan, long suspicious that Crook had become too soft, accepted Crook's offer and transferred him back to the Department of the Platte. Nelson Miles, whose military successes outshone every other officer of the Indian-fighting army, replaced Crook in the Department of Arizona. "He [Sheridan] does not wish to embarrass you by undertaking at this distance to give specific instructions, but it is deemed advisable to suggest the necessity of making active and permanent use of the regular troops of your command," explained Adjutant General Richard C. Drum with the flexibility that typified orders throughout the period. Miles, delighted about the opportunity to upstage Crook, nonetheless maintained that he "never had any desire to go to this section of country." He added, "in fact it was a most undesirable duty."[3]

Whatever his private reservations, General Miles arrived at Fort Bowie, the center for operations in southern Arizona, on April 11. Following an uneasy conference between Miles and Crook, Crook departed the next day, leaving Miles a tangled political and military situation. One of his major supporters in the Southwest, Edmund G. Ross, was the first Democratic governor of New Mexico Territory in over two decades; Ross's quarrels with the Santa Fe Ring, a loose coalition of individuals and companies that dominated the territorial economy, generated powerful opposition among the territory's elites. In Arizona Territory, Governor Conrad M. Zulick, another recently ap-

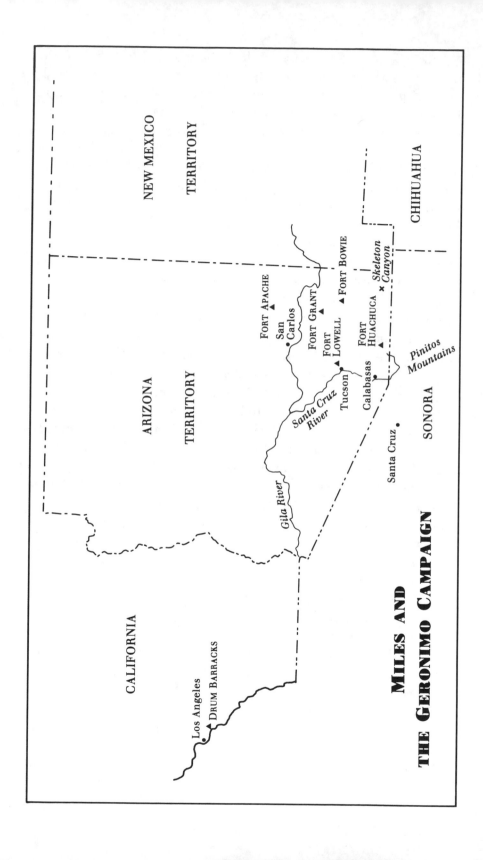

NEW MEXICO
TERRITORY

CHIHUAHUA

FORT APACHE ▲
San
Carlos •
FORT GRANT ▲
FORT
LOWELL ▲
▲ FORT BOWIE
FORT
HUACHUCA ▲
× Skeleton
Canyon
Pinitos
Mountains

ARIZONA

TERRITORY

Santa Cruz
River

Tucson •
Calabasas •

SONORA

Santa Cruz •

Gila River

CALIFORNIA

Los Angeles
• ▲ DRUM BARRACKS

**MILES AND
THE GERONIMO CAMPAIGN**

pointed Democrat who had made no secret about his desire to see the Indians annihilated, had also blasted Crook's failure to crush Geronimo. But their interparty skirmishing with local Republicans made it difficult to distinguish routine politics from more general attacks against Indian policy.[4]

Life near Forts Bowie and Apache was equally uncertain. On Sheridan's orders, the army sent seventy-eight Chiricahuas, including those who had refused to join Geronimo's latest break, to Fort Marion, Florida. Another four hundred Chiricahua and Warm Springs Apaches had since 1884 lived near Fort Apache; white developers now lusted for their lands. These Indians recently seemed quiet, but Miles deemed their presence a genuine threat. "A more turbulent and dissipated body of Indians I have never met," he later declared.[5]

A solution depended on the army's handling of Geronimo and his twenty to thirty warriors who still defied the government's restrictions. Although the difficult terrain and the fighting abilities of his adversaries presented a daunting challenge, Miles enjoyed overwhelming superiority in numbers and resources. Yet their past failures to bring in these Indians had demoralized many of the troops. And the presence of Crook's staff, many of whom remained loyal to their old commander, further complicated Miles's task. The proximity of the Mexican boundary added another dangerous ingredient; all remembered that Mexican troops had killed Captain Emmet Crawford only that January.[6]

Nine days after coming to Fort Bowie, Miles began to set up his plans. He divided New Mexico and Arizona into districts of observation, and oversaw the construction of twenty-seven heliograph stations, each with its component of guards, telescope, water supply, and field glasses. Infantry detachments would guard mountain passes, water holes, and supplies. Yuma Indians would replace the Chiricahua auxiliaries favored by Crook. As per Sheridan's instructions, regular troops would assume the brunt of the field campaigning. The regulars were admonished "to capture or destroy any band of hostile Apache Indians" by following every conceivable trail. Indeed, Miles seemed to be everywhere, scaling mountains to help place heliograph stations, inspecting troops to improve morale, restoring confidence among junior officers with a quiet word of praise, and reorganizing administrative lines to improve command control.[7]

But the Chiricahuas struck before Miles's preparations were complete. Sweeping northward from Mexico, they thundered down the

Santa Cruz Valley in late April before splitting up into small bands, killing and stealing stock along the way. After a two-hundred-mile pursuit south into Sonora, Mexico, Captain Thomas C. Lebo and a squad of Tenth Cavalrymen brushed against one group in the Pinito Mountains on May 3. In another fight twelve days later, Captain Charles A. Hatfield surprised a small band east of Santa Cruz, in Sonora, temporarily seizing the group's camp equipage and horses. Although the Indians recaptured most of their stock in a subsequent ambush, the twin skirmishes forced the Chiricahuas farther south.[8]

As Lebo and Hatfield criss-crossed northern Sonora, Miles organized what he presumed would be a knockout blow. Thirty-five men of the Fourth Cavalry and twenty selected foot soldiers of the Eighth Infantry, supported by thirty packers and one hundred mules, were formed into an elite strike force at Fort Huachuca. Miles insisted that the effort feature regular soldiers; even so, twenty Indian scouts would guide the expedition. He selected Captain Henry W. Lawton, a hard-drinking, hard-driving veteran of Ranald Mackenzie's old Fourth Cavalry. A contract surgeon, Leonard Wood, a cocky, athletic New Englander with barely one year's frontier experience, won a spot as the medical expert; his insistence that "the right sort of white men could eventually break these Indians up and compel them to surrender" had endeared him to Miles.[9]

On May 10, Lawton's force set out under orders "to follow constantly the trail, locate their main camp, and destroy or subdue them." The blistering heat and cactus-filled terrain dismounted the cavalry in five days. After fourteen hundred miles of pursuit had yielded no immediate results, the captain reorganized his force in early July. Replacements took over for the exhausted infantrymen and Indian scouts while at Calabasas, Arizona Territory, Miles and Lawton reviewed the situation. On July 6 Lawton resumed operations, leaving the cavalry and most of the officers behind at a Sonora base camp. The soldiers snatched most of the Chiricahua food supplies and animals shortly thereafter, but the band escaped without human loss. Summer rains and intense heat forced Lawton, with but fourteen regulars fit for duty, to call off the pursuit. Their prison-made army-issue shoes in shreds, his men could only await reinforcements.[10]

By the end of July, nearly three months' campaigning had exhausted the soldiers and produced only three minor skirmishes. One crusty rancher deemed the officers "either grossly inefficient . . . or damnably culpable." Lieutenants James Parker and Charles B. Gatewood, the best of the company officers, complained that the new Indian auxiliaries could scarcely hope to replace the Apaches Miles had dismissed that spring.[11]

Yet Miles remained confident, despite a bout with the flu. He had been working on other ideas that might produce more direct results. In early May, he had met with Lieutenant Colonel James F. Wade, commander of Fort Bowie, and Captain Francis E. Pierce, head of the San Carlos Agency, sharing with both his view that disarmament and removal of the Chiricahua and Warm Springs Apaches was a necessary ingredient to peace. Crook, declared Miles, had been too lenient with the Indians, a mistake he would not make. The Indian Territory seemed a suitable area for relocation, he argued, although Secretary of War Endicott, Secretary of the Interior Lucius Q. C. Lamar, and General Sheridan all opposed that site.[12]

Undaunted, Miles called on his wide array of political connections. He convinced Secretary Lamar to send his son, L.Q.C. Lamar, Jr., to investigate the situation. Miles hoped that by winning over the presumably more malleable son, to whom he had once extended "cordial and generous consideration," the father would change his mind. In mid-July, Miles defied his superiors' intent and sent a group of Warm Springs and Chiricahua leaders, accompanied by his trusted subordinate Captain Joseph H. Dorst, east for direct negotiations.[13]

On July 17, the Indians arrived in Washington. Present on an unrelated staff assignment was Captain John G. Bourke, a former aide to George Crook, who seized the opportunity to renew old acquaintances among the delegation. Other government officials, however, did their best to poison the process by lodging the group at a squalid hotel and delaying meetings with Secretary Lamar and President Cleveland. After finally hearing out the Apache grievances, Cleveland, the two Lamars, Dorst, and Bourke met at the White House on July 31. Bourke and Dorst soon clashed, Bourke arguing that the bands represented by the delegates had been peaceful since surrendering to Crook three years earlier, Dorst representing Miles's cause for removal.[14]

The Indians received a silver medal and certificate but no promises. Bourke, too, emerged disheartened. "He [Cleveland] impressed me as being self-opinionated, stubborn, and not too tenacious of the truth; a man of great sinuosity of morals, narrow in his views, fond of flattery," he wrote. Miles, though his vaunted Indian delegation had been shunted aside by the Cleveland administration, was smugly satisfied at having blocked his army rivals. Although Bourke had attempted to do much mischief, Dorst had promptly checked the former's harmful influence, declared Miles.[15]

Letters to the younger Lamar and Sheridan on the first and second of August, respectively, reflected Miles's continued desire for negotiated settlements. The eastern section of the Indian Territory remained in his view the ideal spot for removal of the Apaches. Sheridan proposed an alternative solution: "The Secretary wishes me to ask what you think of the proposition to forcibly remove all on the reservation and send them to [Fort] Marion, Florida."[16]

By this point, a flurry of contradictory telegrams was causing confusion between Arizona Territory and Washington. No one seemed to know exactly what had or had not been promised to the various Indian groups, now scattered between Carlisle Barracks, Pennsylvania; Fort Leavenworth, Kansas; the San Carlos Reservation, Arizona Territory; and northern Mexico. Miles and his junior officers remained unsure as to how much room they had to maneuver. Lawton, for instance, told Lieutenant Parker that he received his orders "from President Cleveland direct. I am ordered to hunt Geronimo down and kill him. I cannot treat with him." Parker, on the other hand, presumed that Miles was still willing to negotiate.[17]

Parker's hunch proved correct. Hounded by cries for action by local residents and Washington officials alike, Miles had reluctantly dispatched Lieutenant Gatewood and two Chiricahua auxiliaries, Kayitah and Martine, to speak with Geronimo. The move suggested some desperation, for Gatewood's health was poor and he was widely associated with the Crook camp. But the lieutenant was known and respected by Geronimo and his followers, and more traditional measures had not yet borne fruit. Possibly, reasoned Miles, the long campaign had worn down Geronimo's resolve. In mid-August Gatewood reached Lawton's camp, then found and spoke with Geronimo on the twenty-fifth and the twenty-sixth just across the Mexican border. He delivered Miles's ultimatum: "Surrender, and you will be sent with your families to Florida, there to await the decision of the President as to your final disposition. Accept these terms or fight to the bitter end."[18]

Gatewood sympathized with the Indians' reluctance to go to Florida. "They really want to surrender, but they want their families with [them]," he wrote. "Can anyone blame a man for wanting to see his wife and children?" But his revelation that their friends and relatives at San Carlos were also to be moved came as a crushing blow. Wanting to have nothing to do with the two hundred Mexican soldiers also in the vicinity, Geronimo came in to Lawton's camp on the twenty-seventh. After "a hugging match" with the captain, Geronimo requested an interview with Miles.[19]

Miles had in the meantime undertaken negotiations of his own, for the administration rejected his plan for removing the reservation Chiricahuas to the Indian Territory. By August 25, Sheridan had told Miles, "As a preliminary step they [the San Carlos Indians] must go to Fort Marion." There was even less flexibility when it came to Geronimo. President Cleveland ordered, "Nothing . . . [is to] be done with Geronimo which will prevent our treating him as a prisoner of war, *if we cannot hang him, which I would much prefer.*"[20]

Miles, with Gatewood's discussions hinting at a solution, stubbornly opposed sending the reservation peoples to Florida. Privately, he admitted the injustice of such a transfer and complained that his enemies in Washington seemed more dangerous than the Indians. Miles's eleventh-hour telegrams to Washington the following day proposed disarmament of the Indians near Fort Apache, their removal "at least 1200 miles east," and placement of the children in vocational schools. But Miles warned that any reports that their kin would "be banished [all the way] to sickley Florida" would in his view "only strengthen the will of the defiant."[21]

Events soon tested his theory. On August 29, Colonel Wade rounded up 382 Indians at San Carlos, marched them under heavy guard to the railroad station at Holbrook, and packed them off on a Florida-bound train. Even so, Miles continued to balk at direct negotiations with Geronimo, fearing that a premature meeting risked a repeat of Crook's failure that spring, when several dozen Indians had bolted their guards. Peace must be imminent before he would talk to Geronimo. With the tension mounting on September 2, an apprehensive Captain Lawton begged Miles to intervene. "I could try treachery perhaps kill one or two of them," related Lawton, "but it would only make everything much worse."[22]

Miles's fears that Lawton might lose control of the situation outweighed his reluctance about direct talks. On the afternoon of the third, the general, suspicious that war-office rivals were seeking to embarrass him by suppressing information, arrived to meet with Geronimo. The backdrop—an old Indian haunt known as Skeleton's Canyon, which Miles described as "well suited by name and tradition to witness the closing scenes of such an Indian War"—fit the dramatic nature of the encounter. Although the stocky Geronimo bore his perpetual scowl, his intelligence and purpose of mind impressed the general. His sharp eyes, Miles later remembered, compared with those of General Sherman in his prime.[23]

Crucial to the negotiations was the confirmation that the people at San Carlos had been removed. Miles tried to explain that if Geronimo and his compatriots surrendered, they would be sent to Florida, where they would be reunited with their families. To better illustrate his point, Miles bent down and began moving pebbles about on the ground. One rock, he explained, denoted the Apaches already in Florida. Another represented those recently at San Carlos. A third stood for Geronimo and his followers. Moving the markers together, Miles reported that the president wanted to collect all the Apaches in one spot. "So long as you are our prisoners," Miles told Geronimo, "we shall not kill you but shall treat you justly." Miles's later recollection of these events is similar to a version accepted by Geronimo.[24]

Exhausted by the recent campaigns and demoralized by the removal of his fellow tribespeople, Geronimo agreed to these conditions. Natchez, another Apache leader, although still fearing treachery, led another band in on the afternoon of the fourth as late summer rain clouds formed over the southern Arizona mountains. With a keen sense of the occasion's import as well as a desire to avoid a repetition of Crook's fiasco, the following day Miles hustled Geronimo, Natchez, and four other Indian hostages sixty-five miles back to Fort Bowie. As Lawton and the others made their way at a more leisurely pace, a triumphant Miles notified superiors on the sixth that the Indians expected "banishment from this country." He continued, "For reasons of economy, safety, and health, I still believe Fort Riley and Leavenworth would be suitable places of confinement. But unless I receive instructions to the contrary, I shall ship these . . . souls to Fort Marion Florida."[25]

"It is a brilliant ending of a difficult problem," gloated Miles on September 7. But the Geronimo affair had just begun. Unknown to Miles, President Cleveland had that day been informed, through Oliver O. Howard, commander of the Division of the Pacific and now Miles's immediate superior, that the surrender had been "unconditional." Although Miles had used no such word in his correspondence, Howard later claimed to have based his remarks on the "general tenor" of a message from Miles dated the sixth, which explained that the Indians had been "wholly submissive." Assuming that there had been no terms, Cleveland thus accepted Sheridan's recommendation that Geronimo and the other warriors be held in Arizona for civil prosecution. Differing markedly from normal policy that excluded Indians from regular judicial proceedings, the sudden decision "astonished" the younger Lamar.[26]

Matters were confused by the absence of both the president and Secretary of War Endicott from Washington—Cleveland at Bloomingdale, New York, and Endicott in the White Mountains of New Hampshire. On the seventh, Adjutant General Drum told Howard of Cleveland's intentions. Apparently oblivious to the new plan, that same day Miles informed Sheridan that he hoped to get the prisoners away within twenty-four hours. Perplexed, Sheridan directed Miles, "Hold them in close confinement at Fort Bowie until the decision of the President is communicated to you." At 8:10 that evening, Miles replied that Bowie had no place to hold the prisoners securely. "Everything is arranged for moving them and I earnestly request permission to move them out of this mountain country, at least as far as Fort Bliss, Union, or Fort Marion, Fla., for safety. I ask this in behalf of the troops and myself," he wrote.[27]

Miles's latter message was not forwarded to Cleveland until the eighth. The president then reiterated his earlier instructions: "I think Geronimo and the rest of the hostiles should be immediately sent to the nearest fort or prison where they can be securely confined. The most important thing now is to guard against all chances of escape." But events were already in motion. That morning at Fort Bowie, a heavy escort had hustled Geronimo and the others to a waiting train. The Fourth Cavalry band struck up "Auld Lang Syne" and the locomotive chugged away from the station. Kayitah and Martine, the emissaries who had helped Gatewood begin the talks, were among the departing Chiricahuas. Miles later maintained that he did not see the president's final message for another six weeks. Leonard Wood, who as a favorite of Miles hardly represented an unbiased observer, supported this contention, asserting that one of Miles's aides, Captain William A. Thompson, had pigeonholed the telegram so as not to place his commander in the embarrassing situation of having to renege on his promises to Geronimo. Wood recalled that Thompson, "patting his pocket and acting under the confidence bred by several drinks and old friendship," whispered his remarkable secret to Wood. "I have got something here which would stop this movement, but I am not going to let the old man [Miles] see it until you are gone, then I will repeat it to him."[28]

Furious at this apparent disregard for orders, Adjutant General Drum recounted a different version. Drum insisted that Miles had referred to the demand to hold the warriors in Arizona in a September 8 message, thus showing his protestations of ignorance to be false. Though both Wood and Drum might have embellished the truth to serve their own separate purposes, the disposition of the telegram seems less important than its contents. Previous discussions had centered upon the place of removal; the last-minute decision to attempt a civil prosecution of the Chiricahua warriors would break the conditions of previous Gatewood-Miles-Geronimo negotiations. Further, the super-charged atmosphere among the territory's white citizens made a fair hearing highly unlikely.[29]

The president's determination to hold the Apaches in Arizona had also surprised Howard, who was commanding the Division of the Pacific. But Howard, still bitter over the Chief Joseph affair, concluded that Miles's embarkation of the Chiricahuas was "certainly not a compliance with the President's orders." In what Adjutant General Drum called "a savage telegram," Howard charged that Miles had challenged the president's instructions on three occasions. Complaining that he had been left out of the chain of command, Howard asked for the authority "to enforce obedience."[30]

President Cleveland ordered that the rail cars bearing the Apaches be stopped at San Antonio, Texas, while government officials scrambled to decide on the prisoners' fate. Their suspicions heightened by the delay, the Chiricahuas wondered about the trustworthiness of General Miles and his government. Only on October 25 would the men reach their new station at Fort Pickens, across the bay from Pensacola, Florida. The women and children were taken to Fort Marion. Drum seemed equally skeptical of Miles's promises. On September 25, he asked Miles if he had offered Geronimo any unauthorized terms. Miles requested permission to come to Washington to speak with the president; Drum dashed those hopes and demanded an official telegraphic response "without delay."[31]

"They are strictly prisoners of war . . . now entirely under the control of the President," answered Miles. But shaken by the reproaches from Howard and Drum, Miles lashed out in his typical fashion, professing his own innocence, blaming others, and taking his case directly to the press. Contrasting the treatment accorded Sitting Bull and Joseph with that of Geronimo, Miles maintained that he could not have prevented the escape of the Apaches from Fort Bowie. To Mary, he explained that he was honor-bound to prevent the Indians from falling into the hands of an Arizona mob, even if that group met under the auspices of a civilian court. Publicly, he charged that a secret cabal had suppressed his telegrams; privately, he insisted that Howard, Drum, and Crook lay behind this coalition of mean-spirited rivals. Drum, who was alleged to have leaked information to the Associated Press and to the *Washington Evening Star* as well as being a potential rival for promotion, was in Miles's view particularly culpable. Drum "is my personal enemy," wrote Miles indignantly. "I am treated more like a dog than a man." He alleged that Drum, in his capacity as acting secretary of war, had in a September 4 telegram authorized the Apaches' removal to Fort Marion; the adjutant general's office, however, denied this claim.[32]

Miles counted on his well-placed connections in hopes of retaliating against his perceived enemies. His request for a leave was denied, so Mary, instead, went east to lend a bit of personal diplomacy with the influential Camerons of Pennsylvania, the family of her brother-in-law. L.Q.C. Lamar, Jr. was asked to press Miles's case in the Interior Department. Within the army, Quartermaster General Samuel B. Holabird and Major George Baird were called on for support. Through the latter Miles released his self-promoting 1886 annual report to the press. To Governor Ross of New Mexico Territory, Miles dispatched a special cipher for sending back confidential information from Washington—"President, No. 1, Lamar, No. 2, Endicott, No. 3, Sheridan, No. 4, Drum, No. 5"—designed to ferret out which of his "secret enemies" were issuing "lying statements" from the capital.[33]

But Nelson Miles was a far better fighter than public relations manager. His blunt publicity campaign lacked the polish to attract genuine support. Senator Cameron, Miles's brother-in-law, failed to secure a meeting with Cleveland, and the much-vaunted Lamar connection also proved negligible. Unknown to Miles, Secretary Lamar, on learning of Miles's role as Jefferson Davis's jailer, had pledged to oppose him. As a final blow, Adjutant General Drum delivered a stinging reprimand to Miles for having released his annual report.[34]

Miles thus failed to capitalize on the Geronimo surrender. Rather than a promotion, he had won the enmity and distrust of several important officials. Many perceived him as a dogmatic, self-righteous schemer who defied presidential orders without even the hint of apology. His attempts to block the removal of the Chiricahuas to Florida were futile; instead of then seizing the moral high ground, Miles squandered any advantage with his clumsy attacks against those he presumed conspired against him.[35]

The controversies would linger for years, fed in no small measure by Miles's rivalry with George Crook. Unseemly verbal skirmishing broke out concerning their roles in securing Geronimo's defeat. The two took to accusing one another of tampering with the official letterbooks of the Department of Arizona; in Arizona, the pro-Miles *Arizona Daily Star* in Tucson engaged in a bitter editorial battle with the *Prescott Weekly Courier*, which favored Crook. Indeed, the publicity given to the campaign and the fate of the Chiricahuas would soon lead Congress to take up its own investigation.[36]

The repercussions of the controversial campaign against Geronimo affected a wide variety of officers. Miles appointed the invaluable Gatewood to his staff. Temporarily playing down his own importance to the campaign and having fallen out of favor with Crook several years earlier, Gatewood seemed bound for a bright future under Miles's sponsorship. But the lieutenant spoiled his chances. One evening in Prescott, Arizona, he and a civilian packer, H. W. Daly, fortified by heavy doses of alcohol, were discussing the circumstances surrounding Geronimo's surrender, undoubtedly minimizing Miles's role. "Somebody must have called up Gen Miles," recalled Daly some years later, "for the first thing we knew, Miles drove up in his ambulance in front of us and said, 'Mr. Gatewood get into this ambulance with me.'" Gatewood's defiance—he "would return when he got good and ready"—caused the general to hop out of the buggy, push the inebriated lieutenant inside, and drive back to nearby Whipple Barracks. Daly remembered, "As he drove off, I thought—Gatewood you made the mistake of your life."[37]

Gatewood grew increasingly alienated. He charged that his refusal to go along with a scheme of Miles's to employ personal servants as official "packers" and his opposition to a contractor sponsored by Miles, named Amos Kimball, led the general to ostracize him. His health broken by the strenuous campaigning in Arizona and Sonora, the lieutenant retired from the army after an accidental injury in 1892. Four years later Gatewood died, his exploits ignored among official army circles. Miles had never officially recognized Gatewood's full contribution to Geronimo's surrender, for to do so would have admitted that Crook's use of Apache scouts and negotiated peaces had worked. Miles instead emphasized the importance of Lawton, Wood, and the regulars. Gatewood's widow and son Charley—a West Point graduate whose military experiences often resembled those of Miles's son Sherman—never forgave the general. For the next half century, the indefatigable Charley Gatewood attempted to document his father's importance.[38]

Nelson Miles rarely acknowledged the services of anyone who impugned his motives or diminished any of his limelight. In his 1886 annual report he had indeed deemphasized Gatewood's role in the Geronimo surrender. Yet Miles was not as guilty as the Gatewoods imagined. Gatewood's assignment as aide-de-camp was significant, particularly given the importance Miles placed on such a position. And in 1895 Miles backed a recommendation that Gatewood be awarded a Medal of Honor; two years later the general endorsed young Charley as the son of a "distinguished" officer who had performed "faithful and gallant service on the frontier against Indians." Private observers also maintained that they heard Miles admit Gatewood's primacy in the Geronimo talks.[39]

More unseemly was Miles's renewed feuding with Howard. The latter's assistant adjutant general, Chauncey McKeever, opened the skirmishing on November 18, 1886, by defending Howard's annual report against Miles's criticism. Miles countered by asking about the disposition of his September 6 telegram to the Division of the Pacific, which had outlined the terms of the Apache surrender. Howard admitted that he had forwarded to Washington only a brief dispatch, on the assumption that Miles had been ignoring lines of authority and corresponding directly with Washington anyway. On April 16, 1887, Miles quizzed Howard about the latter's allegation that he had on three occasions asked to be excused from presidential instructions. "Of course such a grave charge as yours without my knowledge or an opportunity to reply must have prejudiced the President against me," complained Miles.[40]

Not to be outdone, Howard fired back. Labeling Miles's most recent letter "a disappointment," Howard blamed their personal clash on Miles's actions after the Nez Perce campaign. "It was then, from what motives you know best, that you turned away from me." Miles responded in early May 1887. "You seem unable to comprehend the fact that you have done me a grievous wrong," he answered, demanding Howard's official apology.[41]

Their tempers cooled a bit until September, when a division inspector examined Miles's Arizona department headquarters. The timing could not have been worse; Miles had just broken his right leg in a carriage accident near Santa Monica, California. The special investigation infuriated him, and he wrote to Howard, reminding him of the time he had held Howard's shattered arm as it was amputated at Fair Oaks. It seemed more than a coincidence, speculated Miles, that the inspection was announced on the very day that San Francisco newspapers published the news of his accident. Howard's explanation that the acting secretary of war had ordered the investigation led Miles to shift his attentions back to the Nez Perce war. He closed his letter with a veiled threat—an obtuse reference to a "personal note from you [written during the Nez Perce campaign] *which you requested me to burn,* but which fortunately I happen still to have in my possession."[42]

But the fallout from the Geronimo scandal would not go away. In February 1887 the Senate had requested copies of all of Miles's dispatches regarding Geronimo's surrender. Trying to fend off potential political attacks, the general explained to Herbert Welsh, an aristocratic Philadelphian and leader in the Indian reform movement, the need to remove the Apaches from the Southwest.[43] Miles also blasted the "misrepresentations" made regarding his efforts during the Geronimo campaign and asked Senator Sherman to wangle him an invitation to Washington. His old comrade Francis C. Barlow also rallied to Miles's side. "You have got only one real friend & he is F.C.B.," wrote Barlow, who asked Miles to compile a "brief" summary of the case for President Cleveland. "*But make it short,*" Barlow insisted.[44]

Such efforts failed to placate Miles, who was angered over the publication by the Senate of what he believed to be tainted documents. He insisted that the Senate's official report omitted key portions of his communications with the War Department, thus altering their original meanings. John Sherman conferred with Senator Dawes about the problem. Acknowledging the "bad intent" of the report, both concluded that it was "hardly worth complaining about." Miles, however, would continue to worry that the publication had sullied his reputation.[45]

On December 16, 1886, a group of Tucson citizens had met to discuss a means of expressing their gratitude to General Nelson A. Miles. As one old-timer recalled, "Miles was the only general we ever had any respect for. Old Crook would let the Indians do anything." An honorary sword seemed a suitable gift. That day, seventy-nine persons or groups contributed between fifty cents and fifty dollars, for a total of just over four hundred dollars, to the Miles fund. Subsequent donations trickled in during the following year; by August 1887 the New York Times reported that two thousand contributors had raised one thousand dollars for a Tiffany-designed sword. Editors of one Tucson paper hailed Miles as the next Republican candidate for president.[46]

Originally scheduled for the first anniversary of the Geronimo surrender, the official presentation was delayed by Miles's broken leg until November 8, 1887. The affair displayed all the pomp and circumstance befitting the personality of its honoree. Accompanied by Mary and a few staff officers, but still hobbling about on crutches, Miles was honored by a parade of local dignitaries, representatives from the Mexican government, army officers, schoolchildren, and one hundred Papago Indians. The ladies of Yuma presented flowers to the beaming general. Upon receiving his sword (which boasted fanciful if somewhat incongruous engravings of scenes of the San Carlos River, the cavalry, and Geronimo's bust), Miles offered a few words of thanks, described by the local Democratic press as "broad, practical, generous, and statesmanlike." A ball at the San Xavier Hotel concluded the day's ceremonies.[47]

Two days later, the Society of Arizona Pioneers hosted another reception for Miles at the local Masonic hall. Here Miles called for vastly increased federal spending in the territories. Perhaps influenced by the growing criticism of John Wesley Powell, the U.S. Geological Survey director whose negative reports about the agricultural prospects of some western areas had engendered strong opposition from western farmers, Miles proposed that the government sponsor massive new irrigation projects. A party given by a prominent local jurist provided a glittering conclusion to the conquering hero's tour. Here Mary reveled in her status as a general's wife. Outfitted in a dress of "white Ottoman silk, decolette waist, skirt dancing length, and many brilliant diamonds," her "pleasing and unaffected manner" especially impressed the fawning editors of the *Arizona Daily Star*.[48]

However gratifying the support of the territory's citizens was to Miles, the Geronimo affair would not go away, for the well-publicized deterioration of the tribe at Fort Marion was patently obvious. Many accused Miles of having offered unauthorized concessions to the Chiricahuas. Others blamed him for disobeying presidential instructions or for mistreating Lieutenant Gatewood. His open breech with Crook and Drum merely fueled the flames, as did a rivalry between officers and men of the Fourth and Sixth Cavalry regiments over their respective roles in the campaign.[49]

"I have written a volume upon this subject in answer to the efforts of others to destroy the fruits of a single victory in the Geronimo campaign," sighed Miles in 1888. He charged that petty War Department bureaucrats had rejected even routine requests for minor rewards for his subordinates. These complaints were not unjustified. President Cleveland's last-minute attempt to prosecute the Chiricahuas in Arizona courts had come without warning and had placed Miles in an untenable position. His rivalry with Crook, Drum, and Howard—at least in part attributable to their jealousy over Miles's long string of military successes—was real and did, as Miles suspected, adversely affect his relations with the government.[50]

Miles was fairly honest in his personal treatment of Geronimo. In telling the warriors that he would remove them to Florida, the general was obeying orders as he then understood them and following standard procedure. In actually putting them aboard the train for Florida, two scenarios are possible. One is that Wood was indeed correct, and that Miles never received the message ordering the Chiricahuas to be held for trial in Arizona. The other is that Miles did receive the new instructions and risked personal censure in order to keep his promise to Geronimo.

Miles was, however, naive in his discussions with Geronimo and the others. Miles's assurance that the past would "be considered smooth and forgotten" failed to fairly represent his own knowledge of the government's Indian policies. In an 1894 interview with Marion Maus, one of Miles's aides, Geronimo explained: "I remember all Genl Miles told me & I think he will do what he promised." But the old warrior grew bitter as his efforts to return home proved fruitless. Later press reports declared that Geronimo even refused to admit that he had surrendered. And in a series of interviews published in 1906 as Geronimo's autobiography, editor Stephen M. Barrett quoted the warrior as saying: "I looked in vain for General Miles to send me to that land of which he had spoken; I longed in vain for the implements, house, and stock that General Miles had promised me."[51]

The treatment of Martine, Kayitah, Noche, and the other Chiricahua auxiliaries who had fought for the government was even more unjust. The scouts, who had been removed to Florida along with the very Indians they had helped defeat, made various claims as to the unpaid rewards promised by Miles and other officers in exchange for their services. Gatewood and Miles both denied having given any such assurances, but admitted that some compensation was due. "By some mistake," allowed Miles, Noche "was mixed up with the hostiles . . . which I have always regarded most unfortunate and a great injustice to him." But subsequent employment (again as a scout, in the case of Noche) and a small pension could hardly make up for their lost years.[52]

Even allowing for duplicity on the part of the government, Miles had brought many of his problems upon himself. His propensity to go to the press antagonized civilian and military authorities alike. Particularly maddening to them was his delusion that he had not stooped to the negative tactics of his opponents. He once explained in criticism of Crook's efforts to secure promotion, "I have no desire to get a reputation of that sort like Mr. Crook." He was obsessed by a need to defend his honor against any challengers, and his disputes with fellow officers further sullied his reputation. Although he had with great fanfare employed regulars in the early stages of the recent campaigns, in the end the Apache scouts and Lieutenant Gatewood deserved the most credit for having brought Geronimo.[53]

After years of often brilliant military service, Miles found himself viewed in many circles as an uncooperative schemer who could be relied upon only to serve his own interests. It was perhaps to be expected that administration officials would brush aside Miles's recommendations concerning Indian policy. Although he knew much about Indians, and had tried diligently, within the unquestioned limits mandated by his own racial views, to act with justice and compassion toward his former enemies, Miles found that Washington officials shunted his opinions. Indian policy had become bureaucratized and ossified; even a man as prominent as Nelson A. Miles could exert only limited influence. That his recommendations were ignored was but a preface to the passing of the old army.

10 : PACIFIC COAST COMMANDER

The stormy finale to the Geronimo campaign would have left a less energetic man eager to settle into the mundane tasks of a routine bureaucracy and raising a family in Los Angeles, where a previous commander, anxious to avoid the Far Southwest, had established the headquarters of the Department of Arizona. A black nurse helped Mary with household chores and their son Sherman, a precocious five-year-old whom Leonard Wood remembered as "rather hard to handle." Like the children of many officers of means, Cecilia, now eighteen, attended school in the East. She returned home between semesters and visited with one or both of her parents during their frequent sojourns to Washington, D.C. She also spent time with her great-uncle John and his family. "Cecilia is enjoying herself here," wrote a doting Sherman from his home in Mansfield, Ohio, "and I think you better let her remain."[1]

But family life and office affairs could not satisfy Miles's boundless ambition. He took a keen interest in the rapid growth of Los Angeles. "Life was extremely pleasant," wrote Wood. "The streets . . . were unpaved, and the mud was literally knee-deep in the rainy season. Interest in the country was growing apace, and speculation was at fever heat, prices jumping over night." For part of his tour, Miles and his family lived at the fashionable Raymond Hotel in Pasadena. Horseback rides, trips to the opera, and meetings with visiting luminaries punctuated their West Coast life. A widening circle of contacts and acquaintances, including the future secretary of state John Hay, the historian John Bigelow, the artist Frederic Remington, the showman Buffalo Bill Cody, and editors of the *Forum, Harper's Weekly,* and the *Army and Navy Journal,* also marked Miles's personal correspondence.[2]

Though scornful of the proverbial schoolbook soldier, General Miles took greater interest in his and his junior officers' professional development during his Department of Arizona tenure. In September 1886, noting Lieutenant Powhatan H. Clarke's "very important and meritorious service in the field" against Geronimo, Miles had supported the lieutenant's unsuccessful request for leave to attend the French Army Cavalry School. The following spring he expressed interest in going abroad himself to witness European military maneuvers, but, like Clarke, was denied this opportunity.[3]

Despite the rebuffs, he joined others in making rudimentary comparisons between U.S. and foreign military equipment and organization. In 1887, Miles also introduced to his troops innovative training exercises. "Designed to develop skill in following Indian and outlaw trails, to familiarize both cavalry and infantry with the country, and to teach the cavalry to march long distances without injury to the animals," the exercises were practiced by small parties attempting to elude pursuit while crossing the vast expanses of the Arizona and New Mexico territories. Miles pronounced the results "most pleasing"; Lieutenant John J. Pershing, a favorite of Miles's who commanded one chase team, remembered the proceedings as "fine sport" that engendered "the liveliest interest."[4]

That spring, violence among Indians in Arizona Territory again threatened the white-dominated peace. At the behest of the reformer Herbert Welsh, Miles supported Secretary of War William Endicott's decision to send troops to protect the Hopi Indians from Navajo incursions. Potentially more dangerous was the San Carlos Reservation, where one evening in late May five intoxicated Indian scouts killed the alleged murderers of a kinsman. A scuffle ensued when their commander, Captain Francis E. Pierce, ordered the men to lay down their arms. The insurgents, later joined by fellow tribespeople, fled the agency into the mountains to the east. Several detachments of regulars set out in pursuit. The complex task bewildered Captain Pierce. "Some days I am full of hope, and everything looks prosperous and favorable, other days I am in despair, and it appears as if everything were going wrong," he wrote. "Sometimes it seems as though the whole Apache Nation is about to break loose, and the next day appearances are entirely different."[5]

On June 13, Miles and his staff left headquarters to assess the outbreak. They found that about a thousand Indians had fled their government-designated camps at San Carlos; though the disaffected were rounded up in short order, conditions on the reservation shocked Miles and his party. "What a dreary, desolate country," groaned one aide. Miles reported, "I found on that mountainous, arid reservation more than five thousand degraded and barbarous Indians, a mass of ignorance and superstition." He deemed it a mistake to have placed the Yuma, Mojave, Tonto, San Carlos, Pima, and White Mountain Indians on a single reservation. The Yumas and Mojaves, living in "a sickly country" devoid of wood or grass along the Gila River near Fort Thomas, seemed in the worst straits; a hundred children had died within the last few months. "The further these Indians are moved west the better for them and the country, even if they are moved to the Pacific Coast," Miles concluded. Separating the Yumas, Mojaves, and a few Tontos would in his view relieve demands on scarce resources and quell the threat of a major confrontation at San Carlos. In addition to his removal program, he advised that Pierce be replaced and he organized a delegation of Indian leaders to convey their grievances outside the territory.[6]

Such proposals received little support from Miles's superiors. On August 15 the adjutant general ruled that Pierce and the delegations must return to San Carlos. Arguing that "the sickness . . . has been much exaggerated," the division commander, Howard, also opposed any transferal of San Carlos Indians. When Miles warned of a possible Indian outbreak, Howard, with Sheridan's support and once again backed by the erratic Pierce, remained firm in his antiremoval posture.[7]

Miles returned to Los Angeles, but affairs at San Carlos simmered until late July 1888, when complaints from non-Indian residents triggered another army investigation. Panicky Washington officials, concerned about the political ramifications of another Indian war, demanded "decisive and instant measures . . . to prevent the Indians breaking away from San Carlos." Secretary of War Endicott ordered Miles and Howard to take "every measure" to prevent "another Geronimo raid." The next day, July 31, Miles boarded a train for Arizona.[8]

After sizing up the situation at San Carlos, Miles attributed the outbreaks to the hot weather, poor land, and those inebriated by "tiswin," an alcoholic drink. Other reports of depredations were in his view mere fabrications. Interviews with Mojave, Yuma, and Tonto chiefs who wanted to return to their lands in the Verde River valley reinforced his earlier convictions. Captain John L. Bullis, the recently appointed Indian agent at San Carlos, who boasted years of experience leading Seminole scouts in West Texas and northern Mexico, strongly backed such conclusions. In September, Howard reversed his position on Indian removal, and he and Miles both called attention in their annual reports to the miserable treatment accorded the tribes.[9]

Eastern officials remained dubious, despite Howard's change of heart. The expense of large-scale removal and the opposition by local citizens who thrived on the reservation market concerned both War and Interior department administrators, who sought out the advice of George Crook. "Certainly no commanding officer in Arizona has had the good of the Indians and of the people of Arizona more at heart than he has," went the official army line. Perhaps influenced by his rivalry with Miles, Crook left no doubt as to his opposition to further removal. Knowledgeable officers, he reasoned, could play different tribes against one another to maintain peace on a unified reservation. But despite Crook's recommendations, the abandonment of Forts McDowell and Verde by the military eventually allowed the peaceful return of many Yumas and Mojaves to their homelands.[10]

Through the recent controversies, Miles remained obsessed with promotion. The situation looked promising. Schofield was slated for retirement in 1895. By then, all those with seniority—Howard, Crook, Benet, Drum, and Robert Macfeely—would have reached the legal age limit on military service. "In due time you will rise to the top of the pile, unless by inordinate ambition you spoil your own chances," cautioned an observant William Sherman. Schofield also believed that Miles was destined to command. An undated memo in Schofield's files read, Miles "must as a matter of course at no distant day be assigned to command of the Army," due to his "very distinguished services" and "the great influence of his many friends."[11]

As always, Miles's career remained his top priority. He longed to return to the Department of the Missouri, where Fort Leavenworth promised cooler weather and closer proximity to Washington. He complained that, in transferring him to the Department of Arizona, the army had "disregarded [his] personal interests" and forced him to endure severe "pecuniary losses." Declaring that his efforts against the Apaches and the settlement of Cheyenne grievances in Indian Territory had saved the army $450,000 per annum, he pressed for a transfer even as the dust from the Geronimo campaign was still settling.[12]

In March 1887, mindful of the impending retirement of commander Orlando B. Willcox, then commander of the Department of the Missouri, Miles had taken up his case with President Cleveland's personal secretary, Daniel S. Lamont. Certain parties, charged Miles, "have endeavored to create a prejudice against me and to my disadvantage." April passed without a transfer, so Mary broached the issue with her uncle, John Sherman. She blamed Philip Sheridan for the delay. "[He] hates the whole Sherman family," ranted Mary, who complained about "banishment to this far away country." In her view, Sheridan was trying to ensure that his personal favorite, Wesley Merritt, received the coveted Department of the Missouri. Adopting her husband's exaggerated style, she charged that Sheridan had poured millions of federal dollars into selected regions in the hope of guaranteeing the next Republican presidential nomination. "A more outrageous act of injustice never was attempted," she argued.[13]

"[I] am [at] quite a loss what to do for you," responded Sherman, who admitted that his poor relations with Secretary of War Endicott precluded his personal lobbying. George Jones, editor of the *New York Times* and a staunch ally of Miles's, tried to rally public support by linking War Department opposition to Miles's criticisms of the quality of army shoes. But Jones soon admitted failure. His letters to the president on Miles's behalf had been fruitless; Secretary Endicott's negative influence proved too strong to overcome.[14]

In December 1887, Major General Alfred Terry's poor health and impending retirement renewed Miles's hopes for advancement. Still angry at Terry for having credited David Brotherton with ending the wars against the Sioux, Miles believed that Terry, once his choice to be best man at his wedding, had joined the conspiracy to appoint Adjutant General Drum or one of Sheridan's friends to Terry's position. Miles took some solace in that fact that among the growing list of real and presumed rivals, only George Crook, who had been promoted directly from lieutenant colonel to brigadier general, enjoyed seniority over him.[15]

Experienced in the ways of army lobbying, Miles's supporters swung into action. Francis C. Barlow, who was now the reform-minded attorney general of New York, wrote a letter protesting Miles's ill treatment for George Jones to sign and send to President Cleveland. A bipartisan coalition of Pacific Coast congressmen also petitioned the president. Reminding Sherman of the nation's traditional suspicion of West Point–trained officers, Miles pointed out that Terry had been the ranking soldier who had been a volunteer. Miles contended, "It would only be fair and just," that another citizen-soldier succeed Terry. In an unusually astute political judgment, Miles declined John Sherman's offer to intercede, reasoning that other supporters who enjoyed friendlier relations with Cleveland might be more productive.[16]

By early February 1888, the contest for Terry's major generalship had narrowed to Crook and Miles. Army gossips buzzed about the rivalry, whose combatants were busily accusing one another of having doctored official letterbooks after the Geronimo campaigns. Senator Sherman remained confident. "I believe if [Senator James Don] Cameron will join heartily with me, we can secure your promotion." But Crook enjoyed a good reputation as an Indian fighter as well as eight years' seniority in rank—however tarnished by charges of favoritism, his 1873 appointment easily overshadowed that of Miles's 1881 brigadier generalship. And Miles's conduct during and after the Geronimo campaign still alienated Cleveland administration officials. So, effective April 6, 1888, the Senate conferred a second star on George Crook.[17]

Undaunted, Miles continued his behind-the-scenes jockeying. His attentions now focused on Sheridan, the crusty and often uncooperative commanding general, who was still seven years shy of the mandatory retirement age of sixty-four. Miles feared that Congress would allow Sheridan to remain in that position at the "pleasure of the

President," truly an unhappy prospect for an ambitious brigadier who had done little in the past decade to endear himself to his superiors. "I regard it [the legislation that would have extended Sheridan's military tour] as an insult and an outrage upon General Sherman," fumed Miles, going out of his way to remind Senator Sherman about his brother's retirement. "Besides," he added revealingly, "it will destroy all my prospects of ever being the senior officer of the Army."[18]

Miles's anxieties proved unnecessary. Sheridan, in declining health, suffered a series of heart attacks on May 26. Congress honored the stricken hero with a promotion to the grade of full general—previously reserved for George Washington, Ulysses S. Grant, and William T. Sherman. Sheridan died that August; Miles's acerbic comments now seemed in poor taste when judged against his antagonist's Civil War record.[19]

Sheridan's death triggered a plethora of transfer requests from disgruntled officers. Jockeying for appointments was hardly confined to Miles. For example, Benjamin Grierson, another veteran of the Civil War and nearly two decades of western service, whined that three of the six brigadiers were dissatisfied with their present commands. Miles hoped for command of the Department of the Atlantic, but to his dismay, Major General Howard, a fellow New England native who also longed to return to the East Coast, received the posting by virtue of his seniority. Though unable to honor Miles's top choice, the newly appointed commanding general, Schofield, did help him secure the Division of the Pacific, which encompassed the Departments of Arizona, California, and the Columbia, effective November 23, 1888.[20]

With its headquarters at San Francisco, the new division was a fine consolation prize indeed, especially when combined with the election of Benjamin Harrison as president. "We have been anxious to reach this point [San Francisco] for many years," Miles admitted to William Sherman. Anticipating the possibility of his appointment, he had already launched a Pacific Coast promotional campaign. Logic demanded such boosterism—larger garrisons and new federal military projects often generated political support for the responsible officer. He hailed Harrison's victory as "the opening of a new era in the political history of our country." Never loath to flout protocol, Miles offered Harrison perfunctory congratulations and a much longer essay on the importance of the West. Information regarding Indians, Mormons, statehood, and mineral resources could only be gleaned through a personal visit by the president, declared Miles. "You will find the true American pioneer spirit in this western country," he predicted.[21]

Miles thus sought to ingratiate himself with politicians and to keep his name before the public. He made speeches at various Pacific ports to stress the need for a modern naval presence, which would prove a boon to local economies. The rounds of obligatory social engagements would have seemed onerous to many but they appealed to Mary and Nelson's love of being in the limelight. In an exchange of letters, he congratulated Supreme Court Justice Stephen Field, the former guardian of Lieutenant Leonard Wood's new bride, on his "eminent ability." He took care to make the visit of Senator Eugene Hale a memorable one. Lewis Wolfley, appointed territorial governor of Arizona in 1889, received Miles's warm endorsement. And a year later, in his essay, "Our Unwatered Empire," published by the *North American Review*, Miles again called for major new federal irrigation projects.[22]

The prospect of cementing political alliances as well as his genuine concern for military preparedness led Miles to request increased army appropriations for his division. In 1885, Secretary of War Endicott had organized a blue-ribbon panel to assess the nation's crumbling coastal defenses. Although the Endicott Board had proposed a major new building program, Congress did little to modernize the decaying system until September 1888, when it provided for the establishment of a Board of Ordnance and Fortifications. Miles promptly requested five hundred thousand dollars for military construction at San Diego, San Francisco, Puget Sound, and the mouth of the Columbia River to ameliorate the region's "defenseless condition." Areas west of the Rocky Mountains, he explained, had received less than 1 percent of the money spent on barracks in the past fifteen years. Schofield supported these requests, pointing out, "Seaboard cities cannot be defended without adequate defensive works and trained garrisons."[23]

Reprising an old theme, Miles also sought to mount new explorations into Alaska. In his 1883 trip, Lieutenant Frederick Schwatka had found "a universal desire at all points in Alaska for the military to reoccupy it." Hoping to exploit these perceived needs, Miles queried his former aides Henry T. Allen and Leonard Wood about their interest in outfitting such a mission. Wood seemed particularly keen on the idea.[24] But in early 1889, Adjutant General John C. Kelton rejected Miles's proposal out of hand. Further, he informed Miles, the shortage of quarters precluded any troop transfers to California. Finally, Kelton reminded Miles that the army's financial shortfalls meant that only specially designated artillery officers were to conduct harbor defense inspections; those submitted under Miles's tenure, implied Kelton, were totally unacceptable. The adjutant general instead emphasized the more positive reports compiled by another board of officers that July. Miles's criticisms had again engendered the enmity of staff officers, whose well-placed political connections boded ill for Miles's ambitions.[25]

Apparently still haunted by his demotion in the early days of the Civil War, Miles was unwilling to leave his advancement to chance. He coveted not only the commanding generalship but also the three stars befitting a lieutenant general. The problem seemed simple. Despite having been named to head the army, Schofield remained but a major general. Miles risked a similar fate should Schofield fail to make lieutenant general. Perceiving his own destiny to be intertwined with that of Schofield, Miles threw his full support behind Schofield's quest for a third star. In the second session of the Fiftieth Congress, the House Military Affairs Committee drafted a bill to revive the grade of lieutenant general. The committee's handiwork, however, failed to suit Miles. In addition to leaving the choice of the appointment to the president's discretion, the measure cut the number of major generals from three to two. The prospect of a delayed promotion dictated by this reduction rankled Miles, who demanded that the lieutenant general be selected according to "seniority from the Line of the Army."[26]

In fiery letters to Schofield, both Shermans, and Senator Daniel W. Voorhees, Miles blamed the faulty House bill on "the intrigues of Crook and some of those creatures in Washington." He insisted, "It is a scheme, plot or intrigue . . . not only to prevent my promotion, but to deprive me of the command I now have." Staff officers, who by virtue of their proximity to Congress and their baronial control over army bureaus had seized undue influence, had, in Miles's view, meddled in the proposed legislation. Schofield sought to assuage his fears, but Miles demurred with his usual suspicions. The lieutenant general's bill was, Miles believed, "simply a trick and a scheme to put either Crook or Howard at the head of the Army and keep him there as long as he lives."[27]

The Senate blocked the House proposal, so Miles laid ambitious plans for the Fifty-first Congress, slated to convene in fall 1889. Arguing to Schofield that they must "take one step at a time," Miles submitted a draft bill to "be introduced in the Senate and House during the first hour of any business session." Miles fantasized that Congress might pass his measure, then reestablish a Division of the South and the Departments of the Gulf and the Lakes. Such a move would allow the army to create another major generalship and two additional brigadier generalships to fill the new commands. He reasoned: "This would give commands to Generals [John] Gibbon and [David S.] Stanley . . . and we could all work for it."[28]

In the meantime, Miles worked to establish closer relations with the newly appointed secretary of war, Redfield Proctor, a Civil War veteran and Vermont businessman. "Your points are strong," acknowledged Proctor, who supported Miles's belief that Civil War soldiers deserved special consideration when it came to promotion. When later summing up his six months' association with Miles, whose irascible personality had gained almost legendary status, the secretary wrote in September: "It is said that he is not easily satisfied, but I have not found it so. . . . I think the plan to which Gen. Miles alludes of giving full consideration to war service in making promotions is right and will commend itself to others as well as Gen. M."[29]

Miles pressed his presumed advantage of having Proctor's support as he fended off attempts to transfer Arizona and New Mexico from his own Division of the Pacific. But he believed that he must lay the groundwork for a favorable bill with careful preparation. A trip to Washington would enable him to influence key congressmen and to see the president. To avoid the appearance of lobbying, Miles hoped to procure an official congressional invitation to testify on some other subject. Coastal defense or a new equipment board, surmised the general, would provide the perfect cover. Miles then asked Senator Sherman to introduce "during the *first* hour of the first business session" legislation reviving the grade of lieutenant general.[30]

Miles indeed secured an invitation to testify on coastal defense. But a more complex investigation soon took precedence. In early 1890 the House Committee on Indian Affairs had reopened investigations into the fate of Geronimo and the other Chiricahua prisoners. Pressured by the publicity that had been given to the atrocious conditions at Fort Marion, the government had in 1887 reunited the warriors with their families at Mount Vernon Barracks, Alabama, thirty miles north of Mobile. The new site proved almost as bad as the first; appallingly high numbers of prisoners fell sick and died. Crook, assisted by Lieutenant Lyman V. Kennon, now pressed for the transfer of the survivors to Fort Sill, Indian Territory. As the man responsible for Geronimo's capture, Miles was asked to testify.[31]

Nelson Miles had opposed the original decision to move the Apaches to Florida, describing Fort Marion as "a second black hole of Calcutta." He had originally planned to relocate them instead in the Indian Territory. Now, however, he dubbed Fort Sill too unhealthy and too close to Arizona; North Carolina, he suggested, was a better location. Fearing the Chiricahuas would break for their old homes if moved to Sill, southwesterners joined Miles in the opposition. Crook pounced on his old rival's inconsistency. Lambasting the "false impressions" generated by Miles's "Literary Bureau," he also blasted Miles's attempts to magnify his role in the capture of Geronimo. "Full justice [could not] be done the Indians," wrote Crook, unless all the facts concerning the surrender came to light.[32]

"The large majority of people of Arizona & N.M. know the truth but want to curry favor with M[iles]," Crook argued, noting the absurdity of the presumed threat to the Far Southwest. He authorized Lieutenant Kennon "to let all the stink out of" any pro-Miles press releases and coached him to hint in his congressional testimony at Miles's well-known jealousy of Crook. Crook also called on a fellow antagonist of Miles's, Oliver O. Howard, whose sympathies for the plight of the Chiricahuas mirrored Crook's own. "In as much as the location is the same as proposed and urged by this officer [Miles] in 1886," explained Crook to Howard on February 27, 1890, "it would appear that his opposition is based rather on personal grounds, than a desire that these Indians should be treated with humanity and justice."[33]

From his Atlantic command headquarters at New York City, Howard, long suspicious of conditions faced by the Apaches in Florida, leaped aboard the Crook bandwagon. Having already dispatched his son, Lieutenant Guy V. Howard, to compile what would be a scathing report on the condition of the Apaches, Howard convinced Schofield and Secretary Proctor that Miles's objections had been based on personal feelings. "A judicious Associated Press item or paragraph started from here or from Boston might help," he advised Crook. Still, Howard warned, "the adverse influence of our friend seems to be great." Crook accepted this logic and lined up the Washington correspondent H. V.

Boynton, a former Civil War general and noted critic of anything remotely associated with William Sherman. Boynton, thought Crook, "enjoys a row & thinks he would like to pitch into Miles."[34]

The Crook-Miles rivalry had thus reached new heights. Miles testified before the House Committee on Indian Affairs, "The Chiricahua Apaches are the lowest, most brutal, and cruel of all the Indian savages on this continent. They kill for the pleasure of killing, and they take fiendish delight in the most cruel tortures." Miles explained his original suggestion that the tribe be removed to Indian Territory: "I did not suppose at that time I would be able to get them farther." He was poised to take on his prime antagonist, but the steam went out of the transfer movement with Crook's unexpected death, following a heart attack, on March 21.[35]

After pausing in feigned homage, Miles joined those seeking the vacated major generalship. Divisiveness seemed the rule among the officers of the old army. Continuing budget crises, boredom, and rivalries over Civil War records had nearly ruined morale; a sizable number refused to acknowledge service against Indians, whom they deemed an inferior enemy, as legitimate military experience. Stagnation had further embittered those who sought promotion in partial compensation for their service. Miles had become especially proficient in maneuvering for promotion, despite his steadfast protestations to the contrary. On March 27, 1890, for instance, he asked Senator Dawes, in connection with the vacancy left by Crook's death, to remind the president of his record. "I have not thought it necessary to write or use my influence," blustered Miles with either an astonishing lack of honesty or an abundance of self-delusion, "but every man has some enemies."[36]

Congressmen and governors bombarded the president's office with professions of support for Nelson Miles. On April 4, John Sherman sent a strong recommendation. "I have known Miles now for twenty-four years, and have never known him to do anything but what is honorable, and I believe his record will compare with that of any officer of the army," he wrote. "If he has sometimes been wilful," Sherman reasoned, "it is the fault of most men who have been successful."[37]

With his senior rivals retired or dead, Miles finally won his second star. "The top round of the ladder gives me more pleasure I think than any of the others," he told Mary smugly. Though he deserved the appointment, his constant self-aggrandizement rankled many colleagues. "I had no hopes of beating Miles," concluded one disgruntled contender, General Stanley. "He has made a business of looking after the advancement of himself, and I cannot match him." Even John Sherman admonished Miles. "I got the impression from my conversations both with the President and Secretary [of War], that you were a little too urgent and strong in supporting your own opinion rather than yielding pleasantly and gracefully to theirs."[38]

But Miles's colossal appetite for power would not be easily satisfied. He now lobbied for the Division of the Missouri. William Sherman again warned Miles to control his ambitions: "I advise that you do not enter any controversy. Let the War Dept. do what it pleases only giving an opinion if asked for. Do well and cheerfully whatever post is allotted to you, sure that your own time will come, when you will be equally jealous of outside suggestions."[39]

Even though Proctor had begun to question the size of the sprawling Division of the Missouri and Congress was considering legislation that did not suit his purposes on the lieutenant general bill, Miles mustered enough self-control to remain inconspicuous in the summer of 1890. His barrage of requests and demands slacked off. The tactic worked; Miles was appointed to command the Division of the Missouri on September 1. Two weeks later he made a triumphant final stop in old Fort Keogh where the adoring garrison entertained his party—including Mary, Cecilia, Miles's aides Lieutenant Marion P. Maus and Captain Eli Lundy Huggins, and two of Mary's nieces—with a gala "hop" that brought back memories of frontier days past.[40]

They reached Chicago on the sixteenth and Miles began setting up his new headquarters in the Pullman Building. The dinners, dances, banquets, and military ceremonies accompanying his new position appealed to the general's vanity and provided a glittering welcome. Even the recent decision to remove the Department of Texas from his jurisdiction could not dim his rosy optimism. After twenty years west of the Missouri River, he viewed the prospect of life in Chicago, the commercial center of the Midwest and in the midst of a massive building boom, as a long-overdue opportunity. Miles found it convenient to ignore the squalor of the city's slums in favor of its imposing Gilded Age architectural grandeur. "A wonderful city," this Chicago, which Miles predicted might "in time become the largest in this country if not in the world."[41]

11 : THE GHOST DANCE

While stopping off at Fort Keogh en route to Chicago in September 1890, Miles had learned of the plight of his old enemies, the Northern Cheyennes. The federal government had again failed to live up to its treaty obligations with them. Most of the tribe lived at the Tongue River Reservation in southeastern Montana, but Little Chief led about five hundred people at the Pine Ridge Agency, South Dakota. Reductions in food shipments had forced them to slaughter their cattle herds. With winter approaching, the Northern Cheyennes resorted to stealing from nearby whites.[1]

Blasting the incompetence of the civilians who ran the Indian agencies, Miles asked for an immediate emergency appropriation. He got some money, plus the authority to take a commission to investigate and negotiate with the Northern Cheyennes. Combining this business with his insatiable quest for publicity, General Miles invited the illustrator and author Frederic Remington to accompany the official entourage. Remington's long bouts with the bottle slowed the column and proved a tremendous burden for Miles's overworked staff, especially Captain Baldwin. But for Miles, the ploy worked as designed: Remington's laudatory essay, "Chasing a Major-General," was published by *Harper's Weekly* in early December. "The escort strings out behind," wrote Remington, who was amazed that Miles's increasing girth seemed not to slow him. That he was outpacing his followers was "observed with a grim humor by the general [Miles], who desire[d] nothing so much as to leave his escort far in the rear."[2]

Miles tore himself away from Remington long enough to meet with assorted Indian delegations. At Pine Ridge, home of the Oglala Sioux as well as Little Chief's Northern Cheyennes, he listened to Little Chief's reasons as to why he should be allowed to reunite his people in Montana, then Miles heard out the fears of the worried agent, Daniel F. Royer. Royer's case exemplified much of what was wrong with the nation's methods of dealing with Indians. A physician, newspaperman, and sometime territorial legislator from Alpena, South Dakota, Royer knew nothing about Indians, but needed a government job. His ties with the state's congressional delegation far outweighed his lack of qualifications. The skittish Royer, whom his charges dubbed "Young-Man-Afraid-of-Indians," had already notified his Indian Bureau superiors that troops might be necessary to quell the disturbances.[3]

Miles, on the other hand, oozed confidence. To Red Cloud, the Oglala chief who stubbornly worked to defend tribal ways against white influence, the major-general's visit seemed at least a dim hope that better times awaited. Miles was a hard campaigner but was reputed to be fair and honest. "I and my people have heard a great many times of you. We are very glad to have you come," he told Miles. "It is like a person coming out of darkness into light to meet a good man." Aware that false alarms greatly outnumbered actual violent outbreaks, the general sought to reassure Royer and cautioned the chiefs to prevent their people from precipitating a conflict. Despite his outward calm, Miles worried about his inability to agree to terms with the Cheyennes. Should the Indians remain armed and on their reservations, he feared, war remained a distinct possibility. Also disconcerting to representatives of the government was the popularity of the new religion sweeping through the tribes of the northern Plains—the Ghost Dance.[4]

The Ghost Dance had been popularized by an obscure Paiute mystic named Wovoka. To its adherents, bewildered and confused by the changes wrought by the whites' expansion, it promised a millennium of peace and prosperity, and offered a blend of traditional Indian beliefs and Christianity. Bliss could be achieved, taught Wovoka, through pacifism, virtue, and performing the Ghost Dance. But as the movement spread, new converts altered the shaman's original message. Recent cutbacks in government rations and reductions in their reservations had embittered the Sioux and Northern Cheyennes. Crop failures in 1890 only increased their misery. The Ghost Dance began to symbolize a means for them to strike back against their white antagonists.[5]

Caught up in the rumors circulating from the Standing Rock, Cheyenne River, and Pine Ridge reservations, panic-stricken whites in the Dakotas and Nebraska unleashed a flood of telegrams, letters, and petitions for help to a variety of military and government officials. As a friend told Miles on October 22, "The Pine Ridge Indians are having their '*Ghost*' dance & the agent is doing his best to stop it. The Indians say it is part of their religion & they claim the right to dance." If troops intervened, he feared, "there [would] surely be trouble." On the thirty-first, President Harrison instructed the army to send either Miles or Brigadier General Thomas H. Ruger, commanding the Department of the Dakota, to investigate the Sioux crisis. Ruger thus toured the Standing Rock and Cheyenne River agencies, resolving to prevent any potential conflict by arresting Sitting Bull, whom many whites feared as a symbol of military resistance, and by reinforcing the garrison at Fort Bennett, which lay between the Cheyenne River Reservation and the Pine Ridge and Rosebud reservations.[6]

Agent Royer, on the other hand, wanted more forceful action. The local Indian police had defied his orders and joined the Ghost Dance. "I have carefully studied the matter for nearly six weeks and have brought all the persuasion through the chiefs to bear on the leaders that was possible, but without effect, and the only remedy for this matter is the use of the military," Royer wrote on October 30. A similar telegram followed two weeks later. The acting secretary of the interior, George Chandler, formally requested military assistance for his terrified Pine Ridge agent on November 13. President Harrison approved military intervention the same day.[7]

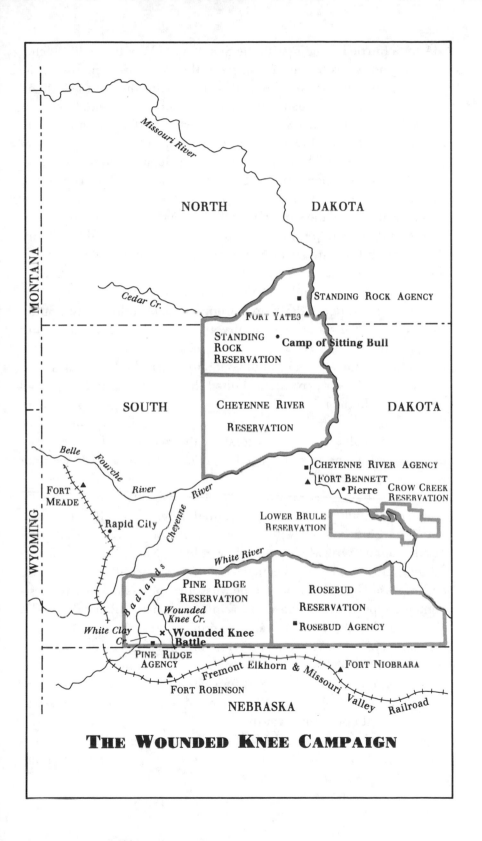

THE WOUNDED KNEE CAMPAIGN

After a hurried meeting with the Secretary of War, Redfield Proctor, in St. Louis, Miles began mapping out the military's response to the crisis. Initially, he concurred with Ruger's conclusion that the Indians' disaffection would not lead to immediate violence. But reinforcements seemed only prudent. Experience suggested that if the army were indeed to occupy an Indian reservation, an overwhelming display of force was advisable. The commander of the Department of the Platte, Brigadier General John R. Brooke, was to occupy Pine Ridge and Lieutenant Colonel A. T. Smith, commander of Fort Niobrara, Nebraska, would head the garrison at the Rosebud Agency. In a display of timing and cooperation rarely equaled by the Indian-fighting army, Brooke, with three troops of Ninth Cavalrymen and one company of the Eighth Infantry from Fort Robinson, four companies of the Second Infantry from Omaha, a Hotchkiss cannon, and a Gatling Gun, rumbled into Pine Ridge at dawn on November 20. Simultaneously, Smith led two troops of the Ninth Cavalry, three companies of the Eighth Infantry, and a Hotchkiss gun onto the Rosebud Reservation.[8]

Stunned by the efficiency of the operation, hundreds of well-armed tribesmen and their dependents bolted the agencies and disappeared onto the northern prairies. As Brooke and Smith struggled to maintain the uneasy peace, Miles urged caution. "One thing should be impressed upon all officers, never to allow their commands to be mixed up with the Indians," he instructed Brooke on November 18. A similar reminder came five days later: "Do not allow your command to become mixed up with the Indians friendly or otherwise." And on the seventh: "I must call your attention to my original order not to allow the commands to be mixed up with Indians in any way, or to be taken at disadvantage." Overwhelming force would be available should peaceful measures fail. Having been given authority over all the areas once encompassed by the Division of the Missouri and assured of full presidential support, Miles poured in reinforcements. Colonel James W. Forsyth and the Seventh Cavalry Regiment rode into Pine Ridge, as did Colonel Frank Wheaton and four companies of the Second Infantry, another troop of Ninth Cavalrymen, and an artillery battery. Lieutenant Colonel J. A. Poland and four companies of the Twenty-first Infantry marched into the Rosebud Agency. A reserve cavalry force was assembling at Fort Leavenworth, Kansas.[9]

Miles briefed his staff the day after Thanksgiving, warning them of the messianic movement and reiterating his hope that the military would be given full control over Indian affairs. The general also initiated two efforts at personal diplomacy. One of the leading Indians living at the Cheyenne River Agency was Hump, who had scouted for Miles during the Nez Perce campaign. Miles knew that Captain Ezra P. Ewers, now stationed in Texas, had during years of work with the tribe earned Hump's confidence. Ewers was called in and sent to Hump's camp; shortly thereafter, Hump and most of his followers came in to Fort Bennett.[10]

A second envoy came straight out of vaudeville. While at a recent banquet, Miles had run into an old crony and former scout—William F. Cody. A showman, entrepreneur, and supposed friend of Sitting Bull (the chief had once been a star attraction in his Wild West Show), Buffalo Bill might be just the man to diffuse the crisis. Resplendent in patent leather shoes and dress suit, Cody appeared at Fort Yates, on the Standing Rock Reservation, on November 27 with three companions, five journalists, and a scribbled message from Miles.[11]

Written on the back of a calling card, the note instructed officers to provide Cody with transportation and an escort. Buffalo Bill was "to secure the person of Sitting Bull and deliver him to the nearest com'g officer of U.S. Troops." Startled officials at Fort Yates—Lieutenant Colonel William F. Drum and Agent James McLaughlin—feared the impromptu emissary would get himself killed and start a full-fledged war. Convinced that Cody must not be allowed to leave, Drum and McLaughlin spelled out the gravity of the situation by telegraph to General Ruger, who promptly passed word along to Washington.[12]

In the meantime, Cody had to be delayed. Three officers plied the showman with whiskey. "They did their duty nobly and Cody was retired for the night amid general rejoicing at the success of the scheme," remembered one. But Cody proved remarkably resilient; the following morning, "great indeed was everybody's surprise to see the latter emerge from his temporary quarters sweet, smiling and happy, ready for the start to Sitting Bull's camp and asking for transportation and escort." Quick-thinking Fort Yates personnel directed Cody down the wrong trail. While Cody backtracked, President Harrison, who had gotten wind of the scheme, forbade Sitting Bull's arrest.[13]

General Miles received a further jolt when he read the November 21 issue of the *Washington Evening Star.* "A prominent army officer" stationed in Washington had in a sensational interview charged that Miles was using the crisis to promote his own presidential candidacy.

"Miles is predicting a general Indian war and virtually asks that the command of the entire army be turned over to him. He wants to create a scare and pose as the savior of the country," explained the unnamed source. "I have no doubt in the world that he is honest in his candidacy. He has shrewdly enlisted the favor of nearly every newspaper man in California, and has by his agreeable manners and the expenditure of his means managed to make himself very popular in a certain way in the west. He is one [of] the most ambitious men in the army and he is pulling the wires shrewdly."[14]

Furious at both the accusation and the sabotaging of his plan to seize Sitting Bull, Miles deemed a quick trip to Washington to be in order. There, he repeated a common theme—the military must be given control over the tribes of the northern plains. Army officers should man the troubled agencies and have "absolute central control." Further, the Indians' rations must be restored to full treaty levels. Though the President, Secretary Proctor, and Commanding General Schofield opposed any more attempts to arrest individual Indian leaders, they promised to leave the matter to Miles's discretion. Miles also made a hit with the press and Congress, several members of which quoted him in speeches before both chambers. The pressure forced the Interior Department to accede to Miles's wishes; rations would be increased and Sioux agents were to abide by military orders. Only the reluctance shown by Schofield and Proctor in ferreting out the source of the scandalous *Evening Star* story marred Miles's junket.[15]

Miles did not forget the incident, but had to delay his investigation pending the resolution of the Ghost Dance crisis, which he characterized as "serious" in a December 1 letter to Herbert Welsh. He set up temporary headquarters at Rapid City, South Dakota, so as to better direct field operations. Careful diplomacy augured well around the Cheyenne River Agency, where the army seemed prepared to manage the situation. Hump had come out against the Ghost Dancers and Big Foot, the leader of those Minneconjou Sioux who remained recalcitrant, continued to profess peaceful intent.[16]

Such was hardly the case at Pine Ridge, where several hundred excited Brule Sioux from the Rosebud Agency had joined the Oglalas in the northwestern quarter of the reservation. There the Indians occupied a natural fortress, the Stronghold, an elevated plateau that seemed impervious to all but the most determined assaults. Reinforcements continued to stream in; a mixed squadron of four troops of cavalry under Lieutenant Colonel George B. Sanford, eight companies of Colonel Eugene A. Carr's Sixth Cavalry, and seven companies of the Seventeenth Infantry had assumed positions to block the Indians' escape from the Stronghold. To alleviate the administrative imbroglio, Miles temporarily assigned Brooke, as head of the Department of the Platte, to control all troops from Pine Ridge to the west; Ruger, from the Department of the Dakota, would lead those east of that line.[17]

Hesitant to storm the Oglala-Brule stronghold, Brooke opted for negotiations. On the morning of December 6, he joined Colonels Wheaton and Forsyth in meeting a delegation of six chiefs. Despite contemporary newspaper reports that suggested that the Indians had made no agreement, Brooke was optimistic about the meeting: "The result of the council . . . is very satisfactory, and I think there will be no further trouble with the indians of these agencies," he wired his headquarters. Critical of Brooke's independent talks, Miles referred his subordinate to the press reports, which seemed to indicate that Brooke was "not master of the situation at that place." He again reminded Brooke of his "original order not to allow the command to be mixed up with the Indians in any way."[18]

Indian emissaries sent by the army, on the other hand, enjoyed greater success, and Two Strike and some nine hundred other Brule Sioux returned to Pine Ridge. Brooke proposed using military force to bring in those who remained out. Colonel Carr, a decorated Civil War veteran with long years of experience fighting Indians, would block the north with his Sixth Cavalry and Brooke himself would lead an assault on the Stronghold from the south. Miles vetoed this scheme, arguing that such a massive force would scatter the Indians. He instead proposed to lay siege and wait for the effects of the bitter plains winter. By continuing to promise that the government would fulfill its treaty obligations, argued the general, peace might still be preserved.[19]

Brooke protested the delay. "I believe I have done all things possible to avert a war or an outbreak here and have no hopes of any further efforts at pacification being successful." Though disappointed in Miles's decision, on December 16 Brooke obediently hatched another plan. This time, he theorized that several hundred Indians still at the Pine Ridge Agency might go out and convince the others to give themselves up. Planning and implementation of this effort would take about a week.[20]

As Brooke struggled to master the situation at Pine Ridge, Miles determined that he must seize Sitting Bull, despite the objections of Washington officials. On December 10, he set the process in motion. At Fort Yates, Drum and McLaughlin decided that a detachment of about forty Indian policemen could best handle the delicate capture. Captain E. G. Fechet, two companies of regulars, a Hotchkiss cannon, and a Gatling gun provided close support. The Indian police arrested Sitting Bull at his camp on the morning of the fifteenth, only to be jumped by his followers. The resulting melee left Sitting Bull, seven supporters, and six Indian policemen dead or mortally wounded. Several cannon volleys and the intercession of Fechet's troopers rescued the remaining policemen but caused about four hundred of Sitting Bull's people to flee the agency.[21]

Miles had regarded the Minneconjou chief Big Foot as posing a threat almost as great as that of his old foe Sitting Bull. Widely respected, even venerated, for his skillful diplomacy and keen interest in retaining traditional ways, Big Foot had in the fall of 1890 briefly accepted the Ghost Dance. Though he later rejected the movement, many of those at Cheyenne River remained ardent disciples of the faith. Further, his presence along the Cheyenne River, some sixty miles west of Fort Bennett and the Cheyenne River Agency, attracted militant refugees from other agencies. On December 16, General Ruger suggested that Big Foot's arrest would be "desirable." Lieutenant Colonel Edwin V. Sumner, who had been monitoring the situation there for nearly two weeks, began herding the 333 Indians west toward Camp Cheyenne, which the army had established to monitor the actions of Big Foot and his people.[22]

Sumner doubted the advisability of arresting Big Foot, with whom he had established a working relationship. But the chief's followers chafed under the supervision of Sumner's bluecoats. Ruling out the use of direct force, Sumner permitted the tribespeople to return to their homes on condition of Big Foot's promise that he and any refugees from Sitting Bull's band would later return to their reservations. Sumner anxiously counted the hours; "if Big Foot does not keep his promise and come in to-day with those people," he wrote on the twenty-third, "I think I will have temporized to keep peace with him long enough, and would like to go down and capture his village." Subsequent investigation found the Indian camp deserted. Miles was livid. "You have missed your opportunity," he admonished Sumner.[23]

At Rapid City, the intense pressures had kept Miles from writing

Mary until the nineteenth. He did, however, fire off letters to Senator Dawes and General Schofield reiterating his criticisms of the government's failure to fulfill its treaties. He demanded that Congress restore confidence among the tribes by appropriating the proper rations and turning the agencies over to the military. On a wintry Christmas Day, good news from Brooke eased his anxieties: a Pine Ridge delegation of Indians had convinced their fellow Oglalas to return to the agency. Optimistically, Miles repeated for Mary's benefit Brooke's observation that the Indians were turning themselves in. Violence might still be avoided. But even this personal note betrayed the emotional roller coaster that characterized the campaign, for while writing the letter Miles received another dispatch that seemed much less encouraging.[24]

The latter message undoubtedly recounted the unknown whereabouts of Big Foot. Stricken with a severe case of pneumonia, the leader had crept along more slowly than the army anticipated. But Big Foot could no longer ignore the hopelessness of the situation; he finally opted to make his way to Pine Ridge. Four troops of the Seventh Cavalry, led by Major Samuel M. Whitside and supported by two Hotchkiss guns, cautiously approached the tormented Minneconjou's camp on the afternoon of December 28. The joint column made camp that evening at Wounded Knee Creek, where Colonel Forsyth and the rest of the Seventh came up about 8:45 P.M. Forsyth, whose trim gray mustache and goatee gave him an appearance befitting the dashing Civil War cavalryman he was, assumed command. He had led Custer's rebuilt regiment since 1886 and was well regarded by his men. Brooke later recalled his verbal orders to Forsyth: "To disarm Big Foot's band, take every precaution to prevent the escape of any; if they fought to destroy them."[25]

Fighting had as yet been limited, although Forsyth faced a delicate task on the twenty-ninth. The Seventh Cavalry, its 438 men augmented by a squad of Oglala scouts and four Hotchkiss cannon, easily outnumbered Big Foot's 120 warriors and 230 women and children. But the colonel's demands that the Indians give up their weapons had produced only a smattering of broken carbines. Forsyth determined that more direct action was necessary and moved Troops B and K to a position between the main Indian camp and the council meeting site. Two officers and thirty men began searching the lodges, a direct violation of instructions Miles had given Brooke.[26]

The tension mounted as the soldiers turned up caches of rifles. One of the frustrated tribesmen discharged a shot into the air. Several other Indians, followed in short order by the soldiers, fired with more deadly intent. Troops B and K, caught between those Minneconjous at the council and in the camp, fell back in a hail of volleys. Four Hotchkiss cannons and the rest of the regiment fired into the village as the Indians scrambled into the snow-covered ravines surrounding the campsite. When the smoke cleared, 84 Indian men and boys, 44 women, and 16 children lay dead; 7 of the 51 known to have been wounded died later. Of Forsyth's men, 25 were killed and 39 wounded.[27]

Word of the carnage spread quickly. Thousands of Brules and a lesser number of Oglalas at Pine Ridge, enraged and frightened, left the agency and thundered down White Clay Creek. Short Bull and Kicking Bear, prominent disciples of the Ghost Dance who were en route to Pine Ridge to surrender, instead joined the excited Brules, bringing the total number of refugees up to about four thousand persons. On the thirtieth, Indians set fire to a small cabin at the Drexel Mission, four miles from the army's base at Pine Ridge. To challenge them, Brooke dispatched Forsyth with eight troops of his Seventh Cavalry and a Hotchkiss cannon. The column raced helter-skelter down a valley in pursuit, only to find itself ambushed by Indians occupying the overlooking bluffs. Pinned down by the crossfire, Forsyth struggled to extricate his command and called for reinforcements. Major Guy V. Henry's battalion of Ninth Cavalry, their mounts nearly disabled from the effects of a one-hundred-mile march the day before, rode up from Pine Ridge to drive the Indians away.[28]

Sketchy reports of the fight at Wounded Knee had led Miles, exhausted by the lack of sleep, to begin transferring his headquarters from Rapid City to the Pine Ridge Agency just before midnight on December 30. His plan of action was simple; he would assemble overwhelming numbers to block escape avenues and to tighten the noose around the Indians, dig in at Pine Ridge, and reopen diplomatic channels with key chiefs. Miles now had over thirty-five hundred men at his immediate disposal, with another two thousand on call—fully one-fifth of the entire army. Several hundred Indian auxiliaries further augmented his forces.[29]

From his new headquarters at the Pine Ridge agent's comfortable residence, Miles tightened the circle and renewed his demands for total army control. Ignoring minor skirmishes on December 30, January 3, and January 7, he stepped up the diplomatic pressure in communiqués to influential Indian leaders, many of whom—Broad Tail, Little Hawk, Kicking Bear, and Short Bull being among the most prominent—had first surrendered to him years before during the Great Sioux War. His messages were firm. They must give themselves up to the army, which would in turn attempt to guarantee their treaty privileges. "You know that I did what was right by you before; I shall do what is right by you now," he assured his former enemies. "I must be Chief. I know I can do you good. If you expect me to help you, you must help me by doing what I want you to do." He wanted their immediate surrender; nothing less would do.[30]

Rumors of another impending massacre swept the Indian camps as it became increasingly evident that their escape was impossible. In the incessant cold, the Oglalas wavered, and despite Brule taunts began defecting back to Pine Ridge. Still, the situation remained tense; the soldiers' wives were "in constant anxiety and horror about their husbands," wrote Colonel Carr. Brooke shared these anxieties as the rebel camp slowly moved back toward the mission. "The situation is so delicate that any premature move might cause a stampede [and] I have been exceedingly cautious and at the same time watching them closely."[31]

By January 13, the Indian camp, still nearly four thousand strong, was squarely between Brooke's command and the troops at Pine Ridge. Miles jubilantly proclaimed success that day in a private letter to Mary. But only on the fifteenth did the still-defiant Kicking Bear throw down his rifle; other tribesmen would be disarmed throughout the month. Miles packed Kicking Bear, Short Bull, and twenty other warriors off to Fort Sheridan, Chicago, to guarantee the peace. The other tribesmen were escorted back to their reservations.[32]

The major figures in the Wounded Knee campaign met various fates. Buffalo Bill Cody got wind of Miles's scheme to take the hostages back to Chicago; wouldn't it be equally effective and much more profitable, argued the showman, if they joined his Wild West entourage and went on a European tour instead? Miles concurred, and Cody overrode the protests of Commissioner of Indian Affairs Thomas J. Morgan to organize a popular tour. Cody wrote Miles several months later: "The hostiles say if you had not scared them with so many soldiers last winter they would have been fighting still. They looked for only a few soldiers at a time, and they would whip them by detail, but you brought more than they ever saw before, and it frightened them."[33]

The other Indians returned to their reservations. Miles made a special case for the transfer of the Northern Cheyennes, many of whom had "rendered most heroic and valuable service" in the recent campaign, back to their tribal homeland along the Yellowstone River. After intensive lobbying from Miles and over the objections of Interior Secretary John Noble, Captain Ewers escorted Little Chief's band to Montana.[34]

But the army's conduct at Wounded Knee remained a matter of concern. Initially, Miles distributed the blame equally on Sumner, who had allowed Big Foot to escape, and Forsyth, who had botched the disarmament process. Only on January 1 did the general begin to focus upon Forsyth's "fatally defective dispositions" and the "very large number of women and children" killed. Schofield urged Miles to use his best judgment in investigating the tragedy.[35]

Miles promptly relieved Forsyth of command and appointed a military court of inquiry. "Tony" Forsyth's past record bothered him. A staff officer for much of his career, Forsyth had been an ally of Sheridan and had spoken out against George Custer during the Belknap scandal fifteen years before. To Miles, a line officer who revered Custer and had grown distant from Sheridan, this seemed a perfect example of the personal intrigues that weakened the army. Privately, he attributed the massacre to "blind stupidity or criminal indifference."[36]

To many, the military tribunal looked like another of the general's familiar gambits. Schofield declared that Miles, by organizing the court on his own authority, had exceeded his orders. When pressed by reporters, a confused Secretary of War Redfield Proctor muttered, "Gen. Miles did it. It is a very mixed up matter and I may explain it later." From his retirement, William Sherman added a stern warning to Mary. "If Forsyth was relieved because some squaw was killed, somebody has made a mistake, for squaws have been killed in every Indian war." He advised Miles to "say little and write less, but create success."[37]

Miles ignored these admonitions. Colonel Carr was named to the court but could not serve, because he was needed with his regiment. The division inspector general, Jacob Ford Kent, and Miles's trusted friend and ally, the acting assistant inspector general, Captain Frank Baldwin, would thus handle the investigation. The latter appointment called into question the court's objectivity—Forsyth, for example, later made repeated reference to the long-time relationship between Baldwin and Miles, charging that Miles had forced his opinions and wishes on the court through his old subordinate.[38]

One line of investigation centered on Forsyth's placement of his troops at Wounded Knee, which Miles claimed to have been remarkably poor. A fresh second lieutenant, argued the general, could surely have deployed the nearly five hundred troops and auxiliaries on hand more effectively. The one hundred-odd Indian warriors, encumbered by two hundred fifty women and children, should have been disarmed by the threat of force alone. Kent and Baldwin dutifully grilled the regiment's junior officers about the deployment of forces. Emphasizing that they had not expected any violence, most were reluctant to criticize their colonel.[39]

The second line of questioning focused on the high number of noncombatant deaths. Miles always contended that the soldiers had been close enough to distinguish their targets, and that many casualties bore telltale traces of short-range gunpowder burns. Responses to close questioning seemed to indicate that although the vast majority of soldiers had tried to avoid taking needless casualties, the incredible confusion had rendered exact aim impossible. The testimony of Lieutenant S.R.H. Tompkins, D Company, captured the sentiments of those officers who testified. "Generally speaking," concluded Tompkins, "men and women were so mingled together that it was impossible to destroy the bucks without endangering the women and children." He insisted that, as the fighting continued, they "took particular pains not to fire on women and children."[40]

Torn between their loyalty to Miles, on whose staff they served, and their empathy with the situation Forsyth had encountered, Kent and Baldwin on January 13 wrote a mixed report. They acknowledged that all officers needed to be ready for any contingency, but the sudden turn to violence at Wounded Knee had come as a complete surprise to virtually every officer on the field. Both criticized Forsyth's deployment of forces, especially the detached placement of Troops B and K among the Indians. But Kent in particular gave the colonel every benefit of the doubt. "Unavoidable and unfortunate circumstances" in his view were the cause of the high number of noncombatant casualties.[41]

On January 16, Miles requested that the court reopen the case. They should procure testimony from General Brooke as to whether or not he had forwarded Miles's repeated injunctions to his subordinates against mixing the troops with the Indians. Although Brooke first insisted that he did not remember these instructions, under closer questioning he admitted that he had "impressed upon Major Whitside and General Forsyth [Forsyth had been appointed major general of volunteers shortly after the Civil War] the importance of capturing and holding Big Foot's people at a distance." In light of this evidence, Kent admitted that "Forsyth's command was not held at a safe distance," but he still defended the colonel. "It seems impossible to me that he could then calculate that the Indians would deliberately plan their own destruction." Baldwin was more critical: the order to avoid stationing regulars among the Indians "was entirely disregarded and lost sight of by Colonel Forsyth."[42]

For his part, Forsyth discounted the matter, concluding that Kent and Baldwin were too closely associated with their sponsor to render fair judgments. The colonel decided not to even dignify the charges with a defense. He did assert, however, that Brooke told Miles that Brooke had not forwarded any injunctions to his subordinate because the messages had been marked confidential.[43]

The court finished its work on January 18, but Miles waited until the thirty-first to compose his endorsements. His aide-de-camp, Eli L. Huggins, though he understood Miles's fury towards Forsyth, pleaded with his superior to tone down the initial draft. "Two lines, the most pernicious ones in the paper," were finally omitted. "[Miles] apparently cares nothing for the hatred of his enemies," marveled Huggins, "but his indignation at the mismanagement and worse of the Big Foot affair, and his disgust at the butchery there left him no other course to pursue." What remained were "savage" attacks on Forsyth, who, in Miles's words, left "unheeded and disregarded" Miles's warnings that he remain on the alert. Forsyth's failure to maintain basic security measures was "incomprehensible and inexcusable." Miles continued, "It is in fact difficult to conceive how a worse disposition of troops could have been made." Forsyth had demonstrated "incompetence" and "entire inexperience" throughout the operation. A formal letter on February 14 demonstrated Miles's utter contempt: "I have no hesitation in saying, that I would not jeopardize the lives of officers and men in the hands of such an officer."[44]

Weary of Miles and anxious to divert public attention from the Wounded Knee fiasco, Schofield and Proctor concluded that the investigation had gone on long enough. "The interests of the military service do not . . . demand any further proceedings in this case," commented Schofield. Proctor agreed and restored Forsyth to command. Frazzled by the agonizing campaign and subsequent political maelstrom, Miles took the judgment as a personal affront. Assistant Adjutant General Henry Corbin undoubtedly understated sentiments around division headquarters when he noted that Miles was "very much put out by the treatment given him by the folks in Washington." Huggins feared for Miles's health. "The General says little, but chafes terribly," he wrote on February 17. "He has made several remarks . . . which convince me that he thinks sudden death not unlikely."[45]

Miles continued to associate Forsyth with a War Department conspiracy. His annual report for 1891 reflected poorly on the colonel; fearing that Forsyth's friends would expunge critical documents from his official file, the general detached an aide to transcribe the records for use at a later date. But despite Miles's best efforts, Forsyth stayed in the army, eventually advancing to the rank of major general.[46]

Meanwhile, friends of General Miles were tracking down the source of the November 1890 *Washington Evening Star* release that had accused him of manufacturing an Indian war in order to further his presidential ambitions. By January 8, 1891, the pro-Miles *New York Times* had identified the source as Colonel Chauncey McKeever, a West Point graduate, a long-time member of the adjutant general's department, and a sharp critic of Miles's handling of the Geronimo affair. An unauthorized publication in the *Army and Navy Journal* of one of Miles's official reports only intensified the search. The *Journal* reporter, it turned out, was also a War Department clerk. Furious at the leaks and anxious to quell the furor over the Wounded Knee affair, Secretary of War Proctor dismissed the clerk and transferred McKeever to the adjutant general's office of the Division of the Missouri. There, Miles, as commanding officer, could make McKeever's life miserable.[47]

Satisfied with this turn of events, Miles pressed for major revisions in Indian policy. His feelings were well known, having been stated in numerous past reports, in letters to Senator Dawes and General Schofield during the Wounded Knee campaign, and in an article in the January 1891 issue of the *North American Review.* The timing of this piece, titled "The Future of the Indian Question," could not have been more convenient for the general's purposes. Several years earlier, he had composed an essay on Indian policy in response to a request from the publisher Allen Thorndike Rice, but the latter's death in 1889 had delayed printing. Altered to take into account the Sioux crisis, the essay blasted civilian agents and demanded "judicious, humane, and patriotic treatment" of Indians.[48]

Miles believed that "a positive, strong government" must initiate major changes. He insisted on full funding for treaty obligations, a switch in emphasis from farming to stockraising, tribal self-sufficiency, and military control over the reservations. To the latter end he appointed officers to duty at the Tongue River, Rosebud, Pine Ridge, and Cheyenne River agencies. The general, as he had done so many times before, also began organizing a delegation of chiefs to meet government officials in Washington.[49]

Congress moved swiftly. In January 1891, it appropriated $465,000 to make good treaty promises concerning rations to, the use of ponies by, and education to the Sioux. With public sympathy for the Sioux still running high, Congress then passed measures for the next fiscal year. The resulting Indians Appropriations Act included nearly $1.4 million for the Sioux, plus another $100,000 to compensate "friendly Sioux" for property damages incurred during the outbreak.[50]

Miles's vaunted Indian delegation met a different fate. The Harrison administration, though it had gone along with the congressional appropriation, seemed bent on forgetting the Ghost Dance and Wounded Knee controversies. Proctor sought to wash his hands of the entire episode and refused to authorize a military officer as escort. Hats in hands, the emissaries finally secured a February 7 meeting with Secretary Noble. Flanked by a collection of minor bureaucrats and their gawking families, the white-haired secretary listened to the Indian grievances "with an expression of alternate amusement and concern." The Indians, sympathized one observer, looked "absurdly out of place" in their "cheap, ill-fitting store clothes, white shirts, old-fashioned collars, curious neck-ties." Their deliberate style of presentation frustrated the impatient whites, whose cold efficiency in turn infuriated their guests. The nation's press, briefly intrigued by the plight of the Sioux and the Northern Cheyennes soon moved on to better copy.[51]

The administration's indifference was painfully obvious to Miles. Proctor responded to a rejoinder by the general with a haughty profession of innocence; to President Harrison, the Secretary explained that the "soft and soothing" reply was intended only "to 'turn away wrath' even such as his [Miles's]." Miles's aide, Huggins, concluded, "It is hard to believe that the Secretary read the evidence at all." Huggins attributed the anti-Miles feeling to the influence of Forsyth and the jealousy of Schofield and Proctor. "The President was made to fear Miles as a probable rival," charged Huggins.[52]

Miles's innate paranoias, stirred up in the aftermath of Wounded Knee, were kindled through the summer of 1891. Colonel Sumner protested Miles's criticisms of his failure to catch Big Foot. Others, quick to seize the moment, raised the old questions surrounding the Geronimo campaign. And friends of Sheridan and Forsyth (the former had lived in Chicago for fourteen years while commanding the Division of the Missouri; Forsyth had been on his staff for much of that time) forced Miles to endure several social slights. Petty retribution continued. Miles wanted to set up headquarters at Fort Sheridan so that his son, Sherman, in poor health, might be closer to medical attention. Proctor, however, ruled out such a move, assuring the general that he could find a nice place in a Chicago suburb "suitable for an invalid." And an investigation of Forsyth's alleged mishandling of the Drexel Mission fight went nowhere, bottled up by Schofield and Proctor.[53]

Miles's attempts to institutionalize reform also went down to defeat. Indian agents howled at his determination to replace them with army officers. Protective of his own turf, Commissioner of Indian Affairs Morgan protested Miles's "excess of zeal," and argued that the military must absolve itself of all civil duties, especially Indian affairs. And Miles got no support from within the War Department. "I do not endorse the criticism made by General Miles upon the management of these Indians by the officials of the Department of the Interior," wrote Secretary Proctor.[54]

The final blow came in early July 1891, when the War Department announced long-awaited administrative reorganizations. The old divisions were abolished; though Miles would keep the Department of the Missouri, he was stripped of the Departments of the Platte, Texas, and Dakota, which were given independent status. The new system was widely interpreted as a means by which the administration could vent its displeasure with General Miles, who also lost control of the strategic Standing Rock, Tongue River, Cheyenne River, and Pine Ridge agencies in the process. "I believe that Forsyth business is at the bottom of it all," charged one army wife who supported Miles. Miles, who accepted the reductions with an unusually philosophical spirit, wrote, "My command is cut down to what one paper called a gerrymandered district."[55]

Miles privately suspected that the Mormons had been behind the Ghost Dance and concluded on November 30, "I have never heard of a more brutal, cold-blooded massacre than that at Wounded Knee." His own record in the campaign reflected his long experience in Indian affairs; Robert Utley, the foremost expert on the subject, has credited Miles with "combining force and diplomacy in just the right proportions." Leading reform groups of the time, including the Indian Rights Association, adopted Miles's suggestion that army officers be appointed as Indian agents. The president was given the power to make such selections in 1892; by the second administration of Theodore Roosevelt, the civil service system had been extended to cover most jobs associated with the Indian agencies.[56]

Though Miles could take some satisfaction in these developments, his handling of the political reverberations had not endeared him to his civilian superiors. A perfunctory word of thanks in President Harrison's State of the Union message for 1891 seemed a mere sop. Many saw Miles's interest in Indian reform as simply meddling in business better left to the Interior Department. The War Department reorganization reduced, rather than enlarged, his responsibilities. Forsyth, the target of his bitterest attacks, emerged with his reputation tarnished but his career intact.[57]

"The old theory that the destruction of a vast herd of buffalo had ended Indian wars, is not well-founded," wrote Miles after the campaign. His fear of another Indian outbreak, combined with his genuine concern about the welfare of his former enemies, lead Miles to keep a close watch on Indian affairs, despite the criticisms his controversial positions often encouraged. With so little support from within the army or the government, occasional praise from leading chiefs must have been especially gratifying. "I know that you never say anything false," wrote the Sioux chief Short Bull in 1892, "you keep every one of the promises you make."[58]

12 : COMMANDING GENERAL

After watching a spirited dance troupe number at a Chicago theater shortly after Wounded Knee, Nelson Miles noted wryly that "he preferred the performance to a ghost dance." He was clearly ready for a break, as was Mary, whose bulging scrapbook of her husband's exploits probably did not feature press coverage of the recent funeral of General William Sherman, who had died on February 14, 1891. An impressive procession of dignitaries attended the ceremony; the *New York Times*'s discussion of the antics of an unaccompanied Newfoundland dog before mentioning General and Mrs. Miles might have been an unintended indication of the pair's tarnished image. That March the family, accompanied by Frederic Remington and one of Nelson's aides, Marion Maus, traveled to Mexico where they met

President Porfirio Diaz and reviewed the Mexican army. Sherman became ill in Mexico City, forcing the group to remain ten days longer than expected. During this time Nelson visited the coastal port of Vera Cruz.[1]

The vacation proved an excellent restorative. The general now focused on Chicago's upcoming Columbian Exposition, which would honor the four hundredth anniversary of Columbus's voyage to America. Miles, who always loved military pomp and circumstance, determined that the exposition must have its fair share of such activities. Working closely with the event's planners, he joined the entrepreneurial giants Marshall Field, George Pullman, and Philip Armour in sponsoring an inaugural reception and ball at the Exposition Auditorium. Nearly fifteen thousand regulars and state troops participated in opening-day parades and drills. Later, in 1893, as the World's Fair dragged on, Miles organized a massive encampment of national guardsmen.[2]

Miles continued to dabble in politics. Western newspapers had mentioned him as a presidential candidate as early as 1887, but even Miles recognized that it was still too early to throw his hat in the political ring. But he saw no danger in using his political connections to help his uncle-in-law, John Sherman, who desperately wanted to be president and had requested Miles's support for his bid for the 1888 Republican nomination. Chronically addicted to machinations of this type, Miles counted the journalist George Jones and the railroad magnate Frederick Billings as among those he had swung to Sherman's camp.[3]

But that year the Republicans by-passed party stalwarts like Sherman and James G. Blaine in favor of the dark-horse candidate, Benjamin Harrison, a Civil War veteran who won the electoral college despite having lost a majority of the popular vote. However, Sherman mounted another determined effort four years later, when the higher tariff and extravagant public spending turned many against the incumbent Republican president. Only too happy to oppose Harrison, who had not supported him in the aftermath of Wounded Knee, Miles again joined the Sherman bandwagon. Quiet lobbying among his friends and acquaintances, though, yielded fewer allies than he anticipated. Miles could only hope that President Harrison and Blaine would deadlock the Republican National Convention, at which time exhausted delegates would turn to Sherman. But Harrison received the Republican nomination, only to lose to a resurgent Grover Cleveland in an election notable for the strong showing of the People's Party.[4]

Although the political pendulum had not swung in Miles's direction, various official and semi-official duties at least gave him ample opportunity to enjoy the great outdoors. A trip with his daughter Cecilia and Captain Huggins for a naval review in New York City marked the spring of 1893 and the general organized an expedition to hunt grizzly bears that October. The hunting party—including his son Sherman, Frederic Remington, and officers Hugh Scott, Francis Michler, and Leonard Wood—traveled in grand style in the general's private railroad car, replete with a special dining room and sleeping berths. The following year, John Sherman joined another pilgrimage that combined Miles's official inspection tour of his department with ten days of hunting.[5]

Miles loved travel and saw these trips, like his continued affiliation with various Civil War veterans' associations, as a good way of making powerful friends. In addition to his publicity value to Miles, for example, Remington enjoyed inside connections with the newly appointed Secretary of War, Daniel Lamont. Lamont, however, proved an elusive quarry. Miles hoped he and President Cleveland would accompany him on a tour of the Indian Territory in 1894; hunting birds and investigating the reservations seemed to Miles an irresistible inducement. Failing in this, he invited the secretary to watch military maneuvers in Evanston, Illinois, only to be rebuffed again by Lamont's instructions that Miles devote his "personal attention" to ongoing tests of magazine rifles.[6]

During this brief era of national peace, General Miles was quick to grab any chance to gain a little publicity. A minor wrangle ensued in late 1892, when several newspapers attributed to Miles certain inflammatory statements concerning the British and Canadian naval presence on the Great Lakes. Long an advocate of U.S. expansion to the north, he had often lamented the U.S.'s failure to occupy more Canadian territory. But Miles, although quite willing to berate Canada, had no intention of disturbing the unusual harmony he enjoyed with his superiors, and denied having made any derogatory statements. Government officials accepted this explanation.[7]

Miles also joined a parade of fellow Civil War veterans in seeking out new recognition. Twenty-five Medals of Honor were awarded in 1890 for Civil War valor; another forty-one soldiers secured the tribute the following year. In June 1892, the industrialist Albert Pope, a long-time friend of Miles's, helped initiate a campaign on Miles's behalf with a strong letter of praise. Darious Crouch, one of Miles's former superiors, chipped in with an equally effusive recommendation. Along with sixty-five other applicants that year, the War Department awarded Nelson Miles the Medal of Honor. His own reputation thus protected, the general sponsored the causes of several junior officers who had performed with gallantry during the Indian wars. With his help, men like Marion Maus, Myles Moylan, Edward S. Godfrey, and George W. Baird received their medals in 1894; Frank Baldwin was awarded two medals (one for Civil War service at Peach Tree Creek, Georgia, and the other for his role in rescuing the German girls). As was the case for the Civil War veterans, however, the sheer number of citations for Indian service somewhat tainted the meaning of the honor.[8]

Throughout the 1890s a few well-timed efforts by Miles on behalf of a bill to recreate a lieutenant general's position seemed in order. Miles knew that Schofield's acquisition of a third star would establish a useful precedent, but he wanted the bill to contain a special type of language that neither the House nor the Senate seemed inclined to accept. The proposal to appoint "only those who commanded armies during the [Civil] war . . . is unjust and class legislation," he protested to Schofield. Miles preferred a measure that would appoint as lieutenant general the army's senior major general. Miles, who had not commanded an army during the Civil War and stood to be the ranking officer after Schofield's retirement, would be the obvious benefactor of such legislation. But a fickle Congress delayed Schofield's promotion, and Miles's continued aspersions against the deceased George Crook merely antagonized uncommitted politicians.[9]

Major civil disorders in Chicago briefly tore Miles's attention from the lieutenant general's bill. South of the city proper, George Pullman had reduced the pay of his workers in his effort to overcome the depression of 1893. In May 1894 the Pullman workers went on strike, an action supported by Eugene V. Debs and the fledgling American Railway Union. In retaliation the management-dominated General Managers' Association began dismissing workers sympathetic to the strike, thus paralyzing rail traffic in and out of Chicago.

Under the pretext of protecting the mails, the federal government intervened. On July 2, officials in Washington began a frantic search for

Miles, who, unknown to his superiors, had left his department offices near Chicago to go on leave to New York and New England. Belatedly, he reported to the White House for a meeting with President Cleveland, Attorney General Richard Olney, Secretary of War Lamont, Secretary of State Walter Q. Gresham, and commanding general Schofield the following day. Seeking to crush the union and humble Debs, Olney persuaded the president, over the objections of Miles and Governor John Altgeld of Illinois, to use regular soldiers. The general was dispatched to Chicago to reopen the rail lines.[10]

Back in Chicago by noon of the fourth, Miles soon forgot his earlier hesitation, for the large number of foreign-born strikers rankled his nativist prejudices. "I have directed all commanding officers not to allow crowds or mobs to congregate about the commands in a menacing or threatening manner and to keep out pickets and guards and after due warning if the mobs approach the commands in a threatening manner, they must be dispersed even if fire arms have to be used," read his first breathless report back to Washington. Additional reinforcements were needed. On the fifth, he saw the situation as having deteriorated further. U.S. troops, federal and company marshals, city policemen, and strikebreakers, each responsible to a separate authority, battled the booing, hissing working-class mobs. "Shall I give the order for troops to fire on mob obstructing trains?" Miles asked his superiors.[11]

Shaken, the general tallied forty-one rail cars overturned or destroyed, thirty-four cars and locomotives wrecked, five buildings burned, forty-four trains stoned or fired on, and twenty men killed or injured. A mob was reportedly moving into the city center, destroying railroad cars and property in its wake. "The riot will soon embrace all the criminals of the city and vicinity," concluded Miles on the sixth. "Unless very positive measures are taken, the riot will be beyond the control of my small force."[12]

Although detachments could push away the surly crowds from any single point, the general had too few regulars to guard every rail line. Clearly under the influence of the General Managers' Association, he set aside a special fund to hire spies to infiltrate union meetings. His accounts, like those of most journalists, took on an ominous tone: "The agitators are very ugly and say they may have to have civil war," read one wire of July 7; "Rioters or anarchists have 6000 Winchester rifles and bushels of dynamite bombs," he reported three days later, even as regulars streamed in from forts Riley and Robinson to crush the strike. Instead of keeping to the instructions given him—to reopen the rail lines—Miles allowed himself to be drawn into the complex business of attempting to restore order in the city as a whole.[13]

Olney, Schofield, and Cleveland refused to give Miles authorization to open fire. At Schofield's behest, the regulars began to concentrate on opening interstate rail traffic. A full company escorted trains departing from each of the city's six main depots. Meanwhile, the militia and police focused their efforts on restoring order. Quiet had returned by the twelfth, but Miles rejected Lamont's suggestion two days later that federal troops be withdrawn. "Many new employes have . . . been employed," he wrote. "The idle strikers threaten revenge and violence." Lamont responded on the sixteenth, "We don't want to jeopardize the good opinions we have won by outstaying our welcome."[14]

Supported by railroad managers, Miles still balked at removing the troops and asked permission to send an aide to Washington to explain the situation. Fed up with the general's exaggerated posturing, Schofield refused. Miles renewed his request on the seventeenth, with a warning that the strikers might attack a subtreasury building. The following day, he compiled a nine-page analysis that again argued for the necessity for troops. He did not trust the state militia or the local police and maintained that if an outbreak similar to those that had "occurred in other cities, particularly in Paris in 1790 and 1791, there would be great danger of the armed forces of the United States coming in conflict with those of the city and state." With over half a million "foreigners" living in abject poverty, argued Miles, Chicago contained "more anarchists and socialists than any city on earth."[15]

Miles went on to say that "entirely reliable" sources had told him that the mob leaders would remain quiet only while federal troops remained. Once the regulars left, strikers and lawbreakers would again launch "a reign of terror." "Fiendish plots to blow up bridges, buildings, and railroad property were about," he warned. "The rebellious and communistic element has been very intense and hostile. The anarchists have been very active in plotting methods for destruction, plunder and terror."[16]

Miles's latest communication forfeited any remaining credibility he had with Schofield. The commanding general concluded that he had attempted to shirk his duty by leaving Chicago in the opening days of the strike and by hiding many subsequent reports behind the guise of confidentiality. Indeed, Miles had displayed none of the talents that had marked his leadership against the Confederates and the Indians. An essay for the *North American Review* made his prejudices abundantly clear. Miles labeled Eugene V. Debs a "dictator" and unequivocally backed the interests of corporate America. "Men must take sides either for anarchy, secret conclaves, unwritten law, mob violence, and universal chaos under the red or white flag of socialism on the one hand," the general argued, "or on the side of established government, the supremacy of the law, the maintenance of good order, universal peace, absolute security of life and property, the rights of personal liberty, all under the shadow and folds of 'Old Glory,' on the other." His bigotry against immigrants and his admiration for big business colored his judgment and, if his requests to open fire had been honored, might have led to a massacre in the streets of Chicago.[17]

Despite Miles's threats and fears, further bloodshed was largely avoided. But he was by no means alone in voicing such concerns. The myriad new immigrants from Eastern Europe frightened many conservatives, as did the socialism advocated by men like Eugene Debs. Any attempt to chastise the general for his words or deeds during the Chicago strikes would have antagonized the most powerful elements of American society. Miles, therefore, suffered no immediate professional ramifications from the Pullman strike—other than further straining his relationship with Schofield.

In November 1894, on Oliver O. Howard's retirement, Miles assumed command of the Department of the East, comprising most of the Atlantic seaboard. Thrilled at the prospect of being at Governors Island, strategically situated between Long Island and Manhattan, he and Mary decorated their new home with relics of the general's career: battle flags, with the old Second Corps standard displayed in a prominent place; a stuffed buffalo head; a quiver and arrows; and the war bonnet of Iron Star, pierced by the bullet that killed its original owner in the Lame Deer fight.[18]

The ceremonial tasks and personal inspection tours that accompanied the new position delighted Miles. He retained his full military bearing, even at age fifty-six. Graying hair and mustache now topped his solid two-hundred-pound frame, which was highlighted by his blue-gray eyes and jutting chin. Reviews of New York City parades excited his own martial ardor as well as that of adoring crowds, who thrilled to see a man of such stature. Receptions in his honor at the local chapters of the Grand Army of the Republic and the United Service Club, a professional officers' organization, delighted his immense ego. Speeches and magazine articles also kept him in the spotlight; the allure of politics remained keen, a viable option, perhaps, for a career after the army.[19]

Nelson maintained his busy social schedule in New York. Charles Ayer Whipple painted a life-sized portrait of him in full-dress uniform, his arms folded defiantly. "Lovely young women in fashionable gowns" formed the receiving line at the catered unveiling ceremonies at Whipple's studio. Dinners and parties with men like Frederic Remington and Theodore Roosevelt, where all could regale one another with boastful tales of hunting and Indians, also accentuated his stay in New York. Neither the glamor of high society nor an extensive tour of eastern seaboard defenses in March 1895 could prevent Miles from expanding his list of outdoor activities. Sailing and the new-fangled sports of bicycling and football seemed ideal tonics to the bureaucratic frustrations of the peacetime army. Horseback riding remained a favorite pastime of his. And to his father's great glee, even Sherman, a sickly child, grew in strength as he matured.[20]

Miles also completed his personal reminiscences during this time. Civil War veterans had seized on the public's thirst for tales of the conflict, and publishers turned the practice of writing memoirs into a veritable cottage industry. For Miles, the long-delayed project gained momentum during the late spring and summer of 1895, as a legion of friends, acquaintances, and assistants collected materials. His former staff member Marion P. Maus gathered official reports, checked out books on Indians from the Interior Department library and assisted in the writing. From the scout Ben Clark, Miles requested information on Indian history, tradition, and culture; in return, he saw to it that Clark's government salary was increased from sixty-eight to seventy-five dollars per month. Henry T. Allen, Miles's aide who explored Alaska, secured photographs from the Smithsonian Institution and copies of official military reports. The railroad president and retired General Grenville M. Dodge chipped in with his recollections of post–Civil War Indian campaigns. Miles's personal secretary, Noble E. Dawson, assisted in writing the preface.[21]

Miles had secured a publisher by August 1895: the Werner Company of Chicago. Seeking additional fame and fortune, however, proved more difficult, as his efforts to publish extracts in *Harper's Weekly* and the *Army and Navy Journal* did not reach fruition. But such setbacks seemed minor as he scrambled to collect a few final photographs and illustrations. Clark, with whom Miles had apparently contracted to write sections of the book, failed to complete this work on time but did send in several last-minute photographs of Indians. Fortunately, Frederic Remington came through with fifteen black-and-white paintings that added markedly to the book's value.[22]

Miles's handiwork, *Personal Recollections and Observations of General Nelson A. Miles, Embracing a Brief View of the Civil War; or, From New England to the Golden Gate, and the Story of His Indian Campaigns, with Comments on the Exploration, Development and Progress of Our Great Western Empire*, appeared the following year. A rambling hodgepodge of anthropology, ethnology, history, personal reminiscences, travel accounts, and extracts from official reports, the book was written with an eye toward advancing the author's political future. He called slavery "a blot upon our history," but wrote that it should have been ended by appropriating "a sufficient sum to have paid liberally for every slave on the American continent." In case he was mistakenly identified as espousing full equality for blacks, the book contained enough Sambo-like characters and mocking references to black dialect to satisfy the most avid racist. It avoided remarks that former Confederates might have found offensive, omitted the author's role in the imprisonment of Jefferson Davis, and skipped Reconstruction. Presenting a sympathetic though paternalistic view of Indians, the work sought to portray Miles as a wise, self-effacing individual whose only wish was to serve his country.[23]

The volume did contain one potential bombshell. Long known for his advocacy of George Custer, Miles insisted he possessed an anonymous affidavit that purported to recount the last conversation between Custer and Alfred H. Terry before the Battle of the Little Bighorn. According to this account, Terry had on the evening of June 21 or the morning of June 22 instructed Custer: "Use your own judgment and do what you think best if you strike the trail."[24]

If Miles's claim were true, it would do much to clear Custer of charges that he had exceeded his instructions in taking the initiative along the Little Bighorn. Miles later revealed that the affiant had been Mary Adams, a devoted servant to the Custers. Because it was long believed that Mary had not accompanied the expedition, the testimony was for many years disputed. Mary is now thought to have been present on the specified day, making the affidavit seem much more reliable than Miles's contemporaries generally believed. Although Miles, long an advocate of the fallen Custer, hardly seems an unbiased source, the tenor of Terry's purported instructions is well in line with general army practice throughout the Indian campaigns. As a relative newcomer to the Indian wars, Terry surely placed great faith in the abilities of his more experienced subordinate.[25]

Whatever the veracity of the Adams affidavit, *Personal Recollections and Observations* failed to sell well. Much of the failure was attributable to the unwieldy organization and sheer length of the massive tome. But the Werner Company shared part of the blame. Having recently been capitalized at an impressive $3.5 million, the publishing house also boasted an experienced manager, Alexander Belford. But it did little advertising, and its decision to print, under the banner of the American News Company, several of the original Remington sketches under the title of "Remington's Frontier Sketches," suggests that the Werner Company was hoping to squeeze out a few more dollars. Miles and Remington secured an injunction for copyright infringement, and the fact that a London publishing house filed a similar claim against Werner suggests a pattern of abuse. The company declared bankruptcy in 1898.[26]

Although the literary world had not been as kind as Miles hoped, his professional advancement awaited; General Schofield, who had finally received the lieutenant general's three stars, neared retirement. Though Miles was known as a " 'prominent' Republican," President Cleveland, a Democrat, could hardly refuse him the chance to be commanding general. Friendly editorials in the *New York Times*, which had championed Miles's career for years, guarded his reputation against allegations by the *St. Louis Republican* that attributed his success to his marriage into the Sherman family. Only a minor rebuke from Secretary Lamont—that Miles had been indiscreet in discussing his appointment with the press—marred the actual appointment. The official announcement came on October 2, 1895. "By direction of the President," read General Order Number 53, "Major General Nelson A. Miles is assigned to the command of the Army of the United States."[27]

The new job promised untold opportunity. Mary, who was sympathetic to the burgeoning women's rights movement, became a popular Washington society figure, an avid charity worker, and an active supporter of animal rights, despite having been weakened by a heart attack in 1895. For temporary living quarters, she selected a modest brick house on the corner of Twentieth and G Streets, northwest of the capitol. When plans by the National Society of New England Women to raise one hundred thousand dollars to purchase a house for Miles fell through, the family moved in 1897 to a massive four-thousand-square-foot home on 1723 Rhode Island Avenue. Two years later they bought an even more prestigious brick residence at 1736 N Street NW, one-and-a-half blocks west of Scott Circle. Sherman was enrolled in the Friends School and Cecilia adapted to the glamour of Washington life, attending a variety of social events with her parents, the Shermans, and a bevy of young gentlemen callers. Whenever a formal date could not be arranged, the general's handsome aide, John J. Pershing, was pressed into service.[28]

Nelson thrived on the excitement of the capital. He and Mary were noted for their "brilliant entertainments." The Army and Navy Assembly, a social club for commissioned personnel of all service branches, elected him president. His second-floor office in the sprawling State-War-Navy Building next to the White House was "the coolest place in Washington," boasted Miles to his sister-in-law Lizzie Cameron. Miles made a flurry of recommendations on behalf of friends and old army comrades; he received an honorary degree from Harvard, and invitations to the White House were among the perquisites of office. Of course, "slight changes" in his uniform were essential for such occasions. The *Army and Navy Register* detailed these alterations:

General Miles . . . added gold embroidery to the sleeves and collar of the full-dress coat. The design is a delicate tracery of oak leaves in gold. The familiar epaulets have been abandoned in favor of the flat Russian shoulder knot, without fringe, bearing the coat of arms of the United States and the two stars indicative of the rank of major general. To this is added a belt of Russian leather piped with gold bullion and embroidered in oak leaves to match the design on the collar and cuffs of the coat. The new features of the uniform are completed by a sash of alternate stripes of yellow and gold, which extends from the right shoulder to the left side.[29]

His penchant for annoying his superiors continued unabated. Though rightfully indignant about the bureaucratic red tape involved in securing staff officers of his choice, Miles made frequent complaints that peeved civilian officials, and minor snubs by all concerned poisoned relations with the Cleveland administration. It was galling to Miles that the Cleveland administration stubbornly resisted awarding him a third star. Miles was keenly interested in China and wanted to take charge of arrangements for the 1896 visit of Viceroy Li Huang Chang to the United States. That honor, however, was bestowed on "an officer of lesser rank," General Thomas Ruger.[30]

Miles continued to pay close attention to the Indians. In 1895 he had warned: "Only a few years have elapsed since the country was threatened by the most serious hostile conspiracy ever known in its history." He used his position to champion a more active role for the army in Indian affairs. But he believed several potential problems remained. The non-Apache Indians at Fort Apache deserved a separate agency and "liberal allowances." He asked that the "Mexican" Kickapoos, in the Indian Territory, be allowed to keep their reservation free of white intrusion. And Miles again pressed, unsuccessfully, for the return of Chief Joseph and his followers to their old Lapwai Reservation. There were still minor outbreaks in Arizona and Minnesota; they, along with restlessness on the Kiowa-Comanche Reservation in Indian Territory, continued to threaten western peace.[31]

The army's increased involvement in Alaska mirrored his long interest in the region. The discovery of gold along the Yukon River had sparked a frantic scramble to the fields and rekindled public interest. Thousands ventured north, often neglecting to prepare themselves for the frigid wilderness conditions. In an attempt to allay the suffering, Congress approved, with Miles's full support, two hundred thousand dollars in relief appropriations. The commanding general applauded the white migration to Alaska, but predicted that it would prompt resistance among the native peoples. "Such has been the history of nearly all the tribes in other Territories," he warned. Though such a challenge never materialized, army exploring teams ventured into the region in 1898 and again in 1899, and a separate military Department of Alaska was created the following year.[32]

A trip to Europe was also in the offing for Miles. Unofficially, it would fulfill his lifelong dream to see England and the Continent. Such a tour also promised professional dividends, for the commanding general of the United States Army obviously needed to review military developments abroad. In 1897 the war between Greece and Turkey and regular summer maneuvers of the major European powers provided the perfect opportunity. So diplomats abroad scrambled to arrange inspection tours with the armies of Greece, Turkey, Italy, Austria-Hungary, England, Germany, Russia, and France.[33]

Miles's entourage included his wife, his aide Marion Maus, and his personal secretary Noble Dawson. In early May they booked passage from New York City aboard the American Line steamship, *St. Paul*, then rode the Orient Express from England to Constantinople, where they debarked on May 19, 1897. Miles reviewed the Turkish army, which left a favorable impression, and the Greek military forces, which seemed by comparison to the Turks demoralized and backward. "I came away from the country feeling that the glory of Greece had departed, that she is living to-day on the past," he wrote.[34]

After whirlwind trips through Italy and Austria-Hungary, Miles headed for England, where he represented the army at Queen Victoria's Diamond Jubilee Celebration. The pomp and circumstance surrounding the royal family and the endless military processions left the general, always young at heart on such occasions, breathless with excitement and more than willing to spend government money in a regal fashion. Russia was next; here he got a good taste of the country's glittering aristocracy and stoically determined soldiers. "The Russian army is, I think, capable of greater endurance in the field than any other in Europe," Miles concluded perceptively.[35]

Germany and France served as the final stops for the group, although poor health forced Mary to remain behind at Carlsbad in Germany. Kaiser Wilhelm's interest in military affairs, the great Krupp manufacturing works at Essen, and the efficiency of the German army convinced Miles of that young nation's awesome strength. At St. Quentin, France, he observed French army maneuvers and emerged from that country a Francophile. The American people, believed Miles, must always support the French, who "have maintained in the heart of Europe a liberal government similar to our own, against the prejudices of their surrounding neighbors."[36]

Miles quickly published a book concerning his travels, *Military Europe: A Narrative of Personal Observation and Personal Experience*, along with an analysis, "The Political Situation in Europe and the East" for the *Forum*. Although neither created the sensation the general hoped, he returned to the United States full of continental culture and smugly confident that he could handle whatever challenges the future might bring. But Henry Allen, a former aide to Miles and now the military attaché to Germany, pointed out that the trip had not fully compensated for Miles's inadequate education and egotistic nature: "I am always astonished at the lack of knowledge of Genl. M," wrote Allen on August 10, 1897. "It is a painful fact that notwithstanding his stay in Europe, he did not know the names of the reigning houses of Germany and Austria. He reads a minimum and his opinions are not at all well founded, although he has a natural intelligence of a high order. This absence of general knowledge, his great vanity, and the unfortunate selection of an aide [Marion P. Maus] are sufficient to cause friction wherever he goes."[37]

Indeed, his narrow background limited Miles's vision of military reform. In December 1897, to improve morale he ordered post commanders to encourage their garrisons to prune their shrubbery, plant vines and trees, and protect "native singing birds." He insisted that promotion among general officers be made according to seniority. Reducing the influence of Washington-based staff officers, argued Miles, would resolve most if not all of the army's problems. He believed the role of the adjutant general to be particularly inflated. He also introduced a system of "*practical* instruction" similar to the one that he had employed in Arizona during the late 1880s and he stressed the importance of physical training. Like many of his predecessors, he sought to concentrate several cavalry regiments so as to improve tactical instruction and to serve as a ready reserve should another Indian war erupt. Modernized artillery and better information-collecting agencies were also in order.[38]

An army of more than twenty-five thousand was also necessary, argued Miles. Infantry regiments should each be allotted two additional companies, thus allowing each regiment to be organized into three four-company battalions. "If the shell of twenty-five thousand is ever broken the army may in time grow as the nation grows," believed Miles. It seemed only natural to link the size of the army with that of the general population. He thus submitted in January 1897 a bill that set the minimum number of troops at one to every two thousand persons; in case of emergency, this proposal would have allowed the president to increase that proportion to one per thousand.[39]

Long fascinated by technological advances, Miles foresaw the decline of the cavalry. In his opinion, automobiles held the key to increasing mobility, but until such machines became readily available, the bicycle seemed an ideal stopgap measure. While still in the Department of the Missouri, he had, over the initial objections of the Adjutant General's Office, detached squads to test bicycles as early as 1892. During Miles's New York tour, the general careening about on his high front-wheeled bicycle alongside his children had become a familiar sight. In his first annual report as commanding general he recommended that an entire regiment be equipped with bicycles and motor wagons. Miles also encouraged regular and National Guard units to take part in various long-distance tours and races. That Albert Pope, who had sponsored the effort to secure the general's Medal of Honor, was a prominent bicycle manufacturer only added to the potential for Miles's professional and personal gain.[40]

Miles had no delusions about soldiers pedaling into combat. But the bicycle showed promise as a vehicle for couriers, and with certain modifications, such as punctureless tires and a capability to fold up, they might extend a heretofore unknown mobility to infantrymen. Miles's trip to Europe, where armies used such equipment extensively, had confirmed this interest. "The value of the wheel to an army is beginning to be recognized everywhere," he concluded in 1897. "Whoever first places 25,000 or 50,000 men on bicycles in the next war will have a decided advantage over his opponent."[41]

But Congressional parsimony rendered any steps toward modernization faltering at best. Even if the army had reached a consensus on the importance of mobility and the limited reforms proposed by Miles, a few thousand bicyclists could scarcely have competed in the public's imagination with the navy's gleaming modern warships. Too, the army had no theorist to compete with Alfred Thayer Mahan, whose advocacy of a powerful modern navy promised lucrative economic benefits and world power for the United States.

The army got little help from the White House. In 1896, William McKinley had won a smashing victory over the Democratic-Populist coalition headed by the silver-tongued William Jennings Bryan. McKinley, a Civil War veteran interested in expanding American overseas markets rather than the army, implicitly accepted the navy's ascendance by naming John Long, the able, popular, and respected Republican from Massachusetts, as secretary of the navy. With little thought about his qualifications for dealing with a future war, the president selected Russell A. Alger of Michigan to head the War Department. But McKinley and the rest of the nation would soon discover that Alger was a man whose paper credentials and former Civil War experience as a colonel of cavalry hid his indolence and incapacity to handle great responsibility. McKinley's choice of John Sherman as secretary of state promised great personal benefits to Miles; unfortunately for Miles, however, the aging Sherman's diminishing faculties quickly reduced his cabinet-level influence.[42]

The army thus lay unprepared for a major power conflict. It had practically ignored discussions of grand strategy; although a Military Information Division had been formed in 1889 in part to assess the geography, economy, and military forces of potential rivals, budgetary constraints and general complacency had limited its effectiveness. In early 1898 the old army stood as it had for twenty years—some 25,000 men organized into five artillery, ten cavalry, and twenty-five infantry regiments. Official figures set the organized state militias at about 114,000 men, but the latter institutions were poorly equipped and indifferently trained.

Deteriorating relations with Spain soon highlighted this lack of readiness. Long dissatisfied with their position within the crumbling Spanish empire, Cuban insurgents had renewed their struggle for independence in 1895. Aroused by strategic, economic, and humanitarian interests, McKinley's escalating diplomatic pressures against Spain had not secured satisfactory results. In February 1898, two events pushed the United States closer to war. On the ninth, the *New York Journal* published a critical letter about McKinley, written by the Spanish minister to the United States, Enrique Dupuy de Lome. Six days later, the battleship *Maine*, sent to Cuba as a show of U.S. force, blew up in Havana harbor. Widely believed at the time to be the work of Spanish agents, the disaster intensified the American public's demands for Spain's withdrawal from Cuba.[43]

With war clouds on the horizon, Congress authorized a special $50 million for military appropriations in early March 1898. Of that money, 60 percent was earmarked for the navy; not wishing to upset his continuing negotiations with Spain, McKinley devoted the army's share to defensive measures. Over 80 percent of the army's $19 million thus went to coastal defense, with the remainder dispersed among the Medical, Quartermaster, and Signal bureaus.[44]

Long troubled by Congress's failure to implement the old Endicott Board's recommendations, General Miles happily concurred with the decision to strengthen national defenses. Fewer than 150 of the 2,362 guns and mortars originally called for were in place. In his 1895 inspection tour of the eastern seaboard, he had complained that the approaches to most Atlantic and Gulf ports were "practically unguarded." In a whirlwind lobbying campaign to drum up more money for coastal defenses, Miles had appeared before three congressional committees in 1896 and 1897 and written an article for the *Forum* in January 1898. His March warning to Secretary Alger that it was "quite probable" that small Spanish raiders would strike U.S. ports if war broke out was thus consistent with Miles's previous policy statements.[45]

In addition to the defensive build-up, War Department officials pressed to increase the regular army. Even assuming, as did virtually all planners that spring, that the army would play a supporting role to the navy, current land forces could not possibly carry out national policy should war break out. Working closely with Representative John A. T. Hull, the chairman of the House Committee on Military Affairs, Adjutant General Henry C. Corbin and Secretary Alger drew up a plan to increase the regular army to 104,000. Champions of the volunteer tradition and the state militias, however, saw the Hull bill as a threat to their respective institutions, which so large a standing force would render superfluous. Combining their political might with that of Southern Democrats still resentful about the army's role in Reconstruction and Populists angry over the use of the military in civil disorders, opponents of an expanded regular establishment sent the Hull proposal back to committee by a large margin.[46]

On April 1, Miles wrote, "No one can tell at this moment whether we will have war or peace, or in case of war whether it will be confined to Spain alone." Pressured from critics on both sides, President McKinley intensified the diplomatic pressure as the army struggled to prepare a semblance of a workable strategy. On the ninth, Miles and his staff drew up plans for an expeditionary column under Major General John R. Brooke to gather at Chickamauga Battlefield Park, Georgia. With the manpower at his disposal still undecided, Miles recommended that fifty thousand volunteers join all available regulars in comprising the strike force. Miles slated another forty thousand volunteers to provide coastal defense and a reserve. As the nation mobilized, Generals William R. Shafter, John J. Coppinger, and James F. Wade would oversee preparations for military camps at New Orleans, Mobile, and Tampa, respectively.[47]

But if war came, how would the expanded army help defeat Spain? Cuba remained the cornerstone of Spain's Caribbean empire. Lieutenant Colonel Arthur L. Wagner, a staff assistant and the army representative on the two-man army-navy board, identified the crucial issues in an April 11 memo. Delaying an assault on Cuba invited foreign intervention, left the long American coastline vulnerable to Spanish attack, and might be interpreted as a sign of weakness. A blockade would cost millions of dollars and might starve civilians rather than the Spanish soldiers. Finally, argued Wagner, the British had proved that an invasion was possible when they captured Havana in the summer during the early 1800s; American troops could surely match the exploits of the British.[48]

Having acknowledged these points, Wagner then picked apart the case of an immediate offensive against Cuba. He predicted that organizational problems, similar to the Union's clumsy efforts at First Bull Run in 1861, would plague any hastily expanded army. A direct assault against a strong foe would endanger thousands of American lives. A summer offensive in the tropics invited the ravages of yellow fever; who could ever forget the disastrous French attempt to retake Haiti in the early 1800s, when tens of thousands of Napoleonic veterans died of yellow fever.[49]

Miles may or may not have instructed Wagner to draw these conclusions. From the outset, however, he opposed a premature invasion of Cuba. Intelligence reports set Spain's forces there at eighty thousand men and 183 guns, truly a formidable threat to the inexperienced American recruits. Miles worried that the navy might not be able to protect supply lines back to the U.S. Disease posed an even greater danger: "I think it would be injudicious to put an army on that Island at this season of the year," concluded Miles in an April 18 letter to Secretary Alger. Miles advised a safer course: "By mobilizing our force and putting it in healthful camps, *and using such force as might be necessary to harrass the enemy and doing them the greatest injury with the least possible loss to ourselves*, if our Navy is superior to theirs, in my judgment, we can complete the surrender of the Army on the Island of Cuba with very little loss of life, and possibly avoid the spread of yellow fever over our own country."[50]

Rear Admiral William T. Sampson, commander of a powerful armored squadron assembling at Key West, called for a more aggressive strategy. Like most observers, Sampson deemed Havana the key to controlling Cuba. He believed that his cruisers and battleships could pierce the port's harbor defenses and force the town to surrender under the threat of their eight-, twelve-, and thirteen-inch guns. But the Navy Department overruled this ambitious scheme—the precious men-of-war must not be risked against land-based batteries and underwater mines. And even if the bombardment worked, the army could not exploit a quick landing. The navy opted instead for a close blockade against Cuba and an attack against Spain's Pacific fleet, harbored in the Philippines at Manila.[51]

On the afternoon of April 20, McKinley met with Secretaries Alger and Long, Miles, retired General John Schofield, and two senior naval officers. The president seemed resigned to a patient campaign of harassment and military build-up until autumn. But the army's evident disorganization distressed all those present. As Secretary Long scoffed, "at present it seems as if the army were ready for nothing at all." The naval secretary predicted, "If war actually comes, the country will demand that our soldiers make a landing and do something." Miles, observed one Washington wife that same day, was "accused of being strongest on millinery." Poking fun at his well-documented passion for military fashion and publicity, she teased, " 'The situation is serious enough to warrant General Miles in getting a new uniform' and 'When in doubt, Miles has his photograph taken.' "[52]

13 : THE SPANISH-AMERICAN WAR

The lack of a clear strategic vision had long haunted the United States army. During the Civil War, Abraham Lincoln, Ulysses Grant, and William Sherman, combining shrewd judgment with hard-won personal experience, had finally cobbled together a winning plan during the early months of 1864. Against the Indians of the frontier, the bluecoats had fought bravely, but the U.S. victory was attributable to the nation's overwhelming superiority of men and material, the railroads, and the flood of immigration to the West rather than any effective strategic consensus. Having inherited the old army from his Civil War predecessors Sherman, Phil Sheridan, and John Schofield, Nelson Miles saw little need for military reform. After all, reasoned Miles complacently, the army had never lost a war. Courage, endurance, and close attention to tactics would surely suffice in any future conflict. Besides, the Atlantic and Pacific oceans provided the ultimate protection. Should war break out, the army would have ample time for planning.

The impending conflict of 1898 shattered these time-honored assumptions. The regular army, less than 30,000 strong, was insufficient to force a military solution to the Spanish problem. The administration and the army had initially envisioned an orderly build-up of regulars under the Hull bill, supplemented by a volunteer force of 50,000 to 60,000 men. But on April 21, under heavy pressure from state militias, the National Guard, and proponents of a volunteer army, President McKinley doubled the latter figure to 125,000. Only then did Congress pass an emaciated version of the Hull bill, which included an enlisted component of 61,000 regulars. On the twenty-fifth, the United States declared war on Spain.[1]

The increase in volunteers boded ill for a bureaucracy already stretched well beyond normal capacity. "The governmental machinery was altogether inadequate to immediately meet the emergency," confessed Secretary of War Alger. Raising the troops was easy enough; training, equipping, feeding, clothing, and organizing this many men proved beyond the immediate resources of the creaky War Department's bureau system. Recognizing the potential for disaster, Miles suggested that the recruits remain in their home states for thirty days, during which time they might be given equipment and initial training, while the army selected its main camp sites. He also made numerous recommendations for volunteer commissions, basing his decisions on his wide personal connections and experiences. Four men he suggested be made generals were members of Congress. He also included eleven prospective staff members who had served in the Second Corps, Army of the Potomac, during the Civil War. By coincidence or collusion, the Second Army Corps Association had only that March sponsored a resolution supporting Miles's promotion to lieutenant general.[2]

But incompetence permeated the War Department, and Miles's attempts to delay new recruits in their home states were ignored. Alger's inept performance in cabinet meetings dumbfounded most observers. Engulfed by office-seekers, the chaos at the Adjutant General's headquarters reminded one officer of "the foyer of a cheap Washington hotel." The open personal antipathy between Alger and Miles merely exacerbated traditional rivalries between the Secretary of War and the commanding general. One confidant asserted, "He [Miles] assured me that Alger is crazy." No wonder, then, that one journalist concluded, "The army is utterly unfit."[3]

Enormous logistical and organizational problems accompanied the drive to double the size of the regular army and to raise, equip, and train 125,000 volunteers. The National Guard, from which the bulk of the recruits was to have been drawn, was unprepared for mobilization. Between one-third and one-half of its members refused to enlist or failed their physicals, and the individual states could neither feed nor clothe their men. Bound by tradition and handcuffed by interbureau rivalries, the War Department eventually worked out most of the egregious problems. But the learning process took several months; in the meantime, the army's improvisations impressed no one.[4]

According to design, camps at Chickamauga, San Francisco, San Antonio, and Washington, D.C., would supplement the original expeditionary-force launching points at New Orleans, Tampa, and Mobile. Inadequate sanitation facilities at these sites, however, left the army open to sensational charges by a news-hungry press. Though some exaggeration occurred, the stories usually stemmed from real problems. As one young officer at Chickamauga complained: "The condition of some or rather most of the troops here is enough to make a martyr's flesh to creep and writhe in anguish. There is a sanitary condition existing which would cause a microbe to rub its hands in anticipation of a feast of Moloch."[5]

President McKinley, who had taken a personal interest in the frenetic mobilization effort, recognized the War Department's inadequacies. Aides transformed a White House clerk's second-floor filing office into a war room replete with maps and twenty telegraph wires. Fifteen telephone lines allowed the president heretofore unknown influence and coordination with Congress and his executive departments. McKinley soon determined that Alger was hopelessly overmatched. The president's former association with George Crook had instilled in McKinley certain negative images about Miles, whose pretentious obstructionism only reinforced these biases. In late March, searching for a dependable military advisor, the president invited the sixty-six year old Schofield to Washington.[6]

But Schofield also failed to meet McKinley's needs. The cantankerous old general clashed with the bumbling Alger and seemed unable to comprehend the difficulties of the present war; by his own admission,

Schofield was soon "kept in absolute ignorance" and left the capital in June. And Miles's star sank progressively lower. In McKinley's view, his excuses, inordinate meddling, uncooperative nature, and inability to grasp the political need to initiate some front against Spain outweighed any advantages his long experience might have brought.[7]

Even on purely military affairs Miles often offered poor counsel. His decision to ship to the war front one hundred massive metal shields, each mounted on wheeled carriages, proved a ludicrous failure. Equally dubious was Miles's eleventh-hour attempt to replace the standard infantry arm, the Krag-Jorgensen rifle. On April 18, he insisted that the government order ten thousand Winchester rifles, at a cost of two hundred thousand dollars. Unfortunately, the Winchesters failed to meet government standards. General Miles also suggested the purchase of ten "dynamite guns" for coastal defense. Remembering that Miles himself had nearly been killed when such a cannon exploded during a trial demonstration, Alger attributed the recommendations to Miles's attempts to repay his personal loans by granting favorable weapons contracts to his cronies.[8]

Adjutant General Henry Corbin, on whom McKinley eventually depended for military matters, believed the president broke with Miles after reading the commanding general's cautious note of April 18, in which he advised that the Cuban invasion be delayed. "God willing . . . we shall end the war before the General would have us begin operations," proclaimed McKinley, whose finely tuned political skills accurately gauged American public opinion. "He little understands me, no more does he know the temper of our people. I deplore the war, but it must be short and quick to the finish." After that, insisted Corbin, whom Miles later blamed for interfering in his relationship with the president, McKinley "never sought his [Miles's] advice and never gave it any weight when offered."[9]

But events would not wait for the army to restore its own house. McKinley determined to strike Cuba as quickly as possible; the gradual mobilization envisioned by Miles was swept aside in the wartime excitement. On the twenty-fourth, Alger summoned Miles and Adjutant General Corbin to his home to explain the president's wishes and select a commander for the Cuban invasion. Two surviving accounts of this conversation, each written after the fact, are in sharp conflict. At Alger's later request, Corbin recalled the events in a letter dated November 16, 1900. According to this version, Miles first suggested William R. Shafter, "without any hesitation whatever." Alger was called away to confer with Senators Redfield Proctor and William B. Allison; upon the secretary's return, Miles said that he wanted to lead it. Corbin then held that Alger placed a grateful hand on the commanding general's sturdy shoulder and exclaimed: " 'General, I wish you would.' " The following day, according to Corbin, Miles again changed his mind and deferred to Shafter.[10]

Alger, however, recalled a far different scenario. According to the secretary, Miles first suggested that John J. Coppinger lead the Cuban expedition. Alger nominated James Wade and Miles, after an initial assent, eventually demurred. Then someone alluded to Shafter. Although Alger could not remember exactly which of the three (he, Miles, or Corbin) first mentioned the name, all assented that afternoon. The secretary also insisted that Miles could have taken personal command at any time.[11]

Miles left no accounting of the meeting, but later asserted that he had never been offered the expedition. One of his aides, John Pershing, declared that Miles "would have been the choice of the Army," and attributed the decision to keep him home "to a fear that Miles might become too strong politically after the war." Others speculated that Shafter owed his appointment to the fact that both he and the secretary hailed from Michigan. Regardless of the circumstances, the choice of Shafter engendered great jealousy among general officers.[12]

Shafter's gout, varicose veins, and three-hundred-pound carriage hardly suited him to the rigors of tropical campaigning. Still, he was a Civil War veteran whose self-taught military education and lack of regard for George Crook undoubtedly endeared him to Miles. Indeed, Miles had recommended Shafter for promotion on at least three occasions. On receiving his first star, a grateful Shafter, whose good but unspectacular record against the Indians seemed no threat to Miles's standing as the nation's preeminent living warrior, had thanked Miles profusely. The two had become fairly good friends, Shafter having boarded several of Miles's horses in California during the mid 1890s.[13]

On April 29, Adjutant General Corbin, McKinley's de facto chief military adviser given the inadequacies of Alger, Miles, and Schofield, issued Shafter's marching orders. With an expeditionary force of five thousand men, Shafter was to sail from Tampa to Tunas, on the southern Cuban coast. From there he was to go inland and furnish rebel forces under Máximo Gómez with weapons and supplies. Shafter would then return to Tunas, sail to Cuba's northwest coast, supply other insurrectionists, then return to the United States. "This expedition is in the nature of a reconnaissance in force, to give aid and succor to the insurgents, to render the Spanish forces as much injury as possible, and avoiding serious injury to your own command," explained Corbin.[14]

"No branch of the public service was so well prepared for war as the navy," bragged Admiral Sampson after the war. Though the navy was hardly the invincible juggernaut sometimes portrayed in contemporary literature, it had at least drawn up contingency plans in case of a war against Spain. On receiving McKinley's approval of the navy's strategy, Commodore George Dewey sailed into Manila Bay on May 1 and annihilated the outdated Spanish Pacific fleet. The victory transformed America's wartime goals; McKinley, a strong supporter of the nation's expanding economic interests, now seized the opportunity afforded by the victory at Manila Bay to counter the growing European presence in the Far East.[15]

Unofficial reports of Dewey's victory, along with news that Admiral Pascual de Cervera's Spanish Atlantic squadron had sailed from the Cape Verde Islands, led McKinley to meet with Alger, Long, Miles, and Rear Admiral Montgomery Sicard to discuss policy. To expand the war to the Pacific they agreed to begin organizing a Philippines occupation force, but as this mobilization might take weeks, the army's immediate focus must remain on Cuba. But Cervera's movement forced a change in Shafter's planned raid. Rather than landing at the exposed southern coast, Shafter would alight at Mariel, twenty-five miles west of Havana on the northwest coast. Here the U.S. fleet could maintain the blockade and at the same time shield the transports needed to supply the American troops.[16]

After a cabinet meeting on May 6, naval secretary Long ridiculed the "striking lack of promptness" among his army rivals. He was forced to recant his criticism four days later, when he learned that the army had suddenly set the Mariel landing date at May 11. "We must at least have short notice when and where they [the naval forces] are wanted," bleated Long. McKinley thus postponed the effort for a week, then abandoned the raid altogether when Cervera's fleet slipped away from American patrol boats.[17]

The delay gave Miles, still in the capital, the opportunity to bolster coastal defenses and to press for alternate strategies. His new scheme, elaborated on May 26 and 27, depended on Cervera's actions. If the Spanish squadron had made harbor at Santiago, on Cuba's southern coast, American troops should land at Daiquirí, fifteen miles to the east. The army could then link up with eight thousand rebels under General Calixto García and lay siege to Santiago. The strike force should consist solely of regulars, the volunteers being "neither equipped nor instructed, or even supplied with ammunition to fight a battle." A cavalry raiding party, working in conjunction with other insurgents already in contact with American officers, could further confuse the Spanish on Cuba by landing at Puerto de Nuevitas, on the northeast coast.[18]

If, on the other hand, Cervera's fleet had sailed from Santiago or been destroyed by the U.S. Navy, Miles proposed an indirect approach—the invasion of Puerto Rico (known at the time as Porto Rico). Conditions on the smaller island seemed ideal for Miles's anaconda strategy, which envisioned the slow strangulation of Spanish ground forces in the Caribbean. The twenty-five thousand men slated for this attack could overwhelm the twenty-one thousand Spanish defenders there, scattered as they were across the island. With Puerto Rico's fall, the navy could interdict all relief efforts bound for Cuba. Cooler fall weather would allow a direct strike against Spanish defenses weakened by the blockade.[19]

Alger dismissed any notion of invading Puerto Rico, disagreed with Miles's proposed assault on Cuba, and denounced his general's insubordination. Plans for a cavalry landing at Puerto de Nuevitas, argued the Secretary, failed to take into account the distance between there and Havana. Further, the operation depended on the capture of the strongly fortified Puerto Príncipe (the present city of Camagüey) as a base of supplies, a move Alger dubbed hazardous at best. Miles's refusal to inspect troops at Chickamauga, Tampa, and Mobile completed the break between the commanding general and the secretary of war. "Orders not obeyed," read a cursive memo at the bottom of one Alger directive retained in the secretary's personal files, "Gen. Miles saying he was in the habit of issuing his own orders."[20]

After repeated starts and stops, the War Department wired Shafter instructions on May 31. Cuba, not Puerto Rico, would be the first objective of American ground forces. Shafter was to use his Fifth Corps to take possession of the high ground overlooking Santiago harbor, neutralize the city's garrison, and assist the navy in destroying Cervera's fleet. "When will you sail?" queried Corbin impatiently. Miles, who had visited Tampa to look at matters firsthand, attempted to regain the president's confidence. "Everything is being pushed as rapidly as possible to embark troops," he assured Washington. "Men are working night and day."[21]

Despite Miles's optimism, monumental fiascoes were plaguing operations at Tampa. With initial plans having called for a five-thousand-man expeditionary force, the decision to more than treble this number left the War Department staff unprepared to handle the onslaught. And Shafter had ignored Miles's May 17 directive to find a point where "the government [would] not be subjected to a monopoly of any one railroad." One track fed the entire port complex; army logisticians poured in men and material but failed to link up the troops with their heavy equipment. Mules and men struggled to bring order to the incredible chaos. More than three hundred rail cars—without record of their contents—lined the tracks. Enterprising officers took to breaking open the cars until they stumbled upon the items their men required.[22]

If nerves were strained in Tampa, they were frazzled in Washington. Desperate for a thrust into the Caribbean, McKinley asked Miles on June 4 when the latter could debark for Puerto Rico. Miles promised that he could sail in ten days and again suggested that it might be wise to allow him to take that island while Shafter waited until the fall to strike Cuba. "The President says no," replied Alger; Shafter's expedition retained top priority. Seeking to spark the beefy Shafter, the secretary wired Tampa on June 7: "The President directs you to sail at once with what forces you have ready." Shafter promised to move the following day, only to be ordered to delay pending the investigation of a purported sighting of a Spanish cruiser. With a lack of ferries rendering initial attempts to board the troops impossible, Alger nervously wondered if the men might be moved to a more suitable port. Miles again pressed the need to strike against Puerto Rico. While most of the navy combat fleet chased the phantom Spanish raiders, Miles suggested that the army help protect the convoy by mounting its artillery on transport vessels.[23]

Miles had infused his typical energy into the proceedings at Tampa. "He looks well and active," wrote Colonel John T. Weston of the Subsistence Department. But the imbroglio cast a chaotic shadow over everything. As usual, Miles believed he had friends, connections, and ideas sufficient to render all previous plans obsolete. But the situation at Tampa demanded organization and efficiency rather than new sets

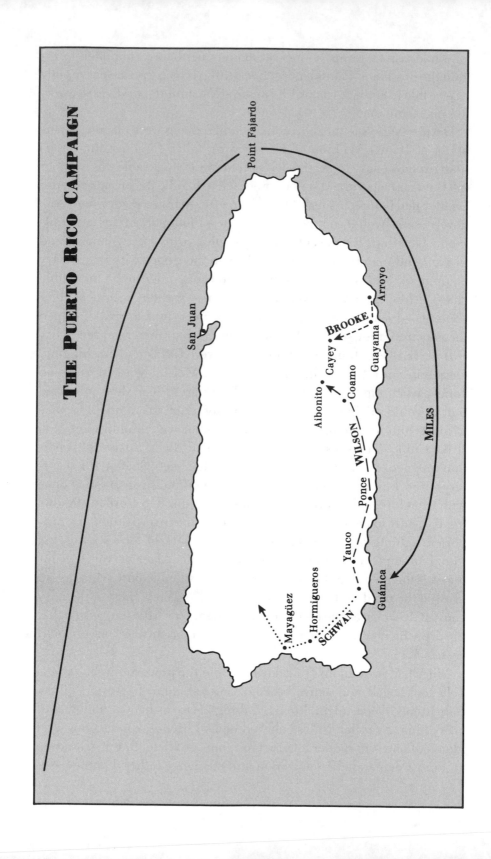

THE PUERTO RICO CAMPAIGN

Point Fajardo

San Juan

Aibonito

Cayey

BROOKE

Coamo

Guayama

Arroyo

WILSON

Ponce

MILES

Yauco

Guánica

Mayagüez

Hormigueros

SCHWAN

of blueprints and contractors. His last-minute attempts to hire private firms to improve the roads and docks and to supply construction materials only added to the confusion.[24]

While their superiors haggled and the navy scrambled to organize a protective convoy for the invasion flotilla, soldiers crammed aboard the transports, dazed by the incompetence they had witnessed. One of those sweltering in the Florida heat was Lieutenant Colonel Theodore Roosevelt, the charismatic former assistant secretary of the navy who had resigned on May 6 to help raise the First Volunteer Cavalry Regiment. Roosevelt's colonel, Leonard Wood, was a favorite of Miles who had assured Roosevelt that the commanding general could, if given full control, "straighten things out." By June 12, however, Roosevelt was skeptical: "I most earnestly wish the experiment could be tried, though personally I cannot help feeling that Miles might have remedied a great deal that has gone wrong if only he had chosen or had known how."[25]

The repeated orders and counterorders had left the regiments with little of their organic equipment or support services. Further, only about seventeen thousand men had been able to crowd aboard the overloaded transports. "The whole thing is beyond me," wrote one journalist. "It is the most awful picnic that ever happened, you wouldn't credit the mistakes that are made." But the time for action was at hand as the navy assembled off Key West. Bombarded by anxious telegrams from Alger, the last of Shafter's transports sailed on June 14.[26]

The fleet dropped anchor off Santiago six days later. Exhausted by their long journey aboard the cramped steamers, the lead echelons of Shafter's expeditionary force splashed ashore at Daiquiri, a few miles east of Santiago Bay, on June 22. Plagued with severe shortages of supplies and transport, Shafter followed a suggestion of Miles's and marched inland to seize the high ground overlooking Santiago. Uncoordinated attacks against fierce opposition left the Americans bloodied but in possession of San Juan Hill and El Caney on July 1. Shafter, shaken by a thousand casualties and a near-debilitating attack of gout, contemplated abandoning the newly won positions until he was overruled by a unanimous vote of his division commanders. The latter decision proved wise, for with food, water, and ammunition already running low in Santiago, the besieged Spanish forces there soon realized that their position was untenable.[27]

As Shafter's force was assembling outside Santiago, Miles scurried north to Washington, where the publication of one of his telegrams criticizing the War Department bureaus had again left him in hot water. His aide, Francis Michler, tried to stop the unfavorable press coverage by launching a stinging attack on one Florida newspaper. Though Representative Hull stood behind Miles and even revived the lieutenant general's bill on his behalf, the incident further soured Miles's already low standing among politicians and government officials. Senator William Lindsay, for example, found him "very vain and fond of adulation." Miles finally received orders on June 26 to assemble five divisions for a second operation against the enemy "in Cuba and Puerto Rico." The force was to set forth "with the least possible delay."[28]

On July 3, Sampson's Atlantic Squadron annihilated Cervera's decrepit fleet as it steamed out of Santiago Harbor. Shafter had in the meantime opened negotiations with General José Toral, commander of the besieged Spanish garrison at Santiago. Shafter advised Washington to accept Toral's offer of July 8, in which he proposed to evacuate the city if his men were allowed to keep their weapons. Worried about Shafter's health, his willingness to fight, and his incessant calls for reinforcements, McKinley dispatched General Miles to assess the military situation on Cuba. Miles had been dispatched strictly as an observer, Corbin assured Shafter, "[He is] not to in any manner supersede you as commander of forces in the field near Santiago as long as you are able for duty."[29]

Shafter, who well knew Miles's proclivity for satisfying his own purposes, seemed to recover his health as the perilousness of the Spanish position became more obvious. He resented the fact that Miles, who had done none of the fighting, was now poised to grab some of the glory from a quick Spanish capitulation. Shafter further insisted that his own staff seemed rife with informants and he later accused Joseph C. Breckinridge, the inspector general, and Arthur Wagner of having accompanied the Cuban foray "for the sole purpose of taking notes for General Miles."[30]

Miles was relieved to be back in the field, far from the cutthroat bureaucracy of Washington and the overcrowded piers of Tampa. Self-assured and superior, he did nothing to calm Shafter's fears. In Miles's view, he was in command. As Grant had held authority over Meade and the Army of the Potomac in 1864–65, Miles, as commanding general, automatically supplanted all others. His message to Shafter, dated July 18, outlined these views: "Your command is a part of the United States Army which I have the honor to command." Miles went on to assert that Secretary Alger had left the decision to take command of the army on Cuba to his discretion.[31]

As the two generals staked out their positions, negotiations with the Spanish progressed. A War Department concession—safe conduct to Spain for those troops who surrendered—sparked new hopes for a peaceful settlement. Miles and Shafter advised that a truce be concluded along these lines. A continued siege, reasoned Miles, would last a minimum of two months; any such delay would render thousands of refugees destitute. More important, over one hundred American soldiers had already contracted yellow fever, a number predicted to grow dramatically within the next few days. Miles and Shafter thus met with Toral on July 13. With Spain still defiant, despite the impending surrender at Santiago, Miles looked ahead to additional conquests. Six days earlier, the industrialist Andrew Carnegie had cabled Miles his view that Santiago was "worthless." The capture of Puerto Rico, on the other hand, "would tell heavily [in] Spain and Europe." The advice of this "patriotic philanthropist" renewed Miles's determination to take Puerto Rico. The island's fall might drive the final nail into the coffin of the Spanish empire. And a dramatic triumph might convince Congress to recreate the position of lieutenant general.[32]

On the seventeenth, twenty thousand Spanish troops surrendered to the Fifth Corps. Sampson's fleet had remained in limbo throughout the negotiations. Although Miles had tried to keep the navy informed and had even invited Sampson to send a representative to army headquarters, Shafter refused to allow the navy's delegate to sign the capitulation. Because the army had made no assertions as to its role in the naval victory at Santiago, reasoned Shafter, the navy should stake no claims about its part in the surrender of ground forces. In a scene befitting a slapstick comedy, which characterized deteriorating interservice relations, the army and the navy each sent boarding parties to seize a prize vessel lying in Santiago harbor, the *Alvarado*.[33]

Alger had already ordered Miles to return to the states and assume command of an expeditionary force against Puerto Rico. Officials now scurried to coordinate regiments scattered from Charleston to Mobile with those troops already in Cuba. Transports were still in short supply. Miles, who had the good sense to insist that vessels carrying his troops be properly ventilated and equipped with hammocks, reported that he and twenty-five hundred men aboard ships in Guantánamo Bay were ready to sail on July 17. Hoping ultimately to assemble thirty thousand men for his invasion, Miles, upon the advice of Admiral Sampson, planned to land at Point Fajardo, on the eastern end of Puerto Rico.[34]

Alger deemed the timing premature. Miles stressed the virtues of a quick strike; rather than exposing the troops to yellow fever, better that they sail to Puerto Rico and establish a beachhead as reinforcements were readied. He also requested that the navy, which longed to sail against Spain and whose officers were fuming about Shafter's repeated snubs, be required to cooperate. "The experience of the last few weeks should not be repeated," he warned. Miles asked that Winfield Scott Schley, rather than the resentful Sampson, be designated to lead the naval forces.[35]

McKinley followed with a stern admonition to Long that the navy assist Miles, and on the evening of July 21 the convoy sailed. Miles's force now consisted of thirty-three hundred soldiers on nine transports, escorted by the battleship *Massachusetts* and two smaller craft. But he began to question the landing at Point Fajardo. Aware that his cables had passed over foreign lines, he feared that the Spanish would discern his intentions and fortify the area. Further, the lighters and tugs needed to disembark the troops had not yet rendezvoused with the fleet.[36]

Miles shared his fears with Captain Francis J. Higginson, commanding the naval convoy, on July 22. "As it is always advisable not to do what your enemy expects you to do," he explained, "I think it advisable, after going around the northeast corner of Porto Rico, to go immediately to Guanica and land this force." The alternate plan, reasoned the general, offered many advantages. The fleet could make a demonstration at Point Fajardo until dusk, then sail under cover of darkness to Guánica, where deeper water and harbor facilities would support a landing. After the surprise strike at Guánica, the troops could occupy Ponce; at fifty thousand inhabitants it was the largest city on Puerto Rico and the site of another fine harbor.[37]

On the twenty-third, Captain Higginson invited Miles to confer aboard the battleship *Massachusetts*. The skeptical captain pointed out that the Guánica harbor was too shallow for three of the major escorts, a problem they would not encounter if they attacked Point Fajardo. Better navigational charts and a nearby coal station at St. Thomas lent additional advantages to the original site. Miles departed to a fifteen-gun salute and, indifferent to the problems, signaled his determination to land at Guánica. "All right," replied Higginson, "Guanica it is."[38]

The following day aboard the USS *Yale*, Miles wrote the first of a series of letters to Mrs. E. M. Heintzelman, the mother of Lieutenant Stuart Heintzelman, then a cadet at West Point. The origins and eventual outcome of this relationship are cloudy, but the first note relayed in very personal terms his jubilation about the prospects of landing on Puerto Rico. Smooth seas, clear skies, and the "magnificent steamer" had made it a "remarkable journey." His servant had brought along a spunky English terrier named Jubilee. Delighted at the prospect of outfoxing his enemy, Miles confided: "I presume every one believes we are going to the Cape St. de Juan on the north east corner of Porto Rico and I hope the Spaniards think we are going there but it is to Guanica about fifteen miles from Ponce that we are going."[39]

It seems particularly revealing both of Miles's willingness to disregard regular lines of authority and of his poor relations with Alger that the general would outline his plans as to the landing site in a private letter (which was presumably mailed only after the operation began) rather than in an official message to the War Department. To maintain secrecy, Captain Higginson had been instructed not to relay the change of plan back to the transports carrying the bulk of the expeditionary force, which had not yet joined the lead convoy. Instead, one of the escorts would remain at Fajardo and guide the reinforcements to Guánica.[40]

Despite the ad hoc arrangements, the landing proceeded without a hitch. They entered the harbor without opposition about daylight on the twenty-fifth, and the navy's brief bombardment scattered the few surprised Spanish soldiers in the area. Troops landed and after a brief skirmish seized the port and ten small lighters. Miles expanded the beachhead the following day. Seven companies of volunteer infantry under Brigadier General George A. Garretson routed a Spanish force near Yauco, giving the Americans control of the key railroad between Guánica and Ponce. Through it all, Miles kept his own counsel. News trickling in from Puerto Rico bewildered Washington officials. "Conflicting reports here as to your place of landing," wired Alger on the twenty-sixth, who "doubted" the truth of an Associated Press dispatch concerning the strike against Guánica. "Why did you change?"[41]

"Circumstances were such that I deemed it advisable," went Miles's cryptic explanation later that evening. The following day the bulk of the fleet steamed into Ponce and began unloading General James H. Wilson's division. Welcomed by a cheering populace at Ponce, U.S. troops now moved inland. On the twenty-eighth, with an eye toward ensuring the continued support of the island's residents, Miles issued a public proclamation. The Americans, he explained, came "not to make war upon the people of a country that for centuries has been oppressed," but "bearing the banner of freedom" against the Spanish tyrants.[42]

With the enemy in full retreat, Miles plotted a lightning campaign calculated to exploit the rout. His subordinates were to avoid frontal assaults, relying instead on flanking maneuvers and speed to secure their objectives. Brigadier General Theodore Schwan, a former enlisted man and recipient of a Medal of Honor, landed twenty-eight hundred regulars at Guánica on the thirty-first and began moving west. With five thousand volunteer infantrymen, Major General Brooke disembarked to the east at Arroyo, overcoming light resistance to seize Guayama on August fifth. His troops won another minor engagement three days later as they continued their advance toward Cayey.[43]

On August 9, elements of Wilson's division clashed with Spanish troops at Coamo, east of Ponce. Scaling a difficult mountain trail, the Sixteenth Pennsylvania Volunteer Infantry skirted the enemy line and cut off its retreat. Six United States soldiers were wounded, but the two ranking Spanish officers were killed and 167 prisoners taken. Wilson then continued toward Aibonito, held by a more sizeable Spanish garrison. General Schwan's column was also making good progress in a push from Guánica toward Mayagüez. On the tenth Schwan used combined arms to defeat a fortified enemy line near Hormigueros. The march resumed as the advance guard, led by Colonel Daniel W. Burke, ambushed a Spanish column attempting to cross the Rio Prieto, inflicting heavy losses.[44]

The fall of San Juan seemed assured when President McKinley and Spanish Ambassador Jules Cambon signed an armistice on August 12. Spain relinquished its sovereignty over Cuba and Puerto Rico, leaving the fate of the Philippines to be decided in peace talks that fall. Save for a staged attack against Manila the following day, during which American troops occupied the capital after a cursory skirmish, the Spanish-American War had ended. Miles wrote to Mrs. Heintzelman, "In some respects it has been a romance and not much tragedy except for the Spaniards. They have been outmanuevered at every point."[45]

Though resistance had been light, Miles was justified in taking pride in his Puerto Rican campaign. At his insistence, his troops had been given adequate quarters aboard the transports; a strict quarantine and improved medical services had also protected the bulk of his command from yellow fever. He had matched the men with their equipment on the transports, caught the enemy off guard by landing at Guánica, and exploited his advantage before his foes could regain their balance. Buoyed by a cadre of regulars, Miles and his aides "managed every detail methodically and efficiently," raved General Wilson. The expedition was "the most instructive of any I ever accompanied," wrote the journalist Richard H. Davis, "and without any question the best conducted, and planned." "Not a lisp of criticism," wrote Senator Redfield Proctor, Miles's old nemesis from the Wounded Knee days.[46]

For Miles, the biggest problems now seemed to be finding his eyeglasses (he preferred not to wear them unless absolutely necessary) and ferreting out the sources of the "low intrigue" operating against him. That intrigue, whether it be "low" or not, was very real. From Washington, Captain Alfred Thayer Mahan, whose theories of naval power had taken the public by storm, questioned the "military stupidity" of having landed so far from San Juan, Puerto Rico's capital.[47]

A more serious challenge to Miles's authority had come from the Caribbean. In an August 2 message to Sampson, the commander of the auxiliary cruiser uss Dixie, Captain C. H. Davis, had suggested that the American fleet could "by a coup de main without the assistance of the army" sail into San Juan and capture the city. Eight days later, Miles got wind of the scheme and wrote a "personal and confidential" note to Secretary Alger. "I am fully convinced that Sampson has sent orders to the Commander of this fleet," wrote Miles, that as "soon as [the] Army leaves the south coast to take his fleet, go round to San Juan, and demand the surrender of the Capital or bombard the city, and not to waste ammunition on any of the batteries." Miles protested both the threat to shell noncombatants as well as the navy's meddling in his campaign. "Am assured there is no cause for your apprehension," comforted Alger the following day. But unlike many of Miles's imagined conspiracies, the interservice rivalry was real. The short Caribbean conflict had exacerbated army-navy jealousies, and Miles and Sampson were and would remain bitter opponents.[48]

Miles also pressed for the United States' annexation of Puerto Rico, which he believed would aid national growth as well as his career. By controlling the island, argued Miles, the U.S. could dominate the Caribbean. The paternalism that characterized his dealings with Indians also applied to the inhabitants of Puerto Rico. He argued that these dark-skinned peoples would prosper with the presence of American government and civilization. He also hoped the campaign would prove an important addition to his political arsenal. The name of Nelson A. Miles, he thought, would forever be associated with the acquisition.[49]

Getting back to the American mainland quickly seemed vital to these imperial designs. His personal lobbying could only help, he reasoned. And private matters also merited his presence. Mary, Cecilia, and Sherman were spending August on Long Island and would surely provide the conquering hero with a suitable reunion. Mrs. Heintzelman also awaited. Letters from Miles to the latter on August 13 and 21 conveyed innocent expressions of goodwill and hopes that they might see one another after his return. A note dated August 15, however, suggested a deeper affinity, and is the only shred of evidence that even hints that Miles engaged in any extramarital affairs. "Will you please in your next tell me . . . where are you going to be and what your plans are? You ought to make me your confidant when I have been your very good friend for such a *very long time*," purred the general.[50]

None of the other correspondence implies that Miles carried out such designs. And more immediate matters awaited, affairs that had a much greater bearing on his future. His invasion of Puerto Rico had attracted distressingly little press coverage. Improvements in army readiness, weak Spanish defenses, and that expedition's secondary importance had provided few of the juicy materials rife in Shafter's Cuban campaign. But on August 23, Miles granted a sensational interview with a *Kansas City Star* correspondent, J. D. Whelpley. Without bothering to obtain promises of anonymity, the general leveled serious charges against Shafter and the War Department. Alger's assurances to Shafter that the commanding general had not gone to Cuba to supersede him were, according to Miles, "based on an impossibility." Warming to the occasion, he continued: "I no more superseded Gen. Shafter than a Colonel supersedes a Captain. If a Captain was sent ahead with a company of soldiers, and was later on joined by his Colonel with the rest of the regiment, the Colonel would not supersede the Captain, he would simply take command of the entire force, as I did at Santiago."[51]

Miles went on to assert that the War Department had ignored his advice and leaked his plans to land at Fajardo to the press. Showing Whelpley a copy of one cable, Miles asserted that his suggestions for the Cuban enterprise—that the troops select fresh campsites daily and move inland into the mountains—would have prevented the spread of yellow fever that threatened to destroy the American army. Finally, he believed that Washington press releases had endangered thousands of American lives. His intentions, he declared, "were given out there in manifest detail long before I was ready to move, and the whole thing was thoroughly exploited before the public and the press of the entire world."[52]

As Miles observed, much of the war had indeed been botched. Secretary Alger had displayed an alarming lack of ability and understanding and aging War Department bureaucrats had been unprepared for the onslaught of volunteers. Likewise, the sudden call-up proved the much-vaunted state militias virtually impotent. But as commanding general, Miles shared much of the blame. The war had caught his army without contingency plans and he had failed to advise President McKinley effectively. The insufferable general seemed a throwback to the bygone days of the Civil War rather than a modern military strategist. Only when freed from the administrative and tactical arenas had he flourished; his invasion of Puerto Rico seemed a model of efficiency when compared to the Cuban landing. Time would tell if this combat leadership could quiet the calls for military reform aroused by the war.

14 : BEEF, ROOT, AND ROOSEVELT

On September 1, 1898, Nelson Miles left Puerto Rico. That same day, the *New York Times* reported that Secretary of War Russell Alger was "angry and troubled" over the general's recent statements. Into New York and the controversy strode Miles on the seventh, escorted by his family, his staff, and the Second Wisconsin Volunteers. Comfortably ensconced at the posh Waldorf-Astoria Hotel, Miles relished the attention surrounding his arrival; the men of the Second Wisconsin, however, muttered about the absence of a parade. "Say, what's the meaning of it all?" wondered one disappointed volunteer.[1]

The sentiments of the men of the Second Wisconsin were lost amid the excitement concerning the rift between Miles and the War Department. The general had planned to go to the theater, but the press of callers convinced him to hold an impromptu press conference in the hotel lobby instead. In hopes of embarrassing the administration, Democratic newspapers like Joseph Pulitzer's *New York World* strongly backed Miles. When asked if he wanted to retract any of the *Kansas City Star* quotes, he replied: "Nothing." He distributed a lengthy prepared statement that defended his actions. "Any pretense" that Miles had gone to Cuba "disrobed of his authority or official capacity is too childish to be considered by sensible men. . . . Gen. Miles . . . now returns to Washington where he believes he can be most useful."[2]

The following day a large crowd at Washington's Union Station welcomed Miles back to the capital. Outfitted in a sporty blue serge suit and a broad-brimmed white hat, the general chatted freely with reporters as he made his way through the throngs. He thought Puerto Rico, which could be garrisoned by a mere twelve thousand troops, would be a magnificent addition to the American empire. Spoiling for a fight with the War Department, he was assembling evidence to support his contention that Cuban insurgents had followed his rather than Shafter's instructions. Under great public pressure, Alger called for an inquiry.[3]

McKinley named retired General Grenville M. Dodge to head the investigation. As the Dodge Commission began its work, Miles set out to capitalize on his new-found notoriety. Frederic Remington came through with a stinging indictment of the War Department in an essay for *Harper's Weekly*. And along with the former Rough Rider Theodore Roosevelt, Miles proved a popular speaker on the dinner circuit. Each was abundant in his praise for the other. "It was not his [Roosevelt's] taste to remain at a desk, but he drew his sword among the bravest of the brave on the field of battle," lauded Miles. Roosevelt returned the compliment, warning a captive audience not to allow the advancement of "broken-down and aged Brig.-Generals, men who never commanded three companies before"—an obvious slap at Shafter.[4]

Managing to tear his attention from the speaker's circuit to army affairs, Miles also analyzed potential military reforms. When compared with the navy's spectacular successes, the army's initial mobilization effort seemed a national embarrassment. Fears of conspiracies, however, consumed Miles, who on December 12 proposed only limited reforms before the House Committee on Military Affairs. Combined with the traditional demands of the Indian frontier, the new American empire—Cuba, the Philippines, and Puerto Rico—necessitated a one-hundred-thousand-man army. Miles also stumped for the restoration of the rank of lieutenant general. And in a furious assault on his antagonists within the various bureaus, he opposed any notion of creating specialized staff officers or a general staff. "You may have a very efficient staff officer," he testified, "but if you have an inefficient commanding officer it does not mean a thing."[5]

Rumors that Miles, a favorite among some anti-imperialist circles for his opposition to the continued occupation of the Philippines, would stand as the Democratic Party's next candidate for president were heightened when the Dodge Commission called him in for questioning. Declining verbal invitations to testify, Miles appeared on December 21 only after a written request. Miles, accompanied by his personal stenographer, defended his plan to strike Puerto Rico rather than Cuba. He followed with a barely concealed attack on the navy. Then he delivered his bombshell. The canned beef sent to troops in the Caribbean had been unfit; even worse, an unhealthy chemical process had "embalmed" 327 tons of refrigerated meat. Miles aired his concerns to the press later that week, while visiting in-laws in Cincinnati. "I believe that the action of these chemicals was largely responsible for the sickness in the army. I have medical authority for this statement, and I believe it to be true."[6]

The sensational charges represented an open attack against the commissary department; indirectly, they challenged the competency of the entire McKinley administration. Miles later wrote, "My attention was first particularly directed to the bad quality of this article by an official report of Colonel Theodore Roosevelt . . . dated September 3, 1898, in which he stated that it was 'unfit to eat.' " Dr. William H. Daly, a member of the general's wartime staff, reported that the fresh beef was "preserved with secret chemicals which destroy its natural flavor." Boric acid, concluded Daly, had been injected into the meat to compensate for inadequate refrigeration.[7]

The objects of Miles's attacks sprang to the defense. Several wondered why the general had not complained earlier. Others charged that Daly had accepted kickbacks from War Department contractors. And suppliers of the refrigerated beef vigorously denied the allegations. Secretary of War Alger demanded Miles's removal. The president shared this distrust but decided to defer action until after Dodge's investigating commission had rendered its verdict. But with Miles submitting additional reports of tainted meat, a reluctant War Department formed another board to study the allegations.[8]

Colonel Roosevelt supported Miles's charges. Although the corned beef "was good," wrote the colonel on January 9, 1899, "the so-called canned roast beef . . . was practically worthless. Unless very hungry, the men would not touch it, and even when suffering from lack of food, they never ate a fifth of it. At the best it was tasteless; and at worst, it was nauseating." A shipment at Tampa, he continued, "was supposed to be fitted by some process to withstand tropical heat. It at once became putrid and smelt so that we had to dispose of it for fear of its creating . . . disease."[9]

But while other officers complained that the beef tasted bad and was ill-suited for tropical climates, they refused to condemn the meat issues. Leonard Wood blamed the problem on poor preparation. Another war veteran, Colonel William J. Powell, described the canned beef as "a stringy, unwholesome looking mass, more like wet sea weed than anything else I can think of." Theodore Roosevelt believed that fear of army retribution was preventing his fellow officers from supporting Miles. "I have . . . found that very naturally even brave and good officers are most reluctant to testify when their testimony may get them into trouble and may ruin their future careers."[10]

The commissary general, Charles P. Eagan, with the most to lose from a court condemnation, delivered a blistering counterattack. Miles, he declared, "lies in his throat, he lies in his heart, he lies in every hair of his head and every pore of his body, he lies wilfully, deliberately, intentionally, and maliciously. . . . I wish to force the lie back into his throat, covered with the contents of a camp latrine." Though damaging to Miles's ego, Eagan's outburst diverted attention from Miles, and in early 1899 a military court found the commissary general guilty of conduct unbecoming an officer.[11]

Foolishly, however, Miles again went to the press, reiterating his claims on the beef issue in a January 31 interview outside New York's Waldorf-Astoria Hotel. A legion of Miles's enemies circled for the kill. Rumor held that Secretary Alger, his own performance also under serious scrutiny, now sought to prefer charges against Miles for his having granted unauthorized press releases. Shafter, too, had broken with Miles. Among the bureau chiefs, only Inspector General Joseph C. Breckinridge remained loyal to him. Stung by his criticisms of Admiral Sampson; many in the navy refused to sympathize with Miles. Southerners remembered Miles's treatment of Jefferson Davis; as Georgia governor Allen D. Chandler, himself a Confederate veteran, wrote: "Miles is a brute no one who knows the man personally can doubt. He has neither brains nor soul." General James H. Wilson, who had commanded a division under Miles in the Puerto Rico campaign, suspected that Miles's abilities had deteriorated as he aged. Even the *New York Times* admitted that Miles, in his attacks on Alger, "might" have omitted "one or two expressions . . . on the score of good taste."[12]

Miles's propensity to air his grievances before the press and his well-known presidential ambitions merely worsened his image. The popular satirist Finley Peter Dunne (alias Mr. Dooley) joined the ranks of Miles's detractors. Miles's sister-in-law, Elizabeth Cameron, called upon her family's powerful political allies, but to little avail. Henry Adams, perhaps the Gilded Age's most perceptive observer, wrote, "He is too big a fool to live." And Miles's past critics reemerged. Former Attorney General Richard Olney, to whom Miles had scarcely endeared himself during the rail strikes of 1894, wrote, "Miles is here to my disappointment in plain clothes and not in his gold uniform. . . . I think I found out that the Presidential bee in his bonnet has swelled to the size of a full-grown peacock."[13]

On February 9, the Dodge Commission submitted its report to President McKinley. On the beef question, it concluded that the mass of testimony contradicted the claims of Miles and Daly. Inspections of private packing facilities had turned up no evidence of chemical injections. The canned meat, though rendered objectionable by the tropical climate, was not intrinsically unhealthy when properly prepared. Dodge urged McKinley to destroy Miles. "This attack is not on beef," reasoned Dodge, "it is on the administration."[14]

With the Dodge report completed, the army beef board also considered Miles's charges. Chaired by Major General James F. Wade but often referred to as the Miles Court of Inquiry, the committee called as its first witness the center of the controversy—Nelson Miles. Seeking to tone down his image as a "peacock" and to appear as the champion of the common soldier, Miles, whose stately bearing still reflected a lifetime of outdoor activity, wore a fatigue uniform in lieu of his dress blues. Initial questioning focused on the canned beef and the general's statements to the press. Why, asked one member, had Miles not first reported his suspicions to the commissary general's office? Leaning forward imperiously and furrowing his eyebrows, Miles retorted: "I am not required, sir, to report to the Commissary General." He had delayed sending his complaints to the Adjutant General in hopes of collecting additional evidence. Subsequent inquiries about his public pronouncements, however, found Miles more prone to compromise. He disclaimed having intended to impute fraud upon any individual and he did admit to having on occasion uttered "an unfortunate expression."[15]

As the investigation continued, it became clear that little evidence would come forth to support Miles's "embalmed beef" theory. His counsel, former aide Major Jesse Lee, attributed the lack of supportive witnesses to the problem previously observed by Roosevelt. As Lee explained it, "Our worthy President it is said has promised immunity to those testifying, but he can not . . . save an officer from disfavor with his own department." Even a public relations campaign in Massachusetts, featuring speeches by Miles at Harvard University, Fitchburg, and Springfield, failed to sway board members. By mid-May, the Miles Court of Inquiry had completed its survey. Miles was censured for not reporting his suspicions to the Secretary of War, as was Eagan for making a "colossal error" in purchasing large quantities of canned beef without first testing its suitability as an army ration. But the refrigerated beef had not been "embalmed."[16]

Undaunted by this slap on the wrist, a confident Miles basked in two personal triumphs as the twentieth century opened. On January 10, 1900, his daughter Cecilia married her second cousin, Captain Samuel Reber, in a Washington ceremony. A former aide to his father-in-law, Reber was a West Point graduate and specialist in electricity and later became a high-ranking official in the Radio Company of America. Highlighting the wedding was a quintessentially Milesian celebration breakfast for several hundred diplomats, officers, government representatives, and assorted friends.[17]

General Miles also received his third star, after lobbying by Senator Henry Cabot Lodge and Congressman William H. Moody, both Massachusetts Republicans. Exploiting the residual sentiment from the Spanish-American War to piece together a bipartisan coalition of Republicans and non-Southern Democrats, these two men secured the administration's support by tying the creation of the lieutenant general's rank to a major generalship for Henry Corbin. Though bitter sparring ensued—Miles was attacked yet again for having placed Jefferson Davis in chains, and Corbin was alleged to have deserted his wife and children, to have been blackballed by several social clubs, and to have cheated at cards—effective June 6, 1900, Nelson Miles was appointed lieutenant general.[18]

Although personally gratifying to Miles, these victories did nothing to silence the nation's calls for military reform. The war had demonstrated the old army's outmoded bureaucracy and absence of strategy. Its senior officers, aging veterans of the Civil and Indian wars, were as a whole brave but not inclined toward cerebral activity. Secretary Alger seemed helpless. The bureau chiefs operated independently of Miles, who was a fine tactician but too bound by tradition and personal ambition to implement corrective measures in the army. Henry Adams succinctly summarized the paralysis. "Alger is very little regarded by anybody. Corbin is much disliked. As for Miles, he can be quite unconsulted and unconsidered." Sharing these convictions, McKinley forced Alger's resignation on July 19, 1899. To fill the vacant cabinet post, the president selected Elihu Root, a reform-minded corporation lawyer who by his own admission knew little about the military (the army had refused to accept his volunteer application during the Civil War on account of his frail health) but much about people, institutional modernization, and the governance of the new colonies of Puerto Rico and the Philippines.[19]

As the strong-willed Root assumed his new post, Nelson Miles blithely continued the practices that had antagonized so many. On August 3, 1899, he lodged a formal complaint with the new secretary of war. Before leaving office, Alger had removed the Inspector General's Department from the commanding general's line of authority. Miles's frustration at his inability to control the bureaus was understandable, but his filing of the complaint reinforced his litigious image. Miles also badgered Root on behalf of his son, Sherman, whose astigmatism of the left eye threatened to prevent his entrance into West Point. Root rallied to Miles's side, but the incident sustained the widely held impression that personal sentiment rather than professional judgment dictated the general's decisions. And when called on to recommend officers for the new army, now triple the size of the older frontier constabulary, Miles submitted names chosen almost entirely on the men's seniority. In so doing, he was following a time-honored tradition. Root, however, found the choices a political embarrassment and drew up his own list. Rumors of a bid for president by Miles did nothing to allay concerns within the administration about the loyalty of the nation's ranking army officer.[20]

Secretary Root soon signaled his intention to take an active role in army affairs. A minor "difference of opinion" between Miles and officers in Cuba over the proper procedure for withdrawing U.S. forces there was brought to the secretary's attention. "I have decided it," wrote Root firmly. But only after establishing a system for bringing Puerto Rico and the Philippines under the federal government's control did Root consider serious military reform. On the advice of Assistant Adjutant General William H. Carter, he turned to the work of the late Emory Upton, a noted military thinker whose unpublished manuscript, "Military Policy of the United States," recommended sweeping organizational changes.[21]

Still unsure of the magnitude of the problem, Root's initial proposals were relatively minor. In February 1900, he had presented legislation "designed to secure some reasonable opportunity for selection in line promotions, to secure flexibility in the staff, and break up the excessive bureaucratic tendency and to reorganize the artillery on modern lines." He also hoped to enlarge West Point and to create an army war college for strategic studies. Miles, who had long demanded the rotation of staff and line officers, found the plan's modest provisions eminently acceptable, and in 1901 Congress approved the measure.[22]

President McKinley had in the meantime breezed to another victory over William Jennings Bryan. The election was particularly notable for the rise of Theodore Roosevelt, who filled a G.O.P. vacancy created by the death of Vice President Garret A. Hobart. Roosevelt, who would settle for nothing less than the presidency, seemed at first to bear no hard feelings about Miles's ill-timed intimation, made several years earlier, that he run as a vice-presidential candidate on a Miles ticket for the presidency. However, Miles committed the unforgivable when he suggested in a speech in June 1901 that Roosevelt had not led the charge up San Juan Hill. Perhaps it was an inadvertent slip of the tongue made during a routine address; perhaps it was a jealous slight against the man who had stolen the war's spotlight and catapulted himself into national prominence. Whatever the motivation, Miles had made another powerful enemy. "What a scoundrelly hypocrite the man is!" wrote Roosevelt.[23]

Miles's falling out with Roosevelt took on major proportions in September 1901, when McKinley was assassinated at the Pan-American Exposition in Buffalo, New York. Roosevelt had no qualms about using the imperial presidency against an uncooperative commanding general, especially one who had maligned his honor. Though he had earlier supported another candidate for the office of secretary of war, as president, Roosevelt soon warmed to Root's immense talents.[24]

The relationship between Root and Miles also soured that fall. The secretary vetoed Miles's suggested reductions in Cuban occupation forces, but even more serious was a dispute regarding army stations in the continental United States. Chronic shortages of barracks made routine transfers difficult; Miles proposed that the War Department alter its plans to better accommodate several of his favorite colonels. He then issued a paternalistic corrective to what he felt to be Secretary Root's ignorance of weather conditions near certain bases. Subsequently, Miles protested Root's proposal to enlarge the role and scope of the army's Leavenworth schools instead of pressing for a new military institute on the Pacific Coast. At the heart of each disagreement, of course, remained the traditional dispute between the secretary of war and the commanding general over control of the army.[25]

In late 1901 a rift over the proper location of the Fourteenth Cavalry widened the breach. After some preliminary sparring, Miles recommended the transfer of part of the regiment from Fort Logan, Colorado, to Arizona Territory. He argued that Fort Logan's proximity to Denver made it a poor post for mounted troops. "The place of the cavalry is supposed to be near the frontier . . . near the reservations of semi-hostile Indians, or where it can readily give protection and security to settlers." Recently, however, he declared, "some influence seems to have prevailed in congregating a large portion of the cavalry near large cities." Root, irked by the challenges to his authority and tired of the general's obstreperous behavior, rebuked Miles for having allowed politics to interfere with his judgment.[26]

In December, Miles's reaction to a court of inquiry's denunciation of Commodore Winfield Schley completed the break. A naval tribunal had attributed several tactical errors before and during the Battle of Santiago to Schley. While in Cincinnati visiting one of his wife's in-laws, Frank Wiborg, Miles defended Schley (who by rivaling Miles's nemesis, Sampson, seemed to the general a convenient foil) and publicly lambasted the court: "I have no sympathy with the efforts which have been made to destroy the honor of an officer under such circumstances." Root demanded an explanation; Miles contended that his personal views were "in no sense intended as a criticism of any action taken by a co-ordinate branch of the service." The minority opinion of Admiral Dewey, the board president, who had refused to condemn Schley, seemed to Miles reason enough to question the court's judgment. Miles subsequently made an even more vigorous defense. "I request that this note be laid before the President," concluded Miles, "and have no objection to it being made public."[27]

Root responded, "Your explanation of the public statement made by you is not satisfactory. You are in error if you suppose that you have the same right as any other citizen to express publicly an opinion regarding official questions pending in the course of military discipline. . . . You had no business in the controversy and no right, holding the office which you did, to express any opinion." President Roosevelt shared Root's anger, ruling, "General Miles is to be reprimanded severely." The *New York Times* printed an unsubstantiated story that the president, in front of twenty amazed onlookers, had shaken his finger angrily in Miles's face and demanded: "This thing must stop."[28]

Roosevelt swore that Miles should have been court-martialed three years before and called upon friendly journalists to turn public opinion against Miles. The general vowed to resist. At the twenty-ninth annual meeting of the New York Press Club on January 18, 1902, Miles noted wryly, "Unlike the newspaper men, the soldiers may not talk back!" Six days later he lodged a formal protest against Root's reprimand. The members of the armed forces "do not cease to be citizens," proclaimed Miles, who requested that all correspondence relating to the issue be forwarded to the appropriate congressional committees.[29]

A nasty sleigh-ride accident in early February, during which his horse-drawn vehicle rammed another, did not slow Miles. On the seventeenth, he requested permission to go to the Philippines, hoping to repeat a standard gambit of his. Noting the benefits of having sent various Indian delegations to Washington for negotiations, he proposed to find Filipinos for a similar purpose. But his allegations of army atrocities in the archipelago infuriated Roosevelt, as did Miles's demands that the islands be granted independence. According to Roosevelt, Miles had couched his request "in language which amounted to an endorsement by the head of the army of some of the most offensive and most unfounded slanders which have been put forth on the stump and in Congress by the violent traducers of the army and of the nation."

He continued, "General Miles has made it abundantly evident by his actions that he has not the slightest desire to improve or benefit the army . . . his desire is purely to gratify his selfish ambition."[30]

In March Miles further diminished his stature by coming out against Secretary Root's new reform package. Attempting to expand the limited changes secured the previous year, Root had introduced a general staff bill to Congress. The new proposal would have abolished the commanding general's position and consolidated the Quartermaster, Subsistence, and Pay departments into a single Department of Supply. More significant was its attempt to institutionalize and rationalize army planning by creating a general staff. In essence, Root sought to apply progressive theories of public management to the military.[31]

Root's military reforms were but a part of more widespread changes. Improving efficiency and creating order in the War Department were natural outgrowths of efforts to apply new principles of corporate leadership to public administration. Urban industrial forces seemed to be wresting control of government from the agrarian interests that had dominated the eighteenth and nineteenth centuries. Understandably, the threat of such a transformation frightened many Americans, who were products of their experiences in the Civil and Indian wars and were more attuned to the problems of the frontier west than the modern American empire.[32]

Miles made no secret of his opposition to the Root reforms. In his view, incompetent individuals rather than a defective system of administration had caused the army's recent problems. Consolidating the pay, quartermaster, and commissary departments into a single agency was unworkable, he testified in March 1902 before the Senate Military Affairs Committee. The general staff proposal seemed equally misguided. Its proposed composition, he argued at the hearing and in a letter to the editor of the *Army and Navy Journal,* ignored Civil War veterans, whose "invaluable" service gave "tone and character to the Army." Miles concluded, "I trust that the office which [Winfield] Scott and Sherman held with so much distinction will not be destroyed while any of their comrades and friends still survive."[33]

In the short term, references to the Civil War proved effective, for Grand Army veterans, including Senator Joseph Hawley, the chair of the Senate's Committee on Military Affairs, still held enormous congressional influence. Sympathetic to Miles's calls to oppose Root's reforms, they informed Colonel Carter, Root's point man at the hearings, that the current measure would not pass. But Miles sought to crush Root's sweeping reforms forever. Overcentralizing power in a small general staff "would seem to Germanize and Russianize the small army of the United States," he declared. Setting a prepared statement aside, he launched into a passionate attack. One newspaper reported his finale: "Warming up somewhat, he asserted that the bill was calculated to accomplish no purpose except to allow the Secretary of War and the Adjutant General to promote the interests of their personal favorites."[34]

Although the general staff bill stood little chance of passing the present Congress, reaction to Miles's latter charges were swift. The *New York Tribune* labeled his attacks as "sensational"; Henry Adams concluded that Miles had "at last given himself his coup-de-grace." Realizing himself that he had perhaps gone too far, the commanding general, using the privileges generally granted such witnesses, had the most egregious statements deleted from the official record. But the damage was done. The administration sent Generals Schofield and Merritt to testify before the Senate Military Affairs Committee in favor of the reforms, and Roosevelt discussed Miles's fate at a tense March 21 meeting with his advisors. "Of course General Miles' usefulness is at an end and he must go," wrote the president, but Republican senators warned against immediate action. As Miles's testimony was privileged, they explained, he should not be punished for these statements. In addition, an attack on Miles might delay passage of the general staff bill and risk a political backlash.[35]

Miles's allies attempted to limit the damage. Sympathetic members of the House Committee on Insular Affairs requested copies of all papers relating to his request to go to the Philippines. Supporters in and out of Congress tried various means of deflecting criticism— suggesting that he take an extended tour of Europe, reminding an increasingly prohibitionist public of his strong stance against the abuse of alcohol, stressing his anti-imperialist position—all of which hinted that Miles would run for president at the next opportunity. His coy denials of interest in the White House only heightened such rumors.[36]

But in opposing Root's latter reforms, Miles had committed a colossal blunder. The *Independent*, a Boston-based magazine, blasted the "spectacular self-glory which General Miles was so foolishly seeking" in the Philippines. Secretary Root proclaimed him "a rather annoying obstacle to pretty much every movement for reform of army organization and administration." Even the *New York Times* turned against him. His "extremely crude and ill-considered" proposition to go to the Philippines impugned the reputation of government officials already there. Instead of allowing the matter to drop, Miles then submitted another document—an act considered "very serious misconduct" committed in "a spirit unworthy of his profession and his rank," according to the *Times*. The newspaper blamed Miles's shenanigans on his presidential ambitions and called for his resignation.[37]

"Dismissal of Army's head said to be certain," proclaimed the *New York Tribune* on April 14, 1902. In a move that could only embarrass Miles, retired General Schofield came out in favor of the general staff bill. Miles's few remaining friends within the War Department found themselves stripped of influence. In June, the administration recalled him from an inspection at Fort Riley to discuss military secrets leaked by Senator Charles A. Culberson, an ally of Miles's.[38]

Miles was cleared of charges of official misconduct and joined Root and Roosevelt to form an uneasy speaker's trio at the West Point graduation ceremonies that June. With each camp threatening recriminations, Miles's subsequent renewal of his request to go to the Philippines (confining himself to purely military affairs and inspection duties), seemed a way to relieve the tension. He and his entourage, including his wife, Captain and Mrs. Maus, a stenographer, a messenger, and three personal friends, sailed from San Francisco aboard the recently refurbished transport, the uss *Thomas*, on October 1. Other than the robbery of Maus's hotel room during the group's brief stay in Honolulu, the voyage went off without a hitch. While they were en route Roosevelt announced that Samuel B. M. Young, the head of the newly formed War College Board and formerly Roosevelt's division chief during the Spanish-American War, would upon Miles's sixty-fourth birthday become commanding general.[39]

Other than a few of Miles's old Indian-fighting comrades, most notably John J. Pershing, Jesse Lee, and Frank Baldwin, officials in the Philippines were none too pleased about the general's arrival. William Howard Taft, head of the second Philippines Commission, wrote "The prospect of a visit from the Lieutenant General of the Army does not awaken that enthusiasm, either in civil or military circles, which might be expected." The party nonetheless anchored off Manila Bay on October 30, accepting Taft's unenthusiastic invitation to stay at the Malacanan Palace.[40]

After the Treaty of Paris was signed on December 10, 1898, the Philippines conflict had taken an ugly turn when Americans sought to stamp out all opposition to their new regime. Both Filipino "rebels" and American "liberators" resorted to scorched-earth tactics and tortured noncombatants and prisoners to procure information. Assisted by Baldwin, Miles investigated alleged atrocities. His activities, particularly his meetings with the captured Apolinario Mabini, a former advisor to the rebel Emilio Aguinaldo, infuriated most of the occupying Americans; Taft, for example, maintained that Baldwin was, "like Miles[,] . . . entirely insubordinate," and had "stirred up the Filipinos in Miles' behalf." Undeterred by any criticism, Miles in late November began compiling charges of cruelty against members of the American armed forces.[41]

With advance warning about the charges from Taft, the War Department refused to publish any general reports, instead advising Miles to send specific information. The general complied on December 9, 1902, citing orders issued by Frederick Funston, Adna Chaffee, J. Franklin Bell, Jacob Smith, and Robert P. Hughes "which justifie[d] use of any means for certain purposes." Subsequent letters from Miles identified six junior officers alleged to have tortured prisoners. War Department officials, however, labeled the data "meager" and noted that many of Miles's charges were already under investigation.[42]

Officers in the Philippines breathed collective sighs of relief as Miles departed for Hong Kong and Japan. Brigadier General Bell "needs a long vacation," remarked Governor Taft. Miles, however, needed no such rest. He made a hasty inspection of Russian forces at Port Arthur, on the Liaotung Peninsula, before securing an audience with the empress dowager of China. He then took an eighteen-day journey to Moscow on the Trans-Siberian Railroad. St. Petersburg, Berlin, Paris, and London awaited; in a minor embarrassment, an invitation that Miles dine with King Edward VII at Windsor Castle did not include Mary. The group returned to New York on February 15, 1903.[43]

Rather than easing tensions, the tour intensified the mutual animosity between Miles and the Roosevelt administration. Many found Miles's reports from abroad to be tainted by self-righteousness, self-promotion, and self-aggrandizement. The avidly imperialist *New York Times* appealed to American jingoism by reminding readers of "the proverb about the manner of bird which fouls its own nest." In his analysis of actions in the Philippines, Miles had criticized Bell's campaign in the Batangas Province; he had accused Major Edwin F. Glenn of wrongdoing in one report, although subsequent courts-martial against Glenn and others acquitted the defendants on the grounds that they were following orders. And Miles's scathing condemnations of U.S. defenses along the Pacific Coast precipitated a host of angry replies, especially from Major General Robert P. Hughes of the Department of California. Dismissing any counterattacks, Miles labeled Hughes's remarks "disrespectful, unsoldierly, and unworthy."[44]

Though Roosevelt yearned to punish Miles, the president opted instead for the safer solution of waiting for Miles's retirement on his sixty-fourth birthday. Roosevelt thus limited his outbursts about the general to diatribes to trusted friends. The War Department did transfer Baldwin, who had been particularly troublesome to Taft, from the Philippine Islands. After a series of complaints from anti-imperialists such as Miles's old crony Herbert Welsh, the War Department released Miles's Philippines reports to the press. But as Root and Roosevelt predicted, these papers failed to generate much sensation. "Instead of being filled with dynamite," cracked one editor, "it proves to have been stuffed with sawdust." Taft felt vindicated. "I see that Miles has emitted another bad smell and that the newspapers generally have treated his report as it deserves to be treated."[45]

Within the War Department, however, Miles's assessment of the Philippines stimulated bitter comment. Roosevelt and Root fumed about charges by "swine" like Welsh that they had "suppressed" army reports. And in a twenty-two-page typewritten response, a staff officer pointed out numerous inaccuracies in Miles's report. Referring to this rejoinder as "specious, self-laudatory, unnecessary, often irrelevant and impertenent," Miles retorted with his own analysis, which counted no less than twenty-five errors in the response.[46]

But though Miles might have derived some perverse satisfaction from these petty skirmishes, the major questions about army reform had already been settled. Stymied by a Congress reluctant to act before November elections, Root had marshaled his forces for another reform push in the winter of 1902–03. To mold a consensus, he dropped the plan to consolidate the supply bureaus and retained a separate Inspector General's Department. Only after the general staff system proved its worth would it be filled on a permanent basis. Most important, the chief of staff would supervise rather than command the bureau chiefs.[47]

In December 1902, President Roosevelt urged Congress to create a general staff. With the careful management of Speaker David B. Henderson, the general staff bill passed the House in early January 1903. Senator Hawley bottled up the measure in the upper chamber until ill health forced him to relinquish his chairmanship of the Senate Committee on Military Affairs. Redfield Proctor, who as a former secretary of war appreciated better than most the need for reform, succeeded Hawley as chair. Root pulled every political string he could muster; in a final concession, he agreed to delay implementation of the general staff system until after Miles's scheduled retirement later that year. The measure became law in mid-February. "It is not in as good shape as I would like," admitted Corbin, "but it is a solid rock upon which we can lay a corner-stone for the building of a staff organization that we have needed so long."[48]

Miles continued to grandstand while Root and Roosevelt plotted revenge. When his retirement was less than a month away, the commanding general displayed his conditioning by riding the ninety miles from Fort Sill to Fort Reno in nine hours, ten minutes, exhausting a squad of horses but arriving none the worse for wear himself. The spectacle seemed especially ludicrous in light of Miles's final recommendations for the army, which called for the replacement of five regiments of cavalry with troops equipped with bicycles, automobiles, and motorcycles.[49]

Miles's final day in the army came on August 8, 1903—his sixty-fourth birthday. Following precedent, fellow officers, wearing full-dress uniforms, dropped in to pay their respects as he finished up odds and ends around the office. Root and Roosevelt then played their trump card, in the hope of humiliating the troublesome general. They released an official announcement about Miles's departure: "The retirement from active service by the President, Aug. 8, 1903, of Lieut. Gen. Nelson A. Miles, United States Army, by operation of law, under the provision of Congress approved June 30, 1882, is announced," read Root's icy notation, sent through Adjutant General Corbin's office. "Lieut. Gen. Miles will proceed to his home. The travel enjoined is necessary for the public service." No platitudes, no letter of commendation, no official recognition of the general's forty-two years of service to his country would be forthcoming from the Roosevelt administration.[50]

The curt statement provoked a stormy response. Newspapers that supported Miles, like the *Springfield* (Mass.) *Republican,* howled; even the *New York Times,* which had recently turned against him, believed that Roosevelt had committed "a frightful blunder." Miles enjoyed a triumphal cross-country tour to the annual encampment of the Grand Army of the Republic in San Francisco, where his fellow veterans hailed him as one of their own. Others, however, rejoiced at the dismissal. Georgians contemplated decorating their state capitol with Confederate memorabilia to commemorate the great day. The *Atlanta Constitution* explained: "Concerning General Miles and his past services it is difficult to speak acceptably from the Southern point of view." And Roosevelt stood firm. "Nothing will hire me to praise him," he vowed.[51]

15 : TWILIGHT

Embittered by the shabby treatment doled out by the Roosevelt administration, Miles left Washington for a western vacation in September 1903. With only mundane tasks like securing a license for his automobile entrusted to his son-in-law Samuel Reber occupying him, Miles relaxed with a few rounds of golf and a little hunting with his prize pointers. Financial opportunities provided another welcome diversion from the recent humiliation. He and the former governor of Texas, James Hogg, whom he had met that spring at a convention in St. Louis, had invested in Louisiana and Texas oil fields. In early October, the two partners attended the Texas State Fair and toured Beaumont, the scene of the immense Spindletop gusher. From Dallas, Miles admitted: "I am so favorably impressed with the state that I have assumed some material business interests in it. These affairs are such that I may have to spend much of my time in Texas hereafter."[1]

Although Miles later denied having become involved in Texas oil, correspondence between him and Hogg suggested otherwise. Miles's financial empire continuously expanded—real estate investments in California, Washington, and Missouri; mineral interests on Puget Sound; western timber properties; scattered packets of land and buildings in the District of Columbia; legacies from wealthy relatives; and joint ventures in the Westminster area with his brother Daniel had freed him from financial strain. Inside connections with his brother-in-law Colgate Hoyt, who was a Wall Street broker, allowed the general access to lucrative investment opportunities. He and Mary retained four black servants and continued to live in grand style.[2]

But tangible comforts were not enough, for his ambition rivaled even his immense talents on the battlefield. President Roosevelt and Secretary of War Root had driven him from the army; by entering politics he might fulfill his own desires and at the same time even the score. But Roosevelt's iron hand doomed any chance Miles might have had within the G.O.P. Too, the party's association with the Philippines adventure, its broad construction of the constitution, and its refusal to oppose labor unions seemed anathema to the conservative Miles.[3]

Democratic party bosses, meanwhile, were searching for fresh talent. Though William Jennings Bryan had managed to fuse old-line Democrats with their angrier Populist cousins, his defeats in 1896 and 1900 stamped Bryan as a perennial loser. Roosevelt's attacks on private monopolies and his past reputation as a reformer siphoned away many moderates from the Democratic Party. A smattering of Democrats, most notably the semiliterate boss of the Tammany machine, Richard Croker, began to look toward Miles for leadership. His military fame might be the ideal stimulus to a party searching to define its identity.[4]

Roosevelt was "mortally afraid of him," chortled one optimistic backer of Miles, "on one hand [we have] Roosevelt and war, on the other hand Miles and peace." Miles hoped to make forays into the South to quell the old Reconstruction bitterness, and he offered simple platform promises—peace, state sovereignty, internal development, and Philippines independence. Instead of wasting money on the Philippines and the Panama Canal, argued the retired general, the government should build a comprehensive system of public roads and western dams. "We need not cultivate an appetite for the horizon when we have the best country on earth, with undeveloped resources that will occupy our people for hundreds of years," he declared.[5]

Miles also became a darling of the Prohibition Party. For several years, he had eschewed all forms of alcohol. When asked if he would stand for the party's nomination, however, he fell back upon false modesty: "It remains with my friends to say what service I shall render further to my country." John D. Woolley, who had been the party's candidate in 1900, strongly backed Miles, whose name recognition surely augured well for the prohibitionists. As editor of the party organ, the *New Voice*, Woolley commanded wide support. But Miles was well aware that the Prohibition Party had received less than 2 percent of the popular vote in the last presidential election. Assuring his Prohibition-ist Party supporters that temperance was "one of the seven cardinal virtues," he advised the group to delay naming him as their candidate until after the major parties had made their selections.[6]

While attempting to hold the Prohibitionists at arm's length, Miles stumped hard for the Democratic nod, making a series of appearances before political clubs, veterans' associations, and "good roads" conven-tions (held to pressure the government into improving roads). On June 26, 1904 he informed Senator Charles A. Towne that he would sacrifice his own modest ambitions in order to serve the public as the Democratic nominee. This maneuvering led skeptical Prohibitionists, already divided over whether they should broaden their party platform, to reconsider Miles. He initially vetoed a potential Prohibition bid, then hinted that he would accept an offer if the party would support the direct election of senators, civil-service reform, and state sovereignty. Prohibitionists who opposed Miles, like Dan R. Sheen and W.P.F. Ferguson, chipped away at the general, whose contradictory state-ments and blatant desire to secure the Democratic candidacy alienated Prohibition hard-liners. The party instead selected Silas C. Swallow, an acerbic Methodist firebrand noted for his attacks on slavery, alcohol, dancing, card playing, and roller-skating.[7]

The Democrats convened that July at the St. Louis Coliseum. Ever the optimist, Miles hoped for strong support from Pennsylvania, New England, the South, and the West. David Overmyer, a lawyer influen-tial in the Kansas party machinery, nominated Miles for president. His candidate's wartime service, anti-imperialist stance, strict constitutional construction, and opposition to labor unions made him the ideal candidate. According to Overmyer, Roosevelt's ruthless efforts to destroy Miles indicated the Republicans' fear of his candidacy. Overmyer minimized the threat of Southern dissent over Miles's decision to place Jefferson Davis in irons. "Any honest Democrat can carry the South," he reasoned.[8]

Overmyer's arguments failed to sway his fellow Democrats, who opted for Alton B. Parker, a respected though somewhat colorless New York attorney who steadfastly refused to take the campaign trail until the late stages of the contest. One of nine nominees at the convention, Miles garnered only two votes, both from Kansas. Despite Overmyer's optimism, few party stalwarts wanted to risk the enmity of Southerners, who continued to lambast Miles. Reeling from his poor showing but still determined to see Roosevelt humbled, Miles swung loyally into line behind Parker. Indeed, the Democrats adopted one of his speeches protesting the occupation of the Philippines into their official campaign literature.[9]

As the campaign developed, however, a personal tragedy dealt Miles a more permanent blow. Mary's health had long been deteriorating; on January 7, 1904, Samuel Reber had noted: "Mrs. Miles is far from well, and I am afraid never will be strong again as her heart has gone completely back on her." By March, George Baird, a long-time family friend, described her condition as "critical." A temporary recovery allowed her to accompany Nelson to their summer cottage at Cold Spring, New York, and to see their son Sherman, now a cadet at nearby West Point. In late July, Miles left for a brief side-trip; he returned on August 2, a day after Mary had succumbed to a fatal heart attack.[10]

Funeral ceremonies were held on the fifth at the Military Academy chapel. Two private railroad cars carried friends and relatives from West Point to Washington, D.C., where Mary's body was interred in the family plot at Arlington National Cemetery. Old friends and comrades, including Frank Baldwin, Carl Schurz, James Wilson, and Eli Huggins, rallied to the grieving general's side. Libbie Custer wrote a particularly memorable consolation letter. "It is a great thing for a wife to have her heart filled with pride and her ambition gratified by the distinguished success of her husband," she confided, noting the limited opportunities open to nineteenth-century women. "But if she could speak, she would say that it was a greater triumph to have you come to her when your enemies assailed you and find in her your solace, and from her gain new courage to go forth and meet those whose jealousy will never leave you alone."[11]

Stunned by Mary's death, Miles did not rejoin the campaign until late September, when he blasted Roosevelt's "extravagant ideas of expansion." Repeating familiar themes, Miles pledged that the Democratic Party would enforce laws restricting illegal combinations and divert monies being spent on the Philippines and the Panama Canal to internal projects like roads and irrigation. But the Parker campaign failed to capture the imagination of the American people. Roosevelt, "amused" at the political antics of Nelson Miles, swept to a landslide victory.[12]

Bloodied but more defiant than ever, Miles, now sixty-six, struggled to upgrade his public image. He wrote a rebuttal of Southern claims regarding his treatment of Jefferson Davis, which appeared in the *Independent*. His hopes for the presidency temporarily shattered, he tried to develop grassroots political support in his native Massachusetts. Governor-elect William L. Douglas, the first Democratic governor of Massachusetts in twelve years, asked Miles to serve as adjutant general of the state militia. Using a recently passed law that allowed retired officers to serve with militias at full federal pay plus their state allotments, the job promised handsome financial benefits in addition to its political attractions.[13]

Critics howled over the sweetheart deal. Turn-of-the-century morals did not allow for an officer to draw two government stipends. In late December 1904, Miles attempted to deflect criticism by resigning his adjutant general's position in favor of an unpaid job as state inspector general. He continued to take an active role in militia affairs, however, changing its annual state encampment from Farmington to Westfield and suggesting that its numbers be reduced in the name of efficiency. But the House of Representatives, despite the protests of the Massachusetts delegation, deemed the former commanding general's actions undignified and voted 201 to 50 to prohibit retired officers over the rank of major from receiving full pay if they entered state service. The measure was openly directed against one man—Nelson Miles. Only the intervention of Senators Henry Cabot Lodge, Orville H. Platt, and Redfield Proctor saved Miles from further assaults; their compromise allowed such officers to draw retired rather than active duty salaries. The gambit having proved more trouble than it was worth, Miles tendered his resignation in December 1905.[14]

"Miles wanders like a restless Hamlet over the earth, satisfied to rest nowhere and I fear with the ignus fatuus of the [presidential] 'bee in his bonnet' and probably no more chance to attain it than you who have it not," wrote one long-time acquaintance. The description was entirely accurate. Scornful enemies ridiculed suggestions that he run for governor of New York or Massachusetts. Miles, denying rumors that he was planning to marry again, made extended automobile tours through Europe with his brother-in-law Colgate Hoyt in 1906 and again in 1909.[15]

Although he broke two ribs when thrown from his horse in April 1910, Miles completed a second set of memoirs—*Serving the Republic: Memoirs of the Civil and Military Life of Nelson A. Miles, Lieutenant-General, United States Army*. It was published in 1911 by Harper and Brothers, with a series of excerpts also appearing in *Cosmopolitan* magazine. Reviewers panned the new account, a dull, unimaginative monologue with little of the personal flair or insights essential to such a genre. As in his earlier books, Miles appeared too bent on appealing to everyone in what seemed little more than a crude attempt to drum up political support.[16]

Undaunted by the setbacks, Miles kept up a vigorous schedule. In 1909, he had moved from his old place at 1736 N Street in Washington, D.C., to a temporary residence on Seventeenth Street; the following year, he took up life at the fashionable Rochambeau Apartments, a seven-story complex of eighty apartments built at a cost of five hundred thousand dollars. Its location, two blocks north of the State-War-Navy Building and the White House, gave Miles convenient access to army friends and government officials. He often spent the winter at Boston's Hotel Somerset and whiled away many hours with friends and financiers at the Union League Club or the Waldorf Hotel in New York City. Secretive business deals and interminable lobbying on behalf of his allies still fired his interest. He made frequent speeches before Civil War veterans' associations, which brought forth in him mixed emotions—pride at being so much in demand and sadness at reviewing the diminishing numbers of fellow comrades in arms.[17]

His children offered emotional support, with Cecilia and her sons spending a good deal of time in Washington. In 1911, Samuel Reber's transfer to Governors Island provided Miles with an excuse to visit that city and play golf on a regular basis. As always, Miles provided unstinting support for Reber's military career. And the general took comfort in the fact that Sherman seemed to be thriving on army life. In 1909, he married Yulee Noble, the daughter of Nelson's long-time personal secretary, William Noble. Only the sudden death of Nelson's brother Daniel disrupted family harmony. A bank president and minor industrialist in Westminster, Daniel died in mid-February 1912 of a massive heart attack while visiting Washington. By coincidence, Nelson was motoring along Pennsylvania Avenue at the time. Seeing a man collapse on the street, an astonished Miles stopped, hopped nimbly out of his car, and declared, "It's my brother."[18]

Upon his retirement from active duty, Miles frequently returned to his boyhood haunts in Westminster, where as the village's most famous son he received almost imperial acclaim. The "Gen. Miles Sporting Co." stood proudly among the village's preeminent businesses. His brother's former home on Main Street became the local Baptist parsonage. Of course, local ceremonies—the opening of the Forbush Library, the town's sesquicentennial, the anniversary of the Baptist church—often featured Nelson Miles as a guest speaker.[19]

Miles still dabbled in public affairs and politics. He served as a member of the Oliver H. Perry Victory Centennial Commission as well as the Jefferson Memorial Association. Assiduously courting the friendship of the elusive Andrew Carnegie, he participated in the receiving committee for president-elect Woodrow Wilson's triumphant entry into the capital. But Miles never grasped the value of party loyalty. Once a Republican but more recently a Democrat, he had returned to the G.O.P. by 1913. That September, Miles announced his candidacy for the Republican nomination in Massachusetts' Third Congressional District, where a seat had been made vacant by the death of William H. Wilder. Basing his campaign at his ancestral home, Miles lost the party's nod to the eventual victor in the general election, Calvin D. Paige.[20]

Miles's politics had taken an increasingly conservative bent. A 1912 letter of his to Carnegie had hinted at Miles's plans: "I am interested in organizing what may be the largest body of patriots ever organized in this country." Dubbing themselves the Guardians of Liberty, the group assumed a virulent anti-Catholic, anti-immigrant stance. Miles became the society's leader ("chief guardian"). Plagued by political infighting, the Guardians failed to fulfill Miles's predictions but provided a good deal of excitement. In one 1916 gathering in New York City, for example, Miles warned the group against allowing Catholic proselytizing in the public schools. Catholics, having infiltrated the meeting, promptly drowned him out with their jeers. A quick-thinking janitor forestalled a possible riot by turning out the lights; outside, the winter night cooled tempers more effectively than anything the keynote speaker might have offered.[21]

In late 1912, Miles's career took another exciting twist. His son Sherman was serving as the U.S. military attaché in the Balkans when Bulgaria, Serbia, and Greece launched simultaneous attacks against the crumbling Ottoman Empire. Nelson became an impromptu "expert" on the conflict, attributing the initial Bulgarian success to good training and swift mobilization. Although he predicted a Turkish recovery, Miles, in comparing the Bulgarian soldier to the American Civil War volunteer, declared, "A new first-class fighting power has arisen at the storm center of Europe."[22]

Interested in the ongoing Balkan crisis and anxious to see Sherman, Miles left for Sofia in June 1913. But events soon turned against the Bulgarians. Dissatisfied by the spoils secured in the Treaty of London (which had ended the First Balkan War in May 1913), they launched a preemptive strike against their former allies, the Serbs and the Greeks. Intervention by Romania and Turkey brought about a near-collapse of the Bulgarian war effort and briefly trapped General Miles in Sofia. The Bulgarians gave up their recent territorial gains in the Treaty of Bucharest; still enamored with their cause, Miles defended their interests in the United States and sought out Red Cross assistance for Balkan refugees.[23]

After his return to the United States from Europe, Miles undertook an unusual project in the fall of 1913. His old friend William Cody, short on cash after the enforced disbandment of the Buffalo Bill's Wild West and Pawnee Bill's Far East show, considered making a moving picture. Investors included Fred Bonfils and Harry Tammen, owners of the Sells-Flots Circus and publishers of the *Denver Post*. George K. Spoor and G. M. Anderson, heads of the Essanay Film Company, also joined what seemed to be a sure-fire financial bonanza. Cody's proposal: a movie, or a series of film shorts, about the American West, replete with cowboys, Indians, and soldiers. It seemed to have the potential for vast audience appeal. The spectacular Buffalo Bill would be the feature attraction and a proven drawing card. Cody could attract wide support for the project, which promised a faithful portrayal of the nation's conquest of the American West. In September 1913, excited associates pooled their resources to form the Colonel W. F. Cody (Buffalo Bill) Historical Pictures Company.[24]

Cody secured approval from the secretary of the interior, who seized on the project as a way to display the "progress" of the nation's Indian wards. The War Department saw the movie as a first-rate recruiting tool and assigned three troops of cavalry to serve as extras. Theodore Wharton, who went on to shoot a number of World War I government propaganda films, seemed an ideal choice as director. Vernon Day was the production manager and promised to pay any claims by Indians against Cody. Among the cameramen was D. T. Hargan, who later shot wildlife footage in Central Africa. Hundreds of Indians agreed to participate and Ryley Cooper, who had ghost-written an autobiography of Cody's wife, accompanied the entourage to the northern plains for filming. "The reunion between the Indians and their old time enemies will be as amiable as the recent reunion at Gettysburg," wrote one supporter.[25]

The epic was slated to include several battle scenes, including that of Wounded Knee. To ensure historical accuracy, Cody brought in veterans like Jesse M. Lee, Frank Baldwin, Charles King, and Marion P. Maus. And Nelson Miles, whose reputation might lend an air of authenticity, seemed a natural complement. When he was asked to participate, the general proved a fine negotiator, expressing just enough reluctance to make the producers even more eager to attract his presence. On September 13, he outlined his conditions to Baldwin. "If the parties are responsible and really desire to reproduce an important and historic event, in a truthful and accurate manner, then we could very properly assist them."[26]

The general received the necessary assurances. He would be the chief technical advisor. Real-life participants would reenact their roles rather than use prepared scripts. His reservations assuaged, Miles became actively involved. On September 30, 1913, he presented another formidable list of recommendations. Color rather than black and white film seemed "essential" in making the movie historically correct. "The Indians are neither white or black, but are the noted copper-colored race that is disappearing forever," he argued. His other ideas concerned the movie's very subject, which he declared should be "peace—the transformation of the Indians from war tribes to civilized, progressive, peaceful Indians."[27]

That October, the crew gathered at Pine Ridge, South Dakota. On his way to join them, Miles outlined his role to a reporter. "They want me there to make sure that everything they do is historically correct," he explained. "I shall take active part in it, too, perhaps." The reunion seemed a splendid opportunity to visit old friends and former enemies, as well as a chance to showcase his exploits in a permanent pictorial fashion.[28]

Theodore Wharton had his hands full. Thousands of Indians, soldiers, and horses milled about waiting for action. The Oglala Sioux adopted Vernon Day's wife as a daughter of the tribe, but most found it difficult to grasp their roles as extras. The Indians often refused to remain "dead" on film. Rumors swept the location; the tribesmen were purportedly planning to use live ammunition during the reenactment of the Battle of Wounded Knee. Cody, known in the industry as something of a prima donna, seemed the most practical of the participants and averted the potential crisis during an impromptu late-night meeting with several chiefs.[29]

But the mystified Indians hardly compared with the cantankerous Miles, who insisted that every detail be accurate. A minor dispute arose over the recreation of the final army review at Pine Ridge, in which over thirty-five hundred troops had been present. But the film company had fewer than three hundred soldiers at its disposal. Anguished discussions produced a compromise; General Miles would lead the troopers around and around the cameras until thirty-five hundred soldiers were captured on film. The scene wasted a few hours but not much film, for although the cameramen continued to crank their machines as the soldiers made their circuits, they allowed no exposures after the first three rounds.[30]

Of greater concern was Miles's determination to have scenes reenacted on the sites at which they had actually occurred. Events that had occurred in the Badlands must be filmed in the Badlands. Such an exercise threatened to add weeks to production and cost thousands of dollars. Cody defended pragmatism; Miles demanded realism. To break the impasse, the Indians and troopers left for three days of filming on the Badlands. But this gesture did not meet the demands of Miles, who stormed off the set upon their return. A relieved crew completed the final shooting, with Buffalo Bill Cody filling in as historian. On October 28, a great feast celebrated the final day's filming, when the Brule Sioux named Wharton an honorary chief.[31]

Armed with thirty thousand feet of film, the editors began their task, which took six months. Miles demanded that his name be expunged from the project entirely. His seventy-five years had made him neither compromising nor self-deprecating. He vented his anger to George Spoor of Essanay. "I am obliged to enter a solemn protest against the misrepresentation and misleading statements made in regard to those pictures," he wrote. Not only had the project been undertaken in October rather than midwinter, but several events had been filmed out of sequence. There was no "War of the Messiah," as one of the title frames suggested; "barring the bad English it would be impossible to know what that refers to. Possibly some of the Roman wars or Crusades," Miles complained. Finally, Cody had deemphasized the army's role. "You can consider this confidential and act accordingly," he warned, "or you can publish it in any way advisable."[32]

The general's boycott failed to prevent the film's gala sneak preview—a special exhibition for congressmen, cabinet members, and other Washington dignitaries. But "The Last Indian Wars for Civilization" drew less-than-rave reviews, and its government sponsors withheld it from public release for six months. Known by a variety of titles— "The Indian Wars Refought," "The Last Indian Battles; or, From Warpath to the Peace Pipe," "The Wars for Civilization in America," "Buffalo Bill's Indian Wars," "Indian War Pictures," "The Adventures of Buffalo Bill"—one version was finally shown in New York. Cody and a band of Indian warriors introduced a Denver opening. Another brief run followed Cody's death in 1917.[33]

Unofficial comment was mixed. Baldwin gave the film his blessing; King exuberantly proclaimed: "Nothing like this has ever been done before. Nothing to equal it will, perhaps, ever be done again." Ben Black Elk, the son of one of the Indian performers, also attested to the movie's authenticity. But Chief Chauncey Yellow Robe of the Sioux decried the picture's attempt to transform Indian-killers into heroes. In particular, critics argued that the reenactment of Wounded Knee had been a desecration of those persons killed in the disaster.[34]

Whatever the movie's authenticity, the government sought to minimize its publicity and distribution. Allegedly, the official copies decomposed in the dank files of the Bureau of Indian Affairs during the 1920s. The lack of official enthusiasm seems attributable not to the opposition from Nelson Miles, but to the film's less than glowing portrayal of the nation's Indian policy. Interior Secretary Franklin Lane had hoped the film would portray "the advance of the Indians under modern conditions"; the failure of either Cody or the Essanay Company to immediately provide the Interior Department with copies further rankled Lane. Indeed, it would have been difficult for early twentieth-century cinematographers to transform the miserable Indian reservations of reality into the cradles of civilization they were espoused by government spokesmen to be.[35]

Miles, though immutable in some situations, such as the filming of "Indian Wars," had not lost his grasp of the changing ways of warfare. His continued insistence on using flanking attacks and maneuvers during the Puerto Rico campaign suggested a healthy respect for the defensive power of modern weapons. His condemnation of direct frontal assaults against entrenched defenders, issued in November 1912, seemed especially prescient as the First World War began. On August 3, 1914, even before Britain had joined the conflict, Miles warned: "I am afraid that one of the most terrible wars in the history of the world is at hand."[36]

President Wilson, although pressed by sporadic U-boat attacks on ships carrying American citizens and the U.S.'s financial ties to the Allies, charted a precarious course of official neutrality. As America sought to maintain a pretense of normalcy, Miles remained an outspoken advocate of prohibition and a harsh critic of Pancho Villa's Mexican revolutionaries. Restoration of a statue of William Sherman in New York's Central Park, a furtive meeting with Henry Ford, and a speech before a large crowd of Harlem blacks each attracted at least passing interest by the press.[37]

Meanwhile, the secretary of war, Lindley Garrison, and the general staff sought to formulate contingency plans should the nation enter the war. Post-1898 reforms had improved army preparedness, but national apathy, inadequate appropriations, and the failure to fully resolve the extent of the federal government's authority over the National Guard left critical gaps. Seeking to craft a politically viable solution, Garrison proposed an increase in regular forces to 140,000. Another 400,000 citizens would be raised over a period of three years to form a "Continental" army. Independent of the National Guard, these soldiers, who would undergo two months' military training every year, would compose something akin to a nationalized militia.[38]

A strange coalition opposed the Continental army. Ignored by Garrison's scheme, the National Guard massed its formidable political resources to resist the plan. But those who advocated a large professional army blasted the plan's alleged deemphasis of a regular force. During congressional testimony in February 1916, Miles damned the Garrison plan. He offered instead a traditional approach: Form a skeleton army of 140,000 to 150,000 that would expand to about 400,000 in case of emergency. "You can't Germanize the American people," he told senators. Congress should instead be funding "the new American engines of war"—submarines and airplanes. His testimony before the House made clear Miles's everlasting bitterness over his own stormy departure from active duty. He complained, the army "was in better condition when I left it than it has ever been since," and general staff officers "could be better employed if serving with troops."[39]

"I was glad to see that you opposed that miscalled-continental-by conscription-germanic-goosestep army," wrote Miles to a long-time correspondent on February 17. Garrison resigned in protest over the president's refusal to support his measure; that summer, Congress passed the National Defense Act of 1916. A far cry from establishing the Continental army, the new measure provided for a four-tiered system of land power. The regular army of 175,000 would be supplemented by a 457,000-man National Guard, a reserve, and the volunteers. The act, which included deep cuts in the General Staff, undoubtedly pleased the tradition-bound Miles.[40]

From his posh Washington apartment, the general chafed for action as the nation edged toward war. Service on the government-sponsored Medal of Honor Board and speeches to groups like the National Guard Association only whetted his insatiable appetite. On March 17, 1917, young at heart if not in body, Miles offered his military services to Secretary of War Newton D. Baker. The official declaration of war came on April 6; only eighteen days later the seventy-eight-year-old Miles proposed that he organize and lead an expeditionary force into Russia. Wracked by disorder from within and without, Aleksandr Kerenski's new government, which had overthrown Czar Nicholas II only a month earlier, had but a tenuous foothold. The United States needed to infuse massive amounts of aid to Russia, argued Miles, or that country's nascent democratic movement would collapse. To expedite the process, native-born Russians now living in the United States could be recruited. American engineers and workers could revitalize the Trans-Siberian railway. Miles listed nine trusted men—veterans of the Civil, Indian, and Spanish conflicts—who should be instructed to report for duty as his staff to put this scheme into effect.[41]

The War Department had enough to do without handling a septuagenarian's fantasies. But Miles was determined to serve. Russia's turn towards Bolshevism and the various Allied misadventures in Siberia and Murmansk sparked renewed requests by him for an assignment. All military attaché posts in that country were filled, replied the War Department. "I had in mind . . . an enterprise of far greater magnitude," retorted Miles on November 24, "the accomplishment of which could involve action quite out of the ordinary." His subsequent proposals suggested that an expeditionary force of twenty-five thousand officers and noncommissioned personnel led by Miles would attract half a million volunteers in Russia and save the country from the Kaiser and socialism.[42]

Though Miles's services were not employed directly in the war effort, it was of some gratification to him that his former aide John J. Pershing was appointed to lead the American Expeditionary Force in Europe. Subsequent events, especially Warren G. Harding's election to the presidency in 1920 and the Senate's rejection of the League of Nations, also pleased Miles. Woodrow Wilson's misguided attempt to create a League "super-government," argued Miles, threatened to endanger American independence, whereas the victorious Harding's "experience, disposition and principle" rivaled those of Abraham Lincoln, and Vice President Calvin Coolidge seemed a second John Hancock.[43]

"A familiar figure" at patriotic functions along the mid-Atlantic seaboard, Miles also composed introductions for autobiographies written by his old friends Anson Mills, a veteran Indian-fighter, and "Yellowstone" Kelly. In 1922, he recovered from a bout with pneumonia in time to help direct the Grant Memorial Parade in the nation's capital. The American Patriotic League made Miles a life member the following year, and the Military Order of the Loyal Legion of the United States named him its commander in chief. In 1924, he dedicated a war memorial on Long Island and raised thirty thousand dollars as chairman of the Washington district of the American Committee for the Relief of German Children. One newspaper even reported that he was attempting to persuade Congress to appropriate forty thousand dollars for a monument to George Custer.[44]

A changing world notwithstanding, Miles remained an unreconstructed Indian wars buff. In 1909, he had met with several friends—Frederic Remington, Leonard Wood, the photographer Rodman Wanamaker, and William Cody—to discuss a suitable tribute to the native peoples. A huge Indian statue at the mouth of the Hudson River seemed appropriate. Miles strongly backed the idea; it should consist, in his view, of "a group of figures that would express the emotions of surprise, alarm, and curiosity, as well as the stoic apathy, strong defiance and cordial welcome of the Indian character." The project did not come to pass, but Miles often attended meetings of a veterans' group, the Order of Indian Wars, which gathered annually to recount tales of the old frontier. And in 1917, he had joined others in demanding government compensation for the survivors of Wounded Knee.[45]

Miles seemed a living symbol of a bygone era. As the author Forrestine Hooker proclaimed: "Miles will never die. The West is his monument!" Museums and galleries coveted his exotic collection of scalps, headdresses, blankets, bearskin rugs, and weapons once belonging to Joseph, Geronimo, and Lame Deer. But true to his character, Miles proved a finicky patron, and withdrew an offer to the Smithsonian when that institution refused to guarantee that his entire collection would be placed on permanent display. Better, thought Miles, that it remain in private storage.[46]

Though his shaky handwriting betrayed signs of his increasing age, Miles remained unusually vigorous. Double pneumonia could not keep him from serving as the grand marshal of ceremonies at the unveiling of a statue honoring Ulysses S. Grant. "I will lead or bust," he told an assistant. Miles still enjoyed playing golf or whizzing about in a powerful automobile, and had become an avid chess player. An active clubman and thirty-second-degree Freemason, he visited Washington's Metropolitan Club nearly every day. His old friends Lizzie Cameron and Frank Wiborg, his children, and his grandchildren—Sherman and his wife had named a son after him in October 1917—were welcome visitors. Miles Reber, the son of Cecilia and Samuel, graduated from West Point in 1923, with his stately grandfather in proud attendance. Samuel Reber, Jr., attended Harvard. Unfortunately, the brood's far-flung military obligations precluded all but occasional meetings. "All of my fathers family have gone," complained Miles in

July 1924, "and my children and grandchildren are scattered in distant stations. They have left me alone and I miss them very very much."[47]

The year 1925 opened routinely, with speeches to groups ranging from the Chicago Press Club to the District of Columbia chapter of American War Mothers. Miles still haunted the State-War-Navy Building, chatting with bureaucrats and pressing the causes of friends and relatives. A confirmed advocate of military aviation, he testified before the House Special Committee investigating Billy Mitchell, who was court-martialed for insubordination for criticizing the War and Navy Departments' handling of aviation service. Although gratified to learn of a group's interest in placing commemorative markers for the Puerto Rico campaign, he reacted in a customary manner—by protesting their use of July 17, 1898, as the date of General Toral's surrender. Not so, explained Miles. Toral had capitulated three days earlier.[48]

On the morning of May 16, 1925, Miles ambled over to the home of Mrs. William E. Noble, his son's mother-in-law. After lunch, he escorted her and the grandchildren to a performance of the Barnum and Bailey Circus. Miles loved circuses, and met the owner John Ringling before the show began. "You know I never miss the circus," roared Miles. "I have been coming for years." His distinguished military carriage belying his advanced years, he ushered his party to third-row seats under the big top.[49]

The crowd rose as one as the band struck up the "Star-Spangled Banner." As Miles settled back into his seat, a heart attack killed him instantly. Only a few onlookers even knew that anything was amiss. Dr. A. E. Craig caught the lifeless figure as it slumped backwards. There was a temporary Red Cross station just outside the tent, but it was too late. The body was taken to Casualty Hospital on Capitol Hill, where the coroner certified "myocarditis and acute dilation of the heart" as the cause of death.[50]

On May 17, General John J. Pershing and Acting Secretary of War Dwight F. Davis gave the eulogies at a memorial service. Final services were held two days later at St. John's Church in Washington. After the ceremony, six black horses pulled an artillery caisson that bore a flag-draped coffin holding Miles's body. A color guard and Army, Navy, and Marine detachments totaling twenty-five hundred men, escorted the long procession, which wound its way across the Potomac River to Arlington National Cemetery. As a bugler played taps, a fifteen-gun salute boomed farewell to one of the nation's greatest fighting soldiers.[51]

EPILOGUE

Following their father's death, Cecilia and Sherman donated his collection of Indian memorabilia to the Museum of the American Indian, operated by the Heye Foundation. It was placed on public display in New York City that November. Cecilia, who lived long enough to see her sons, Miles and Samuel Reber, enjoy success in the army and the foreign service respectively, died in 1952. Sherman Miles, who was sailing home from Europe at the time of his father's death, served out his military career as a staff officer. A long-time correspondent of George S. Patton and a witness at the congressional hearings concerning the Japanese attack on Pearl Harbor, he died in 1966.[1]

"Old soldiers never die, they just fade away," lamented the twentieth-century military figure Douglas MacArthur, whose career often paralleled that of Nelson Miles. Miles had yearned to avoid such a fate, but like MacArthur, he failed to do so. Bemused observers found the retired general's forays into public affairs sadly ludicrous. Even in death the bittersweet dénouement continued. President Calvin Coolidge attended the graveside ceremonies, a gesture that the status-conscious Miles would surely have taken as a final vindication. An ornate family mausoleum served as his final resting place. He had hoped the grand monument would be a permanent symbol of the services he had rendered to his country. But, alas, the location—on a low bluff at the end of a quiet cul-de-sac off the beaten path at Arlington National Cemetery—proved unlucky. Nearly forgotten, the memorial lies far away from the sites normally frequented by visitors.

About Miles's retirement from the military the *New York Tribune* had commented: "It marks . . . the end of a regime. It signals the abandonment of an outworn and obsolete army system. It is the last step toward newer models of organization and administration—toward genuine and lasting military reforms." The practical effects of these reforms had not been immediately apparent; early chiefs of staff (Samuel B. M. Young, Adna R. Chaffee, John C. Bates, and J. Franklin Bell) were hesitant to assert command. But Fred C. Ainsworth, who by virtue of his previous service in the Pension Office had not been liable to the mandatory rotation of staff and line officers appointed after the passage of Root's general staff measure, easily extended his authority over the army's day-to-day affairs in 1907, when Congress recreated the position of adjutant general.[2]

In taking control, Ainsworth was in practice nullifying many of the Root reforms. Ainsworth's rise seemed the last gasp of the old guard, for he was as much a product of the old bureaucratic army as Miles himself had been of the frontier army. He was formerly a contract surgeon and lacked combat experience, but was a master at pleasing Congress. The scheming Ainsworth seemed the quintessential Washington staff officer so detested by Miles and his frontier colleagues.[3]

Leonard Wood, the Harvard-educated medical doctor whose military career Miles had helped to launch during the Geronimo campaigns, challenged the Ainsworth regime when he was appointed chief of staff in 1910. With the selection of the reform-minded Henry L. Stimson as secretary of war the following year, Wood determined to confront the adjutant general. Ainsworth enjoyed close ties with the chairmen of both the House and Senate Military Affairs Committees and his caustic defense of a bureaucratic tool—the traditional muster roll—impugned the ability and authority of Secretary Stimson as well as Wood. Supported by Root, the latter duo persuaded President William Howard Taft to threaten court-martial proceedings in response to the adjutant general's intemperate response to Wood's plan to abolish the muster roll system. Ainsworth opted instead to retire. As one historian has concluded, the dismissal represented "a turning point in the vexed history of the Army's command."[4]

The similarities between Miles and Wood, the man who by asserting the chief of staff's authority had done so much to destroy Miles's army were ironic. Wood was notorious for his own political machinations and his lack of formal military training and obsessive ambition embittered many of his colleagues, much as Miles's background and scheming had alienated his own peers. But Wood was a product of a vastly different country. Intuition and bravery alone would not suffice in the more cerebral, scientific world espoused by the Progressives. In contrast to Miles, Wood owed his rise not to his battlefield exploits (although he had been given a Medal of Honor for his service against Geronimo) but to his administration of Cuba and the Philippines as a military governor.[5]

The quest for efficiency dominated Wood's career. One West Pointer put it this way: "Everybody is looking forward to increased professionalism under Wood. . . . He will force out, they say, the backward, the old and the incompetent in the higher grades of the army." Wood's comment as chief of staff seems even more damning to the enduring legacy of Nelson Miles and the old ways: "The Army's worst enemies were within itself," he wrote of the "stupid fools" who were not "sufficiently intelligent enough to see beyond their own noses."[6]

Like most institutions of its size, influence, and bureaucratic longevity, the old army died a lingering death. At Ainsworth's urging, Congress passed a bill in 1912 excluding Wood as a future candidate as chief of staff, reducing the number of general staff officers, and placing military post consolidation in the hands of a congressional committee. Only a presidential veto checked this counteroffensive, the enactment of which would have been a major triumph for the old regime. Even with the veto, the continued military service, often in the Philippines, of men who had once patrolled the American frontiers invited frequent comparisons of the post-1898 army with that of the late nineteenth century.[7]

The twilight of the old army was indeed long. The poor food, inadequate quarters, and bitter racism of the Philippines War often resembled problems the army had faced during its earlier struggles against the Indians, as did the American army's haphazard strategical and tactical responses to the military resistance found in the Philippines.[8] But the nation's ground forces changed in style and composition, albeit slowly and unsteadily. The regular army, once numbering just over twenty-five thousand, nearly quadrupled in size. The old model 1873 single-shot Springfields had been replaced, first by the Krag-Jorgensen and later by the deadlier bolt-action magazine model 1903 Springfield. New three-inch field guns equipped with optical sights, brought into service in 1902, fired smokeless powder and had recoilless carriages and were a far cry from the old frontier mountain howitzers. More comprehensive post-graduate schools for officers; the new War College; and the Dick Act of 1903, which began the slow process of coordinating the state militias and the regular army, all heralded significant change. Perhaps most symbolic of the new age was the creation, at the behest of Stimson and Wood, of division-sized units, the peacetime army's first attempts to organize so large a tactical body.[9]

Rather than encouraging schoolbook learning or professional development, the officer corps of the old army had emphasized personal leadership, bravery, and instinct, qualities that made the army resistant to change, poorly organized, and prone to internecine jealousies. Such problems, of course, were hardly unique to the American army of the late nineteenth and early twentieth centuries. But their pervasive effects, combined with the continued emphasis by older veterans on Civil War exploits, did much to set this army apart. Consumed with their generation's quest for honor and manhood, aging veterans fought and refought the battles of their youths. The long international peace— broken, of course, by the wars against the Indians, which many regulars believed to be beneath their dignity—gave younger men little opportunity to prove themselves against the standards set by their peers in "real" warfare.

Yet for all of its faults, the old army had suited the nation's purposes. Congress demanded that it protect the frontiers inexpensively, which it did. Though much maligned, it also provided a wide range of important (and often controversial) nonmilitary services—enforcing Reconstruction in the South, protecting the national parks, encouraging a number of scientific endeavors, providing relief to drought-stricken frontier settlers, and asserting federal authority against strikers.

Nelson Miles symbolized the best and worst of the old army. Thrice wounded during the Civil War and having repeatedly risked his life during the Indian conflicts, his bravery was unquestioned, as was his ability to motivate those under his immediate command. Miles developed into a skilled tactician who won every major engagement in which he enjoyed autonomy. The diversity of his military foes—Confederates, Comanches, Sioux, Northern Cheyennes, Apaches, Bannocks, Nez Perces, and the Spanish—demanded that Miles master a flexible approach to warfare. He was "a truly great soldier," concluded one admiring subordinate.[10]

But Miles was less adaptable during times of peace. As a junior officer, his restless, unbending pursuit of excellence had seemed a fine attribute. But his climb to the top left him badly scarred. Always fearful of conspiracies, Miles divided the world into two clearly distinguishable factions: those wise enough to agree with him and those mean-spirited enough to allow their jealousies to affect their judgment. In a simple truth akin to a battlefield maneuver against his enemies, he was right and his foes were wrong. Ambition and the pursuit of power came to dominate his life. Miles always suspected that his rivals permitted their envy to guide their actions; for his own part, he was equally guilty for having allowed jealousy to cloud his professional judgment.

His views on national expansion also reflected an egocentric world view. During the 1870s and 1880s, many Americans dreamed of annexing huge chunks of Canada. Miles, who as commander of the District of the Yellowstone and the Department of the Columbia would have been directly involved in the move, counted himself within the expansionist camp. And during the 1890s, he supported the acquisition of Puerto Rico, an island captured by virtue of his skillful leadership. But the general adopted a different stance when it came to regions in which he had no personal involvement. He sought, unsuccessfully, to limit American interests in Cuba, an island the invasion of which he had hoped to delay. More strident was his opposition to continued U.S. involvement in the Philippines, a position which made him the darling of many anti-imperialists.

Miles's views on army reform reflected a similar approach. In 1876 he had supported the consolidation of the Quartermaster, Commissary, and Pay departments into one corps; later, as a commanding general, he resisted such a move, which, by upsetting the army's traditional bureaucratic structure, might weaken the forces that opposed substantive changes. His reasoning was simple. Having risked his life for his country, he was not about to allow anyone to deprive him of his hard-won recognition or the nation of his practical wisdom and experience. In the process, Colonel Miles the advocate of reform became General Miles the outdated traditionalist.[11]

"In this and similar aversions to new-fangled military notions," remarked the editors of the *Nation* on the occasion of his retirement, "Gen. Miles has been merely one of a number of civil-war veterans who could never be brought to see that the methods of 1865 were not those of 1885, and much less those of 1898." A product of his own experiences, Miles could understand the need for fundamental army reform no more than he could see any virtues in the progressive movement as a whole. Rather than remodeling the army to meet the new century, the general opted to reward Civil War cronies and use troops to guard Indian reservations.[12]

Miles knew and understood the old frontier army, an institution shaped by its experiences in fighting Confederates and Indians. Its officers, proud of their record of service, found it difficult to accept society's reluctance to recognize or repay their efforts. Slow promotions and boredom threatened to stifle the most promising officers. Understandably disappointed by their relative loss of status after the Civil War, they scrapped among themselves for scarce crumbs. After repeated disappointments, Miles concluded that loud and frequent complaints best served his ambitions. As his former aide Jesse M. Lee explained when applying for a new post: "I don't suppose it will be granted, but as our dear friend General Miles used to say, 'I will put myself on record.'"[13]

Influence-peddling, corruption, and shady dealings were common in American society during the Gilded Age. Though much more complex than the celebrated "great barbecue" of lore in which greedy politicians feasted on the profits of corrupt government, the late nineteenth century seemed plagued by such activities. Miles recognized this phenomenon, and assiduously sought to exploit his personal connections. William and John Sherman, the Cameron family, Francis

Barlow, assorted Massachusetts politicians—indeed, all who would listen—were courted by him with deliberate, calculated forethought.

The ambition that fired such efforts as Miles's did not preclude all innovation by army officers. Many refused to fall victim to the stagnation that loomed so dangerously close. Miles, despite his opposition to the Root reforms, was by no means a traditionalist on all counts. "The future historian . . . will look in vain for any stirring utterance against favoritism within the army and will find few if any searching reforms due to Gen. Miles's advocacy," wrote the editors of the *Nation*. But, "if the historian then turn[s] to this officer's purely military services he will find much to praise." He had been one of few post-bellum officers to use infantry and artillery effectively against Indians, depending on greater firepower, longer-ranged weapons, and longer resiliency in the field to overcome his mounted foes. More than most, he recognized that dogged pursuit, whatever the weather, often held the key to military success against the Indians. As early as 1899 Miles had predicted that the automobile would supplant the horse in military operations. His successful use of troops in the Civil War and of Indian auxiliaries in the west, his advocacy of military aviation and increased mobility, and his recognition that the rapid-firing weapons of the early twentieth century had fundamentally changed warfare marked Miles as an imaginative military thinker.[14]

But an unflinching sense of righteousness, bred in his boyhood and reinforced by his military experience, consumed Miles's persona. His search for publicity antagonized almost all of his peers, many of whom resented his success and honors. "Too much circus, too little brain!" exclaimed Frederick Benteen, a leader of the anti-Custer faction within the Seventh Cavalry. Even Colonel George B. Sanford, who appreciated Miles's military talents, found him "the most ambitious officer" in the army.[15]

More serious than the criticism of his personality were charges that ambition and jealousy influenced his handling of Indian affairs. "Miles was never honest with officer or Indian, unless it suited his policy," insisted one of his enemies. "If Crook was disliked, you should know how much more bitterly Miles was hated; he was regarded as a coward, a liar, and a poor officer," added an Apache. The general's changing stance as to the proper location for Geronimo and the captured Apaches seemed to confirm such judgments. His suggestion in 1890

that they be moved to North Carolina rather than the Indian Territory—his original choice in 1886—was carefully suited to his political
ambitions. He knew the Arizonans feared that the Chiricahuas' transfer to the Indian Territory would encourage them to attempt to return
to their tribal homeland.[16]

Others came to Miles's defense. One Bannock campaign veteran
argued that Miles was always "just and firm in his treatment of Indians." From the Northern Cheyenne reservation, Captain Oscar Long
told Miles, "[The Indians] speak of you every day and wherever else
they differ, they blend harmoniously in warm praise of you." Buffalo
Bill Cody reached a conclusion similar to Long's. During one Wild
West performance at Madison Square Garden, General Miles came up
to pay his respects. Cody later recalled, "The Indians came crowding
around him, and followed him wherever he went. This Indian escort at
last proved to be almost embarrassing, for the general could not go to
any part of the Garden without four or five of the braves silently
dogging his footsteps and drinking in his every . . . word."[17]

Miles's determination to stamp out corruption in the Indian Bureau,
along with his long record of support for Chief Joseph and the survivors
of Wounded Knee, also suggests a genuine interest in the welfare of
certain tribes. But following the popular theory of his time, he believed
that humankind gained "civilized" status only after passing through
several stages of development. Some Indians—particularly the Plains
tribes—were nearer to this lofty goal than others. Others, however, had
a long way to go. The Apaches, he wrote in 1911, "excelled in activity,
cunning, endurance, and cruelty. . . . An account of their atrocities and
raids would fill a volume." Why risk losing political support, he reasoned, on behalf of a group whose culture and belief systems differed
so greatly from those of most Americans?[18]

Although his wife's involvement in the women's suffrage movement
distinguished both her and her husband from societal norms on that
issue, Miles mirrored his nation's inconsistency on matters of race. On
the one hand, he advocated just treatment for Indians; on the other, he
rejected traditional tribal values and urged the tribes' assimilation into
white-dominated society. He fought for the abolition of slavery, worked
to assist freedmen, and spoke to black groups. But he refused to accept
blacks as equals and left his black regiment at the earliest opportunity
after the Civil War.

Nelson Miles was a poorly educated, extraordinarily vain man who exasperated each and every one of his superiors. His boorish drive for power lacked the sophistication or refinement that a longer formal education might have provided. This trait, combined with his tendency to associate with those who echoed rather than refined his judgments and his well-known fondness for ornate military regalia, made him a popular subject for contemporary lampoons. Teddy Roosevelt labelled Miles a "brave peacock." "Seize Gin'ral Miles' uniform," teased the satiric Mr. Dooley. "We must strengthen th' gold reserve."[19]

Thus Miles the enigma, a certifiable hero in wars against three very different enemies, but one whose personality threatened to obscure his military success. Without the advantages often resulting from a formal education, he was ill equipped to handle the multiple demands of a general officer, particularly one who was given so many delicate assignments. He adapted well to the changing nature of the battlefield, but found that dealing with Jefferson Davis, Sitting Bull, Chief Joseph, the army bureaucracy, industrial unrest, William T. Sampson, William McKinley, Elihu Root, and Theodore Roosevelt required more than the courage demanded by the Civil War generation's code of honor. A deft touch, diplomacy, a willingness to share credit was essential. Miles, like his army, could not escape the controversies of the times. Criticism of his efforts to resolve national crises—of his decision to place the former president of the Confederacy in irons; of his treatment of Indians, which some felt too harsh and others too lenient; of his inconsistent attitudes toward military reform and national expansion—left him convinced that only through loud and constant self-promotion could he secure recognition.

And who could blame Miles for his frustration? When he was an ambitious teenager the limited opportunities in Westminster had driven him from his family's farm. A political decision had stripped him of his first captain's bars before he even took the field. Despite a splendid Civil War record, this man, who at twenty-six led a corps of twenty-five thousand veterans, seemed doomed to lead a regiment of five hundred infantrymen for most of his adult life. So he worked and persevered, defeating Grey Beard, Sitting Bull, Joseph, and Geronimo.

Ungrateful superiors, concluded Miles, had conspired against him. Though appointed a general, he had not been selected as secretary of war or even chief signal officer. In his opinion, others with inferior records, such as George Crook and Richard Drum, had by virtue of personal contacts or seniority remained ahead of him on the army list.

After several years' banishment in Arizona, he returned to the Midwest just in time to check the Sioux and Northern Cheyenne outbreak of 1890–91, only to see his responsibilities then reduced. Four years later, Miles believed that he had prevented the socialists and anarchists from seizing control of Chicago, only to be criticized by the Cleveland administration. Equally misguided, in his view, was McKinley, who ignored his advice that might have prevented the near-disaster in Cuba and who forgot his brilliant victory in Puerto Rico. Root and Roosevelt, rather than bestowing on him the honors he deserved, retired him without even a hint of thanks.

But times had changed during Miles's career. After he died only two Civil War generals in blue were still alive.[20] From a raw second-rate regional power, the United States had emerged as a major force in a complex global community. The responsibilities that accompanied the nation's burst of international activity demanded a new type of military leader, one who could get along with politicians, bureaucrats, and admirals who cared little about the Civil or Indian wars. Politically naive and educationally limited, Miles never mastered the nuances of personal diplomacy. A man on the battlefield, he seemed but a boy during times of peace. Courage and military success alone were not enough to equip Nelson Miles, or the old army, for the twentieth century.

NOTES

ABBREVIATIONS

ACP DOC.	Appointments, Commissions, and Personal Branch Document File, RG 94
AGO DOC.	Adjutant General's Office Document File, RG 94
LC	Library of Congress, Washington, D.C.
LR, AGO, 1871–80	Letters Received by the Office of the Adjutant General (Main Series), 1871–1880, M 666
LR, AGO, 1881–89	Letters Received by the Office of the Adjutant General (Main Series), 1881–89, M 689
LR, CB	Letters Received by the Commission Branch of the Adjutant General's Office, 1863–70, M 1064 roll 525
LR, NC	Letters Received by the District of North Carolina, RG 393
LR, NM	Letters Received by Headquarters, District of New Mexico, Sept. 1865–Aug. 1890, M 1088
LR	Letters Received
LS	Letters Sent
LS, AGO	Letters Sent by the Office of the Adjutant General (Main Series), 1800–1890, M 565
LS, ARIZ.	Letters Sent by the Department of Arizona, RG 393
LS, COLUMBIA	Letters Sent by the Department of the Columbia, RG 393
LS, EAST	Letters Sent by the Department of the East, RG 393
LS, HQA	Letters Sent by the Headquarters of the Army (Main Series), 1828–1903, M 857
LS, MO.	Letters Sent by the Department of the Missouri, RG 393
LS, N.C.	Letters Sent by the District of North Carolina, RG 393
LS, PLATTE	Letters Sent by the Department of the Platte, RG 393
LS, SW	Letters Sent by the Secretary of War Relating to Military Affairs, 1800–1889, M 6

LS, YELLOWSTONE	Letters Sent, Yellowstone Command, RG 393
MS(S)	Manuscript(s)
NARA	National Archives and Records Administration
RG	Record Group
SI	Secretary of the Interior
SW	Secretary of War

CHAPTER ONE

1. Nelson A. Miles, *Personal Recollections and Observations of General Nelson A. Miles* (1896; reprint, New York: Da Capo Press, 1969), 21–22; Systematic History Fund, *Vital Records of Westminster, Massachusetts, to the End of the Year 1849* (Worcester, Mass.: Franklin P. Rice, 1908), 61–62.

2. Miles, *Personal Recollections*, 21; *New York Times*, Nov. 11, 1894.

3. Miles, *Personal Recollections*, 21; *New York Times*, May 16, 1925.

4. Miles, *Personal Recollections*, 22; *Celebration of the One Hundredth Anniversary of the Incorporation of Westminster, Mass.* . . . (Boston: T. R. Marvin & Son, 1859), 30; Brian C. Pohanka, ed., *Nelson A. Miles: A Documentary Biography of His Military Career, 1861–1903* (Glendale, Calif.: Arthur H. Clark, 1985), 19; Systematic History Fund, *Vital Records of Westminster*, 61–62; U.S. Census, Manuscript Returns, 1850, roll 340, Worcester County, Massachusetts.

5. Miles, *Personal Recollections*, 20–23.

6. *Celebration of the . . . Incorporation of Westminster*, 97, 122; Miles, *Personal Recollections*, 23; A. Judson Rich, *Historical Discourse Delivered on Occasion of the One-hundred and Twenty-fifth Anniversary of the Congregational Church . . . in Westminster, Mass., September 9, 1868* (Springfield, Mass.: Samuel Bowles and Co., 1869), 37, 80, 96; Pohanka, *Documentary Biography*, 19 (quotation); U.S. Manuscript Census, 1860, roll 531, Worcester County, Massachusetts; William Sweetzer Heywood, *History of Westminster, Massachusetts, (first named Narragansett No. 2) from the Date of the Original Grant of the Township to the Present Time, 1728–1893* . . . (Lowell, Mass.: Vox Populi Press, 1893), 781.

7. *Celebration of the . . . Incorporation of Westminster*, 57; Virginia Weisel Johnson, *The Unregimented General: A Biography of Nelson A. Miles* (Boston: Houghton Mifflin Co., 1962), 4; Miles, *Personal Recollections*, 23; Peter R. Knights, *The Plain People of Boston, 1830–1860: A Study in City Growth* (New York: Oxford University Press, 1971), 20, 21, 37, 40; Miles to Brother, July 26, 1857 (quotations), May 6, 1860, Nelson A. Miles Collection, U.S. Army Military History Institute, Carlisle Barracks, Pennsylvania (hereafter cited as Miles Collection).

8. *Boston Directory for the Year ending June 30, 1860, Embracing the City Record, a*

General Directory of the Citizens, and a Business Directory (Boston: Adams, Sampson and Co., 1859), 91; Johnson, *Unregimented General*, 5; Miles to Brother, Mar. 7, 1858, Miles Collection (quotations).

9. Unidentified newspaper clipping, May 20, 1925, Nelson A. Miles materials, Forbush Memorial Library, Westminster, Mass. (hereafter cited as Miles materials, Forbush Library); Miles to Brother, July 26, 1857 (quotation), Jan. 6, 1859, Aug. 10, 1861, Miles Collection; Knights, *Plain People*, 16, 41; *The Boston Directory, Embracing the City Record, a General Directory of Its Citizens, and a Business Directory, for the Year Commencing July 1, 1860* (Boston: Adams, Sampson and Co., 1860), 301.

10. Johnson, *Unregimented General*, 5; Nelson A. Miles, *Serving the Republic: Memoirs of the Civil and Military Life of Nelson A. Miles, Lieutenant-General, United States Army* (New York: Harper and Brothers, 1911), 10–11; Miles to Brother, Jan. 6, 1859, May 6, 1860 (quotation), Miles Collection.

11. Miles to Brother, Mar. 7, 1859, Miles Collection; Miles, *Personal Recollections*, 21–22 (quotations); Miles to Brother, May 6, 1860, Miles Collection; Miles to Uncle and Aunt, Oct. 25, 1861, ibid.; Miles to Aunt, Dec. 12, 1861, ibid.; *Progressive Men of the State of Montana* (Chicago: A. W. Bowen and Co., n.d.), 1164.

12. Miles, *Serving the Republic*, 11–12; Pohanka, *Documentary Biography*, 20; Miles to Brother, Jan. 6, 1859 (quotation), May 6, Aug. 10, 1860, Miles Collection.

13. Miles to Brother, May 6, 1860, Miles Collection; Miles, *Personal Recollections*, 24.

14. Miles to Brother, Apr. 18, 1861, Miles Collection.

15. Miles, *Personal Recollections*, 30; Miles, *Serving the Republic*, 25; Miles to Church, Aug. 8, 1890, box 2, William C. Church Papers, LC (hereafter cited as Church Papers); Miles to Uncle, Dec. 18, 1861, Miles Collection; Miles to Aunt, Dec. 12, 1861, ibid. (first quotation); John L. Parker and Robert G. Carter, *Henry Wilson's Regiment: History of the Twenty-Second Massachusetts Infantry, the Second Company Sharpshooters, and the Third Light Battery, in the War of the Rebellion* (Boston: Rand Avery Co., 1887), 11; Massachusetts Adjutant General's Office, *Massachusetts Soldiers, Sailors, and Marines in the Civil War* (Norwood: Norwood Press, 1931), 2:679; Arthur J. Amchan, *The Most Famous Soldier in America: A Biography of Lt. Gen. Nelson A. Miles, 1839–1925* (Alexandria, Va.: Amchan Publications, 1989), 6 (second quotation).

16. Miles to Brother, Mar. 7, 1858, Miles Collection; Miles, *Serving the Republic*, 28; *Official Army Register of the Volunteer Force of the United States Army for the Years 1861, '62, '63, '64, '65*, part 1, *New England States* (1865; reprint, Gaithersburg, Md.: Ron R. Van Sickle Military Books, 1987), 181; Parker and Carter, *Wilson's Regiment*, 48–49.

17. Parker and Carter, *Wilson's Regiment*, 3, 24–27; Miles to Brother, Sept. 24, 1861, Miles Collection; Miles, *Personal Recollections*, 31.

18. Miles to Uncle and Aunt, Oct. 5, 1861, Miles Collection (quotation); Parker and Carter, *Wilson's Regiment*, 33–44.

19. Parker and Carter, *Wilson's Regiment*, 44–49, 50.

20. Ibid., 47, 60; Miles to Uncle and Aunt, Oct. 5, 25 (quotation), 1861, Miles Collection.

21. Miles, *Serving the Republic*, 28; Parker and Carter, *Wilson's Regiment*, 67 (quotation); General Orders no.8, Nov. 10, 1861, Miles Collection.

22. Miles to Uncle, Dec. 11, 12, 18 (first quotation), 1861, Miles Collection; Miles to Uncle and Aunt, Oct. 5 (second quotation), 25 (third quotation), 1861, ibid.; Oliver O. Howard, *Autobiography of Oliver Otis Howard, Major General, United States Army*, 2 vols. (New York: Baker and Taylor Co., 1908), 1:181; Parker and Carter, *Wilson's Regiment*, 54.

23. Miles to Aunt, Dec. 12, 1861, Miles Collection (first, second, and third quotations); La Mountain to Butler, Aug. 10, 1861, *War of the Rebellion: A Compilation of the Official Records of the Union and Confederate Armies*, 129 vols. (Washington, D.C.: GPO, 1880–1901) (hereafter cited as *War of the Rebellion* and unless otherwise noted all citations are from series 1) 4:600–601.

24. Miles to Aunt, Dec. 12, 1861, Miles Collection; Miles to Uncle, Dec. 18, 1861, ibid.; Miles to Uncle and Aunt, Dec. 29, 1861, ibid.

25. Mark M. Boatner III, *The Civil War Dictionary*, rev. ed. (New York: David McKay, 1988), 44; Stephen W. Sears, *Landscape Turned Red: The Battle of Antietam* (New Haven: Ticknor and Fields, 1983), 247; Barlow to Mother, Jan. 30, 1862, roll 1, Francis C. Barlow Papers, Massachusetts Historical Society, Boston (hereafter cited as Barlow Papers) (first three quotations); Barlow to Morgan, May 1, 1862, War 1861–65 Letters B, box 1, Miscellaneous Manuscripts, New-York Historical Society, New York City (fourth and fifth quotations).

26. Miles to Uncle, Dec. 18, 1861, Miles Collection (first two quotations); Miles to Uncle and Aunt, Dec. 29, 1861, ibid. (third and fourth quotations).

27. Report of Howard, June 3, 1862, *War of the Rebellion*, vol.2, pt.1, pp.769–70; Report of Richardson, June 6, 1862, ibid., 766.

28. Report of Howard, June 3, 1862, ibid., 769 (quotation); Francis A. Walker, *History of the Second Army Corps in the Army of the Potomac* (New York: Charles Scribner's Sons, 1886), 53.

29. Miles, *Serving the Republic*, 31 (quotation); Miles to Howard, Sept. 26, 1887, Oliver O. Howard Papers, Bowdoin College Library, Brunswick, Maine (hereafter cited as Howard Papers); Howard, *Autobiography*, 245–52.

30. Miles, *Serving the Republic*, 35.

31. Report of Caldwell, July 6, 1862, *War of the Rebellion*, vol.2, pt.2, p.62.

32. Barlow to Edward and Richard, July 12, 1862, roll 1, Barlow Papers (quotation); Barlow to Mother, July 4, 1862, ibid.; Barlow to Edward, July 8, 1862, ibid.

33. Report of Caldwell, July 6, 1862, *War of the Rebellion*, vol.2, pt.2, p.62 (quotation); Report of Barlow, July 5, 1862, ibid., 68; Miles, *Personal Recollections*, 31; Miles, *Serving the Republic*, 39–40; Miles to Church, Aug. 8, 1890, box 2, Church Papers; George E. Pond, "Major-General Nelson A. Miles," *McClure's Magazine* 5 (Nov. 1895): 564; Barlow to Wilson, Nov. 28, 1863, box 2, Nelson A. Miles Papers, Library of Congress, Washington, D.C. (hereafter cited as Miles Papers).

34. John Gibbon, *Personal Recollections of the Civil War* (New York: G. P. Putnam's Sons, 1928), 73.

35. Charles A. Fuller, *Personal Recollections of the War of 1861, Sixty-first Regiment New York Volunteer Infantry* (Sherburne, N.Y.: News Job, 1906), 57; Miles, *Serving the Republic*, 44 (quotation).

36. Sears, *Landscape Turned Red*, 247–52; Miles, *Serving the Republic*, 45; E. P. Alexander, *Military Memoirs of a Confederate*, ed. T. Harry Williams (Bloomington: Indiana University Press, 1962), 262.

37. Report of Caldwell, Sept. 24, 1862, *War of the Rebellion*, vol.19, pt.2, p.286 (first two quotations); Barlow to Mother, Sept. 18, 1862, roll 1, Barlow Papers (third quotation); Report of Barlow, Sept. 22, 1862, *War of the Rebellion*, vol.19, pt.1, p.290 (fourth quotation).

38. Shelby Foote, *The Civil War: A Narrative, Fort Sumter to Perryville* (New York: Random House, 1958), 765.

39. Report of Miles, Dec. 14, 1862, *War of the Rebellion*, 21:236–37 (first quotation); Report of Caldwell, Jan. 21, 1863, ibid., 233 (second quotation); Report of Hancock, Dec. 25, 1862, ibid., 227.

40. Report of Caldwell, Jan. 21, 1863, *War of the Rebellion*, 22:233–34; Fuller, *Personal Recollections*, 81; Howard, *Autobiography*, 1:340–42.

41. Report of Caldwell, Jan. 21, 1863, *War of the Rebellion*, 22:234 (first quotation); Report of Hancock, Dec. 25, 1862, ibid., 230 (second and third quotations).

42. Surgeon's Certificate, Jan. 5, 1863, Miles Collection; Report of Miles, Dec. 14, 1862, *War of the Rebellion*, 21:238 (first quotation); Fuller, *Personal Recollections*, 81 (second and third quotations), 36 (fourth quotation); Francis A. Walker, *General Hancock* (New York: D. Appleton and Co., 1894), 67; Report of Hancock, Dec. 25, 1862, *War of the Rebellion*, 21:230.

43. Miles to Brother, Feb. 26, 1863, Miles Collection (first quotation); Miles to Uncle and Aunt, Feb. 7, Mar. 8, 20 (second quotation) 1863, ibid.; Pohanka, *Documentary Biography*, p.34, n.18; Howard to Assistant Adjutant General, Apr. 13, 1863, 2220 ACP 1879, box 570, ACP Doc., RG 94, NARA.

44. Miles to Uncle and Aunt, Mar. 8, 20, 1863, Miles Collection.

45. Peter R. DeMontravel, "The Career of Lieutenant General Nelson A. Miles: From the Civil War through the Indian Wars" (Ph.D. diss., St. John's University, 1983), 43–45.

46. Report of Miles, May 5, 1863, *War of the Rebellion*, vol.25, pt.1, p.322; Miles to Hancock, May 2, 1863, ibid., vol.51, pt.1, pp.1034–35; Walker, *General Hancock*, 79, 82 (quotation); Walker, *Second Army Corps*, 62; Report of Hancock, May 19, 1863, *War of the Rebellion*, vol.25, pt.1, pp.311–13; Report of Caldwell, May 12, 1863, ibid., 319; David M. Jordan, *Winfield Scott Hancock: A Soldier's Life* (Bloomington: Indiana University Press, 1988), 70; Darius N. Couch, "The Chancellorsville Campaign," *Battles and Leaders of the Civil War*, vol.3 (New York: Century Co., 1888), 161.

47. Report of Miles, May 5, 1863, *War of the Rebellion*, vol.25, pt.1, p.323.

48. *New York Times*, Aug. 1, 1899; Report of Vogell, Feb. 5, 1866, Miles Collection; Miles, *Serving the Republic*, 55 (quotation). Miles later met the soldier who allegedly shot him (see *New York Times*, May 16, 1925).

49. Miles, *Serving the Republic*, 55; J. W. Muffly, ed., *The Story of Our Regiment: A History of the 148th Pennsylvania Volunteers* (Des Moines: Kenyon Printing Co., 1904), 184.

50. Report of Caldwell, May 12, 1863, *War of the Rebellion*, vol.25, pt.1, pp.320–21 (first quotation); Caldwell to Miles, May 19, 1863, box 1, Miles Papers (second quotation); Report of Hancock, May 19, 1863, *War of the Rebellion*, vol.25, pt.1, p.315 (third quotation); Walker, *General Hancock*, 82 (fourth quotation); Report of K. O. Broady, May 7, 1863, *War of the Rebellion*, vol.25, pt.1, p.325 (fifth quotation).

In 1892, Miles was awarded the Medal of Honor for his gallantry at Chancellorsville (see below, chap.12).

51. Gerald F. Linderman, *Embattled Courage: The Experience of Combat in the American Civil War* (New York: Free Press, 1987), 7–8, 21–22, 43–44; Bruce Catton, *The Army of the Potomac: Glory Road* (Garden City, N.Y.: Doubleday and Co., 1962), 199–200; Fuller, *Personal Recollections*, 107 (quotation); Pond, "Miles," 64–66.

52. Howard, *Autobiography*, 1:187; Sears, *Landscape Turned Red*, 243 (quotation).

CHAPTER TWO

1. Boatner, *Civil War Dictionary*, 204.

2. H. C. Vogell to Miles, June 10, 1863, Miles Collection (quotation); Miles to Brother, June 28, 1863, ibid.; Miles, *Personal Recollections*, 33.

3. Miles to Aunt, July 19, 1863, Miles Collection (first quotation); Miles to Uncle and Aunt, July 29, 1863, ibid. (second quotation); Troops in the Department of the Susquehanna, July 10, 1863, *War of the Rebellion*, vol.27, pt.3, pp.641–43;

Report of Couch, July 15, 1863, ibid., pt.2, p.214; Miles, *Serving the Republic*, 61.

4. Miles to Uncle and Aunt, July 29, 1863, Miles Collection; Miles to Uncle Nelson, Aug. 26, 1863, ibid.; Miles to Wilson, Aug. 12, 1863, LR, CB, NARA; Pohanka, *Documentary Biography*, 38 n.23; Barlow to Miles, May 26, 1863, box 1, Miles Papers; Hancock to S. Williams, June 23, 1863, *War of the Rebellion*, vol.27, pt.3, p.274; ibid., p.796.

5. Miles to Uncle and Aunt, July 29, 1863, Miles Collection; Miles to Brother, Aug. 4, 1863, ibid. (first quotation); Miles to Uncle and Aunt, July [presumably Aug.] 3, 1863, ibid.; Miles to Uncle Nelson, Aug. 26, 1863, ibid. (second quotation).

6. Miles to Brother, Aug. 4, Sept. 8, 1863, ibid.; Miles to Aunt, Aug. 22, 1863, ibid. (first quotation); Miles to Uncle and Aunt, Sept. 21, 1863, ibid. (second quotation); Heywood, *History*, 781.

7. Miles to Brother, Sept. 8, 19, 1863, Miles Collection; Miles to Uncle, Oct. 28, 1863, ibid.; Miles to Aunt, Nov. 5, 1863, ibid.; B. F. Powelson, *History of Company K of the 140th Regiment Pennsylvania Volunteers (1862–'65)* (Steubenville, Ohio: Cornahan Co., 1906), 30–31 (quotations).

8. Miles to Aunt, Nov. 5, 1863, Miles Collection.

9. Miles to Uncle Nelson, Aug. 26, Oct. 28, 1863, ibid.; Miles to Uncle and Aunt, Oct. 19, Nov. 15 (first quotation), 1863, ibid.; Miles to Brother, Nov. 20, 1863, ibid. (second quotation).

10. Miles to Brother, Dec. 9, 1863, ibid. (first quotation); Miles to Uncle and Aunt, Dec. 1863, ibid. (second, third, and fourth quotations).

11. Miles to Uncle, Oct. 28, 1863, ibid.; Miles to Aunt, Nov. 5, 1863, ibid.; Miles to Uncle and Aunt, Nov. 15 (first quotation), Dec. (second quotation) 1863, ibid.

12. Miles to Uncle and Aunt, Dec. 29, 1863, ibid.; Miles to Brother, Feb. 5, 1864, ibid.; General Orders no.11, Mar. 25, 1864, *War of the Rebellion*, 33:735; Miles to Whittier, Mar. 28, 1864, ibid., vol.40, pt.1, p.196. The Sixth Minnesota, originally a part of Miles's brigade, would soon be transferred.

13. Miles to Uncle and Aunt, Nov. 15, 1863, Miles Collection.

14. Report of Miles, Oct. 30, 1864, *War of the Rebellion*, vol.36, pt.1, p.360; Jordan, *Hancock*, 110–25.

15. Return of Casualties, *War of the Rebellion*, vol.36, pt.1, p.120; Report of Hancock, Sept. 21, 1865, ibid., 329 (quotation); Report of Miles, Oct. 30, 1864, ibid., 370; Jordan, *Hancock*, 126; William D. Matter, *If It Takes All Summer: The Battle of Spotsylvania* (Chapel Hill: University of North Carolina Press, 1988), 78, 81–82.

16. Report of Hancock, Sept. 21, 1865, *War of the Rebellion*, vol.36, pt.1, pp.331–33; Report of Miles, Oct. 30, 1864, ibid., 370.

17. Report of Hancock, Sept. 21, 1865, *War of the Rebellion*, vol.36, pt.1, pp.331–33; Report of Miles, Oct. 30, 1864, ibid., 370; Francis G. Barlow, "The Capture

of the Salient, May 12, 1864," in *The Wilderness Campaign May–June 1864*, vol.4, *Papers of the Military Historical Society of Massachusetts* (Boston: Military Historical Society of Massachusetts, 1905), 247 (quotation); Jordan, *Hancock*, 137.

18. Report of Hancock, Sept. 21, 1865, *War of the Rebellion*, vol.36, pt.1, p.335; Report of Miles, Oct. 30, 1864, ibid., 370; Robert Laird Stewart, *History of the One Hundred and Fortieth Pennsylvania Volunteers* (privately published, 1912), 197; Barlow, "Capture of the Salient," 250–59; Grady McWhiney and Perry D. Jamieson, *Attack and Die: Civil War Military Tactics and the Southern Heritage* (University: University of Alabama Press, 1982), 92, 95.

19. Report of Hancock, Sept. 21, 1865, *War of the Rebellion*, vol.36, pt.1, p.335; Report of Miles, Oct. 30, 1864, ibid., 370; Stewart, *History*, 197; Barlow, "Capture of the Salient," 250–59; McWhiney and Jamieson, *Attack and Die*, 92, 95.

20. Ibid.; Miles, *Serving the Republic*, 67 (first quotation); extract of Miles to Barlow, Jan. 6, 1879, in Barlow, "Capture of the Salient," 259–62 (second quotation); Miles to M. J. Wright, Feb. 3, 1896, Miscellaneous Files, EG, box 41, Huntington Library, San Marino, California.

21. George A. Armes, *Ups and Downs of an Army Officer* (Washington, D.C.: privately printed, 1900), 98 (first quotation); Barlow to Wilson, Nov. 28, 1863, box 2, Miles Papers; Barlow to Walker, May 13, 1864, *War of the Rebellion*, vol.36, pt.2, p.710; Report of Hancock, Sept. 21, 1865, ibid., pt.1, p.339; Meade to Bowers, May 16, 1864, ibid., pt.2, p.812 (second quotation).

22. Grant to Halleck, May 11, 1864, *War of the Rebellion*, vol.36, pt.1, p.4 (quotation); Jordan, *Hancock*, 132–33.

23. Report of Miles, Oct. 30, 1864, *War of the Rebellion*, vol.36, pt.1, p.370; Miles to Brother and All, May 25, 1864, Miles Collection (quotations).

24. Report of Miles, Oct. 30, 1864, *War of the Rebellion*, vol.36, pt.1, pp.371–72; William Child, *A History of the Fifth Regiment New Hampshire Volunteers in the American Civil War, 1861–1865* (Bristol, N.H.: R. W. Musgrove, 1893), 253.

25. Jordan, *Hancock*, 137–39; Report of Miles, Oct. 30, 1864, *War of the Rebellion*, vol.36, pt.1, p.372; Report of J. E. Larkin, Aug. 9, 1864, ibid., 375–76.

26. Report of Hancock, Sept. 21, 1865, *War of the Rebellion*, vol.36, pt.1, pp.344–46 (quotations); Jordan, *Hancock*, 139–40; Miles to Brother, June 8, 1864, Miles Collection.

27. Miles to Uncle, June 28, 1864, Miles Collection.

28. Miles to Driver, Oct. 30, 1864, *War of the Rebellion*, vol.40, pt.1, p.333; Barlow to Walker, June 25, 1864, ibid., 330 (first quotation); Jordan, *Hancock*, 147; James M. McPherson, *Battle Cry of Freedom: The Civil War Era* (New York: Oxford University Press, 1988), 735–36; Miles to Brother, June 22, 1864, Miles Collection (second and third quotations).

29. Miles to Uncle, June 28, 1864, Miles Collection (first quotation). Casualty figures compiled from *War of the Rebellion*, vol.36, pt.1, pp.120, 137, 153, 166, and vol.40, pt.1, p.219. Miles to Aunt Mary, June 27, 1864, Miles Collection (second quotation); Miles to Howard, Aug. 11, 1864, ibid.

30. Jordan, *Hancock*, 146–49; Armes, *Ups and Downs*, 111; Miles to Brother, July 26, 1864, Miles Collection (quotations).

31. Jordan, *Hancock*, 152–54; Miles to Driver, Oct. 30, 1864, *War of the Rebellion*, vol.40, pt.1, p.333; Report of Fleming, n.d., ibid., 335; Barlow to Wilson, n.d., ibid., 331; General Orders no.25, July 31, 1864, ibid., 324–25.

32. Jordan, *Hancock*, 152–54; Child, *Fifth Regiment*, 209 (quotation); Special Orders no.258, Aug. 3, 1864, *War of the Rebellion*, vol.40, pp.42–43. The Crater board's report may be found in ibid., 125–29, 171–76.

33. Barlow to Wilson, n.d., *War of the Rebellion*, vol.42, pt.1, pp.247–48 (quotation); Hancock to Williams, Nov. 12, 1864, ibid., 217; Miles to Bingham, Oct. 10, 1864, ibid., 250; *War of the Rebellion*, vol.42, pt.1, pp.116–17; Jordan, *Hancock*, 155–56; Boatner, *Civil War Dictionary*, 44.

34. Barlow to Wilson, n.d., *War of the Rebellion*, vol.42, pt.1, p.249; Miles to Wilson, Aug. 30, 1864, ibid., 251; Walker, *Second Army Corps*, 231; Hancock to Grant, Aug. 19, 1864, *War of the Rebellion*, vol.42, pt.2, p.301; Grant to Hancock, Aug. 19, 1864, ibid., 301; Miles to Wilson, Aug. 30, 1864, ibid., pt.1, pp.250–51; Jordan, *Hancock*, 160–61.

    Miles had briefly assumed division command in late July, when Barlow's wife, a nurse, died of typhoid (Pohanka, *Documentary Biography*, 48).

35. Hancock to Humphreys, Aug. 24, 1864, *War of the Rebellion*, vol.42, pt.2, p.448 (quotation); Miles to Wilson, ibid., pt.1, p.251; Jordan, *Hancock*, 160.

36. Miles to Wilson, Aug. 30, 1864, *War of the Rebellion*, vol.42, pt.1, pp.251–53 (quotation); Miles to Uncle, Sept. 12, 1864, Miles Collection; Hancock to Humphreys, Aug. 26, 1864, *War of the Rebellion*, vol.42, pt.2, p.525.

37. Jordan, *Hancock*, 162; Miles to Wilson, Aug. 30, 1864, *War of the Rebellion*, vol.42, pt.1, p.253; Gibbon to Wilson, Aug. 30, 1864, ibid., 293–94; Hancock to Williams, Sept. 12, 1864, ibid., 226.

38. Hancock to Williams, Sept. 17, 1864, *War of the Rebellion*, vol.42, pt.2, p.886; Hancock to Williams, Sept. 12, 1864, ibid., pt.1, p.227; Miles to Uncle, Sept. 12, 1864, Miles Collection (first quotation); Miles to General, Sept. 3, 1864, ibid. (second and third quotations); Hancock to Williams, Aug. 30, 1864, *War of the Rebellion*, vol.42, pt.2, p.594; Meade to Stanton, Nov. 2, 1864, ibid., pt.3, p.483.

39. Circular, Sept. 6, 1864, *War of the Rebellion*, vol.42, pt.2, p.722; Hancock to Williams, Sept. 24, 1864, ibid., 993–94; Miles to Bingham, Sept. 25, 1864, ibid., 1018; circular, Oct. 3, 1864, ibid., pt.3, p.57; Miles to Carncross, Oct. 17, 1864, ibid., 258.

40. Hancock to Humphreys, Oct. 23, 1864, ibid., 310; circular, Oct. 24, 1864, ibid., 323–34; Williams to Miles, Oct. 27, 1864, ibid., 383; Muffly, *Story of Our Regiment*, 50–53.

41. Husk to Mitchell, Oct. 31, 1864, *War of the Rebellion*, vol.42, pt.1, pp.259–60; MacDougall to Driver, Nov. 1, 1864, ibid., pt.1, p.256; Miles to Carncross, Nov. 2, 1864, ibid., 255; Milliken to Mitchell, Oct. 31, 1864, ibid., 257; Delavan S. Miller, *Drum Taps in Dixie: Memories of a Drummer Boy, 1861–1865* (Watertown, N.Y.: Hungerford-Holbrook Co., 1905), 143.

42. Miles to Uncle, Sept. 12, Oct. 21 (quotations), 1864, Miles Collection.

43. Miles to Uncle and Aunt, Sept. 21, 1863, Dec. 7, 1864, ibid.; Miles to Uncle, Sept. 12 (quotation), Oct. 21, 1864, ibid.

44. Miles to Uncle, Sept. 12, Oct. 21 (first quotation), Dec. 7, 1864, ibid.; Miles to Brother, Nov. 9, 1864, ibid. (second quotation); Hancock to Meade, Nov. 8, 1864, *War of the Rebellion*, vol.42, pt.3, p.561; Meade to Stanton, Nov. 11, 1864, ibid., 595–96.

45. Hancock to Williams, Nov. 10, 1864, *War of the Rebellion*, vol.42, pt.3, p.586; Pond, "Miles," 565; Jordan, *Hancock*, 169–72; Boatner, *Civil War Dictionary*, 417.

46. Humphreys to Meade, Dec. 6, 1864, *War of the Rebellion*, vol.42, pt.3, pp.823–24; Miles to Uncle, Oct. 21, 1864, Miles Collection (quotation); Miles to Carncross, Dec. 20, 1864, *War of the Rebellion*, vol.42, pt.3, pp.1046–47.

47. See exchanges between Grant and Meade, Dec. 9, 1864, *War of the Rebellion*, vol.42, pt.3, pp.889–91, 901 (first quotation); Armes, *Ups and Downs*, 121–27; Miles to Carncross, Dec. 13, 1864, *War of the Rebellion*, vol.42, pt.1, pp.260–61; Miles to Humphreys, Dec. 9, 1864, ibid., pt.3, p.900; Miles to Assistant Adjutant General, Dec. 9, 1864, ibid., pt.3, pp.907–08; Miles to Carncross, Dec. 20, 1864, ibid., pt.3, pp.1046–47 (second quotation).

48. Miles to Carncross, Jan. 5, 1865, *War of the Rebellion*, vol.46, pt.2, p.42; Hancock to Warren, Oct. 31, 1864, ibid., vol.42, pt.3, p.450; Humphreys to Williams, Dec. 27, 1864, ibid., 1083 (quotation); Humphreys to Webb, Feb. 14, 1865, ibid., vol.46, pt.2, p.555; Ruggles to Miles, Feb. 15, 17, 1865, ibid., pp.563, 577. The previous October, Meade had suggested minor changes in the dates of brevet ranks so that Miles would not outrank his long-time and equally deserving superior, Francis Barlow (Meade to Stanton, Oct. 31, 1864, ibid., vol.42, pt.3, pp.443–44).

49. Meade to Grant, Feb. 22, 1865, ibid., vol.46, pt.2, p.631; Miles to Webb, ibid., 635 (first quotation); Webb to Miles, ibid. (second quotation); Miles to Whittier, Mar. 14, 1865, ibid., 969.

50. Humphreys to Webb, Mar. 25, 1865, ibid., pt.3, p.126; Orders, ibid., 129; Miles to Whittier, ibid., vol.51, pt.1, p.1205; Miles to Whittier, Mar. 28, 1865, ibid., vol.46, pt.1, p.197 (quotation).

51. Miles to Aunt, Mar. 28, 1865, Miles Collection (first and second quotations);

General Orders no.28, Mar. 27, 1865, *War of the Rebellion*, vol.46, pt.3, p.201 (third quotation); Orders, Mar. 30, 1865, ibid., 297.

52. Miles to Whittier, Mar. 30, 1865, *War of the Rebellion*, vol.51, pt.1, p.1209; Miles to Whittier, Mar. 31, 1865, ibid., pt.3, p.355; Miles to Whittier, Apr. 20, 1865, ibid., vol.46, pt.1, p.710 (quotation); Humphreys to Webb, Mar. 31, 1865, ibid., pt.3, p.351; Humphreys to Webb, Apr. 21, 1865, ibid., pt.1, p.677.

53. Miles to Whittier, Apr. 20, 1865, ibid., pt.1, pp.710–11; Humphreys to Webb, Mar. 31, 1865, ibid., pt.3, p.348; Meade to Humphreys, ibid., 349–50. Warren spent the next seventeen years attempting to clear his name. In 1882, the Warren Court of Inquiry exonerated the accused on three of the four charges Sheridan had made against him. Miles played but a minor role in the hearings; characteristically, his testimony credited his own men for having forced Rebel troops in front of Warren to retreat (*New York Times*, June 29, 1880).

54. Grant to Meade, Apr. 1, 1865, *War of the Rebellion*, vol.46, pt.3, p.396; Miles to Whittier, Apr. 20, 1865, ibid., pt.1, p.711; Whittier to Miles, Apr. 1, 1865, ibid., pt.3, p.408; Sheridan to Rawlins, May 16, 1865, ibid., pt.1, p.1106; Miles to General, Apr. 2, 1865, Alexander Stewart Webb Papers, Manuscripts and Archives, Yale University Library, New Haven (hereafter cited as Webb Papers) (first quotation); Miles to Humphreys, Apr. 2, 1865, *War of the Rebellion*, vol.46, pt.3, p.469 (second quotation).

55. Miles to Whittier, Apr. 20, 1865, *War of the Rebellion*, vol.46, pt.1, pp.711–12 (quotation); Meade to Bowers, Apr. 30, 1865, ibid., 603; Meade to Grant, Apr. 2, 1865, ibid., pt.3, p.457.

56. Sheridan to Rawlins, May 16, 1865, ibid., pt.1, p.1106; Miles to Whittier, Apr. 2, 1865, ibid., pt.3, p.470; Meade to Bowers, Apr. 30, 1865, ibid., pt.1, p.605 (first quotation); Grant to Meade, Apr. 2, 1865, ibid., pt.3, p.459 (second quotation).

57. Orders, Apr. 4, 1865, ibid., pt.3, p.552.

58. Humphreys to Webb, Apr. 21, 1865, ibid., pt.1, p.682 (first quotation); Miles to Whittier, Apr. 20, 1865, ibid., 712; Miles, *Personal Recollections*, 39–40 (second quotation).

59. Miles to Whittier, Apr. 7, 1865, *War of the Rebellion*, vol.46, pt.3, p.627 (quotations), Miles to Whittier, Apr. 20, 1865, ibid., pt.1, pp.712–13.

60. Miles to Whittier, Apr. 7, 1865, *War of the Rebellion*, vol.46, pt.3, p.627; Miles to Whittier, Apr. 20, 1865, ibid., pt.1, pp.712–13; Douglas Southall Freeman, *R. E. Lee: A Biography* (1935; reprint, New York: Charles Scribner's Sons, 1947), 4:120–23 (quotation).

61. Miles, *Personal Recollections*, 45 (quotations); Miller, *Drum Taps*, 183; Miles to Wright, Feb. 3, 1896, Miscellaneous Files, EG, box 41. Huntington Library. For a slightly different version of the oak tree story, see Matter, *If It Takes All Summer*, 373.

62. Miles, *Personal Recollections*, 34; Linderman, *Embattled Courage*, 156–255.

63. Pond, "Miles," 564 (first quotation); Howard to whom it may concern, Dec. 14, 1865, Miles Collection (second quotation); Barlow to Wilson, Nov. 28, 1863, box 2, Miles Papers (third quotation); Humphreys to Ruggles, Apr. 21, 1865, *War of the Rebellion,* vol.46, pt.3, pp.878–79; Boatner, *Civil War Dictionary,* 550.

CHAPTER THREE

1. Proclamation of Johnson, May 2, 1865, Miles Collection; Report of Pritchard, May 25, 1865, *War of the Rebellion,* vol.49, pt.1, pp.536–38.

2. Pohanka, *Documentary Biography,* 66; Orders, May 14, 1865, *War of the Rebellion,* vol.46, pt.3, p.1150; Grant to Meade, May 19, 1865, ibid., 1175 (quotation); Grant to Halleck, ibid., 1174.

3. Richard P. Weinert, Jr., and Colonel Robert Arthur, *Defender of the Chesapeake: The Story of Fort Monroe* (Annapolis, Md.: Leeward Publications, 1978), 128–29; Grant to Halleck, May 19, 1865, *War of the Rebellion,* vol.46, pt.3, p.1174; Dana to Stanton, May 22, 1865, ibid., ser.2, pt.8, pp.563–64 (quotation).

4. Halleck to Miles, May 22, 1865, *War of the Rebellion,* ser.2, vol.8, pp.565–66 (quotation); Dana to Stanton, ibid., 564.

5. Dana to Stanton, May 22, 1865, ibid., 564 (first quotation); Halleck to Miles, ibid., 564–65 (second quotation).

6. Miles to Townsend, Oct. 30, 1878, Miles Collection; Dana to Miles, May 23, 1865, *War of the Rebellion,* ser.2, vol.8, p.569; Report of Dana, May 22, 1865, ibid., 565 (quotation); Dana to Leslie J. Perry, Sept. 3, 1895, Miles Collection; Miles to Dawes, Dec. 28, 1896, Henry L. Dawes Papers, LC (hereafter cited as Dawes Papers).

7. Davis to Miles, [May 23, 1865], Miles Collection (quotation); Miles to Townsend, Oct. 30, 1878, ibid.; Weinert and Arthur, *Defender of the Chesapeake,* 131–32.

8. John J. Craven, *Prison Life of Jefferson Davis, Embracing Details and Incidents in His Captivity, Particulars Concerning His Health and Habits, Together with Many Conversations on Topics of Great Public Interest* (1866; reprint, Marceline, Mo.: Walsworth Publishing Co., 1979), 33–39; William Hanchett, "Reconstruction and the Rehabilitation of Jefferson Davis: Charles G. Halpine's *Prison Life,*" *Journal of American History* 56 (Sept. 1969): 287 (first quotation); *New York Tribune,* May 27, 1865; Miles to Dana, May 24, 1865, *War of the Rebellion,* ser.2, vol.8, pp.570–71 (second quotation).

9. General Orders no.60, May 20, 1865, *War of the Rebellion,* vol.46, pt.3, p.1184; Special Orders, May 25, ibid., 1213; Miles affidavit, Sept. 22, 1865, attached to Booker to Johnson, Aug. 22, 1865, section 1, Schilling Papers, Virginia Histor-

ical Society, Richmond (hereafter cited as Schilling Papers); Miles to Senator, Sept. 13, 1865, Miles Collection (quotation); Nugent to Miles, May 25, 1865, ibid.

10. Dana to Stanton, May 22, 1865, *War of the Rebellion*, ser.2, vol.8, p.564; Craven, *Prison Life* (quotation), 43, 51–52; Miles to Halleck, May 24, 1865, *War of the Rebellion*, ser.2, vol.8, p.570; Halleck to Miles, ibid.

11. Craven, *Prison Life*, 65; *New York Tribune*, May 27, 1865; Letter from A. A. Wiley, Feb. 14, fragment, *Montgomery Journal*, in Miles Collection; Stanton to Miles, May 28, 1865, *War of the Rebellion*, ser.2, vol.8, p.577 (first quotation); Miles to Stanton, ibid. (second quotation).

12. Miles to Townsend, June 6, 1865, *War of the Rebellion*, ser.2, vol.8, p.642; Townsend to Miles, ibid.; Townsend to Miles, June 8, 1865, ibid., 647; Stanton to Miles, July 14, 1865, ibid., 706 (quotation).

13. Craven, *Prison Life*, 96, 116–17; Davis to Mrs. Davis, Oct. 11, 1865, in Dunbar Rowland, *Jefferson Davis, Constitutionalist: His Letters, Papers and Speeches*, 10 vols. (Jackson: Mississippi Department of Archives and History, 1923), 7:50; Miles to Townsend, Oct. 23, 1865, *War of the Rebellion*, ser.2, vol.8, pp.769–70 (quotation).

14. Miles to Townsend, June 27 (quotation), July 20, 1865, *War of the Rebellion*, ser.2, vol.8, pp.673, 710, 769–70; Craven, *Prison Life*, 183–84; Stanton to Miles, July 22, 1865, *War of the Rebellion*, ser.2, vol.8, pp.710–14.

15. Craven, *Prison Life*, 191; Miles to Townsend, Aug. 15, 1865, *War of the Rebellion*, ser.2, vol.8, pp.716–17; Townsend to Miles, Aug. 18, 1865, ibid., 719 (quotation); Hudson Strode, ed., *Jefferson Davis: Private Letters, 1823–1889* (New York: Harcourt, Brace and World, 1966), 168; Miles to T. T. Eckert, Sept. 14, 1865, *War of the Rebellion*, ser.2, vol.8, p.748; Eckert to Miles, ibid., 747.

16. Davis to Mrs. Davis, Oct. 2, 11, 1865, in Rowland, *Jefferson Davis*, 7:42, 51–52; Lloyd Brice to Davis, Oct. 30, 1889, Ibid., 157–58 (first quotation); statement of July 1, 1898, attached to Varina Davis to [James Henry Morgan], June 30, 1898, MSS 2 D2987, Virginia Historical Society; Miles to Senator, Sept. 13, 1865, Miles Collection (second quotation); Clay to unknown, Oct. 25, 1865, Clement Claiborne Clay Papers, Perkins Memorial Library, Manuscript Department, Duke University, Durham, North Carolina (hereafter cited as Clay Papers).

17. Craven to Miles, Aug. 20, Sept. [n.d.] (quotations), 1865, *War of the Rebellion*, ser.2, vol.8, pp.720, 740; Miles to Townsend, Sept. 2, 12, Oct. 2, 1865, ibid., 740, 746, 761; Townsend to Miles, Sept. 4, 1865, ibid., 740; Townsend to L. H. Pelouze, Sept. 25, 1865, ibid., 755.

18. Miles to E. W. Smith, June 17, 25, 1865, ibid., 657, 673; Miles to Mrs. Clay, June 20, 1865, Clay Papers (first and second quotations); Miles to Townsend, July 4, Aug. 11, 1865, *War of the Rebellion*, ser.2, vol.8, pp.695, 715–16; Clay to

Miles, July 27, 1865, Miles Collection; Miles to Madam, July 29, 1865, Clay Papers; Clay to Wife, Aug. 11, Sept. 18, 1865, ibid. (third quotation).

19. Clay to unknown, [Oct. 1865], Clay Papers (first quotation); Clay to unknown, Oct. 25, 1865, ibid. (second quotation).

20. Mrs. John T. Broadnax to Davis, Mar. 13, 1889, in Rowland, *Jefferson Davis*, 9:535; Davis to Mrs. Davis, Oct. 11, 1866, ibid., 7:49 (first quotation); Hanchett, "Reconstruction," 280–81 (second quotation); Craven, *Prison Life*, 362.

21. Pelouze to Townsend, Sept. 29, 1865, *War of the Rebellion*, ser.2, vol.8, pp.755–60; Miles to Townsend, Dec. 29, 1865, ibid., 841 (first and third quotations); Muhlenberg to J. S. McEwan, ibid. (second quotation).

22. Townsend to Miles, Dec. 30, 1865, ibid., 841–42 (quotation); Miles to Townsend, Jan. 11, 1866, ibid., 846; Townsend to Miles, Jan. 11, 1866, ibid., 847; Miles to Townsend, Jan. 19, 1866, ibid., 869.

23. Unknown to Johnson, Mar. 16, 1866, Clay Papers; Miles to Wilson, Oct. 1, 1865, LR, CB, NARA; Wilson to Stanton, Oct. 9, 1865, ibid.; Miles to Howard, Dec. 12, 1865, Howard Papers (quotation); DeMontravel, "Nelson A. Miles," 127–28; *Arizona Weekly Star*, Oct. 13, 1887; Miles to Townsend, Apr. 10, 1866, Miles Collection; Humphreys to Miles, Jan. 7, 1866, box 2, Miles Papers; Halleck to Miles, Jan. 16, 1866, box 7, ibid.

24. Statement of July 1, 1898, attached to Davis to [Morgan], June 30, 1898, MSS 2 D2987, Virginia Historical Society (quotations). For reports of Davis's health, see *War of the Rebellion*, ser.2, vol.8, pp.871, 875, 886, 892–93, 904. Townsend to Miles, Apr. 26, 1866, ibid., 901. For treatment of Clay, see Johnson to Commander, Dec. 20, 1865, Jan. 12, Mar. 13, 1866, Fair Copy, vol.2, pp.91, 96, 104, roll 43, Andrew Johnson Papers, LC (hereafter cited as Johnson Papers); Miles to Townsend, Mar. 17, 1866, *War of the Rebellion*, ser.2, vol.8, pp.889–90; Townsend to Miles, Apr. 17, 1866, ibid., 899.

25. Cooper to Adj. Genl., May 9, 1866, *War of the Rebellion*, ser.2, vol.8, p.908.

26. Miles to Townsend, May 16, 26 (first, second, and third quotations), 28 (fourth quotation), 1866, ibid., 914, 919.

27. Halpine to Johnson, Mar. 20, 1866, roll 21, Johnson Papers (quotation); Hanchett, "Reconstruction," 280–82; Mrs. J. T. Brodnax to Davis, Mar. 13, 1889, in Rowland, *Jefferson Davis*, 9:535.

28. Barnes to Stanton, June 6, 1866, *War of the Rebellion*, ser.2, vol.8, p.924 (first, second, and third quotations); Cooper to Miles, June 6, 1866, ibid., 925; Cooper to Commanding Officer, July 18, 1866, ibid., 947 (fourth quotation). For another dispute, see the conflicting reports of Cooper to Miles, Aug. 15, 1866, ibid., 952–53; and C. H. Crane and J. Simpson to Barnes, Aug. 14, 1866, ibid., 953–54.

29. Miles to Wilson, July 31, 1866, LR, CB, NARA.

30. Stanton to Miles, Aug. 2, 1866, box 5, Miles Papers (first quotation); Stanton to Miles, Aug. 3, 1866, roll 11, Edwin Stanton Papers, LC (hereafter cited as

Stanton Papers) (second quotation); Miles to Stanton, Aug. 24, 1866, *War of the Rebellion*, ser.2, vol.8, p.955 (third and fourth quotations).

31. Miles to Stanton, Aug. 30, 1866, *War of the Rebellion*, ser.2, vol.8, p.956 (quotation); DeMontravel, "Nelson A. Miles," 125–26; Miles to Howard, Aug. 29, 1866, Howard Papers; Townsend to Miles, Sept. 3, 1866, *War of the Rebellion*, ser.2, vol.8, p.961.

32. Fortieth Infantry Returns, Nov. 1866, roll 295, Returns from Regular Army Infantry Regiments, June 1821–Dec. 1916, NARA; Sheridan to Miles, Sept. 29, 1866, box 9, Miles Papers; Meade to Miles, Oct. 1, 1866, box 3, ibid.; Hancock to Miles, Oct. 15, 1866, box 2, ibid. (quotation).

33. Fortieth Infantry Returns, Dec. 1866–Mar. 1867, roll 294, Returns from Regular Infantry Regiments, June 1821–Dec. 1916, NARA.

34. Ibid., Mar.–Apr. 1867.

35. James E. Sefton, *The United States Army and Reconstruction, 1867–1877* (Baton Rouge: Louisiana State University Press, 1967), 25–60, 113, 144; Michael Perman, *Emancipation and Reconstruction 1862–1879*, The American History Series (Arlington Heights, Ill.: Harlan-Davidson, 1987), 54–55.

36. Miles to Howard, Mar. 8, 19 (first quotation), Aug. 24 (second quotation), 1866, Howard Papers; Miles to Senator, Mar. 15, 1867, LR, CB, NARA (third quotation); Miles to Caziari, Apr. 18, 1867, Miles Collection (fourth quotation). See also George R. Bentley, *A History of the Freedmen's Bureau* (Philadelphia: University of Pennsylvania Press, 1955), 72.

   In 1888, Miles again criticized Grant for having recognized too many former Confederates, arguing that Southern loyalists could have created the nucleus of a strong anti-Democratic party (Miles to Sherman, Nov. 12, 1888, roll 39, William T. Sherman Papers, LC [hereafter cited as W. Sherman Papers]).

37. Circular no.8, Apr. 26, 1867, Miles Collection (first three quotations); circular letter, ibid. (fourth quotation).

38. *Raleigh Weekly Standard*, May 1, 1867 (first and second quotations); Worth to J. L. Orr, May 3, 1867, in J. G. de Roulhac Hamilton, *The Correspondence of Jonathan Worth*, 2 vols. (Raleigh: North Carolina Historical Commission, 1909), 2:942–43 (third quotation); Worth to George Howard, May 11, 1867, ibid., 950–51 (fourth quotation); Worth to C. A. Cilley, May 16, 1867, ibid., 955; Richard L. Zuber, *Jonathan Worth: A Biography of a Southern Unionist* (Chapel Hill: University of North Carolina Press, 1965), 265–66; W. A. Swanberg, *Sickles the Incredible* (New York: Charles Scribner's Sons, 1956), 284–86, 289, 292–93.

39. Circular letter, May 23 (quotation), Nov. 6, 1867, Miles Collection; circular no.13, July 1, 1867, ibid.; circular no.14, July 22, 1867, ibid.; circular no.8, Aug. 17, 1868, ibid.; circular no.19, Oct. 10, 1867, ibid.

40. Gray to Miles, et. al., May 13, July 8, 1867, roll 19, Records of the Assistant Commissioner for the State of North Carolina, Bureau of Refugees, Freedmen,

and Abandoned Lands, 1865–1870, M 843, NARA; J. F. Churr to A. S. Morton, July 2, 1867, ibid. (first quotation); Alvord to Churr, Sept. 13, 1867, ibid.; E. D. Morgan to Miles, May 28, 1867, box 8, Miles Papers; Miles letter of May 9, 1868, James S. Henry Harris Private Collection, North Carolina State Archives, Raleigh; Miles, Holden, and Pulliam letter of May 12, 1868, ibid.; circular no.9, May 22, 1867, Miles Collection; circular no.10, June 10, 1867, ibid.; circular no.15, July 23, 1867, ibid.; Miles to Howard, Oct. 15 (second and third quotations), Dec. 20, 1867, Howard Papers.

41. Otto Olsen, "North Carolina: An Incongruous Presence," in *Reconstruction and Redemption in the South*, ed. Otto Olsen (Baton Rouge: Louisiana State University Press, 1980), 165–78; James L. Lancaster, "The Scalawags of North Carolina, 1850–1868" (Ph.D. diss., Princeton University, 1974), 259–61, 315.

42. Constitutional Convention of North Carolina, Feb. 10, 1868, Miles Collection (quotation); circular no.6, May 21, 1868, ibid.; John Alfred to Holden, Apr. 24, 1868, W. W. Holden Private Collection, North Carolina State Archives; *North Carolina Standard*, Aug. 19, 1868; Jesse Parker Bogue, Jr., "Violence and Oppression in North Carolina during Reconstruction, 1865–1873" (Ph.D. diss., University of Maryland, 1973), 212.

43. Miles to Howard, Nov. 1, Dec. 17, 1867, Howard Papers; Miles to Howard, undated, Miles Collection; circular no.1, Jan. 17, 1868, ibid.; circular no.4, May 18, 1868, ibid. (quotations).

44. Miles to Howard, Dec. 17, 1867, Howard Papers; Howard to Miles, Dec. 20, 1867, box 2, Miles Papers (first quotation); Pohanka, *Documentary Biography*, 73 (second quotation).

45. Miles to Brother, July 20, 1865, Miles Collection; Miles to General, July 10, 1866, ibid.; Miles to Townsend, July 12, 1866, *War of the Rebellion*, ser.2, vol.8, p.946; Miles to Howard, Oct. 15, 1867, Howard Papers.

46. J. Sherman to Mary, Aug. 23 (first quotation), Nov. 22, 1867, box 4, Miles Papers. For the courtship, see Johnson, *Unregimented General*, 32–33 (second quotation).

47. J. Sherman to Mary, Nov. 22, 1867, box 4, Miles Papers; Miles to Howard, Feb. 4, Apr. 8, 1868, Howard Papers; Johnson, *Unregimented General*, 33–34 (quotation).

48. Johnson, *Unregimented General*, 34 (second quotation); Miles to Howard, June 17, 1868, Howard Papers (first quotation); Sheridan to Miles, May 21, 1868, box 9, Miles Papers; J. Sherman to Mary, June 22, 1868, box 4, ibid.; *Cleveland Plain Dealer*, June 27, July 1, 1868.

49. Laura Holden to Ida H. Cowles, Aug. 9, 1868, Calvin J. Cowles Papers, no.3808 Southern Historical Collection, Library of the University of North Carolina at Chapel Hill (quotations).

50. Raphael P. Thian, *Notes Illustrating the Military Geography of the United States, 1813–1880*, ed. John M. Carroll (1881; reprint, Austin: University of

Texas Press, 1979), 95; Fortieth Infantry Returns, Aug. 1868, roll 295, Returns from Regular Army Infantry Regiments June 1821–Dec. 1916, NARA; Meade to Grant, July 30, 1868, LR, NC, NARA (quotation); Holden to Meade, Sept. 14, 1868, ibid.; Drum to Miles, Sept. 16, 1868, ibid.

51. Drum to Miles, Sept. 24, 29 (quotation), 1868, LR, NC, NARA; Miles to Drum, Sept. 25, 1868, LS, NC, NARA; Miles to Howard, Sept. 26, 1868, roll 60, Registers and Letters Received by the Commissioner of the Bureau of Refugees, Freedmen, and Abandoned Lands, 1865–1872, M 752, NARA.

52. Miles to Drum, Oct. 4, 1868, LS, NC, NARA (quotations); Miles to Holden, Oct. 9, 1868, ibid.; Holden to Miles, Oct. 7, 1868, in *North Carolina Standard*, Oct. 9, 1868.

53. Meade to Grant, Oct. 9, 1868, LR, NC, NARA.

54. Meade to Adj. Genl., Oct. 13, 1868, Miles Collection; circular no.10, Oct. 14, 1868, ibid.; Townsend to Meade, Oct. 23, 1868, vol.48, p.513; roll 35, LS, AGO, NARA; Miles to Drum, Oct. 22, 1868, LS, NC, NARA (quotation).

55. General Order no 9, Oct. 14, 1868, Miles Collection (first quotation); Holden to Miles, Oct. 24, 1868, William H. Holden Papers, Governors' Letter Books, North Carolina State Archives; Holden to Sheriff of Cumberland Co., Oct. 24, 1868, LR, NC, NARA; Holden to Miles, Oct. 27, 1868, ibid.; J.C.L. Harris to Miles, Oct. 28, 1868, ibid.; *Raleigh Weekly Standard*, Nov. 4, 1868; Drum to Miles, Oct. 31, 1868, LR, NC, NARA; *Army and Navy Journal*, Nov. 7, 1868; DeMontravel, "Nelson A. Miles," 149 (second quotation).

56. DeMontravel, "Nelson A. Miles," 150–51; *New York Times*, Nov. 13, 1868 (quotation).

57. General Order no.7, District of North Carolina, Oct. 9, 1868, Miles Collection; Anonymous to sw, Sept. 14, 1868, LR, NC, NARA (first quotation); Miles to Howard, Dec. 19, 1868, Howard Papers (second quotation). For the army's inability to solve problems in the Second Military District, see Bogue, "Violence and Oppression in North Carolina," 125.

58. W. Sherman to Mary, Sept. 18, Oct. 21, 1868, box 4, Miles Papers.

59. Holden to North Carolina Representatives and Senators, Jan. 20, 1869, Miles Collection; Scott to Miles, Jan. 20, 1869, box 9, Miles Papers; Miles to W. Sherman, Mar. 12, 1869, roll 14, W. Sherman Papers.

60. Miles later considered retiring in North Carolina, where he would have faced a less-than-gracious welcome (*New York Times*, Apr. 21, 1900).

61. J. Mitchell to Miles, Aug. 21, 1865, Miles Collection; Petition to Miles, Sept. 2, 1866, ibid.; Roberts to Miles, Feb. 15, 1867, ibid. (first quotation); Statement of J. S. McEwan, May 31, 1866, ibid. (second quotation); M. J. Morton to Miles, Feb. 8, 1891, ibid.; McEwan to Miles, Feb. 9, 1891, ibid.; *New York Times*, Feb. 24, Mar. 12, 1905; Miles to Mrs. Clay, Dec. 16, 1865, Clay Papers; V. C. Clay to Miles, Dec. 20, 1865, Miles Collection; Miles to Madam, Mar. 2, 1866, Clay Papers. To compare the treatment of Davis and Clay with other Confeder-

ate prisoners, see J. A. Dix to H. A. Allen, May 25, 1865, *War of the Rebellion,* ser.2, vol.8, p.575. Miles insisted that he had done everything within his power to protect Davis's health, noting that "he walked out of the prison in excellent condition, lived thereafter twenty-two years, and finally died of old age. Any effort to make him a martyr is simply maudline sentimentality" (Miles to Dawes, Dec. 28, 1896, box 20, Dawes Papers).

62. Clay to Jennie, Apr. 19, 1866, Clay Papers (quotation); Statement of July 1, 1898, attached to Varina Davis to [James Henry Morgan], June 30, 1898, MSS 2 D2987, Virginia Historical Society.

63. Miles to Mrs. Clay, Sept. 29, 1866, Clay Papers.

CHAPTER FOUR

1. Miles, *Personal Recollections,* 59–61.

2. Fifth Infantry Returns, Apr. 1869, roll 57, Returns from Regular Army Infantry Regiments, June 1821–Dec. 1916, NARA.

3. Ibid. Mar., Apr. 1869. Service records compiled from Francis B. Heitman, *Historical Register and Dictionary of the United States Army, from Its Organization, September 29, 1789, to March 2, 1902,* 2 vols. (Washington, D.C.: GPO, 1903). For unit organization, see Gregory J. W. Urwin, *The United States Infantry: An Illustrated History, 1775–1918* (New York: Blandford Press, 1988), 120–21.

4. Fifth Infantry Returns, Mar. 1869, roll 57, Returns from Regular Army Infantry Regiments, June 1821–Dec. 1916, NARA; Schofield to Adj. Genl., Apr. 27, May 21, 1869, LS, Mo., NARA; "Memoirs," box 1, pp.255–56, Frank D. Baldwin Papers, Huntington Library (hereafter cited as Baldwin Papers) (first quotation); D. Swift to Mrs. Baldwin, Jan. 10, 1874, box 14, ibid. (second quotation).

5. Elizabeth B. Custer, *Following the Guidon* (1890; reprint, Norman: University of Oklahoma Press, 1966), 80. On Custer, see Robert M. Utley, *Cavalier in Buckskin: George Armstrong Custer and the Western Military Frontier* (Norman: University of Oklahoma Press, 1989).

6. Miles, *Personal Recollections,* 152 (quotation); Miles to Schofield, Apr. 22, 1869, box 6, John M. Schofield Papers, LC (hereafter cited as Schofield Papers); Medical Records, Fort Harker, pp.121, 122, 125, roll 2, Selected Records of Kansas Army Posts, T 837, NARA. On the early relationship between Miles and Custer, much exaggerated by biographers of Miles, see Minnie Dobbs Hollbrook, "Big Game Hunting with the Custers, 1869–1870," *Kansas Historical Quarterly* 41 (Winter 1973): 434 n.18, 442, 443.

7. Armes, *Ups and Downs,* 298, 301; Miles, *Personal Recollections,* 151; Custer, *Following the Guidon,* 195–203; Cecilia Sherman to Mary, July 26, 1869, box

4, Miles Papers; L. Custer to Mrs. Miles, July 10, [n.d.], box 1, ibid.; W. Sherman to Mary, July 22, [n.d.], ibid.; Johnson, *Unregimented General*, 42.

8. U.S. Census, Manuscript Returns, 1870, Ellsworth County, Kansas; Heywood, *History*, 359; Hancock to Miles, Mar. 28, 1870, box 2, Miles Papers; Miles to Schofield, Apr. 29, 1870, box 37, Schofield Papers; J. Sherman to Miles, Dec. 21, 1869, box 4, Miles Papers.

9. W. Sherry to Miles, n.d. [Aug. 5, 1869], LS, Mo., NARA; Mitchell to Commanding Officer, Fort Harker, Oct. 28, Dec. 13, 1869, Jan. 3, 1870, ibid.; Miles to W. Sherman, June 18 (first quotation), July 22, 1870, roll 28, W. Sherman Papers; W. Sherman to Miles, June 18, 1870, box 4, Miles Papers (second quotation); W. Sherman to Miles, Nov. 12 (third quotation), 15, 1870, roll 40, LS, AGO, NARA; Miles to Sherman, Nov. 15, 1870, LR, CB, NARA; Miles to Sherman, Nov. 19, 1870, roll 16, W. Sherman Papers (fourth and fifth quotations).

10. Medical Records, Fort Harker, p.213, roll 2, Selected Records of Kansas Army Posts, T 837, NARA; Miles, *Personal Recollections*, 61–62 (first quotation); Pope to J. Fry, Jan. 4, 1872, LS, Mo., NARA; Asst. Adj. Genl. to Miles, Oct. 24, Dec. 5, 1871, ibid.; Special Orders no.29, Feb. 26, 1872, Miles Collection; General Orders no.10, Oct. 4, 1871, ibid.; Miles to W. Sherman, Nov. 15, 1872, roll 18, W. Sherman Papers (second and third quotations); W. Sherman to Miles, Nov. 19, 1872, box 4, Miles Papers (fourth quotation).

11. Miles to Howard, May 26, 1873, Howard Papers (first quotation); Miles to W. Sherman, Nov. 8, 1873, roll 19, W. Sherman Papers (second quotation).

12. Sheridan to Pope, Dec. 4, 11, 1872, box 92, Philip Sheridan Papers, LC (hereafter cited as Sheridan Papers).

13. George Walton, *Sentinel of the Plains: Fort Leavenworth and the American West* (Englewood Cliffs, N.J.: Prentice-Hall, 1973), 152; General Orders no.10, Oct. 4, 1871, Miles Collection; Vincent to Miles, July 5, 1873, roll 43, LS, AGO, NARA; Miles to Sherman, Nov. 8, 1873, roll 19, July 4, 1876, roll 20, W. Sherman Papers; Jack D. Foner, *The United States Soldier Between Two Wars: Army Life and Reforms, 1865–1898* (New York: Humanities Press, 1970), 56–57; Miles to Adj. Genl., Apr. 18, July 14, 1874, LR, CB, NARA; Adj. Genl. to Miles, May 6, 1874, ibid.

14. General Orders no.10, Oct. 4, 1871, Miles Collection; Adj. Genl. to Miles, July 5, 1873, roll 43, LS, AGO, NARA; Miles to W. Sherman, Nov. 8, 1873, roll 19, W. Sherman Papers; Special Orders no.134, July, 1873, House Exec. Doc. 19, 43d Cong., 1st sess., serial 1606, p.5; Report of Miles, Thomas F. Barr, and George P. Andrews, n.d., ibid., pp.5–10; "Rules and Regulations," ibid., pp.18–25 (quotations).

15. Miles to Howard, Dec. 29, 1873, May 15, 1874, Mar. 6, 1875 (quotation), Howard Papers; Howard to Miles, May 16, 1874, ibid.; John A. Carpenter, *Sword and Olive Branch: Oliver Otis Howard* (Pittsburgh: University of Pitts-

burgh Press, 1964), 226–33; Miles to Sherman, July 4, 1874, roll 20, W. Sherman Papers.

16. Sheridan to Sherman, Sept. 5, 1874, box 11, Sheridan Papers; Report of Pope, Sept. 7, sw, *Annual Report, 1874*, 31; Report of Augur, Sept. 28, ibid., 40–41.

17. Report of Augur, Sept. 28, sw, *Annual Report, 1874*, 40–41; Report of Pope, Sept. 7, ibid., 29–31.

18. Pope to Sheridan, July 16 (first quotation), 22, 1874, LS, Mo., NARA; Sheridan to C. Augur, Aug. 24, 1874, box 11, Sheridan Papers; Pope to Miles, July 29 (second quotation), Aug. 3, 5 (third quotation), 1874, ibid.; Pope to Price, Aug. 12, 1874, ibid.

19. Miles to his wife, Aug. 2, 7, 10, 1874, Nelson A. Miles letters assembled by Sherman Miles and held by Robert M. Utley (hereafter cited as Sherman Miles MSS); Miles, *Personal Recollections*, 164; Baird to Baldwin, Aug. 11, 1874, Baldwin Papers (quotation); J. T. Marshall, *The Miles Expedition of 1874–1875: An Eyewitness Account of the Red River War*, ed. Lonnie J. White (Austin: Encino Press, 1971), 7–12; Report of Miles, Mar. 4, sw, *Annual Report, 1875*, 78.

20. Miles to his wife, Aug. 10, 14, 18, 25, 1874, Sherman Miles MSS; Hunt to Miles, Dec. 12, 1878, Miles Collection (quotation); Miles, *Personal Recollections*, 163–66; "Indian Territory Expedition," Aug. 14, 1874, typescript, George W. Baird Papers, Kansas State Historical Society, Center for Historical Research, Topeka (hereafter cited as "Indian Territory Expedition," Baird Papers, Kansas).

21. Miles, *Personal Recollections*, 167–71 (quotation); Miles to his wife, Sept. 1, 6, 1874, Sherman Miles MSS; Marshall, *Miles Expedition*, 15–19; "Indian Territory Expedition," Baird Papers, Kansas; Adjutant General's Office, *Chronological List of Actions &c., with Indians from January 15, 1837 to January, 1891* (Fort Collins, Colo.: Old Army Press, 1979), 58. Secondary accounts of the battle differ widely. James L. Haley, *The Buffalo War: The History of the Red River Indian Uprising* (Garden City, N.Y.: Doubleday and Co., 1976), is critical of Miles; Robert M. Utley, *Frontier Regulars: The United States Army and the Indian, 1866–1891* (New York: Macmillan Co., 1973), presents a more convincing interpretation.

22. Baldwin to G. Baird, Sept. 10, 1874, in Joe F. Taylor, ed., *The Indian Campaign on the Staked Plains, 1874–1875: Military Correspondence from War Department Adjutant General's Office, File 2815-1874* (Canyon, Tex.: Panhandle-Plains Historical Society, 1962), 28–31; Miles to Pope, Sept. 14, 1874, ibid., 34–35; W. Lyman to Commanding Officer, Camp Supply, Sept. 10, sw, *Annual Report, 1874*, 86; Miles, *Personal Recollections*, 172–74; Marshall, *Miles Expedition*, 20, 24 (quotation).

23. Miles to Asst. Adj. Genl., Oct. 12, 1874, in Taylor, *Indian Campaign*, 60–63; Pope to Miles, Sept. 13 (first quotation), 15, 18, 24 (second and third quota-

tions), 1874, LS, Mo., NARA; Miles to his wife, Sept. 14, 1874, Sherman Miles MSS.

24. Miles to his wife, Aug. 25, Sept. 14, 18, 24, 27, Oct. 1, 5, 1874, Sherman Miles MSS; Dunn to Miles, Nov. 3, 1874, LS, Mo., NARA; R. Williams to Commander, District of New Mexico, Mar. 16, 1875, file M 156, roll 25, LR, NM, NARA; Donald F. Schofield, *Indians, Cattle, Ships and Oil: The Story of W.M.D. Lee* (Austin: University of Texas Press, 1985), 32; Miles to Pope, Oct. 7, 1874, Miles Collection; Miles to W. Sherman, Sept. 27, 1874, roll 20, W. Sherman Papers (quotation).

25. Pope to Sheridan, Sept. 18, 1874, in Taylor, *Indian Campaign*, 41–42 (quotation); Robert C. Carriker, *Fort Supply, Indian Territory: Frontier Outpost on the Plains* (Norman: University of Oklahoma Press, 1970), 101–2; Miles to Pope, Oct. 5, 1874, Miles Collection; Miles to his wife, Oct. 5, 1874, Sherman Miles MSS.

26. Miles to his wife, Oct. 5, 1874, Sherman Miles MSS; Utley, *Frontier Regulars*, 230–31; R. C. Drum to W. Whipple, Oct. 24, 1874, in Taylor, *Indian Campaign*, 80–81.

27. Marshall, *Miles Expedition*, 36; Miles to his wife, Oct. 13, 27, 1874. Sherman Miles MSS.

28. Farnsworth to Field Adj., Nov. 7, 1874, in Taylor, *Indian Campaign*, 102–3; Adjutant General's Office, *List of Actions*, 59; Utley, *Frontier Regulars*, 233; "Indian Territory Expedition," Nov. 4–9, 1874, Baird Papers, Kansas; Report of Miles, Mar. 4, SW, *Annual Report, 1875*, 79–81.

29. Miles, *Personal Recollections*, 175; Baldwin's diary, Nov. 4–9, 1874, in Baird Papers, Kansas (first quotation); Baldwin to Alice, Dec. 27, 1874, box 11, Baldwin Papers; Miles to his wife, Dec. 2, 1874, Sherman Miles MSS; Miles to Sheridan, Nov. 25, 1874, Miles Collection (second and third quotations).

30. Miles to his wife, Nov. 2, 16, 1874, Sherman Miles MSS; Davidson to Augur, Nov. 28, 1874, in Taylor, *Indian Campaign*, 109; Carriker, *Fort Supply*, 100–101.

31. Miles to Asst. Adj. Genl., Dec. 5, 1874, in Taylor, *Indian Campaign*, 128–29; Miles to Forsyth, Dec. 9, 1874, Miles Collection; Miles to Pope, Dec. 13, 1874, ibid.; Miles to his wife, Dec. 17, 1874, Jan. 5, 11, 1875, Sherman Miles MSS; Miles to W. Sherman, Dec. 27, 1874, roll 30, W. Sherman Papers; Report of Miles, Mar. 4, SW, *Annual Report, 1875*, 81–82; Miles, *Personal Recollections*, 176.

32. Neill to R. Williams, Feb. 7, 1875, in Taylor, *Indian Campaign*, 169–70; Pope to R. Drum, Feb. 23, 1875, ibid., 180–82; Neill to Pope, Mar. 6, 1875, ibid., 190; Neill to Asst. Adj. Genl., Mar. 7, 1875, ibid., 190–92; Utley, *Frontier Regulars*, 235.

33. Report of Miles, Mar. 4, SW, *Annual Report, 1875*, 80–85.

34. Miles to Adj. Genl., Mar. 11, 1875, box 4, Baldwin Papers; Miles to Asst. Adj.

Genl., Mar. 22, 1874, file 4914, box 552, AGO Doc., NARA. On Baldwin, see Robert C. Carriker, "Frank D. Baldwin," in *Soldiers West: Biographies from the Military Frontier*, ed. Paul Andrew Hutton (Lincoln: University of Nebraska Press, 1987), 228–43. Before the campaign, Baldwin had assured his wife that Miles "has done everything for me that he could" (Baldwin to Mary, Aug. 14, 1874, box 11, Baldwin Papers).

35. Miles to his wife, Nov. 16, 1874, Sherman Miles MSS; Grace E. Meredith, ed., *Girl Captives of the Cheyennes* (Los Angeles: Gem Publishing Co., 1927), 17–19, 81, 91–95, 104–5, 112–13; Miles, *Personal Recollections*, 181; Garfield to Miles, Mar. 15, 1875, box 2, Miles Papers; Alice to Baldwin, Sept. 3, 1876, box 9, Baldwin Papers; Miles to Probate Court, Apr. 5, 1877, Miles Collection; J. Sherman to Miles, Apr. 30, 1877, box 4, Miles Papers.

36. Miles to Pope, Dec. 25, 1874, Miles Collection; Miles to W. Sherman, Dec. 27, 1874, roll 20, W. Sherman Papers (quotation).

37. Miles to Pope, Dec. 1874, Miles Collection (quotation). Anderson, a West Point graduate of 1871, was serving as acting engineer of the campaign (George W. Cullum, *Biographical Register of the Officers and Graduates of the U.S. Military Academy* . . . , 3 vols. 3d ed. (Boston: Houghton Mifflin, 1891), 3:168–69).

38. Pope to Miles, Mar. 12, 1877, Sept. 23, 1885, box 3, Miles Papers.

39. Thian, *Military Geography*, 76–77; Haley, *Buffalo War*, 206–7 (quotation).

40. W. Sherman to Miles, Mar. 25, 1875, box 4, Miles Papers; Miles to W. Sherman, Apr. 26, 1875, roll 20, W. Sherman Papers.

41. Miles, *Personal Recollections*, 180; Richard Henry Pratt, *Battlefield and Classroom: Four Decades with the American Indian, 1867–1904*, ed. Robert M. Utley, Yale Western Americana Series, no.6 (New Haven: Yale University Press, 1964), 109 (quotation); Miles, *Serving the Republic*, 130; Utley, *Frontier Regulars*, 239. Grey Beard was later killed while trying to escape (Pratt to Asst. Adj. Genl., May 21, 1875, in Taylor, *Indian Campaign*, 285).

42. Dunn to Miles, Nov. 3, 1874, LS, Mo., NARA; Miles to W. Sherman, Dec. 27, 1874, roll 20, W. Sherman Papers; R. Williams to Commander, District of New Mexico, Mar. 16, 1875, file M 156, roll 25, LR, NM, NARA; Special Orders 27, Apr. 3, 1875, ibid.; Heitman, *Historical Register*, 1:807; DeMontravel, "Nelson A. Miles," 170–71.

43. B. Cowen to SW, June 12, 1875, pp. 118–19, roll 16, Letters Sent by the Indian Division of the Office of the Secretary of the Interior, 1849–1903, M 606, NARA; J. McNulta to Smith, May 13, 1875, file M 469, Sept. 6, 1875, file M 775, roll 564, Letters Received by the Office of Indian Affairs, 1824–1881, New Mexico Superintendency, M 234, NARA; Irvine to Smith, Nov. 17, 1875, file I 1573, ibid.; W. Mills to Smith, Nov. 18, 1875, file M 1038, ibid. (quotation); Edward Hill, *The Office of Indian Affairs, 1824–1880: Historical Sketches* (New York: Clearwater Publishing Co., 1974).

44. Pyle to Smith, Dec. 2, 1875, file P 552, roll 564, Letters Received by the Office

of Indian Affairs, M 234, NARA; Pope to Drum, Dec. 9, 1875, file W 1823, roll 565, ibid.; Pope to Townsend, Dec. 10, 1875, ibid.; Miles, *Personal Recollections*, 182–84; G. Cornish to Asst. Adj. Genl., Dec. 26, 1875, roll 26, LR, NM, NARA; Crosby to SI, Jan. 3, 1876, roll 72, LS, SW, NARA; Asst. Adj. Genl. to Commanding Officer, District of New Mexico, Jan. 15, 1876, LS, Mo., NARA.

45. Miles to Brother, Dec. 25, 1875, Miles Collection.
46. Harry James Brown and Frederick D. Williams, eds., *The Diary of James A. Garfield*, 4 vols. (East Lansing: Michigan State University Press, 1973), 3:98–100.
47. Sheridan to R. Williams, Oct. 6, 1874, box 11, Sheridan Papers.
48. Testimony of Miles, Feb. 8, 1876, House Report 356, 44th Cong., 1st sess., serial 1709, pp.80–82.
49. Miles to Howard, May 26, 1875, Howard Papers (quotation); letters of testimony in House Report 354, 44th Cong., 1st sess., vol.2, serial 1709; J. Sherman to Miles, Feb. 26, 1876, box 4, Miles Papers; Miles to Church, Jan. 20, 1876, box 1, Church Papers.
50. Report of Miles, Mar. 4, sw, *Annual Report, 1875*, 84–85.
51. Buell to Miles, Oct. 18, 1874, in Taylor, *Indian Campaign*, 79–80.
52. Custer to Merritt, Dec. 15, 1875, roll 7, Sheridan Papers.

CHAPTER FIVE

1. Utley, *Frontier Regulars*, 60–61; Robert Wooster, *The Military and United States Indian Policy, 1865–1903* (New Haven: Yale University Press, 1988), 86.
2. Report of Sheridan, Nov. 25, sw, *Annual Report, 1876*, 440–41; Report of Terry, Nov. 21, ibid., 459.
3. Reynolds to Sherman, Apr. 11, 1876, roll 23, W. Sherman Papers (first and second quotations); Report of Sheridan, Nov. 25, sw, *Annual Report, 1876*, 441; Subreport of Crook, May 7, 1876, ibid., 502–3; Miles to Sherman, Apr. 14 (third quotation), June 15, 1876, ibid. (fourth quotation).
4. Johnson, *Unregimented General*, 84–85.
5. Sherman to Sheridan, July 22, 1876, roll 46, LS, AGO, NARA; Sheridan to Sherman, July 7, 1876, roll 72, LS, SW, NARA.
6. "Notes," George P. Miles Papers, Montana Historical Society, Helena (hereafter cited as George Miles Papers); Miles, *Personal Recollections*, 212–13; Alice to Baldwin, July 20, 1876, box 9, Baldwin Papers (first quotation); Pope to Miles, Sept. 15, 1876, box 3, Miles Papers; W. Sherman to Miles, July 29, 1876, box 4, ibid. (second quotation).
7. Miles to his wife, July 23, 1876, Sherman Miles MSS; Diary, July 23, 1876, Miles Collection; Miles, *Personal Recollections*, 212–15.

8. Miles to his wife, July 16, 20, 22, 29, 1876, Sherman Miles MSS; Diary, July 22, 1876, Miles Collection (quotation).

9. Miles to his wife, July 29, Aug. 4, 1876, Sherman Miles MSS.

10. Sheridan to Terry, May 16, 1876, box 58, Sheridan Papers (quotation); Utley, *Frontier Regulars*, 252; John S. Gray, *Centennial Campaign: The Sioux War of 1876* (Fort Collins, Colo.: Old Army Press, 1976), 110–24, 308–57; John W. Bailey, *Pacifying the Plains: General Alfred Terry and the Decline of the Sioux, 1866–1890*, Contributions in Military History, no.17 (Westport, Conn.: Greenwood Press, 1979), 135; Utley, *Cavalier in Buckskin*, 169–75.

11. Miles to his wife, July 29, Aug. 4, 1876, Sherman Miles MSS.

12. Sherman to Sheridan, Feb. 21, 1877, roll 47, LS, AGO, NARA; Miles to Mary, Aug. 2, 1876, Sherman Miles MSS; Bailey, *Pacifying the Plains*, 163–64; Sheridan to Terry, Feb. 8, 1876, box 14, Sheridan Papers; Utley, *Cavalier in Buckskin*, 169–70.

13. Miles to his wife, Aug. 12, 1876, Sherman Miles MSS; Bailey, *Pacifying the Plains*, 164; W. Donald Horn, *Witnesses for the Defense of George Armstrong Custer* (Short Hills, N.J.: Horn Publications, 1981), 76–77; Sherman to Cameron, Aug. 19, 1876, roll 46, LS, AGO, NARA.

14. Miles to his wife, Aug. 12, 1876, Sherman Miles MSS (quotations); Bailey, *Pacifying the Plains*, 164; Horn, *Witnesses*, 76–77; Sherman to Cameron, Aug. 19, 1876, roll 46, LS, AGO, NARA; M. Carroll diary, Aug. 11, 1876, p.238, Montana Historical Society.

15. Report of Terry, Nov. 21, SW, *Annual Report, 1876*, 466–67; Miles to his wife, Aug. 20, 1876, Sherman Miles MSS. For additional criticism of Crook, see E. Carr to his wife, Sept. 25, 1876, box 3, Eugene A. Carr Papers, U.S. Army Military History Institute, Carlisle Barracks (hereafter cited as Carr Papers).

16. "Notes," Aug. 21, 1876, George Miles Papers; Miles to Mary, Aug. 20, 1876, Sherman Miles MSS.

17. "Notes," Aug. 23, 1876, George Miles Papers; Fort Keogh, Brief Histories of U.S. Army Commands (Army Posts) and Descriptions of Their Records (microfilm T 912), NARA; Report of Terry, Nov. 21, SW, *Annual Report, 1876*, 468; Report of G. Gibbon, Oct. 21, SW, *Annual Report, 1877*, 540; Utley, *Frontier Regulars*, 270–71; Jerome A. Greene, *Slim Buttes, 1876: An Episode in the Great Sioux War* (Norman: University of Oklahoma Press, 1982).

18. Johnson, *Unregimented General*, 109–11; Report of Terry, Nov. 12, SW, *Annual Report, 1877*, 488; Miles, *Personal Recollections*, 217–19 (quotation); Miles to Sherman, Oct. 2, 16, 23, 1876, roll 23, W. Sherman Papers.

19. Luther S. Kelly, *"Yellowstone Kelly": The Memoirs of Luther Sage Kelly*, ed. M. M. Quaife (New Haven: Yale University Press, 1926), xii; Miles to Asst. Adj. Genl., Nov. 18, 1876, LS, Yellowstone, NARA.

20. Kelly, *"Yellowstone Kelly,"* xii; Fort Keogh, Post Returns, Sept., Oct. 1876, roll 572, Returns from U.S. Military Posts, 1800–1916, M 617, NARA; Report of

Terry, Nov. 12, 1877, sw, *Annual Report, 1877,* 488; Miles to Sherman, Oct. 2, 16 (quotation), 1876, roll 23, W. Sherman Papers.

21. Report of Terry, Nov. 21, sw, *Annual Report, 1876,* 470; Miner to Post Adj., Oct. 12, 1876, ibid., 486–87; Report of Otis, Oct. 13, 1876, ibid., 485; Report of Otis, Oct. 27, 1876, in sw, *Annual Report, 1877,* 490–91; Report of Miles, Oct. 25, 1876, ibid., 482; Utley, *Frontier Regulars,* 273; Adjutant General's Office, *List of Actions,* 63.

22. Miles, *Personal Recollections,* 194 (first quotation); Report of Miles, Oct. 25, sw, *Annual Report, 1876,* 482 (second and third quotations); Jerome A. Greene, "The Beginning of the End: Miles versus Sitting Bull at Cedar Creek," *Montana: The Magazine of Western History* 41 (Summer 1991): 20–21.

23. Report of Miles, Oct. 25, 1876, sw, *Annual Report, 1876,* 483 (quotations); Miles to his wife, Oct. 25, 1876, Sherman Miles mss. The dream is outlined in George W. Baird, "Indian Campaigning with General Miles in Montana," George William Baird Letters and Official Papers, Western Americana Collection, Beinecke Rare Book and Manuscript Library, Yale University, New Haven, Connecticut (hereafter cited as Baird, "Indian Campaigning," Baird Papers, Beinecke); Miles to his wife, Dec. 15, 1876, Sherman Miles mss; Miles to Baird, Feb. 28, 1890, Baird Papers, Kansas.

24. Report of Miles, Oct. 25, 1876, sw, *Annual Report, 1876,* 483 (quotation); Edwin M. Brown, "Terror of the Badlands," 9–11, Montana Historical Society (hereafter cited as Brown, "Terror of the Badlands"); Greene, "Beginning of the End," 24–26; Pohanka, *Documentary Biography,* 95.

25. Report of Miles, Oct. 25, 1876, sw, *Annual Report, 1876,* 483; Brown, "Terror of the Badlands," 9–11; Greene, "Beginning of the End," 24–26; Pohanka, *Documentary Biography,* 95; Miles to his wife, Oct. 25, 1876, Sherman Miles mss; Adjutant General's Office, *List of Actions,* 63.

26. Miles to his wife, Oct. 25, 1876, Sherman Miles mss; Miles to Sherman, Oct. 23, 1876, roll 23, W. Sherman Papers (quotations).

27. Report of Miles, Oct. 27, 1876, sw, *Annual Report, 1876,* 484; Miles to Terry, Oct. 28, 1876, ibid., 484–85; Miles to Sherman, Oct. 27, 1876, roll 23, W. Sherman Papers; Miles to Commanding Officer, Cheyenne Agency, Nov. 2, 1876, ls, Yellowstone, nara (quotation).

28. Miles to Terry, Oct. 28, sw, *Annual Report, 1876,* 485; Fort Keogh, Nov. 1876, roll 572, Returns from U.S. Military Posts, 1800–1916, M 617, nara; Frank D. Baldwin Diary, 1–2, Montana Historical Society (hereafter cited as Baldwin Diary); Miles to Sherman, Nov. 1, 1876, roll 23, W. Sherman Papers (quotations).

29. Miles to his wife, Nov. 13, 1876, Sherman Miles mss; Alice to Baldwin, Nov. 3, 1876, box 9, Baldwin Papers (first quotation); W. Sherman to Drum, Nov. 1, 1876, roll 46, ls, ago, nara; W. Sherman to Sheridan, Nov. 10, 1876, ibid. (second quotation).

30. W. Sherman to Miles, Aug. 23, 1876, box 4, Miles Papers (quotation); Miles to his wife, Nov. 13, 1876, Sherman Miles MSS; "Notes," George Miles Papers; Kelly, *"Yellowstone Kelly,"* 148–49.

31. Report of Miles, Dec. 27, 1877, SW, *Annual Report, 1877,* 524; Miles to his wife, Nov. 13, 1876, Sherman Miles MSS; Miles to Sherman, Nov. 18 (quotation), Dec. 25, 1876, roll 23, W. Sherman Papers.

32. Sherry L. Smith, *Sagebrush Soldier: Private William Earl Smith's View of the Sioux War of 1876* (Norman: University of Oklahoma Press, 1989), is a superb account of the Powder River expedition.

33. Baldwin Diary, Nov. 21, 27 (first quotation), 29 (second quotation), 1876; Brown, "Terror of the Badlands," 20 (third and fourth quotations). The episode explains Miles's subsequent request for lightweight rubber boats (Townsend to Commander, Division of the Missouri, May 25, 1877, roll 47, LS, AGO, NARA).

34. Baldwin Diary, Dec. 1, 1876, Montana; Miles to Clendenning, Nov. 30, 1876, LS, Yellowstone, NARA; Report of Miles, Dec. 27, 1877, SW, *Annual Report, 1877,* 524; Report of G. Gibson, Oct. 1, 1877, ibid., 541.

35. Miles to Asst. Adj. Genl., Dec. 17, 1876, Jan. 22, 1877, LS, Yellowstone, NARA (quotations); Miles to Terry, Dec. 20, 1876, ibid.; Miles to L. Carpenter, Dec. 23, 1876, ibid.; Miles to Sherman, Dec. 25, 1876, roll 23, W. Sherman Papers.

   In a subsequent report, Miles gave the date as the sixteenth (Report of Miles, Dec. 21, 1876, SW, *Annual Report, 1877,* 524). However, his report to Terry of the twentieth (see above) fixed the date as the seventeenth.

36. M. Carroll Diary, 240; "Notes," 65–66, George Miles Papers (quotation); Miles to the Traders, Dec. 24, 1876, LS, Yellowstone, NARA; Miles to his wife, Nov. 30, 1876, Sherman Miles MSS.

37. Report of Miles, Dec. 21, 1876, SW, *Annual Report, 1877,* 524; Miles, *Personal Recollections,* 236–38; Miles to Sherman, Dec. 25, 1876, roll 23, W. Sherman Papers; Miles to his wife, Dec. 27, 1876, Sherman Miles MSS.

38. Miles to Sherman, Jan. 4 (first quotation), 20 (second quotation), 1877, roll 23, W. Sherman Papers; Miles, *Personal Recollections,* 218–19; Report of Miles, Dec. 21, 1876, SW, *Annual Report, 1877,* 524; Margot Liberty and John Stands in Timber, *Cheyenne Memories,* Yale Western Americana Series, no.17 (New Haven: Yale University Press, 1967), 220; Thomas B. Marquis, *A Warrior Who Fought Custer* (Minneapolis: Midwest Co., 1931), 289–92.

39. Report of Miles, Dec. 21, 1876, SW, *Annual Report, 1877,* 524–25; Miles to Terry, Jan. 20, 1877, Oscar F. Long Papers, Huntington Library (hereafter cited as Long Papers, Huntington); Utley, *Frontier Regulars,* 285; Miles to Sherman, Mar. 29, 1877, roll 24, W. Sherman Papers; Don Rickey, Jr., "The Battle of Wolf Mountain," *Montana: The Magazine of Western History* 13 (Spring 1963): 47–54; Miles to Baird, Feb. 28, 1890, Baird Papers, Kansas.

40. Pope to Baird, Mar. 1, 1880, July 10, [1891] (first quotation), Baird Papers,

Kansas; depositions of Henry Rodenburg and John McHugh, Aug. 4, 1891, ibid.; Butler to Baird, July 6, 1891, ibid.; Baird to Butler, Aug. 21, 1891, ibid.; Baldwin to Baird, Feb. 20, 1890 [enclosure B], ibid. (second quotation).

Casey and Butler received Medals of Honor on Miles's recommendation seventeen years later (see file 4914, box 552, AGO Doc., NARA).

41. George Hyde, *Red Cloud's Folk: A History of the Oglala Sioux Indians* (Norman: University of Oklahoma Press, 1937), 289; Miles to his wife, Jan. 19, Feb. 19, 1877, Sherman Miles MSS; Miles to Hazen, Jan. 22, 1877, LS, Yellowstone, NARA; Miles to Baldwin, Jan. 23, 1877, ibid.; Miles to Sherman, Mar. 29, 1877, roll 24, W. Sherman Papers.

42. Miles to Sherman, Jan. 20 (first quotation), Feb. 1 (second quotation), 5 (third quotation), and 1 (fourth quotation), 1877, roll 23, W. Sherman Papers.

43. Sheridan to Sherman, Feb. 10, 1877, roll 21, Sheridan Papers. See also Sheridan's letter of March 17, 1877, ibid.

44. Sherman to Sheridan, Feb. 10, 21, 1877, roll 47, LS, AGO, NARA; Sherman to Miles, Dec. 18, 1876; Feb. 28 (quotations), 1877, box 4, Miles Papers.

45. Smith, *Sagebrush Soldier*, 129–31; Liberty and Stands in Timber, *Cheyenne Memories*, 222; Marquis, *Warrior Who Fought Custer*, 295; Report of Miles, Dec. 27, 1876, SW, *Annual Report, 1877*, 525; Report of Terry, Nov. 12, 1876, ibid., 496; Peter J. Powell, *Sweet Medicine: The Continuing Role of the Sacred Arrows, the Sun Dance, and the Sacred Buffalo Hat in Northern Cheyenne History*, 2 vols. (Norman: University of Oklahoma Press, 1969), 1:182–88; John S. Gray, "What Made Johnnie Bruguier Run?" *Montana: The Magazine of Western History* 14 (Spring 1964): 34–49; Miles, *Personal Recollections*, 239–40.

46. Miles to his wife, Feb. 19, 1877, Sherman Miles MSS; Miles to Asst. Adj. Genl., Mar. 24, 1877, SW, *Annual Report, 1877*, 496; Report of Crook, Aug. 1, 1877, ibid., 84; Utley, *Frontier Regulars*, 279; Liberty and Stands in Timber, *Cheyenne Memories*, 222–23; Smith, *Sagebrush Soldier*, 131.

Sheridan was skeptical of Crook's negotiations. "Gen. Crook is a little more confident than I am, but I have thought it best to defer to his opinion for a little while yet" (Sheridan to Sherman, Mar. 17, 1877, box 17, Sheridan Papers).

47. Miles to his wife, Mar. 20, 22, 24, 1877, Sherman Miles MSS; Miles to Asst. Adj. Genl., Mar. 24, 1877, SW, *Annual Report, 1877*, 496; Liberty and Stands in Timber, *Cheyenne Memories*, 224; George B. Grinnell, *The Fighting Cheyennes* 2d ed. (Norman: University of Oklahoma Press, 1956), 384–85; Powell, *Sweet Medicine*, 188–89.

48. Miles to his wife, Mar. 22, 24, 31, 1877, Sherman Miles MSS; Miles to Sherman, Apr. 8, 1877, roll 24, W. Sherman Papers (quotation).

49. Report of Terry, Nov. 12, 1877, SW, *Annual Report, 1877*, 497; Report of Sheridan, Oct. 25, 1877, ibid., 55; Liberty and Stands in Timber, *Cheyenne Memories*, 223.

50. Miles to Asst. Adj. Genl., May 16, 1877, sw, *Annual Report, 1877*, 497–98; Grinnell, *Fighting Cheyennes*, 387–90.

51. Jerome A. Greene, "The Lame Deer Fight: Last Drama of the Sioux War of 1876–1877," *By Valor and Arms* 3, no.3 (1978): 11–21; Miles, *Personal Recollections*, 248–51; Grinnell, *Fighting Cheyennes*, 390–97; Utley, *Frontier Regulars*, 280; Report of Miles, Dec. 27, 1877, sw, *Annual Report, 1877*, 525–26 (quotation); Miles to Asst. Adj. Genl., May 16, 1877, ibid., 497; G. McCrary to Secretary of the Interior, June 7, 1877, roll 74, LS, SW, NARA.

Upon Miles's recommendation, Privates William Leonard and Samuel D. Phillips, Second Cavalry, received Medals of Honor for their "conspicuous bravery" in the Lame Deer fight. In 1894, Miles requested that Lieutenant Edward W. Casey, Twenty-second Infantry, receive such an award. But as Casey was by then deceased, it was not granted. (Miles to Adj. Genl., July 4, 1877, 4141 AGO 1877, roll 358, LR, AGO, 1871–80, NARA; Townsend to Miles, Aug. 8, 1877, roll 47, LS, AGO, NARA; file 4914, box 552, AGO Doc., NARA.)

The newly mounted infantrymen, composing companies B, F, G, and I, were formed as a battalion under the command of Captain Simon Snyder and dubbed "the Eleventh Cavalry" (George W. Baird, "General Miles's Indian Campaigns," *Century Magazine* 42 (July 1891): 359).

52. Baird, "General Miles' Indian Campaigns," 359–60; Report of Gibson, Oct. 1, 1877, sw, *Annual Report, 1877*, 543–46; Terry to Sherman, June 9, 1877, roll 24, W. Sherman Papers (quotation); Report of Miles, Dec. 27, 1877, sw, *Annual Report, 1877*, 526–27; "Memoranda of movements of, and events in, Yellowstone Command," June 1877, Baird Papers, Kansas; Report of Lazelle, Sept. 5, 1877, sw, *Annual Report, 1877*, 574–75; Report of Sheridan, Oct. 25, 1877, ibid., 55–56.

53. Utley, *Frontier Regulars*, 284–85; Hyde, *Red Cloud's People*, 297–303.

54. Smith, *Sagebrush Soldier*, 132–34; Grinnell, *Fighting Cheyennes*, 398–427.

55. Devins to Miles, Apr. 26, 1877, box 1, Miles Papers; Pope to Miles, Mar. 12, 1877, box 3, ibid. (first quotation); Report of Sheridan, Oct. 25, 1877, sw, *Annual Report, 1877*, 55 (second quotation); Sherman to McCrary, Aug. 3, 1877, roll 47, LS, AGO, NARA (third quotation); Terry to Miles, June 4, 1877, Miles Collection (fourth quotation).

56. Report of Gibson, Oct. 1, 1876, sw, *Annual Report, 1877*, 545.

CHAPTER SIX

1. Sheridan to Sherman, Feb. 10, 1877, roll 23, W. Sherman Papers.

2. Miles to Sherman, Mar. 29 (first quotation), Apr. 8 (second quotation), 1877, ibid.

3. Miles to Sherman, Nov. 18, 1876, Apr. 8, 1877 (quotations), roll 24, ibid.

4. Sherman to Miles, Dec. 4, 1876 (quotations), Apr. 23, June 1, 1877, box 4, Miles Collection.

5. Sherman to McCrary, Aug. 3, 1877, roll 47, LS, AGO, NARA; Sherman to Miles, Aug. 17, 1877, box 4, Miles Papers.

6. I have used Alvin M. Josephy, Jr., *The Nez Perce Indians and the Opening of the Northwest*, Yale Western Americana Series, no. 10 (New Haven: Yale University Press, 1965). For a slightly different interpretation, see Merrill D. Beal, *"I Will Fight No More Forever": Chief Joseph and the Nez Perce War* (Seattle: University of Washington Press, 1963).

7. Josephy, *Nez Perce*, 450–526; Report of Howard, Dec. 26, 1877, SW, *Annual Report, 1877*, 586–90, 602.

8. Utley, *Frontier Regulars*, 301–5; Report of Howard, Dec. 26, 1877, SW, *Annual Report, 1877*, 603–7.

9. Utley, *Frontier Regulars*, 306–7; Josephy, *Nez Perce*, 553–88; Report of Gibbon, Sept. 1, 1876, SW, *Annual Report, 1877*, 68–71.

10. Utley, *Frontier Regulars*, 306–7; Josephy, *Nez Perce*, 553–89; Report of Gibbon, Sept. 2, 1877, SW, *Annual Report, 1877*, 68–71.

11. Baird to Sturgis, Aug. 11, 16, 1877, Baird Papers, Kansas; Miles to Sturgis, Aug. 12, 16, 19, 26, 27, 1877, ibid.

12. Sturgis to Miles, Sept. 13, 1877, SW, *Annual Report, 1877*, 73–74.

13. Howard to W. Sherman, Aug. 24, 1877, ibid., 13; Wooster, *Military and Indian Policy*, 177.

14. Report of Howard, Dec. 26, 1877, SW, *Annual Report, 1877*, 621–23; Howard to Miles, Sept. 12, 1877, Miles Collection (quotation).

15. Utley, *Frontier Regulars*, 311; Miles to Howard, Sept. 17, 1877, Miles Collection.

16. Howard to Miles, Sept. 20, 1877, Miles Collection (quotations); Charles Anders Fee, *Chief Joseph: The Biography of a Great Indian* (New York: Wilson-Erickson, 1936), 245; Howard to Headquarters, Sept. 26, 1877, Senate Exec. Doc. 257, 56th Cong., 1st sess., serial 3867. Howard also claimed to have "slowed" his command in his report of action to Sheridan (Oct. 17, 1877, SW, *Annual Report, 1877*, 76).

17. Miles to Asst. Adj. Genl., Oct. 6, 1877, SW, *Annual Report, 1877*, 74; Josephy, *Nez Perce*, 613–15.

18. Miles to Asst. Adj. Genl., Oct. 6, 1877, SW, *Annual Report, 1877*, 74; Miles to Howard, Sept. 29, 1877, Miles Collection (quotation).

19. Miles to Asst. Adj. Genl., Oct. 6, 1877, SW *Annual Report, 1877*, 74; Josephy, *Nez Perce*, 616–19; Lucullus V. McWhorter, *Yellow Wolf: His Own Story* (Caldwell, Idaho: Caxton, 1940), 205; Report of Miles, Dec. 27, 1877, SW, *Annual Report, 1877*, 528.

20. Utley, *Cavalier in Buckskin*, 194–205.

21. Utley, *Frontier Regulars*, 312–13; Josephy, *Nez Perce*, 618–19 (quotation); Re-

port of Miles, Dec. 27, 1877, sw, *Annual Report, 1877*, 528; Chief Joseph, "An Indian's View of Indian Affairs," *North American Review* 128 (Apr. 1879): 428–32; Henry Romeyn, "The Capture of Chief Joseph and the Nez Perce Indians," *Historical Society of Montana Collections* 2 (1896): 287–88.

22. Utley, *Frontier Regulars*, 312–13; Josephy, *Nez Perce*, 618–19; Report of Miles, Dec. 27, 1877, sw, *Annual Report, 1877*, 528; Chief Joseph, "An Indian's View," 428–32; Romeyn, "Capture of Chief Joseph," 287–88; McWhorter, *Yellow Wolf*, 206–7.

23. Romeyn, "Capture of Chief Joseph," 287–88 (quotation); Report of Miles, Dec. 27, 1877, sw, *Annual Report, 1877*, 528.

24. Baird, "Indian Campaigning" (quotation); Joseph, "An Indian's View," 428. For Miles's efforts to secure Medals of Honor for his subordinates, see file 4914, box 552, AGO Doc., NARA.

25. Report of Miles, Dec. 27, 1877, sw, *Annual Report, 1877*, 528.

26. Ibid.; Pohanka, *Documentary Biography*, 110–11; Romeyn, "Capture of Chief Joseph," 289; McWhorter, *Yellow Wolf*, 210–11.

27. McWhorter, *Yellow Wolf*, 211–13; Josephy, *Nez Perce*, 621; Baird to Sturgis, Sept. 3, 1877, Baird Papers, Kansas; Miles to Terry, Oct. 3, 1877, sw, *Annual Report, 1877*, 514–15; Miles to Asst. Adj. Genl., Oct. 6, 1877, ibid., 515–16.

28. Josephy, *Nez Perce*, 622; Liberty and Stands in Timber, *Cheyenne Memories*, 228 (quotation). Chief Joseph's account, "An Indian's View," 428, corroborates the Cheyenne peace initiative.

29. Josephy, *Nez Perce*, 623. Yellow Wolf held that Miles ordered Joseph bound, rolled up in a blanket, and taken to the army mule herd. Joseph did not mention the incident; Wood denied its validity. "The account that General Miles hobbled Joseph and held him corralled with the mules until after the surrender is absolute rot without slightest foundation whatever. I can't imagine how it came into being, except that more fairy tales and lies originated about the Chief Joseph campaign, probably, than about the Civil War" (Wood to H. S. Howard, Feb. 20, 1942, WD box 234 (1), Charles E. S. Wood Collection, Huntington Library [hereafter cited as Charles Wood Collection]). For Yellow Wolf's account, see McWhorter, *Yellow Wolf*, 217.

30. Miles to Terry, Oct. 3, 1877, sw, *Annual Report, 1877*, 514–15 (quotation); Joseph, "An Indian's View," 429. Lieutenant Jerome later maintained that he had accompanied Joseph after a preliminary parley with Miles, and had waited there while the two leaders opened negotiations (Fee, *Chief Joseph*, 337–39). Josephy, *Nez Perce*, 624, has a fine summary of the historiographical problems. In 1942, Wood recalled that Lieutenant Jerome had gone over to the Indian camp "on his own volition" to inspect their defenses (Wood to H. S. Howard, Feb. 20, 1942, WD box 234 (1), Charles Wood Collection).

31. Miles to Asst. Adj. Genl., Oct. 6, 1877, sw, *Annual Report, 1877*, 516; Josephy,

Nez Perce, 625; Miles, *Personal Recollections*, 273–75 (first quotation); Miles to Terry, Oct. 3, 1877, sw, *Annual Report, 1877*, 515 (second quotation).

32. Report of Howard, Dec. 26, 1877, sw, *Annual Report, 1877*, 629–30.

33. Report of Howard, Dec. 26, 1877, ibid., 628–30; Howard to Adj. Genl., Oct. 4, 1877, Senate Exec. Doc. 257, 56th Cong., 1st sess., serial 3867 (second quotation). Wood's account is in his "The Pursuit and Capture of Chief Joseph," in Fee, *Chief Joseph*, 325. In a 1929 interview, Wood gave a slightly different version of Howard's conversation. "Wood, Miles was my aide-de-camp in the Civil War; as you all know I got him his first command. I trust him as I would trust you" (Interview in *Spectator*, Sept. 14, 1929, Order of Indian Wars Collection, I-15, U.S. Army Military History Institute [hereafter cited as Order of Indian Wars Collection]).

34. McWhorter, *Yellow Wolf*, 220–25; Josephy, *Nez Perce*, 625–26; Utley, *Frontier Regulars*, 313–14; Joseph, "An Indian's View," 429.

35. Josephy, *Nez Perce*, 526–29, 632; Joseph, "An Indian's View," 429 (quotation); Report of Howard, Dec. 26, 1877, sw, *Annual Report, 1877*, 630; Report of Miles, Dec. 27, 1877, ibid., 529.

36. Josephy, *Nez Perce*, 628–30; Utley, *Frontier Regulars*, 313–14.

37. Miles to Terry, Oct. 5, 1877, sw, *Annual Report, 1877*, 515 (first quotation); General Orders no.3, Oct. 7, 1877, Senate Exec. Doc. 257, 56th Cong., 1st sess., serial 3867 (second quotation); Miles to Howard, Jan. 31, 1878, Howard Papers.

38. Howard to Miles, Oct. 7, 1877, sw, *Annual Report, 1877*, 631–32.

39. *Spectator*, Sept. 14, 1929, I-15, Order of Indian Wars Collection (first quotation); Howard to Wood, June 5, 1897, wD box 153 (23), Charles Wood Collection (second quotation). See also *Chicago Tribune*, Oct. 19, 1877.

40. DeMontravel, "Nelson A. Miles," 261 (first and second quotations); Report of Howard, Dec. 26, 1877, sw, *Annual Report, 1877*, 633 (third quotation); General Field Orders no.8, Dec. 1, 1877, ibid., 634–35.

41. DeMontravel, "Nelson A. Miles," 258–62; Report of Howard, Dec. 26, 1877, sw, *Annual Report, 1877*, 633; General Field Orders no.8, Dec. 1, 1877, ibid., 634–35; Wood, "Pursuit and Capture of Chief Joseph," in Fee, *Chief Joseph*, 333 (quotation); Miles to his wife, Oct. 14, 1877, Sherman Miles MSS.

42. Paul Andrew Hutton, *Phil Sheridan and His Army* (Lincoln: University of Nebraska Press, 1985), 333; Report of Sherman, Nov. 7, 1877, sw, *Annual Report, 1877*, 15; W. Sherman to Miles, Nov. 13 (quotations), 1877, Jan. 9, 1878, box 4, Miles Papers.

43. Miles to Howard, Jan. 8 (first and second quotations), 31 (third quotation), 1878, Howard Papers.

44. Wood to Miles, Feb. 21, 1878, ibid.; Howard to Miles, Mar. 29, 1878, ibid. (first and second quotations); Miles to Howard, June 8, 1878, ibid. (third quotation).

45. Carpenter, *Sword and Olive Branch*, 263, 289; Miles, *Personal Recollections*, 267, 275; Miles, *Serving the Republic*, 178; Wood to Adj. Genl., Dec. 11, 1883, WD Box 235 (7), Charles Wood Collection; fourth endorsement, Dec. 13, 1883, ibid. (quotations); Wood notations on Special Orders no.175, Dec. 14, 1883, box 225 (14), ibid.

46. Miles to his wife, Oct. 14, 1877, Sherman Miles MSS; Miles to Terry, Oct. 17, 1877, Miles Collection (first quotation); Miles to Sherman, Oct. 28, 1877, roll 24, W. Sherman Papers (second quotation).

47. Francis Paul Prucha, *American Indian Policy in Crisis: Christian Reformers and the Indian, 1865–1900* (Norman: University of Oklahoma Press, 1976), 125; McCrary to SI, Oct. 12, 1877, roll 74, LS, SW, NARA; Report of Sherman, Nov. 7, 1877, SW, *Annual Report, 1877*, 15; Joseph, "An Indian's View," 431 (quotations).

48. Josephy, *Nez Perce*, 638–40 (first quotation); Fee, *Chief Joseph*, 269–70; Miles to Hayes, Jan. 28, 1881, Rutherford B. Hayes Papers, Hayes Library, Fremont, Ohio (hereafter cited as Rutherford B. Hayes Papers); *New York Daily Tribune*, Feb. 26, 1881 (second quotation).

49. Josephy, *Nez Perce*, 642–43; Utley, *Frontier Regulars*, 315; Fee, *Chief Joseph*, 295–96, 300; Miles to SI, Apr. 7, 1900, Miles Collection.

CHAPTER SEVEN

1. Warren to Miles, Oct. 11, 1877, box 5, Miles Papers (first quotation); Gibbon to Miles, Oct. 21, 1877, box 2, ibid.; Report of Hayt, Nov. 1, 1877, SI, *Annual Report, 1877*, 409 (second and third quotations).

2. Alice to Frank, July 9, 25 (quotation), 1876, box 9, Baldwin Papers; "Notes," July 14, 15, 1876, George Miles Papers.

3. Pope to Miles, Sept. 14, 1876, box 3, Miles Papers; Sherman to Mary, Sept. 5, 1876, box 4, ibid. (quotation).

4. Sherman to Miles, Oct. 20 (first quotation), Dec. 18, 1876, box 4, Miles Papers; Sherman to Howard, Mar. 29, 1877, Howard Papers (second quotation).

5. Miles to his wife, Feb. 5, 1877, Mar. 31, Apr. 5, 1877, Sherman Miles MSS.

6. Alice to Baldwin, Apr. 14, 1877, box 9, Baldwin Papers; Sherman to Miles, Feb. 18, Apr. 23, 1877, box 4, Miles Papers; Baird to Miles, May 19, 1877, Baird Papers, Beinecke; J. D. McBride to Baird, Apr. 27, 1885, ibid.

7. Utley, *Frontier Regulars*, 62; Sherman to Miles, June 9, 1877, box 4, Miles Papers (quotation).

8. Report of Gibson, Oct. 1, 1877, SW, *Annual Report, 1877*, 545; Sherman to J. Cameron, July 17, 1877, box 4, Miles Papers (first quotation); Miles, *Personal Recollections*, 256; Baird to Commanding Officer, Cantonment, Feb. 18, 1877,

LS, Yellowstone, NARA; Ruggles to Miles, Apr. 14, 1877, U.S. War Department Collection, Montana Historical Society; Alice to Frank, July 31, box 9, Baldwin Papers (second quotation).

9. Alice to Frank, Nov. 4, 11, 1877, box 9, Baldwin Papers; "Notes," 70–71, George Miles Papers (first quotation); Miles, *Personal Recollections*, 330 (second quotation). On the feud between Brotherton and Miles, see Alice to Baldwin, July 12, 1876, box 9, Baldwin Papers; and J. W. Pope to Baldwin, Jan. 30, 1907, box 3, ibid.

10. Alice to Baldwin, Nov. 4 (first quotation), 11 (second quotation), 1877, box 9, Baldwin Papers.

11. Miles to his wife, Oct. 21, 1877, Sherman Miles MSS; Ord to Shafter, May 15, Aug. 14, 1876, roll 1, William Rufus Shafter Papers, M 072, Department of Special Collections, Stanford University Libraries (hereafter cited as Shafter Papers); Ord to Sherman, June 27, 1876, roll 23, W. Sherman Papers; Sherman to Ord, Nov. 22, 1876, vol.60, LS, AGO, NARA; Miles to J. Sherman, Nov. 25, 1877, box 150, John Sherman Papers, LC (hereafter cited as J. Sherman Papers) (quotation). In late November, William Sherman quietly sought out Sheridan's views on a series of administrative changes, one of which included the transfer of Miles to Arizona (Sherman to Sheridan, Nov. 29, 1877, roll 45, W. Sherman Papers).

12. Terry to Miles, Oct. 25, 1877, box 4, Miles Papers; Utley, *Frontier Regulars*, 284–85; John P. Turner, *The North-West Mounted Police, 1873–1893*, 2 vols. (Ottawa: Ed Cloutiers, King's Printer and Controller of Stationery, 1950), 1:320–73; Bailey, *Pacifying the Plains*, 172–74; Harry Anderson, "A Sioux Pictorial Account of General Terry's Council," *North Dakota History* 22 (July 1955): 92–116.

13. Gibbon to Miles, Oct. 21, 1877, box 2, Miles Papers; Townsend to Commander, Div. of Missouri, Dec. 12, 1877, roll 48, LS, AGO, NARA; Miles to Sherman, Jan. 8, 1878, roll 24, W. Sherman Papers (quotations); Miles to Chiefs of the Hostile Camp, Mar. 18, 1878, Miles Collection; "Memoranda of Movements of and Events in, Yellowstone Command . . ." Baird Papers, Kansas. Miles's testimony of December 13, 1877, is in House Committee on Military Affairs, H Mi 45A, U.S. Congressional Hearings Supplement.

14. McCrary to SI, Jan. 29, 1878, roll 77, LS, SW, NARA; McCrary to Secretary of State, Mar. 14, 1878, roll 76, ibid.; Sherman to Sheridan, Feb. 9, 1878, roll 48, LS, AGO, NARA; Sherman to Miles, Feb. 9, 1878, roll 45, W. Sherman Papers; Lord Dufferin to Sherman, Mar. 27, 1878, box 7, Miles Papers; Sherman to Miles, Mar. 30, 1878, box 4, ibid. (quotations).

15. Sherman to Miles, Apr. 23, May 12 (first quotation), 1878, box 4, Miles Papers; Miles to Sheridan, July 23, 1878, box 19, Sheridan Papers; Miles to Sherman, May 22, 1878, roll 25, W. Sherman Papers (second and third quotations).

16. Sherman to Miles, Apr. 23, 1878, box 4, Miles Papers (first quotation); Sherman to Sheridan, July 25, 1878, roll 17, Sheridan Papers (second quotation); Sherman to Miles, July 30, 1878, box 4, Miles Papers (third quotation).

17. Miles to Asst. Adj. Genl., Aug. 15, 1878, 6445 AGO 1878, roll 427, LR, AGO 1871–80, NARA (first quotation); Townsend to Commander, Dept. of the Missouri, Oct. 10, 1878, roll 49, LS, AGO, NARA (second quotation).

18. Miles to his wife, Aug. 7, 20, 1876, Sherman Miles MSS; Miles to Sherman, Oct. 23, 1876, roll 23, W. Sherman Papers; Libbie Custer to Miles, Sept. 18, 1877, box 1, Miles Papers; Miles, *Personal Recollections*, 286, 294–95.

    Though Miles did not fully elaborate his views on the Little Bighorn for some twenty years, there is no reason to believe his perceptions changed substantially in the intervening years, especially considering his lifelong support for Custer. He wrote Sherman on October 18, 1878: "I visited a second time the Custer battleground and learned from the lips of the actors in that fight many facts not known before, if there is any investigation of that affair I want to be on the court" (Miles to Sherman, Oct. 18, 1878, roll 25, W. Sherman Papers). Miles later alleged to have in his possession affidavits that would clear Custer of any charges that he had disobeyed orders (see below, Chap. 12).

19. Correspondence on the Bannock conflict may be found in SW, *Annual Report, 1878*, 127–92.

20. Kelly, *"Yellowstone Kelly,"* 223; Report of Gibbon, Oct. 4, 1878, SW, *Annual Report, 1878*, 67; Miles, *Personal Recollections*, 294–300; Crosby to SI, Sept. 16, 1878, roll 76, LS, SW, NARA; Miles to Sherman, Oct. 18, 1878, roll 25, W. Sherman Papers. Casualty figures are taken from Gibbon's report. The Adjutant General's Office, *List of Actions*, 68, lists one officer and one citizen killed, along with two regular soldiers wounded.

21. S. D. Hauser to Maginnis, Dec. 11, 1877, box 2, Martin Maginnis Papers, Montana Historical Society (hereafter cited as Maginnis Papers); W. J. McCormick to Maginnis, Dec. 30, 1877, ibid.; F. D. Pease to Maginnis, Jan. 19, 1877, ibid.; Potts to J. Sherman, Dec. 20, 1869, J. Sherman Papers; Potts to Miles, Jan. 17, 1877, box 9, Miles Papers (first quotation); Potts to Maginnis, Mar. 30, 1877, box 2, Maginnis Papers; McCrary to Governor of Montana, Aug. 8 (second quotation), Oct. 14, 1878, roll 76, LS, SW, NARA.

22. Potts to Sherman, Sept. 12, 1878, LR, CB, NARA (first quotation); Potts to Miles, Aug. 27, Oct. 7, 1878, box 3, Miles Papers; Potts to President, Dec. 26, 1877, Miles Collection (second quotation); testimony of Miles, Dec. 13, 1877, House Committee on Military Affairs, H Mi 45A, U.S. Congressional Hearings Supplement (third quotation); Miles to Maginnis, Mar. 16, Oct. 18, Nov. 8, 1878, box 2, Maginnis Papers; Miles to Cameron, Oct. 18, 1878, box 3, ibid.

23. Miles to Sherman, Oct. 18, 1878, roll 25, W. Sherman Papers.

24. Sherman to Sheridan, Nov. 4, 1878, roll 17, Sheridan Papers (first quotation); Sheridan to Sherman, Nov. 9, 1878, box 20, Sheridan Papers (second quota-

tion); Sherman to Miles, Nov. 8, 12 (third quotation), 1878, box 4, Miles Papers; Sherman to Mary, Nov. 8, ibid.

25. Potts to Miles, Nov. 19 (quotations), Dec. 5, 1878, box 9, Miles Papers; Message of Potts, Jan. 13, 1877, *Council Journal of the Eleventh Session of the Legislative Assembly of Montana* (1879), 19; *Laws, Resolutions and Memorials of the Territory of Montana Passed at the Eleventh Regular Session of the Legislative Assembly,* Feb. 5, 1879, p.119, Montana Historical Society; Maginnis to Hauser, Jan. 5, 29, box 4, Samuel T. Hauser Papers, Montana Historical Society; Potts to Maginnis, Feb. 5, 1879, box 2, Maginnis Papers; McCrary to Governor of Montana, Jan. 9, 1879, roll 78, LS, SW, NARA; Miles to Maginnis, Mar. 1, 1880, box 2, Maginnis Papers.

26. Sherman to Mary, Nov. 8, 1878, box 4, Miles Papers (quotation); Miles to Maginnis, Oct. 18, 1878, box 2, Maginnis Papers; Ward Thoron, ed., *The Letters of Mrs. Henry Adams* (Boston: Little, Brown, and Co., 1936), 256–57; H. Adams to J. Lowell, May 15, 1883, in J. C. Levenson et al., eds., *The Letters of Henry Adams,* 3 vols. (Cambridge: Belknap Press of Harvard University Press, [1982–]), 3:500–501.

27. Post Returns, Fort Keogh, Nov. 1878, roll 572, Returns from U.S. Military Posts, 1800–1916, M 617, NARA; Special Orders no.244, Nov. 11, 1878, 7721 AGO 1878, roll 437, LR, AGO, 1871–80, NARA; Ord to Adj. Genl., Dec. 11, 1878, ibid.; Miles to Adj. Genl., Dec. 16, 1878, ibid.; W. Kobbe to Adj. Genl., Dec. 20, 1878, ibid.; Board Proceedings, Jan. 2, 1879, p.14, ibid.; Sherman to Sheridan, Jan. 1, 1879, roll 49, LS, AGO, NARA.

28. Board Proceedings, Jan. 3, 1879, p.16, 7721 AGO 1878, roll 438, LR, AGO, 1871–80, NARA; Board Report, ibid.; Williams to Miles, Nov. 6, 1867, roll 33, LS, AGO, NARA; W. Mitchell to Miles, Dec. 10, 1869, LS, Mo., NARA; Asst. Adj. Genl. to Commanding Officer, Fort Leavenworth, Mar. 11, 1872, ibid.; Crosby to Miles, Mar. 21, 1874, roll 68, LS, SW, NARA; Townsend to Miles, Oct. 13, Nov. 12, 1875, roll 45, LS, AGO, NARA.

29. Miles to Sheridan, Nov. 25, 1874, Miles Collection; Miles to Sherman, July 8, 1876 (first and second quotations), roll 23, W. Sherman Papers; Sherman to Miles, July 29, 1876, box 4, Miles Papers; testimony of Miles, Feb. 8, 1876, House Report 356, 44th Cong., 1st sess., serial 1709 (third quotation).

30. Miles to Adj. Genl., Mar. 4, 8, 1879, 7721 AGO 1878, roll 437, LR, AGO, 1871–80, NARA; Board Proceedings, Mar. 21, 1879, ibid.; McCrary, endorsement of Mar. 10, 1879, ibid. (quotation); Sherman, endorsement of Mar. 6, 1879, ibid.

31. Miles to Adj. Genl., Jan. 17, 1879, ibid.; Board Proceedings, Feb. 1, Mar. 8, 1879, pp.56, 117–18, roll 438, ibid.; Board Report, pp.68–69, 73–74, ibid.; Sherman to McCrary, July 15, 1879, roll 63, LS, AGO, NARA (quotations).

32. Miles to Adj. Genl., Apr. 24, 1879, 2521 AGO 1879, roll 470, LR, AGO, 1871–80, NARA (quotation); Sherman, third endorsement, ibid.; Benet to General of the Army, Apr. 29, 1879, ibid.

33. Miles to Asst. Adj. Genl., June 16, 1879, ibid.

34. Benet to Adj. Genl., July 12, 1879, ibid. (first, second, and third quotations); Miles to Asst. Adj. Genl., Nov. 15, 1879, ibid. (fourth, fifth, and sixth quotations).

35. Sherman, endorsement of July 15, 1879, ibid. (first quotation); Townsend to Commander, Div. of the Missouri, Jan. 9, 1880, roll 51, LS, AGO, NARA (second and third quotations).

36. Post Returns, Fort Keogh, June, 1879, roll 572, Returns from U.S. Military Posts, 1810–1916, M 617, NARA; Certificate of Apr. 30, 1879, LR, CB, NARA; Utley, *Frontier Regulars*, 294–95 n.40 (first quotation); Sherman to Sheridan, Mar. 9, 1879, roll 17, Sheridan Papers; Sherman to Miles, Mar. 10, 1879, box 4, Miles Papers (second and third quotations).

37. Terry to Adj. Genl., May 30, 1879, sw, *Annual Report, 1879*, 60; Terry to Miles, June 5, 1879, ibid., 61 (quotations); Miles to Asst. Adj. Genl., Sept. 1879, ibid., 61–62.

38. Miles to Asst. Adj. Genl., Sept. 1879, sw, *Annual Report, 1879*, 62–63; *New York Times*, July 23, 25, Aug. 1, 5, 1879; Huggins to Dear Home Folks, July 25, 1879, Eli Lundy Huggins Papers, Bancroft Library, University of California, Berkeley (hereafter cited as Huggins Papers); McCrary to Secretary of State, July 30, Aug. 12, 13, 15, 20, 23, 1879, roll 78, LS, SW, NARA; John F. Finerty, *War-Path and Bivouac; or, The Conquest of the Sioux* (Norman: University of Oklahoma Press, 1961), 255–98.

39. Post Returns, Fort Keogh, Aug. 1879, roll 572, Returns from U.S. Military Posts, 1810–1916, M 617, NARA; Report of Terry, Dec. 1, 1879, sw, *Annual Report, 1879*, 64 (first quotation); Sherman to Sheridan, July 19, (second and third quotations), 25, 1879, roll 45, W. Sherman Papers; Sherman to Sheridan, July 24, 1879, box 59, Field Dispatches and Telegrams Sent, Sheridan Papers; *New York Times*, July 25, 1879; J. Sherman to Mary, Aug. 14, 1879, box 4, Miles Papers; Miles to his wife, July 30, Aug. 9, 1879, Sherman Miles MSS.

40. Post Returns, Fort Keogh, Apr. 30, 1878, roll 572, Returns from U.S. Military Posts, 1810–1916, M 617, NARA; Miles to his wife, July 30, Aug. 9, 1879, Sherman Miles MSS; Miles, *Personal Recollections*, 333; Alice to Baldwin, Nov. 4, 1877, box 9, Baldwin Papers (quotation).

41. Miles, *Personal Recollections*, 132, 306, 333.

42. Ibid., 330–35; Demontravel, "Nelson A. Miles," 262; Finerty, *War-Path and Bivouac*, 244; Huggins to Hattie, Sept. 21, 1879, Huggins Papers (quotations); Huggins to Sister, Feb. 14, 1880, ibid.; U.S. Census, Manuscript Returns, 1880, roll 742, Custer County, Montana Territory.

43. Michael P. Malone and Richard B. Roeder, *Montana: A History of Two Centuries* (Seattle: University of Washington Press, 1976), 127; Miles to Baldwin, recd. May 11, 1878, box 16, Baldwin Papers (quotation); Miles to Potts, Dec. 22, 1876, LS, Yellowstone, NARA; "Notes," George Miles Papers; *New York Times*, May 16, 1925.

44. A. R. Mininger to Maginnis, Dec. 1, 1877, box 2, Maginnis Papers; Crosby to Adj. Genl., Oct. 17, 1879, roll 78, LS, SW, NARA; Post Returns, Fort Keogh, Nov. 1879, roll 572, Returns from U.S. Military Posts, 1810–1916, NARA; "Notes," pp.68–69, George Miles Papers (first quotation); Malone and Roeder, *Montana*, 127 (second quotation).

45. Miles to Saunders, Sept. 17, 1878, Miles Collection (quotation); Lewis H. Morgan, *Ancient Society*, ed. Leslie A. White (1877; reprint, Cambridge: Belknap Press of Harvard University Press, 1964). I thank James E. McClellan, professor emeritus of the State University of New York and visiting professor of philosophy at Corpus Christi State University, for bringing Morgan to my attention.

46. Testimony of Miles, Dec. 13, 1877, pp.235, 237, House Committee on Military Affairs H Mi 45A, U.S. Congressional Hearings Supplement (quotations); Miles to Ramsey, Apr. 13, 1880, Miles Collection.

47. Miles to Saunders, Sept. 17, 1878, Miles Collection (first quotation); testimony of Miles, Feb. 8, 1876, House Report No. 356, 44th Cong., 1st sess., serial 1709, p.81; Miles, "Our Indian Question," *Journal of the Military Service Institution of the United States* 2, no.7 (1881): 284, 286 (second quotation); *New York Times*, Dec. 23, 1880; *New York Daily Tribune*, Dec. 23, 1880 (third quotation).

48. Miles, "Our Indian Question," 309 (first quotation), 312; testimony of Miles, Dec. 13, 1877, House Committee on Military Affairs H Mi 45A, U.S. Congressional Hearings Supplement (second quotation); *New York Times*, Jan. 14, 1880.

49. Pratt to Miles, July 11, 1885, box 1, Long Papers, Bancroft; *New York Daily Tribune*, Dec. 23, 1878; J. Sherman to Miles, Apr. 30, 1877, box 4, Miles Papers; Dawes to Endicott, Jan. 22, 1886, LR, CB, NARA; A. Smiley to Hayes, Aug. 8, 1885, Rutherford B. Hayes Papers; Schurz to Miles, Oct. 29, 1880, box 3, Miles Papers.

50. Sherman to Sheridan, Aug. 2, 1879, box 59, Field Dispatches and Telegrams Sent, Sheridan Papers (quotation); Miles to Asst. Adj. Genl., Mar. 16, 1880, LS, Yellowstone, NARA; Ramsey to Secretary of State, Feb. 19, Mar. 16, Apr. 14, 1880, roll 80, LS, SW, NARA; Miles to Ramsey, Apr. 13, 1880, Miles Collection; Report of Miles, Sept. 21, 1880, SW, *Annual Report, 1880*, 74–76; Turner, *North-West Mounted Police*, 510–20.

51. Turner, *North-West Mounted Police*, 519–20; Huggins to Sister, Aug. 28 (first quotation), Sept. 9, 26, 1880, Huggins Papers; Miles to Ramsey, Apr. 13, 1880, Miles Collection; Schurz to Miles, Dec. 26, 1878, roll 86, Carl Schurz Papers, LC (hereafter cited as Schurz Papers); H. Crosby to SI, Oct. 2, 1880, roll 80, LS, SW, NARA; Miles to Schurz, Oct. 17, 1880, roll 31, Schurz Papers; Schurz to Miles, Oct. 29, 1880, box 3, Miles Papers (second quotation).

52. Turner, *North-West Mounted Police*, 539–40; Report of Terry, Oct. 6, 1881, SW,

Annual Report, 1881, 100; Everette to Miles, Nov. 15, 1882, Miles Collection (quotation); Crosby to Secretary of State, Nov. 4, 1880, roll 80, LS, SW, NARA. On Everette's lack of reliability, see Morgan B. Sherwood, *Exploration of Alaska, 1865–1900* (New Haven: Yale University Press, 1965); *New York Daily Tribune*, Feb. 21, 1881.

53. Report of Terry, Oct. 6, 1881, SW, *Annual Report, 1881*, 107–8; Turner, *North-West Mounted Police*, 567–75, 579–87. Early suggestions of a break between Terry and Miles are in Benteen to Goldin, Apr. 3, 1892, John M. Carroll, ed., *The Benteen-Goldin Letters on Custer and His Last Battle* (New York: Liveright, 1974), 221.

54. Sherman to Miles, Apr. 23, 1877, box 6, Miles Papers; Sheridan to Sherman, July 21, 1879, roll 26, W. Sherman Papers.

55. See, for example, testimony of Miles, Feb. 8, 1876, House Report 356, 44th Cong., 1st sess., serial 1709, p.83.

56. Upton to F. Greene, Oct. 3, 1879, box 2, Francis Vinton Greene Papers, New York Public Library, Rare Books and Manuscripts Division (hereafter cited as Greene Papers) (quotation); Edward M. Coffman, *The Old Army: A Portrait of the American Army in Peacetime, 1884–1898* (New York: Oxford University Press, 1986), 271–74.

57. "Enclosure C," Baird Papers, Kansas; Woodruff to Baird, Feb. 13, 1890, ibid.; Miles to his wife, July 29, 1876, Sherman Miles MSS; Miles to SW, Feb. 28, 1877, LS, Yellowstone, NARA (first quotation); Miles to Sherman, Oct. 23, 1876, roll 23, W. Sherman Papers (second and third quotations).

58. Townsend to Quartermaster General, Apr. 16, 1877, roll 60, LS, AGO, NARA; Miles to Maginnis, Mar. 22, 1880, box 2, Maginnis Papers; Alice to E. Knightley, June 19, 1884, box 2, Baldwin Papers; Miles to President, Jan. 22, 1886, box 4, ibid.

CHAPTER EIGHT

1. W. Sherman to Miles, May 26, 1880, LR, CB, NARA; Miles to W. Sherman, May 27, 1880, ibid.; Sherman to Howard, Apr. 13, 1881, roll 9, LS, HQA, NARA; Miles to Maginnis, Mar. 22, 1880, box 2, Maginnis Papers.

2. J. B. Hubbell to Maginnis, Apr. 11, 1880, box 1, Maginnis Papers (first quotation); Miles to J. Sherman, Aug. 12, 1880, box 228, J. Sherman Papers; J. Sherman to Miles, Aug. 21, 1880, box 4, Miles Papers (second quotation); Miles to J. Sherman, Sept. 7, 1880, box 229, ibid. (third, fourth, and fifth quotations); Pope to President, Aug. 28, 1880, Miles Collection.

3. J. Sherman to Miles, Sept. 13, 1880, box 4, Miles Papers (quotation); Cameron to Miles, Sept. 17, 1880, box 1, ibid.; Miles to J. Sherman, Sept. 19, 1880, box 230, J. Sherman Papers; Sheridan to Miles, Sept. 12, 1880, roll 12, Sheridan

Papers; J. Sherman to Hayes, Sept. 26, 1880, Rutherford B. Hayes Papers; Miles to Schurz, Oct. 17, 1880, roll 31, Schurz Papers. Assorted recommendations may be found in LR, CB, NARA.

4. Sherman to Mackenzie, Sept. 28, 1882, roll 47, W. Sherman Papers; L. Hayes to W. C. Hayes, Nov. 20, 1880, Webb C. Hayes Papers, Hayes Library (hereafter cited as Webb C. Hayes Papers); Marian to Pater, Nov. 21, 1880, in Thoron, *Letters of Mrs. Adams,* 236.

5. *New York Times,* Nov. 19, 1880; B. F. Fisher to R. B. Hayes, Nov. 19, Rutherford B. Hayes Papers; Hazen to Garfield, July 28, Sept. 24, Oct. 28, Nov. 3, 5, 1880, James Garfield Papers, LC; W. C. Hayes to R. B. Hayes, Nov. 26, 1880, Webb C. Hayes Papers; Garfield to Hayes, Dec. 25, 1880, Rutherford B. Hayes Papers. Some asserted that Miles had at the last minute opted not to accept the signal officer's position.

6. T. Harry Williams, *Hayes: The Diary of a President, 1875–1881, Covering the Disputed Election, the End of Reconstruction, and the Beginning of Civil Service* (New York: David McKay Co., 1964), 307; Sherman to Pope, Oct. 24, 1881, roll 47, W. Sherman Papers (first quotation); Logan to Grierson, Jan. 6, 1881, roll 10, Benjamin Grierson Papers, Illinois State Historical Library, Springfield (second quotation).

7. Miles, *Personal Recollections,* 352–53; Marian to Pater, Dec. 12, 1880, in Thoron, *Letters of Mrs. Adams,* 243; Clover to Pater, Dec. 19, 1880, ibid., 244; Coffman, *Old Army,* 227–28; *New York Times,* Jan. 14, 1880. For a fine secondary study, see John F. Marszalek, Jr., *Court-Martial: A Black Man in America* (New York: Charles Scribner's Sons, 1972).

8. Coffman, *Old Army,* 227–28; Marszalek, *Court-Martial,* 140–41, 163; Gardner to Adj. Genl., Jan. 20, Mar. 17, 1881, 7836 AGO 1880, roll 584, LR, AGO, 1871–80, NARA; Adj. Genl. to Miles, Jan. 22, 1881, ibid.; Miles to Adj. Genl., Apr. 27, 1881, ibid.; C. McKeever to J Craig, Feb. 15, 1881, ibid.; Sherman to Miles, May 16, 1881, roll 9, LS, HQA, NARA (quotation); Asst. Adj. Genl. to Dept. of the Columbia, June 1, 1881, LS, Columbia, NARA; George L. Andrews, "West Point and the Colored Cadets," *International Review* (Nov. 1880): 477–98.

For Miles's defense of individual blacks, see J. F. Weston to Gatewood, Nov. 11, 1886, box 7, Charles B. Gatewood Papers, Arizona State Historical Society/Tucson (hereafter cited as Gatewood Papers).

9. Coffman, *Old Army,* 228; Marszalek, *Court-Martial,* 240–50; Whittaker to Arthur, Mar. 26, 1882, 2208 ACP 1882, box 772, ACP Doc., NARA. For the charges and the court's original finding, see 7836 AGO 1880, roll 584, LR, AGO, 1871–80, NARA.

10. Francis Paul Prucha, *The Great Father: The United States Government and the American Indians,* 2 vols. (Lincoln: University of Nebraska Press, 1984), 1:566–67.

11. Ibid., 570–71; Hayes to Miles, Jan. 28, 1881, box 2, Miles Papers; Schurz to

Dawes, Feb. 7, 1881, in Frederic Bancroft, ed., *Speeches, Correspondence and Political Papers of Carl Schurz* (New York: G. P. Putnam's Sons, 1913), 106–8. For the hearings, see Senate Exec. Doc. 30, 46th Cong., 3d sess., serial 1941, and testimony of Miles, Feb. 26, 1881, Senate Select and Special Committee, S S 46A, U.S. Congressional Hearings Supplement.

12. Prucha, *Great Father*, 1:570–71; *New York Daily Tribune*, Feb. 21, 1881 (quotations).

13. "Nelson A. Miles on Prohibition," Miles Collection; Marian Adams to Pater, Apr. 17, 1881, in Thoron, *Letters of Mrs. Adams*, 284; John Jacob Astor to Miles, [1881], box 6, Miles Papers; Miles to T. Nash, Apr. 19, 1881, HM 15527, Huntington Library.

14. Miles, *Personal Recollections*, 352–53, 371; Thian, *Military Geography*, 56, 187; Report of Miles, Oct. 2, 1884, sw, *Annual Report, 1884*, 136–39.

15. Miles to Asst. Adj. Genl., Sept. 11, 1882, LS, Columbia, NARA; Endicott to Attorney General, Mar. 9, 1885, roll 94, LS, SW, NARA; Ericsson to Miles, Jan. 16, 1883, Long Papers, Huntington; Miles, *Serving the Republic*, 215; Ericsson to Miles, Sept. 24, 1885, Jan. 5, 1887, box 1, Miles Papers; Marian Adams to Pater, Feb. 25, 1883, in Thoron, *Letters of Mrs. Adams*, 426; Edison to Miles, June 7, 1882, box 1, Miles Papers. For a description of the Hotchkiss "revolving cannon," which boasted a range of twenty-five hundred yards, see Finerty, *War-Path and Bivouac*, 250–51.

16. Asst. Adj. Genl. to Wheaton, Nov. 3, 1881, LS, Columbia, NARA; Miles to Asst. Adj. Genl., Sept. 23, 1882, LR, CB, NARA (first quotation); Asst. Adj. Genl. to Miles, Sept. 27, Oct. 3, Dec. 13, 1882, Jan. 25, Feb. 1, 1883, LS, Columbia, NARA; Marian Adams to Pater, Feb. 25, 1883, in Thoron, *Letters of Mrs. Adams*, 425; Miles to W. Sherman, Apr. 5, 1883, LR, CB, NARA (second quotation); Committee of Arrangements to Miles, July 18, 1883, Miles Collection; E. Robins to Miles, Sept. 22, 1883, ibid.; Long to Miles, Sept. 4, 1883, LS, Columbia, NARA; McKeever to Adj. Genl., Sept. 17, 1885, LR, CB, NARA; Miles to Adj. Genl., Nov. 25, 1885, ibid. (third quotation); Tweedale to Second Comptroller, Jan. 12, 1888, roll 105, LS, SW, NARA.

17. Crook to Miles, Feb. 13, 1882, box 1, Miles Papers; Miles to Dawes, May 5, 1882, box 26, Dawes Papers; Coffman, *Old Army*, 232; J. Ropes to Miles, Aug. 22, 1883, box 8, Miles Papers; Clark C. Spence, *Territorial Politics and Government in Montana, 1864–1889* (Urbana: University of Illinois Press, 1975), 164; Miles to J. Sherman, May 15, 1884, box 323, J. Sherman Papers; J. Sherman to Miles, May 23, 1884, box 4, Miles Papers.

18. Miles to W. Sherman, Dec. 12, 1881, roll 30, W. Sherman Papers (quotation); Miles to J. Sherman, May 15, 1883, box 323, J. Sherman Papers; Miles, *Personal Recollections*, 398–403.

19. Nelson A. Miles, "Northern Pacific Railroad: Its Character and Importance to the Government," March 6, 1880, William R. Coe Collection, Beinecke; Miles

to Maginnis, Mar. 1, 1880, box 2, Maginnis Papers; Billings to Miles, Mar. 29, Aug. 5, Oct. 11, 1880, box 1, Miles Papers; Miles to J. Sherman, Jan. 3, 1884, box 309, J. Sherman Papers; J. Sherman to Miles, Jan. 4, 14, 1884, box 4, Miles Papers; Miles, *Personal Recollections*, 430–31.

20. Miles to Asst. Adj. Genl., Sept. 21, 1884, LS, Columbia, NARA; Miles to Asst. Adj. Genl., Nov. 9, 1881, 6265 AGO 1881, roll 58, LR, AGO, 1871–80, NARA; Drum to McDowell, Oct. 22, Nov. 22, 1881, roll 56, LS, AGO, NARA; Lincoln to Attorney General, Oct. 11, 27, 1881, roll 83, LS, SW, NARA; Lincoln to Speaker of the House, Dec. 5, 1881, ibid.; Miles to Sherman, Dec. 12, 1881, roll 30, W. Sherman Papers; Miles to Endicott, June 26, 1885, William Endicott Papers, Massachusetts Historical Society (hereafter cited as Endicott Papers); Drum to Commander, Div. of the Pacific, May 31, 1882, roll 55, LS, AGO, NARA; Drum to Miles, Jan. 12, 1882, roll 54, ibid.; Miles, endorsement of June 15, 1882, LS, Columbia, NARA; Asst. Adj. Genl. to Miles, Feb. 17, ibid. Troop strengths are in SW, *Annual Report, 1881*, 59; and SW, *Annual Report, 1884*, 69.

21. Ted C. Hinckley, *The Americanization of Alaska, 1867–1897* (Palo Alto, Calif.: Pacific Books, 1972), 147; Miles to W. Sherman, Dec. 12, 1881, roll 30, W. Sherman Papers; Schwatka to Miles, Oct. 26, 1881, 6247 AGO 1881, roll 58, LR, AGO, 1881–89, NARA; Miles to Asst. Adj. Genl., Nov. 2 (first and second quotations), Dec. 21 (third quotation), 1881, ibid.; Drum to Miles, Dec. 1, 1881, roll 53, LS, AGO, NARA; Sherwood, *Exploration of Alaska*, 99.

22. Drum to SW, Jan. 28, 1882, roll 54, LS, AGO, NARA; J. Sherman to Miles, Apr. 8, 1882, ser.3, vol.7, J. Sherman Papers; Sherwood, *Exploration of Alaska*, 99; Miles to W. Sherman, Feb. 13, 1882, roll 30, W. Sherman Papers; Miles, *Personal Recollections*, 420 (quotation). Copies of the bills (H.R. 1363 and S. 360) may be found in 6247 AGO 1881, roll 58, LR, AGO, 1881–89, NARA. Schwatka's report and accompanying documents are in Senate Exec. Doc. 2, 48th Cong., 2d sess., serial 2261.

23. Sherwood, *Exploration of Alaska*, 99–102 (quotations); Schwatka to Miles, June 1, 1883, box 5, Miles Papers.

24. Sherwood, *Exploration of Alaska*, 103–18; Miles, *Personal Recollections*, 419–25; Allen to Miles, Dec. 31, 1884, box 1, Miles Papers; Diary, pp.55–59, box 1, Henry T. Allen Papers, LC (hereafter cited as Allen Papers); Miles to Allen, Oct. 24 (quotation), Dec. 17, 1885, July 18, 1886, box 5, ibid.

25. Sherwood, *Exploration of Alaska*, 115–18; Miles to Sherman, Dec. 12, 1881, roll 30, W. Sherman Papers (quotations); Miles, *Personal Recollections*, 429. Miles also believed that Allen enjoyed strong support from Kentucky politicians (Miles to Allen, Mar. 6, 1886, box 5, Allen Papers).

26. Constance McLaughlin Green, *Washington: Capital City, 1879–1905* (Princeton: Princeton University Press, 1963), 47; J. Sherman to Miles, Apr. 8, 1882, ser.3, vol.7, J. Sherman Papers (quotation); J. Sherman to Miles, Mar. 20, 1883, box 4, Miles Papers.

27. J. Sherman to Miles, Apr. 20, 1882 [should be 1883], Jan. 4, 14, Feb. 5, 14, Apr. 17, May 9, 1884, box 4, Miles Papers; Miles to J. Sherman, Jan. 3, 1884, box 309, Jan. 15, 1884, box 310, May 19, 1884, box 326, J. Sherman Papers.

28. J. Sherman to Miles, May 23 (first and second quotations), 29, Sept. 1 (third quotation), 1884, Apr. 16, July 8, 31, Aug. 11, Nov. 3, 1885, box 4, Miles Papers; Miles to J. Sherman, Apr. 8, 1885, box 344, July 1885, box 347, Oct. 24, 1885, box 353, J. Sherman Papers; J. Sherman to Miles, June 21, 1884, Aug. 14, Aug. 1885, ser.3, vol.7, ibid.

29. J. Sherman to Miles, July 8, 1885, box 4, Miles Papers; W. S. Ladd to Miles, Jan. 31, 1884, box 8, ibid.

30. Schurz to President, Jan. 19, 1881, Miles Collection; Lincoln to si, Nov. 23, 1881, roll 83 (quotation), Mar. 10, 1882, roll 84, ls, sw, nara; Josephy, *Nez Perce*, 641–42.

31. For information on the Yakima controversy, see miscellaneous correspondence in sw, *Annual Report, 1882*, 121–40. On the controversies surrounding the Colville and Columbia River reservations, see Miles to Lamar, Mar. 22, 1884, box 20, Baldwin Papers; Report of Miles, Oct. 2, 1884, sw, *Annual Report, 1884*, 139; George W. Fuller, *A History of the Pacific Northwest, with Special Emphasis on the Inland Empire*, 2d ed. (New York: Alfred A. Knopf, 1958), 275–76.

32. *New York Daily Tribune*, Feb. 21, 1881 (first quotation); Report of Miles, Sept. 12, 1885, sw, *Annual Report, 1885*, 153–54 (second quotation).

33. Hutton, *Phil Sheridan*, 346 (quotation); Miles to W. Sherman, Dec. 12, 1883, roll 32, W. Sherman Papers; Mary to J. Sherman, May 2, 1887, box 402, J. Sherman Papers; Miles to J. Sherman, Apr. 9, 1888, box 439, ibid.

34. Hancock to Miles, Dec. 24, 1880, box 2, Miles Papers.

35. Lincoln to Cameron, Aug. 16, 1882, ibid.; Sheridan to Lincoln, Sept. 25, Oct. 7, 1883, box 34, Sheridan Papers; J. Sherman to Miles, Apr. 17, 1884, box 4, Miles Papers; Miles to W. Sherman, Nov. 25, 1884, roll 33, W. Sherman Papers; Miles to Endicott, June 26, 1885, Endicott Papers; Sherman to Augur, July 4, 1885, Christopher C. Augur Papers, Illinois State Historical Library (hereafter cited as Augur Papers) (quotation); Miles to his wife, July 12, 1885, Sherman Miles mss.

36. General Order no.75, July 10, 1885, lr, cb, nara; Miles to President, July 20, 1885, Miles Collection (quotations); Donald J. Berthrong, *The Cheyenne and Arapaho Ordeal: Reservation and Agency Life in the Indian Territory, 1875–1907* (Norman: University of Oklahoma Press, 1976), 99–105.

37. Berthrong, *Ordeal*, 106–9; J. Tweedale to si, June 23, 1885, roll 94, ls, sw, nara; Tweedale to P. Plumb, Aug. 22, 1885, roll 95, ibid.; Drum to Endicott, June 28, 1885, ser.2, roll 15, Grover Cleveland Papers, lc (hereafter cited as Cleveland Papers) (first quotation); Armstrong to si, July 5, 1885, subject file, "Cheyenne Outbreak 1885," box 72, Schofield Papers (second quotation).

38. Endicott to President, July 11, 1885, roll 94, ls, sw, nara; Pratt to Miles,

July 11, 1885, box 1, Long Papers, Bancroft; Corbin to Hayes, July 27, 1885, Rutherford B. Hayes Papers; Miles, *Personal Recollections*, 432; Pohanka, *Documentary Biography*, 127 (quotations); Sheridan to President, July 24, 1885, sw, *Annual Report, 1885*, 65–71; Report of Miles, Sept. 12, 1885, ibid., 153; Miles to his wife, July 12, 18, 1885, Sherman Miles mss.

39. Pohanka, *Documentary Biography*, 127; Asst. Adj. Genl. to Mrs. Miles, Sept. 2, 1885, ls, Columbia, nara; Miles to W. Sherman, Oct. 6, 1885, roll 35, W. Sherman Papers; Miles to J. Sherman, Oct. 24, 1885, box 353, J. Sherman Papers; W. Sherman to Miles, Sept. 7, 1885, box 4, Miles Papers (quotations).

40. Hutton, *Phil Sheridan*, 363–64; Utley, *Frontier Regulars*, 380–96; Howard R. Lamar, *The Far Southwest, 1846–1912: A Territorial History* (New Haven: Yale University Press, 1966), 176–85; Report of Crook, Sept. 9, 1885, sw, *Annual Report, 1885*, 169–79. Dudley Acker has compiled a fine summary of criticism of Crook in the Arizona press in his unpublished manuscript, "A War between Two Generals," (1985) which he generously shared with the author.

41. Pope to Miles, Sept. 23, 1885, box 3, Miles Papers, Barlow to Miles, Dec. 18, 1885, box 1, ibid.; Pope to Mary, Mar. 5, 1886, box 6, ibid.; *New York Times*, Apr. 3, 1886; Barlow to Fish, Feb. 25, 1886, box 151, Hamilton Fish Papers, lc; Miles to Long, Dec. 15 (first quotation), Nov. 2 (second quotation), 1885, Long Papers, Huntington; Ross to Miles, Dec. 8, 1885, Apr. 6, 1886, box 3, Miles Papers; assorted letters of recommendation, Dec. 1885–Jan. 1886, Long Papers, Huntington; Howard R. Lamar, "Edmund G. Ross as Governor of the New Mexico Territory: A Reappraisal," *New Mexico Historical Review* 36 (July 1961): 197–98.

Miles's allies also sought, unsuccessfully, to secure from the former Confederate president Jefferson Davis a denial of mistreatment by Miles (W. French to Davis, Feb. 16, 1886, in Rowland, *Jefferson Davis*, 9:407–8.

42. *New York Times*, Sept. 21, Oct. 4, 1885, Jan. 9, 10, 1886; Miles to Sherman, Jan. 6, 1886, roll 36, W. Sherman Papers (quotations).

43. Joseph C. Porter, *Paper Medicine Man: John Gregory Bourke and His American West* (Norman: University of Oklahoma Press, 1986), 174–75.

44. Report of Sheridan, Oct. 24, 1885, sw, *Annual Report, 1885*, 60; Miles to Long, Jan. 12, 1886, box 2, Long Papers, Huntington; Ross to Miles, Jan. 20, 1886, box 3, Miles Papers; Hancock to Miles, Jan. 20, 1886, box 2, ibid.

45. Barlow to C. Codman, Jan. 29, 1886, lr, cb, nara (first quotation); Miles to Long, Feb. 5 (second quotation), 9, 1886, box 1, Long Papers, Bancroft.

46. Walker, *General Hancock*, 314. Terry also enjoyed strong Democratic support (see J. Sherman to Miles, Mar. 19, 1886, box 4, Miles Papers).

47. Miles to Allen, Dec. 17, 1885, box 5, Allen Papers; Barlow to Miles, Mar. 11, 1886, box 1, Miles Papers; Miles to Endicott, Mar. 23, 1886, Endicott Papers; Endicott to Parkman, Feb. 4, 1886, Francis Parkman III Papers, Massachusetts Historical Society (quotations).

CHAPTER NINE

1. Utley, *Indian Frontier*, 196–201.

2. Robert Utley, forward to Britton Davis, *The Truth About Geronimo*, ed. M. M. Quaife (1929; reprint, Lincoln: University of Nebraska Press, 1976).

3. Drum to Miles, Apr. 2, 1886, Press Copies, Department of Arizona, RG 393, NARA; Drum to Miles, Apr. 3, 1886, LS, Arizona, NARA (first quotation); Miles, *Personal Recollections*, 476 (second quotation).

4. Miles to his wife, Apr. 11, 1886, Sherman Miles MSS; Lamar, *Far Southwest*, 176–85, 473–74; Miles to Ross, Nov. 11, 1885, Jan. 11, 12, 1886, Edmund G. Ross Collection, Kansas State Historical Society, Center for Historical Research (hereafter cited as Ross Collection); Ross to Miles, Jan. 15, 1886, box 3, Miles Papers.

5. Porter, *Paper Medicine Man*, 211; Charles R. Lummis, *General Crook and the Apache Wars* (Flagstaff, Ariz.: Northland Press, 1985), 30–49; Report of Miles, Sept. 18, 1886, SW, *Annual Report, 1886*, 171 (quotation).

6. Miles to his wife, Apr. 11, 1886, Sherman Miles MSS; Miles, *Personal Recollections*, 476; Miles to Lamont, Apr. 18, 1895, box 50, Daniel Lamont Papers, LC (hereafter cited as Lamont Papers). Most sources cite thirty-six Indians still being out. Dan L. Thrapp, *The Conquest of Apacheria* (Norman: University of Oklahoma Press, 1967), 350.

7. General Field Orders no.7, Apr. 20, 1886, SW, *Annual Report, 1886*, 166 (quotation); C. B. Gatewood, comp., "A Short Outline of the Apache Indian Campaign of 1885–86," box 3, Gatewood Collection; James L. Parker, *The Old Army Memories, 1872–1912* (Philadelphia: Dorrance and Co., 1929), 169–71; Miles, *Personal Recollections*, 478–82; Bruno J. Rolak, "General Miles' Mirrors: The Heliograph in the Geronimo Campaign of 1886," *Journal of Arizona History* 16 (Summer 1975): 145–60. Robert M. Utley, "The Surrender of Geronimo," *Arizoniana* 4 (1963): 1–9, provides a concise account of the campaign.

8. Report of Miles, Sept. 18, 1886, SW, *Annual Report, 1886*, 167–68; Endicott to Secretary of State, May 18, 1886, roll 97, LS, SW, NARA; Utley, *Frontier Regulars*, 397.

9. Orders no.58, May 4, 1886, SW, *Annual Report, 1886*, 176–77; Utley, *Frontier Regulars*, 397; Diary, May 4, 1886, box 1, Leonard Wood Papers, LC (hereafter cited as Leonard Wood Papers) (quotation).

10. Report of Lawton, Sept. 9, 1886, SW, *Annual Report, 1886*, 177–81 (quotation); Diary, May–June, 1886, box 1, Leonard Wood Papers; Miles to Mary, May 24, 30, 1886, Sherman Miles MSS; Report of Miles, Sept. 18, 1886, SW, *Annual Report, 1886*, 170.

11. F. J. Heney to Miles, May 29, 1886, box 5, Gatewood Collection (quotation); Gatewood to his wife, June 25, 1886, box 7, ibid.; Parker, *Old Army Memories*,

173; Dan L. Thrapp, *Encyclopedia of Frontier Biography*, 3 vols. (Glendale, Calif.: Arthur H. Clark Co., 1988), 3:543.

12. Miles, *Personal Recollections*, 494–95; Miles to his wife, June 15, July 21, Aug. 4, 1886, Sherman Miles MSS; Report of Miles, Sept. 18, 1886, SW, *Annual Report, 1886*, 168–71; Sheridan to Miles, July 15, 1886, Miles Collection.

13. Miles to his wife, May 23, June 21, 1886, Sherman Miles MSS; Miles, *Personal Recollections*, 495–97; Miles to Asst. Adj. Genl., July 7, 12, 1886, Miles Collection; Miles to Dawes, July 13, 1886, box 27, Dawes Papers; Report of Miles, Sept. 18, 1886, SW, *Annual Report, 1886*, 170; Lamar to Miles, Aug. 4, 1879, box 8, Miles Papers (quotation).

14. Porter, *Paper Medicine Man*, 213–16. A transcript of a July 26 meeting with Secretary Endicott may be found in Senate Exec. Doc. 83, 51st Cong., 1st sess., serial 2686, pp.41–43.

15. Porter, *Paper Medicine Man*, 215–16 (quotation); Miles to his wife, July 31, 1886, Sherman Miles MSS; Miles to Barlow, Mar. 30, 1888, Miles Collection.

16. Miles to Lamar, Aug. 1, 1886, Miles Collection; Miles to Sheridan, Aug. 2, 1886, ibid.; Sheridan to Miles, July 31, 1886, ibid. (quotations); Miles to his wife, Aug. 2, 1886, Sherman Miles MSS.

17. Miles to Barlow, Mar. 30, 1888, Miles Collection; Parker, *Old Army Memories*, 178 (quotation).

18. Miles to his wife, July 31, 1886, Sherman Miles MSS; Davis, *The Truth About Geronimo*, 223; Jack C. Lane, ed., *Chasing Geronimo: The Journal of Leonard Wood, May–September, 1886* (Albuquerque: University of New Mexico Press, 1970), 88, 135 n.4; Charles Byars, ed., "Gatewood Reports to His Wife from Geronimo's Camp," *Journal of Arizona History* 7 (Summer 1966): 81 n.6 (quotation); Gatewood to his wife, Aug. 26, 1886, box 7, Gatewood Collection.

19. Gatewood to his wife, Aug. 26, 1886, box 7, Gatewood Collection (quotations); H. W. Daly to Gatewood, June 18, 1928, box 9, ibid.; Utley, *Frontier Regulars*, 399.

20. Miles to Lamar, Aug. 13, 25, 1886, Miles Collection; Lamar to Miles, Aug. 14, 16, 1886, ibid.; Drum to Endicott, Aug. 14, 1886, ser.2, roll 38, Cleveland Papers; Miles to Mary, Aug. 15, 1886, Sherman Miles MSS; Miles to Adj. Genl., Aug. 20, 1886, Miles Collection; Sheridan to Miles, Aug. 25, 1886, ibid. (first quotation); Drum to Miles, Aug. 25, 1886, roll 98, LS, SW, NARA (second quotation).

21. Miles to his wife, Aug. 27, 1886, Sherman Miles MSS; Miles to Drum, Aug. 28, 1886, Miles Collection (first quotation); Drum to President, Aug. 30, 1886, container 96, Lamont Papers (second and third quotations).

22. Miles to his wife, Aug. 29, Sept. 2, 1886, Sherman Miles MSS; Utley, *Frontier Regulars*, 399; Lawton to Wilder, Aug. 30, 1886, box 5, Gatewood Collection; Lawton to Miles, Sept. 2, 1886, ibid. (quotations); Parker, *Old Army Memories*, 184–86.

23. Parker, *Old Army Memories*, 186; Report of Miles, Sept. 18, 1886, sw, *Annual Report, 1886*, 173; Miles to Lamar, Sept. 2, 1886, Miles Collection; Gatewood to Miles, Oct. 15, 1886, House Committee on Indian Affairs, H In 51-1, pp.9–10, U.S. Congressional Hearings Supplement; Miles to Adj. Genl., Division of the Pacific, Sept. 24, 1886, Senate Exec. Doc. 117, 49th Cong., 2d sess., serial 2449, p.19; Miles, *Personal Recollections*, 520–21 (quotation).

24. D. Stanley to Adj. Genl., Oct. 27, 1886, Senate Exec. Doc. 117, 49th Cong., 2d sess., serial 2449, p.22; Miles, *Personal Recollections*, 521 (quotation).

25. Miles, *Personal Recollections*, 521–27; Report of Miles, Sept. 18, 1886, sw, *Annual Report, 1886*, 173; Miles to Asst. Adj. Genl., Sept. 6, 1886, Miles Collection (quotations); Thrapp, *Conquest of Apacheria*, 365–66.

26. Miles to his wife, Sept. 7, 1886, Sherman Miles mss (first quotation); Howard to Adj. Genl., Sept. 7, 1886, Senate Exec. Doc. 117, 49th Cong., 2d sess., serial 2449, pp.7–8 (second quotation); Howard to Drum, Oct. 2, 1886, ibid., p.23 (third and fourth quotations); Lamar to Miles, n.d., Miles Collection (fifth quotation).

27. Senate Exec. Doc. 117, 49th Cong., 2d sess., serial 2449, pp.8–13, 23.

28. Drum to President, Sept. 8, 1886, ibid., p.10; Drum to Miles, Sept. 8, 1886, ibid., p.11 (first quotation); Drum to Endicott, Sept. 7, 1886, Miles Collection; Diary, Sept. 8, 1886, box 1, Leonard Wood Papers (second and third quotations); Thrapp, *Conquest of Apacheria*, 365.

29. Miles to Baird, Oct. 9, 30, 1886, Baird Papers, Beinecke; Miles to Asst. Adj. Genl., Nov. 3, 1886, Miles Collection; Miles to Ross, Oct. 1, 1886, ibid.; Drum to Howard, Sept. 9, 1886, roll 99, ls, sw, nara; Drum to President, Sept. 8, 1886, box 96, Lamont Papers.

30. Howard to Adj. Genl., Sept. 9, 1886, Miles Collection (first quotation); Drum to Endicott, Sept. 10, 1886, ser.2, roll 38, Cleveland Papers (second quotation); Howard to Adj. Genl., Sept. 9, 1886, Miles Collection (third quotation).

31. John A. Turcheneske, Jr., "Arizonans and the Apache Prisoners at Mount Vernon Barracks, Alabama: 'They Do Not Die Fast Enough,'" *Military History of Texas and the Southwest* 11, no.3 (1973): 197–226; Report of Endicott, Nov. 30, 1886, sw, *Annual Report, 1886*, 13; G. W. Wratten to Miles, Sept. 23, 1886, box 7, Gatewood Collection; Drum to Miles, Sept. 25, 1886, ser.2, roll 38, Cleveland Papers; Miles to Cameron, Oct. 4, 1886, Miles Collection; Drum to Miles, Sept. 26, 1886, roll 98, ls, sw, nara (quotation).

32. Report of Endicott, Nov. 30, 1886, sw, *Annual Report, 1886*, 13 (first quotation); Miles to Acting sw, Sept. 29, 1886, Senate Exec. Doc. 117, 49th Cong., 2d sess., serial 2449, pp.20–21; Miles to Mary, June 24, Oct. 4, 19, 1886, Sherman Miles mss; Miles to Ross, Oct. 1, 1886, Miles Collection (second quotation); Miles to "Senator," Oct. 1, 1886, ibid. (third quotation); Miles to Cameron, Oct. 4, 1886, ibid.; Miles to Baird, Oct. 9, 1886, Baird Papers, Beinecke; W. J. Worth to Miles, Oct. 11, 1886, box 5, Miles Papers; Miles to Barlow, Mar. 30,

1888, Miles Collection. For references to the mysterious telegram of September 4, see Howard to Adj. Genl., Sept. 17, 1886, Senate Exec. Doc. 117, 49th Cong., 2d sess., serial 2449, p.16; and Kelton to Commanding General, Division of the Pacific, Sept. 18, 1886, ibid.

33. Kelton to Miles, Sept. 24, 1886, Miles Collection; Worth to Miles, Oct. 11, 1886, box 5, Miles Papers; Miles to Welsh, Apr. 12, 1887, Miles Collection; Miles to Cameron, Oct. 4, 1886, ibid.; Miles to Mrs. Miles, Oct. 15, 1886, ibid.; Miles to Ross, Oct. 1 (first quotation), 4, 1886, ibid.; Miles to Ross, Nov. 1, 1886, Ross Collection (second and third quotations); Ross to Miles, Aug. 14, Oct. 3, Nov. 15, 1886, box 3, Miles Papers; Holabird to Miles, Nov. 12, Dec. 6, 1886, box 2, ibid.; Miles to Baird, Oct. 30, 1886, Baird Papers, Beinecke; Baird to Miles, Nov. 11, 1886, box 6, Miles Papers; Report of Miles, Sept. 18, 1886, sw, *Annual Report, 1886*, 164–76; O. Poe to Miles, Nov. 6, 1886, box 7, Miles Papers.

34. Report of Sheridan, Oct. 10, 1886, sw, *Annual Report, 1886*, 73; Report of Endicott, Nov. 30, 1886, ibid., 12–17; Crook to W. Hayes, Apr. 2, 1887, George Crook Papers, Hayes Library (hereafter cited as Crook Papers, Hayes Library); *New York Times*, June 20, 1887; L.Q.C. Lamar [Sr.] to Davis, Jan. 1, 1881, in Rowland, *Jefferson Davis*, 8:544–45; Drum to Commanding Officer, Dept. of Arizona, Nov. 6, 1886, Miles Collection; excerpts from *Army and Navy Register*, Sept. 26, Oct. 2, 1886, ibid.; C. Zulick to Miles, Apr. 8, 1887, box 9, Miles Papers.

35. For his protests against the removal to Florida, see for example Miles to Lamar, Sept. 2, 1886, Miles Collection.

36. Worth to Miles, Feb. 2, 1887, box 5, Miles Papers; Crook to Adj. Genl., May 16, July 28, 1888, Crook Papers, Hayes Library; Kelton to Miles, July 30, 1888, roll 62, ls, ago, nara; Kelton to Commander, Division of the Missouri, Aug. 1, 1888, ibid. For the newspaper war in Arizona, see Turcheneske, "Arizonans and the Apache Prisoners," 212–26.

37. Daly to Gatewood, Feb. 6, 1924, box 10, June 18, 1928 (quotations), box 9, Gatewood Collection. Miles's appointment of Gatewood as an aide was of particular importance because Miles valued aides as trusted allies (see J. Weston to Gatewood, Nov. 11, 1886, box 7, ibid.; Baird to Gatewood, Sept. 21, 1886, ibid.; Miles to Mary, Apr. 17, 1886, Sherman Miles mss).

38. Byars, "Gatewood Reports to His Wife," 76–77. See the Gatewood Collection, particularly boxes 7, 8, and 10.

39. Daly to Gatewood, Feb. 6, Apr. 25, 1924, box 10, Gatewood Collection; W. C. Brown to Gatewood, Sept. 11, 1925, box 7, ibid.; Corbin to Miles, June 26, 1895, ibid.; Miles, endorsement of Dec. 2, 1897, ibid. (quotations); Brown to E. A. Brininstool, June 4, July 9, 1925, ibid.

40. McKeever to Miles, Nov. 18, 1886, box 5, Gatewood Papers; Miles to Howard, Feb. 10, 1886 [1887], Howard Papers; Howard to Miles, Feb. 12, 1887, ibid.; Miles to Howard, Apr. 16, 1887, Miles Collection.

41. Howard to Miles, Apr. 22, 1887, Miles Collection (first and second quotations); Miles to Howard, May 12, 1887, ibid. (third quotation). In 1890, Miles charged that his message of September 6 "went . . . into a pigeon-hole at division headquarters in San Francisco, and remained there for a month" (testimony of Miles, Feb. 15, 1890, House Committee on Indian Affairs, H In 51-1, p.10, U.S. Congressional Hearings Supplement).

42. Diary, Sept. 1887, box 1, Leonard Wood Papers; Howard to Miles, May 16, 1887, Miles Collection; Miles to Howard, May 28, 1887, Jan. 26, 1888 (quotations), ibid.; Howard to Miles, June 1, 1887, ibid.; Howard to Miles, Sept. 2, 29, 1887, box 2, Miles Papers; Miles to Howard, Sept. 19, 26, Oct. 11, 1887, Howard Papers.

43. Endicott to President pro temp of Senate, Feb. 28, 1887, M 6, roll 101, vol.188, Letters Sent by the Secretary of War Relating to Military Affairs, NARA; Miles to Welsh, Apr. 12, 1887, Miles Collection. On Welsh, see William T. Hagan, *The Indian Rights Association: The Herbert Welsh Years, 1882–1904* (Tucson: University of Arizona Press, 1985).

44. Miles to J. Sherman, Dec. 30, 1887, box 420, J. Sherman Papers (first quotation); Barlow to Miles, Jan. 24, 1888, box 1, Miles Papers (second, third, and fourth quotations).

45. Miles to J. Sherman, Feb. 1, 1888, box 426, J. Sherman Papers; J. Sherman to Miles, Feb. 28, 1888, box 4, Miles Papers (quotations); Miles to Barlow, Mar. 20, 1888, Miles Collection.

46. "Reminiscences of an Arizona Pioneer," p.7, Mattie Riggs Johnson, biographical file, Arizona Historical Society/Tucson (quotation); *Arizona Daily Star*, Dec. 19, 1886; *New York Times*, Aug. 9, 1887; *Arizona Weekly Star*, Aug. 4, 1887.

47. *New York Times*, Sept. 1, Nov. 9, 1888; *Arizona Daily Star*, Nov. 9, 15 (quotation), 1888; *Tucson Daily Citizen*, Nov. 8, 1888; Miles, *Personal Recollections*, 532; Diary, Sept.–Nov. 1888, box 1, Leonard Wood Papers.

48. Miles, *Serving the Republic*, 229; *Arizona Daily Star*, Nov. 10, 11, 13 (quotations), 1887.

49. H. Carr to Gatewood, May 1, 1934, box 10, Gatewood Collection; Diary, May 4, 1889, box 1, Leonard Wood Papers; Miles to Barlow, Mar. 30, 1888, Miles Collection; Gatewood to Brown, Sept. 7, 1925, box 7, Gatewood Collection.

50. Miles to Barlow, Mar. 30, 1888, Miles Collection (quotation); Miles to Mary, Aug. 27, 1886, Sherman Miles MSS. James Parker believed Miles deserved "the real credit" for capturing Geronimo (Parker, *Old Army Memories*, 190).

51. Report of Stanley, Oct. 22, 1886, in S. M. Barrett, ed., *Geronimo's Story of His Life* (1905; reprint, Williamstown, Mass.: Corner House Publishers, 1973), 159 (first quotation); interview with Maus, Aug. 29, 1894, box 6, Hugh Scott Papers, LC (second quotation); Barrett, *Geronimo's Story of His Life*, 178 (third

quotation); *Tucson Daily Citizen*, May 17, 1904; Angie Debo, *Geronimo: The Man, His Time, His Place* (Norman: University of Oklahoma Press, 1976), 295.

52. Gatewood to editor, *Army and Navy Register*, Apr. 4, 1887, Lyman Walter Kennon Papers, Perkins Memorial Library, Manuscript Department; "Office of Apache Prisoners of War," May 2, 1911, file 1791876, box 6548, LR, AGO, NARA; Miles, fourth endorsement, June 28, 1911, ibid. (quotation); Maus, sixth endorsement, Aug. 11, 1911, ibid.; Adj. Genl. to Commanding Officer, Fort Apache, Nov. 14, 1911, ibid.; C. Martine to Gatewood, Mar. 24, 1926, box 8, Gatewood Collection.

53. Miles to Long, Mar. 31, 1886, box 1, Long Papers, Bancroft.

CHAPTER TEN

1. Diary, 1887, box 1, Leonard Wood Papers (first quotation); J. Sherman to Mary, May 13, 1887, Sept. 16, 1890 (second quotation); Allen to Miles, Mar. 6, 1889, box 1, Miles Papers.

2. Diary, Feb. 6, 15, 18, Mar. 1 (quotation), 1887, box 1, Leonard Wood Papers; Miles to Miss Strong, Mar. 25, 1887, HS 232, Huntington Library; Anson Mills, *My Story*, ed. C. H. Claudy (Washington, D.C.: Press of Byron S. Adams, 1918), 190; Worth to Miles, Dec. 19, 1886, box 5, Miles Papers; Bigelow to Miles, Dec. 25, 1886, box 6, ibid.; L. Metcalf to Miles, Sept. 14, [1886], box 8, ibid.; Hay to Miles, May 18, 1887, box 2, ibid.; Frederic Remington, *The Collected Writings of Frederic Remington*, ed. Peggy and Harold Samuels (New York: Doubleday and Co., 1979), 601; Fields to Miles, Apr. 13, 1888, box 1, Miles Papers; Cody to Miles, Feb. 7, 1889, ibid.; A. Lefevre to Miles, June 24, 29, 1889, box 8, ibid.; Miles to Church, Aug. 13, 1889, box 2, Church Papers.

3. Clarke to Adj. Genl., Sept. 26, 1886, file 3760, box 908, AGO Doc., NARA; Lamont to Miles, Mar. 21, 1887, box 2, Miles Papers; P. Bigelow to Miles, Dec. 18, 1888, box 1, ibid.; J. Sanger to Miles, May 15, 1889, box 3, ibid.

4. Memoirs, chap.4, pp.9–10, box 380, John J. Pershing Papers, LC (hereafter cited as Pershing Papers) (first, third, and fourth quotations); Miles, *Personal Recollections*, 538–44 (second quotation).

5. Hagan, *Indian Rights Association*, 68; Miles, *Personal Recollections*, 533–36; "Brief," July 28, 1887, 3267 AGO 1887, roll 536, LR, AGO, 1881–89, NARA; Miles to Asst. Adj. Genl., Aug. 3, 1887, ibid. (quotations). For another incident, see J. Speedy to E. Shaw, Mar. 4, 1887, 1220 AGO 1887, roll 519, ibid.; Lawton to Adj. Genl., Mar. 7, 1887, ibid.; Howard to Adj. Genl., Mar. 7, 1887, ibid.

6. Gatewood to his wife, June 17, 1887, box 7, Gatewood Collection (first quotation); Miles to Asst. Adj. Genl., June 25, 1887, LS, Ariz., NARA (second, third, and fourth quotations).

7. Adj. Genl. to Howard, Aug. 15, 1887, LS, Ariz., NARA; Howard to Adj. Genl.,

Sept. 3, 1887, ibid. (quotation); Miles to Asst. Adj. Genl., Sept. 18, 1887, ibid.; Howard to Miles, Sept. 18, 1887, ibid.; Report of Miles, Sept. 3, 1887, sw, *Annual Report, 1887*, 160; Report of Howard, Sept. 22, 1887, ibid., 157; Report of Sheridan, Nov. 1, 1887, ibid., 75; Pierce to si, Oct. 8, 1887, Removal of Certain Indians from the San Carlos Agency, 1887, file 69, box 1, Miscellaneous Records, Indian Division, RG 48, NARA.

8. Kelton to Howard, July 30, 1888, roll 62, LS, AGO, NARA (quotations); Diary, July 26–Aug. 2, 1888, box 1, Leonard Wood Papers; Kelton to sw, Aug. 1, 2, 1888, roll 62, LS, AGO, NARA.

9. Diary, Aug. 2–7, 1888, box 1, Leonard Wood Papers; Miles to Commanding Officer, Fort Bowie, Aug. 2, 1888, Press Copies, Department of Arizona, RG 393, NARA (quotation); Bullis to Commissioner of Indian Affairs, Aug. 17, 1888, 3264 AGO 1887, roll 536, LR, AGO, 1881–89, NARA; Miles endorsement, Sept. 25, 1888, ibid.; Howard endorsement, Sept. 27, 1888, ibid.; Report of Miles, Sept. 8, 1888, sw, *Annual Report, 1888*, 128; Report of Howard, Sept. 22, 1888, ibid., 123; Miles to Grierson, Mar. 14, 1889, roll 2, Benjamin Grierson Papers, Newberry Library, Chicago, Illinois (hereafter cited as Grierson Papers, Newberry).

10. Miles to Grierson, Mar. 14, 1889, roll 2, Grierson Papers, Newberry; Report of Grierson, Sept. 1, 1889, sw, *Annual Report, 1889*, 181–82; Miles, *Personal Recollections*, 536–37; Kelton endorsement, May 11, 1889, 3264 AGO 1887, roll 536, LR, AGO, 1881–89, NARA (quotation); Crook to Adj. Genl., May 18, 1890, ibid.; Report of Grierson, July 1, 1890, sw, *Annual Report, 1890*, 167–69.

11. *The United States Military List . . . January 1889* (Washington, D.C.: United Service Co., 1889); W. Sherman to Miles, Nov. 21, 1888, box 4, Miles Papers (first quotation); unsigned, undated "Memorandum," Command of the Army subject file, box 72, Schofield Papers (second, third, and fourth quotations).

12. Miles to his wife, Apr. 2, 1886, Long Papers, Huntington; Miles to Endicott, Oct. 9, 1886, Endicott Papers (quotation).

13. Miles to Lamont, Mar. 19, 1887, ser.2, roll 47, Cleveland Papers (first quotation); Miles to Adj. Genl., Mar. 24, 1887, LR, CB, NARA; Lamont to Miles, Apr. 2, 1887, box 2, Miles Papers; Mary to Uncle, May 2, 1887, box 403, J. Sherman Papers (second, third, and fourth quotations); Miles to Schurz, Mar. 2, 1887, roll 44, Schurz Papers.

14. J. Sherman to Mary, May 13, 27, 1887, box 4, Miles Papers (quotation); Mary to Uncle John, May 15, 1887, box 403, J. Sherman Papers; *New York Times*, June 11, 1887; Jones to Miles, Sept. 9, 1887, box 2, Miles Papers.

15. Miles to Baird, Dec. 17, 1887, Baird Papers, Kansas; Miles to Grierson, Dec. 17, 1887, roll 2, Grierson Papers, Newberry; Miles to J. Sherman, Dec. 19, 1887, box 419, J. Sherman Papers.

16. Jones to President, Dec. 29, 1887, LR, CB, box 1, NARA; Barlow to Miles, Dec. 31,

1887, Miles Papers; J. Sherman to Miles, Dec. 22, 1887, Jan. 10, 1888, box 4, ibid.; J. Ropes to Barlow, Dec. 30, 1887, box 8, ibid.; Miles to J. Sherman, Dec. 19, 1887, box 419 (quotation), Dec. 30, 1887, box 420, Feb. 1, 1888, box 426, J. Sherman Papers; Petition of Jan. 5, 1888, LR, CB, NARA.

17. *New York Times*, Feb. 5, 1888; Miles to Church, Feb. 24, 1888, box 21, Church Papers; Shafter to Miles, Mar. 16, 1888, box 4, Miles Papers; J. Sherman to Miles, Apr. 2, 1888, ibid. (quotation); Miles to Cameron, Apr. 11, 1888, Miles Collection; Crook to Adj. Genl., May 16, July 28, 1888, Crook Papers, Hayes Library; Kelton to Miles, July 30, Aug. 1, 1888, roll 62, LS, AGO, NARA; Kennon Diary, Aug. 3, 1888, Crook-Kennon Papers, U.S. Army Military History Institute (hereafter cited as Crook-Kennon Papers).

18. Miles to J. Sherman, Mar. 19, box 435 (quotations), Apr. 9, 1888, box 439, J. Sherman Papers; J. Sherman to Miles, Apr. 2, 1888, box 4, Miles Papers.

19. Hutton, *Phil Sheridan*, 371–72.

20. Grierson to Schofield, July 28, 1888, box 11, Schofield Papers; Shafter to Miles, May 27, 1888, box 4, Miles Papers; Miles to Schofield, Aug. 11, Nov. 27, 1888, Special Correspondence, box 41, Schofield Papers; Schofield to Miles, Aug. 15, 1888, LS, box 54, ibid.; Schofield to SW, Nov. 9, 1888, ibid.

21. Miles to W. Sherman, Jan. 14, 1889 (first quotation), Nov. 12, 1888 (second quotation), roll 39, W. Sherman Papers; Miles to Harrison, Nov. 10, 1888, ser. 1, roll 12, Benjamin Harrison Papers, LC (hereafter cited as Harrison Papers) (third quotation).

22. S. Field to Miles, Oct. 18, 1889, box 1, Miles Papers; Miles to Field, Aug. 27, 1889, Stephen J. Field Collection, Bancroft Library (quotation); Mabel E. Deutrich, *The Struggle for Supremacy: The Career of General Fred C. Ainsworth* (Washington, D.C.: Public Affairs Press, 1962), 108; Hale to Miles, Oct. 26, 1889, box 2, Miles Papers; endorsement of Mar. 6, 1889, LS, box 54, Schofield Papers; Wolfley to Miles, Apr. 19, 1889, box 9, Miles Papers; Glenn S. Dumke, "Advertising Southern California before the Boom of 1887," *Quarterly of the Historical Society of Southern California* 24 (Mar. 1942): 22; *New York Times*, Dec. 13, 1888; Miles to "My dear Alvord," Aug. 28, 1890, William Alvord Papers, Bancroft Library; Nelson A. Miles, "Our Unwatered Empire," *North American Review* 150 (Mar. 1890): 370–81.

23. Russell F. Weigley, *Towards an American Army: Military Thought from Washington to Marshall* (New York: Columbia University Press, 1962), 141–44; A. Perry to Asst. Adj. Genl., Nov. 24, 1888, Special Correspondence, box 41, Schofield Papers; Miles to Adj. Genl., Dec. 26, 1888, ibid. (first quotation); Miles to Adj. Genl., Dec. 26, 1888, 6155 AGO 1888, roll 658, LR, AGO, 1881–89, NARA; Schofield endorsement, Jan. 11, 1889, ibid. (second quotation).

24. Schwatka to Miles, June 1, 1883, box 5, Miles Papers (quotation); Allen to Miles, May 28, 1888, box 1, ibid.; Miles to Allen, June 5, Dec. 29, 1888, box 5,

Allen Papers; Miles to Wood, Jan. 29, 1889, box 26, Leonard Wood Papers; Wood to Miles, Feb. 4, 11, Mar. 13, 1889, box 5, Miles Papers.

25. Kelton to Commanding Officer, Division of the Pacific, Feb. 23, July 15, 1889, roll 63, LS, AGO, NARA; Miles to Allen, Mar. 29, 1889, box 5, Allen Papers; Wood to Miles, Apr. 11, 1889, box 5, Miles Papers; Miles to Schofield, June 20, 1889, Special Correspondence, box 42, Schofield Papers.

26. Report of Spinola, Jan. 12, 1889, House Report 3677, 50th Cong., 2d sess., serial 2673; Schofield to Miles, Jan. 9, 14, 1889, LS, box 54, Schofield Papers; Miles to W. Sherman, Nov. 12, 1888, Jan. 14, 1889, roll 39, W. Sherman Papers; Miles to Schofield, Sept. 21, Dec. 31, 1888, Jan. 15, 1889 (quotation), Special Correspondence, box 41, Schofield Papers.

27. Miles to W. Sherman, Jan. 14, 1889, roll 39, W. Sherman Papers (first quotation); Miles to J. Sherman, Jan. 25, 1889, box 469, J. Sherman Papers (second quotation); Miles to Vorhees, Jan. 16, 1889, Special Correspondence, box 41, Schofield Papers; Miles to Schofield, Jan. 17, 1889, ibid.; Schofield to Miles, Jan. 24, 1889, LS, box 54, ibid.; Miles to Schofield, Jan. 26, 28 (third quotation), Special Correspondence, box 41, ibid.; Miles to Grierson, Mar. 14, 1889, roll 2, Grierson Papers, Newberry.

28. J. Sherman to Miles, Jan. 29, 1889, box 4, Miles Papers; unsigned, undated, untitled typescript, Rank of Lieutenant General file, box 86, Schofield Papers; Schofield to Miles, Mar. 23, 1889, box 54, ibid.; Miles to Schofield, Nov. 18, 1889 (first quotation), Apr. 17, 1889 (second and third quotations), Special Correspondence, box 41, ibid.

29. Proctor to Miles, Apr. 13, July 2 (first quotation), Dec. 10, 1889, Jan. 6, 1890, Redfield Proctor Papers, Proctor Free Library, Proctor, Vermont (hereafter cited as Proctor Papers); Schofield to Miles, Mar. 23, 1889, LS, box 54, Schofield Papers; Worth to Miles, May 5, 1890, box 5, Miles Papers; Proctor to President, Sept. 16, 1889, ser.1, roll 22, Harrison Papers (second quotation). The best study of Proctor is Chester Winston Bowie, "Redfield Proctor: A Biography" (Ph.D. diss., University of Wisconsin-Madison, 1980).

30. Sanger to Miles, May 15, 1889, box 3, Miles Papers; Miles to Schofield, Oct. 31, Nov. 4, 18, 1889, Special Correspondence, box 41, Schofield Papers; Miles to J. Sherman, Nov. 22, 1889, box 495, J. Sherman Papers (quotation).

31. J. Sherman to Miles, Nov. 28, Dec. 16, 1889, box 4, Miles Papers; Martin F. Schmitt, ed., *General George Crook: His Autobiography* (1946; reprint, Norman: University of Oklahoma Press, 1960), 294; Debo, *Geronimo*, 313–14; Jason Betzinez with Wilber Sturtevant Nye, *I Fought with Geronimo* (Harrisburg, Pa.: Stackpole Co., 1959), 165. See also Senate Exec. Doc. 35, 51st Cong., 1st sess., serial 2682.

32. Miles to Baird, Oct. 9, 1886, Miscellaneous Manuscripts, Beinecke Rare Book and Manuscript Library (first quotation); *Washington Evening Star*, Feb. 22,

1890; Crook to Kennon, Feb. 3 (fourth quotation), 5 (second and third quotations), 1890, George Crook Papers, Special Collections, Knight Library, University of Oregon, Eugene (hereafter cited as Crook Papers, Oregon); Schmitt, *General George Crook*, 292.

33. Crook to Kennon, Feb. 5, 18, 1890, Crook Papers, Oregon; Crook to Kennon, Feb. 24 (first and second quotations), 25, 26, 1890, Crook-Kennon Papers; Crook to Howard, Feb. 27, 1890, ibid. (third quotation).

34. G. Howard to Adj. Genl., Dec. 23, 1889, Senate Exec. Doc. 35, 51st Cong., 1st sess., serial 2682, pp.9–11; Harrison to Senate and House, Jan. 20, 1890, ibid., p.1; Schmitt, *General George Crook*, 292; Howard to Crook, Mar. 1, 1890, Crook Papers, Oregon (first and second quotations); Crook to Kennon, Mar. 15, 1890, Crook-Kennon Papers (third quotation); James M. Merrill, *William Tecumseh Sherman* (Chicago: Rand McNally and Co., 1971), 386.

35. Testimony of Miles, Feb. 15, 1890, House Committee on Indian Affairs, H In 51, pp.6–13, U.S. Congressional Hearings Supplement (quotations); W. Lyman to Baird, Feb. 18, 1890, Baird Papers, Kansas; Kelton to Miles, Jan. 25, 1890, LR, CB, NARA; Schmitt, *General George Crook*, 294–300.

36. Miles to Dawes, Mar. 27, 1890, box 29, Dawes Papers.

37. R. Littlefield to Hayes, Mar. 28, 1890, Rutherford B. Hayes Papers; J. Campbell to President, Apr. 1, 1890, box 6, Miles Papers; J. Sherman to Harrison, Apr. 4, 1890, ser.1, roll 26, Harrison Papers (quotations). Miscellaneous letters of support may also be found in LR, CB, NARA.

38. Pohanka, *Documentary Biography*, 185 (first quotation); *New York Times*, Apr. 7, 1890; Stanley to Schofield, Apr. 14, 1890, Special Correspondence, box 42, Schofield Papers (second and third quotations); J. Sherman to Miles, Mar. 31, 1890, Miles Collection (fourth quotation).

39. Miles to Schofield, Apr. 12, 28, 1890, box 41, Schofield Papers; Alger to Miles, Apr. 24, 1890, box 6, Miles Papers; Schofield to Miles, May 6, 1890, box 24, Schofield Papers; W. Sherman to Miles, May 19, 1890, box 3, Miles Papers (quotation). Sherman had refused to assist Miles in this latest gambit (see W. Sherman to Miles, Apr. 4, 1890, box 4, Miles Papers).

40. Report of Wheeler, July 11, 1890, House Report 2686, 51st Cong., 1st sess., serial 2814; *Congressional Record*, 51st Cong., 1st sess., 21:10194; Proctor to Miles, July 14, 1890, Proctor Papers; Miles to Schofield, July 22, 1890, Special Correspondence, box 41, Schofield Papers; Oct. 6, 1890 entry in Alvin Humphrey Sydenham Journal, 1889–1890, U.S. Army Collections, New York Public Library (hereafter cited as Sydenham Journal).

41. Pohanka, *Documentary Biography*, 185; Huggins to Mabel, Oct. 20, 1890, Huggins Papers; Miles to J. Sherman, Oct. 5, 1890, box 529, J. Sherman Papers (quotation). For Chicago during the period, see David F. Burg, *Chicago's White City of 1893* (Lexington: University Press of Kentucky, 1975).

CHAPTER ELEVEN

1. Report of Miles, Sept. 14, 1891, sw, *Annual Report, 1891*, 133–34.
2. G. Chandler to Miles, Oct. 3, 1890, Miles Collection; Peggy and Harold Samuels, *Frederic Remington: A Biography* (Austin: University of Texas Press, 1985), 148–51; Remington, *Collected Writings*, 51–55 (quotations).
3. Robert M. Utley, *The Last Days of the Sioux Nation* (New Haven: Yale University Press, 1963), 102–5; Report of T. J. Morgan, Oct. 1, 1891, excerpts in Wilcomb E. Washburn, ed., *The American Indian and the United States: A Documentary History*, 4 vols. (New York: Random House, 1973), 1:562.
4. "Conversation between General Miles and Sioux Indian Chiefs Red Cloud and Little Wound at Pine Ridge Agency," Oct. 27, 1890, Miles Collection (quotations); Utley, *Last Days*, 104–5; Nov. 3, 1890, Sydenham Journal.
5. Report of A. L. Chapman, Dec. 6, 1890, sw, *Annual Report, 1891*, 191–94; Utley, *Last Days*, 60–83.
6. W. Worth to Miles, Oct. 22, 1890, box 5, Miles Papers (quotations); Utley, *Last Days*, 110–11; Ruger to Asst. Adj. Genl., Nov. 16, 26, 1890, sw, *Annual Report, 1890*, 189–91; S. Breck to Commander, Div. of the Missouri, Oct. 31, 1890, roll 1, Reports and Correspondence Relating to the Army Investigations of the Battle of Wounded Knee and to the Sioux Campaign of 1890–1891, M 983, NARA (hereafter cited as Wounded Knee Investigations).
7. Royer to Belt, Oct. 30, 1890, roll 1, Wounded Knee Investigations; Royer to Commissioner of Indian Affairs, Nov. 13, 1890, ibid.; Chandler to President, Nov. 13, 1890, ibid.; Report of Miles, Sept. 14, 1891, sw, *Annual Report, 1891*, 144–45; Report of Morgan, Oct. 1, 1891, in Washburn, *American Indian*, 1:562; Harrison to sw, Nov. 13, 1890, roll 1, Wounded Knee Investigations.
8. Report of Miles, Sept. 14, 1891, sw, *Annual Report, 1891*, 144–48; Utley, *Last Days*, 113–16; Miles to Schofield, Nov. 14, 1890, roll 1, Wounded Knee Investigations. On the mobilizations, see the exchange of telegrams between Ruger, Brooke, and R. Williams, Nov. 16–18, in roll 1, ibid.
9. Miles to Schofield, Nov. 17, 1890, roll 1, Wounded Knee Investigations; Williams to Brooke, Nov. 18 (first quotation), 23 (second quotation), 1890, ibid.; Miles to Brooke, Dec. 7, 1890, ibid. (third quotation); Miles to Adj. Genl., Nov. 20, 1890, ibid.
10. Charles Richard Williams, ed., *Diary and Letters of Rutherford Birchard Hayes, Nineteenth President of the United States* (Columbus: Ohio State Archaeological and Historical Society, 1926), 617; Report of Miles, Sept. 14, 1891, sw, *Annual Report, 1891*, 147.
11. William Frederick Cody, *Autobiography of Buffalo Bill Cody* (New York: Cosmopolitan Book Corp., 1920), 273, 304–5; Utley, *Last Days*, 123–24; Col. Peter E. Traub, "Sioux Campaign, Winter of 1890–'91," *The Papers of the Order of Indian Wars* (Fort Collins, Colo.: Old Army Press, 1975), 57–58.

12. Don Russell, *The Lives and Legends of Buffalo Bill* (Norman: University of Oklahoma Press, 1960), 358–61; Traub, "Sioux Campaign," 57–58.

13. Traub, "Sioux Campaign," 58 (quotations); Cody, *Autobiography*, 308; Kevin Brownlow, *The War, the West, and the American Wilderness* (New York: Alfred A. Knopf, 1979), 227; Schofield to Miles, Nov. 29, 1890, roll 1, Wounded Knee Investigations.

14. DeMontravel, "Nelson A. Miles," 345–46; *Washington Evening Star*, Nov. 21, 1890 (quotations); M. Bundy to Miles, Nov. 22, 1890, box 6, Miles Papers. Rumors concerning Miles's presidential ambitions were widespread (see Hagan, *Indian Rights Association*, 117).

15. Miles to Adj. Genl., Nov. 23 (quotation), 28, 1890, roll 1, Wounded Knee Investigations; Noble to sw, Nov. 25, ibid.; Proctor to Miles, Dec. 1, 1890, Proctor Papers; Schofield to Miles, Dec. 6, 1890, Special Correspondence, box 41, Schofield Papers; *Washington Evening Star*, Dec. 1, 2, 4, 1890; *Congressional Record*, 51st Cong., 2d sess., vol.22, pt.1, pp.44–48, 68–74, 200; Utley, *Last Days*, 129–30.

16. Hagan, *Indian Rights Association*, 117 (quotation); Utley, *Last Days*, 129–30; Report of Miles, Sept. 14, 1891, sw, *Annual Report, 1891*, 148.

17. Utley, *Last Days*, 179; Report of Ruger, Oct. 19, 1891, sw, *Annual Report, 1891*, 181.

18. Brooke to Asst. Adj. Genl., Dept. of the Platte, Dec. 6, 1890, Telegrams Sent, Headquarters in the Field, Dept. of the Platte, RG 393, NARA (first quotation); Brooke to Asst. Adj. Genl., 11 A.M. 4:20 P.M., Dec. 6, 1890, ibid.; Corbin to Brooke, Dec. 6, 1890, p.262, LS, Division of the Missouri, RG 393, NARA; Miles to Brooke, Dec. 7, 1890, p.264, ibid. (second and third quotations).

19. Brooke to Asst. Adj. Genl., Div. of the Missouri, Dec. 15, 1890, Telegrams Sent, Headquarters in the Field, Dept. of the Platte, RG 393, NARA; Brooke to Miles, Dec. 16, 1890, ibid.; Miles to Brooke, Dec. 16, 1890, LR, Headquarters in the Field, Dept. of the Platte, RG 393, NARA; Utley, *Last Days*, 140–45; Report of Miles, Sept. 14, 1891, sw, *Annual Report, 1891*, 148–50; "Memoirs," chap.5, p.5, box 380, Pershing Papers; Brooke to Miles, Dec. 16, 1890, p.88–90, Letters and Endorsements Sent, Headquarters in the Field, Dept. of the Platte, RG 393, NARA; Thrapp, *Encyclopedia*, 1:230–31.

20. Brooke to Miles, Dec. 16 (quotation), 18, 20, 1890, LS, Platte, NARA; Report of Brooke, Mar. 2, 1891, roll 2, Wounded Knee Investigations. Reports from Indian delegations may be found in LR, Headquarters in the Field, Dept. of the Platte, RG 393, NARA.

21. Report of Merritt, Sept. 1, 1891, sw, *Annual Report, 1891*, 167–68; Report of Ruger, Oct. 19, 1891, ibid., pp.181–82; Report of Drum, Feb. 27, 1891, ibid., pp.194–95; Fechet to Post Adj., Dec. 17, 1891, ibid., pp.197–99; Miles to Adj. Genl., Dec. 13, 1890, roll 1, Wounded Knee Investigations; McLaughlin to Morgan, Dec. 24, 1890, ibid.

22. Utley, *Last Days*, 173–74; Report of Sumner, Feb. 3, 1891, sw, *Annual Report, 1891*, 223–25; Sumner to Miles, Dec. 8, 1890, ibid., 228; Barber to Sumner, Dec. 16, 1890, ibid., 229 (quotation).

23. Report of Sumner, Feb. 3, 1891, sw, *Annual Report, 1891*, 224–27; Sumner to Miles, Dec. 19, 21, 22, 23 (first quotation), ibid., 232–34; Sumner to Miles, Feb. 21, 1891, box 5, Miles Papers; Miles to Commanding Officer, Fort Bennett, Dec. 24, 1890, sw, *Annual Report, 1891*, 209–10; Sumner to H. Merriam, Dec. 26, 27, 1890, ibid., 210; Miles to Sumner, Dec. 24, 1890, ibid., 235 (second quotation); Miles to Adj. Genl., Dec. 24, 1890, roll 1, Wounded Knee Investigations; unsigned "Confidential Report," Division of the Missouri, Mar. 4, 1891, Miles Collection.

24. Miles to his wife, Dec. 19, 20, 22, 25, 1890, Sherman Miles MSS; Miles to Schofield, Dec. 19, 1890, sw, *Annual Report, 1891*, 149; Miles to Dawes, Dec. 19, 1890, ibid.; Brooke to Miles, 2:30 P.M., 8:20 P.M., Dec. 25, 1890, Telegrams Sent, Headquarters in the Field, Dept. of the Platte, RG 393, NARA; Miles to Adj. Genl., Dec. 27, 1890, roll 1, Wounded Knee Investigations.

25. Utley, *Last Days*, 192–97; testimony of Whitside, Jan. 7, 1891, "Report of Investigation," roll 1, Wounded Knee Investigations; testimony of Forsyth, Jan. 11, 1891, ibid.; testimony of Brooke, Jan. 11, 1891, ibid. (quotation). See also Brooke to Miles, Dec. 31, 1890, pp.52–53, Letters and Endorsements Sent, Headquarters in the Field, Dept. of the Platte, RG 393, NARA.

26. Utley, *Last Days*, 200–207; testimony of Whitside, Jan. 7, 1891, "Report of Investigation," roll 1, Wounded Knee Investigations.

27. Utley, *Last Days*, 200–207; testimony of Whitside, Jan. 7, 1891, "Report of Investigation," roll 1, Wounded Knee Investigations.

28. Report of Miles, Sept. 14, 1891, sw, *Annual Report, 1891*, 150; Kay Graber, ed., *Sister to the Sioux: The Memoirs of Elaine Goodale Eastman, 1885–91*, Pioneer Heritage Series, vol.7 (Lincoln: University of Nebraska Press, 1978), 160; Utley, *Last Days*, 231–41; Miles to Baird, Nov. 20, 1891, Baird Papers, Beinecke; Henry to Miles, Jan. 27, 1892, box 2, Miles Papers.

29. Miles to his wife, Dec. 30, 1890, Sherman Miles MSS; Utley, *Last Days*, 251–55; Miles to Adj. Genl., Dec. 29, 30, 1890, roll 1, Wounded Knee Investigations.

30. Miles to Schofield, Jan. 3, 1891, roll 1, Wounded Knee Investigations; Miles to Adj. Genl., Jan. 5, 1891, ibid.; Miles to Big Road, et. al., Jan. 6, 1891, pp. 201–2, LS, Headquarters in the Field, Division of the Missouri, RG 393, NARA (quotations); *Washington Evening Star*, Jan. 17, 1891; Miles to his wife, Jan. 8, 1891, Sherman Miles MSS; Report of Miles, Sept. 14, 1891, sw, *Annual Report, 1891*, 152.

31. Merriam to Miles, Jan. 11, 1891, sw, *Annual Report, 1891*, 219; Carr to Sister, Jan. 7, 1891, box 4, Carr Papers (first quotation); Brooke to Asst. Adj. Genl., 8:00 A.M., Jan. 11, 1891, pt.3, Letters and Endorsements Sent, Headquarters in

the Field, Dept. of the Platte RG 393, NARA (second quotation); Miles to Adj. Genl., Jan. 11, 12, 1891, roll 1, Wounded Knee Investigations.

32. Miles to his wife, January 13, 15, 1891, Sherman Miles MSS; Miles to Adj. Genl., Jan. 27, 1891, roll 2, Wounded Knee Investigations; Report of Miles, Sept. 14, 1891, SW, *Annual Report, 1891,* 152–53.

33. Miles to Cody, Jan. 16, 1891, LS, Headquarters in the Field, Division of the Missouri, RG 393, NARA; Miles to Adj. Genl., Mar. 14, 19, 1891, roll 2, Wounded Knee Investigations; Russell, *Buffalo Bill,* 369; Utley, *Last Days,* 271–72; G. Chandler to Morgan, Mar. 6, 1891, Letters Sent, Indian Division, RG 48, NARA; Cody to Miles, May 4 (quotation), June 24, 1891, box 1, Miles Papers.

34. Miles to Schofield, Jan. 16, 1891, Special Correspondence, box 41, Schofield Papers (quotation); Miles to Adj. Genl., Jan. 18, roll 2, Wounded Knee Investigations; Williams to Miles, Jan. 19, 1891, ibid.; Morgan to SI, Jan. 20, 1891, ibid.; Special Orders no.24, Jan. 21, 1891, ibid.; Miles to SW, Jan. 21, 1891, ibid.

35. Miles to his wife, Dec. 30, 1890, Sherman Miles MSS; Miles to Schofield, Jan. 1, 1891, roll 1, Wounded Knee Investigations (quotations); Schofield to Miles, Jan. 2, 1891, ser.1, roll 30, Harrison Papers.

36. Miles to Forsyth, Jan. 4, 1891, LS, Headquarters in the Field, Division of the Missouri, RG 393, NARA; Miles to Schofield, Jan. 5, 1891, roll 1, Wounded Knee Investigations; Miles to Mary, Jan. 6, 1891, Sherman Miles MSS (quotation); Forsyth to Lamont, Dec. 31, 1896, in James W. Forsyth, "Statements in Defense of the Seventh Cavalry while under His Command against the Sioux," Rare Books and Manuscripts Division, New York Public Library (hereafter cited as Forsyth, "Statements"); Utley, *Cavalier in Buckskin,* 100; Special Orders no.8, Jan. 4, 1891, "Report of Investigation," pp.1–2, roll 1, Wounded Knee Investigations. Note also the request by division headquarters that Forsyth detail his Indian-fighting experience (Forsyth to Asst. Adj. Genl., Jan. 18, 1891, pp.78–79, ibid.).

37. Miles to his wife, Jan. 6, 1891, Sherman Miles MSS; Schofield to Miles, Jan. 6, 1891, roll 1, Wounded Knee Investigations; *Washington Evening Star,* Jan. 5, 1891 (first quotation); Forsyth to Lamont, Dec. 31, 1896, Forsyth Statement; W. Sherman to Mary, Jan. 7, 1891, box 4, Miles Papers (second and third quotations).

38. Special Orders no.10, Jan. 6, 1891, roll 1, Wounded Knee Investigations; Forsyth to Lamont, Sept. 1, 1895, Forsyth Statement.

39. Miles to his wife, Jan. 6, 1891, Sherman Miles MSS; "Report of Investigation," roll 1, Wounded Knee Investigations.

40. See testimony of Moylan, p. 14, W. Nicholson, p. 19, E. Godfrey, p.27, S. Rice, p.28, C. Ilsley, p.33, S. Tompkins, p.43–44 (quotation), in "Report of Investi-

gation," roll 1, Wounded Knee Investigations; Miles, second endorsement, Mar. 21, 1891, Baird Letters, Beinecke.

41. "Memoirs," chap.5, p.7, box 380, Pershing Papers; Report of Kent, Jan. 13, 1891, "Report of Investigation," pp.74–76, Wounded Knee Investigations; Report of Baldwin, Jan. 13, 1891, pp.76–77, ibid.

42. Corbin to Kent and Baldwin, Jan. 16, 1891, "Report of Investigation," roll 1, Wounded Knee Investigations; testimony of Brooke, ibid.; Brooke to Asst. Adj. Genl., Jan. 23, 1891, ibid. (first quotation); Report of Kent, Jan. 18, 1891, ibid. (second and third quotations); Report of Baldwin, Jan. 18, 1891, ibid. (fourth quotation). See also Brooke to Miles, [Dec. 31, 1890], pt.2, Letters and Endorsements Sent, Headquarters in the Field, Dept. of the Platte, RG 393, NARA.

43. Forsyth to Lamont, Sept. 1, 1895, Forsyth Statement. See also Forsyth's testimony, "Report of Investigation," roll 1, Wounded Knee Investigations.

44. Huggins to Sister and Home Folks, Feb. 17 (first quotation), Jan. 31 (second and third quotations), 1891, Huggins Papers; F. Edmund to Father, Feb. 10, 1891, Frank Edmund Papers, Special Collections, U.S. Military Academy Library, West Point, New York; Endorsement of Miles, Jan. 31, 1891, "Report of Investigation," pp.114–15, roll 1, Wounded Knee Investigations (fourth, fifth, sixth, seventh, and eighth quotations); Miles to Adj. Genl., Feb. 4, 1891, roll 2, Wounded Knee Investigations (ninth quotation).

45. Endorsement of Schofield, Feb. 4, 1891, "Report of Investigation," roll 1, Wounded Knee Investigations (first quotation); Proctor to Schofield, Feb. 12, 1891, roll 2, ibid.; Bowie, "Redfield Proctor," 245; Forsyth to Lamont, Sept. 1, 1895, Forsyth Statement; Miles to Proctor, Feb. 13, 1891, ser.1, roll 30, Harrison Papers; Proctor to Miles, Feb. 17, 1891, ibid.; Miles to Baird, Nov. 30, 1891, Baird Papers, Beinecke; Corbin to R. Hayes, Feb. 4, 16 (second quotation), 1891, Rutherford B. Hayes Papers; Huggins to Sister, Feb. 17, 1891, Huggins Papers (third and fourth quotations).

46. Miles to Huggins, Sept. 21, 1891, Huggins Papers.

47. McKeever to Miles, Nov. 18, 1886, box 5, Gatewood Collection; McKeever to Kennon, Dec. 12, 1890, LR, CB, NARA; *New York Times*, Jan. 8, 22, 1891; Bowie, "Redfield Proctor," 245–28; *Washington Evening Star*, Jan. 24, 1891; J. McEwan to Miles, Feb. 9, 1891, box 3, Miles Papers; Miles to Baird, Nov. 20, 1891, Baird Papers, Beinecke; undated newspaper clipping, p.89, untitled scrapbook, Augur Papers.

48. Rice to Miles, July 12, 1888, box 8, Miles Papers; Miles to Sherman, Feb. 7, 1889, roll 39, W. Sherman Papers; Sherman to Miles, Sept. 12, 1889, box 4, Miles Papers; W. Ridering to Miles, Sept. 16, 1889, box 8, ibid.; Miles, "The Future of the Indian Question," *North American Review* 152 (Jan. 1891): 10 (quotation).

49. Miles to Schofield, Jan. 7, 1891, ser.1, roll 30, Harrison Papers; General Orders

no.2, Jan. 12, 1891, ibid.; Miles to Adj. Genl., Feb. 9, Mar. 20 (quotation), 1891, ibid.; Report of Miles, Sept. 14, 1891, sw, *Annual Report, 1891*, 153–54; "Memoirs," chap.5, pp.4–5, box 380, Pershing Papers; Schofield to Miles, Jan. 7, 1891, roll 1, Wounded Knee Investigations; Miles to Adj. Genl., Jan. 14, 1891, ibid.; Brock to Miles, Jan. 15, 1891, ibid.; Schofield to Miles, Jan. 16, 1891, ibid.; Miles to Adj. Genl., Mar. 13, 1891, roll 2, ibid.

50. Utley, *Last Days*, 274; *Statutes at Large*, 51st Cong., 26:720–21, 1001–2.

51. Proctor to Noble, Jan. 17, 1891, roll 1, Wounded Knee Investigations; Kelton to Miles, Jan. 23, 1891, roll 2, ibid.; David Graham Phillips, "The Sioux Chiefs before the Secretary," *Harper's Weekly* 35 (Feb. 21, 1891): 142 (quotations); "Indian Truth and Eloquence," ibid., 131; *New York Times*, Feb. 9, 1891.

52. Proctor to Miles, Feb. 17, 1891, ser.1, roll 30, Harrison Papers; Proctor to President, Feb. 18, 1891, box 3, Proctor Papers (first and second quotations); Huggins to Sister and Home Folks, Feb. 13, 1891, Huggins Papers (third quotation); Huggins to Sister, Feb. 17, 1891, ibid. (fourth quotation).

53. Sumner to Miles, Feb. 21, 1891, box 5, Miles Papers; Huggins to Sister, Feb. 17, 1891, Huggins Papers; Schofield to Miles, Feb. 27, 1891, box 54, Schofield Papers; Proctor to Miles, May 16, 1891, box 3, Proctor Papers (quotation).

54. Morgan to si, Feb. 24, 1891, ser. 1, roll 30, Harrison Papers (first quotation); Proctor to Miles, Feb. 24, 1891, ibid. (second quotation).

55. Report of Miles, Sept. 14, 1891, sw, *Annual Report, 1891*, 132; *New York Times*, July 6, 12, 1891; Alice to Baldwin, June 9, 1891, box 9, Baldwin Papers (first quotation); Miles to Baird, July 9, 1891, Baird Papers, Kansas (second quotation).

56. Miles to Baird, Nov. 20, 1891, Baird Papers, Beinecke (first quotation); Robert M. Utley, *The Indian Frontier of the American West, 1846–1890* (Albuquerque: University of New Mexico Press, 1984), 257 (second quotation); Diary, chap.5, pp.7–8, box 380, Pershing Papers; Prucha, *Great Father*, 2:731–36.

57. Harrison to Congress, Dec. 9, 1891, in James D. Richardson, ed., *A Compilation of the Messages and Papers of the Presidents, 1789–1908*, 10 vols. (Washington, D.C.: Bureau of National Literature and Art, 1908), 9:202; Miles to Harrison, Dec. 16, 1891, roll 33, Harrison Papers.

58. Report of Miles, Sept. 14, 1891, sw, *Annual Report, 1891*, 144 (first quotation); Cody to Miles, May 4, 1891, box 1, Miles Papers; American Horse to My Friend General Miles, Sept. 10, 1891, Miles Collection; Short Bull to Miles, July 15, 1891, ibid. (second quotation); Miles to Adj. Genl., Mar. 16, 1893, ibid.; Report of Miles, Sept. 14, 1892, sw, *Annual Report, 1892*, 102; Report of Miles, Aug. 25, 1893, sw, *Annual Report, 1893*, 122; Miles to Adj. Genl., Nov. 10, 1894, Miles Collection.

CHAPTER TWELVE

1. Huggins to Sister and Home Folks, Jan. 31, 1891, Huggins Papers; Miles to Adj. Genl., Feb. 9, 14, 1891, LR, CB, NARA; *New York Times,* Feb. 19, 1891 (quotation); *St. Louis Post-Dispatch,* Feb. 21, 22, 1891; H. Merriam to Miles, May 17, 1891, box 8, Miles Papers; J. Sherman to Miles, Mar. 8, 1891, box 4, ibid.; *San Antonio Daily Express,* Mar. 24, 1891; Miles to J. Sherman, May 14, 1891, box 542, J. Sherman Papers; Remington, *Collected Works,* 78–79.

2. Barlow to Miles, Aug. 23, 1891, box 1, Miles Papers; H. Washburn to Miles, July 19, 1902, box 9, ibid.; J. Kirkland to Miles, Oct. 22, 1892, box 7, ibid.; Miles to Baird, Nov. 20, 1891, Baird Papers, Beinecke; Pratt, *Battlefield and Classroom,* 296–97; Adj. Genl. to C. Culp, Dec. 23, 1892, LR, CB, NARA; E. Williams to Miles, Jan. 17, 1893, ibid.; Burg, *Chicago's White City,* 100; Miles to Adj. Genl., Jan. 26, 1893, in Pohanka, *Documentary Biography,* 235–39.

3. T. Livermore to Miles, Sept. 3, 1887, box 8, Miles Papers; J. Sherman to Miles, May 31, 1886, Apr. 4, 1887, box 4, ibid.; Miles to J. Sherman, Mar. 25, 1887, box 399, Feb. 25, 1888, box 431, Jan. 21, 1889, box 469, J. Sherman Papers.

4. Miles to J. Sherman, Jan. 9, 1892, box 566, June 1, 1892, box 582, J. Sherman Papers.

5. Miles to Elizabeth, Apr. 23, 1893, box 3, Miles Papers; Peggy and Harold Samuels, *Frederic Remington,* 197–98; John Sherman, *John Sherman's Recollections of Forty Years in the House, Senate and Cabinet: An Autobiography,* 2 vols. (Chicago: Werner Co., 1895), 2:1210–12.

6. Miles to Adjutant General, June 8, 1894, LR, CB, NARA; Robin McKnown, *Painter of the Wild West: Frederic Remington* (New York: Julian Mesner, 1959), 113, 177; Peggy and Harold Samuels, *Frederic Remington,* 183, 200; Lamont to Miles, Jan. 2, 1894, box 2, Miles Papers; Miles to Lamont, Aug. 22, 1894, box 41, Sept. 21, 1894, box 42, Lamont Papers; Lamont to Miles, Aug. 24 (quotation), Sept. 29, 1894, letterbook 7, box 91, ibid.

7. J. Ropes to Miles, Feb. 26, 1892, box 8, Miles Papers; J. Medill to Miles, Oct. 22, 1892, box 3, ibid.; Miles to Adj. Genl., Dec. 23, 1892, LR, CB, NARA; E. Williams to Miles, Jan. 17, 1893, ibid.

8. Joseph L. Schott, *Above and Beyond: The Story of the Congressional Medal of Honor* (New York: G. P. Putnam's Sons, 1963), 61–63; DeMontravel, "Nelson A. Miles," 54–56; Pope to Elkins, June 13, 1892, Miles Collection; Couch to Elkins, May 16, 1892, ibid.; E. St. John to Baldwin, Jan. 29, 1892, box 16, Baldwin Papers; Carriker, "Frank D. Baldwin," 236–37. For Miles's efforts on behalf of others, see file 4914, box 552, AGO Doc., NARA.

9. Report of Wheeler, Jan. 6, 1891, House Report 3370, 51st Cong., 2d sess., serial 2885; Miles to Newberry, Jan. 9, Dec. 28, 1892, Jan. 4, 9, 1893, Miles Collection; Elkins to Senate Chairman, Committee on Military Affairs, Mar. 26, 1892, Rank of Lieutenant General file, box 86, Schofield Papers;

Lamont to Chairman, House Committee on Military Affairs, Jan. 10, 1894, ibid.; J. Sherman to Miles, Jan. 12, 1893, box 4, Miles Papers; D. Davis to Miles, Dec. 29, 1893, box 6, ibid.; Miles to Schofield, Mar. 13, 1894, Jan. 29, 1895, LR, box 31, Schofield Papers (quotation); D. Goldin to E. Brininstool, Apr. 3, 1928, box 9, Gatewood Collection.

10. Allen Nevins, *Grover Cleveland: A Study in Courage* (New York: Dodd, Meade, and Co., 1964), 620–21; Ruggles to J. Sherman, Maus, and Huggins, July 2, 1894, Chicago Riots file, box 72, Schofield Papers; L. Hoyt to Ruggles, July 2, 1894, ibid.; Jerry M. Cooper, *The Army and Civil Disorder: Federal Military Intervention in Labor Disputes, 1877–1900*, Contributions in Military History, no. 19 (Westport, Conn.: Greenwood Press, 1980), 144–46.

One observer tied Miles's opposition to using regular soldiers to his alleged association with the People's Party. See Mrs. Gresham to Gresham, in Matilda Gresham, *Life of Walter Quinton Gresham 1832–1895*, 2 vols. (Chicago: Rand McNally and Co., 1919), 1:418–19.

11. Miles to Adj. Genl., July 4 (first quotation), 5 (second quotation), 1894, Chicago Riots file, box 72, Schofield Papers; J. Ropes to Miles, Aug. 22, 1883, box 8, Miles Papers.

12. Schofield to Miles, July 5, 1894, Chicago Riots file, box 72, Schofield Papers; Miles to sw, July 6, 1894, ibid.; Miles to Schofield and sw, July 6, 1894, ibid.; Miles to Adj. Genl., July 6, 1894, ibid. (quotations).

13. Cooper, *Army and Civil Disorder*, 146–55 (first quotation); Miles to Lamont, July 7, 10 (second quotation), 1894, Chicago Riots file, box 72, Schofield Papers; Crofton to Conrad, July 8, 1894, ibid.; Miles to Schofield, July 10, 1894, ser.2, roll 85, Cleveland Papers; Nevins, *Grover Cleveland*, 622.

14. Cooper, *Army and Civil Disorder*, 147–55; Schofield to Miles, July 14, 1894, Chicago Riots file, box 72, Schofield Papers; Miles to Schofield, July 14, 1894, ibid. (first and second quotations); Asst. Adj. Genl. to Schofield, July 16, 1894, ibid.; Lamont to Miles, July 16, 1894, box 2, Miles Papers (third quotation).

15. Asst. Adj. Genl. to Schofield, July 16, 1894, Chicago Riots file, box 72, Schofield Papers; J. Hopkins to Miles, July 16, 1894, ibid.; L. Troy to Miles, July 17, 1894, ibid.; Miles to Lamont, July 17, 1894, ibid.; Miles to Adj. Genl., July 18, 1894, ibid. (quotations); S. Fish to Schofield, July 19, 1894, ibid.; Cooper, *Army and Civil Disorder*, 153.

16. Miles to Adj. Genl., July 18, 1894, Chicago Riots file, box 72, Schofield Papers.

17. Unsigned, undated typescript, Command of the Army file, box 72, Schofield Papers; Index-Digest Diaries, p.461, box 17, Charles S. Hamlin Papers, LC; Miles, *Serving the Republic*, 256–57; Nelson Miles, "The Lesson of the Recent Strikes," *North American Review* 159 (Aug. 1894): 184–87 (quotations).

18. Nevins, *Grover Cleveland*, 624; Miles to Adj. Genl., Feb. 16, 1894, LR, CB, NARA; Pond, "Miles," 562; *New York Times*, Nov. 20, 1894.

19. Pond, "Miles," 562; *New York Times*, Dec. 11, 1894, Jan. 17, Apr. 28, May 19, 1895; circular, Feb. 14, 1895, LS, East, NARA; Ridering to Miles, Feb. 21, 1895, box 8, Miles Papers.

20. *New York Times*, Mar. 19, May 18 (quotation), 1895; Remington to Wister, Apr. 1895, in Ben Merchant Vorpahl, *My Dear Wister: The Frederic Remington-Owen Wister Letters* (Palo Alto, California: American West, 1972), 120; Miles to M. Handy, Feb. 3, 21, 1895, Moses Purnell Handy Papers, William L. Clements Library, University of Michigan, Ann Arbor; Asst. Adj. Genl. to Miles, Mar. 6, 1895, LS, East, NARA; Miles to Adj. Genl., May 1, 1895, ibid.; Miles to Governor of Massachusetts, May 7, 1895, ibid.; Nita to Papa, May 29, 1893, box 13, Baldwin Papers; "Memoirs," chap.6, box 380, Pershing Papers; Wood to Miles, July 29, 1895, box 5, Miles Papers; Pond, "Miles," 574.

21. Maus to Miles, May 13, 1895, box 8, Dec. 15, 1895, box 9, Miles Papers; Daly to Gatewood, Apr. 6, 1927, box 10, Gatewood Collection; Clark to Miles, July 6, 1895, box 1, ibid.; Allen to Miles, July 18, 1895, box 1, ibid.; Miles to Allen, July 19, 1895, box 5, Allen Papers; Dodge to Miles, July 19, 1895, Miles Collection.

22. H. Nelson to Miles, Aug. 5, 1895, box 8, Miles Papers; Miles to Church, Oct. 2, 1895, box 2, Church Papers; Clark to Miles, Aug. 26, 1895, box 1, Miles Papers.

23. E. Brininstool to Gatewood, June 8, 1925, box 10, Gatewood Collection; Miles, *Personal Recollections*, 12 (first quotation), 13 (second quotation), 215.

24. Robert M. Utley, *Custer and the Great Controversy: The Origin and Development of a Legend* (Pasadena, Calif.: Westernlore Press, 1962), 72–74.

25. Utley, *Cavalier in Buckskin*, 195; John S. Manion, *General Terry's Last Statement to Custer: New Evidence on the Mary Adams Affidavit* (Monroe, Mich.: Monroe County Library System, 1983); Wooster, *Military and Indian Policy*, passim. I am particularly grateful to my readers, Gregory Urwin and Robert Utley, for their suggestions on the Adams affidavit.

26. *New York Times*, Nov. 17, Dec. 11, 1898; B. Colby to Miles, Feb. 23, 1900, box 1, Miles Papers; John Tebbel, *The Expansion of an Industry, 1865–1919*, vol. 2 of *A History of Book Publishing in the United States* (New York: R. R. Bowker, 1975), 447–48; *Publishers' Weekly* (Dec. 3, 1898): 1034; ibid. (Dec. 17, 1898): 1105; ibid. (Dec. 9, 1899): 1245.

   For a favorable review of *Personal Recollections and Observations*, see "Reviews and Exchanges," *Journal of the Military Service Institution of the United States* 20 (Jan. 1897): 219–20.

27. Report of Hull, June 22, 1898, House Report 1610, 55th Cong., 2d sess., serial 3722, p.2; *New York Times*, May 8, 1895 (first quotation), Sept. 6, 1895; Pope to Miles, July 27, 1895, box 3, Miles Papers; Miles to Allen, July 19, 1895, box 5, Allen Papers; N. Lieber to Miles, Sept. 17, 1895, box 2, Miles Papers; H. Merriam to Miles, Oct. 4, 1895, box 8, ibid.; W. Reid to Miles, Sept. 18, 1895, box 3,

ibid.; Lamont to Miles, Sept. 29, 1895, box 2, ibid.; Pohanka, *Documentary Biography*, 27 (second quotation).

28. *New York Daily Tribune*, Aug. 3, 1904; *Washington Post*, Aug. 3, 1904; *New York Times*, Apr. 9, 1895; Van Vliet to Miles, June 18, 1895, box 9, Miles Papers; Johnson, *Unregimented General*, 309; Boyd's *Washington City Directory*, 1896, p.667; ibid., 1897, p.658; ibid., 1899, p.725; *Baist's Real Estate Atlas Surveys of Washington* (Philadelphia, 1903), vol.1, pl.14; General Assessment Books, 1893–94, pp.91, 131, General Assessments, Records of the Government of the District of Columbia, RG 351, NARA; J. Sherman to Miles, Jan. 12, 1893, box 4, Miles Papers; K. Fields to Mrs. Miles, Jan. 31, 1894, box 1, ibid.; Miles to Lizzie, Aug. 12, 1896, box 3, ibid.; "Memoirs," chap.6, p.15, box 380, Pershing Papers.

On the efforts of the National Society of New England Women, which later turned the work over to the General Miles Testimonial Association, see *New York Times*, Mar. 1, May 3, 1896, Feb. 9, 1897. The lot was later acquired by the General Federation of Women's Clubs (see "Commemorating the Centennial of the Nelson A. Miles Mansion . . ." in Miles materials, Forbush Library). Contemporary sources indicate that Miles owned the home at 1736 N Street, although the Federation of Women's Clubs refers to it as 1734 N Street.

29. A. Niblack to Miles, Dec. 7, 1895, box 3, Miles Papers; *New York Times*, Aug. 23, 1897, Mar. 23, 1899; *Washington Post*, Aug. 3, 1904 (first quotation); Miles to Lizzie, Aug. 12, 1896, box 3, Miles Papers (second quotation); Miles to sw, Mar. 31, 1897, roll 14, LS, HQA, NARA; *Washington Evening Star*, Mar. 5, 1897; Miles to sw, May 1, 1897, box 1, Miles Papers (third quotation); Edward Ranson, "Nelson A. Miles as Commanding General, 1895–1903," *Military Affairs* 39 (Winter 1966): 181 (fourth quotation).

30. Diary, 1895, pp.316–17, box 1, Allen Papers; Miles to Lamont, Apr. 18, 1895, box 50, Lamont Papers; Miles to sw, Mar. 6, 1897, roll 14, LS, HQA, NARA; *New York Times*, June 19, 1896; J. McCook to Olney, July 10, 1896, roll 21, Richard Olney Papers, LC (hereafter cited as Olney Papers); J. Walker to Miles, July 14, 1896, box 5, Miles Papers; Lamont to Olney, Aug. 7, 1896, roll 21, Olney Papers; Lamont to Miles, Aug. 17, 1896, roll 14, LS, HQA, NARA (quotation); H. Squires to Miles, May 2, 1898, box 9, Miles Papers.

31. Report of Miles, Nov. 5, 1895, sw, *Annual Report, 1895*, 63–64 (first quotation); Report of Miles, Nov. 10, 1896, idem, *Annual Report, 1896*, 75; Breck to Commanding General, Department of the Colorado, Nov. 13, 1895, roll 14, LS, HQA, NARA; Miles to C. Bliss, Mar. 31, 1897, file 11, box 1, Miscellaneous Records, Indian Division, RG 48, NARA; Miles to Commissioner of Indian Affairs, May 16, 1896, roll 14, LS, HQA, NARA; Miles to Commanding General, Department of Colorado, May 18, 1896, ibid.; Miles to Baldwin, Jan. 6, 1897, ibid.; H. Scott to Miles, Apr. 3, 1897, box 4, Miles Papers; Miles to SI, Apr. 16, 1897, roll 14, LS, HQA, NARA; Miles to sw, Oct. 9, 1898, roll 15, ibid.

32. Report of Miles, Oct. 21, 1897, sw, *Annual Report, 1897*, 90–91 (quotation); Miles to Hawley, Dec. 15, 1897, roll 14, LS, HQA, NARA; Miles to Allen, Dec. 29, 1897, box 6, Allen Papers; Sherwood, *Exploration of Alaska*, 154–68.

33. Miles to sw, Aug. 24, 1891, 4143 ACP 1873, box 204, ACP Doc., NARA; Nelson A. Miles, *Military Europe: A Narrative of Personal Observations and Personal Experiences* (New York: Doubleday and McClure, 1898), 3; A. Terrell to Sherman, May 14, 1897, roll 63, Despatches from U.S. Ministers to Turkey, 1818–1906, M 46, NARA; E. Alexander to Sherman, May 17, 1897, roll 11, Despatches from U.S. Ministers to Greece, 1868–1906, T 159, NARA.

34. J. Sherman to Diplomatic and Consular Officers, Apr. 30, 1897, Miles Collection; *New York Times*, May 5, 6, 1897; Terrell to Sherman, May 20, 1897, roll 63, Despatches from U.S. Ministers to Turkey, 1818–1906, NARA; Miles, *Military Europe*, 4–29 (quotation).

35. J. Sherman to Hay, June 1, 1897, *Papers Relating to the Foreign Relations of the United States, with the Annual Message of the President, Transmitted to Congress December 6, 1897* (1898; reprint, New York: Kraus Reprint Co., 1968), 251; R. Buller to Miles, July 9, 1897, box 6, Miles Papers; Miles, *Military Europe*, 33–35, 42, 74 (quotation), 104–7. For expense accounts of the trip, see Letters and Records of Captain M. P. Maus, box 6, Records of the Headquarters of the Army, RG 108, NARA.

36. Miles to sw, Aug. 4, 1897, Russell Alger Papers, William L. Clements Library (hereafter cited as Alger Papers); Miles, *Military Europe*, 94, 107 (quotation); *New York Times*, Aug. 8, 1895; H. Porter to Miles, Sept. 2, 1897, box 3, Miles Papers; Diary, Aug. 9, 1897, box 1, Allen Papers.

37. Baird to Barlow, Aug. 10, 1897, box 2, Baldwin Papers; Nelson A. Miles, "The Political Situation in Europe and the East," *Forum* 25 (Apr. 1898): 159–65; Diary, Aug. 10, 1897, box 1, Allen Papers (quotations).

38. General Order 71, Dec. 1897, roll 14, LS, HQA, NARA (quotation); "Memorandum for the Adjutant General," May 1, 1896, ibid.; Breck to Ruger, June 15, 1896, ibid.; Breck to Adj. Genl., Dec. 12, 1896, ibid.; *Washington Evening Star*, Jan. 1, 1897; Miles to sw, Mar. 19, Apr. 23, May 3, 1897, Alger Papers; Miles to Newcomb, Dec. 31, 1892, Miles Collection; Miles to Lamont, Mar. 19, 1894, box 35, Lamont Papers; Miles to Adj. Genl., Aug. 25, 1894, Miscellaneous Manuscripts, New-York Historical Society; Miles to Adj. Genl., Aug. 22, 1895, file 24798, box 181, AGO Doc., NARA. For other proposals, see Miles to sw, Jan. 3, 1897, roll 14, LS, HQA, NARA.

39. Miles to sw, Jan. 3, 1896, Jan. 4, 1897, roll 14, LS, HQA, NARA; Miles to Allen, Dec. 29, 1897, box 6, Allen Papers (quotation); *Washington Evening Star*, Jan. 28, 29, 1897.

40. *Washington Evening Star*, Dec. 14, 1896; *New York Times*, June 20, 1899; Pond, "Miles," 562; F. Michler to Commanding General, Department of California, Oct. 11, 1895, roll 14, LS, HQA, NARA; Report of Miles, Nov. 5, 1895, sw, *Annual*

Report, 1895, 69; Miles to Ruger, Nov. 26, 1895, roll 14, LS, HQA, NARA; Breck to G. Stevens, Dec. 26, 1895, ibid.; Pope to Proctor, Jan. 23, 1897, "Bicycle" papers, box 8, Correspondence on Subjects of Concern to the Army Headquarters, Special File, RG 108, NARA. See also letters from bicycle enthusiasts sparked by Miles's pronouncements, ibid.

For a good summary of early military cycling, see Charles M. Dollar, "Putting the Army on Wheels: The Story of the Twenty-fifth Infantry Bicycle Corps," *Prologue* 17 (Spring 1985): 7–23.

41. Asst. Adj. Genl. to Commanding Officer, Each Post in Department, Mar. 28, 1895, LS, East, NARA; *New York Times,* Jan. 5, 1896; Adj. Genl. to Commanding Generals of all Departments, May 3, 1897, roll 14, LS, HQA, NARA; Miles, *Military Europe,* 111–12 (quotations).

42. Lewis L. Gould, *The Spanish-American War and President McKinley* (Lawrence: University Press of Kansas, 1982), 6–11; H. Wayne Morgan, *William McKinley and His America* (Syracuse: Syracuse University Press, 1963), 260–61; Jasper B. Reid, Jr., "Russell A. Alger as Secretary of War," *Michigan History* 43 (June 1959): 225–39.

43. Gould, *Spanish-American War and President McKinley,* 19–42.

44. David R. Trask, *The War with Spain in 1898,* The Wars of the United States (New York: Macmillan Co., 1981): 144–48; Graham A. Cosmas, *An Army for Empire: The United States Army in the Spanish-American War* (Columbia: University of Missouri Press, 1971), 73, 82–83.

45. Russell A. Alger, *The Spanish-American War* (New York: Harper and Bros., 1901), 7–11; *New York Times,* Jan. 22, 1898; Miles to Ruggles, May 23, 1895, LS, East, NARA (first quotation); testimony of Miles, Jan. 28, 1896, Senate Committee on Coastal Defense S Cod 54A, p.50, U.S. Congressional Hearings Supplement; testimony of Miles, Mar. 5, 1896, House Committee on Appropriations, H Ap 54C, pp.47–55, ibid.; testimony of Miles, Jan. 30, 1897, House Committee on Appropriations, H Ap 54D, p.18, ibid.; Miles to SW, May 4, 1897, Miles Collection; Gould, *Spanish-American War and President McKinley,* 38; Miles to SW, Mar. 18, 1898, Alger Papers (second quotation); Nelson Miles, "Our Coast Defenses," *Forum* 24 (Jan. 1898): 513–19.

46. Trask, *War with Spain,* 150–51; Stephen Skowronek, *Building a New American State: The Expansion of National Administrative Capacities, 1877–1920* (Cambridge: Cambridge University Press, 1982), 113–14; John Hull, "The Army Appropriation Bill," *Forum* 25 (May 1898): 399.

47. Miles to Allen, Apr. 1, 1898, box 6, Allen Papers (quotation); Report of Miles, Nov. 5, 1898, SW, *Annual Report, 1898,* 5–7; Cosmas, *Army for Empire,* 99; Miles to SW, Apr. 9, 11, 15, 1898, Miles Collection; Orders of Apr. 15, 1898, in *Correspondence Relating to the War with Spain and Conditions Growing out of the Same, . . . between the Adjutant General of the Army and Military Commanders in the United States, Cuba, Porto Rico, China, and the Philippines*

Islands, from April 15, 1898 to July 30, 1902, 2 vols. (Washington, D.C.: GPO, 1902), 1:7–8; Miles to Hull, Apr. 7, 1898, roll 15, LS, HQA, NARA.

48. Memorandum prepared by Col. Wagner, Apr. 11, 1898, Miles Collection.

49. Ibid.

50. Miles to sw, Apr. 18, 1898, roll 15, LS, HQA, NARA.

51. Rear Adm. French Ensor Chadwick, *The Relations of the United States to Spain: The Spanish-American War*, 2 vols. (New York: Charles Scribner's Sons, 1909), 1:63–64, 70; Trask, *War with Spain*, 89–90; Sampson to Secretary of the Navy, Mar. 29, 30, 1898, file 8, roll 227, Area File of the Naval Records Collection, 1775–1910, M 625, NARA; Long to Sampson, Apr. 6, 1898, p.171, Secretary of the Navy, *Annual Report, 1898*.

52. Journal, Apr. 20, 1898, John Long Papers, Massachusetts Historical Society (hereafter cited as John Long Papers) (first and second quotations); Chadwick, *Relations of the United States to Spain*, 1:63–64, 70–88; *Washington Wife: Journal of Ellen Maury Slayden, from 1897–1919* (New York: Harper and Row, 1962), 17 (third and fourth quotations).

CHAPTER THIRTEEN

1. Cosmas, *Army for Empire*, 109; *New York Times*, Apr. 22, 23, 24, 25, 26, 1898; Miles to sw, Apr. 9, 1898, sw, *Annual Report, 1898*.

2. Alger, *Spanish-American War*, 7 (quotation); Trask, *War with Spain*, 158; Armes, *Ups and Downs*, 706; Miles to sw, Apr. 26, 1898, roll 15, LS, HQA, NARA; Miles to Alger, May 3, 1898, file 310015, box 2061, AGO Doc., NARA.

3. Journal, May 13, 26, 1898, John Long Papers; Allen to Jeannie, May 28, 1898, box 6, Allen Papers (first quotation); "Autobiography," p.87, Corbin Papers, LC (hereafter cited as Corbin Papers); Alger to Corbin, Nov. 11, 19, 1900, box 1A, ibid.; Alger to Hoar, Feb. 8, 1902, Alger Papers; Diary, May 27, 28, 29 (second quotation), 1898, box 1, Allen Papers; H. Seckendorff to Reid, May 23, 1898, roll 178, Reid Family Papers, LC (hereafter cited as Reid Papers) (third quotation).

4. Cosmas, *Army for Empire*, 127–28. Two years earlier *Cosmopolitan* had asked Miles to describe the effects of a war with a European power. One point of special interest to the magazine was mobilization. Miles instead took the opportunity to discuss the need for coastal defense and the frequency of attacks made prior to a formal declaration of war (Nelson A. Miles, "War," *Cosmopolitan* 21 [June 1896]: 142–48; John Brisbane Walker, "In Case of War with England—What?" ibid., 149–51).

5. Cosmas, *Army for Empire*, 116–17; Parker, *Old Army Memories*, 212–13; Lucian to Mama, Aug. 4, 1898, box 605, Breckinridge Family Papers, LC (hereafter cited as Breckinridge Papers) (quotation).

6. Gould, *Spanish-American War and President McKinley*, 55–60, 68; Seckendorff to Reid, Aug. 8, 1898, roll 178, Reid Papers; Cosmas, *Army for Empire*, 58. For a less critical assessment of Alger, see Rodney Ellis Bell, "A Life of Russell Alexander Alger, 1836–1907" (Ph.D. diss., University of Michigan, 1975), 386–87.

7. Journal, Feb. 5, 1898, John Long Papers. For Schofield's work in the McKinley Administration, see "Some of my experiences with the Administration of President McKinley," box 93, Schofield Papers (quotation); Cosmas, *Army for Empire*, 140; Gould, *Spanish-American War and President McKinley*, 102.

8. Miles to sw, Apr. 18, 1898, Miles Collection; Chief of Ordnance, "Report," May 2, 1898, Alger Papers; *New York Times*, Apr. 14, 1896; Cosmas, *Army for Empire*, 144; undated, unsigned memorandum, Alger Papers.

9. "Autobiography," pp.87–89, Corbin Papers.

10. Corbin to Alger, Nov. 16, 1900, box 1A, ibid. See also *New York Times*, Nov. 23, 1898.

11. Alger to Corbin, Nov. 19, 1900, Corbin Papers.

12. Miles, *Serving the Republic*, 279; "Memoirs," chap.7, p.10, box 380, Pershing Papers; Corbin to Alger, Nov. 16, 1900, box 1A, Corbin Papers; Cosmas, *Army for Empire*, 193; Wade to Miles, May 8, 1898, box 9, Miles Papers.

13. Miles to President, Oct. 31, 1891, box 570, 2220 ACP 1879, ACP Doc., NARA; Miles to Adj. Genl., Mar. 25, 1893, ibid.; Shafter to Miles, Oct. 10, 1886, Mar. 20, June 24, Sept. 10, 1895, Oct. 5, 1897, box 4, Miles Papers; Miles to sw, Mar. 19, 1897, Alger Papers; Paul H. Carlson, *"Pecos Bill": A Military Biography of William R. Shafter* (College Station: Texas A & M University Press, 1989), 136, 162–63.

14. J. Weston to Wilson, Aug. 16, 1899, box 26, James Henry Wilson Papers, LC (hereafter cited as J. Wilson Papers); Corbin to Shafter, Apr. 29, in Alger, *Spanish-American War*, 44–45 (quotation).

15. William T. Sampson, "The Atlantic Fleet in the Spanish-American War," *Century Magazine* 57 (Apr. 1899): 886 (quotation); Gould, *President McKinley and the Spanish-American War*, 60–63, 94–97.

16. Alger, *Spanish-American War*, 46–47; Journal, May 2, John Long Papers.

17. Journal, May 6 (first quotation), 10 (second quotation), 1898, John Long Papers; Corbin to Wade, May 9, 10, 11, 1898, in *Correspondence Relating to the War with Spain*, 11–12; Corbin to Brooke, May 10, 1898, ibid.; Alger, *Spanish-American War*, 47–48.

18. Miles to sw, May 26, 27, 1898, in *Correspondence Relating to the War with Spain*, 261–63 (quotation); Miles to sw, May 8, 1898, Miles Collection.

19. Miles to sw, May 26, 27, 1898, in *Correspondence Relating to the War with Spain*; Miles to sw, May 8, 1898, Miles Collection; "Notes Regarding the Island of Puerto Rico and the Spanish Forces There," May 27, 1898, Miles

Collection; testimony of Miles, Dec. 21, 1898, Senate Doc. 221, 56th Cong., 1st sess., serial 3865.

20. Alger to Miles, May 26, 1898, Alger Papers (quotation); Alger to Hoar, Feb. 8, 1902, ibid.

21. Breckinridge to Sweet Charm, May 15, 1898, box 605, Breckinridge Papers; *World* to Breckinridge, May 21, 1898, ibid.; Corbin to Shafter, May 30, 1898 [sent in cipher May 31], in *Correspondence Relating to the War with Spain*, 18– 19 (first quotation); Miles to Alger, June 1, 1898, ibid., 21 (second and third quotations).

22. Miles to Shafter, May 17, 1898, Miles Collection (quotation); W. Ludlow to Miles, May 22, 1898, ibid.; Miles to sw, June 4, 1898, ibid. See also correspondence, May 31 to July 8, 1898, ls, hqa, nara.

23. McKinley to Miles, June 4, 1898, in *Correspondence Relating to the War with Spain*, 263; Miles to Alger, June 6, 1898, ibid., 264; Alger to Miles, June 6 (first quotation), 7, 8, 1898, ibid., 32–34, 264; Alger to Shafter, June 7, 1898, ibid., 30 (second quotation); Miles to Alger, June 2, 5, 1898, pt.1, Letters and Telegrams Sent from Florida and Puerto Rico, May 31–September 7, 1898, rg 108, nara; Hanna to Moore, June 6, 1898, roll 231, Area File of the Naval Records Collection, 1775–1910, M 625, nara; Shafter to Alger, June 7, 1898, in *Correspondence Relating to the War with Spain*, 31.

24. Weston to Wilson, June 7, 1898, box 26, J. Wilson Papers (quotation); Remington, *Collected Works*, 338–39; D. Van Allen to Miles, June 20, July 2, 1898, Frank Hecker Papers, William L. Clements Library; Miles to Ludington, July 6, 1898, ibid.

Theodore Roosevelt offered this view of Miles's role: "[Colonel Leonard] Wood thinks that if Miles could be given absolute control he would straighten things out and I most earnestly wish the experiment could be tried, though personally I cannot help feeling that Miles might have remedied a great deal that has gone wrong if only he had chosen or known how" (Roosevelt to Lodge, May 12, 1898, in Henry Cabot Lodge and Charles F. Redmond, *Selections from the Correspondence of Theodore Roosevelt and Henry Cabot Lodge, 1884– 1918*, 2 vols. [New York: Da Capo Press, 1971], 1:306–7).

25. Roosevelt to Lodge, June 12, 1898, Elting E. Morison, ed., *The Letters of Theodore Roosevelt*, 8 vols. (Cambridge: Harvard University Press, 1951–54), 2:840.

26. Charles Belmont Davis, *Adventures and Letters of Richard Harding Davis* (New York: Charles Scribner's Sons, 1917), 246–47.

27. Cosmas, *Army for Empire*, 206–25; Alger, *Spanish-American War*, 84–90.

28. Michler to Duval, June 24, 1898, Letters, Cablegrams, and Telegrams Sent from Florida and Cuba, June 5–July 1, July 7–20, 1898, Headquarters in the Field, rg 108, nara; Hull to J. Wheeler, June 13, 1898, box 2, Miles Papers; Report of Hull, June 22, 1898, House Report 1610, 55th Cong., 2d sess., serial

3722; S. Harrill to W. Hayes, July 21, 1898, Webb C. Hayes Papers; Diary, May 29, 1898, Allen Papers (first quotation); Alger to Miles, June 26, 1898, in *Correspondence Relating to the War with Spain*, 268–29 (second and third quotations).

29. Trask, *War with Spain*, 289–304 (quotation); Gould, *Spanish-American War and President McKinley*, 110–11; *New York Times*, Aug. 30, 1898.

30. "Confidential Report of Observations made by Lieutenant Colonel Marion P. Maus . . .," Sept. 18, 1898, Miles Collection; Breckinridge to Lindsay, July 10, 1898, box 605, Breckinridge Papers; Shafter to Corbin, Aug. 16, 1898, box 1, Corbin Papers (quotation); Shafter to Miles, July 17, in *New York Times*, Aug. 30, 1898.

31. Miles to Shafter, July 18, in *New York Times*, Aug. 30, 1898.

32. Trask, *War with Spain*, 304–11; Gould, *Spanish-American War and President McKinley*, 110–12; Chadwick, *Relations of the United States to Spain*, 2:233; Carnegie to Miles, July 7, 1898, Miles Collection (first and second quotations); Miles, *Serving the Republic*, 274 (third quotation). In subsequent accounts, Miles referred to Carnegie as having advised against an attack on Havana (see Miles to Carnegie, Apr. 11, 1911, box 191, Andrew Carnegie Papers, LC [hereafter cited as Carnegie Papers]). On the status of the lieutenant general bill, see Senate Report 670, 55th Cong., 2d sess., serial 3622; Allen to Jeannie, May 1, 1898, box 6, Allen Papers; Diary, May 29, 1898, box 1, ibid.; Wheeler to Miles, July 18, 1898, box 5, Miles Papers. For a valuable analysis of the army's problems, see Dick to McKinley, July 13, 1898, box 68, G. B. Courtleyou Papers, LC (letter courtesy of Lewis L. Gould, University of Texas at Austin).

33. Trask, *War with Spain*, 312–16, 320–21; Chadwick, *Relations of the United States to Spain*, 2:235–48; W.A.M. Goode, *With Sampson through the War; Being an Account of the Naval Operations of the Atlantic Squadron during the Spanish American War of 1898* (New York: Doubleday and McClure Co., 1899), 261–62; Shafter to Sampson, July 23, 1898, roll 236, Area File of the Naval Records Collection, 1775–1910, M 625, NARA; Shafter to Sampson, Aug. 1, 1898, roll 237, ibid.; Sampson to Long, Aug. 4, 1898, ibid.

34. Alger to Miles, July 14, 1898, in *Correspondence Relating to the War with Spain*, 272; Miles to Alger, June 14, July 16, 17, 1898, ibid., 267, 280; Hanna to Moore, June 6, 1898, Miles Collection. For the disrepair in other military camps, see Asst. Adj. Genl. Cecil to Miles, June 7, 1898, ibid.; Brooke to Miles, June 10, 1898, ibid.

35. Alger to Miles, July 17, 1898, in *Correspondence Relating to the War with Spain*, 281; Miles to Alger, July 17, 18 (quotation), 1898, ibid., 277, 281–82, 285; Miles to sw, July 18, 20, 22, 1898, Letters, Cablegrams, and Telegrams Sent from Florida and Cuba, June 5–July 1, July 7–20, 1898, box 1, Headquarters in the Field—Cuba and Puerto Rico, RG 108, NARA; Corbin to Miles, July 18, 1898, in *Correspondence Relating to the War with Spain*, 283.

36. McKinley to Long, July 20, 1898, Miles Collection; Corbin to Miles, July 19, 1898, in *Correspondence Relating to the War with Spain*, 287; Alger to Miles, July 19, 1898, ibid.; Wilson to Corbin, July 19, 1898, ibid.; Miles to Alger, July 20, 21, 1898, ibid., 293, 297, 301; Report of Miles, Nov. 5, 1898, sw, *Annual Report, 1898*, 26–29.

37. Miles to Higginson, July 22, 1898, sw, *Annual Report, 1898*, 29–30; *New York Times*, Aug. 24, 1898. H. H. Whitney offered the following intelligence report: Guánica "is the best harbor on the island. It is not guarded or torpedoed, only a few hundred men guarding this section" (Memo of Whitney, July 24, 1898, 2:95–96, Letters Received During the Cuban Expedition, May 28–September 1, 1898, RG 108, NARA).

38. Higginson to Sampson, Aug. 2, 1898, roll 237, Area File of the Naval Records Collection, 1775–1910, M 625, NARA; Chadwick, *Relations of the United States to Spain*, 2:285–87 (quotation).

39. Miles to Mrs. Heintzelman, July 24, 1898, Miles Miscellaneous Manuscripts, Hayes Library.

40. Miles to Higginson, July 24, 1898, sw, *Annual Report, 1898*, 30; Huse to Captain, USS *Gloucester*, July 25, 1898, roll 236, Area File of the Naval Records Collection, 1775–1910, M 625, NARA; Report of Miles, Nov. 5, 1898, sw, *Annual Report, 1898*, 30–31.

41. Report of Miles, Nov. 5, 1898, sw, *Annual Report, 1898*, 31; Alger to Miles, July 26, 1898, Alger Papers (first quotation); Corbin to Brooke, July 26, in *Correspondence Relating to the War with Spain*, 321 (second quotation); Alger to Miles, July 26, 1898, Alger Papers (third quotation).

42. Miles to Alger, July 26 (first quotation), 29, 1898, in *Correspondence Relating to the War with Spain*, 322, 330; Miles to inhabitants of Puerto Rico, July 28, 1898, sw, *Annual Report, 1898*, 31–32 (second quotation).

43. Miles to Alger, July 31, Aug. 6, 1898, in *Correspondence Relating to the War with Spain*, 341, 365; Report of Miles, Nov. 5, 1898, sw, *Annual Report, 1898*, 34–35; Pohanka, *Documentary Biography*, 287 n.273.

44. Report of Miles, Nov. 5, 1898, sw, *Annual Report, 1898*, 34–36; Miles to Alger, Aug. 9, 11, 1898, in *Correspondence Relating to the War with Spain*, 372, 380, 381.

45. Miles to Mrs. Heintzelman, Aug. 15, 1898, Miles Miscellaneous Manuscripts, Hayes Library.

46. General Orders no.2, July 13, 1898, Miles Collection; James Harrison Wilson, *Under the Old Flag: Recollections of Military Operations in the War for the Union, the Spanish War, the Boxer Rebellion, etc.* (New York: D. Appleton and Co., 1912), 449–50 (first quotation); Davis to Miles, Apr. 13, 1901, box 1, Miles Papers (second quotation); Proctor to Miles, Aug. 29, 1898, box 8, Proctor Papers (third quotation).

Wilson did, however, criticize the disposition of the troops in Puerto Rico.

"While well-calculated to confuse the Spaniards, [troop placements] made it almost impossible to synchronize and coordinate our own movements" (Wilson, *Under the Old Flag*, 443).

47. Miles to Mrs. Heintzelman, Aug. 15, 1898, Miles Miscellaneous Manuscripts, Hayes Library (first quotation); Mahan to Long, Aug. 5, Nov. 16 (second quotation), 1898, Robert Seager II, and Doris D. Maguire, *The Letters and Papers of Alfred Thayer Mahan*, 3 vols. (Annapolis: Naval Institute Press, 1975), 2:573, 612.

48. C. Davis to Sampson, Aug. 2, 1898, Miles Collection (first quotation); Miles to sw, Aug. 10, 1898, ibid. (second and third quotations); Alger to Miles, Aug. 11, 1898, ibid. (fourth quotation). See also the partially decoded message from Sampson to Senior Naval Officer, Aug. 10, 1898, ibid.

49. Miles to Mrs. Heintzelman, Aug. 13, 15, 1898, Miles Miscellaneous Manuscripts, Hayes Library; "Miles to the Inhabitants of Puerto Rico," July 28, 1898, in Pohanka, *Documentary Biography*, 285; Report of Miles, Nov. 5, 1898, sw, *Annual Report, 1898*.

50. Morton to Pershing, Aug. 10, 1898, box 316, Pershing Papers; Miles to Mrs. Heintzelman, Aug. 13, 15 (quotation), 21, 1898, Mar. 24, 1899, Miles Miscellaneous Manuscripts, Hayes Library; Miles to S. Heintzelman, July 18, 1899, ibid.

51. *New York Times*, Aug. 24 (quotations), 30, 1898.

52. Ibid.

CHAPTER FOURTEEN

1. Testimony, Special File, box 9, RG 108, NARA; *New York Times*, Sept. 1 (first quotation), 2, 6, 8 (second quotation), 1898.

2. *New York Times*, Sept. 8, 1898 testimony, Special File, box 9, RG 108, NARA (quotations); Amchan, *Most Famous Soldier*, 125.

3. Ibid., Sept. 8, 9, 1898; A. Rowan to Miles, July 22, 1922, Miles Collection; Miles, *Serving the Republic*, 277–80; Edward Ranson, "The Investigation of the War Department, 1898–99," *Historian* 34 (Nov. 1971): 81–82; Dodge to H. Gallagher, Feb. 15, 1899, Grenville Dodge Papers, State Historical Society of Iowa, Des Moines (hereafter cited as Dodge Papers).

4. Remington, *Collected Works*, 327–31; *New York Times*, Oct. 2 (first quotation), Nov. 12 (second quotation), 1898; Roosevelt to H. Lodge, Dec. 6, in Morison, *Letters of Roosevelt*, 2:892. On the composition of the committee, see Ranson, "Investigation."

5. *New York Times*, Sept. 10, 18, Dec. 15, 1898; Lee to Breckinridge, Nov. 26, 1898, box 606, Breckinridge Papers; Breckinridge to Willie, Dec. 12, 1898, box 605, ibid.; Miles to sw, Dec. 5, 1898, Senate Committee on Military Affairs,

S Mi 55A, U.S. Congressional Hearings Supplement; testimony of Miles, Dec. 12, 1898, House Committee on Military Affairs, H Mi 55A, ibid. (quotation).

6. Ranson, "Investigation," 90; testimony of Miles, Dec. 21, 1898, Senate Doc. 221, 56th Cong., 1st sess., serial 3865, pp.3240–64, 3795–98; *Nation*, Jan. 2, 1896; Nevins, *Grover Cleveland*, 720; Adams to E. Cameron, Dec. 18, 1898, in Worthington Chauncey Ford, ed., *Letters of Henry Adams (1892–1918)* (Boston: Houghton Mifflin Co., 1938), 197; Mahan to Long, Dec. 28, 1898, John Long Papers; Edward F. Keuchel, "Chemicals and Meat: The Embalmed Beef Scandal of the Spanish-American War," *Bulletin of the History of Medicine* 98 (Summer 1974): 252; *New York Times*, Dec. 22 (first quotation), 24 (second quotation), 1898.

7. Shafter to Corbin, Oct. 23, 1898, box 1, Corbin Papers; Draft reply to Alger, Miles Collection (first quotation); Daly to Asst. Adj. Genl., Sept. 21, 1898, in *New York Times*, Dec. 31, 1898 (second quotation); testimony of Daly, Jan. 20, 1899, Senate Doc. 221, 56th Cong., 1st sess., serial 3865, pp.3707–36. See also "Proceedings of the Commission to Investigate the Conduct of the War Dept., Testimony of Dr. Wm. H. Daly & of Maj. Genl. Miles," box 9, Correspondence on Subjects of Concern to Army Headquarters, Special File, RG 108, NARA.

8. Dodge to Corbin, Feb. 21, 1899, box 34, Dodge Papers; Boynton to Dodge, May 26, 1899, ibid.; Alger to Shafter, Nov. 28, 1898, roll 6, Shafter Papers; *New York Times*, Dec. 28, 31, 1898; Alger to Hoar, Feb. 8, 1902, Alger Papers; J. Lewis to Miles, Dec. 29, 1898, box 8, Miles Papers.

9. Roosevelt to Miles, Jan. 9, 1899, in Morison, *Letters of Roosevelt*, 2:903 (quotations); Roosevelt to P. Dana, Jan. 14, 1899, ibid., 912–13; Roosevelt to Mrs. Cameron, Feb. 27, 1899, box 3, Miles Papers. See also Adams to E. Cameron, Mar. 5, 1899, in Ford, *Henry Adams*, 225.

10. *New York Times*, Jan. 14, Feb. 21 (first quotation), 1899; Roosevelt to Miles, Jan. 14, 1899, in Morison, *Letters of Roosevelt*, 2:911 (second quotation).

11. Ranson, "Investigation," 91 (quotations); Lewis L. Gould, *The Presidency of William McKinley*, American Presidency Series (Lawrence: Regents Press of Kansas, 1980), 173; "Autobiography," p.85, Corbin Papers; G. Lodge to Miles, n.d., box 2, Miles Papers.

12. S. Brice to Shafter, Jan. 19, 1901, roll 6, Shafter Papers; Breckinridge to Mrs. Breckinridge, Jan. 23, 1899, box 608, Breckinridge Papers; Adams to E. Cameron, Jan. 15, Feb. 5, 12, 1899, in Ford, *Henry Adams;* W. Wise to Long, Nov. 1, 4, 1898, John Long Papers; T. Oglesby to Chandler, Jan. 21, 1899, Thaddeus K. Oglesby Papers, Perkins Memorial Library; Chandler to Oglesby, Jan. 23, 1899, ibid. (first quotation); Wilson to H. Biddle, Dec. 17, 1898, box 43, J. Wilson Papers; Wilson to A. Huggins, Aug. 14, 1899, box 44, ibid.; *New York Times*, Sept. 8, 1898 (second and third quotations), Feb. 1, 3, 4, 8, Mar. 18, 1899.

13. Adams to E. Cameron, Jan. 13, Feb. 5, 1899 (first quotation), in Ford, *Henry Adams*; Foraker to E. Cameron, Feb. 20, 1899, box 2, Miles Papers; W. Frye to E. Cameron, Feb. 21, [1899], ibid.; H. Lodge to Mrs. Cameron, Feb. 26, 1899, box 2, ibid.; Olney to Cleveland, Mar. 22, 1899, roll 59, Olney Papers (second quotation).

14. *New York Times*, Feb. 9, 1899; Dodge to Boynton, Mar. 23, 1899, box 1A, Corbin Papers; Boynton to Dodge, Mar. 27, 1899, box 34, Dodge Papers; Dodge to Boynton, Mar. 28, 1899, roll 6, ser. 1, William McKinley Papers, LC (hereafter cited as McKinley Papers) (quotation); Dodge to McKinley, Apr. 20, 1899, ibid.; Boynton to McKinley, Apr. 25, 1899, ibid.

15. *New York Times*, Feb. 8, 21, 1899.

16. Ibid., Feb. 4, 21, Mar. 4, 23, 24, 26, May 2, 4, 11, 1899; Lee to Breckinridge, Nov. 26, 1898, box 606, Breckinridge Papers (first and second quotations); *New York Times*, May 8, 1899 (third quotation); Weston to Wilson, Apr. 28, 1899, box 26, J. Wilson Papers; *New York Tribune*, June 10, 1901. Historians have generally accepted the board's conclusions. See Keuchel, "Chemicals and Meat," 258–64; and Gould, *Presidency of McKinley*, 172–73. Three years later, Surgeon Daly, Miles's lone supporting witness, committed suicide.

17. *New York Times*, Jan. 11, 1900, Mar. 28, 1902, Apr. 18, 1933; Miles to sw, Nov. 16, 1895, roll 14, LS, HQA, NARA; Miles to Lizzie, Sept. 6, 1899, box 3, Miles Papers; Wilson to Root, Oct. 5, 1899, box 45, J. Wilson Papers. For a brief résumé of Reber's career, see Miles to Taft, Jan. 9, 1913, file 4244, roll 450, William Howard Taft Papers, LC (hereafter cited as Taft Papers).

18. *Congressional Record*, 56th Cong., 1st sess., 33:2694, 2873, 2918, 3024, 3063, 6742–44; T. Bingham to Drum, Mar. 31, 1900, box 8, Corbin Papers. Ironically, Theodore Roosevelt, who as president feuded almost constantly with Miles, later named Moody his secretary of the navy (Lewis L. Gould, *The Presidency of Theodore Roosevelt*, American Presidency Series (Lawrence: Regents Press of Kansas, 1991), 48.

19. Adams to E. Cameron, Jan. 22, 1899, in Ford, *Henry Adams*, 206 (quotation); Gould, *Spanish-American War and President McKinley*, 121–23; James Hewes, *From Root to McNamara: Army Organization and Administration, 1900–1903*, Special Studies Series (Washington, D.C.: Center for Military History, 1975), 3–8; Corbin to C. Grosvenor, Feb. 4, 1907, box 1, Corbin Papers; Ronald James Barr, "American Military Reform, 1898–1904: The Reasons for Reform and the Eventual Outcome" (M.A. thesis, Louisiana State University, 1989), 32; Alger to Root, July 21, 1899, vol. 3, Elihu Root Collection, New York Public Library (hereafter cited as Root Collection, New York); McKinley to Root, n.d., July 22, 1899, vol. 1, ibid.

20. *New York Times*, 9, 11, 12, Sept. 27, 1899; Miles to Root, Aug. 3, 1899, Feb. 7, 14, Mar. 16, 1901, box 4, 16, Elihu Root Papers, LC (hereafter cited as Root Papers, LC); Philip C. Jessup, *Elihu Root* (New York: Dodd, Mead and Co.,

1938), 244; Allan R. Millett, *The General: Robert L. Bullard and Officership in the United States Army, 1881–1925*, Contributions in Military History, no.10 (Westport, Conn.: Greenwood Press, 1975), 113–14; H. L. Nelson, "Secretary of War Root and His Task," *Harper's Weekly* 43 (Sept. 2, 1898): 858. See also A. Pope to Root, July 24, 1899, vol.1, Root Collection, New York.

21. Root to President, Aug. 15, 1899, roll 7, McKinley Papers (quotations); Barr, "American Military Reform," 33–35.

22. Root to Church, Feb. 20, 1900, box 2, Church Papers (quotation); William R. Roberts, "Loyalty and Expertise: The Transformation of the Nineteenth-Century American General Staff and the Creation of the Modern Military Establishment" (Ph.D. diss., Johns Hopkins University, 1980), 235–37; Miles to sw, May 13, 1878, LR, CB, NARA; Miles to sw, May 10, Nov. 15, 1900, Miles Collection; testimony of Miles, Dec. 11, 1900, pp.7–12, Senate Committee on Military Affairs, S Mi 56A, U.S. Congressional Hearings Supplement.

23. Roosevelt to Wood, Apr. 9, 1900, in Morison, *Letters of Roosevelt*, 2:1252; Roosevelt to G. Lyman, June 18, 22 (quotation), 1901, ibid., 3:96; Jessup, *Elihu Root*, 245.

Miles explained the incident concerning a possible Miles-Roosevelt ticket for president as follows: "In the autumn of 1895 a man in Kansas wrote to General Miles saying that his political ticket was MILES and ROOSEVELT. On meeting then Colonel Roosevelt in Washington not long afterwards, General Miles mentioned this fact, not considering it of any importance or worthy of any serious consideration. That evening, as he was about to start on a journey west, he happened to meet in the Pennsylvania depot Colonel Roosevelt, who was going to New York. Lest the brief conversation during the day should be repeated or misunderstood, he asked the Colonel to consider it in the strictest of confidence, and received the assurance from him that it would be so considered. The published accounts which have been sent broadcast over the country, and especially about General Miles following Colonel Roosevelt down to the depot and dragging him out of bed . . . are wholly unwarranted" (see undated memorandum, Miles Collection).

24. Roosevelt to Greene, July 25, 1899, box 2, Greene Papers; Roosevelt to Root, July 25, 1899, vol. 1, Root Collection, New York.

25. Miles to Root, July 27, Aug. 6, Nov. 15, 1901, box 19, Root Papers, LC; Miles to sw, July 23, 1901, file 523783, box 3640, LR, AGO, 1890s and 1900s, NARA; Varnum to Adj. Genl., Nov. 16, 1901, box 19, Root Papers, LC; Miles to sw, Nov. 22, 1901, Miles Collection; Wheeler to Root, Dec. 2, 1901, box 23, Root Papers, LC; Root to Wheeler, Dec. 10, 1901, ibid. For Root's new system of military education, see "Memorandum for a General Order—Subject: Instruction of Officers," Nov. 27, 1901, in sw, *Annual Report, 1901*, 93–98.

26. Corbin to Miles, Nov. 25, 1901, box 19, Root Papers, LC; Miles to sw, Nov. 25, 1901, ibid. (quotations); Root to Miles, Dec. 3, 1901, pt.2, letterbook 175, ibid.;

Root to Wheeler, Dec. 10, 1901, box 23, ibid.; Root to Miles, Dec. 18, 1901, box 19, ibid.; Report of Root, Dec. 1, 1902, sw, *Annual Report, 1902,* 20.

27. *New York Times,* Dec. 17, 1901; *New York Tribune,* Dec. 17, 1901 (first quotation); Root to Miles, Dec. 19, 1901, box 19, Root Papers, LC; Diary of Mrs. G. Dewey, Dec. 15, 1901, box 86, George Dewey Papers, LC; Miles to Root, Dec. 20 (second quotation), 21 (third quotation), 1901, box 19, Root Papers, LC. See also "Military Views of the Schley Verdict," *Literary Digest* 23 (Dec. 28, 1901): 825.

Miles befriended Dewey, and upon Dewey's death, his body was kept in the Miles family mausoleum at Arlington until a separate vault was completed (Mildred Dewey to Miles, Apr. 6, 1919, box 1, Miles Papers).

28. Root to Miles, Dec. 21, 1901, box 19, Root Papers, LC (first quotation); Roosevelt to R. Patterson, Dec. 21, 1901, in Morison, *Letters of Roosevelt,* 3:210 (second quotation); *New York Tribune,* Dec. 22, 1901; *New York Times,* Dec. 29, 1901 (third quotation); Jessup, *Elihu Root,* 245.

29. Roosevelt to J. Matthews, Dec. 31, 1901, in Morison, *Letters of Roosevelt,* 3:213; Gould, *Presidency of Theodore Roosevelt,* 48; H. Watterson to Miles, Jan. 3, 1902, box 5, Miles Papers; *New York Daily Tribune,* Jan. 19, 1902; *New York Times,* Jan. 19, 1902; Miles to sw, Jan. 24, 1902, Miles Collection (quotations).

30. *New York Tribune,* Feb. 4, 1902; Miles to sw, Feb. 14, 1902, Miles Collection; Miles to sw, Feb. 17, 1902, House Doc. 518, 57th Cong., 1st sess., serial 4361; Roosevelt to Root, Feb. 18, Mar. 7 (quotations), 19, 1902, in Morison, *Letters of Roosevelt,* 3:232–33, 240–42, 244–47.

31. Roosevelt to Root, Mar. 15, 1902, box 19, Root Papers, LC; Roberts, "Loyalty and Expertise," 238–45; Russell F. Weigley, "The Elihu Root Reforms and the Progressive Era," in *Command and Commanders in Modern Warfare: The Proceedings of the Second Military History Symposium, U.S. Air Force Academy, 2–3 May 1968,* ed. William Geffen (Office of Air Force History and U.S. Air Force Academy, 1971), 13.

32. Weigley, "Elihu Root Reforms," 12–13.

33. "Extract of Statement from Lieut. Gen. Nelson A. Miles before the Committee on Military Affairs," box 1A, Corbin Papers; Miles to Church, Mar. 26, 1902, box 2, Church Papers (first and second quotations); Philip L. Semsch, "Elihu Root and the General Staff," *Military Affairs* 27 (Spring 1963): 23 (third quotation).

34. "Extract of Statement from Lieut. Gen. Nelson A. Miles before the Committee on Military Affairs," box 1A, Corbin Papers; Miles to Church, Mar. 26, 1902, box 2, Church Papers; Semsch, "Elihu Root and the General Staff," 23; *New York Tribune,* Mar. 23 (first quotation), 21 (second quotation), 1902.

35. *New York Tribune,* Mar. 21 (first quotation), 22, 25, Apr. 19, 1902; Adams to E. Cameron, Mar. 23, 1902, in Ford, *Henry Adams,* 380 (second quotation);

New York Times, Mar. 23, 25, 1902; Miles to Church, Mar. 21, box 2, Church Papers; Roosevelt to O. Villiard, Mar. 22, 1902, in Morison, *Letters of Roosevelt,* 3:247 (third quotation); G. Hoar to Miles, Apr. 14, 1902, box 2, Miles Papers; A. Moot to Root, Apr. 22, 1902, box 28, Root Papers, LC; Gould, *Presidency of Theodore Roosevelt,* 48–49.

Official records of the testimony before the Senate Military Affairs Committee suggest that Miles was saved by Senator Edmund Winston Pettus. "The report of the proceedings should be submitted to General Miles, with permission to strike out such portions as might not be published," stated Pettus. "I do not know that there is anything to be stricken out—," blurted Miles. Senator Pettus responded: "There are some things that he said which he may desire to strike out, and I think he should be allowed that privilege. . . . He should be allowed the liberty of striking out anything which ought not to be published, even if it is stated correctly in the report." The tame language of the official report suggests that Miles took full advantage of this opportunity. (See testimony of Miles, Mar. 20, 1902, Senate Committee on Military Affairs, S Mi 57B, pp.33–51, U.S. Congressional Hearings Supplement. For the testimony of Schofield and Merritt, see ibid., pp.93–115.)

36. Henry Beach Needham, "Mr. Root and the State Department," *World's Work* 11 (Nov. 1905): 6835–40; *Congressional Record,* 57th Cong., 1st sess., 35:3283, 3404; *New York Tribune,* Jan. 26, Mar. 21, 27, Apr. 24, May 24, 1902; Adams to E. Cameron, Apr. 13, 1902, in Ford, *Henry Adams,* 385; *Arizona Daily Star,* Sept. 26, 1902; *New York Times,* Jan. 26, 1902.

37. *Independent,* 54 (Apr. 3, 1902): 831 (first quotation); Root to J. Bishop, Apr. 10, 1902, pt.1, letterbook 180, Root Papers, LC (second quotation); *New York Times,* Mar. 21, 31 (third, fourth, and fifth quotations), Apr. 19, 1902.

38. *New York Tribune,* Apr. 9, 12, 14 (quotation), June 6, 7, 1902; *New York Times,* Apr. 4, May 24, June 6, 7, 1902; Roosevelt to H. Kohlsaat, June 10, 1902, in Morison, *Letters of Roosevelt,* 3:271; Jessup, *Elihu Root,* 246; "General Miles and the Administration," *American Monthly Review of Reviews* 25 (Jan.–June 1902): 532.

39. *New York Daily Tribune,* June 13, Aug. 27, 29, Sept. 3, 12, Oct. 2, 28, 1902; *New York Times,* July 5, Aug. 19, Oct. 22, Dec. 26, 1902; Roosevelt to Hay, July 22, 1902, in Morison, *Letters of Roosevelt,* 3:300; Roosevelt to Crane, July 31, 1902, ibid., 3:308; Miles to sw, Aug. 7, 1902, LR, CB, NARA; W. Sanger to Miles, Aug. 26, Sept. 3, 1902, ibid.; Roosevelt to McKinley, Jan. 29, 1900, S.B.M. Young Papers, U.S. Army Military History Institute.

40. Speech of Miles to troops at Camp Vigars, Nov. 15, 1902, box 136, Pershing Papers; "Memoirs," chap.12, pp.10–11, box 380, ibid.; Taft to Root, Oct. 4, 1902, box 164, Root Papers, LC (quotation); *New York Tribune,* Oct. 31, Nov. 1, 1902; Taft to Miles, Oct. 30, 1902, box 4, Miles Papers.

41. Baldwin to Alice, Dec. 2, 1902, box 11, Baldwin Papers; Miles, *Serving the Republic*, 306; Roosevelt to G. Hoar, Dec. 23, 1902, in Morison, *Letters of Roosevelt*, 3:394; *New York Tribune*, Nov. 13, 22, 1902; *New York Times*, Nov. 22, 1902; Taft to Root, Nov. 22, 1902, box 164, Root Papers, LC (quotations); "Memorandum," [1902], Miles Collection.

42. Taft to Root, Nov. 22, 1902, box 164, Pershing Papers; Davis to Adj. Genl., Nov. 26, 1902, LR, CB, NARA; Corbin to Davis, Nov. 28, 1902, ibid.; Miles to SW, Dec. 9, 1902, ibid. (first quotation); Davis to Adj. Genl., Jan. 5 (second quotation), 22, 1903, ibid.; Miles to Root, Feb. [19], Apr. 24, 1903, Miles Collection.

43. Taft to Root, Jan. 25, 1903, box 165, Root Papers, LC (quotation); Miles to Reber, Dec. 10, 1903, box 28, ibid.; *New York Tribune*, Dec. 28, 29, 1902, Jan. 20, 27, 30, Feb. 3, 16, 1903; Miles, *Serving the Republic*, 308–10; *New York Times*, Jan. 20, Feb. 16, 1903; H. White to Miles, Jan. 29, 1903, box 5, Miles Papers; Roberts to Miles, Feb. 4, 1903, box 8, ibid.; White to Knollys, Feb. 6, 1903, Miles Collection; Miles to SW, Mar. 23, 1903, file 481301, box 3369, LR, AGO, 1890s and 1900s, NARA; Hay to SW, May 16, 1903, ibid.

44. *New York Times*, Apr. 28, 1903 (first quotation); Report of Inspection, Nov. 28, 1902, file 481301, box 3369, LR, AGO, 1890s and 1900s, NARA; Endorsement of Miles, Mar. 13, 1903, ibid. (second quotation).

    Stuart Creighton Miller, *"Benevolent Assimilation": The American Conquest of the Philippines, 1899–1903* (New Haven: Yale University Press, 1982), though incorrectly identifying Miles as chief of staff, provides a good survey of newspaper coverage.

45. Roosevelt to Hoar, Dec. 23, 1902, in Morison, *Letters of Roosevelt*, 3:394; Roosevelt to Taft, Sept. 3, 1903, ibid., 3:585; Taft to Root, Mar. 2, 1903, box 165, Root Papers, LC; Root to J. Palfrey, Apr. 25, 1903, pt.3, letterbook 176, ibid.; Miles to SW, Apr. 24, 1903, Miles Collection; *New York Times*, Apr. 28, May 14, 16, 1903; Root to J. Ecob, May 6, 1903, pt.3, letterbook 176, Root Papers, LC; Taft to Root, May 13, 1903, box 165, ibid.; circular letter sent by Herbert Welsh, May 14, 1903, file 481301, box 3369, LR, AGO, 1890s and 1900s, NARA; *New York Tribune*, May 15, 16 (first quotation), 1903; Taft to Root, June 15, 1903 (second quotation), box 165, Root Papers, LC; "General Miles's Report," *Outlook* 74 (May 9, 1903): 99–100.

46. Roosevelt to Root, May 23, 1903, box 19, Root Papers, LC (first and second quotations); Davis to Adj. Genl., May 17, 1903, file 481301, box 3369, LR, AGO, 1890s and 1900s, NARA; Miles, statement of May 17, 1903, ibid. (third quotation); Roosevelt to Root, May 23, 1903, box 19, Root Papers, LC. See also miscellaneous letters received in regards to publication of the report, in file 481301, boxes 3369–70, LR, AGO, 1890s and 1900s, NARA.

47. Barr, "American Military Reform," 77; Roberts, "Loyalty and Expertise," 245–50. For internal army debate, see Allen to Carter, Nov. 25, 1902, box 7, Allen

Papers; Young to sw, Dec. 12, 1902, Young Papers; Young to Chaffee, Dec. 29, 1902, ibid.; Corbin to Allen, Jan. 12, 1903, box 8, Allen Papers; Weston to Wilson, Jan. 22, 1903, box 26, J. Wilson Papers.

48. Gould, *Presidency of Theodore Roosevelt*, 122–23; Corbin to Allen, Jan. 12, 1903, box 8, Allen Papers (quotation); Root to Dodge, Jan. 22, 1903, pt.2, letterbook 180, Root Papers, LC; Barr, "American Military Reform," 77; Bowie, "Redfield Proctor," 414–22.

49. *New York Times*, July 15, Aug. 28, 1903; H. Rouse to Allen, July 22, 1903, box 9, Allen Papers; Miles to sw, Aug. 7, 1903, Miles Collection.

50. *New York Times*, Aug. 8, 1903.

51. *New York Times*, Aug. 10 (first quotation), 14, 22, 27, 1903; *Atlanta Constitution*, Aug. 9, 1903 (second quotation); *New York Tribune*, Aug. 4, 10, 1903; memorandum of J. B. Hodge, received Aug. 21, 1903, box 35, Root Papers, LC; Roosevelt to Wood, Aug. 1, 1903, in Morison, *Letters of Roosevelt*, 3:539; Roosevelt to Lodge, Aug. 6, Sept. 3 (third quotation), 1903, ibid., 3:545; Roosevelt to L. Davis, Aug. 20, 1903, ibid., 3:567; Roosevelt to Taft, Sept. 3, 1903, ibid., 3:585; Roosevelt to G. Harvey, Jan. 22, 1904, ibid., 3:705.

Surveys of contemporary newspaper editorials on Miles's retirement may be found in *Literary Digest* 27 (Aug. 15, 22, 1903); and *Public Opinion* 35 (Aug. 13, 1903).

CHAPTER FIFTEEN

1. Reber to Miles, Sept. 2, 17, Nov. 11, 1903, Reber-Miles Papers; Reber to George, May 29, ibid.; Miles to J. Wise, Feb. 15, 1901, Wise Family Papers, Virginia Historical Society; *New York Tribune*, Apr. 29, July 9, 10, 17, Sept. 30 (quotation), 1903; oral interview, Robert Cotner and Ima Hogg, July 31, 1954, tape 159, Pioneers in Texas Oil, Oral History of the Oil Industry Collection, Barker Texas History Center, Austin.

2. Miles to Hogg, Aug. 1, 1903, box 31, Oct. 23, 1904, box 32, Hogg Collection, Barker Texas History Center; *New York Tribune*, Oct. 29, 1903; I. Lewis to Miles, Sept. 29, 1903, box 3, Miles Papers; Miles to Alger, Aug. 21, 1891, Alger Papers; J. Sherman to Miles, May 16, 1891, box 4, Miles Papers; Miles to J. Sherman, June 1, 1892, box 582, J. Sherman Papers; S. Reber to C. Reber, Dec. 26, 1901, Reber-Miles Papers; "General Miles Given $5,000," undated clipping, Miles materials, Forbush Library; Miles to A. Hoyt, Apr. 6, July 20, 1900, Miles Collection; Miles to G. Curtis, Aug. 5, 1902, ibid.; U.S. Census, Manuscript Returns, 1900, enumeration district 41, roll 160, District of Columbia, vol. 4; *New York Times*, Aug. 3, 1904; *Washington Post*, Aug. 3, 1904.

3. Adams to E. Cameron, Feb. 19, 1899, in Ford, *Henry Adams*, 218–19; Reber to Hawley, Apr. 22, 1902, Reber-Miles Papers.

4. Lothrop Stoddard, *Master of Manhattan: The Life of Richard Croker* (New York: Longmans, Green and Co., 1931), 216–22; Harry Wilson Walker, "The Trail of the Tammany Tiger," *Saturday Evening Post* 186 (Apr. 1914): 20.

5. *New York Tribune*, Nov. 9, 1903; *New York Times*, Mar. 14, 1904 (first and second quotations); Gamaliel Bradford, "To the Delegates to the Democratic National Convention of July 6th," [1904], in *The Campaign Text Book of the Democratic Party of the United States, 1904* (New York: Democratic National Committee, 1904) (third quotation); Miles to Atkinson, May 6, 1904, Edward Atkinson Papers, Massachusetts Historical Society (hereafter cited as Atkinson Papers).

Miles had initially supported the canal (see "The Necessity of the Isthmus Canal," *Independent* 52 [Feb. 15, 1900]: 409).

6. Baird to Baldwin, June 1, 1904, box 2, Baldwin Papers; *New York Daily Tribune*, Mar. 15 (first quotation), 24 (second quotation), 1904; Jack S. Blocker, Jr. *Retreat from Reform: The Prohibition Movement in the United States, 1890–1913*, Contributions in American History, no.51 (Westport, Conn.. Greenwood Press, 1976), 144–83; Mark Edward Lender, *Dictionary of American Temperance Biography: From Temperance Reform to Alcohol Research, the 1600s to the 1980s* (Westport, Conn.: Greenwood Press, 1984), 530–31.

7. *New York Daily Tribune*, Mar. 29, June 26, 29, 30, 1904; *New York Times*, Mar. 29, May 24, 26, June 29, 1904; Miles to Atkinson, May 6, 1904, Atkinson Papers; Blocker, *Retreat from Reform*, 183–85; Lender, *Dictionary of American Temperance Biography*, 477–78.

8. Miles to Overmyer, June 5, 18, 1904, David Overmyer Collection, Kansas State Historical Society, Center for Historical Research; Walker, "Trail of the Tammany Tiger"; *Official Report of the Proceedings of the Democratic National Convention . . .*, reported by Milton W. Blumenberg (New York: Publisher's Printing Co., 1904), 200–207 (quotation). For a sketch of Overmyer, see *The National Cyclopedia of American Biography . . .*, 54 vols. (New York: James T. White and Co., 1924), 8:248–49.

9. *Official Report of the Proceedings*, 247; Parker to Miles, July 16, 1904, box 3, Miles Papers; *New York Times*, Aug. 16, 20, 23, 1904; *Campaign Text Book of the Democratic Party*, 183–84.

For the continued dispute regarding Jefferson Davis, see "A Statement of the Facts Concerning the Imprisonment and Treatment of Jefferson Davis . . ." in Miles Collection; "Open Letter to the Press from Lieutenant General Nelson A. Miles," Feb. 1905, ibid.; *New York Times*, Feb. 3, 1905; and G. Hopper to Miles, Feb. 25, 1906, Miles Collection.

10. Reber to E. Patterson, Jan. 7 (first quotation), 21, 1904, Reber-Miles Papers; Baird to Baldwin, Mar. 14 (second quotation), 23, 1904, box 2, Baldwin Papers; *New York Times*, Mar. 18, Aug. 3, 1904; *Washington Post*, Aug. 3, 1904.

11. *New York Times*, Aug. 3, 1904; Miles to Baldwin, Aug. 8, box 3, Baldwin

Papers; Miles to M. Finch, Aug. 8, 1904, Miscellaneous Manuscripts, New-York Historical Society; Miles to Schurz, Aug. 8, 1904, roll 79, Schurz Papers; Miles to Wilson, Aug. 2, 1904, box 16, J. Wilson Papers; Huggins to Cousin, Dec. 24, 1904, Huggins Papers; Custer to Miles, Aug. 23, [1904], box 1, Miles Papers (quotations).

12. *New York Times*, Sept. 24, Oct. 24, 1904; "Letter of Nelson A. Miles to Comrade," Miles Collection (first quotation); Baird to Baldwin, Nov. 1, 1904, box 2, Baldwin Papers; Roosevelt to Wood, Oct. 6, 1904, in Morison, *Letters of Roosevelt*, 4:974 (second quotation).

13. Nelson A. Miles, "My Treatment of Jefferson Davis," *Independent* 58 (Feb. 23, 1905): 413–17; *New York Tribune*, Nov. 11, 1906; *New York Times*, Dec. 4, 1904, Feb. 24, Mar. 5, 1905; Michael E. Hennessy, *Four Decades of Massachusetts Politics, 1890–1935* (Norwood, Mass.: Norwood Press, 1935), 88–91.

14. *New York Times*, Jan. 12, 21, 26, Feb. 3, 26, 1905; *Congressional Record*, 58th Cong., 3d sess., 39:1106–7, 1136, 1333–43, 1393–96, 1670, 3472; Miles to Douglas, Dec. 11, 18, 1905, Miles Collection.

15. J. Pope to Baldwin, Jan. 30, 1907, box 3, Baldwin Papers (quotation); Lodge to Roosevelt, Aug. 21, 1905, Lodge and Redmond, *Correspondence of Roosevelt and Lodge*, 2:177; *New York Times*, June 24, 1905, Jan. 10, 19, 1909; Mills, *My Story*, 312.

16. Butt to Clara, Apr. 28, 1910, in *Taft and Roosevelt: The Intimate Letters of Archie Butt, Military Aide* (Garden City, N.Y.: Doubleday, Doran and Co., 1930), 340; Miles to Baldwin, June 4, 1910, box 3, Baldwin Papers; *New York Times Review of Books*, Nov. 19, 1911; *Independent* 71 (Nov. 30, 1911): 1206. An exception to Miles's attempt to appeal to everyone was his biting criticism of Roosevelt (see Miles, *Serving the Republic*, 269).

17. *Boyd's Washington City Directory*, 1909, p.913; ibid., 1910, p.951; ibid. 1911, p.1021; Permit 2034, June 19, 1903, roll 277, microcopy M 1116, District of Columbia Building Permits, 1877–1949, NARA; *Baist's Real Estate Atlas Surveys of Washington*, 1919, vol.1, plan 15; Miles to Baldwin, Feb. 17, 1907, Feb. 18, 1908, box 3, Baldwin Papers; Miles to My Dear General, Feb. 20, 1907, Miles Collection; Miles to R. Aguilera, Oct. 9, 1906, box 136, Carnegie Papers; Miles to L. Donaldson, Sept. 25, 1907, Miles Collection; Miles to Maxwell, Feb. 10, 1901, ibid.; Miles to Mrs. Robinson, May 5, 1912, S. G. Flagg Collection, Manuscripts and Archives, Yale University Library; *New York Times*, May 8, Oct. 1, 1915; Miles to Nicholson, Feb. 4, 1911, NI 852, Miscellaneous Manuscripts, Huntington Library; Miles to P. Whitcomb, Jan. 6, 1914, CW 312, ibid.; Miles to J. Nagle, Mar. 23, 1915, NI 853, ibid.; Miscellaneous materials on the death of Eugene Carr, box 2, Carr Papers; Miles to Wilson, Mar. 15, ser.4, roll 202, Woodrow Wilson Papers, LC (hereafter cited as Woodrow Wilson Papers); Miles to President, Mar. 30, 1912, Clay Papers; Stewart, *History*, 402, 407, 497; interview with Robert Cotner and Ima Hogg, June 20, 1949, box 3, N 395,

Robert Cotner Collection, Barker Texas History Center; Baldwin to Miles, Mar. 25, 1915, box 1, Baldwin Papers.

18. Miles to Carnegie, Apr. 11, 1911, box 191, Carnegie Papers; Adams to E. Cameron, Feb. 18, 1912, in Ford, *Henry Adams*, 586; Miles to Baldwin, Feb. 25, 1908, box 3, Baldwin Papers; Miles to Taft, Jan. 9, 1913, file 4244, roll 450, Taft Papers; S. Miles to J. Williams, July 22, 1909, James T. Williams Papers, Perkins Memorial Library; Remington to My Dear General, n.d., Remington Papers, New-York Historical Society; Peggy and Harold Samuels, *Frederic Remington*, 433–34; Newton F. Tolman, ed., *A History of Westminster, Massachusetts, 1893–1958* (Petersborough, N.H.: Richard R. Smith, 1961), 59, 114; *New York Times*, Feb. 23, 1912 (quotation); *New York Daily Tribune*, Feb. 22, 23, 1906.

19. Tolman, *History of Westminster*, 21, 38; *The Dedication of the Forbush Memorial Library Building in Westminster, Massachusetts, August 22, 1902* (Gardner, Mass.: Press of Whiting & Whitaker, n.d.); Wilbur F. Whitney, *An Account of the Exercises Connected with the 150th Anniversary Celebration of the Town of Westminster Massachusetts, 1909* (Gardner, Mass.: Meals Printing Co., n.d.), 23, 27, 29; Miles to P. Loughlin, Aug. 10, 1922, Miles materials, Forbush Library.

20. Correspondence on the Perry Commission is in the Webb C. Hayes Papers; *Congressional Record*, 57th Cong., 2d sess., vol.36, pt.2, p.1396; Miles to Taft, Jan. 9, 1913, file 4244, roll 450, Taft Papers; Miles to Carnegie, Mar. 31, 1911, box 190, Nov. 8, 1911, box 199, Dec. 11, 1911, box 201, Apr. 25, 1912, box 201, Carnegie Papers; Miles to T. Page, Feb. 26, 1913, Thomas Nelson Page Papers, Perkins Library; *New York Times*, Sept. 21, 1913, Oct. 28, 1920.

21. Miles to Carnegie, Apr. 19, 1912, box 205, Carnegie Papers (quotation); Gleason, Secor, and Gregory to Miles, 1912, roll 778, Index to General Correspondence of the Office of the Adjutant General, 1890–1917, M 698, NARA; *New York Times*, Jan. 7, 1913, Jan. 21, 1916; W. Harding to Miles, Aug. 9, 1029, box 2, Miles Papers. For a brief survey, see "The Guardians of Liberty," *Literary Digest* 45 (July 27, 1912): 152–53.

22. *New York Times*, Nov. 2, 1912.

23. Wilson to Miles, May 21, 1913, ser.3, roll 133, Woodrow Wilson Papers; *New York Times*, June 13, July 23, 25, Aug. 7, 16, 1913, July 24, 1914; Miles to M. Boardman, Sept. 7, 1913, Miles Collection, "A Monsieur le General Nelson A. Miles," Mar. 30, 1914, ibid.

24. Brownlow, *The War, the West*, 227–30; George N. Fenin and William K. Everson, *The Western: From the Silents to the Seventies* (New York: Grossman, 1973), 53; L. Laylin to Attorney General, Aug. 4, 1913, pt.2, file 5-70, "Indian Office: Indians for Show and Exhibition Purposes," Central Classified File, 1907–1936, RG 48, NARA.

25. Brownlow, *The War, the West*, 227–30; Fenin and Everson, *The Western*, 53;

L. Laylin to Attorney General, Aug. 4, 1913, pt.2, file 5-70, "Indian Office: Indians for Show and Exhibition Purposes," Central Classified File, 1907–1936, RG 48, NARA; F. Belford-Wayne to Lane, Aug. 27, 1913, file 5-2, "Indian Office: Moving Pictures," Central Classified File, 1907–1936, RG 48, NARA (quotation); Cody to Garrison, Aug. 24, 1913, ibid.; Lane to Sells, Aug. 24, 1913, ibid.; "Buffalo Bill Picture Shown," *Moving Picture World* 19 (Mar. 14, 1914): 1370; L. Laylin to Attorney General, Oct. 27, 1913, pt.2, file 5-70, "Indian Office: Indians for Show and Exhibition Purposes," Central Classified File, 1907–1936, RG 48, NARA.

In 1908, the Interior Department had not objected to the use of Indians at the Crow Reservation to film, for educational purposes, a re-creation of the fighting at Little Bighorn (J. Wilson to sw, Aug. 29, 1908, pt.1, ibid.).

26. Brownlow, *The War, the West*, 228; "Buffalo Bill Picture Shown," 1370; Miles to Baldwin, Sept. 15, 1913, box 3, Baldwin Papers (quotation).

27. "Buffalo Bill Picture Shown," 1370; Miles to Baker, Sept. 30, 1913, box 5, Baldwin Papers (quotations); Miles to Baldwin, ibid.

28. "Battle of Pine Ridge Made Realistic in Pictures," *Moving Picture World* (Oct. 25, 1913): 362.

29. "Theodore Wharton's Big Job," ibid., 368 (quotation); "Director Wharton Talks About 'Buffalo Bill' Series," *Moving Picture World* (Nov. 22, 1913): 851; "Buffalo Bill Picture Shown," 1370; Louisa Frederici Cody and Courtney Ryley Cooper, *Memories of Buffalo Bill* (New York: D. Appleton and Co., 1919), 306–9; Brownlow, *The War, the West*, 230–31.

30. Brownlow, *The War, the West*, 230.

31. Ibid., 232–33; "Theodore Wharton's Big Job," 368; Miles to Baldwin, undated letter in envelope postmarked Oct. 1913, box 3, Baldwin Papers.

32. Miles to Spoor, Jan. 24, 1914, Baldwin Papers (quotations); Miles to Baldwin, Jan. 26, 1914, ibid.; "Buffalo Bill Picture Shown," 1370.

33. Cody to Baldwin, Jan. 29, 1914, Baldwin Papers; Day to Baldwin, Feb. 13, 1914, ibid.; printed invitation dated Feb. 27, 1914, ibid.; Brownlow, *The War, the West*, 233–35; "Buffalo Bill Picture Shown," 1370. The opening title is cited in Cody to Baldwin, Feb. 28, 1914, Baldwin Papers.

34. Baldwin to Cody, Mar. 9, 1914, Baldwin Papers; *Moving Picture World* 21 (Sept. 12, 1914) (quotation): 1500; Brownlow, *The War, the West*, 228, 235.

35. Brownlow, *The War, the West*, 233–35; Lane to Bonfels, Aug. 28, 1913, Moving Pictures file, RG 48, NARA (quotation); E. Ayers to Cody, Dec. 18, 1915, Jan. 14, 29, 1916, ibid.; Cody to Ayers, Feb. 1, Mar. 31, 1916, ibid.; Day to Ayers, Mar. 21, 1916, ibid.

In a separate incident, the Interior Department confiscated another film of the Snake Dance ceremony, which did not comply with the department's demands that it be used solely for "historical or educational purposes" (A. Jones to Pathe Freres Motion Pictures, Sept. 12, 1913, ibid.).

36. *New York Times*, Jan. 19, 1909, Nov. 2, 1912, Aug. 3, 1914 (quotation).

37. Received Aug. 11, 1914, roll 778, Index to General Correspondence of the Office of the Adjutant General, 1890–1917, M 698, NARA. *New York Times*, Aug. 3, 1914, July 3, 8, 24, 25, Sept. 16, 1915, Mar. 10, 1916; Miles to E. Moore, Nov. 14, 1918, Miles Collection.

38. Russell F. Weigley, *History of the United States Army*, enlarged ed. (Bloomington: Indiana University Press, 1984), 344–47.

39. Miles to Wilson, Feb. 1, 1916, box 16, J. Wilson Papers; *New York Times*, Feb. 1 (first quotation), 9, 1916; testimony of Miles, Feb. 8, 1916, "Bill to Increase the Efficiency of the Military Establishment (1916)," *Congressional Hearings*, 156:1252–60 (second, third, and fourth quotations).

40. Miles to Church, Feb. 17, 1916, box 2, Church Papers.

41. Medal of Honor Board, Jan. 1917, Miles Collection; Miles to SW, July 16, 1916, Mar. 17, 1917, ibid.; *New York Times*, Mar. 28, 1917, May 16, 1925; Miles to SW, Apr. 24, 1917, box 3, Baldwin Papers.

42. Miles to SW, Nov. 13, 24 (quotations), 1917, Miles Collection; SW to Miles, Nov. 17, 1917, ibid.; Miles to Lewis, Mar. 8, June 15, 1918, ibid.

43. J. T. Schneider to Hughes, Oct. 1, 1919, box 136, Pershing Papers; Frank E. Vandiver, *Black Jack: The Life and Times of John J. Pershing*, 2 vols. (College Station: Texas A & M University Press, 1977), 2:133, 155–56, 173; Harding to Miles, Feb. 2, June 15, 1920, box 2, Miles Papers; *New York Times*, Oct. 27, 1920 (quotations); Miles to Mrs. A. Cook, July 28, 1924, Miles Collection. Ironically, in 1918, Miles had supported the concept of "a Congress of Nations . . . and an impartial high court of justice created, with ample power accorded to adjudicate international controversies" (Nelson A. Miles, *An Address Delivered at the Stated Meeting of May 1, 1918, by the Commander Lieutenant-General Nelson A. Miles, United States Army, on his Election as Commander of the Commandery* [Washington, D.C., 1918], 52).

44. *New York Times*, Sept. 2, 1920, June 7, 1921, Apr. 27, 1922, Nov. 18, 1924, May 16, 1925 (quotation); Kelly, *"Yellowstone Kelly"*; Mills, *My Story*; Miles to Taft, Apr. 24, 1922, roll 241, Taft Papers; "minutes, extracts of . . . ," Oct. 24, 1923, Miles Collection; Miles to Commanders and Companions of the Military Order of the Loyal Legion, Aug. 30, 1924, ibid.; "Remarks of Lieut. General Nelson A. Miles . . . , Nov. 11, 1921," ibid.; Allen to Miles, July 7, 1924, ibid.; Miles, *Address Delivered at the Stated Meeting of May 1, 1918*; Logan to Miles, May 16, 1920, box 8, Miles Papers; *Liberty* (Texas) *Vindicator*, Mar. 21, 1924.

45. Peggy and Harold Samuels, *Frederic Remington*, 426; Miles to Wanamaker, July 9, 1909, file 4006, roll 350, Taft Papers (quotation); *The Papers of the Order of Indian Wars* (Fort Collins, Colo.: Old Army Press, 1975); DeMontravel, "Nelson A. Miles," 372; Utley, *Last Days*, 249.

46. Hooker to Alice, Feb. 5, 1923, box 14, Baldwin Papers (quotation); *New York Times*, Aug. 11, Nov. 27, 1925.

47. Miles to W. Hayes, Jan. 1, 1924, Webb C. Hayes Papers; Miles to D. Boshy-shell, Nov. 13, 1920, NI 854, Miscellaneous Manuscripts, Huntington Library; George W. Baird, "Prominent Americans Who Are Masons," *Master Mason* 1 (Jan. 1924): 53–55; Pohanka, *Documentary Biography*, 318 (first quotation); Miles to Alice, July 21, 1923, box 14, Baldwin Papers; *New York Times*, May 16, 25, June 13, 1925; Miles to A. Long, Oct. 7, 1919, Miles Collection; W. Bowen to Baldwin, Sept. 12, 1920, box 2, Baldwin Papers; Miles to Lizzie, Dec. 30, 1923 (second quotation), July 7, 1924, box 3, Miles Papers; S. Miles to Pershing, Oct. 19, 1917, box 136, Pershing Papers.
48. *Washington Evening Star*, May 16, 1925; *New York Times*, Feb. 13, Mar. 3, May 16, 1925; Webb C. Hayes to Miles, Jan. 26, 1925, Webb C. Hayes Papers; Miles to Hayes, Apr. 2, 1925, ibid.
49. *New York Times*, May 16 (quotations), 28, 1925.
50. *New York Times*, May 16, 28, 1925.
51. Ibid., May 17, 20, 1925.

EPILOGUE

1. *New York Times*, May 16, Nov. 27, Dec. 6, 1925, Oct. 9, 1966.
2. *New York Tribune*, Aug. 8, 1903 (quotations); "Memoirs," chap.14, box 380, Pershing Papers; Miles to Wood, June 11, 1894, box 26, Leonard Wood Papers; Weigley, *History of the Army*, 322–41; James Hewes, "The United States Army General Staff, 1900–1917," *Military Affairs* 38 (Apr. 1974): 67–72.
3. Deutrich, *Struggle for Supremacy*, 98–122.
4. Skowronek, *Building a New American State*, 223–25; Deutrich, *Struggle for Supremacy*, 105–22; Ainsworth memorandum, Feb. 3, 1902, in House Report 508, 62d Cong., 2d sess., serial 6131, pp.5–13; Weigley, *History of the Army*, 332.
5. Jack C. Lane, *Armed Progressive: General Leonard Wood* (San Rafael, Calif.: Presidio Press, 1978).
6. Ibid., 149, 158.
7. Skowronek, *Building a New American State*, 222–34; Brian Linn, "The Long Twilight of the Frontier Army" (presented at "Soldiers and Explorers: The Military and the History of the American West," Yale University, May 4, 1991).
8. Brian McAllister Linn, *The U.S. Army and Counterinsurgency in the Philippine War, 1899–1902* (Chapel Hill: University of North Carolina Press, 1989), 163–70.
9. Weigley, *History of the Army*, 318–35.
10. Pope to Baird, July 10, 1891, Baird Papers, Kansas.
11. For Miles's early discussions of reform, see unsigned letter to Garfield, 1868,

Miles Collection; and testimony of Miles, Feb. 8, 1902, House Report 356, 44th Cong., 1st sess., serial 1709, pp.81–82.

12. "The Passing of the Commanding General," *Nation* 77 (Aug. 13, 1903): 126–27; Report of Miles, Oct. 1, 1901, sw, *Annual Report, 1901*, 6.

13. Lee to Baldwin, Jan. 6, 1906, box 2, Baldwin Papers.

14. Testimony of Miles, Dec. 13, 1877, pp.237–41, House Committee on Military Affairs H Mi 45A, U.S. Congressional Hearings Supplement; "Passing of the Commanding General," 126–27 (quotations); *New York Times*, June 20, 1899.

15. Benteen to Goldin, Apr. 3, 1902, in Carroll, *Benteen-Goldin Letters*, 220–21 (first quotation); E. R. Hagermann, ed., *Fighting Rebels and Redskins: Experiences in the Army Life of Colonel George B. Sanford, 1861–1898* (Norman: University of Oklahoma Press, 1969), 100–101 (second quotation).

16. Daly to Gatewood, May 15, 1925 (first quotation), Mar. 2, 1926, box 10, Gatewood Collection; Eve Ball, *Indeh: An Apache Odyssesy* (Provo, Utah: Brigham Young University Press, 1980), 111 (second quotation).

17. *New York Times*, Nov. 11, 1878 (first quotation); Long to Miles, Dec. 18, 1887, Miles Collection (second quotation); Cody, *Autobiography*, 280 (third quotation).

18. Miles, *Serving the Republic*, 219.

19. Diary, Aug. 10, 1897, box 1, Allen Papers; Henry F. Pringle, *Theodore Roosevelt: A Biography* (New York: Harcourt, Brace and Co., 1931), 446 (first quotation); Finley Peter Dunne, *Mr. Dooley in Peace and in War* (1898; reprint, New York: Greenwood Press, 1968), 32 (second quotation).

20. Pohanka, *Documentary Biography*, 318.

BIBLIOGRAPHICAL ESSAY

A variety of manuscript and published sources made this book possible. Essential were the various collections of Nelson Miles's papers. I had already begun the project when the staff at the U.S. Army Military History Institute, Carlisle Barracks, Pennsylvania, made available to me a newly acquired trunk of Miles's papers and documents. These did much to explain his life before and during the Civil War. The Nelson A. Miles Papers in the Library of Congress, Washington, D.C., are a particularly good source on his post–Civil War career. Also critical was a typescript copy of letters to his wife, assembled by his son Sherman and made available to me by Robert M. Utley. The Nelson A. Miles Miscellaneous Manuscripts in the Rutherford B. Hayes Presidential Center, Fremont, Ohio, though a small collection, must also be consulted by the serious biographer of Miles. The Forbush Memorial Library, Westminster, Massachusetts, also has a few materials.

Miles did not keep all of his papers, but other manuscript collections help to complete his story. In the Library of Congress, the William T. Sherman (microfilm), John Sherman, Henry T. Allen, and Leonard Wood papers include numerous letters to and about Miles. For understanding the army after the Civil War, the Philip Sheridan (microfilm) and John M. Schofield papers are essential. Only slightly less important are the William C. Church, John J. Pershing, and Hugh Scott papers. Among the Rare Books and Manuscripts Division collections at the New York Public Library (Astor, Lenox, and Tilden foundations), see the Francis Vinton Greene Papers and the Alvin Humphrey Sydenham Journal, 1889–1890 for often-overlooked insights.

Miles's aides also kept many useful documents. These may be found in the Eli Lundy Huggins and Oscar Long papers, Bancroft Library, University of California, Berkeley; the George William Baird materials in the Western Americana Collection, Beinecke Rare Book and Manuscript Library, Yale University, New Haven, Connecticut; the Frank D. Baldwin and Oscar F. Long papers, Huntington Library, San Marino, California; the George W. Baird Papers, Kansas State Historical Society, Center for Historical Research, Topeka; and the Frank D. Baldwin Diary, Montana Historical Society, Helena. The William Rufus Shafter Papers (M 072), Department of Special Collections, Stanford University Libraries; the Sherman Miles Collection, Eugene Carr Papers, Order of Indian Wars Collection, Reber-Miles Papers, and S.B.M. Young Papers, all at the rapidly expanding U.S. Army Military History Institute, are also significant.

Miles's legions of enemies assembled reams of evidence that present an unfavorable impression of the general. The Southern viewpoint may be found in the

Clement Claiborne Clay Papers and the Thomas Nelson Page Papers, both at the Perkins Memorial Library, Manuscript Department, Duke University, Durham, North Carolina; the Calvin J. Cowles Papers, no. 3808, Southern Historical Collection, Library of the University of North Carolina at Chapel Hill; and the Schilling Papers, along with various materials relating to Varina Davis, especially MSS 2 D2987, in the Virginia Historical Society, Richmond.

Miles also had more than his share of detractors within the army. For George Crook's perspective, see the collections of George Crook, Rutherford B. Hayes, and Webb C. Hayes, Hayes Library; the Charles E. S. Wood Collection, Huntington Library; the Lyman Walter Kennon Papers, Perkins Library; the George Crook Papers, Special Collections, Knight Library, University of Oregon, Eugene; and the Crook-Kennon Papers, U.S. Army Military History Institute. Miles's relationship with Oliver O. Howard is documented most thoroughly in the Oliver O. Howard Papers, Bowdoin College Library, Brunswick, Maine. The remarkable Charles B. Gatewood Collection, Arizona Historical Society Collections/Tucson, is essential for assessing Miles's years in Arizona. At the Rare Books and Manuscripts Division, New York Public Library (Astor, Lenox, and Tilden foundations), James W. Forsyth's "Statements in Defense of the Seventh Cavalry while under His Command against the Sioux" adds another dimension to the Wounded Knee tragedy.

Various politicians held strong opinions on the career of Nelson Miles. At the Library of Congress, the papers of each of the presidents during Miles's adult life, available on microfilm, shed insights into Miles's political machinations. The Henry L. Dawes, Hamilton Fish, Charles S. Hamlin, Daniel C. Lamont, and Richard Olney papers contain other useful materials. At the Massachusetts Historical Society, Boston, the John A. Andrews, Francis C. Barlow (microfilm), William Endicott, and John D. Long papers are important for assessing Miles's life. The Robert Cotner Collection, Hogg Collection, and Oral History of the Oil Industry Collections at the Barker Texas History Center, University of Texas, Austin, give evidence of Miles's oil investments. His political activities during the 1880s, 1890s, and 1900s are seen in the Grenville Dodge Papers, State Historical Society of Iowa, Des Moines, and the David Overmyer and Edmund G. Ross collections, Kansas State Historical Society. At the Montana Historical Society, Miles's associations with people who lived in Montana Territory are documented in the Samuel T. Hauser, Martin Maginnis, and George P. Miles papers.

Miles's controversial service during and after the Spanish-American War receives extensive coverage in the Russell Alger Papers, William L. Clements Library, University of Michigan, Ann Arbor; and the Henry Corbin and Elihu Root papers, Library of Congress. The Breckinridge Family Papers, Andrew Carnegie Papers, George Dewey Papers, Reid Family Papers, and James Henry Wilson Papers, all at the Library of Congress, are also useful for this period, as are the Thaddeus K. Oglesby Papers, Perkins Library.

Additional insights into Miles's story may be found in Edwin M. Brown, "Terror of the Badlands," Montana Historical Society; the Miscellaneous Manuscripts and Frederic Remington Papers, New-York Historical Society, New York; the James S. Henry Harris Private Collection, the Governor Harris's Papers, the W. W. Holden Private Collection, North Carolina State Archives, Raleigh; and the S. G. Flagg Collection and Alexander Stewart Webb Papers, Manuscripts and Archives, Yale University Library.

Of course, the holdings of the National Archives and Record Service, Washington, D.C., are fundamental to understanding the career of any nineteenth-century army officer. Its growing number of microfilm collections is more readily available to researchers outside of the immediate District of Columbia area, and will thus be discussed independently of the manuscript materials. A complete guide to the microfilm collections is available, and users should consult this listing before undertaking their research.

Miles's official military file is on roll 525, Letters Received by the Commission Branch of the Adjutant General's Office, 1863–1870 (M 1064). Other important adjutant general records include the exhaustive Letters Sent by the Office of the Adjutant General (Main Series), 1800–1890 (M 565); the Letters Received by the Office of the Adjutant General (Main Series), 1871–1880 (M 666) and 1881–1889 (M 689); and the Index to General Correspondence of the Office of the Adjutant General, 1890–1917 (M 698). The Letters Sent by the Headquarters of the Army (Main Series), 1828–1903 (M 857) supplement the Letters Sent by the Secretary of War Relating to Military Affairs, 1800–1889 (M 6).

For this study the Records of the Assistant Commissioner for the State of North Carolina, Bureau of Refugees, Freedmen, and Abandoned Lands, 1865–1870 (M 843); the Registers and Letters Received by the Commissioner of the Bureau of Refugees, Freedmen, and Abandoned Lands, 1865–1872 (M 752); and the Area File of the Naval Records Collection, 1775–1910 (M 625) were useful. The Reports and Correspondence Relating to the Army Investigations of the Battle of Wounded Knee and to the Sioux Campaign of 1890–1891 (M 983) is essential. For Miles's recommendations on Indian reservations in New Mexico, a subject largely ignored in the secondary literature, see Letters Received by Headquarters, District of New Mexico, Sept. 1865–Aug. 1890 (M 1088); Letters Received by the Office of Indian Affairs, 1824–1881, New Mexico Superintendency (M 234); Letters Sent by the Indian Division of the Office of the Secretary of the Interior, 1849–1903 (M 606); Letters Sent by the 9th Military Department, the Department of New Mexico, and the District of New Mexico 1849–1890 (M 1072); and Records of the Office of Indian Affairs, Registers of Letters Received 1824–1880 (M 18).

Among manuscript collections at the National Archives, the Records of the Office of the Secretary of the Interior (RG 48), Central Classified File 1907–1936, files 5-2 and 5-70, are crucial to unraveling Miles's involvement in the Buffalo Bill Cody movie scheme. The same record group also includes the Miscellaneous

Records in the Indian Division, files 11, 69, and 137, which document his activities in Indian removal cases.

Massive army records are also available. From the Records of the Adjutant General's Office, 1780s–1917 (RG 94), see the Adjutant General's Office Document File, and Letters Received, Document File, for the 1890s and 1900s. The Records of the Headquarters of the Army (RG 108) were especially good for the information on the war against Spain. See the Correspondence on Subjects of Concern to Army Headquarters, Special File; Letters and Records of Captain Maus; Letters and Telegrams Sent from Florida and Puerto Rico, May 31–September 7, 1898; Letters, Cablegrams, and Telegrams Sent from Florida and Cuba, June 5–July 1, July 7–20, 1898, Headquarters in the Field; and Letters Received During the Cuban Expedition, May 28–September 1, 1898.

Important to this study were materials in the Records of the U.S. Army Continental Commands, 1821–1920 (RG 393). The various letters and telegrams sent and received for each of Miles's commands survey his activities in the Departments of Arizona, Columbia, the East, the Missouri, North Carolina, the Platte, and the South. Those from the Division of the Missouri and the Yellowstone Command were also examined. Researchers studying the Wounded Knee crisis should pay particular attention to materials sent from the field, often organized in separate boxes, files, and letterbooks.

Government documents and investigations offer additional information. Indispensable to the student of military and Indian policy are the annual reports of the Secretary of War (available in bound and microfiche form); more complete bibliographic information and serial numbers may be found in my *The Military and United States Indian Policy, 1865–1903* (New Haven: Yale University Press, 1988). For the present book, I also used House Executive Document 19, 43d Cong., 1st sess., serial 1606 (military prison); Senate Executive Document 2, 48th Cong., 2d sess., serial 2261 (military reconnaissance in Alaska); Senate Executive Document 117, 49th Cong., 2d sess., serial 2449 (surrender of Geronimo); Senate Executive Document 35, 51st Cong., 1st sess., serial 2682 (Apache Indians); House Document 3, 55th Cong., 3d sess., serial 3754 (Secretary of the Navy, *Annual Report*; Appendix); Senate Document 118, 58th Cong., 3d sess., serial 4765 (retired officers detailed for service); House Report 508, 62d Cong., 2d sess., serial 6131 (Relief of the Adjutant General). Numerous congressional committees investigated the question of the rank of lieutenant general. See House Report 3677, 50th Cong., 2d sess., serial 2673; House Report 2686, 51st Cong., 1st sess., serial 2814; House Report 3370, 51st Cong., 2d sess., serial 2885; House Report 1648, 53d Cong., 3d sess., serial 3345; Senate Report 670, 55th Cong., 2d sess., serial 3622; House Report 1610, 55th Cong., 2d sess., serial 3722 for information pertinent to Miles.

Scholars can also find rich materials in the U.S. Congressional Hearings Supplement, also available on microfiche. The testimony provided here, along with the committee members' questions and comments, offers many insights into the army's influence with Congress. For this book, materials from the House Committee on Appropriations (1896 - H Ap 54C; 1897 - H Ap 54D; 1901 - H Ap 56E); House Committee on Indian Affairs (1890 - H In 51); House Committee on Military Affairs (1878 - H Mi 45A; 1898 - H Mi 55A); Senate Committee on Coastal Defense (1896 - S Cod 54A); Senate Committee on Military Affairs (1899 - S Mi 55A; 1900 - S Mi 56A and 56B; 1901 - S Mi 57B); and Senate Select and Special Committee (1881 - S S 46A) were especially illuminating.

Previous biographers have not enjoyed access to all of these collections. Virginia Weisel Johnson's authorized biography, *The Unregimented General: A Biography of Nelson A. Miles* (Boston: Houghton Mifflin Co., 1962) is sympathetic to Miles, as is Peter R. DeMontravel, "The Career of Lieutenant General Nelson A. Miles: From the Civil War through the Indian Wars" (Ph.D. diss., St. John's University, 1983). Both Newton F. Tolman, *The Search for General Miles* (New York: G. P. Putnam, 1968) and Arthur J. Amchan, *The Most Famous Soldier in America: A Biography of Lt. Gen. Nelson A. Miles, 1839–1925* (Alexandria, Va.: Amchan Publications, 1989), offer nonacademic approaches. Brian C. Pohanka's comments in his *Nelson A. Miles: A Documentary Biography of His Military Career, 1861–1903* (Glendale, Calif.: Arthur H. Clark Co., 1985) are valuable, but Robert M. Utley's "Nelson A. Miles," in *Soldiers West: Biographies from the Military Frontier*, edited by Paul Andrew Hutton (Lincoln: University of Nebraska Press, 1987), offered the most insightful analysis of the general's career. Unfortunately, Jerome A. Greene's excellent *Yellowstone Command: Colonel Nelson A. Miles and the Great Sioux War, 1876–1877* (Lincoln: University of Nebraska Press, 1992) was published too late to be of use in the present volume. Contemporary accounts may be found in George W. Baird, "General Miles' Indian Campaigns," *Century Magazine* 42 (July 1891): 351–70, and "Prominent Americans Who Are Masons," *Master Mason* 1 (Jan. 1924): 55–55; and George E. Pond, "Major-General Nelson A. Miles," *McClure's Magazine* 5 (Nov. 1895): 562–74.

Miles left a wealth of published material. His two autobiographies, *Personal Recollections and Observations of General Nelson A. Miles* (1896; reprint, New York: Da Capo Press, 1969), and *Serving the Republic: Memoirs of the Civil and Military Life of Nelson A. Miles, Lieutenant-General, United States Army* (New York: Harper and Brothers, 1911), are each important, particularly in showing how Miles hoped to influence the general public. Less so is his published record of his 1897 European tour, *Military Europe: A Narrative of Personal Observation and Personal Experience* (New York: Doubleday and McClure, 1898).

A daunting array of his essays and speeches are also available. Pamphlets, which are held at the Library of Congress, include *An Address Delivered at the Stated Meeting of May 1, 1918, by the Commander Lieutenant-General Nelson A. Miles, United States Army, on his Election as Commander of the Commandery* (Washington, D.C., 1918); *Letter from Lieutenant General Nelson A. Miles, U.S. Army, Retired, to the Commanders and Companions of the Military Order of the Loyal*

Legion of the United States, Defense Day, September 12, 1924 (Philadelphia, 1924); *Memorial Address of Gen. Nelson A. Miles, at Westminster, Mass.* (May 30, 1876); *The Philippines* (1903; reprint, Boston: Anti-Imperialist League, 1909). Shorter independent essays are found in *How I Served My Apprenticeship As a Soldier* (1896; reprint, Boston: Perry Mason and Co., n.d.); and "Letter of Lieut.-Gen. Nelson A. Miles (Retired) to a Civil War Comrade," (n.p.).

Among his periodical offerings, "Our Unwatered Empire," *North American Review* 150 (Mar. 1890): 370–81; "The Future of the Indian Question," ibid. 152 (Jan. 1891): 1–10; "The Lesson of the Recent Strikes," ibid. 159 (Aug. 1894): 180–88; "Our Indian Question," *Journal of the Military Service Institution of the United States* 2, no. 7 (1881): 278–92; "War," *Cosmopolitan* 21 (June 1896): 142–48; and "My Treatment of Jefferson Davis," *Independent* 58 (February 23, 1905): 413–17, are most revealing. Less important are his "The Ambition of Japan," *Success Magazine* (July 1904): 475–78; "General Meade Anniversary Banquet," *Pennsylvania Magazine of History* 35 (Jan. 1911): 28–31; "Hunting Large Game," *North American Review* 161 (Oct. 1895): 484–92; "Just the Boy That's Wanted," *The Youth's Companion* (Feb. 14, 1889): 85; "The Necessity of the Isthmus Canal," *Independent* 52 (Feb. 15, 1900): 409; "Our Coast Defences," *Forum* 24 (Jan. 1898): 513–19; "The Political Situation in Europe and the East," ibid. (Apr. 1898): 159–65; "Preserve the American Republic," *Lion's Club Magazine* (Oct. 1924): 3–4, 30; "The United States Army, and Its Commanders," *Frank Leslie's Popular Monthly* 48 (May 1899): 3–20.

Boston and Washington city directories provided a few glimpses into Miles's life, as did the United States Census, Manuscript Returns, 1850–1900. The *General Assessment, District of Columbia, 1923–1924*, and *General Assessment, Washington City, 1899–1900* and *1911–1912*, along with *Baist's Real Estate Atlas Surveys of Washington* (Philadelphia, 1903) added perspective on his homes in the capital. For information on Westminster, *Celebration of the One Hundredth Anniversary of the Incorporation of Westminster, Mass. . . .* (Boston: T. R. Marvin & Son, 1859); William Sweetzer Heywood, *History of Westminster Massachusetts (first named Narragansett No. 2) from the Date of the Original Grant of the Township to the Present Time, 1728–1893 . . .* (Lowell, Mass.: Vox Populi Press, 1893); Systematic History Fund, *Vital Records of Westminster, Massachusetts, to the End of the Year 1849* (Worcester, Mass.: Franklin P. Rice, 1908); and Wilbur F. Whitney, *An Account of the Exercises Connected with the 150th Anniversary Celebration of the Town of Westminster Massachusetts, 1909* (Gardner, Mass.: Meals Printing Co., n.d.), were most useful.

Newspapers added immensely to my understanding of Miles and his times. Detailed indexing made the *New York Times* and *New York Tribune* easily accessible. Information on his wedding was gleaned from the *Cleveland Plain Dealer*, and the *Raleigh North Carolina Standard* and *Raleigh Weekly Standard* offered coverage on Reconstruction. Contemporary reaction to his campaigns against Geronimo were in the *Tucson Daily Citizen*, the Tucson *Arizona Daily Star*, and the Tucson *Arizona Weekly Star*. The *Washington Evening Star* was useful in analyzing his life in the capital. For army affairs, see the *Army and Navy Journal*.

Other army officers left their own reminiscences. For the Miles saga, especially useful were George A. Armes, *Ups and Downs of an Army Officer* (Washington, D.C.: privately printed, 1900); John M. Carroll, ed., *The Benteen-Goldin Letters on Custer and His Last Battle* (New York: Liveright, 1974); Oliver O. Howard, *Autobiography of Oliver Otis Howard, Major General, United States Army*, 2 vols. (New York: Baker and Taylor Co., 1908); James L. Parker, *The Old Army Memories, 1872–1912* (Philadelphia: Dorrance and Co., 1929); Richard Henry Pratt, *Battlefield and Classroom: Four Decades with the American Indian, 1867–1904*, ed. Robert M. Utley, Yale Western Americana Series, no. 6 (New Haven: Yale University Press, 1964); Martin F. Schmitt, ed., *General George Crook: His Autobiography* (1946; reprint, Norman: University of Oklahoma Press, 1960); John M. Schofield, *Forty-Six Years in the Army* (New York: Century Co., 1897).

The War of the Rebellion: A Compilation of the Official Records of the Union and Confederate Armies (Washington, D.C.: GPO, 1890–1901) remains the best source for students of the Civil War. For tracing Miles's career, other primary accounts fill in some gaps. See especially Charles A. Fuller, *Personal Recollections of the War of 1861, Sixty-first Regiment New York Volunteer Infantry* (Sherburne, N.Y.: News Job, 1906); John L. Parker and Robert G. Carter, *Henry Wilson's Regiment: History of the Twenty-Second Massachusetts Infantry, the Second Company Sharpshooters, and the Third Light Battery, in the War of the Rebellion* (Boston: Rand Avery Co., 1887); and Francis A. Walker's two volumes, *General Hancock* (New York: D. Appleton and Co., 1894), and *History of the Second Army Corps in the Army of the Potomac* (New York: Charles Scribner's Sons, 1886). Somewhat less important were John Gibbon, *Personal Recollections of the Civil War* (New York: G. P. Putnam's Sons, 1928); J. W. Muffly, ed., *The Story of Our Regiment: A History of the 148th Pennsylvania Volunteers* (Des Moines: Kenyon Printing Co., 1904); B. F. Powelson, *History of Company K of the 140th Regiment Pennsylvania Volunteers (1862–'65)* (Steubenville, Ohio: Carnahan Co., 1906); Robert Laird Stewart, *History of the One Hundred and Fortieth Pennsylvania Volunteers* (privately published, 1912). Francis C. Barlow, "The Capture of the Salient, May 12, 1864," in *The Wilderness Campaign May–June 1864*, vol. 4, *Papers of the Military Historical Society of Massachusetts* (Boston: Military History Society of Massachusetts, 1905), added good background, as did William R. Driver, "The Capture of the Salient at Spottsylvania, May 12, 1864," ibid.

Secondary literature on the Civil War continues to set high standards. Bruce Catton's *The Army of the Potomac: Glory Road* (Garden City, N.Y.: Doubleday and Co., 1962) remains a masterpiece. Gerald F. Linderman's *Embattled Courage: The Experience of Combat in the American Civil War* (New York: Free Press, 1987) does much to explain the remarkable heroism shown throughout this most bloody of

American conflicts. Although not completely convincing, Grady McWhiney and Perry D. Jamieson, *Attack and Die: Civil War Military Tactics and the Southern Heritage* (University: University of Alabama Press, 1982) is often provocative. David M. Jordan, *Winfield Scott Hancock: A Soldier's Life* (Bloomington: Indiana University Press, 1988); and William D. Matter, *If It Takes All Summer: The Battle of Spotsylvania* (Chapel Hill: University of North Carolina Press, 1988) were particularly germane to this study; their well-researched accounts helped me to understand their respective subjects.

Most printed sources dealing with the imprisonment of Jefferson Davis are slanted in favor of the former Confederate president. Surgeon John J. Craven's perspective is available in *Prison Life of Jefferson Davis, Embracing Details and Incidents in His Captivity, Particulars Concerning His Health and Habits, Together with Many Conversations on Topics of Great Public Interest* (1866; reprint, Marceline, Mo.: Walsworth Publishing Co., 1979). Many of Davis's letters are included in Dunbar Rowland, *Jefferson Davis, Constitutionalist: His Letters, Papers and Speeches*, 10 vols. (Jackson: Mississippi Department of Archives and History, 1923); and Hudson Strode, ed., *Jefferson Davis: Private Letters, 1823–1889* (New York: Harcourt, Brace and World, 1966). Erom Rowland, *Varina Howell: Wife of Jefferson Davis* (New York: Macmillan Co., 1931), is very sympathetic to Mrs. Davis. More objective are Richard P. Weinert, Jr., and Colonel Robert Arthur, *Defender of the Chesapeake: The Story of Fort Monroe* (Annapolis, Md.: Leeward Publications, 1978); Chester D. Bradley, "Dr. Craven and the Prison Life of Jefferson Davis," *Virginia Magazine of History and Biography* 62 (Jan. 1954): 72–76; and William Hanchett, "Reconstruction and the Rehabilitation of Jefferson Davis: Charles G. Halpine's *Prison Life*," *Journal of American History* 56 (Sept. 1969): 280–89.

Miles's role in Reconstruction has been subjected to less scrutiny, and a close study of manuscript sources is essential. In addition, a few pertinent primary documents can be found in J. G. de Roulhac Hamilton, *The Correspondence of Jonathan Worth*, 2 vols. (Raleigh: North Carolina Historical Commission, 1909). See also *Speeches of Gov. William W. Holden and Gen. Nelson A. Miles, in Raleigh, N.C., November 6, 1868, at the Grant and Colfax Celebration* (New York: n.p., 1869). For the general situation in North Carolina, best are James E. Sefton, *The United States Army and Reconstruction, 1865–1877* (Baton Rouge: Louisiana State University Press, 1967); and Otto Olsen, "North Carolina: An Incongruous Presence," in *Reconstruction and Redemption in the South*, ed. Otto Olsen (Baton Rouge: Louisiana State University Press, 1980). Jesse Parker Bogue, Jr., "Violence and Oppression in North Carolina during Reconstruction, 1865–1873" (Ph.D. diss., University of Maryland, 1973); and James L. Lancaster, "The Scalawags of North Carolina, 1850–1868" (Ph.D. diss., Princeton University, 1974), should also be consulted. William C. Harris, *William Woods Holden: Firebrand of North Car-*

olina Politics, Southern Biography Series (Baton Rouge: Louisiana State University Press, 1987), is an excellent portrayal of the North Carolina governor.

Robert M. Utley's *Frontier Regulars: The United States Army and the Indian, 1866–1891* (New York: Macmillan Co., 1973) remains the best single volume on the Indian-fighting army, but see also my *Military and United States Indian Policy*. For a broader perspective, see Edward M. Coffman's magisterial *The Old Army: A Portrait of the American Army in Peacetime, 1784–1898* (New York: Oxford University Press, 1986); and Russell F. Weigley's *The American Way of War: A History of United States Military Strategy and Policy*, The Wars of the United States (New York: Macmillan Co., 1973), *History of the United States Army* enlarged ed. (Bloomington: Indiana University Press, 1984), and *Towards an American Army: Military Thought from Washington to Marshall* (New York: Columbia University Press, 1962).

More specialized books include Thomas W. Dunlay, *Wolves for the Blue Soldiers: Indian Scouts and Auxiliaries with the United States Army, 1860–90* (Lincoln: University of Nebraska Press, 1982); and Jerry M. Cooper, *The Army and Civil Disorder: Federal Military Intervention in Labor Disputes, 1877–1900*, Contributions in Military History, no. 19 (Westport, Conn.: Greenwood Press, 1980). For the trials of Cadet Whittaker, see John F. Marszalek, Jr., *Court-Martial: A Black Man in America* (New York: Charles Scribner's Sons, 1972). Joseph G. Dawson III, *The Late Nineteenth Century U.S. Army, 1865–1898: A Research Guide*, Research Guides in Military Studies, no. 3 (Westport, Conn.: Greenwood Press, 1990), is an outstanding resource. Shorter works include John M. Gates, "The Alleged Isolation of U.S. Army Officers in the Late Nineteenth Century," *Parameters: The Journal of the U.S. Army War College* 10 (Sept. 1980): 32–45; and Robert Wooster, "'A Difficult and Forlorn Country': The Military Looks at the American Southwest, 1850–1890," *Arizona and the West* 28 (Winter 1986): 339–56.

Excellent biographies detail the lives of many officers. For this study, John W. Bailey, *Pacifying the Plains: General Alfred Terry and the Decline of the Sioux, 1866–1890*, Contributions in Military History, no. 17 (Westport, Conn.: Greenwood Press, 1979); Mabel E. Deutrich, *The Struggle for Supremacy: The Career of General Fred C. Ainsworth* (Washington, D.C.: Public Affairs Press, 1962); Paul Andrew Hutton, *Phil Sheridan and His Army* (Lincoln: University of Nebraska Press, 1985); Joseph C. Porter, *Paper Medicine Man: John Gregory Bourke and His American West* (Norman: University of Oklahoma Press, 1986); Heath Twitchell, Jr., *Allen: The Biography of an Army Officer* (New Brunswick: Rutgers University Press, 1974); and Robert M. Utley, *Cavalier in Buckskin: George Armstrong Custer and the Western Military Frontier*, Oklahoma Western Biographies Series (Norman: University of Oklahoma Press, 1988) offered significant factual information as well as important analysis. Additional biographies are John A. Carpenter, *Sword and Olive Branch: Oliver Otis Howard* (Pittsburgh: University of Pittsburgh Press,

1964); Richard N. Ellis, *General Pope and the U.S. Indian Policy* (Albuquerque: University of New Mexico Press, 1970); Jack C. Lane, *Armed Progressive: General Leonard Wood* (San Rafael, Calif.: Presidio Press, 1978); Robert H. Steinbach, *A Long March: The Lives of Frank and Alice Baldwin* (Austin: University of Texas Press, 1989). Frank E. Vandiver, *Black Jack: The Life and Times of John J. Pershing*, 2 vols. (College Station: Texas A & M University Press, 1977), should be supplemented with Donald Smythe, "John J. Pershing: Frontier Cavalryman," *New Mexico Historical Review* 38 (July 1963): 220–43.

Paul Andrew Hutton's edited *Soldiers West: Biographies from the Military Frontier* (Lincoln: University of Nebraska Press, 1987), is a model anthology; Sherry L. Smith's *Sagebrush Soldier: Private William Earl Smith's View of the Sioux War of 1876* (Norman: University of Oklahoma Press, 1989) offers insights into the wars against the Indians far larger than the title suggests. Robert M. Utley's *Custer and the Great Controversy: The Origin and Development of a Legend* (Pasadena, Calif.: Westernlore Press, 1962), is still useful, as are *The Papers of the Order of Indian Wars* (Fort Collins, Colo.: Old Army Press, 1975).

The Red River War of 1874–75 is the subject of Joe F. Taylor, ed., *The Indian Campaign on the Staked Plains, 1874–1875: Military Correspondence from War Department Adjutant General's Office, File 2815-1874* (Canyon, Tex.: Panhandle-Plains Historical Society, 1962); and J. T. Marshall, *The Miles Expedition of 1874–1875: An Eyewitness Account of the Red River War*, ed. Lonnie J. White (Austin: Encino Press, 1971). Critical of Miles is James L. Haley's *The Buffalo War: The History of the Red River Indian Uprising of 1874* (Garden City, N.Y.: Doubleday and Co., 1976). On the German sisters, see Grace E. Meredith, ed., *Girl Captives of the Cheyennes* (Los Angeles: Gem Publishing Co., 1927). William W. Haines, *The Winter War* (Boston: Little-Brown, 1961), offers a fictional approach.

On the campaigns on the Northern Plains, John F. Finerty, *War-Path and Bivouac; or, The Conquest of the Sioux* (Norman: University of Oklahoma Press, 1961), provides an interesting perspective, as does Luther S. Kelly, *"Yellowstone Kelly": The Memoirs of Luther Sage Kelly*, ed. M. M. Quaife (New Haven: Yale University Press, 1926). John S. Gray, *Centennial Campaign: The Sioux War of 1876* (Fort Collins, Colo.: Old Army Press, 1976), and "What Made Johnnie Bruguier Run?" *Montana: The Magazine of Western History* 14 (Spring 1964): 34–49, offers marvelous detail, as do a trio of contributions by Jerome A. Greene: "The Lame Deer Fight: Last Drama of the Sioux War of 1876–1877," *By Valor and Arms* 3, no. 3 (1978): 11–21; *Slim Buttes, 1876: An Episode in the Great Sioux War* (Norman: University of Oklahoma Press, 1982); and "The Beginning of the End: Miles versus Sitting Bull at Cedar Creek," *Montana: The Magazine of Western History* 41 (Summer 1991): 18–29. Don Rickey, Jr., "The Battle of Wolf Mountain," *Montana: The Magazine of Western History* 13 (Spring 1963): 44–54; and John S. Manion, *General Terry's Last Statement to Custer: New Evidence on the Mary Adams Affidavit* (Monroe, Mich.: Monroe County Library System, 1983), are also essential. For the situation north of the border, see John P. Turner, *The North-West Mounted Police, 1873–1893*, 2 vols. (Ottawa: Ed Cloutiers, King's Printer and Controller of Stationery, 1950).

Indian perspectives are analyzed in Peter J. Powell, *Sweet Medicine: The Continuing Role of the Sacred Arrows, the Sun Dance, and the Sacred Buffalo Hat in Northern Cheyenne History*, 2 vols. (Norman: University of Oklahoma Press, 1969), but see also Margot Liberty and John Stands in Timber, *Cheyenne Memories*, Yale Western Americana Series, no. 17 (New Haven: Yale University Press, 1967), Frank B. Linderman, *Plenty-coups, Chief of the Crows* (1939; reprint, New York: John Day Co., 1972). Among the voluminous literature on Chief Joseph and the Nez Perces, I depended on Henry Romeyn, "The Capture of Chief Joseph and the Nez Perce Indians," *Historical Society of Montana Collections* 2 (1896): 283–91; Alvin M. Josephy, Jr., *The Nez Perce Indians and the Opening of the Northwest*, Yale Western Americana Series, no. 10 (New Haven: Yale University Press, 1965); and Chief Joseph, "An Indian's View of Indian Affairs," *North American Review* 128 (Apr. 1879): 412–33.

Geronimo and the campaigns against the Indians of the Southwest have generated tremendous interest. For the Indian perspective, I found most useful Eve Ball, *Indeh: An Apache Odyssey* (Provo, Utah: Brigham Young University Press, 1980); S. M. Barrett, ed., *Geronimo's Story of His Life* (1905; reprint, Williamstown, Mass.: Corner House Publishers, 1973); Jason Betzinez with Wilber Sturtevant Nye, *I Fought with Geronimo* (Harrisburg, Pa.: Stackpole Co., 1959); Angie Debo, *Geronimo: The Man, His Time, His Place* (Norman: University of Oklahoma Press, 1976); and Morris E. Opler, "A Chiricahua Apache's Account of the Geronimo Campaign of 1886," *New Mexico Historical Review* 13 (Oct. 1938): 360–86. The army's story is recounted by Britton Davis, *The Truth About Geronimo*, ed. M. M. Quaife (1929; reprint, Lincoln: University of Nebraska Press, 1976); Jack C. Lane, ed., *Chasing Geronimo: The Journal of Leonard Wood, May–September, 1886* (Albuquerque: University of New Mexico Press, 1970); Charles R. Lummis, *General Crook and the Apache Wars* (Flagstaff, Ariz.: Northland Press, 1985); Charles Byars, ed., "Gatewood Reports to His Wife from Geronimo's Camp," *Journal of Arizona History* 7 (Summer 1966): 76–81; Bruno J. Rolak, "General Miles' Mirrors: The Heliograph in the Geronimo Campaign of 1886," ibid. 16 (Summer 1976): 145–60. Three works stand out: Dan L. Thrapp, *The Conquest of Apacheria* (Norman: University of Oklahoma Press, 1967); Robert M. Utley, "The Surrender of Geronimo," *Arizoniana* 4 (1963): 1–9; and Dudley Acker, "A War between Two Generals," (unpublished MS, 1985), shared with me by the author.

On a more general level, U.S. Indian policy has also generated lively scholarly debate. For the present book, William T. Hagan, *The Indian Rights Association: The Herbert Welsh Years, 1882–1904* (Tucson: University of Arizona Press, 1985); and Francis Paul Prucha, *American Indian Policy in Crisis: Christian Reformers and the Indian, 1865–1900* (Norman: University of Oklahoma Press, 1976); were especially insightful. Lewis H. Morgan, *Ancient Society*, ed. Leslie A. White (1877; reprint, Cambridge: Belknap Press of Harvard University Press, 1964) was essential to understanding Miles's views. Robert M. Utley, *The Last Days of the Sioux Nation* (New Haven: Yale University Press, 1963), remains the best account of Wounded Knee, but see also Peter R. DeMontravel, "General Nelson A. Miles and the Wounded Knee Controversy," *Arizona and the West* 28 (Spring 1986): 23–44. Contemporary analysis is in "Indian Truth and Eloquence," *Harper's Weekly* 35 (Feb. 21, 1891): 131; and David Graham Phillips, "The Sioux Chiefs before the Secretary," *Harper's Weekly* 35 (Feb. 21, 1891): 142.

Political and administrative histories helped set Miles within the larger context of the late nineteenth and early twentieth centuries. Stephen Skowronek, *Building a New American State: The Expansion of National Administrative Capacities, 1877–1920* (Cambridge: Cambridge University Press, 1982), develops administrative changes. Among political biographies, the best for this study were Lewis L. Gould's *The Presidency of Theodore Roosevelt*, American Presidency Series (Lawrence: Regents Press of Kansas, 1991), and *The Presidency of William McKinley*, ibid. (1980). Philip C. Jessup, *Elihu Root* (New York: Dodd, Mead and Co., 1938) contains much of value, but needs to be updated. Chester Winston Bowie, "Redfield Proctor: A Biography" (Ph.D. diss., University of Wisconsin-Madison, 1980), is excellent; favorable to its subject is Rodney Ellis Bell, "A Life of Russell Alexander Alger, 1836–1907" (Ph.D. diss., University of Michigan, 1975).

Regional perspectives are best seen in Ted C. Hinckley, *The Americanization of Alaska, 1867–1897* (Palo Alto, Calif.: Pacific Books, 1972); Morgan B. Sherwood, *Exploration of Alaska, 1865–1900* (New Haven: Yale University Press, 1965); Howard R. Lamar, *The Far Southwest, 1846–1912: A Territorial History* (New Haven: Yale University Press, 1966), and "Edmund G. Ross as Governor of the New Mexico Territory: A Reappraisal," *New Mexico Historical Review* 36 (July 1961): 179–209; and Clark C. Spence, *Territorial Politics and Government in Montana, 1864–1889* (Urbana: University of Illinois Press, 1975).

For analysis of Miles's views on events and trends during the late 1890s, see "General Miles' Idea of War," *Review of Reviews: An International Magazine* 14 (July–Dec. 1896): 72; and "This Week," *Nation* 62 (Jan. 2, 1896): 1. The general's interest in bicycles is outlined by Charles M. Dollar, "Putting the Army on Wheels: The Story of the Twenty-Fifth Infantry Bicycle Corps," *Prologue* 17 (Spring 1985): 7–23.

To supplement manuscript materials on the war against Spain, primary documents are found in Russell A. Alger, *The Spanish-American War* (New York: Harper and Bros., 1901); Rear Adm. French Ensor Chadwick, *The Relations of the United States to Spain: The Spanish-American War*, 2 vols. (New York: Charles Scribner's Sons, 1909); Finley Peter Dunne, *Mr. Dooley in Peace and in War* (1898; reprint, New York: Greenwood Press, 1968); W.A.M. Goode, *With Sampson through the War; Being an Account of the Naval Operations of the Atlantic Squadron during the Spanish American War of 1898* (New York: Doubleday and McClure Co., 1899); Robert Seager II, and Doris D. Maguire, *The Letters and Papers of Alfred Thayer Mahan*, 3 vols. (Annapolis: Naval Institute Press, 1975); James Harrison Wilson, *Under the Old Flag: Recollections of Military Operations in the War for the Union, the Spanish War, the Boxer Rebellion, etc.* (New York: D. Appleton and Co., 1912); *Correspondence Relating to the War with Spain and Conditions Growing out of the Same, . . . between the Adjutant General of the Army and Military Commanders in the United States, Cuba, Porto Rico, China, and the Philippine Islands, from April 15, 1898 to July 30, 1902*, 2 vols. (Washington, D.C.: GPO, 1902); and John Hull, "The Hull Army Bill," *Forum* 25 (May 1898): 396–402.

Secondary literature on the war against Spain includes Graham A. Cosmas's then-revisionist *An Army for Empire: The United States Army in the Spanish-American War* (Columbia: University of Missouri Press, 1971), which is best on the prewar period. David R. Trask, *The War with Spain in 1898*, The Wars of the United States (New York: Macmillan Co., 1981), provides a strong survey of the military events. For political considerations, see Lewis L. Gould, *The Spanish-American War and President McKinley* (Lawrence: University Press of Kansas, 1982). Louise Carroll Wade, in "Hell Hath No Fury Like a General Scorned: Nelson A. Miles, the Pullman Strike, and the Beef Scandal of 1898," *Illinois Historical Journal* 79, no. 3 (1986): 162–84, attempts to link Miles's role in the beef scandal to the Pullman strike.

On the Philippines insurrection, see Brian McAllister Linn, *The U.S. Army and Counterinsurgency in the Philippine War, 1899–1902* (Chapel Hill: University of North Carolina Press, 1989); and John Morgan Gates, *Schoolbooks and Krags: The United States Army in the Philippines, 1898–1902*, Contributions in Military History, no. 3 (Westport, Conn.: Greenwood Press, 1973). Stuart Creighton Miller, *"Benevolent Assimilation": The American Conquest of the Philippines, 1899–1903* (New Haven: Yale University Press, 1982), relies heavily on sensational newspaper accounts.

Twentieth century army reforms are described by Russell F. Weigley, "The Elihu Root Reforms and the Progressive Era," in *Command and Commanders in Modern Warfare: The Proceedings of the Second Military History Symposium, U.S. Air Force Academy, 2–3 May 1968*, ed. William Geffen (Office of Air Force History and U.S. Air Force Academy, 1971); and Edward Ranson's excellent essays, "The Investigation of the War Department, 1898–99," *Historian* 34 (Nov. 1971): 78–99, and "Nelson A. Miles as Commanding General, 1895–1903," *Military Affairs* 39 (Winter 1966): 179–200. Philip L. Semsch, "Elihu Root and the General Staff," ibid. 27 (Spring 1963): 16–27; Edward F. Keuchel, "Chemicals and Meat: The Embalmed Beef Scandal of the Spanish-American War," *Bulletin of the History of Medicine* 98 (Summer 1974): 249–64; and James Hewes, "The United States Army General Staff, 1900–1917," *Military Affairs* 38 (Apr. 1974): 67–72, offer other insights. Unpublished scholarship by Ronald James Barr, "American Military Reform, 1898–1904: The Reasons for Reform and the Eventual Outcome" (M.A. thesis, Louisiana State University, 1989), and William R. Roberts, "Loyalty and Expertise: The Transformation of the Nineteenth-Century American General Staff and the Creation of the Modern Military Establishment" (Ph.D. diss., Johns Hopkins University, 1980), fill in many gaps.

Henry Adams offered a number of cogent observations about Miles's relationship with the McKinley and Roosevelt administrations. See Worthington Chauncey Ford, ed., *Letters of Henry Adams (1892–1918)* (Boston: Houghton Mifflin Co., 1938); J. C. Levenson, et al., eds., *The Letters of Henry Adams*, 3 vols. (Cambridge: Belknap Press of Harvard University Press, [1988–]); and Ward Thoron, ed., *The Letters of Mrs. Henry Adams* (Boston: Little, Brown, and Co., 1936). For Roosevelt's view, see Elting E. Morison, ed., *The Letters of Theodore Roosevelt*, 8 vols. (Cambridge: Harvard University Press, 1951–54). Contemporary editorial comment may be found in H. L. Nelson, "Secretary of War Root and His Task," *Harper's Weekly* 43 (Sept. 2, 1898): 857–60; "General Miles's Requests," *Independent* 54 (Apr. 3, 1902): 831; "General Miles's Report," *Outlook* 74 (May 9, 1903): 99–100; "General Miles's Retirement," *Public Opinion* 35 (Aug. 13, 1905): 190; "General Miles and the Administration," *American Monthly Review of Reviews* 25 (Jan.–June 1902): 532; "General Miles Retires," ibid. 28 (July–Dec. 1903): 144–45; "Retirement of Lieutenant-General Miles," *Literary Digest* 27 (Aug. 15, 1903): 187; "The Treatment of General Miles," ibid. 27 (Aug. 22, 1903): 214–15; "The Passing of the Commanding General," *Nation* 77 (Aug. 13, 1903): 126–27. Supportive of the general is a song published in Joseph Hanson, *Frontier Ballads* (Chicago: A. C. McClurg and Co., 1910): 35–37.

Published material on his bid for the presidency is found in *The Campaign Text Book of the Democratic Party of the United States, 1904* (New York: Democratic National Committee, 1904); *Official Report of the Proceedings of the Democratic National Convention . . . ,* reported by Milton W. Blumenberg (New York: Publisher's Printing Co., 1904); Jack S. Blocker, Jr., *Retreat from Reform: The Prohibition Movement in the United States, 1890–1913,* Contributions in American History, no. 51 (Westport, Conn.: Greenwood Press, 1976); and Harry Wilson Walker, "The Trail of the Tammany Tiger," *Saturday Evening Post* 186 (Apr. 1914): 20–21, 68–69.

Miles's involvement in Buffalo Bill Cody's movie is best documented in the Baldwin Papers (see above). *Moving Picture World* 18 (Oct. 25, 1913): 362, 368; ibid. 18 (Nov. 22, 1913): 351, 362; and ibid. 19 (Mar. 14, 1914): 1370, also provide coverage. Kevin Brownlow, *The War, the West, and the American Wilderness* (New York: Alfred A. Knopf, 1979), is the best secondary source. Don Russell, *The Lives and Legends of Buffalo Bill* (Norman: University of Oklahoma Press, 1960), examines the enigmatic showman. Miles's relationship with the artist Frederic Remington is best seen in *The Collected Writings of Frederic Remington*, ed. Peggy and Harold Samuels (New York: Doubleday and Co., 1979); and Peggy and Harold

Samuels, *Frederic Remington: A Biography* (Austin: University of Texas Press, 1985).

For background on the Werner Company, see John Tebbel, *The Expansion of an Industry, 1865–1919*, vol. 2 of *A History of Book Publishing in the United States* (New York: R. R. Bowker, 1975); and *Publishers' Weekly* (1896–1900). "The Guardians of Liberty," *Literary Digest* 45 (July 27, 1912): 152–53, describes the nativist group that Miles supported during the 1910s, and "General Nelson A. Miles on Prohibition," *Manufacturers Record* (Baltimore), Mar. 28, 1923, outlines his continued interest in limiting the distribution of alcohol.

INDEX

Bates, John C.: 266
Bear Paw Mountain, Battle of: 102–8, 141
Beaver, James A.: 20
Beef controversy: 234–37
Belford, Alexander: 204
Belknap, William: 79–80, 128, 130, 188
Bell, J. Franklin: 245–46, 266
Benet, Stephen V.: 81, 120, 127–28, 166
Bennett, Andrew S.: 117
Benteen, Frederick: 271
Biddle, Jonathan W.: 102
Bigelow, John: 164
Big Foot: 182, 184–85, 188, 193
Billings, Frederick: 135, 196
Black Elk, Ben: 259
Blair, Thomas F.: 133
Bloody Angle (Civil War): 24–25
Bonfils, Fred: 256
Boston, Mass.: 1, 2, 3, 9
Bourke, John G.: 142, 149–50
Boynton, H. V.: 173–74
Breckinridge, Joseph C.: 224, 235
Brisbin, James S.: 93
Broad Tail: 187
Broady, Knut O.: 20, 27
Brooke, John R.: and Civil War, 24; and Ghost Dance campaign, 180, 183, 185–89; and Spanish-American War, 211, 228
Brotherton, David H.: 114, 126–27, 168
Bruguier, Johnnie: 91, 104
Brule Sioux: 91, 94, 182, 183, 186, 187, 259. *See also* Sioux Indians
Bryan, William Jennings: 209, 239, 250
Buell, George P.: 63, 68, 69, 74–75
Bull Eagle: 84
Bullis, John L.: 166
Bull Run, Battles of: 5, 12, 212

Bureau of Refugees, Freedmen, and Abandoned Lands: 40, 47–52, 54, 62–63
Burke, Daniel W.: 228
Burnside, Ambrose: 14, 15, 27, 28
Butler, Ben: 27, 28, 45
Butler, Edmund: 89, 301 n.40
Butterfield, Daniel: 58

Caldwell, John C.: 11–18
California, Department of: 169, 245
Cameron, Elizabeth: 113, 199, 205, 236, 263, 270–71
Cameron, James Donald: 119, 155, 168, 270–71
Camp Belcher: 58
Camp Cheyenne: 184
Camp Distribution: 47
Camp McDermit: 138
Camp Robinson: 91, 94
Camp Schouler: 7
Camp Sheridan: 93
Camp Supply: 64, 67, 71
Camp Wilson: 8
Captain John: 105
Card, Benjamin: 90
Carnegie, Andrew: 225
Carr, Eugene A.: 183, 187
Carter, Mason: 103
Carter, William H.: 238, 242–43
Casey, James S.: 89, 301 n.40, 302 n.51
Casey, Thomas L.: 130
Cervera, Pascual de: 207, 219, 220
Chaffee, Adna R.: 66, 68, 245, 266
Chancellorsville, Battle of: 16–18, 21
Chandler, Allen D.: 236
Chandler, George: 178
Chandler, Zachariah: 77
Chapman, Arthur: 105
Chevers, Mark L.: 41
Cheyenne and Arapaho Agency: 63, 140

Halpine, Charles G.: 45

Hancock, Winfield Scott: commands First Division, 15–18; commands Second Corps, 20, 22, 23, 25, 26, 29, 30; and Crater board, 28; and Reconstruction, 46, 51; post-1876 career, 59, 61, 129, 130, 139, 141, 143

Harding, Warren G.: 262

Hargan, D. T.: 257

Harper's Weekly: 164, 177, 202, 233

Harrison, Benjamin: 169–70, 178, 182, 192, 194, 196–97

Hatcher's Run, Battle of: 32–33

Hatfield, Charles A.: 148

Hauser, Samuel T.: 118

Hawley, Joseph: 242, 247

Hay, John: 164

Hayes, Lucy Webb: 130

Hayes, Rutherford B.: 88, 110, 114, 118, 132, 133

Hayt, Ezra A.: 111

Hazen, William B.: 115–16, 130–31

Heintzelman, Mrs. E. W.: 227, 228

Heintzelman, Stuart: 227

Heliographs: 135, 147

Henderson, David B.: 247

Henry, Guy V.: 186

Heth, Henry: 33, 35

Higginson, Francis J.: 226–27

High Wolf: 104

Hill, Tom: 105

Hogg, James: 249–50

Holabird, Samuel B.: 155

Holden, Laura: 51

Holden, William W.: 48, 49, 52–54

Hooker, Forrestine: 263

Hooker, Joseph: 15–17

Hopi Indians: 165

Howard, Guy V.: 173

Howard, Oliver O.: 61, 141, 169, 171; and Civil War, 8, 10, 11, 14, 16–17, 37; and Reconstruction, 44, 47, 50, 62–63; and Nez Perce campaign, 98–101, 104–9, 158; and Bannock campaign, 117; promoted to major-general, 143; and Geronimo campaign, 152–55, 173–74; and San Carlos disputes, 165–66; commands Department of the Atlantic, 169; retirement of, 201

Hoyt, Colgate: 250, 254

Huggins, Eli Lundy: 175, 190, 193, 197, 252

Hughes, Robert P.: 245–46

Hull, A. T.: 211, 215, 224

Hump: 181, 182

Humphreys, Andrew A.: 32, 33, 35, 44

Hunkpapa Sioux: 80, 83

Ilges, Guido: 101–2

Independent: 243, 253

Indian Affairs, Bureau of: 125, 128, 177, 259, 272

Indian Rights Association: 194

Inspector General's Department: 73–74, 238, 246

Interior, Department of the: 62, 63, 155, 166, 182, 194, 256–60

Iron Shirt: 67

Iron Star: 93, 201

Irvine, Alexander G.: 72

Jackson, Thomas E. ("Stonewall"): 16–17

James, Division of the: 39

Jefferson Memorial Association: 255

Jerome, Lovell H.: 105

Jicarilla Apaches: 72

Johnson, Andrew: 38, 42, 44, 45

Johnston, Joseph E.: 10, 11

Jones, George: 167, 168, 196

Judge-Advocate General's Office: 73

Juh: 144

Miles, Nelson A. (*cont.*)
81, 85, 88, 96–97, 115, 141–45,
149–50, 156, 160, 161, 168, 171,
173–74, 198, 273; Jefferson Davis,
39–47, 54–56; Winfield S. Hancock,
15–20, 25, 29–30, 46, 51, 59, 129–
30, 139, 141, 143; Oliver O. Howard,
8, 11, 37, 44, 50, 61–63, 101, 105–9,
154, 157–58, 160, 171, 173–74;
Ranald Mackenzie, 67, 71, 74, 115;
John Pope, 60–61, 63, 66–67, 70–
71, 94, 112, 130, 141; Frederic
Remington, 177, 195–96, 202, 203;
Theodore Roosevelt, 202, 223, 233,
239–41, 244–48, 274; John
Schofield, 32, 59, 167, 169, 188,
199–201; Philip Sheridan, 32, 46,
61, 90, 94, 115, 127, 155, 168–69,
188; John Sherman, 50–51, 60, 126,
130, 137–38, 158–59, 168–69, 172,
174–75, 197, 210, 270–71; William
Sherman, 51, 60–61, 62, 71, 79, 85,
86, 90–91, 94–95, 97, 108, 112,
115–23, 130–32, 139–41, 166–67,
175, 270–71; Alfred Terry, 51, 81,
89, 94, 115, 127, 167–68
Miles, Sherman: childhood of, 134,
163, 193, 196, 197, 202, 205, 230,
263; military career of, 238, 252,
255, 256, 265
Miles, Yulee Noble, 255
*Military Europe: A Narrative of
Personal Observation and Personal
Experience:* 207
Military Information Division: 210
Mills, Anson: 262
Miner, Charles W.: 83
Mine Run, Battle of: 22
Minneconjou Sioux: 80, 83, 85, 88, 92,
182, 184–86. *See also* Sioux Indians
Missouri, Department of the: 60, 63,
97, 139, 142–43, 167, 193

Missouri, Division of the: 61, 81, 175,
193
Mitchell, William: 264
Mobley, Harriet: 123
Modoc Indians: 84
Mojave Indians: 165–66
Montana, District of: 119
Moody, William H.: 237, 347 n.18
Morgan, Edwin D.: 10
Morgan, Lewis Henry: 124–25, 138
Morgan, Thomas J.: 187, 193
Mott, Gershom: 33
Mount Vernon Barracks: 172–73
Moylan, Myles: 102, 103, 198
Muache Utes: 72
Muddy Creek, Battle of: 92–93
Museum of the American Indian:
265
Myer, Albert J.: 130
Myles, John: 1–2
Myles, Samuel: 2

Natchez: 152
Nation: 270, 271
National Defense Act (1916): 261
National Guard: 216, 260–61
National Society of New England
Women: 205
Navajo Indians: 144, 165
Navy, Department of the: 213, 219,
226, 229
Negley, James S.: 8
Neill, Thomas H.: 63, 69
New Mexico, District of: 61, 71, 72
New Voice: 251
New York Daily Tribune: 9, 110, 126,
138, 243, 244, 266
New York Journal: 210
New York Times: 159, 167, 191, 195,
204, 232, 236, 241, 244, 245, 248
New York World: 233
Nez Perce campaign: 98–109. *See also*

Wanamaker, Rodman: 263

War, Department of: 79–80, 160, 166, 193, 223–24, 257–60; organization and reform of, 73–74, 193–94, 208, 215–16, 231, 235–48, 266–68, 270–71. *See also individual bureaus; Army*

Warm Springs Apaches: 147, 149

Warm Springs Reservation: 138

Warren, Gouverneur K.: 34, 111, 285 n.53

Washington Evening Star: 155, 181–82, 191

Washita, Battle of the: 59, 102

Welsh, Herbert: 158, 164, 182, 246

Werner Company: 202–4

Westminster, Massachusetts: 1, 2, 3, 15, 17, 21, 250, 255

Weston, John T.: 221

West Point, Department of: 97

Wharton, Theodore: 257, 259

Wheaton, Frank: 180, 183

Wheelen, James W.: 93

Whelpley, J. D.: 230–31

Whipple, Charles Ayer: 202

Whistler, Joseph: 79, 82

White Bear: 84

White Bird: 104, 106

White Bird Canyon, Battle of: 98

White Bull: 92

White Mountain Apaches: 165

White Oak Swamp, Battle of: 11, 12

Whitside, Samuel M.: 185, 190

Whittaker, Johnson C.: 131–32

Wiborg, Frank: 240, 263

Wilder, William H.: 255

Wilderness, Battle of the: 23

Willcox, Orlando B.: 167

Wilson, Henry: 7, 15, 44, 45, 46, 50

Wilson, James H.: 228, 229, 236, 252

Wilson, Woodrow: 255, 260, 262

Winthrop, Robert C.: 7

Wolfley, Lewis: 170

Wolf Mountains, Battle of: 89, 91, 94

Wood, C. E. S.: 105–9

Wood, Leonard: 163–64, 170, 197, 263; and Geronimo campaign, 148, 153–54, 157, 160, 267; and Spanish-American War, 235; as chief of staff, 266–67

Woodruff, Thomas W.: 103

Woolley, John D.: 251

Worth, Jonathan: 48

Wounded Knee, Battle of: 185–86; recreation of, 257–58

Wovoka: 178

Yakima Reservation: 138

Yellow Robe, Chauncey: 259

Yellowstone, District of the: 117, 119

Young, Samuel B. M.: 244, 266

Yuma Indians: 165–66

Zulick, Conrad M.: 145–47